Advances in Intelligent Systems and Computing

Volume 409

Series editor

Janusz Kacprzyk, Polish Academy of Sciences, Warsaw, Poland
e-mail: kacprzyk@ibspan.waw.pl

About this Series

The series "Advances in Intelligent Systems and Computing" contains publications on theory, applications, and design methods of Intelligent Systems and Intelligent Computing. Virtually all disciplines such as engineering, natural sciences, computer and information science, ICT, economics, business, e-commerce, environment, healthcare, life science are covered. The list of topics spans all the areas of modern intelligent systems and computing.

The publications within "Advances in Intelligent Systems and Computing" are primarily textbooks and proceedings of important conferences, symposia and congresses. They cover significant recent developments in the field, both of a foundational and applicable character. An important characteristic feature of the series is the short publication time and world-wide distribution. This permits a rapid and broad dissemination of research results.

Advisory Board

Chairman

Nikhil R. Pal, Indian Statistical Institute, Kolkata, India
e-mail: nikhil@isical.ac.in

Members

Rafael Bello, Universidad Central "Marta Abreu" de Las Villas, Santa Clara, Cuba
e-mail: rbellop@uclv.edu.cu

Emilio S. Corchado, University of Salamanca, Salamanca, Spain
e-mail: escorchado@usal.es

Hani Hagras, University of Essex, Colchester, UK
e-mail: hani@essex.ac.uk

László T. Kóczy, Széchenyi István University, Győr, Hungary
e-mail: koczy@sze.hu

Vladik Kreinovich, University of Texas at El Paso, El Paso, USA
e-mail: vladik@utep.edu

Chin-Teng Lin, National Chiao Tung University, Hsinchu, Taiwan
e-mail: ctlin@mail.nctu.edu.tw

Jie Lu, University of Technology, Sydney, Australia
e-mail: Jie.Lu@uts.edu.au

Patricia Melin, Tijuana Institute of Technology, Tijuana, Mexico
e-mail: epmelin@hafsamx.org

Nadia Nedjah, State University of Rio de Janeiro, Rio de Janeiro, Brazil
e-mail: nadia@eng.uerj.br

Ngoc Thanh Nguyen, Wroclaw University of Technology, Wroclaw, Poland
e-mail: Ngoc-Thanh.Nguyen@pwr.edu.pl

Jun Wang, The Chinese University of Hong Kong, Shatin, Hong Kong
e-mail: jwang@mae.cuhk.edu.hk

More information about this series at http://www.springer.com/series/11156

Suresh Chandra Satapathy · Amit Joshi
Nilesh Modi · Nisarg Pathak
Editors

Proceedings of International Conference on ICT for Sustainable Development

ICT4SD 2015 Volume 2

 Springer

Editors
Suresh Chandra Satapathy
Department of Computer Science and
  Engineering
Anil Neerukonda Institute of Technology
  and Sciences
Visakhapatnam, Andhra Pradesh
India

Amit Joshi
Sabar Institute of Technology
Sabarkantha, Gujarat
India

Nilesh Modi
Narsinhbhai Institute of Computer Studies
  and Management
Kadi, Gujarat
India

Nisarg Pathak
Narsinhbhai Institute of Computer Studies
  and Management
Kadi, Gujarat
India

ISSN 2194-5357   ISSN 2194-5365   (electronic)
Advances in Intelligent Systems and Computing
ISBN 978-981-10-0133-8   ISBN 978-981-10-0135-2   (eBook)
DOI 10.1007/978-981-10-0135-2

Library of Congress Control Number: 2015955863

Printed on acid-free paper

This Springer imprint is published by SpringerNature
The registered company is Springer Science+Business Media Singapore Pte Ltd.

Preface

These AISC volumes contain the papers presented at the ICT4SD 2015: International Conference on Information and Communication Technology for Sustainable Development. The conference was held during July 3–4, 2015 at Hotel Pride Ahmedabad, India, and communally organized by ASSOCHAM Gujarat Chapter, ACM Professional Chapter, GESIA and Sabar Institute of Technology, Gujarat and Computer Society of India, as Knowledge Partner. The objective of this international conference was to provide an opportunity for researchers, academicians, industry persons, and students to interact and exchange ideas, experience, and expertise in the current trend and strategies for Information and Communication Technologies. Besides this, participants were also enlightened about the vast avenues, current and emerging technological developments in the field of ICT in this era, and its applications. The conference attracted a large number of high-quality submissions and stimulated cutting-edge research discussions among many academic pioneering researchers, scientists, industrial engineers, and students from all over the world and provided a forum for researchers. Research submissions in various advanced technology areas were received and after a rigorous peer-review process with the help of program committee members and external reviewers, 154 (Vol-I: 77, Vol-II: 77) papers were accepted with an acceptance ratio of 0.43. The conference featured many distinguished personalities such as Mr. Job Glas, Head of Mission, NBSO, Netherlands, Mr. Volkmar Blech, Zera Gmbh, Germany, Dr. Mukesh Kumar, TITS, Bhiwani, Dr. Vipin Tyagi, Jaypee University, Guna, Prof. Pravesh Bhadviya, Director, Sabar Education, Mr. Bipin V. Mehta, President CSI, Mr. Hemal Patel, MD, Cyberoam, Ms. Bhagyesh Soneji, Chairperson, ASSOCHAM, and Mr. Jay Ruparel, President, GESIA. Separate invited talks were organized on industrial and academia tracks on both days. The conference also hosted a few tutorials and workshops for the benefit of participants. We are indebted to ASSOCHAM Gujarat Chapter, Sabar Institute of Technology and Computer Society of India, ACM Professional Chapter for their immense support to make this conference possible on such a grand scale. A total of 18 sessions were organized as a part of ICT4SD including 15 technical, 2 plenary, and 1 inaugural session. The Session Chairs for the technical sessions included Dr. Chirag Thaker, GEC, Bhavnagar, India, Dr. Vipin Tyagi, Jaypee University, MP, India, Dr. Munesh Trivedi, ABES Engineering College, Ghaziabad, India, Dr. Ramesh Thakur, DAVV, Indore, India, Dr. Dilip Kumar Sharma, GLA University, Mathura, India, Dr. Bhushan Trivedi, GLS University, Ahmedabad, India, Dr. S.M. Shah, KSV University, India, Dr. Nikita Vats Doohan, Indore, MP, India, Dr. Harshal Arolkar, GlS University, Ahmedabad, India, Dr. Priyanka Sharma, Raksha Shakti University, Ahmedabad, India, Dr. Nilesh Modi, KSV, Ahmedabad, India, Dr. Satyen Parikh, Ganpat University, India, Dr. Sakshi Kaushal, UIET, Punjab University, India, Dr. S.C. Satapathy, Visakhapatnam, India, and Dr. Nisarg Pathak, KSV, Ahmedabad, India.

We express our sincere thanks to the members of the technical review committee for their valuable support in doing critical reviews to enhance the quality of all accepted papers. Our heartfelt thanks are due to the National and International Advisory Committee and CSI Execomm Members for their support in making this a grand success. Our authors deserve big thanks since it is due to them that the conference was such a huge success.

Our sincere thanks to all the sponsors, press, print, and electronic media for their excellent coverage of this convention.

July 2015   Suresh Chandra Satapathy
                                                                                              Amit Joshi
                                                                                              Nilesh Modi
                                                                                              Nisarg Pathak

Contents

Committee

Advisory Committee

Mr. H.R. Mohan, Past President, CSI
Prof. Bipin Mehta, President, CSI
Mr. P.N. Jain, Add. Sec., R&D, Government of Gujarat, India
Dr. Srinivas Padmanabhuni, President ACM India
Dr. Anirban Basu, Vice President, CSI
Prof. R.P. Soni, RVP, Region III, CSI
Dr. Malay Nayak, Director-IT, London
Mr. Chandrashekhar Sahasrabudhe, ACM India
Dr. Pawan Lingras, Saint Mary's University, Canada
Prof. (Dr.) P. Thrimurthy, Past President, CSI
Dr. Shayam Akashe, ITM, Gwalior, MP, India
Dr. S.C. Sathapathy, Visakhapatnam, India
Dr. Dharm Singh, Windhoek, Namibia
Prof. S.K. Sharma, Pacific University, Udaipur, India
Prof. H.R. Vishwakarma, VIT, Vellore, India
Prof. Pravesh Bhadviya, Director, Sabar Education, India
Mr. Mignesh Parekh, Ahmedabad, India
Dr. Muneesh Trivedi, ABES, Gaziabad, India
Dr. Chandana Unnithan, Victoria University, Australia
Prof. Deva Ram Godara, Bikaner, India
Dr. Y.C. Bhatt, Chairman, CSI Udaipur Chapter
Dr. B.R. Ranwah, Past Chairman, CSI Udaipur Chapter
Dr. Arpan Kumar Kar, IIT Delhi, India

Organizing Committee

General Chairs
Ms. Bhagyesh Soneji, Chairperson, ASSOCHAM Gujarat
Mr. Jay Ruparel, President, GESIA
Mr. Bharat Patel, COO, Yudiz Solutions

Organizing Chairs
Dr. Durgesh Kumar Mishra, Chairman, Division IV, CSI
Dr. Rajveer Shekhawat, Chairman, ACM Udaipur Chapter

Organizing Co-chair
Dr. Harshal Arolkar, Associate Professor, GLS Ahmedabad

Members
Dr. Vimal Pandya, Ahmedabad, India
Dr. G.N. Jani, Ahmedabad, India
Mr. Nilesh Vaghela, Electromech, Ahmedabad, India
Mr. Vinod Thummar, SITG, Gujarat, India
Dr. Chirag Thaker, GEC, Bhavnagar, Gujarat, India
Mr. Maulik Patel, SITG, Gujarat, India
Mr. Nilesh Vaghela, Electromech Corp., Ahmedabad, India
Dr. Savita Gandhi, GU, Ahmedabad, India
Mr. Nayan Patel, SITG, Gujarat, India
Dr. Jyoti Parikh, Associate Professor, CE, GU, Ahmedabad, India
Dr. Vipin Tyagi, Jaypee University, Guna, India
Prof. Sanjay Shah, GEC, Gandhinagar, India
Dr. Chirag Thaker, GEC, Bhavnagar, Gujarat, India
Mr. Mihir Chauhan, VICT, Gujarat, India
Mr. Chetan Patel, Gandhinagar, India

Program Committee

Program Chair
Dr. Nilesh Modi, Professor and Head, NICSM, Kadi

Program Co-chair
Dr. Nisarg Pathak, SSC, CSI, Gujarat

Members
Dr. Mukesh Sharma, SFSU, Jaipur
Dr. Manuj Joshi, SGI, Udaipur, India
Dr. Bharat Singh Deora, JRNRV University, Udaipur
Prof. D.A. Parikh, Head, CE, LDCE, Ahmedabad, India
Prof. L.C. Bishnoi, GPC, Kota, India

Mr. Alpesh Patel, SITG, Gujarat
Dr. Nisheeth Joshi, Banasthali University, Rajasthan, India
Dr. Vishal Gaur, Bikaner, India
Dr. Aditya patel, Ahmedabad University, Gujarat, India
Mr. Ajay Choudhary, IIT Roorkee, India
Dr. Dinesh Goyal, Gyan Vihar, Jaipur, India
Mr. Nirav Patel, SITG, Gujarat
Dr. Muneesh Trivedi, ABES, Gaziabad, India
Mr. Ajit Pujara, SITG, Gujarat, India
Dr. Dilip Kumar Sharma, Mathura, India
Prof. R.K. Banyal, RTU, Kota, India
Mr. Jeril Kuriakose, Manipal University, Jaipur, India
Dr. M. Sundaresan, Chairman, CSI Coimbatore Chapter
Prof. Jayshree Upadhyay, HOD-CE, VCIT, Gujarat
Dr. Sandeep Vasant, Ahmedabad University, Gujarat, India

About the Editors

Dr. Suresh Chandra Satapathy is currently working as Professor and Head, at the Department of CSE at Anil Neerukonda Institute of Technology and Sciences (ANITS), Andhra Pradesh, India. He obtained his Ph.D. in Computer Science and Engineering from JNTU Hyderabad and his M.Tech. in CSE from NIT, Rourkela, Odisha, India. He has 26 years of teaching experience. His research interests include data mining, machine intelligence, and swarm intelligence. He has acted as program chair of many international conferences and edited six volumes of proceedings from Springer LNCS and AISC series. He is currently guiding eight scholars for Ph.Ds. Dr. Satapathy is also a senior member of IEEE.

Er. Amit Joshi has experience of around 6 years in academic and industry in prestigious organizations in Rajasthan and Gujarat. Currently, he is working as Assistant Professor in the Department of Information Technology at Sabar Institute in Gujarat. He is an active member of ACM, CSI, AMIE, IEEE, IACSIT-Singapore, IDES, ACEEE, NPA, and many other professional societies. Currently, he is Honorary Secretary of CSI Udaipur Chapter and Honorary Secretary for ACM Udaipur Chapter. He has presented and published more than 40 papers in national and international journals/conferences of IEEE, Springer and ACM. He has also edited three books on diversified subjects including Advances in Open Source Mobile Technologies, ICT for Integrated Rural Development, and ICT for Competitive Strategies. He has also organized more than 25 national and international conferences and workshops including International Conference ETNCC 2011 at Udaipur through IEEE, international conference ICTCS—2014 at Udaipur through ACM, international conference ICT4SD 2015—by Springer recently. He has also served on Organizing and Program Committees of more than 50 conferences/seminars/workshops throughout the world and presented six invited talks at various conferences. For his contribution towards society he has been awarded by The Institution of Engineers (India), ULC, the Appreciation Award on the celebration of Engineers, 2014 and by SIG-WNs Computer Society of India on ACCE, 2012.

Dr. Nilesh Modi has rich experience of around 13 years in academics and in the IT industry. He holds a doctorate in e-Security (Computer Science and Application). Continuing his research on cybersecurity, presently he is pursuing postdoctoral research on Wireless Communication and Security and certification as Ethical Hacking. He has a good number of research papers in his name and has presented more than 75 research papers in international and national journals and conferences. He has delivered a number of expert talks on e-Security and hacking in national and international conferences. Dr. Modi, a person with vibrancy, is an active life member of CSI, ACM IEEE, IACSIT, IACSI, and IAEng apart from his academic and industrial careers. As a consultant, he contributes to different system development projects with the IT industry and has carried out different government projects.

Dr. Nisarg Pathak is an astute and result-oriented professional with 10 years of experience in teaching and carving state, national, and international events like workshops, seminars, and conferences. Being a mathematics scholar and a computer science professional, he is actively involved in the research of data mining and big data analytics. He has a strong list of national and international publications to his name. Dr. Pathak is currently Associate Professor of Computer Science and Application at Narsinhbhai Institute of Computer Studies and Management affiliated to Kadi Sarva Vishvavidyalaya. He received his Ph.D. from Hemchandracharya North Gujarat University in Computer Science and his Master's in Mathematics from the same university. His other tenures include research fellow at Indian Statistical Institute, Kolkata, and Indian Institute of Science, Bengaluru.

Implementing the Logical Security Framework for E-Commerce Based on Service-Oriented Architecture

Ashish Kr. Luhach, Sanjay K. Dwivedi and Chandra K. Jha

Abstract Logical security of the modern E-commerce system is one of the major issues, effecting the growth of sophisticated E-commerce systems. Due to poor designing and configuration of the modern E-commerce's system, they lacked in quality attributes such as logical security. In the last decade, the number of highly equipped and trained intruders is increased significantly, due to increase in availability of computer systems and internet. These highly equipped and trained intruders are serious threat for the growing E-commerce industry. One of the leading Indian newspapers in 2013 reported about bugs on some of the most famous E-commerce websites such as Western Union and Facebook. This paper proposed a logical security framework for the small- and medium-sized E-commerce systems. The proposed logical security framework is inherited the benefits of service-oriented architecture and presents an analysis of the eminent security attacks which can be prevented. The proposed logical security framework is implemented and validated on osCommerce, an open source E-commerce.

Keywords Service-oriented architectures · Web services · Encrypted database · Security attacks · Legacy systems

1 Introduction

With the rapid development in information and communication technology (ICT), computers became the most valuable assets to the governing body. This rapid development in ICT transforms the physical existence of the markets and E-markets

A.Kr. Luhach (✉)
Dronacharya College of Engineering, Gurgaon, Haryana, India
e-mail: ashishluhach@gmail.com

S.K. Dwivedi
BBA University, Lucknow, U.P., India

C.K. Jha
Banasthali University, Jaipur, Rajasthan, India

© Springer Science+Business Media Singapore 2016
S.C. Satapathy et al. (eds.), *Proceedings of International Conference on ICT for Sustainable Development*, Advances in Intelligent Systems and Computing 409, DOI 10.1007/978-981-10-0135-2_1

introduced. Organizations start moving toward fast and dependable systems to cope up with the changing customer's demands from legacy organizations. These legacy systems have established very important tactical elements to the arrangements. The maintenance of legacy systems increased, and outweighs the benefit they generate to the organizations [1]. Legacy systems can prevent enterprises from transforming toward E-commerce, but customers are quick to take over. For instance, an organization implemented a home-grown E-commerce platform 10 years ago, which has already updated its legacy systems numerous times in the final ten. Updating the existing system means patching up new functionality and operability on top of already built legacy systems, now the organization ends up with a scheme which is not upgradable or even difficult to put back. These systems were tightly coupled with their legacy systems, and it is almost impossible to shift from these legacy systems to fast and reliable systems without involving the business [2]. These legacy systems are not compatible with modern days E-commerce systems, as today's E-commerce systems have demands of dynamic commercial enterprise applications, which are developed on the concepts of loose coupling and flexibility.

Service-oriented architecture (SOA) is an information technology advancement in which the already existing applications of an organization employed with the various services available in a network, for example, World Wide Web. These types of services which can be easily integrated with the existing one can be developed using SOA. The main problems for developing sophisticated E-commerce systems are integration and transmission of information but SOA can ease the above-mentioned problem as SOA has the feature of loose coupling. SOA has the feature of open standard protocols and excellent encapsulation; this makes SOA the apt pick to employ E-commerce system [3].

2 SOA and Traditional Software Architecture

At present, lot of research is going on and various conferences being conducted on E-commerce to bring all the academician and researcher together to provide help and support to the organizations, so these organizations can migrate toward modern days E-commerce. The general idea behind developing SOA is to incorporate software into services. SOA applications are embedded into network services using XML. Web services attract organizations and various businesses to get the benefits of connectivity through the networks [4]. Table 1 shows the evaluation of various parameters between SOA and component-oriented software architecture (COSA) [5].

Table 1 Evaluation between SOA and COSA

Service-oriented architecture (SOA)	Component-oriented software architecture (COSA)
Flexible and loose coupling	Tight coupling
Harmonious services	Blocked applications
Information-oriented	Object-oriented
Independent of the implementation details	Deep understanding of the implementation details required
Development of interaction and reusability	Long development cycle
Flow-oriented	Function-oriented
Isomeric technologies	Isomorphic technologies

3 Security Analysis of SOA-Based E-Commerce

For accessing the E-commerce system, the users have to authenticate himself as a transaction or enterprise user. If an attacker bypasses this security mechanism of E-commerce system he will be able to gain access to the core database and product search area of E-commerce system. Figure 1 shows the generic system prototype of E-commerce system [2]. Figure 1 shows that the transaction users get access to the E-commerce platform that consists of various business service components, for example, customer information service, etc. through a web server but the enterprise user can access the business service components by directly communicating with simple object access protocol (SOAP). E-commerce system is not only used for online transactions but also can be practiced as a sequential publication of services such as banking services. Most of the E-commerce systems consist of various business services, for example, a famous E-commerce, Policybazar.com provides various services to their customer such as motor and health insurance. These different business services can be managed by diverse vendor or by different departments within the same organization such as Policybazar.com has different departments for the motor and health insurance which manage their own business services. The different services managed by the different departments make an E-commerce a service-oriented heterogeneous system [6, 7]. On the basis of literature review conducted for this research, it is concluded that this heterogeneous E-commerce system will have design and security issues which are as follows.

3.1 Certificate Duplicity

To gain access to E-commerce system components, user must have a valid certificate of authentication. The authentication certificate is issued by identity management service (IMS) upon the subsequent submission of authorized login credentials by the

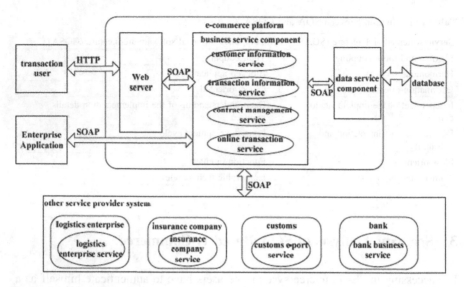

Fig. 1 System architecture of E-commerce platform

user. An intruder or attacker can generate the authorization certificate by gaining some kind of information from the user or through IMS.

3.2 Unsecure Protocols

All kind of communication between the user and E-commerce system is based on the protocols. The most common protocol used for this type of communication is hypertext transfer protocol (HTTP). In contrast, E-commerce requires a more sophisticated protocol for communication, when it comes to handle man-in-middle attacks by the attacker to access the important information from the communication. Man-in-middle attacks can be defined as the form of attacks in which intruder or attacker establishes a network connection with source and destination and relay messages between them giving sender and receiver an illusion that they are communicating directly [8].

3.3 No Filters Mentioned on the Application Level

Code or request filters may be used to block the security threats at the initial entry point of the communication with the E-commerce system. The absence of these kinds of filters at the application level can promote the attackers attempt, which may lead to a security attack. This type of attack which an attacker can perform in the absence of the code or request filters is cross-site scripting and remote file inclusion [9].

3.4 Database Security

Database is the backbone of any E-commerce system and lot of emphasis put on the database security. Attacker can penetrate into E-commerce database without breaking an extra shell of the security which was not there. Infected database may lead to leakage of the sensitive information of the customers and organization [10].

4 The Proposed Security Framework and Implementation for SOA-Based E-Commerce

The proposed logical security framework has the benefits of SOA designing approach. The proposed logical security framework is designed to secure the E-commerce system from known computing threats or attacks. Figure 2 shows the proposed logical security framework. In the proposed logical security framework both the transaction and enterprise users can communicate with the E-commerce system through SOAP instead of earlier or traditional frameworks in which only the enterprise users can directly communicate with E-commerce system through SOAP. The proposed logical security framework consists of a special code or request filtering security layer known as input sanitization and all transaction/enterprise users requesting to access the business service components of the E-commerce system are conceded through this additional security layer. Rule-based plug-in is defined in the proposed logical security framework which implements an additional security layer. For efficient monitoring of the incoming and outgoing packets, intrusion detection system (IDS) and intrusion protection system (IPS) are employed in the proposed logical security framework. With the help of IDS and IPS, each and every packet is monitored and infected packets can be blocked or traced easily. Figure 2 clearly shows that the database of the E-commerce is maintained on a completely different web server named as Server 2 in the proposed logical security framework. All the business service components are maintained on a different web server named as Server 1. The communication between Server 1 and Server 2 is closely monitored by the IDS and IPS, which actually create additional layer of defense from attacker attempt. By placing both business service components and database on different servers, it is very easy to disconnect the database from the E-commerce to ensure the minimal loss of the sensitive information either related to customers or organization.

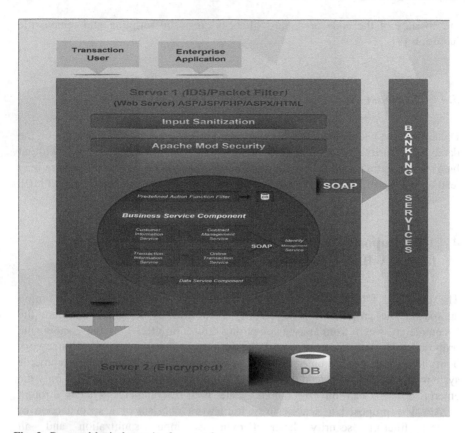

Fig. 2 Proposed logical security framework

5 Usage Scenario

In this part, we look at the usage scenario of the suggested framework. Figure 3 depicts the flow of events in this scenario and the interaction directions between different elements.

- The end user would like to access the E-commerce, for example, a user attempting to buy DVDs from an E-commerce site. He accesses the information related to DVDs under the movies section using his login credentials.
- The web application running on the E-commerce websites uses SOAP messaging and HTTPs for communication.
- The authentication assurance services, which are based on username and password pairs, permit the users to access the DVDs detailed information. The authentication assurance is managed by IMS. To access the business service component uses must be successfully through IMS.

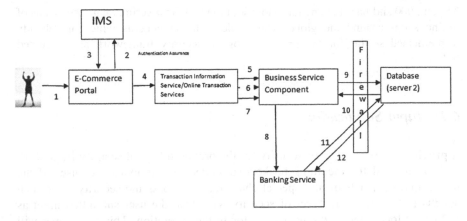

Fig. 3 Usage scenario of the proposed framework

- The user's service requests are first sanitized and then monitored by IDS/IPS before being forwarded to the database.
- The database is maintained on different servers and connected to business service components via firewall.
- Banking services can be accessed through business service components and connected to the database via firewall.

The presented scenario outlines how the proposed framework fulfills the security essential for today's E-commerce system. First, input sanitization solves the risk of certificate duplicity. Predefined actions, filters mentioned in proposed framework, are responsible for separating out the actions specified on web pages. The database is maintained onto a totally different server, which is monitored by IDS/IPS. The presentation of IDS/IPS will avoid the denial of service attempts.

6　Results and Discussion

The proposed logical security framework is validated on an open source E-commerce system, osCommerce. osCommerce provides free of cost online E-commerce solutions for various organizations. osCommerce allows organizations to arrange up their online stores without software costs or license fees. Till now, the osCommerce community provided more than 5,000 add-ons that are absolutely free of cost. osCommerce also provides customized solutions for individual clients equally well. osCommerce implemented with PHP as web scripting language and uses MySQL as database for their server data. The combination of PHP and MySQL allows osCommerce Online Merchant to run on whatever network server environment that supports PHP and MySQL, for example, Linux, Solaris, BSD, Mac OS X, and Microsoft Windows environments. osCommerce was started in

March 2000 and has since matured to a solution that is powering many thousands of online shops around the globe. The implementation benefits which are already implemented so far for the proposed logical security framework are discussed below.

6.1 Input Sanitization

It provides an extra layer of security for the proposed logical security framework as it verifies all the incoming packets submitted by the attacker or user. If the user request consists of any special characters to bypass the security layer such as '#@123*,' this extra layer of security will clean the user submitted input as '123' and forwarded to the next layer for further operation. This extra layer will resolve the issue of certificate duplicity. The highlighted text shown in Fig. 4 is a sample of infected input submitted by the attacker to bypass the security mechanism of an E-commerce system. The input sanitization layer of the proposed logical security framework will clean the infected input submitted by the user as shown in Fig. 5.

Fig. 4 Sample of infected input

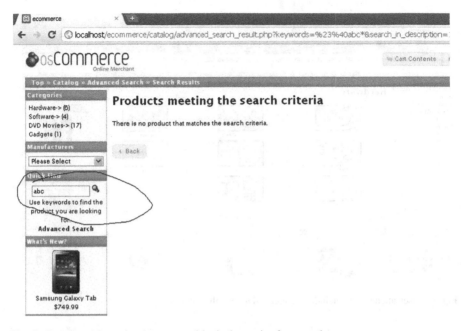

Fig. 5 Sanitizated input by the proposed logical security framework

6.2 Rule-Based Plug-in for Additional Security

This security layer provides an extra layer of security for the proposed logical security framework. This layer comes into play when the attacker successfully bypasses the initial layer of filtration which is input sanitization layer. This additional security layer is created by defining the various rules for accessing the business service component of the E-commerce system. These rules are just another filtering and blocking technique for the input submitted by the user. The user request is matched with the created rules and if matched with the created rules, then the user requested is blocked and rejected. Figure 6 shows the sample user attempt for retrieving the important information without proper means of authentication. Figure 7 shows that the users attempt is filtered and blocked by the proposed logical security framework. The user request was denied and web page remains the same as highlighted.

6.3 Predefined Action Filters

These types of action filters are used to block the attacker attempt of remote code execution or SQL injection. If somehow attacker bypasses the input sanitization and rule-based plug-in for additional security and able to execute his infected code, then

Fig. 6 User attempts to include the local files into their commands

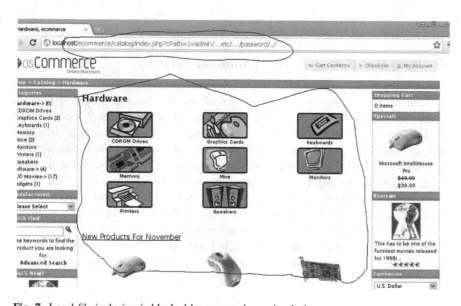

Fig. 7 Local file inclusion is blocked by proposed security design

these predefined action filters block the infected code or program executed by the attacker. Figure 8 shows user attempt of SQL Injection as infected URL and Fig. 9 shows the filtering of the same for the proposed logical security framework and the web page remains the same.

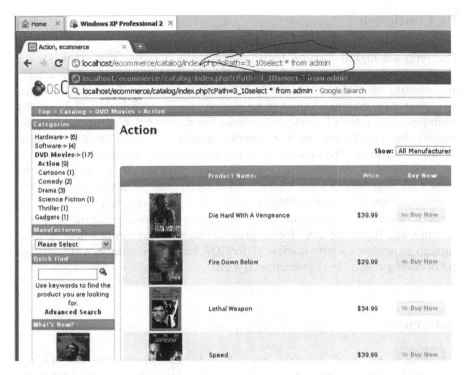

Fig. 8 User attempt of SQL injection

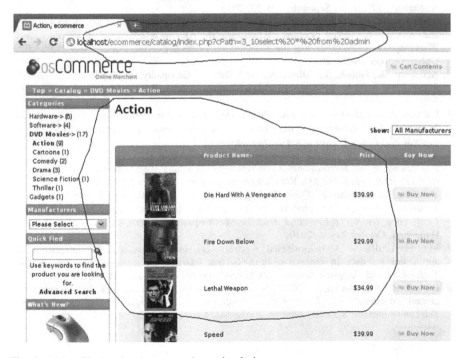

Fig. 9 Action filtering for the proposed security design

7 Conclusion

The proposed logical security framework provides a secure framework for the E-commerce systems from the major computing attacks. The framework is initially implemented on osCommerce, an open source E-commerce system. The implementation of the proposed logical security proves that it accomplishes all the quality attributes of the today's E-commerce system. For the validation of proposed logical security framework, the major computing attacks are tested on the proposed security framework. The main contribution and impact of this research is to align the benefits of SOA with E-commerce system. The proposed logical security framework helps enterprise to organize an absolute suite of amalgamated security architecture which protects SOA-based E-commerce. That place might still be chances of security compromise due to deficiency of protection at the operating system level. The future work for the proposed security framework would be to go through a complete security framework for SOA-based E-commerce, which include the operating system-level protection as well.

References

1. Luhach, A. Kr., Jha, C. K., & Dwivedi, S. K. (2013). Enterprise transformation to service oriented architecture from legacy applications. In *Proceeding of the 4th International Conference on Computer and Communication Technology (ICCCT-2013)* (pp. 39–42). Allahabad, U.P., India, September 20–22, 2013.
2. Al Sheikh, M. A., Aboalsamh, H. A., & Albarrak, A. (2011). Migration of legacy applications and services to service-oriented architecture (SOA). In *International Conference and Workshop on Current Trends in Information Technology (CTIT-2011)* (pp. 137–142). Dubai, October 26–27, 2011.
3. Arsanjani, A., Ghosh, S., Allam, A., Abdollah, T., Ganapathy, S., & Holley, K. (2008). SOMA: A method for developing service-oriented solutions. *IBM Systems Journal, 47*, 377–396.
4. Luhach, A. K., & Dwivedi, S. K. (2014). Designing and implementing a logical security framework for e-commerce system based on service oriented architectures. *International Journal of Advanced Information Technology, 4*(3), 1–10.
5. Xiong-Yi, L. (2009). Research and application of SOA in B2b electronic commerce. In *Proceeding of the International Conference on Computer Technology and Development (ICCTD-2009)* (pp. 649–653), Kota Kinabalu, Malaysia, November 15–18, 2009.
6. Yunliang, J., Xiongtao, Z., Qing, S., Jing, F., & Ning, Z. (2010). Design of e-government information management platform based on SOA framework. In *First International Conference on Networking and Distributed Computing (ICNDC-2010)* (pp. 165–169), Hangzhou, October 21–24, 2010.
7. Ma, H. (2010). A service-oriented e-government support platform for integration of application and data. In *Proceeding of the Second International Conference on Information Technology and Computer Science (ITCS)* (pp. 398–401). Kiev, July 24–25, 2010.
8. Baraka, R., & Madoukh, S. (2012). A conceptual SOA-based framework for e-government central database. In *International Conference on Computer, Information and Telecommunication Systems*. Amman, Jordan, May 14–16, 2012.

9. Trcek, D. (2006). *Managing information systems security and privacy*. Berlin: Springer.
10. Luhach, A. K., Jha, C. K., & Dwivedi, S. K. (2014). Designing a logical security framework for e-commerce system based on service oriented architectures. *International Journal of Soft Computing, 5*(2), 1–10.

Indian Sign Language Translator Using Kinect

Pratik H. Suvagiya, Chintan M. Bhatt and Ritesh P. Patel

Abstract Though Indian sign language (ISL) translation remained under examination for numerous years, still it is very difficult to implement in real-time systems. The background and brightness disturb the skeleton tracing and make the ISL translation very hard. Microsoft Kinect Xbox 360 is capable of giving in-depth vision image and color vision image of everything in front of it, created on which the skeleton body action can be tracked more precise and easier to get depth coordinate of the skeleton. So that nearest matrix matching algorithm of each ISL word is coordinated and matched among input data to get the result.

Keywords Kinect · Sign language · SimpleOpenNI · Indian sign language translator · Sign language translator

1 Introduction

In this world many people live, while some of them are differently abled people, they cannot speak and hear. Also, they have different language to communicate with others, known as sign language.

P.H. Suvagiya (✉) · C.M. Bhatt · R.P. Patel
Chandubhai S. Patel Institute of Technology, Charotar University of Science
and Technology, Changa, Anand, Gujarat, India
e-mail: pratiksuvagia20@gmail.com

C.M. Bhatt
e-mail: bhattchintan70@gmail.com

R.P. Patel
e-mail: riteshpatel.ce@charusat.ac.in

© Springer Science+Business Media Singapore 2016   15
S.C. Satapathy et al. (eds.), *Proceedings of International Conference
on ICT for Sustainable Development*, Advances in Intelligent Systems
and Computing 409, DOI 10.1007/978-981-10-0135-2_2

Fig. 1 Kinect device

Fig. 2 Main functions of the demo system

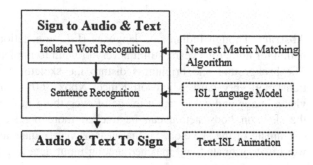

Sign language is a vital communication way among differently abled people. Recently, sign language has been broadly planned to establish on many input devices, such as web camera, data glove, etc. [1, 2]. Though data glove-established ISL translator works better for huge numbers of signs, the data glove is too costly. With a web camera ISL translator, the main advantages are accurateness of the system and body movements. However, it is tough for backgrounds and brightness. On the flip side, ISL translator's goal is to implement good and precise ISL translation using the depth images value acquired by *Microsoft Kinect Xbox 360* Fig. 1.

The simple plan of the ISL translator system is specified in Fig. 2. The nearest matrix matching algorithm characterization comparable to the input ISL word coordinates is recognized by skeleton body tracing facility provide by Kinect software development kit [3]. While dealing with the variance of skeleton movement speed, a pattern matrix is completed to achieve the normalized input pattern matrix coordinates by balancing the acquired size of the entire matrix.

To achieve the final result, an adjustment among the input pattern matrix and storage pattern matrix are required. And finally, the matching results are figured out based on the maximum hit evolution to give the translation output (Fig. 3).

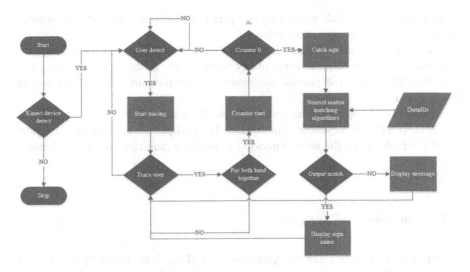

Fig. 3 Flowchart

2 Kinect

Indian sign language translator uses a hardware device called *Kinect for windows.* Kinect device was developed by Microsoft. Microsoft introduced Kinect on November 10, 2010 and is widely used in the Xbox.

Also Microsoft provides Kinect for developing commercial applications. It is a programable device so that we can program it based on our requirement. Kinect gives *x*, *y*, and depth coordinate of 21 joints of human skeleton. Also it is responsible for tracing the human skeleton. Kinect can trace two skeletons at a time.

Through Kinect device we can catch sign, normalize it, and store the sign pattern to the data file. Also, find an input sign into appropriate word through applying *nearest matrix matching* algorithm on the data. Also, we have to use the *SimpleOpenNI 2.2* API of Java, which is responsible to connect Kinect in the system. Moreover, we use the *JavaFX* API for the media player and to play the video of the sign. We use *processing-2* tool for some graphics, and some processing data. For text to voice, we use *speech freetts 1.2.2* API of Java.

3 Proposed ISL Translator System

Our projected nearest matrix matching algorithm, an ISL translator system, is making a strong communication bridge for differently abled people and persons.

The ISL translator system contains two main modules: Sign to Text module, this module is used to translate sign language into text as well as speech and Text to

Sign module, this module is used for any person to communicate with a differently abled person via corresponding video.

Sign to Text module contains single-word translation and sentence translation. In sentence translation, all sign words of any sentence will be the input constantly and after that ISL system will provide the results by maximum hit count of all words of the sentence.

In the Text to Sign module, a video shows the matching ISL word or sentence for the text input by keyboard. The differently abled people give an instant replay via ISL translator. So the normal person can also communicate with the differently abled person.

3.1   Flowchart of System

System flow is once you start the application, it will check the necessity required for the system. When user skeleton is detected, then it will start to trace it. Now you have to put your hands together and wait until the counter reaches down to 0. Once it is completed, it will start to take input for 1.5 s sign.

Apply nearest matrix matching algorithm on that data and give appropriate output. In between, when the user is lost, then the system will start detecting the user. Here the user is an important part of the system, once the user is lost then you have to follow all the process once again. All Indian sign is taken from the Indian web portal.

3.2   Implementation and Result Comparison

The ISL translator system was implemented in Java and *SimpleOpenNI* API of Java Kinect library. We cached data through *Kinect* IR depth sensor and IR Emitter, we apply nearest matrix matching algorithm, match with stored data and display output in string format as well as audio.

The application requires an Kinect device and computer system, USB Kinect adapter. This application does not require any database provider. We will use a text file for a data storage. For text to sign, we have a video file containing all signs.

Note

1. The video file name must be a sign name
2. The video file extension must be .MP4.

3.3 Nearest Matrix Matching Algorithm

```
String Nearest Matrix Matching (String In_Z, String In_Y String In_Z) {
    While (Data_File != Empty){
    Data_X:=Result Set (X);
    Data_Y:=Result Set (Y);
    Data_Z:=Result Set (Z);
    Integer High:=Low:=Med:=0;
    Token Generation (In_X, In_Y, In_Z, Data_X, Data_Z, Data_Z);
    While (Token) {
            If (In_N-30 <= Data_N && IN_N+30 >= Data_N)
                    High++;
            If (In_N-60 <= Data_N && IN_N+60 >= Data_N)
                    Med++;
            If (In_N-100 <= Data_N && IN_N+100 >= Data_N)
                    Low++;
    }
    Array Temp [] [] [] []: =Temp [Result Set No] [High] [Med] [Low];
    High:=Low:=Med:=0;
    Sort (Temp);
    Return Result Set (Temp [0]);
    }
}
```

4 Output

Once you start the application, the home page of the system looks like this.
   In this you have three options.

- Sign to Text translation
- Text to Sign translation
- Exit

   The image (Fig. 4) is the home page of the system.
   Here you have four options, Sign to Text, Text to Sign, about us, and Exit. Once you click on the Sign to Text, you have another four options **Find Sign**, **Insert Sign**, **Text to Sign**, and **Home**.

4.1 Sign to Text

When you click on Find Sign, system checks whether Kinect is connected or not. If connected, then starts to color camera, IR Emitter, IR depth camera of Kinect.

Fig. 4 Home page of the system

The system starts to find user and when the user is found, it starts to trace the user until the user is lost. Now you have to come in the range between the given coordinates, so that you can get maximum accuracy of the system. Your current coordinates display in continually in system, you have to adjust yourself.

When you are in the range of the coordinates, your head is fixed in that position. and then you have to do all signs from the same position.

Now read instructions and follow the given steps.

1. Wait until system detect kinect device, human user, human skeleton.
2. Put your hands together.
3. Get your position and wait until count reaches down to 0.
4. When the system says start, you have to start doing the sign until the system says to stop. If your sign is completed before stop, then you have to stay at the end of you sign position.
5. Wait for output.

Once you complete your sign, the system checks for input, applies nearest matrix matching algorithm on data storage and then finds output of the sign in word format. Whatever output is found will be displayed and given to the Text to Speech converter, which the system will speak.

Note If your output is any symbol, then Text to Speech converter can not speak it.

The image, (Fig. 5), is the output of your inputted sign.

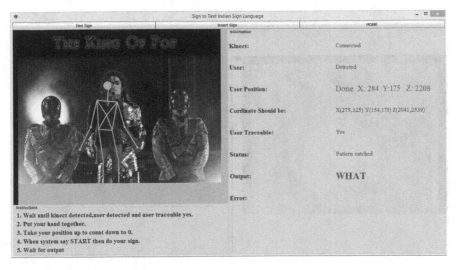

Fig. 5 Output of the sign—Sign to Text module

4.2 Insert Sign

Now you can go to insert sign by click in Insert Sign.

You have to follow the same instruction which you followed in Find Sign module. The only one change is there that you just have to write the name of that sign in the given text box before starting your sign.

Now read the instructions and follow the given steps.

1. Write your sign name in the textbox.
2. Wait until Kinect detect, user detect, and user traceable yes.
3. Put your hands together.
4. Get your position and wait until count reaches down to 0.
5. When the system says start you have to start the sign until the system says to stop If your sign is completed before stop, then you have to stay at the end of you sign position.

4.3 Text to Sign

Now you can go to Text to Sign module by clicking on Text to Sign button. You can also go to the home page and click on Text to Sign button to reach the same module.

This module provides functionality to normal people so that they can communicate with differently abled people. Once you go to Text to Sign module, it will

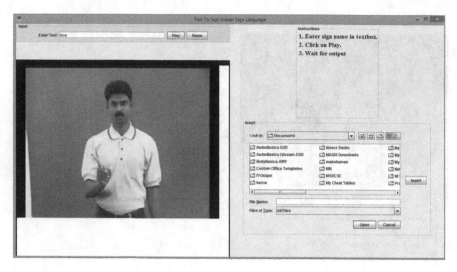

Fig. 6 Text to Text module

play a smiley video in media player with a set of programs. You have to write a sign name in the text box and click on the play button.

The system will find the video for that sign, if found then the media player plays the video. If there is no videos found for that sign name the system says "sign video not found".

4.4 Insert Video for Sign

In the same module, you can also add new video sign through this module. You have to select your video file and click the submit button.

Note

1. Your file name should be your sign name.
2. Your file extension should be .MP4.

The image in (Fig. 6) is for Text to Sign module.

5 Conclusion

The ISL translator fills the huge communication gap between hearing-impaired community and normal persons. Through ISL system, they can communicate with any person and vice versa so that differently abled people will feel good and happy.

This system can be applied in shopping malls, traveling stations, education systems, healthcare systems, etc.

Using this system, differently able people can easily communicate with normal person and vise versa.

References

1. Neha, P., & Shrushti, R. et al. (2015). Study of sign language translation using gesture recognition. *2*, 264–266.
2. Kyatanavar, R.D., & Futane, R.P. (2012). Comparative study of sign language recognition system. *2*, 1–3.
3. Han, J., & Xu, D. (2013). Enhanced computer vison with microsoft kinect sensor: A review. *43*, 1318–1331.

Formal Transformation of UML Diagram: Use Case, Class, Sequence Diagram with Z Notation for Representing the Static and Dynamic Perspectives of System

Monika Singh, A.K. Sharma and Ruhi Saxena

Abstract The two most critical phases of SDLC are the specification and the designing phase as they involve the transformation of the semantics from real world domain to computer software systems. Unified Modelling Language (UML) has been accepted as blue print for design and specification of software critical systems. But, UML structures have the weakness in preciously defining the semantics of a system. Any misinterpretation in safety critical system's specification may risks loss of lives. Formal methods are mathematical tools and techniques which are proven very adequate, principally, at requirement specification and design level. However, formal methods are not welcomed because of rigorous use of mathematics. Therefore, a bridge is required between UML and formal methods to overcome the above insufficiencies. The endeavour of this paper is to propose a new approach by integrating UML and Z notation, a formal specification language. The main focus of this paper is on transforming the UML diagram: use case diagram, class diagram and sequence diagram to Z Schema for capturing both the syntax and semantics, particularly for safety critical system. The resultant formal model of the approach are analyzed and verified by using Z/Eves tool.

Keywords Safety critical system · UML · Z notation · Schema · Z/Eves

M. Singh (✉) · A.K. Sharma
College of Engineering and Technology, Mody University of Science and Technology, Lakshmangarh 332311, India
e-mail: Dhariwal.monika@gmail.com

A.K. Sharma
e-mail: srashok2002@yahoo.com

R. Saxena
Department of Computer Science and Engineering, Thapar University, Patiala 147004, India
e-mail: ruhi.saxena2011@gmail.com

© Springer Science+Business Media Singapore 2016
S.C. Satapathy et al. (eds.), *Proceedings of International Conference on ICT for Sustainable Development*, Advances in Intelligent Systems and Computing 409, DOI 10.1007/978-981-10-0135-2_3

1 Introduction

The advancements of the computing, control and communication technologies increased the complexity of hardware and software systems such as computing critical systems, automated systems, distributed system, networked or embedded systems, etc. Due to the increase in complexity, the likelihood of errors and flaws in the systems grown and design of ultimate bug-free systems becomes more difficult. Design of such a complex system can be possible with the help of advanced mathematical methodologies and step by step design process. One of the best ways of achieving this goal is by using the formal methods. Formal methods are mathematical tool and techniques that use First order predicates, Discrete and set theory. Formal methods are proposed to systematize and introduce stubbornness into all the phases of software development life cycle. This helps us to refrain from overlooking critical issues, form basis for consistency, and provide standard means to record a range of assumptions and decisions, among many related activities. Formal specifications assist the understanding required to integrate the various phases of SDLC by means of providing precise and unambiguous description mechanisms, into a successful venture.

The Unified Modelling Language (UML) is a graphical language for visualizing, specifying, constructing and documenting software-intensive systems. UML facilitate a standard way of writing system's blueprints, covering conceptual things, classes written in a specific programming language, database schemes and reusable software components. It is a standard notation, used by everyone involved in software production, deployment and maintenance. Exploitation of notation language, like UML, may aid communication between all participants in the development process [1].

The graphical modelling elements and relationships defined for UML diagrams are sometimes too limited for certain modelling tasks [2]. The following are the problems with the UML diagrams:

- Due to graphical notation, UML structures are prone to cause errors.
- At design level of software-intensive system, due to hidden semantics of UML, ambiguities might be commenced.
- Since the System Under Test (SUT) may be illustrated by more than one notation or diagram which further cause inconsistency or ambiguity in design of proposed system.
- As the UML model may have multiple elucidations that means, the recipient of the design may not find what exactly the developer(s) want to put in the diagrams [3].

To overcome the above-mentioned issues with UML, an integrated approach is used. The new approach combines two methodologies, i.e. Formal Methods and UML. The initial requirements are captured by using graphical modelling language UML and formal methods are used to verify the three C's, i.e. correctness, completeness and consistency in the design specification of the safety critical system.

Z notation [4] is one of the offsprings in the armoury of formal method which we are going to be used in this research paper. In this paper, three UML diagram namely, (i) Use case diagram, (ii) Class diagram and (iii) Sequence diagram are transformed to Z Schema which would be further verified by using Z/Eves tool for syntax and semantics rules.

2 Literature Review

Lots of work has been done in direction of integration of approaches [5–10] but there does not exist much work on linking UML class diagrams, sequence diagram with Z specification language. This is due to weakness of UML diagram in which the buried semantics cannot be transformed easily into formal notations. In this section, the closely related work is discussed. For instance, in paper [11] Alloy Constraint Analyzer tool is used for supporting the narration of a system in which the relational structures are involved in state space. Another approach is used in [12] where XML is used to analyse visualize Timed Communicating Object Z (TCOZ) models with a multi-paradigm language, into different UML diagrams. The Paper [13] advocates a pathway for creation of SQL tables and code according to UML diagram for Z notation. In article [14], a case study is discussed for Cooperative Composition Modelling Language (CCML) by a formal verification method. Zafar et al. [15] depicts the safety properties of moving block railway interlocking system using Z notation. In paper [16], an integration approach of B method and UML is presented in. The paper [17], explains the reliability issues using fuzzy logic and petri nets. Heiner and Heisel [18], aims on relationship between Z notation and Perti net for safety critical system. In paper [19], a tool is developed which takes UML class diagram in the form of petal files, ASCII format files generated by Rational Rose and evaluates it automatically and produces a list of comments. In article [20], an ontology based formal method is proposed for Activity Model Moreover, a comparative study of Z notation, Fuzzy logic, UML, state-charts and petri nets has been done by taking a simple case study on commerce system in article [17]. Some other related work is mentioned in [13, 21–24].

3 Tools and Methodology

3.1 UML

The Unified Modelling Language (UML) [1, 3, 25] has become a de facto standard notation for analyzing and designing of software system. It has been observed that graphical representation of model is easily accessible and understandable to the user. The primary gap between the developer and the user has been easily fulfilled by the graphical description. In UML, Use Case diagram defines the behaviour of a system. Classes in UML diagrams are used to capture the information about the

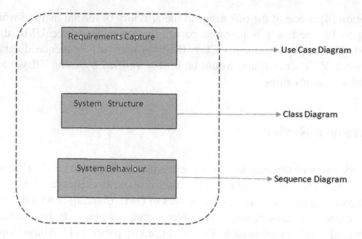

Fig. 1 UML diagram at various stages of software system development

system to be developed. Figure 1, explains the role of use case diagram, class diagram and of sequence diagram in context to the system to be developed.

3.2 Formal Methods

Formal methods are the mathematical based techniques which incorporating accuracy in specification and in development. Consequently, the utter need of formal method is to provide verification of software systems particularly Safety critical System. Numerous of formal languages and techniques exist to treat different types of properties at different levels of the development process, but they are highly recommended especially in the early phases of the development process. There are two techniques to prove the properties of a system [26–30].

3.2.1 Theorem Proving

This technique is used when the system is specified through mathematical definitions. Such system is verified using automatic/semi-automatic theorem provers, which are based on a library of axioms and a set of predefined inference rules. Theorem proving is unrestricted to the size of the state space, and hence consequently can be applied to models with a large number of states, or even to models whose number of states is not determined.

Automated theorem proving allows to prove the properties of the system automatically, without human intervention. This technique is very expensive in terms of time and resources and is not practical for many complex specifications. Therefore, there exist interactive theorem provers which allow the designer to guide the proof.

For example, Z/Eves [31] are a semi-automatic theorem prover, which allows to prove theorems for verifying specifications written in Z notation [4]. After specifying the system using Z Schemas and writing a Z theorem, the designer helps the prover by providing reduction commands (e.g. simplify, reduce, prove by reduce, prove by rewrite), commands for applying theorems, definitions and lemma (e.g. apply, try, invoke, invoke predicate, Use), quantifiers (e.g. Instantiate, Prenex), etc.

3.2.2 Model Checking

In this technique, the desired system is treated as a set of different states which in turns related to each other by a defined set of transitions. Further, Model checking techniques; introduce an algorithm which helps in verifying the satisfaction of a property followed by specifying the list of possible reachable states that a system could enter during its execution. The effectiveness of model checking depends on the size of the space of reachable states.

However, formal methods can also be classified based on application area of method in two categories:

Model-oriented methods: The specification of system consists in defining a model of the system in terms of mathematical structures such as relations, functions, set and sequences. VDM, B and Z notation, Petri net, Communicating Sequential processes (CSP), Calculus of Communicating Systems (CCS) and I/O automata.

Property-oriented methods: The specification of the system consists in defining some properties, usually in terms of axioms that should be satisfied by the system. OBJ and LOTOS are formal languages that belong to this category.

3.3   Z Specification Language

Z Notation is the oldest language in the empire of formal specification languages and has been developed at Oxford University.

The Z notation is based on first order predicate logic [32] and Zermelo-Fraenkel (ZF) set theory [33] used for specifying behaviour of abstract data types and sequential programs. Z language is used for model-oriented specification through special features of the language provided for this reason and called "schemas". Schemas are used to describe both static and dynamic perspectives of a system separately [4].

3.3.1   Terminology Used in Z Notation

- A **data invariant** is a condition that is true throughout the execution of the system.
- In Z specification, the **state** is represented by the system's stored data.

- **Operation** is an action that takes place within a system and read or writes data. Three types of conditions are associated with operation:
- An **invariant** define what is guaranteed not to change.
- A **precondition** defines the circumstances in which a particular operation is valid.
- The **postcondition** of an operation define what is guaranteed to be true upon completion of an operation. This is defined by its effect on data.

3.4 Z/Eves Tool

Z/Eves is an interactive tool which compose, check and analyse Z specifications [31]. This tool proposes two interfaces—a graphical interface and a command-line interface. Both interfaces provide support for type checking, typesetting and theorem proving. Specifications can either be entered manually, or loaded as a Latex file. Once the schema has been drawn, it is saved by using file extension ".zev"; if you are using graphical interfaces or use command-line interface using Latex style.

4 Formal Analysis of UML Diagrams

In this section, the formal analysis of UML diagram: use case diagram, Class diagram and sequence Diagram has been presented. In the first part, the proposed approach is discussed. Then transformation of UML diagram to Z Schema is done in following section.

4.1 Proposed Approach

See Fig. 2.

4.2 Z Schema for UML Diagram

Once the requirements are gathered, by using UML the use case, class and the sequence diagrams are implemented. For capturing the static view, use case and class diagrams are used and that to dynamic view, the sequence diagrams are proposed. (For reference, the UML diagram of the Road Traffic Management System (RTMS) is attached in Appendix: UML diagram).

Fig. 2 Proposed approach for
road traffic management
system using Z notation

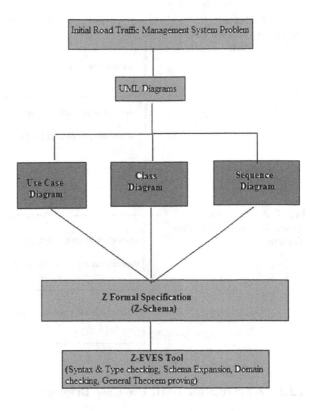

4.2.1 Z Schema of UML Class Diagram

The Class Diagram is composed of the classes and relationship between them.
A class diagram has three constituents; a class name, attributes and the operations.
In our proposed approach, a Z Schema is proposed for a general class having some
attributes and methods associated with it. Here three schemas are shown: for class
diagram, for relationship and the last one is for operations (Figs. 3, 4 and 5).

Fig. 3 Z schema for class
diagram

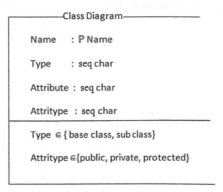

Fig. 4 Z schema for relationship between classes in class diagram

```
——— Relationship ———
reltype       : seq char
cardinality   : ℙℤ
————————————————
reltype ∈ {association, aggregation, generalization, dependency}
cardinality ∈ { (0....1), (1), (0.....*1), (*), (1......*) }
————————————————
```

Fig. 5 Z schema for operations (methods) in class diagram

```
——— Operation ———
Operation Name   : seq char
Visibilitytype   : seq char
————————————————
Visibilitytype ∈ { public, private, protected}
————————————————
```

4.2.2 Z Schema for UML Use Case Diagram

Use case diagram depicts the main functional requirements of the proposed system. It facilitates the functionality that the system will provide and the users who will communicate with the system to use that functionality (Figs. 6 and 7).

In relationship schema, we use two stereotypes; extend and include, where the first one is used when we have to show some alternate behaviour and the later one is used to include common behaviour in use case diagrams.

Fig. 6 Z schema for use case diagram

```
——— Use Case Diagram ———
Actor          : seq char
Relationship   : ℙ ℤ
Event Id       : ℙℤ
————————————————
Relationship Id = dom relationship
Event ID        = dom Event
————————————————
```

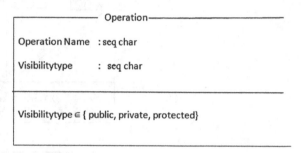

Fig. 7 Z schema for
relationship between various
use cases in use case diagram

```
┌─────────────── Relationship ───────────────
│
│  Actor      :  seq char
│
│  Rel Type   :  seq char
│
│  UC Id      :  ℙZ
│
├─────────────────────────────────────────────
│
│  Rel Type ∈ {⟨⟨extend⟩⟩, ⟨⟨include⟩⟩}; extend ∩ include = ∅
│
│  UC Id   = dom Use Case
│
```

Fig. 8 Z schema for
sequence diagram

```
┌─────────────── Sequence Diagram ───────────────
│
│  Object Name   :   ℙ Object Name
│
│  Link          :   seq char
│
│  MessType      :   seq char
│
├──────────────────────────────────────────────────
│
│   Object Name ∈ dom objectname
│
│   MessType ∈ {simple, synchronous, asynchronous, timeout}
│
│   Link     ∈ {Horizontal, Vertical}
│
```

4.2.3 Z Schema for Uml Sequence Diagram

The sequence diagram depicts the system behaviour. The Sequence diagram consists of the participant's name (More often known as Objectname:) and the type of message through which they communicates with the other objects in given system (Fig. 8).

5 Conclusion and Future Work

The Behavioural specification, i.e. describing how things change is the core characteristic of Z specification but at the same times the loss part of UML. In UML, we can articulate state changes, collaboration and workflow, but we cannot illustrate how objects change in terms of transformations. The positive part of UML is simplicity and the negative side of Z is a lack of graphical notation. Therefore, combining the two approaches for safety critical application to cover ambiguity, identifying consistency and enhancing completeness is indeed needed. This is a part of our project, "Formal analysis of safety critical System: Road Traffic Management System", by making use of Z notation and later on verified by Z/Eves tool for syntax and semantics obligation. In future, we will make schemas for use case diagram, class diagram and sequence diagram particularly for Actors involved in RTMS system, i.e. Traffic police, vehicle owner and admin and later on verified them by theorem prover Z/Eves tool.

Acknowledgments Authors are thankful to College of Engineering and Technology, Mody University of Science and Technology for providing the facility to carry out the research work.

Appendix: UML Diagram

1. Use case Diagram for Road Traffic Management System (RTMS)

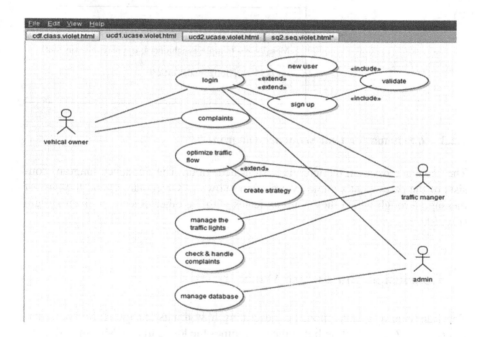

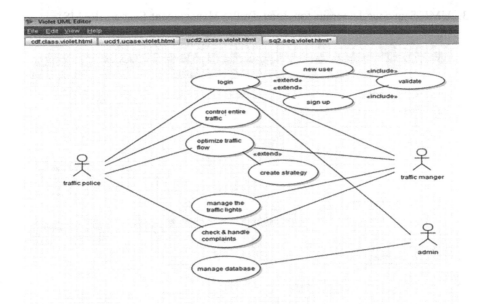

2. Class Diagram for Road Traffic Management System (RTMS)

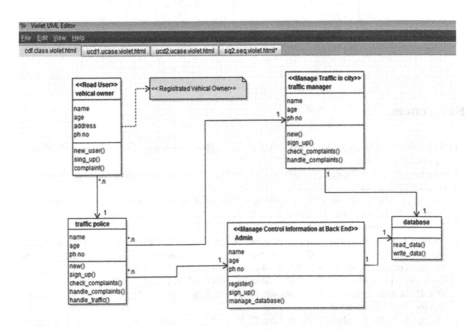

3. UML Sequence Diagram for Road Traffic Management System (RTMS)

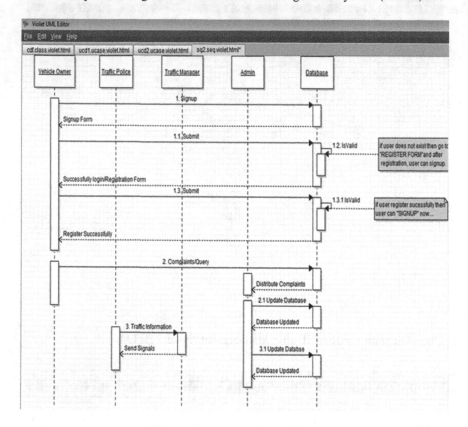

References

1. Selic, B., & Rumbaugh, J. (1998). *UML for modeling complex real-time systems.* Technical report, Object Time.
2. Rumbaugh, J., Jacobson, I., & Booch, G. (2006). *The unified modeling language reference manual* (2nd edn.).
3. Ali, N. H., Shukur, Z., & Idris, S. (2007). A Design of an assessment system for UML class diagram. In *International Conference on Computational Science and Applications* (pp. 539–546). Kuala Lumpur, 26–29 August 2007.
4. Spivey, J. M. (1989). *The Z notation: a reference manual.* Englewood Cliffs: Prentice-Hall.
5. Borges, R., & Mota, A. (2003). Integrating UML and Formal Methods. *Electronic Notes in Theoretical Computer Science, 84,* 97–112.
6. Brendan, M., & Dong, J. S. (1998). Blending object-Z and timed CSP: an introduction to TCOZ. In *Proceedings of International Conference on Software Engineering* (pp. 95-104). Kyoto, 19–25 April 1998.
7. Changchien, W. S., Shen, J. J., & Lin, T. Y. (2002). A preliminary correctness evaluation model of object-oriented software based on UML. *Journal of Applied Sciences, 2*(3), 356–365. doi:10.3923/jas.2002.356.365.

8. Dennis, A., Wixom, B. H., & Tegarden, D. (2005). *Systems analysis and design with UML* (3rd ed., p. 576). New York: Wiley.
9. Derakhshandeh, Z., Ladani, B. T., & Nematbakhsh, N. (2008). Modeling and combining access control policies using constrained policy graph. *Journal of Applied Sciences, 8*, 3561–3571. doi:10.3923/jas.2008.3561.3571.
10. Object-Z/CSP Specification. (2000). In *Proceedings of 2nd International Conference on Integrated Formal Methods* (Vol. 1945, pp. 194–213), London: Springer Verlag.
11. Ehikioya, S. A., & Ola, B. (2004). A comparison of formalisms for electronic commerce systems. In *Proceedings of International Conference on Computational Cybernetics* (pp. 253–258). Vienna, 30 August–1 September 2004.
12. Gervais, F., Frappier, M. & Laleau, R. (2005). Synthesizing B specifications from EB3 attribute definitions. In *Proceedings of 5th International Conference on Integrated Formal Methods*(Vol. 3771, pp. 207–226), Berlin: Springer.
13. Moeini, A., & Mesbah, R. O. (2009). Specification and development of database applications based on Z and SQL. In *Proceedings of International Conference on Information Management and Engineering* (pp. 399–405), Kuala Lumpur, 3–5 April 2009.
14. Hall, A. (2002). Correctness by construction: integrating formality into a commercial development process. *Proceedings of International Symposium of Formal Methods Europe, 2391*, 139–157.
15. Zafar, N. A., Khan, S. A., & Araki, K. (2012). Towards the safety properties of moving block railway interlocking system. *International Journal of Innovative Computing, Information and Control (ICIC International)*, 5677–5690.
16. Hamdy, K. E., Elsoud, M. A., & El-Halawany, A. M. (2011). UML-based web engineering framework for modeling web application. *Journal of Software Engineering, 5*(2), 49–63. doi:10.3923/jse.2011.49.63.
17. Ma, Z. M. (2008). Fuzzy conceptual information modeling in UML data model. In *International Symposium on Computer Science and Computational Technology* (pp. 331-334), Shanghai, 20–22 December 2008. doi:10.1109/ISCSCT.2008.353.
18. Heiner, M., & Heisel, M. (1999). Modeling safety critical systems with Z and petri-nets. In *Proceedings of International Conference on Computer Safety, Reliability and Security* (pp. 361–374), London: Springer-Verlag, 26–28 October 1999. doi:10.1007/3-540-48249-0_31.
19. Leading, H., & Souquieres, J. (2002). Integration of UML and B specification techniques: systematic transformation from OCL expressions into B. In *Proceedings of 9th Asia- Pacific Software Engineering Conference* (p. 495), Gold Coast, 4–6 December 2002. doi:10.1109/APSEC.2002.1183053.
20. Liu, & Chen, C. (2006). An improved quasi-static scheduling algorithm for mixed data-control embedded software. *Journal of Applied Sciences, 6*(7), 1571–1575. doi:10.3923/jas.2006.1571.1575.
21. Hasan, O., & Tahar, S. (2007). Verification of probabilistic properties in the HOL theorem prover. *Proceedings of the Integrated Formal Methods, 4591*, 333–352. doi:10.1007/978-3-540-73210-5_18.
22. He, X. (2000). Formalizing UML class diagrams: a hierarchical predicate transition net approach. In *Proceedings of 24th Annual International Computer Software and Applications Conference* (pp. 217–222), Taipei, 25–28 October 2000.
23. Miles, R., & Hamilton, K. (2006). Learning UML 2.0 (1st ed., p. 288). Sebastopol: O'Reilly Media.
24. Mostafa, A. M., Manal, A. I., Hatem, E. B., & Saad, E. M. (2007). Toward a formalization of UML2.0 meta-model using Z specifications. In *Proceedings of 8th ACIS International Conference on Software Engineering, Artificial Intelligence, Networking and Parallel/ Distributed Computing*, Qingdao (Vol. 3, pp. 694–701). doi:10.1109/SNPD.2007.508.
25. Gherbi, A., & Khendek, F. (2006).UML profile for real-time system and their application. *Journal of Object Technology, 5*.

26. Shroff, M., & France, R. B. (1997). Towards formalization of uml class structures in Z. In 21*st International Conference on Computer Software and Applications* (pp. 646–651). Washington, 11–15 August 1997.
27. Sun, J., Dong, J. S., Liu, J. & Wang, H. (2001). A XML/XSL approach to visualize and animate TCOZ. In *Proceedings of* 8*th Asia-Pacific Software Engineering Conference* (pp. 453–460). Macao, 4–7 December 2001.
28. Than, X., Miao, H., & Liu, L. (2004). Formalizing semantics of UML statecharts with Z. In *Proceedings of* 4*th International Conference on Computer and Information Technology* (pp. 1116–1121). Wuhan, 14–16 September 2004.
29. Wing, J. M. (1990). A Specifier, Introduction to Formal Methods. *Computer Journal, 23*(9), 8–24. doi:10.1109/2.58215.
30. Xiuguo, Z., & Liu, H. (2011). Formal Verification for CCML Based Web Service Composition. *Information Technology Journal, 10*(9), 1692–1700.
31. Saaltink, M. (1999). The Z/EVES 2.0 User's Guide.
32. Benveniste, M. Writing operational semantics in Z: A structural approach, pp. 164–188.
33. Spivey, J. M. (1988, January) Understanding Z: a specification language and its formal semantics. In *Cambridge Tracts in Theoretical Computer Science* (Vol. 3). Cambridge: Cambridge University Press.

A Survey of Android Malware Detection Strategy and Techniques

Mohit Sharma, Meenu Chawla and Jyoti Gajrani

Abstract The expeditious growth of Android malwares has posed a serious challenge in front of researchers. The researchers are continuously proposing countermeasures and developing tools to mitigate against such attacks. In this paper, widely used techniques that have been proposed recently by researchers have been explored. The key contributions of each of these techniques along with their limitations have been analyzed. All these techniques were compared based on nine parameters and it was identified that Mobile Sandbox tool is the best when time factor is not considered because it possess the capability of both a static and dynamic analysis, native API call tracking and web accessibility. If time factor is considered, then Dendroid performs best among all. This is due to the reason that it applies text mining to get the signature of malware and it can also classify unknown malware sample through 1-NN classifier.

Keywords Android · Malware · Static · Dynamic · Survey · Comparison of techniques

1 Introduction

The Internet has evolved from a basic communication medium to new forms of interactions and marketplaces for the sale of products and services. In recent years, smartphone sales have tremendously increased due to Android's popularity as its

M. Sharma (✉) · M. Chawla
Department of CSE, Maulana Azad National Institute of Technology, Bhopal, India
e-mail: mohitsharma2507@gmail.com

M. Chawla
e-mail: meenuchawla@manit.ac.in

J. Gajrani
Department of CSE, Government Engineering College, Ajmer, India
e-mail: jyotigajrani@gmail.com

© Springer Science+Business Media Singapore 2016
S.C. Satapathy et al. (eds.), *Proceedings of International Conference on ICT for Sustainable Development*, Advances in Intelligent Systems and Computing 409, DOI 10.1007/978-981-10-0135-2_4

open source and easily customizable operating system (OS) attracts many developers. Android apps are readily available on Google Play, and various third-party app stores. Apps are installed directly on the user's smartphone. Official Android market place and certain popular third-party repositories do not distribute executable code. The increasing popularity of Android OS has attracted malware developers to exploit android vulnerability. Attackers spread malicious content by repackaging (inserting malicious content) common Android applications. A malicious software or malware reflects the harmful intent of an attacker. Third-party app stores distribute Android malware by hosting infected copies of benign applications and malware by inserting obfuscated code, repackaging of popular apps in order to surpass the existing protection mechanisms. The drastic effects of Android malware include privacy compromise, data leakage, spoofing, resource drainage, sending SMS to premium-rated numbers, etc (Fig. 1).

According to F-Secure report April 2014 [2], 97 % of all the new malwares being developed are targeting Android with Android's market share of 79 %. Around 294 new malware variants of known malware families have been discovered. The McAfee threat report November 2014 [1] states that 7.5 lakh new mobile malwares have been discovered.

Google Play relies on Bouncer which is a dynamic analysis tool based on Quick Emulator (QEMU). It only performs dynamic analysis. Malware authors take advantage of such vulnerabilities and disclose the private user information to inadvertently harm the app-store and the developer reputation. To prevent from such attacks, academic researchers are continuously proposing solutions-based research work in this direction. These solutions can be grouped into two major categories namely, **Static** and **Dynamic**.

Static analysis incorporates the application of reverse engineering to the executable code and then performing analysis on the resultant source code without executing it. These include methodologies like code chunks, permissions, function call graphs, API calls, etc.

Fig. 1 McAfee labs report for new mobile malware [1]

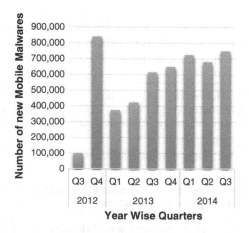

In **Dynamic** analysis, the activities of the application are monitored in a controlled environment and all the activities are analyzed [3]. Dynamic analysis includes key concepts like *Sandbox*, *MonkeyRunner*, etc. In this paper, a detailed analysis of techniques used for Android malware analysis has been covered. A comparison of the analyzed approaches has been provided on the basis of nine parameters. All the tools are critically analyzed and for each, its major contribution and limitations are discussed. The rest of the paper is organized as follows: Section 2 discusses the analysis of various tools/techniques. Section 3 gives a summary view of all the techniques. Further, Sect. 4 covers the related work. Lastly, Sect. 5 draws the conclusion.

2 Analysis of Detection Approaches

2.1 Mining Permission Patterns

Permission analysis can be employed for Maware detection [4]. The technique [5] aims to mine (interpret) the Android permission patterns generated by extracting the required permissions of both benign and malicious applications' dataset. The technique also gains knowledge by analyzing the *used* permissions of various apps. The difference of these permissions will help us to identify the anomalies. There are a total of 130 official Android permissions. Android OS employs "All or None concept" for application installation. The *AndroidManifest.xml* file present under app content folder, contains all the required permissions. The permissions can be classified into four major categories viz. the **Normal** permission category that does not require approval by the user but can be viewed later, the **Dangerous** permission category that requires user confirmation, the **Signature** category that is basically required when the app is signed with the device manufacturer's certificate and installed without user's knowledge, and the last category **SignatureOrSystem** which is same as signature category, but it is granted when the app is in Android system image. The classical technique of permission frequency count is applied on the following four permissions set:

  i. Required permissions for benign apps
 ii. Required permissions for malware apps
iii. Used permissions for benign apps
 iv. Used permissions for malware apps

After comparing the top 20 required permissions from a dataset of 1227 benign applications and 49 malware family dataset, the results obtained are shown in Table 1. The Agglomerative Hierarchical Clustering (AHC) algorithm, a bottom up multilevel approach, is first applied on columns of data and then on the rows of nonclustered dataset matrix. It identifies clusters with sub clusters. The AHC starts with a single data object (cluster) and then merges the two closest clusters by

Table 1 Permission analysis using classic statistical analysis

Permission type	Requested		Used	
	Benign	Malicious	Benign	Malicious
Unique	33	20	9	4
Common	70		28	
Never	5		87	
Frequent permissions	INTERNET, ACCESS_COARSE_LOCATION, WRITE_EXTERNAL_STORAGE and VIBRATE		INTERNET, ACCESS_COARSE_LOCATION, WAKE_LOCK and VIBRATE	

evaluating the distance matrix. The process continues till the hierarchical clustering tree is obtained. The clustering diagram consists of four colors, i.e., black, light gray, dark gray and gray. The result shows different combinations of permissions requested by benign and malicious apps, and thus indicates that the malicious apps request more permissions than benign ones. The next step uses these clusters for contrast detection and treat them as pattern for malicious app detection. For this, the contrast permission pattern mining (CPPM) algorithm is proposed that consists of two process. The first process *"Candidate permission item set generation"* obtains various permissions combinations. Two item dataset is taken that contains either benign or malicious apps. The second step *"Apriori-based itemset generation"* is applied on the itemset having '*n*' number of object (permissions). At each step of iteration, a new item is added to the existing candidate's itemset object. To simplify the process, a support-based pruning is applied which automatically cuts down the cost having value less than predefined threshold value (*supp* (A, B)). The next process, *"Contrast permission pattern selection"* highly contrasts the benign and malicious apps permission pattern. It is based on the concept that if one permission itemset is frequent in one dataset, it is often considered to carry more common features than the infrequent ones.

The permission contrasting difference is calculated on itemset A and B from the support values for benign and malicious dataset which is denoted as "*supp* (A, B)." Its value is governed by Eq. (1):

$$diff(A, B) = supp(A, B)_{benign} - supp(A, B)_{malicious} \tag{1}$$

The summarized observations of the above step are illustrated in Table 2 as following:

Contribution: The contrasting dataset obtained from analyzing required versus used permissions ensures effective classification between benign and malicious apps. Further, the techniques are readily resistant to obfuscation.

Limitation: The various permissions have to be carefully selected on a broad level before using them in making dataset.

Table 2 Permission analysis using CPPM

Permission type	Required		Used	
	Benign	Malware	Benign	Malware
Frequency	103	90	37	31
Unique	N/A	INTERNET, RECEIVE_BOOT_COMPLETED	N/A	INTERNET, READ_PHONE_STATE, ACCESS_FINE_LOCATION
Common (negative support difference)	INTERNET, READ_PHONE_STATE, ACCESS_NETWORK_STATE, ACCESS_WIFI_STATE		INTERNET, READ_PHONE_STATE, ACCESS_NETWORK_STATE, VIBRATE, READ_LOGS	

2.2 Dendroid

It is the text mining-based approach [6] for Android malware analysis which uses the technique of extraction of the code chunks (CC). The CC is basically a control flow graph's (CFG) high level representation using a Context Free Grammar [7, 8]. The CCs are extracted with the help of Androguard [9], an open source tool by Google which applies reverse engineering on the Android executable .apk file and obtains the source code. Each method associated with a class within an app represents a CC. Thus total CCs generated is equal to the number of methods in the app. After extracting the CCs, the following mathematical analysis is performed on them:

$CC(a)$: The set of all different CCs found in an app.
Redundancy R(a): Measures the fraction of repeated CCs present in an app.
Family Code Chunks (FCC): Total CCs of a particular malware family.
Common Code Chunks (CCC): The set of Common CCs found across the malware families.
Fully Discriminant Code Chunks (FDCC): The set of Common CCs of family F that are not found in other families.

The mathematical analysis is performed over the 33 malware families' dataset containing 1249 apps. Next, the Vector Space Modeling (VSM) approach is applied for family feature generation. VSM measures the relevance of a particular term 'T_i' in a document 'D_j'. In context of the paper, VSM is applied to evaluate the popular statistical indicator term frequency-inverse document frequency (tf-idf) as code chunk frequency-inverse Family Frequency (CCF-IFF) and is then stored as Family Feature Vectors. The CCF measures the frequency of a code chunk "c" in a Family F_i. The IFF of a CC 'c' measures how frequent a CC appears in a family F_i and not in all other Family F_j where $i \neq j$. The 1-NN classifier is used for unknown malware characterization. For the purpose of evolution of malware families, single linkage hierarchical clustering is used to evaluate the linkages among various malware families. The working of Dendroid architecture is summarized in Fig. 2 as shown below.

Contribution: Automatic classification of unknown malware samples based on its code structures. The technique is fast, scalable and very accurate. The dendrograms derived, represent phylogenetic trees for malware families.

Fig. 2 Dendroid working flowchart

Limitation: The dimensions of generated family feature vectors grow very high with the addition of new families creating issues to space complexity. Obfuscation strategies are not implemented.

2.3 Crowdroid

This dynamic Android malware analysis tool Crowdroid [10] uses the concept of crowdsourcing. Due to less resources available in the context of smartphones, the whole analysis process is performed on a dedicated server. This tool obtains traces of an application's behavior which can be researched further to analyze the behavior of an application. First, the lightweight client called Crowdroid is developed which is available for download from official Google Play. The concept applied here is that users download the client, install it which in turn tracks the Linux Kernel system calls and other activities of various apps. As more users will use this tool, the system will more robust and accurate. The client uses *Strace*, a command in Linux to collect system calls. While the client is running, an output file is generated which contains all the events generated by various other android apps. This file provides useful information. The generated file is then periodically sent to the dedicated server. At the server, the files generated from various nodes are analyzed and a behavior dataset is created. Finally, the dataset is clustered using *k-means* clustering algorithm. The system gives 100 % accurate results with self-written malware apps, 100 % when analyzed with Steamy Window app and 85 % with Monkey Jump 2 app.

Contribution: The tool hereby separates the installation node and analysis node, which is useful for constrained resource environment like mobiles. The system also analyzes kernel calls and behavior of an app.

Limitation: Being a dynamic analyzer, the suspicious behavior can only be tracked when the application is being installed. This means that if the app is a malware it would have accomplished its job. Also the success of the tool is dependent on more and more malicious reports sent by various Crowdroid clients.

2.4 Androsimilar

Androsimilar [11] detects Android malware that generates signatures through extracting improbable features. The method employs similarity digest hashing scheme on byte stream based on robust statistical malicious features. The method generates signatures by calculating entropy (information unpredictability) on a byte block of 64 byte window. Here the features are the ASCII codes (0–255). The entropy values are then normalized to a scale of 0–1000. The most popular features occurring at regular intervals are extracted and the rest are discarded. After normalizing the entropy, these values are assigned precedence rank which is a measure of occurrence of features obtained by reading the byte block. A window "W" of 64 byte is taken. In that window, the leftmost lowest rank value is taken and assigned popularity 1. The windows and if the same number is selected this time as before, then its popularity is increased by 1. The process continues till features of "B" bytes are investigated. A threshold property for this "B" byte block is selected and features surpassing this threshold are selected. Here the feature values between 100 and 990 are selected and the rest are discarded using Bloom filter. A similarity digest hashing scheme uses this feature to generate a signature for this app. A set of malicious signatures are generated and thus a database of signatures is created. For testing a sample app, its signature is created in the same way as above and is matched against signature database and is considered as malicious if the best matching score crosses 35 %. Although, by employing this methodology for the collected samples, some false positives (2–3 %) were emerged.

Contribution: The technique is resistant against obfuscation and repackaging.

Limitation: Androsimilar works at file level instead of op-code in repackaging, therefore manipulation of shared library is not covered. Also porting the approach to constrained memory and strong database remains a concern still.

2.5 N-Gram Analysis

The N-grams [12] analysis is a probabilistic approach to detect the presence of malware. The reverse engineering tools like DexToJar, Java Decompiler-Graphical User Interface (JD-GUI), and ApkTool are used in this technique to convert executable to source code (High level or Low level language), thereby creating the training dataset. After this, the source code is considered as N-gram signatures. This N-gram model is a popular machine learning algorithm and it is a type of probabilistic language that predicts the next item in the sequence with given datasets of order $(N - 1)$ as in Markov Model. These signatures are then stored in a Comma Separated Values (CSV) file for the reason that signatures occupy huge space. After this, a Common Vulnerability Scoring System (CVSS) is used to assess the vulnerabilities' severity level in software applications. It is a freeware tool. By applying this tool on the apk file under test, the description of all the vulnerabilities and solutions to mitigate the same, is appended to the CSV file.

Contribution: Intuitive use of N-gram machine learning algorithm to analyze android apps.

Limitations: Obfuscation techniques are not implemented.

2.6 Mobile Sandbox

The Mobile Sandboxing [13] is an approach that uses both static and dynamic analysis along with tracking of native Application Programming Interface (API) calls which are a form of obfuscation technique. It works in two steps viz. The first step includes calculating the hash value of app and comparing with VirusTotal database. Next, the app is extracted and the *AndroidManifest* file is read with the *aapt* tool and the intents as well. Further, the compiled dex file is decompiled using *smali* tool and then searched for potentially dangerous functions like *sendTextMessage()*, *getSimCountryIso()*, *exec()*, etc. With this, the available encryption libraries are searched for the sake of obfuscation strategies being implemented. Triggering of certain events are also monitored. At the end of this step, an Extensible Markup Language (XML) file is generated that contains all the activity and logs generated at various processes. The next approach, adopted, is to dynamically analyze the app through the following tools:

1. TaintDroid, that provides real-time privacy information to a user on a private device. This tool supports Android version 2.3.4. Another tool DroidBox, builds logs (DroidBoxlogfile) of all data accessed by the app on the system.
2. For intercepting native API calls, the ltrace of linux is used that generated the ltrace log file.
3. The WireShark tool captures all the networking related logs in a network Packet CAPture (PCAP) file.
4. MonkeyRunner toolkit logs the activities by simulating user interaction activities like touchscreen, key press, etc.

With the above described environment set, 20 malware apps belonging to various Android malware families were analyzed. Various types of malicious activities were logged like Data Leakage, SMS send, etc. The per application analyses time was between 9 and 14 min using Intel 2.4 GHz CPU with 48 GB RAM. The scalability factor states that 36,000 Asian market apps and 4000 malware apps were scanned in a time of 14 days. As of native call were concerned, 24 % of the Asian market apps use native calls. The use of parallel processing can reduce the time of apk analysis. Figure 3 summarizes the working of Mobile Sandbox technique.

Contribution: It implements both Static and Dynamic analysis in one process with appraisable use of various tools. This technique also tracks native API calls.

Limitation: The detection time was quite high and the measure was very weak.

2.7 Embedded Call Graphs

The high level characteristics of Android apps such as function calls graphs [14] which depict the calling relationship among the subroutines can be used to find similarities between samples. This structural detection technique is robust against

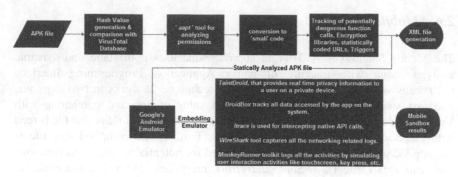

Fig. 3 Mobile sandbox working flowchart

certain obfuscation strategies. The technique first extract function call graphs and then employ an explicit mapping through kernel graph from map call graphs to feature space. Next a support vector machine (SVM) is trained to distinguish benign and malicious applications. The whole process is completed in four steps:

In the first step, the Android apk is disassembled using Androguard framework and function call graphs are extracted. The extracted graph is thus defined as $G = (V, E, L, l)$ where V and E are the vertices and edge set, L is a multiset of labels, and 'l' is a labeling function, depicted as $V \rightarrow L$. For labeling the nodes, a 15-bit field is used where each bit denotes some assembly level operations like move, return, nop, etc. Each node is labeled according to the presence of operation in them, i.e., bit is 0 if not present and 1 if present. After labeling the nodes, all the node labels are replaced by a hash value computed on all the direct neighbors of a particular node by employing a Neighborhood Graph Kernel (NHGK). It is a kernel operating over enumerable set of subgraphs of a labeled graph. Its main advantage is that its operability in linear time is proportional to number of nodes of graph. The hash value is of same length as of original label. The next step is to embed feature space to let the SVM to operate on them. The kernel value of two graphs G and G' is defined as shown in Eq. (2):

$$K\left(G_h, G_h'\right) = S(H, H') \qquad (2)$$

where G_h and G_h' are the graphs obtained by applying hashing function over all nodes of the original graph G. Here S is the size of intersection of histograms of multi-sets L_h and L_h' denoted by H and H', respectively. S is calculated by first sorting the various hash values present in L_h and L_h' and then counting the elements that are common in both multi-sets. Finally, the Kernel functions are calculated as shown in Eq. (3):

$$K\left(G_h, G_h'\right) = S\left(H, H'\right) = \left\langle \emptyset(H), \emptyset(H') \right\rangle \qquad (3)$$

where $\emptyset(H)$ is a P-dimensional vector mapped on each Histogram H containing N bins each having bin size of M. This mapping function $\emptyset$ allows us to embed every call graph in a feature space. After embedding the graph into feature space, the problem can be solved using SVM. The decision function is defined as in Eq. (4):

$$f(G_h) = \langle \emptyset(H), w \rangle + b \tag{4}$$

where $w \in R_p$ is the direction of hyperplane and b is the offset from the origin of vector space. The decision function is defined as shown in Eq. (5):

$$\text{dec(APK)} = \begin{cases} f(G_h) > 0, \text{malicious} \\ f(G_h) \leq 0, \text{benign} \end{cases} \tag{5}$$

The substructures of graph G_h that contributed to above decision is calculated by reversing the above approach and identifying the largest of the aggregated weights 'w_i' and corresponding ith bin means the nodes labeled under this bin influences greatly. The dataset used to test the system consists of 1, 35,792 benign and 12,758 malicious app from Google Play as well as third party markets. The whole process is applied to all apps and detects 89 % of the malwares and at false positive rate of only 1 %. The paper also case studies of FakeInstaller Malware family from app by drawing the Function Control Graph and darkening the malicious structure nodes.

Contribution: The assembly level marking and extracting graphs according to them is a robust approach. The technique has limitable resistant to obfuscation.

Limitation: The construction of static call graph is an undecidable problem; therefore, the attacker can obfuscate by adding unreachable calls. Attackers may also target the decompilation process to evade detection by this method.

3 Related Work

There are a number of tools available for detection and classification of android apps. Both Static and Dynamic analyses are useful for the purpose of malicious code detection. In this regard, [15] has given a summary overview of some of the malware tools or approaches with an appreciable comparison of various approaches.

4 Comparative Study of Malware Tools and Techniques

See Table 3.

Table 3 Comparison table of analyzed tools/techniques

Parameters/properties	Tools/technique used						
	Mining permission patterns [5]	Dendroid [6]	Crowdroid [10]	Androsimilar [11]	N-gram analysis [12]	Mobile sandbox [13]	Embedded call graphs [14]
Publishing year	2013	2013	2011	2013	2014	2013	2013
Static	✓	✓	✗	✓	✓	✓	✓
Dynamic	✗	✗	✓	✗	✗	✓	✗
Hybrid	✗	✗	✗	✗	✗	✓	✗
Time complexity	N/A	Moderate	Low	Moderate	Low	Very high	High
Space complexity	Moderate	Moderate	Less	Large	Moderate	Moderate	Large
Key concept	Permission	Code chunks	Crowd sourcing	Statistical features	N-gram, CVSS	*smali*, emulator	Function call graphs
Major contributions	"Used" permission extraction, informative data from contrast permission patterns	Unknown malware classification, fast and scalable, dendograms	Client APK, behavioral detection	Improbable signature generation, thwart obfuscation and repackaging	Produced N-grams signatures	Both static and dynamic analysis, obfuscation resistance, native API call track, web accessibility	Obfuscation resistance
Observations	Permission type, frequency count, bi-clustering, contrast permission patterns	Malware signatures, VSM, 1-NN, malware evolution	*Strace*, steamy window app, monkey jump 2 app, clustering, System calls	Entropy, signatures, fuzzy hashing	Reverse engineering, CSV signature, vulnerability score	RootSmart to be the most sophisticated and FakeInst to be the most detected family, native calling	Assembly level analysis, SVM implement
Limitation	Careful analysis of permissions, no repackaging resistance	No obfuscation resist, large feature vectors	More clients, dynamic analyzer	Limited malware DB, more false positives	No obfuscation resistance	More detection time	Undecidability of static call graph construction

5   Conclusions

In this paper, a comprehensive analysis of various tools and techniques that are used for Android Malware detection with a comparison study of them is presented. The discussed techniques use tools like Androguard, JD-GUI, ApkTool, DexToJar, and smali for reverse engineering. The Mobile Sandbox tool has the capability to track the native API calls. The techniques viz. mining permission patterns, Mobile Sandbox, Androsimilar, and the embedded call graphs are resistant towards obfuscation techniques. The capabilities of tools Androsimilar, Mobile Sandbox, and embedded call graphs can be used for designing a better system.

References

1. F-Secure, WHITEPAPERS-The latest research from Labs on threats and technology. https://www.f-secure.com/en/web/labs_global/whitepapers
2. McAfee for Business, McAfee Labs Threat Report. http://www.mcafee.com/us/mcafee-labs.aspx
3. Egele, M., Scholte, T., Kirda, E., & Kruegel, C. (2012). A survey on automated dynamic malware-analysis techniques and tools. *ACM Computing Surveys 44*(2), February 6, 2012.
4. Aung, Z., & Zaw, W. (2013). Permission based malware analysis, *International Journal of Scientific and Technology Research 2*(3), March 2013.
5. Moonsamy, V., Rong J., & Liu, S. (2013). Mining permission patterns for contrasting clean and malicious android applications, Future Generation for Computer Systems, Elsevier.
6. Suarez-Tangil, G., Tapiador, J. E., Peris-Lopez, P., & Blasco Alis, J. (2013) Dendroid: a text mining approach to analyzing and classifying code structures in android malware families. Expert Systems with Applications, Elsevier, July 2013.
7. Cesare, S., & Xiang, Y. (2010) Classification of malware using structured control flow. In *Proceedings of the eighth Australasian symposium on parallel and distributed computing* (Vol. 107, pp. 61–70). Australian Computer Society, 2010.
8. Zhou, Y., & Jiang, X. (2012). Dissecting android malware: characterization and evolution, In *IEEE Symposium on Security and Privacy.*
9. Androguard, Reverse engineering, Malware and goodware analysis of Android applications ... and more (ninja!). https://code.google.com/p/androguard/.
10. Burguera, I., Zurutuza, U., & Nadjm-Tehrani, S. (2011) Crowdroid: behavior-based malware detection system for android. In *SPSM'11*, Chicago, Illinois, USA, ACM, 2011
11. Faruki, P., Ganmoor, V., Laxmi, V., Gaur, M. S., & Bharmal, A (2013) AndroSimilar: robust statistical feature signature for android malware detection. In *SIN '13*, Aksaray Turkey, ACM, 2013.
12. Dhaya, R., & Poongodi, M. (2014). Detecting software vulnerabilities using static analysis, In *IEEE ICACCCT*, 2014.
13. Spreitzenbarth, M., Echtler, F., & Hoffmann, J. (2013). *Mobile-Sandbox: having a deeper look into android applications. In SAC'13*. Coimbra Portugal: ACM.
14. Gascon, H., Yamaguchi, F., Arp, D., & Rieck, K. (2013). Structural detection of android malware using embedded call graphs. In *AISec'13*, ACM.
15. Ramteke, M., Sen, P., & Sapate, S. (2014). Comparative study and a survey on malware analysis approaches for android devices. *International Journal of Advanced Research in Computer Science and Software Engineering, 4*, 3rd March 2014.

A Review on Dynamic View Selection

Anjana Gosain and Heena

Abstract Dynamic view selection approach selects materialized view set on runtime and takes into account the changing nature of users' interests and query patterns. This paper provides a review of 24 studies based on this approach and categorizes results on parameters such as constraints, algorithms, and experiment platforms etc.

Keywords Dynamic view selection · Review · Dynamic nature

1 Introduction

Data warehouse is a single, integrated repository gathering information from various heterogeneous data sources to provide support for strategic decision making. Unlike operational databases, data warehouse stores historical information to help managers to analyze and identify trends to gain competitive advantage for their organization. OLAP forms the interface to interact with data warehouse to retrieve answers for the decision support queries that are issued by the top management people to look upon the aggregated data rather than detailed data for the decisions. To execute such complex queries which demand aggregated data from such a voluminous data store requires scanning of large number of records and hence, becomes an expensive and time taking process. As a solution, Data Warehouse provides precomputed data in the form of materialized views which are much smaller than the base tables and thus minimizes the query processing time to several orders of magnitude.

A. Gosain · Heena (✉)
USICT, GGSIPU, New Delhi, India
e-mail: heenamadaan100@gmail.com

A. Gosain
e-mail: anjana_gosain@yahoo.com

© Springer Science+Business Media Singapore 2016
S.C. Satapathy et al. (eds.), *Proceedings of International Conference on ICT for Sustainable Development*, Advances in Intelligent Systems and Computing 409, DOI 10.1007/978-981-10-0135-2_5

Ideally, all views must be precomputed to answer all aggregated queries to obtain lowest query processing time. But, such a setting might exceed storage and cost limits thus arises a need of choosing a set of views to materialize with the aim of minimizing query cost and view maintenance cost remaining within the limits of storage space and maintenance cost constraints. This selection of views has become a challenging problem in data warehouse [1].

View selection can be of two types: static and dynamic view selections. Static view selection approach considers users' query and interaction patterns to be static and select materialized view set on the basis of given workload which are maintained till the execution of queries without any changes [2, 3]. Such an approach cannot predict changes and results in outdated views [4]. This weakness may be overcome by using the dynamic view selection approach which takes into account the dynamic nature of users' interest. It selects set of materialized views on the fly as queries arrive and updates or removes less-beneficial views with better ones as queries get executed [3, 5, 6].

Most of the work and lots of literature surveys [7–10] have been done on static view selection. Little work has been done in dynamic nature of view selection and till date in our knowledge no review work has been published on dynamic view selection. In this paper, we provide a review of the ongoing work on dynamic view selection which can act as a foundation for the future research in this area. Further, the paper is organized as follows: Sect. 2 summarizes the work that has been done to select materialized views dynamically. Section 3 provides the review results focusing on publication, implementation area, applied constraints, and experimental platform. Section 4 concludes our work.

2 Literature Work

To conduct literature review on dynamic view selection in various areas, we searched through various online databases such as Springer, Elsevier, IEEEXplore etc. and found 24 studies relevant for our work. Each of the identified study has implemented the dynamic approach of selecting a set of materialized views by using some framework, applying some algorithm or policy, setting some constraints, selecting some measures to decide the selection of a view and finally conducted an experiment or built some application or simulator or had compared their approach with other proposed approaches. So we provide a summarized view of all these studies considering the parameters such as area of implementation, constraints applied, designed algorithm, measure selected and implementation platform in Table 1 given below.

DW Data warehouse, *QPC* Query processing cost, *SC* Space constraint, *MR* Multidimensional range queries, *Algo* Algorithm, *IMA* Incremental maintenance algo, *EPR* Expected penalty rate, VMC View maintenance cost, *MVMG* Multi-view materialization graph, *CSR* Cost savings ratio, *DS* Dataset, *CRP* Cache replacement policy, *HPSR* Hit prediction savings ratio, *DB* Dataaases, *AST* Automatic Summary

Table 1 Summary of the literature work

Paper	Area	Constraint	Frame work	Algorithm	Measure	Experiment
[11] 1999	DW	QPC + SC	MR queries, hyperplanes	Replace algo, IMA	Goodness-EPR	Prototype
[12] 2000	DW	QPC + VMC	MVMG	–	–	–
[5] 2000	DW	QPC + SC	Data cubes and lattices	DSAMV algo	Benefit	–
[4] 2003	DW	QPC + SC	MDDB with lattice	Partition selection algo	CSR	IBM DB2, TPC-H DS
[13] 2004	DW	QPC + SC	MDDB with lattice	CRP, hit prediction algo	Goodness-HPSR	IBM DB2
[14] 2008	DB	QPC	AST, QGM		Profit	Test App, TPC-H DS
[15] 2008	DW	QPC + VMC + SC		CBDMVS-clustering algo	Similarity function	SQL Server
[6] 2012	DW	QPC + VMC + SC		5 algorithms	Similarity function, BRUF	MATLAB 7.1
[16] 2007	DW	QPC + SC	DAG	Heuristic algo	–	Comparisons
[17] 2006	DW	QPC + SC	Lattice	Randomized algo, BPUS	Benefit per unit space	Comparisons
[18] 2008	DB	QPC + VMC	Materialized query table	Greedy algo-set pruning	Hit ratio, benefit, cache load factor	MQT scheduler, IBM DB2
[19] 2010	P2P system	QPC + VMC + SC + TC	MVMG	View placement policy	Goodness, benefit	–
[20] 2007	DW	QPC + SC	MD lattice	Greedy algo	Benefit–visit frequency per unit space	App of refreshment strategy
[21] 2002	P2P system	QPC + TC		Caching algo-cache benefit, ARA-LBF	Benefit, detailed CSR	Prototype, SYNTH DS

(continued)

Table 1 (continued)

Paper	Area	Constraint	Frame work	Algorithm	Measure	Experiment
[22] 2007	DB	QPC + VMC + SC	Control tables	Cache policy based on 2Q algo	–	MSQL server, TPC-H DS
[23] 1999	DW	QPC + VMC + SC	AND-OR DAG	r-greedy algo, 2 phase algo	–	–
[24] 2011	DW	QPC	–	PR_Q_PS algo., HRU algo	Detailed CSR, TNVR, Benefit	Simulator, headcount DS
[25] 2009	DW	QPC + SC	–	EMVSDIA	Query probability, RUSB	SQL Server
[26] 2003	DW	QPC + VMC + VRC	MVPP	GA, heuristic algo	Fitness function	SUNOS 5.5
[27] 2011	DW	QPC + VMC	–	Dynamic view Materialization Selection algo	Complexity, BRUF, WF, selectivity, ET	–
[28] 2010	DB	QPC + SC	PQ, superior relationship graph	DMV based PQ algo	weight	MATLAB 2007
[29] 2012	DB	QPC	DMV index, ordered tree	VI algo	–	MATLAB 2010
[30] 2013	DB	QPC	DMV index, domain table, ordered tree	VI algo, view search algo, path rename algo, Rebuild path algo	–	MATLAB 2010
[31] 2014	DB	QPC + SC	Superior relationship graph, relationship linked structure	DMV based PQ algo	Weight, access frequency	MATLAB 2007

Tables, *QGM* Query Graph Model, *BRUF* Base Relation Update Frequency, *DAG* Directed Acyclic Graph, *P2P* Peer to Peer, *TC* Transfer Cost, *ARA* Admission and Replacement algo, *LBF* Least Benefit First, *PR_Q_PS* Probabilistic Reasoning Query Prediction System, *TNVR* Total Number of View Replacement, *RUSB* Relative Unit Space Benefit, *VRC* View Reorganization Cost, *GA* Genetic Algorithm, *WF* Weighting Factor, *ET* Execution time, *PQ* Progressive Queries, *DMV* Dynamic materialized view, *VI* View insertion.

3   Review

This section provides a review on dynamic view selection categorizing on the following parameters: publication, area of implementation, constraints applied, and implementation platform.

Figure 1 shows a graph representing the publication trends which indicates that the first paper on dynamic view selection was published in 1999 which initiated the work on this approach. Then most of the work was done after 2006.

Figure 2a classifies the studies as whether published in a conference or a journal and results shows that more than three-fourth of the papers were published in conference and few in journals.

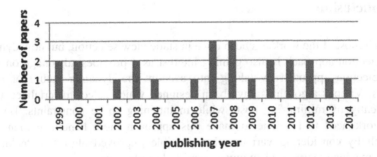

Fig. 1   Publication Trends

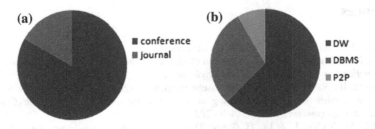

Fig. 2   a Distribution of papers. **b** Distribution according to area of implementation

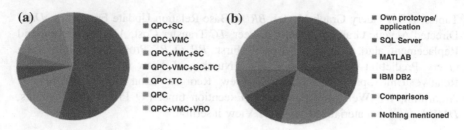

Fig. 3 Distribution of papers **a** according to constraints **b** according to implementation tool

Views are being materialized in every area such as databases, data warehouses, and P2P systems and Fig. 2b figures out that most of the studies found have been implemented in data warehouse, some in databases and very few in P2P systems.

When set of views is to be selected for materialization, the aim is to minimize cost such as query processing cost, view maintenance cost, transfer cost under space constraint, and view maintenance constraint. Thus Fig. 3a represents the distribution of studies on the basis of cost and space constraints.

Many of the works have implemented their approach on some platform or built their own application, simulator, and this distribution is shown in Fig. 3b.

4 Conclusion

Although most of the work has been done in static view selection, but now dynamic view selection approach is also gaining interest as it provides advantage on static view selection approach by taking into account the dynamic nature of users' interests. Various algorithms have been designed which select materialized views dynamically by minimizing costs while maintaining space constraints. But still more work need to be done to make this approach more beneficial than static approach by considering various other possible improved algorithm techniques such as machine learning techniques, hybrid algorithms etc.

References

1. Widom. J. (1995). Research problems in data warehousing. In *CIKM*, pp. 25–30.
2. Gupta, H., & Mumick, I. (2005). Selection of views to materialize in a data warehouse. *IEEE Transactions on Knowledge and Data Engineering, 17*(1), 24–43.
3. Ashadevi, B., Navaneetham, P., & Balasubramanian, R. (2010). A framework for the view selection problem in data warehousing environment. *International Journal on Computer Science and Engineering, 02*(09), 2820–2826.
4. Choi, C.-H., Xu Yu, J., & Lu. H. (2003). Dynamic materialized view management based on predicates. In *Web Technologies and Applications*. Springer Berlin Heidelberg, pp. 583–594.

5. Wang, C., & Bo. X. (2011). Dynamic modulating strategy of materialized views in data warehouse. In *3rd International Conference on Data Mining and Intelligent Information Technology Applications (ICMiA), 2011* IEEE.
6. Chaudhari, M. S., & Dhote. C. (2012). Dynamic materialized view selection algorithm: a clustering approach. In *Data Engineering and Management*. Springer Berlin Heidelberg. pp. 57–66.
7. Mami, I., & Bellahsene, Z. (2012). A survey of view selection methods. *SIGMOD Record, 41* (1), 20–29.
8. Ashadevi, B. (2011). Analysis of view selection problem in data warehousing environment. *International Journal of Engineering and Technology, 3*(6), 447–457.
9. Gosain, A., & Alka. (2013). A comparative study of materialised view selection in data warehouse environment. In *5th International Conference on Computational Intelligence and Communication Networks (CICN)*. IEEE.
10. Thakur, G., & Gosain, A. (2011) A comprehensive analysis of materialized views in a data warehouse environment. In *International Journal of Advanced Computer Science and Applications (IJACSA)* 2.5. (2011).
11. Kotidis, Y., & Roussopoulos, N. (1999). DynaMat: a dynamic view management system for data warehouses. In *Proceedings of the 1999 ACM SIGMOD international conference on Management of data*, pp. 371–382, Philadelphia, Pennsylvania, USA.
12. Bellahsène, Z., & Marot. P. (2000) Materializing a set of views: dynamic strategies and performance evaluation. In *Proceedings of International Database Engineering and Applications Symposium*, IEEE, Yokohoma, Japan.
13. Choi, C.-H., Xu Yu, J., & Lu, H. (2004). A simple but effective dynamic materialized view caching. *Advances in Web-Age Information Management*. Springer Berlin Heidelberg, pp. 147–156.
14. Luebcke, A., Geist, I., Bubke, R. (2008). Dynamic detection and administration of materialized views based on the query graph model. In *Third International Conference on Digital Information Management*. IEEE.
15. Gong, A., & Zhao, W. (2008). Clustering-based dynamic materialized view selection algorithm. In *Fifth International Conference on Fuzzy Systems and Knowledge Discovery. FSKD'08*. Vol. 5. IEEE.
16. Xu, W., Theodoratos, D., Zuzarte, C., Wu, X., & Oria, V. (2007). *A dynamic view materialization scheme for sequences of query and update statements. In Data Warehousing and Knowledge Discovery* (pp. 55–65). Berlin Heidelberg: Springer.
17. Lawrence, M., & Rau-Chaplin, A. (2006). *Dynamic view selection for OLAP. In Data Warehousing and Knowledge Discovery* (pp. 33–44). Berlin Heidelberg: Springer.
18. Phan, T., & Li, W. S. (2008). Dynamic materialization of query views for data warehouse workloads. In *24th International Conference on Data Engineering, ICDE*. IEEE.
19. Bellahsene, Z., Cart, M., & Kadi, N. (2010). A cooperative approach to view selection and placement in P2P systems. In *On the Move to Meaningful Internet Systems. OTM*. Springer, Berlin Heidelberg. pp. 515–522.
20. Yin, G., Yu, X., & Lin, L. (2007). Strategy of Selecting Materialized Views Based on Cache-updating. In *IEEE International Conference on Integration Technology. ICIT'07*.
21. Kalnis, P., Ng, W. S., Ooi, B. C., Papadias, D., & Tan, K. L. (2002). An adaptive peer-to-peer network for distributed caching of olap results. In *Proceedings of the 2002 ACM SIGMOD international conference on Management of data*. ACM.
22. Zhou, J., Larson, P. A., Goldstein, J., & Ding, L. (2007). Dynamic materialized views. In *IEEE 23rd International Conference on Data Engineering, 2007. ICDE*.
23. Theodoratos, D., & Sellis, T. (1999). *Dynamic data warehouse design. In DataWarehousing and Knowledge Discovery* (pp. 1–10). Berlin Heidelberg: Springer.
24. Daneshpour, N., & Barfourosh, A. A. (2012). Dynamic view management system for query prediction to view materialization. In *Developments in Data Extraction, Management, and Analysis*, p. 132.

25. Lijuan, Z., Xuebin, G., Linshuang, W., & Qian, S. (2009). Efficient materialized view selection dynamic improvement algorithm. In *Sixth International Conference on Fuzzy Systems and Knowledge Discovery. FSKD'09* (Vol. 7.) IEEE.
26. Zhang, C., Yang, J., & Karlapalem, K. (2003). Dynamic materialized view selection in data warehouse environment. *Informatica (Slovenia), 27*(4), 451–460.
27. Rashid, A. B., Islam, M. S., & Hoque, A. L. (2011). *Dynamic materialized view selection approach for improving query performance. In Computer Networks and Information Technologies* (pp. 202–211). Berlin Heidelberg: Springer.
28. Zhu, C., Zhu,Q., Zuzarte, & C. (2010). Efficient processing of monotonic linear progressive queries via dynamic materialized views. In *Proceedings of the 2010 Conference of the Center for Advanced Studies on Collaborative Research*. IBM Corp.
29. Zhu, C., Zhu, Q., Zuzarte, C., & Ma, W. (2012). DMVI: a dynamic materialized view index for efficiently discovering usable views for progressive queries. *CASCON*.
30. Zhu, C., & Zuzarte, C. (2013). Developing a dynamic materialized view index for efficiently discovering usable views for progressive queries. *Journal of Information Processing Systems, 9*(4), 511–537.
31. Zhu, C., Zhu, Q., & Zuzarte, C. (2014). Optimization of monotonic linear progressive queries based on dynamic materialized views. *The Computer Journal, 57*(5), 708–730.

Software Project Estimation Using Fuzzy Inference System

V.S. Dhaka, Vishal Choudhary, Manoj Sharma and Madan Singh

Abstract Project estimation using fuzzy inference system is widely accepted and pervasive technique to capture the software development processes as well as requirements of a software application project. The fuzzy inference system on the use cases provides the practical capacity of the project. By investigating the content of use cases we will get valuable insight into the effort, size, and time required to design, test, and implement a project. In general, projects with large, complicated use cases need more effort in designing and implementation in comparison to small projects with less complicated use cases. The time to complete a project is highly effected by technical requirement and environmental factors. In traditional models we take only software size as input parameters and apply the adjustment factors on it to compute the estimates. But in case of object-oriented software development use case plays an important role. Use case is used for early prediction of size, development effort, and cost estimation. In use case point we classify the actors or functions into simple average and complex. The total weight is calculated by multiplying the number of use case point with their weighting factor and adding up the product. In each use case we define the complexity based on the predefined values to segregate in simple average and complex. In this paper methodology adopted for estimation is more reliable than functional point analysis. In this paper it is considered if the complexity of use case is more, time taken to design develop, test, and implement the project will be high. Estimation has great impact on every facet of a software project time cost and qualities are some of them. Analysis of use case points gives an inference of reliable results because estimates are produced

V.S. Dhaka (✉) · V. Choudhary · M. Sharma · M. Singh
School of Engineering and Technology, Jaipur National University, Jaipur, India
e-mail: vishalhim@yahoo.com

V. Choudhary
e-mail: vijaypal.dhaka@gmail.com

M. Sharma
e-mail: manoj186@yahoo.co.in

M. Singh
e-mail: madan.phdce@gmail.com

© Springer Science+Business Media Singapore 2016
S.C. Satapathy et al. (eds.), *Proceedings of International Conference on ICT for Sustainable Development*, Advances in Intelligent Systems and Computing 409, DOI 10.1007/978-981-10-0135-2_6

61

from actual business process. This paper gives the detailed analysis of each parameter involved in the project development.

Keywords Adjustment factor · Estimation techniques · Environment factor · Fuzzy inference · Technical and weighting factor

1 Introduction

The fuzzy inference system on the use cases provides the practical capacity of the project. By investigating the content of use cases we will get valuable insight into the effort, size, and time required to design, test, and implement a project. In general, projects with large, complicated use cases need more effort in designing and implementation in comparison to small projects with less complicated use cases. The time to complete a project is highly effected by technical requirement and environmental factors. In traditional models we take only software size as input parameters and apply the adjustment factors on it to compute the estimates. But in case of object-oriented software development use case plays an important role [1]. Use case is used for early prediction of size, development effort, and cost estimation. In use case point we classify the actors or functions into simple average and complex. The total weight is calculated by multiplying the number of use case point with their weighting factor and adding up the product. In each use case we define the complexity based on the predefined values to segregate in simple average and complex. In this paper methodology adopted for estimation is more reliable than functional point analysis [2–4]. In this paper it is considered if the complexity of use case is more, time taken to design develop, test, and implement the project will be high. In real situation we found that if the size of project is large then project estimation cost is also high still it does not give 100 % guarantee that estimation is correct because many factors influence the estimation does not be taken into account and one of them is human itself. Another factor is technology and environment involved in estimation. In this paper we will analyze all the factors in detail and find the results of project estimation either they are close to real target or not.

2 Fuzzy Logic

Fuzzy logic varies from classical logic in which logics are no longer yes or no, true or false, and on or off. In traditional logics are based on true or false values for zero or one. In fuzzy logic, a statement can be any real value between 0 and 1, like an analog signal which is more accurate than digital signals. The theory of fuzzy logic will be used in the model and the estimation process to remove the ambiguity of the information obtained in early phases of software development projects [5]. It will help us to manage the ambiguity about the specific meaning of linguistic values used by the "professional" when upcoming with an approximation. In fuzzy precise reasoning is viewed as limiting case of approximate reasoning. Every statement has relative degree with which ultimate value be taken into consideration. Any system which can use logic be fuzzyfied. Elasticity is associated with all interpretation of knowledge. Fuzzy inference is a type of mapping for a set of inputs to a set of outputs. Based on this mapping we can make important decision. In this process we take membership functions, operators, and if-then rules. Generally, we use two types if inference system: one is mamdani type and another is sugheno type. Fuzzy inference system can be used in controllers, decision support systems, expert systems, and many advanced AI applications. Mamdani's fuzzy system is first used in control system developed using fuzzy set theory. It is first developed by Ebrahim Mamdani in 1975. In this after aggregation, there is a fuzzy set for every output variable that needs defuzzification.

3 Estimation and Software Engineering

The estimation is very complex and estimation varies with many factors that is taken into consideration generally we use estimation in all fields and day to day activities like how much time a bus will take to reach from one station to another station we always have some approximate ideas of time it will take to reach the destination, but there are some factors which will greatly influence the actual time based on road condition, congestions, and other the same way test estimation in the software engineering is a broad concept. Sometimes, we use the t estimation in cost, and otherwise we use for efforts and we are test to find the errors in the final product. Actual testing is the testing which gives us expected best and worst outputs before deployment of software. We also take into the consideration the testing cost, testing time, and testing efforts. Testing always need experts who know what is right and what is wrong. Even our tools are accurate but final human interpretation will have more importance. The project estimation procedure involves characterizing the factors involved in estimation. This classification then forms the foundation for making the decision of similar or related projects which have been completed, and for them effort is known. These effort data are then used, perhaps with modification, to generate the expected value. A complexity with this method includes finding the correlation and assessing the level of similarity.

4 Functional Point Inference System

Function point analysis is a novel technique for estimating the size of a project based on input and output. Since size of project is calculated based on line of code, we can estimate before the project was completed. FPA methodology for estimating the size of software is devised by IBM [6–10]. The functional point count helps us to estimate the size of project by considering the input and output variables and function they will perform. Counting the functional point gives a better estimate. This methodology validates the individual elements to arrive at the complexity level of low and high mediums. There are five basic function types like external interface file (EIF), inter logical files (ILF), external input (EI), external output (EO), and external query (EQ). The important characteristic of functional point method is that it provides pre-project estimate. These estimates help for an organization to prepare tenders, estimates, and project plans. The functional point method is widely in use but still is under experimentation phase.

The function point method for estimating project size involves the following steps:

1. First compute the crude function point (CFP). In this we identify the software system functional components followed by evolution phase simple, average, and complex. At this point we are able to apply the weighting factor to system component and compute their weighted value.
2. Second phase is to compute the relative complexity adjustment factor (RCAF) for the project under estimation.
3. The third phase is the computing phase where we calculated total deviation in each case, i.e., in simple average and complex by the following formula:

$$TDEV = 2.5^{\times}(\text{Total Points})^{0.38}$$

$$FP = CFP(0.65 + 0.01 \times RCAF).$$

the number of functional point is evaluated by above formula.

The calculations for crude function are based on the following variables.

a. The number of user inputs for distinct input applications.
b. The number of user outputs for distinct applications like batch file, invoices, print files, error message, etc.
c. Number of online queries–distinct queries.
d. Number of different logical files. The files that deal with the input data types.
e. External interface like output screen, CD, transmission media, and recording media, etc.

The fuzzy inference system is developed based on the values present in Table 1 (Figs. 1, 2, 3, 4 and 5).

1. If (*user_input* is simple) and (*useroutput* is simple) and (*onlinequries* are simple) and (*logicalfiles* are simple) and (*externalinterface* is simple), then (output1 is simple) (1)
2. If (*user_input* is average) and (*useroutput* is average) and (*onlinequries* is average) and (*logicalfiles* is average) and (*externalinterface* is average), then (output1 is average) (1)

Table 1 Functional point calculation for system components

System component	Simple				Average				Complex			TDEV	CFP	FP
	Count	Weight factors	Points	TDEV	Count	Weight factor	Points	TDEV	Count	Weight factor	Points			
	A	B	C=AxB		D	E	F=DxE		G	H	I=GxH			
User inputs	10	3	30	9.10429005	15	4	60	11.847793	25	6	150	20.06413	44.016	47.16
User outputs	5	4	20	7.80425420	7	5	35	9.6535236	10	7	70	15.65906	33.11	38.08
User online queries	10	3	30	9.10429005	15	4	60	11.847793	25	6	150	20.06413	41.01	47.16
Logical files	20	7	140	16.3481518	30	10	300	21.839670	50	15	750	36.86785	75.055	86.31
External interfaces	15	5	75	12.8962454	20	7	140	16.348151	25	10	250	25.79717	54.04	63.30
Total			295	55.25723			595	71.5369			1370	118.4523	245.25	282

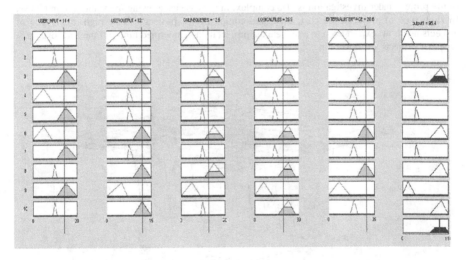

Fig. 1 Fuzzy inferences for different sets of inputs

3. If (*user_input* is complex) and (*useroutput* is complex) and (*onlinequries* is complex) and (*logicalfiles* is complex) and (*externalinterface* is complex), then (output1 is complex) (1)

4. If (*user_input* is simple) and (*useroutput* is average) and (*onlinequries* is average) and (*logicalfiles* is average) and (*externalinterface* is average), then (output1 is average) (1)

5. If (*user_input* is complex) and (*useroutput* is average) and (*onlinequries* is average) and (*logicalfiles* is average) and (*externalinterface* is average), then (output1 is average) (1)

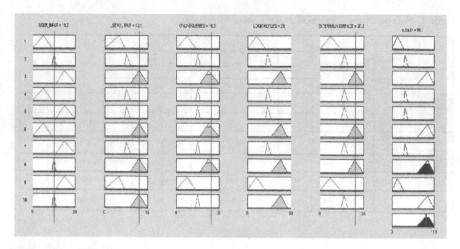

Fig. 2 We found that if all the parameters involved in inference systems are complex then the size of the project under investigation is also complex; in our case its showing the values around 96 %. In such type of projects, the cost, time, and complexity of project will be high. Such type of projects needs the expert team to complete the project in the predefined limit of time and cost. Such types of projects are uncertain

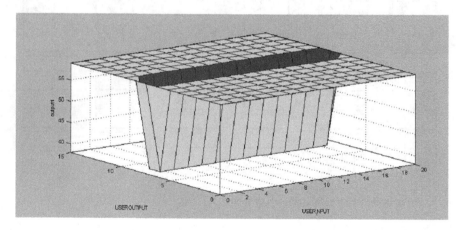

Fig. 3 Variation of user input, output versus project complexity. Range of user inputs varies from 0 to 20 and user outputs range is in-between 5 and 10. Here project complexity is around 15–55 functional points

6. If (*user_input* is simple) and (*useroutput* is complex) and (*onlinequries* is complex) and (*logicalfiles* is complex) and (*externalinterface* is complex), then (output1 is complex) (1)
7. If (*user_input* is complex) and (*useroutput* is average) and (*onlinequries* is average) and (*logicalfiles* is average) and (*externalinterface* is average), then (output1 is average) (1)

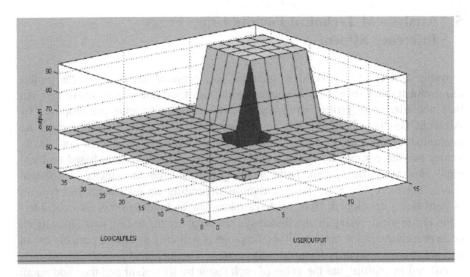

Fig. 4 A graph between user output, logical files, and project complexity

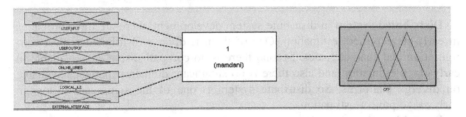

Fig. 5 Mamdani fuzzy inference system for functional point

8. If (*user_input* is average) and (*useroutput* is complex) and (*onlinequries* is complex) and (*logicalfiles* is complex) and (*externalinterface* is complex), then (output1 is complex) (1)
9. If (*user_input* is complex) and (*useroutput* is simple) and (*onlinequries* is simple) and (*logicalfiles* is simple) and (*externalinterface* is simple), then (output1 is simple) (1)
10. If (*user_input* is average) and (*useroutput* is complex) and (*onlinequries* is average) and (*logicalfiles* is complex) and (*externalinterface* is average), then (output1 is complex) (1).

5   Analysis of Technical Factors Using Fuzzy Inference System

Symons (1988) [11] devised a standard for technical factors, i.e., "a project requirement other than those concerned with code t hat affects the size of task but that not arise from project environment"; the constant weights are proposed by Albrecht (1979) [12, 13, 6]. For any project estimation, the technical factors are evaluated by the project estimation team by assigning a predefined complexity value, and the complexity factor is determined by estimation team based on technical aspects of the system. Different people define the complexity in different ways. Therefore, there are wide variations depending on estimators and type of system being developed. Here we have taken few technical factors into consideration either we are using in distributed system, what are the testing tools, how much code reusability in the project, either the projects will easy to install, portable or not and what are the security features in the system. The technical complexity factor is calculated by multiplying the value of each factor by its weight and then adding all these values to get total. The following formula is applied:

$$TCF = 0.6 + (0.01 \times (Technical\,Complexity))$$

Distributed system in distribute system development, there are three problems in early-stage project estimation. One of them is diverse distributed project configuration and characteristics. Second there is no comprehensive data available in early-stage estimation and also there is no significant domain experience available on diverge platforms. So distribute system is one of the significant factors in early-stage project estimation.

Reusable code in reusable code, many factors are associated including domain analysis, reusable components, maintenance and revisions of the reused components documents, etc. So this is again an important technical factor in project estimation.

Easy to install this is also an important technical factor in project estimation. Either the system is easy to configure deploy and run or need the specialized team for its operation.

Easy to use the software needs to be easy to use; the technical complexity increases the operational cost of a software as software needs to be more than functional and reliable. So we also take it as a technical factor.

Portable the use of same software on different environments and platforms gives us the concept of portability. It is an important factor in development cost reduction.

Concurrent this is another factor in the efficiency of a software process. If same software performs the different functions at same time, then we can say the system is concurrent.

Security feature security is the important factor in the software project estimation. If software continues its correct functioning under the malicious attack, and if there is rigorous inbuilt security mechanism, then we can say it is more secure. So we took this factor into consideration under the project estimation and planning.

Here we applied 18 set fuzzy inference rules to check the technical complexity of projects based on Table 2 (Figs. 6, 7 and 8).

1. If (*distributed_system* is simple) and (*reusable_code* is simple) and (*easy_to_install* is simple) and (*easy_to_use is simple*) and (portable is simple) and (*concurrent* is simple) and (*security_feature* is simple), then (output1 is simple) (1)

2. If (*distributed_system* is average) and (*reusable_code* is average) and (*easy_to_install* is average) and (*easy_to_use* is average) and (*portable* is average) and (*concurrent* is average) and (*security_feature* is simple), then (output1 is simple) (1)

3. If (*distributed_system* is complex) and (*reusable_code* is complex) and (*easy_to_install* is complex) and (*easy_to_use* is complex) and (*portable* is complex) and (*concurrent* is complex) and (*security_feature* is simple), then (output1 is simple) (1)

4. If (*distributed_system* is not simple) and (*reusable_code* is simple) and (*easy_to_install* is simple) and (*easy_to_use* is simple) and (portable is simple) and (concurrent is simple) and (*security_feature* is simple), then (output1 is simple) (1)

5. If (*distributed_system* is not average) and (*reusable_code* is average) and (*easy_to_install* is average) and (*easy_to_use* is average) and (*portable* is simple) and (*concurrent* is average) and (*security_feature* is simple), then (output1 is simple) (1)

6. If (*distributed_system* is not complex) and (*reusable_code* is complex) and (*easy_to_install* is complex) and (*easy_to_use* is complex) and (*portable* is complex) and (*concurrent* is complex) and (*security_feature* is simple), then (output1 is simple) (1)

7. If (*distributed_system* is not simple) and (reusable_code is not simple) and (*easy_to_install* is not simple and (*easy_to_use* is complex) and (*portable* is complex) and (*concurrent* is average) and (*security_feature* is simple), then (output1 is simple) (1)

8. If (*distributed_system* is not simple) and (*reusable_code* is not simple) and (*easy_to_install* is not simple) and (*easy_to_use* is not simple) and (*portable* is not simple) and (*concurrent* is complex) and (*security_feature* is simple), then (output1 is simple) (1)

9. If (*distributed_system* is average) and (*reusable_code* is complex) and (*easy_to_install* is complex) and (*easy_to_use* is complex) and (*portable* is complex) and (*concurrent* is complex) and (*security_feature* is simple), then (output1 is simple) (1)

10. If (*distributed_system* is complex) and (*reusable_code* is average) and (*easy_to_install* is complex) and (*easy_to_use* is average) and (portable is complex) and (CONCURRENT is complex) and (*security_feature* is simple), then (output1 is simple) (1)

Table 2 Technical complexity calculation for use cases

Use case	Simple				Average				Complex			
	Weight	No. of use cases	TC	TCF	Weight	No. of use cases	TC	TCF	Weight	No. of use cases	TC	TCF
Distributed system	2	5	10	0.7	2	10	20	0.8	2	15	30	0.9
Reusable code	1	5	5	0.65	1	15	15	0.75	1	30	30	0.9
Easy to install	0.5	4	2	0.62	0.5	6	3	0.63	0.5	8	4	0.64
Easy to use	0.5	3	1.5	0.615	0.5	5	2.5	0.625	0.5	7	3.5	0.635
Portable	2	4	8	0.68	2	5	10	0.7	2	7	14	0.74
Concurrent	1	3	3	0.63	1	6	6	0.66	1	8	8	0.68
Security feature	1	5	5	0.65	1	15	15	0.75	1	20	20	0.8
Total				0.649286				0.702143				0.756429

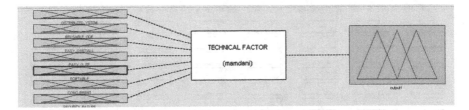

Fig. 6 Mamdani fuzzy inference for technical factors

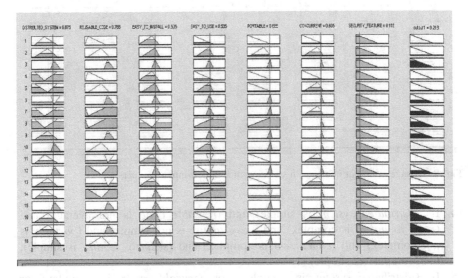

Fig. 7 Output efforts Vs technical input parameters

11. If (*distributed_system* is simple) and (*reusable_code* is not complex) and (*easy_to_install* is simple) and (*easy_to_use* is not complex) and (*portable* is simple) and (*concurrent* is average) and (*security_feature* is simple), then (output1 is simple) (1)

12. If (*distributed_system* is complex) and (*reusable_code* is not average) and (*easy_to_install* is complex) and (*easy_to_use* is not average) and (portable is complex) and (*concurrent* is complex) and (*security_feature* is simple), then (output1 is simple) (1)

13. If (*distributed_system* is average) and (*reusable_code* is not complex) and (*easy_to_install* is simple) and (*easy_to_use* is not complex) and (*portable* is simple) and (*concurrent* is average) and (*security_feature* is simple), then (output1 is simple) (1)

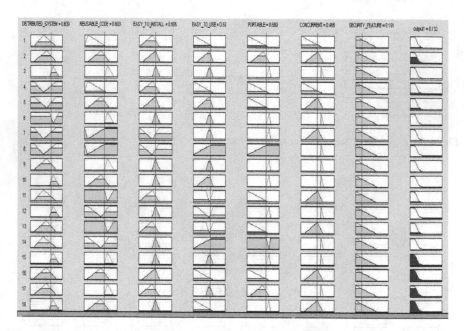

Fig. 8 Change in output efforts with variation in technical input parameters

14. If (*distributed_system* is simple) and (*reusable_code* is not average) and (*easy_to_install* is complex) and (*easy_to_use* is not simple) and (*portable* is not complex) and (*concurrent* is complex) and (*security_feature* is simple), then (output1 is simple) (1)

15. If (*distributed_system* is complex) or (*reusable_code* is complex) or (*easy_to_install* is complex) or (*easy_to_use* is complex) or (*portable* is complex) or (*concurrent* is complex) or (*security_feature* is simple), then (output1 is simple) (1)

16. If (*distributed_system* is average) or (*reusable_code* is average) or (*easy_to_install* is average) or (*easy_to_use* is simple) or (*portable* is SIMPLE) or (*concurrent* is average) or (*security_feature* is simple), then (output1 is simple) (1)

17. If (*distributed_system* is average) or (*reusable_code* is complex) or (*easy_to_install* is SIMPLE) or (*easy_to_use* is complex) or (*portable* is average) or (*concurrent* is complex) or (*security_feature* is simple), then (output1 is simple) (1)

18. If (*distributed_system* is complex) or (*reusable_code* is average) or (*easy_to_install* is complex) or (*easy_to_use* is simple) or (*portable* is complex) or (*concurrent* is average) or (*security_feature* is simple), then (output1 is simple) (1).

6 Analysis of Environmental Factors Using Fuzzy Inference System

The environmental factor is the factor that characterizes a project and its environment. Change in the process gives rise to change in environment and change in environment also gives rise to change in software process. So software process and its environment are complimentary to each other. It indicates that software development process is dynamic. The complexity of software is greatly influenced by the environment used in the development process.

Application knowledge one of the most important factors in project success is the ability of estimator. If the estimator has experienced with similar type of projects, it is easier to predict the right schedule and budget of a software project. Many softwares fail only due to the fact that estimator has no prior experience to handle such type of projects, and there is huge loss of funds and times. It is always preferred experienced and matured professionals to give accurate estimates.

Test environment test environment is a setup of software and hardware on which the testing team is going to perform the test. This is the physical setup which includes types of operating system, server databases, and front-end interface.

Test data in order to test the software we need to enter some data for testing the feature of software. So tester always identifies a set of input data that is used for testing. Some test data is based on the expected output and another set of test data shows the invalid behavior. The test data is generated by tester or by automation tools. It is always expected that the test data should be verified before using it to any kind of test.

Test leader capability Test leader is responsible for planning, monitoring, and controlling the testing activities. They are also responsible for setting the test objectives, test policies, and test plans. Test leader guides, monitors, analyzes, designs, and implements the test cases. Sometimes test leader works as test manger or test coordinator. So project estimation depends upon the test leader capability. If test leader has more experience about the project estimation, then he can plan and design good test case.

Motivation the team motivation is an important factor in testing. The testing team gets motivation if the test leader recognizes the ability of testing team. Testing team should have promotional opportunities. Also, fair and pleasant workplace supports in motivation. The testing team leader should be supportive fair and highly competent. All members like to feel that they are well paid for time and expertise.

Stable requirements it is a metric used in controlling and tracking the changes in the original specification in the requirements of new project. Since the projects begin after consultation with the users or clients, project manager create a requirement document. This document expresses what is the need of clients. However, when the design or development process is underway clients may change their expectation, if that phase is not resolved then there is fear loss of time and money and if the project go beyond the scope results in failed project. Requirement management has become more challenging task with advancements in technology.

Part-time workers part-time workers are recruited for software projects mainly for two reasons either to save time or money. With part-time worker, there are morale and employee relation problems. There is more negligence on the behalf of part-time workers than permanent employees. Part-time workers perform the task without any commitments, but sometimes part-time workers provide the specialized skills than permanent employees. So during project estimation this is an important parameter taken into consideration.

The environment factor is calculated by multiplying the value of each factor by its weight and getting the values called Efac. The following formula is applied:

$$EF = 1.4 + (-0.03 \times (Efac))$$

The seven identified domains are summarized in Table 3, along with an explanation above of why these domains were selected for inclusion.

Here we applied 12 set fuzzy inference rules to check the environment complexity of projects based on Table 3 (Figs. 9, 10, 11, 12 and 13).

1. If (*application_knowledge* is simple) and (*test_environment* is simple) and (*test_data* is simple) and (*leader_capability* is simple) and (motivation is simple) and (*stable_requirment* is simple) and (*part_time_worker* is simple), then (output1 is simple) (1)

2. If (*application_knowledge* is simple) and (*test_environment* is average) and (*test_data* is average) and (*leader_capability* is average) and (*motivation* is average) and (*stable_requirment* is average) and (*part_time_worker* is simple), then (output1 is simple) (1)

3. If (*application_knowledge* is complex) and (*test_environment* is complex) and (*test_data* is complex) and (*leader_capability* is complex) and (motivation is complex) and (*stable_requirment* is complex) and (*part_time_worker* is simple), then (output1 is simple) (1)

4. If (*application_knowledge* is average) and (*test_environment* is average) and (*test_data* is average) and (*leader_capability* is average) and (*motivation* is average) and (*stable_requirment* is average) and (*part_time_worker* is simple), then (output1 is simple) (1)

5. If (*application_knowledge* is average) and (*test_environment* is simple) and (*test_data* is simple) and (*leader_capability* is simple) and (*motivation* is simple) and (*stable_requirment* is simple) and (*part_time_worker* is simple), then (output1 is simple) (1)

6. If (*application_knowledge* is average) and (*test_environment* is complex) and (*test_data* is complex) and (*leader_capability* is complex) and (motivation is complex) and n(*stable_requirment* is complex) and (*part_time_worker* is simple), then (output1 is simple) (1)

7. If (*application_knowledge* is complex) and (*test_environment* is average) and (*test_data* is average) and (*leader_capability* is simple) and (*motivation* is average) and (*stable_requirment* is average) and (*part_time_worker* is simple), then (output1 is simple) (1)

Table 3 Environmental factor calculation for use cases

Use case	Simple				Average				Complex			
	Weight	No. of use cases	Efac	EF	Weight	No. of use cases	Efac	EF	Weight	No. of use cases	Efac	EF
Application knowledge	0.5	7	3.5	1.295	0.5	13	6.5	1.205	0.5	15	7.5	1.175
Test environment	2	7	14	0.98	3	15	45	0.05	5	40	200	-4.6
Test data	0.3	7	2.1	1.337	0.3	15	4.5	1.265	0.3	20	6	1.22
Test leader capability	0.5	8	4	1.28	0.5	18	9	1.13	0.5	25	12.5	1.025
Motivation	0.3	3	0.9	1.373	0.3	40	12	1.04	0.3	20	6	1.22
Stable requirement	1	12	12	1.04	1	14	14	0.98	1	25	25	0.65
Part-time worker	-1	3	-3	1.49	-1	10	-10	1.7	-1	20	-20	2
Total				8.795				7.37				2.69

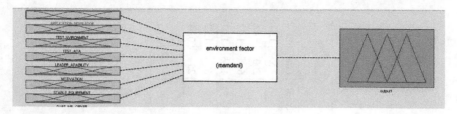

Fig. 9 Fuzzy inference system for environment factors

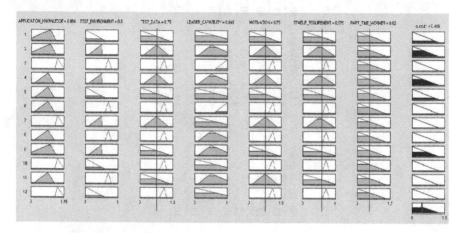

Fig. 10 Graph shows the inference on conditions for application knowledge (80 %), test data under investigation (75 %), leader capability (65 %), and part-time worker (40 %). If we take the average case, then the overall influence is around 46 %

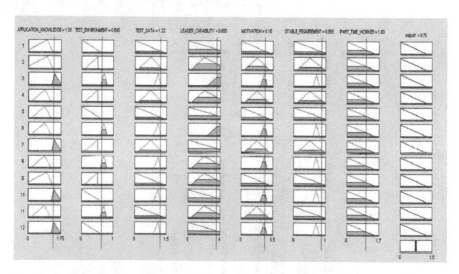

Fig. 11 From the graph above we inference on conditions for application knowledge, test environment, test data under investigation test leader capability, and part-time worker; here overall influence is around 75 %

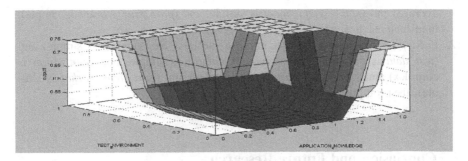

Fig. 12 Variation of test environment with application knowledge

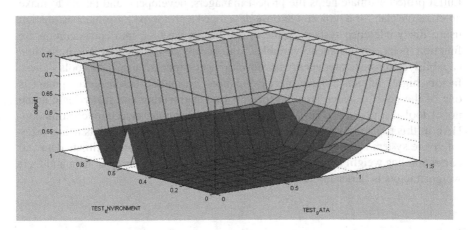

Fig. 13 Variation of test environment with test data

8. If (*application_knowledge* is average) and (*test_environment* is complex) and (test_data is complex) and (*leader_capability* is average) and (*motivation* is complex) and (*stable_requirment* is complex) and (*part_time_worker* is simple), then (output1 is simple) (1)

9. If (*application_knowledge* is simple) and (*test_environment* is average) and (*test_data* is simple) and (*leader_capability* is average) and (*motivation* is simple) and (*stable_requirment* is simple) and (*part_time_worker* is simple), then (output1 is simple) (1)

10. If (*application_knowledge* is complex) and (*test_environment* is simple) and (*test_data* is complex) and (*leader_capability* is simple) and (*motivation* is complex) and (*stable_requirment* is complex) and (*part_time_worker* is simple), then (output1 is simple) (1)

11. If (*application_knowledge* is average) and (*test_environment* is complex) and (test_data is simple) and (*leader_capability* is average) and (*motivation* is

average) and (*stable_requirment* is simple) and (*part_time_worker* is simple), then (output1 is simple) (1)

12. If (*application_knowledge* is complex) and (*test_environment* is simple) and (*test_data* is complex) and (*leader_capability* is simple) and (*motivation* is complex) and (*stable_requirment* is complex) and (*part_time_worker* is simple), then (output1 is simple) (1).

7 Conclusion and Future Research

Initial project estimate helps the project managers, developers, and testers to make an effective plan for a project. Here we developed a prototype for project estimation using fuzzy inference system. Some of the factors we took into consideration are function point, environment variables, and technical factors that are individual capability, domain experience, the development process, size, and tools. These factors highly influence the project estimation. Estimation before development is one of the novel research areas in the software engineering and fuzzy logic is the novel tool that gives use fairly accurate, near to accurate, or accurate estimation. Here in this paper we studied the influence of different use case points using fuzzy inference system for the project estimation. Here we took the approximate data and corresponding weight factors from different sources. The accuracy of data and their weight factors is under investigation.

References

1. Jacobson, I. (1987). Object oriented development in an industrial environment. In *OOPSLA '87 Proceedings*, October 4–8, 1987, pp. 183–191.
2. Garmus, D., & Herron, D. (2000). *Function point analysis: measurement practices for successful software projects*. Boston, Addison Wesley.
3. MacDonell, S. G. (1994). Comparatives review of functional complexity assessment methods for effort estimation. *BCS/IEEE Software Engineering Journal, 9*(3), 107–117.
4. Symons, C. R. (1988). Function-point analysis: difficulties and improvements. *IEEE Transactions on Software Engineering, 14*(1), 2–11.
5. Resource Estimation for Objectory Projects Gustav Karner Objective Systems SF AB Torshamnsgatan 39, Box 1128, 164 22 Kista, September 17, 1993.
6. Factor affecting software maintenance productivity an exploratory study: Carnegie Mellon University by Rajiv D. Banker Journal information technology and management, Issue 1–2, January 2002, pp. 25–41.
7. Clarke, P., & O'Connor, R. V. (2012). The situational factors that affect the software development process: towards a comprehensive reference fra mework. *Journal of Information Software and Technology, 54*(5), 433–447.
8. Armour, P. (2002). Ten unmyths of project estimation. *Communications of the ACM, 45*(11), 15–18.

9. Banker, R., Kauffman, R., et al. (1994). An empirical test of object-based output measurement metrics in a computer-aided software engineering (CASE) environment. *Journal of Management Information Systems/Winter, 1991–92,* 127–150.
10. Banker, R. D., Datar, S. M., et al. (1993). Software complexity and maintenance costs. *Communications of the ACM, 36*(11), 81–94.
11. Furey, S., & Kitchenham, B. (1997). Point/counterpoint: function points. *IEEE Software, 14* (2), 28–31.
12. Albrecht, A. J. (1979). Measuring application development productivity. In *Proceedings of IBM Applications Development Symposium, Monterey,* CA, p. 83, October 14–17, 1979.
13. Albrecht, A. J. (1985). Function points help managers assess application, maintenance values. In *Computer World Special Report on Software Productivity, CW Communications,* pp. SR20–SR21.
14. Nageswaran, S. (2001). Test effort estimation using use case points. In *Quality Week 2001,* San Francisco, California, USA, June 2001.
15. Anda, Bente. (2002). *Improving estimation practices by applying use case models.* PROFES: Rovaniemi, Finland.
16. Fei, Z., & Liu X. (1992) f-COCOMO: fuzzy constructive cost model in software engineering. In *Proceedings of the IEEE International Conference on Fuzzy Systems,* IEEE Press, New York, pp. 331–337.
17. Albrecht, A. J. & Gaffney J. E. (1983). Software function, lines of code and development effort prediction: a software science validation. *IEEETransactions on Software Engineering,* **SE-9** (6): 639–647

Linear and Nonlinear Modeling of Protein Kinase B/AkT

Shruti Jain and D.S. Chauhan

Abstract AkT is the main protein which was frequently occurred in the human cancer. There are several pathways of AkT which were shown in this paper which lead to cell death/survival. In this paper, we have used the mathematical analysis (linear modeling and non linear modeling) to make a best model of the survival/death proteins, i.e., epidermal growth factor, tumor necrosis factor, and insulin using ten different combinations. The model was made using linear modeling using different regression analysis techniques in which different parameters like mean sq error, root mean sq error, mean abs error, relative sq error, root relative sq error, and relative abs error were analyzed. Later on, Kolmogorov–Smirnov, Anderson–Darling, and chi-square tests were done using different distribution functions. Results with half-normal distribution function are the best as their AD and chi-square values are the maximum. Nonlinear modeling was done using neural network with MLP and RBF approaches.

Keywords Akt · Regression analysis · Kolmogorov–Smirnov · Anderson–Darling · Chi-square tests · Neural network

1 Introduction

The protein kinase B/AkT [1–5] is the main protein for the regulation of growth, death, and metabolism [6–10] by TNF [11, 12], EGF [13, 14], and insulin pathway [15–17].

AkT leads to cell survival [18, 19] by activating the proteins like Bad [20], NF-kB, and CREB and inactivating the proteins like FKHR and caspase 9 [21].

S. Jain (✉)
Jaypee University of Information Technology, Waknaghat, Solan 173234, Himachal Pradesh, India
e-mail: jain.shruti15@gmail.com

D.S. Chauhan
GLA Mathura, Mathura 281406, Uttar Pradesh, India

© Springer Science+Business Media Singapore 2016
S.C. Satapathy et al. (eds.), *Proceedings of International Conference on ICT for Sustainable Development*, Advances in Intelligent Systems and Computing 409, DOI 10.1007/978-981-10-0135-2_7

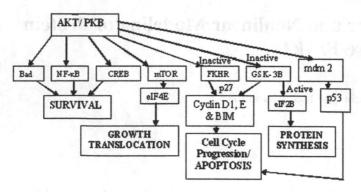

Fig. 1 Block diagram of AkT model [8]

PTEN is a main negative regulator of the AkT pathway. AkT plays main part in cell survival by phosphorylating mTOR. Figure 1, shows the model of AkT.

In this paper, we have calculated different r^2 (predicted, adjusted) values, predicted sum of square value, t-value, p-value etc. [22]. We have also established the regression equation of AkT in terms of different concentrations of different inputs. Mathematical analysis was done by two methods: linear modeling (regression analysis), K–S, AD, chi-square tests, and nonlinear modeling (neural network). Different regression analysis methods like linear, partial least square, k nearest neighbors, random forest, mean and SVM regression were used in calculation of different parameters. After regression analysis, Kolmogorov–Smirnov (K–S), Anderson–Darling (AD), and chi-square tests were done using different distribution functions, i.e., Weibull, normal, log normal, triangular, Rayleigh, half normal, and general pareto. Results with half-normal distribution function are found to be the best. MLP and RBF techniques were used in nonlinear modeling [23–25].

2 System Implementation Using Linear Modeling

For linear modeling, we have used different types of regression analysis like linear, partial least square, k nearest neighbors, random forest, mean, and SVM regression. We have designed a model using regression analysis for cell survival/death. Different parameters are calculated with the different concentrations (ng/ml) of the EGF, TNF and Insulin [7, 8] which was illustrated in Table 1.

(a) For $r^2, r^2_{pred}, r^2_{adj}$: Eq. 1 gives the regression coefficient (r^2) equation.

$$r^2 = 1 - \frac{\sum (y_i - f_i)^2}{\sum (y_i - \bar{y})^2} \ \text{or} \ r^2 = \frac{\sum (f_i - \bar{f})^2}{\sum (y_i - \bar{y})^2} \tag{1}$$

Table 1 Ten combinations of TNF, EGF, and insulin

	i	ii	iii	iv	v	vi	vii	$viii$	ix	x
TNF	0	5	100	0	5	100	0	0.2	5	100
EGF	–	–	–	100	1	100	–	–	–	–
Insulin	0	0	0	–	–	–	500	1	5	500

where y_i are the observed values, f_i are the predicted values, $\bar{y}$ are the means of the observed data and $\bar{f}$ are the means of the predicted values.

The parameters which we have calculated for AkT are: S = 0.006077 r^2 = 91.8 %, r^2 (adj) = 91.5 %, = r^2 (pred) = 91.22 %

We clubbed all the concentrations of TNF, EGF, and Insulin and only the normalized output (AkT) was taken and we get the regression equation as:

$$\begin{aligned} \text{Final Output for AkT} = {}& 0.444 - 0.000048i + 0.000004ii + 0.000170iii \\ & + 0.000002iv - 0.000007v + 0.000006vi - 0.000133vii \\ & + 0.000087viii + 0.000012ix + 0.000257x. \end{aligned}$$

$$(2)$$

We have also calculated: mean sq error (MSE), root mean sq error (RMSE), mean abs error (MAE), relative sq error (RSE), root relative sq error (RRSE), and relative abs error (RAE) for AkT which was given in Table 2.

(b) *PRESS*: The prediction sum of squares value should be smaller for better predictive model. In our case, the PRESS value for *AkT* is coming out to be 0.011475.

(c) The variance was shown in Table 3, which shows the sum of squares and mean squares of the regression and residual error for AkT.

Table 2 Various analysis parameters using diff regression methods for AkT

	MSE	RMSE	MAE	RSE	RRSE	RAE
PLS regression	0.0000	0.0062	0.0050	0.0893	0.2989	0.2646
Linear regression	0.0000	0.0062	0.0050	0.0893	0.2989	0.2646
SVM regression	0.0005	0.0216	0.0207	1.0755	1.0371	1.0969
K nearest neighbours regression	0.0000	0.0066	0.0054	0.1001	0.3164	0.2831
Mean	0.0004	0.0210	0.0190	1.0125	1.0062	1.0042
Random forest regression	0.0000	0.0064	0.0052	0.0954	0.3089	0.2771

Table 3 Analysis of variance (ANOVA) for all combinations of AkT

Source	dF	Sum of squares	Mean of squares	F-value
Reg	10	0.120009	0.012001	324.93
Residual error	289	0.010674	0.000037	
Total	299	0.130683		

Table 4 Regression analysis in terms of standard error coefficients, t-value, p value, and VIF for AkT

Predictor	Coeff	SER	t-Val	p-Val	VIF
Const	0.4436	1	0.03117	14.23	0.000
0-0-0	−0.00004778	0.00007015	−0.68	0.496	8.2
5-0-0	0.00000430	0.00006852	0.06	0.950	1.4
100-0-0	0.00016999	0.00007279	2.34	0.020	31.0
0-100-0	0.00000154	0.00006801	0.02	0.982	5.2
5-1-0	−0.00000679	0.00009481	−0.07	0.943	54.6
100-100-0	0.00000625	0.00007477	0.08	0.933	2.1
0-0-500	−0.00013323	0.00006566	−2.03	0.043	20.5
0.2-0-1	0.00008699	0.00006647	1.31	0.192	11.4
5-0-5	0.00001155	0.00003415	0.34	0.736	150.2
100-0-500	0.00025730	0.00003962	6.49	0.000	81.2

(d) *Standard Error Coefficients* (SER): The SER is used to find the precision of the estimate of the coefficient. The value of SER should be small. To get the *t*-value coefficient, values are divided by SER value. Table 4 shows the regression analysis in terms of SER, *t*-value, *p*-value, and VIF for AkT.

3 System Implementation Using Kolmogorov–Smirnov, Chi- Square and Spapiro Wilk Test

Cumulative distribution function specifies the distance of multivariate random variables X. The real-valued random variables X with a given probability distance will found to have a value less than or equal to x. There are different tests performed on different distribution functions: Kolmogorov–Smirnov test, Anderson–Darling test, and chi-square test (Tables 5 and 6).

(a) The Kolmogorov–Smirnov (K–S/KS) test is an equality test using nonparametric. It can also be used as a goodness of fit test. One sample/one dimensional K–S test is used to compare a sample with a prob function while two sample/2-D test is used to compare two samples.
The K–S statistic for a given cumulative distribution function $F(x)$ is

$$D_n = \sup_x |F_n(x) - F(x)| \qquad (3)$$

where sup x is the supremum value of the distances.

Table 6 The output of AkT for different concentration using ANN

S. no	Network name	Training perfection (%)	Test perfection (%)	Validation perfection (%)	Training algorithm	Hidden activation	Output activation
1	MLP 10-9-1	96.3884	96.2563	95.1267	BFGS 14	Tanh	Tanh
2	MLP 10-4-1	96.6091	96.333	95.1007	BFGS 22	Tanh	Identity
3	MLP 10-13-1	96.6275	96.2382	95.1159	BFGS 19	Tanh	Exponential
4	MLP 10-10-1	95.8873	96.3377	95.2907	BFGS 7	Logistic	Logistic
5	MLP 10-8-1	96.5909	96.3153	95.2068	BFGS 24	Exponential	Exponential
6	RBF 10-22-1	95.9533	95.2069	94.1186	RBFT	Gaussian	Identity
7	RBF 10-28-1	96.3238	94.7159	94.6874	RBFT	Gaussian	Identity
8	RBF 10-21-1	96.1945	95.3453	94.3453	RBFT	Gaussian	Identity
9	RBF 10-26-1	95.7076	94.9749	93.941	RBFT	Gaussian	Identity
10	RBF 10-29-1	95.9666	95.6203	94.1033	RBFT	Gaussian	Identity

Table 7 The output of AkT for different concentration using CNS

S. no	Network name	Training perfection (%)	Test perfection (%)	Validation perfection (%)	Training algorithm	Hidden activation	Output activation
1	MLP 10-8-1	96.3622	96.2517	95.0763	BFGS 13	Tanh	Identity
2	RBF 10-15-1	94.687	94.2678	92.5952	RBFT	Gaussian	Identity

(b) The Anderson–Darling (AD) test/Shapiro Wilk test is a statistical test and is based on the distance

$$A = n \int_{-\infty}^{\infty} \frac{(F_n(x) - F(x))^2}{F(x)(1 - F(x))} dF(x) \tag{4}$$

where $w(x) = [F(x)(1 - F(x))]^{-1}$ is a weight function.

c) A chi-squared test, also referred to as χ^2 test (or chi-square test), is any statistical hypothesis test which is used to determine whether there is a significant difference between the observed frequencies and the expected frequencies in one or more categories.

Table 5 shows the KS, AD, and chi-square value of different functions.

4   System Implementation Using Non-linear Modeling

A neural network (ANN) model was developed for the AkT which predicts whether cell will survive or die. For training the ANN model, experimental data form ten different concentrations of each marker proteins was taken as input, and their

Table 5 KS, AD, and chi-square values of different distribution function

	K–S d	K–S	AD stat	AD p-value	Chi-square	Chi-square p-value	Chi-square df
Gaussian mixture (Mixing.Coef.1, Mean 1, Std.Dev 1, Mixing Coef.2,…)	0.026799	0.978501	0.1503	0.998562	6.067	0.108415	3
Weibull (scale, shape)	0.183078	0.000000	18.5049	0.000000	193.533	0.000000	7
Triangular(min, max, mode)	0.210974	0.000000	25.5090	0.000000	232.733	0.000000	6
Normal (location, scale)	0.231571	0.000000	22.6154	0.000000	266.733	0.000000	7
Log normal (scale, shape)	0.236718	0.000000	23.2578	0.000000	279.467	0.000000	7
Rayleigh (scale)	0.568500	0.000000	117.2716	0.000000	1424.267	0.000000	8
Half-normal (scale)	0.640743	0.000000	144.1607	0.000000	1907.267	0.000000	8
General pareto (scale, shape)	0.867025	0.000000	532.6983	0.000000	1555.267	0.000000	7

corresponding possible experimental output. We have implemented the neural network model using STATISTICA data miner software. If the predicted output in the neural network is >0.5, then it will lead to cell survival; otherwise, it leads to cell death. The data from the four treatments were used as test set to validate the predictive accuracy of ANN model.

The training perfection, test perfection, and validation perfection using MLP and RBF methods of 10 possible combinations for AkT using automated neural search (ANS) and custom neural network (CNS) are shown in Tables 6 and 7, respectively.

5 Conclusion

It was found that survival/death of the signals by AkT are temporarily separated and this is reflected in our model by the differences between the values of the parameters used. In this paper, we have used linear and nonlinear modeling. The model was made using linear modeling (different regression analysis like linear, partial least square, k nearest neighbors, random forest, mean and SVM regression) in which different parameters like MSE, RMSE, MAE, RSE, RRSE, RAE, r^2, r^2_{adj}, PRESS, t-values for our 10 data sets which comes out to be correct. K–S, AD, and chi-square test were also done on different functions and the results with half-normal function are the best. Nonlinear modeling was also done using neural network with MLP and RBF approach using two different approaches, i.e,. automated neural search and custom neural network. Models are powerful and flexible which incorporate noise and produce good predictions.

References

1. Staal, S. P. (1987). Molecular cloning of the akt oncogene and its human homologues AKT1 and AKT2: Amplification of AKT1 in a primary human gastric adenocarcinoma. *Proceedings of the National Academy of Sciences of the USA, 84*, 5034–5037.
2. Vanhaesebroeck, B., & Alessi, D. (2000). The PI3K-PDK1 connection: More than just a road to PKB. *Biochemical Journal, 346*, 561–576.
3. Coffer, P. J., Jin, J., & Woodgett, J. R. (1998). Protein kinase B (c-Akt): A multifunctional mediator of phosphatidylinositol 3-kinase activation. *Biochemical Journal, 335*, 1–13.
4. Brazil, D. P., & Hemmings, B. A. (2001). Ten years of protein kinase B signalling: A hard Akt to follow. *Trends in Biochemical Sciences, 26*, 657–664.
5. Hemmings, B. A. (1997). Akt signaling: Linking membrane events to life and death decisions. *Science, 275*, 628–630.
6. Cohen, P., Alessi, D. R., & Cross, D. A. E. (1997). PDK1, one of the missing links in insulin signal transduction? *FEBS Letters, 410*, 3–10.
7. Jain, S. (2012). Communication of signals and responses leading to cell survival/cell death using engineered regulatory networks. *PhD Thesis, Jaypee University of Information Technology, Solan, Himachal Pradesh, India.*

8. Jain, S., Bhooshan, S. V., & Naik P. K., Compendium model of AkT for cell survival/death and its equivalent BioCircuit. *International Journal of Soft Computing and Engineering, 2*(3), 91–97.
9. Weiss, R. (2001). Cellular computation and communications using engineered genetic regulatory networks. *PhD Thesis, MIT.*
10. Gaudet, S., Janes Kevin, A., Albeck John, G., Pace Emily, A., Lauffenburger Douglas, A., & Sorger Peter, K. (2005). *A compendium of signals and responses trigerred by prodeath and prosurvival cytokines Manuscript M500158-MCP200.*
11. Brockhaus, M., Schoenfeld, H. J., Schlaeger, E. J., Hunziker, W., Lesslauer, W., & Loetscher, H. (1990). Identification of two types of tumor necrosis factor receptors on human cell lines by monoclonal antibodies. *Proceedings of the National Academy of Sciences of the USA, 87*, 3127–3131.
12. Thoma, B., Grell, M., Pfizenmaier, K., & Scheurich, P. (1990). Identification of a 60-kD tumor necrosis factor (TNF) receptor as the major signal transducing component in TNF responses. *Journal of Experimental Medicine, 172*, 1019–1023.
13. Ullrich, A., & Schlessinger, J. (1990). Signal transduction by receptors with tyrosine kinase activity. *Cell, 61*, 203–211.
14. Arteaga, C. (2003). Targeting HER1/EGFR: A molecular approach to cancer therapy. *Seminars in Oncology, 30*, 314.
15. Lizcano, J. M., & Alessi, D. R. (2002). The insulin signalling pathway. *Current Biology, 12*, 236–238.
16. White, Morris F. (1997). The insulin signaling system and the IRS proteins. *Diabetologia, 40*, S2–S17.
17. Jain, S., Naik, P. K., & Bhooshan, S. V. (2011). Mathematical modeling deciphering balance between cell survival and cell death using insulin. *Network Biology, 1*(1), 46–58.
18. Kim, D., & Chung, J. (2002). Akt: Versatile mediator of cell survival and beyond. *Journal of Biochemistry and Molecular Biology, 35*(1), 106–115.
19. Brunet, A., Bonni, A., Zigmond, M. J., Lin, M. Z., Juo, P., & Hu, L. S. (1999). Akt promotes cell survival by phosphorylating and inhibiting a Forkhead transcription factor. *Cell, 96*, 857–868.
20. Datta, S. R., Dudek, H., Tao, X., Masters, S., Gotoh, H., & Fu, Y. (1997). Akt phosphorylation of BAD couples survival signals to the cell-intrinsic death machinery. *Cell, 91*, 231–241.
21. Cardone, M. H., Roy, N., Stennicke, H. R., Salvesen, G. S., Franke, T. F., & Stanbridge, F. (1998). Regulation of cell death protease caspase-9 by phosphorylation. *Science, 282*, 1318–1321.
22. Jain, S., & Chauhan, D. S. (2015). Mathematical analysis of receptors for survival proteins. *International Journal of Pharma and Bio Sciences, 6*(3), 164–176.
23. Mandic, D., & Chambers, J. (2001). *Recurrent neural networks for prediction: Learning algorithms, architectures and stability.* New York: John Wiley & Sons.
24. Bishop, C. M. (1995). *Neural networks for pattern recognition.* Oxford, UK: Oxford University Press.
25. Rumelhart, D. E., Williams, R. J., & Hinton, G. E. (1986). Learning representations by back-propagating errors. *Nature, 323*, 533–536.

Lost Connectivity Restoration
in Partitioned Wireless Sensor Networks

Ranga Virender, Dave Mayank and Verma Anil Kumar

Abstract Since low-cost devices have been acclaimed in wireless sensor networks (WSNs), their applications in harsh surroundings, i.e., combat field reconnaissance, border protection, space exploration, etc. have become very common nowadays. Due to an unhealthy and exposed environment in which the proposed network has to be operated, sometimes result in damage of large-scale backbone actor nodes that causes connected network split into multiple disjoint segments. Placement of relay nodes (RNs) is the only way to connect the partitioned network, but the higher cost of RNs then becomes an addressable issue of their placement. A new solution based on concentric Fermat points towards the center of deployment called restore relay lost connectivity using concentric fermat points (RRLC-CFP) for RNs' placements is proposed. The simulation results confirm the potency of our proposed solution.

Keywords Spider Web-1C · Relay node placements · Connectivity restoration · Node failure

1 Introduction

The use of wireless sensor networks (WSNs) has become very useful in the real life in the recent years. The applications such as combat field reconnaissance, border protection, space exploration, etc. operate in the harshest environments, where

R. Virender (✉) · D. Mayank
Department of Computer Engineering, National Institute of Technology,
Kurukshetra, Haryana, India
e-mail: virender.ranga@nitkkr.ac.in

D. Mayank
e-mail: m.dave@ieee.org

V.A. Kumar
Department of Computer Science and Engineering, Thapar University,
Patiala, Punjab, India
e-mail: akverma@thapar.edu

© Springer Science+Business Media Singapore 2016
S.C. Satapathy et al. (eds.), *Proceedings of International Conference
on ICT for Sustainable Development*, Advances in Intelligent Systems
and Computing 409, DOI 10.1007/978-981-10-0135-2_8

89

sensor nodes reduce the danger of the human life [1–3]. Since a sensor node is typically constrained in its energy, computational and communication resources, a large set of sensors is involved to ensure area coverage and increase the fidelity of the collected data. Due to small form factor and limited on board energy supply, a sensor is very susceptible to the failure. Due to hostile environments in which the network operates result in large-scale damage of the nodes that causes network partitioning and converts into disjoint segments as shown in Fig. 1. For e.g., some sensors may be buried under snow or sand after the storm or in the field of battle, a component of the deployment area may be assaulted by the explosives and, thus a set of sensor nodes in the neighborhood would be ruined. Thus, repairing of large-scale partitioned WSN is the latest research topic in the recent years. Deploying RNs in the disconnected network is the solitary path to tie the large-scale damaged network. RN is a more up to node with significantly more energy reserve and longer communication range than sensor nodes. Although RNs can, in principle, be equipped with sensor circuitry; mainly perform data aggregation and forwarding. Unlike sensor nodes, a RN may be mobile and has some navigation capabilities. The RNs are favored in the retrieval process, because these are easily to accurately place relative to the sensor nodes, and their communication range is even larger, which facilitates and expedites the connectivity restoration among the

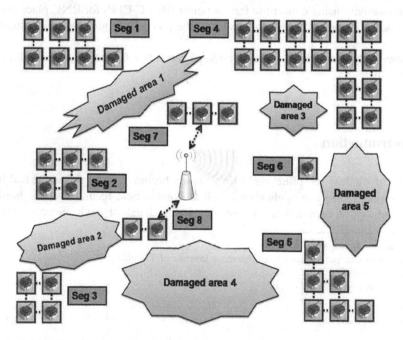

Fig. 1 Articulation of segmented area due to large-scale failure of nodes [3]

disjoint segments effectively and efficiently. Intuitively, RNs are more expensive and thus, minimum number of RNs should to be used for the recovery of the partitioned network. The minimum number of RNs can be found out using Steiner minimum tree (SMT), but it is shown to be NP-hard problem [4]. Therefore, a heuristic is required to find the minimum number of deployed RNs in the partitioned network.

Two major RNs placement heuristics have been published in the recent years. In the first one, the authors proposed a nature-inspired heuristic and use a spider-web-like RNs placement technique called Spider Web-1C approach [4]. The key idea is to form the stronger connectivity, achieve better sensor coverage, and enable balanced distribution of traffic load on the employed relays as well. One of the main advantages of the Spider Web-1C approach that it plugs into the segmented network very efficiently and effectively, but the major problem is the big number of deployed RNs for the recovery. The second approach is based on SMT called ORC-SMT [5]. The idea is the use of SMT by considering three outer segments that are formed after applying the convex hull algorithm recursively in the cyclic fashion. The points thus obtained are then applied recursively to find more Steiner minimum point (SMP) for the RNs placements. The multiple points that come in the radio range of the node, then become a single point for RN placement. In this way, the process repeats itself till all the outer segments for which the run was made are not less than three. Then, RNs are placed on these points by applying minimum spanning tree (MST) algorithm such as Kruskal or Prim algorithm. The main advantage of ORC-SMT that it connects various segments quickly and efficiently with a small number of RNs placements. In this research paper, we consider the similar type of problem, i.e., network partition problem due to failure of a large-scale node with large number of partitions in the network. The distinction of our work as compared with previous proposed works is that in our proposed solution network partition problem is addressed and solved by using of concentric Fermat points, which is not yet seen in other solutions. However, in [9], the authors have considered Fermat point in the data propagation to reduce data transmission distance among the nodes to enhance network lifetime but without considered the partitioned problem. The remainder of the paper is organized as follows: In Sect. 2, related work is described. Section 3 gives the problem statement. Section 4 explains our proposed solution and Sect. 5 shows performance evaluation of our proposed approach through simulations. In Sect. 6, the article is concluded with future scope.

2 Related Works

Many advances have been proposed till last year to endure a large-scale node failure in WSNs. The authors of [1, 2] have given the comprehensive survey of the network partitioning recovery approaches based on different standards. All approaches are classified into two broad categories: (a) centralized approaches, and (b) distributed or semi-distributed approaches. The classification is further divided into three different categories, i.e., proactive, reactive, and hybrid approaches. For proactive schemes, many approaches have been considered to tolerate node's failure in the literature. A similar classification is applied to reactive and hybrid approaches. In all proposed approaches, controlled node mobility has been used to restore the partitioned network. For example, in [5], a robot called Packbot has been used to serve as a mobile RN. The use of robot enables the recovery of partitioned network, or break links. An algorithm is applied to determine the trajectory of a moving robot in the network. A similar type of solution is presented by Wang et al. [6]. The authors have considered mobile RNs within 2-hop of the sink in the network to restore the partitioned network. Unlike [5], the idea is that RNs do not need to travel the long distance in the network. The use of Packbots and similar types of devices is inefficient due to unexpected delays in data delivery even multiple such devices are used in the network. The reason is the slow motion of devices to cover every individual best point in the network. Wang et al. [7] have exploited node controlled mobility in order to cover the coverage holes which are not covered by sensor nodes during their initial deployment. The idea behind this work is to identify some spare nodes from different parts of the network that can be relocated to coverage-hole places. Since moving a node for long distance can drain significant node power, a cascaded movement is proposed if the sufficient number of sensor nodes is available on the way. Another approach is proposed by Sentruk et al. [8] to improve the scalability by reducing the number of candidate locations. A RN placement algorithm is used to find the set of locations which can guarantee the connectivity if RNs are to be deployed to these locations.

3   System Model and Problem Definition

We assume a network in which a large number of sensor nodes are deployed throughout an area of interest. Due to the harsh environment of the application like in a battlefield, where sensor nodes could be destroyed by enemy explosives, thus causing a large scale node's failure which leads to multiple disjoint partitions in the network. Thus, RNs are used to connect this disjoint network. Our problem can be defined as follows: "N sensor nodes that know their location using some localization algorithm are randomly deployed in an area of interest. Let us assume that j disconnected subnetworks are formed as a result of failure of a large-scale node in the network. Each subnetwork G_i has n_i sensor nodes where $0 < n_i \ll N$. Our goal is to implement an algorithm that will ensure the lost connectivity among the disconnected subnetworks G_i by using the minimum number of RNs placements and thus, create a new connected network".

4 Restore Relay Lost Connectivity Using Concentric Fermat Points

Our proposed approach, unlike ORC-SMT, considers three segment groups as a triangle and finds the centroid (CoD) of triangle instead of calculating SMT that behaves like a Fermat point (F_p) of a triangle for angle less than 120°. The Fermat point is a point within a triangle at which the sum of the distances between a point and the three vertices of the triangle is minimal [9]. Our proposed approach exploits the mathematical property of F_p to place the RNs. Figure 2 illustrates an example to calculate F_p The point F_p denotes the Fermat point of Δxyz. It can be defined as follows: first, three equilateral triangles, i.e., $\Delta x'yz$, $\Delta y'xz$, and $\Delta z'xy$ are drawn on each side of. These equilateral triangles are connected with three extended straight lines, i.e., yy' and. The common point of intersection of three straight lines is a Fermat point F_p Three angles, $\angle xF_pz$ and $\angle yF_pz$ will be equal to 120° such that the sum of the distances between F_p and vertices x, y, and z are minimal. Our proposed approach RRLC-CFP adopts the algorithm proposed by Ssu et al. [9] to perform vector calculations which quickly converges to an approximate value of the F_p or the placement of RNs. We also check to see whether F_p existing inside the triangle or not. If it is the case, we use Weiszfeld algorithm proposed in [9] to identify the F_p locations. Otherwise, the center of the triangle is chosen as F_p or convergence. In case multiple segments exist in the network like we have taken in our scenario, then the idea is to place the RNs on the chaining path of the multiple consecutive F_p. Initially, three random segments are taken based on node density function and calculate the first F_p. Consequently, the given segments are sorted in clockwise

Fig. 2 Example of calculation of F_P of three segments

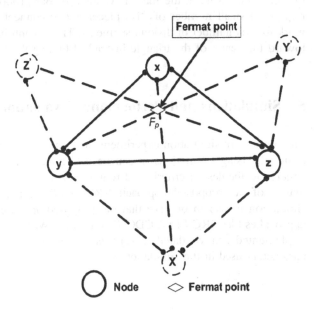

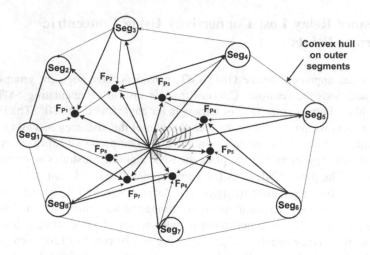

Fig. 3 Example of calculation of concentric F_{p_s}

direction from the first segment. To understand this, let us consider the scenario as shown in Fig. 3 where the first F_p is computed by taking three segments at a time (It is assumed that segments are sorted in descending order as per node density). Indeed, we obtain a chain of connected tree by combining the calculated F_{p_s} Thus, RNs are deployed toward the center of the deployment. Tons of algorithms are available in the literature to find the center of the triangle (in case triangle is not an equilateral triangle) like Napoleon point, Spieker Center, and Nine-point Center etc. However, the Spieker Center is an easy and simple method to find the center of the triangle. Furthermore, the main advantage of our proposed RRLC-CFP is that it requires a small number of RNs placement to connect disjoint network and can work for any number of disjoint segments. The key intubation is to deploy the RNs toward the center of the triangle instead of finding the SPs separately.

5 Simulations and Performance Evaluation

The purpose of simulation experiments acts as a proof of concept for the designed protocol. Using simulations, it can be determined whether the designed protocol adheres to the design criteria and requirements. This section evaluates the performance of our proposed approach RRLC-CFP through simulation. The goal of simulation is also to observe that the proposed approach outperforms over other approaches like ORC-SMT, CDCH, and Spider Web-1C. Our proposed approach is implemented and validated in C++ environment. Table 1 shows the simulation parameters used in the simulation.

The following three parameters are considered in our experiments for simulation:

(a) Number of segments (N_s).
(b) Communication range (r) of an RN.
(c) Number of placed RNs.

In the simulation experiments, we have taken different topologies with the number of outer segments varying from 4 to 8 and inner segments varying from 2 to 5 i.e. total disjoint segments varies from 6 to 13 that are randomly located in an area of interest (i.e. 2000 m × 2000 m). While studying the impact of r on the performance, it varies between 50 and 200 m. The results of the individual experiments are averaged over 30 trials of different topologies. We have observed simulation results within 5–10 % of the sample mean. We consider the number of RNs placed for evaluating the performance of our proposed approach and compare with the existing approaches.

Number of placed RNs. This metric report the total number of required RNs to restore the lost connectivity in the network. As aforementioned, RNs are usually more expensive than sensor nodes. Thus, this metric reflects the total cost of repairing of the partitioned network. Figure 4a, b show the number of required RNs while varying node radio range in the configuration. Therefore, it is clear from the simulation graphs that ORC-SMT performs better than our proposed approach RRLC-CFP only when the number of partitions is less than 5; however, our proposed approach performs well for any number of partitions. Moreover, BD approach shows a large number of RNs placements for the repairing of partitioned network due to deployment of nodes along the border of the convex hull in the circular fashion. Furthermore, Spider Web-1C shows similar result like our proposed approach RRLC-CFP as the node radio range increases due to making of large size web structure for the placement of RNs towards CoM. The ORC-SMT fails when the number of outer segments is more than 5 as shown in Figs. 5 and 6.

Table 1 Simulation parameters	Parameter	Value
	Simulation area	2000 m × 2000 m
	Nodes	100–500
	Radio model	Path loss model
	MAC layer	IEEE 802.15.4
	Communication range (R)	50–200 m
	Node initial energy (E_i)	100 J
	Total number of partitions	6–13
	Channel frequency	2.4 GHz
	Packet size	512 bytes
	Antenna model	Omni-directional
	Mobility model	On-demand mobility
	Failure model	Random
	Data transmission rate	15 packets/s
	Simulation time	1000 s

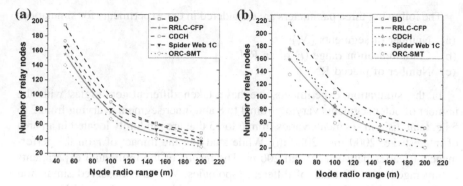

Fig. 4 Number of relay nodes **a** versus node radio range when outer segments are 4 and inner segments varies from 2 to 8, **b** versus node radio range when outer segments are 5 and inner segments varies from 2 to 8

Fig. 5 Number of relay nodes versus number of outer segments with node radio range 100 m

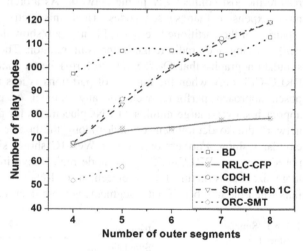

The reason is that in the random topologies, when number of outer segments becomes larger than 5, more than one of the angles of the Steiner triangle of SMT comes out to be greater than 120° (obviously some are less than 120°); therefore, the calculated SPs comes out to be on the segment itself. This questions the convergence ability of the ORC-SMT algorithm toward the center for which the authors have claimed. The situation becomes more intense as the number of segments grows and the algorithm fails in the simulations as we observed in our experiments. In a nutshell, we can say that ORC-SMT behaves best when it serves with a small number of segments (i.e., less than 5), as we have verified in the simulation. Furthermore, the Spider Web-1C heuristics runs almost parallel to the CDCH when the node radio range is smaller. This is because the web formed by Spider Web-1C would be much closer to the CoM as explained earlier, and lesser

Fig. 6 Number of relay
nodes versus number of outer
segments with node radio
range 200 m

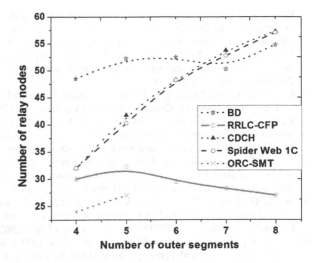

number of nodes is required for the repairing of the lost connectivity. The
RRLC-CFP shows good results as compared with ORC-SMT, Spider Web-1C,
CDCH, and BD as the number of outer segments increases. The reason is the
deployment of a small number of RNs toward the center of damage as explained
earlier. Figures 5 and 6 also confirm the effectiveness of our proposed approach.

6 Conclusion and Future Scope

In this paper, we have proposed a new solution based on concentric Fermat points
for RNs' placements in large-scale partitioned WSN. The main strength of the
proposed approach is the placement of only a small number of RNs and it works for
any number of disjoint segments compared with existing proposed approaches. The
simulation results confirm the goodness of our proposed approach. In the future, our
study can focus on simulation of our proposed solution to evaluate the actual
network performance parameters like throughput, end-to-end delay, packet delivery, loss ratio, etc. with the recovery process.

References

1. Younis, M., Sentruk, I. F., Akkaya, K., Lee, K., & Senel, F. (2013). Topology management
   techniques for tolerating node failures in WSNs: A survey. *Computer Networks* (*Elsevier*), 1–30.
2. Ranga, V., Dave, M., & Verma, A. K. (September 2013). Network partitioning recovery
   mechanisms used in WSANs: A survey. *Wireless Personal Communications* (*Springer*), 72(2),
   857–917.

3. Ranga, V., Dave, M., & Verma, A. K. (April 2015) Realy node placement for lost connectivity restoration in partitioned WSNs. *Proceeding of the International Conference on Recent Advances on Electroscience and Computers, Barcelona, Spain* (pp. 571–575).
4. Senel, F., Younis, M. F., & Akkaya, K. (May 2011). Bio-inspired relay node placement heuristics for repairing damaged wireless sensor networks. *IEEE Transactions on Vehicular Technology, 60*(4), 1835–1848.
5. Lee, S., & Younis, M. (August 2012). Optimized relay node placement for connecting disjoint wireless sensor networks. *Computer Networks (Elsevier), 56*(12), 2788–2804.
6. Kansal, A., Somasundara, A., Srivastava, D. J. M., & Estrin, D. (2004) Intelligent fluid infrastructure for embedded networks. *Proceeding of the 2nd International Conference on Mobile Systems, Applications and Services (MobiSys'04), Boston, MA* (pp. 1–14).
7. Wang, W., Srinivasan, V., & Chu, K. (2005). Using mobile relays to prolong the lifetime of WSNs. *Proceeding of the 11th Annual International Conference on Mobile Computing and Networking (Mobicom'05), Cologne, Germany* (pp. 270–283).
8. Wang, G., Cao, G., Porta, T. L., & Zhang, W. (2005). Sensor relocation in mobile sensor networks. *Proceeding of the 24th International Annual Joint Conference of IEEE Computer and Communication Societies (INFOCOM'05), Miami, FL* (pp. 2302–2312).
9. Ssu, K. F., Yang, C. H., Chou, C. H., & Yang, A. K. (2009). Improving routing distance for geographic multicast with Fermat points in MANETs. *Computer Networks, 53*(15), 2663–2673.

Analysis of Authentication Techniques Adopted by End Users in Real-Life Cloud Implementation

Bansi Khimani and Kuntal Patel

Abstract Security and privacy concerns when using cloud computing services are similar to those of the traditional noncloud services. Cloud Computing represents dynamic area during present days with new security level and trust. In this paper, we have analyzed the authentication techniques adopted by the users. There are various cloud computing issues like security, privacy, trust etc. which should be solved quickly to increase the user trust in cloud-based services. There are so many techniques to secure data in cloud like user id and password, pattern lock system, biometric system, one-time password (OTP) via email or SMS etc. Through this paper, we have tried to analyze how multifactor authentication techniques are adopted by end users. The result obtained after the analysis related to authentication techniques adopted and preferred by the users are given using various visual summaries.

Keywords Authentication · Cloud computing issues · SaaS · PaaS · IaaS · Authentication techniques · Multifactor authentication · One-time password (OTP) · Two-factor authentication

---

The two authors contributed equally to this work.

B. Khimani (✉)
School of Computer Science, RK University, Rajkot, India
e-mail: bansirkhimani@gmail.com

K. Patel
School of Computer Studies, Ahmedabad University, Ahmedabad, India
e-mail: kuntal.patel@ahduni.edu.in

© Springer Science+Business Media Singapore 2016
S.C. Satapathy et al. (eds.), *Proceedings of International Conference on ICT for Sustainable Development*, Advances in Intelligent Systems and Computing 409, DOI 10.1007/978-981-10-0135-2_9

1 Introduction

Nowadays, a user uses cloud technology for various reasons including storing data, transferring data, securing data, entertainment etc., and they are alert while using this technology. Sometimes the user wants high security of data while storing or transferring data; sometimes, users just use it for entertainment purpose. Authentication is one of the security mechanisms for securing data. User authentication is used for restricting unauthorized people to access sensitive data.

Many organizations, educational institutes, industries, and governments also adopted cloud technology for storing and retrieving their data. Now, via laptops and smartphones also one can do all these activities. To secure data in cloud is same as to store data in desktop system. The main difference is that in cloud you do not know where your data is going to be stored and also you have to pay for what you use. Some of the cloud services are free of cost. It may be possible that various resources are shared between several users in cloud, i.e., operating system, hardware sharing, storage etc. In such types of cases, system must allow only authenticated users to use resources.

Authentication means the process of verifying who you are by which you can access something. Logging on to a PC with a username and password is one of the popular authentication mechanisms. Gaining access to a resource (e.g., directory on a hard disk) using the permissions configured on it allow you to access is authorization [1]. In this paper, using a survey, we have analyzed the authentication-related technology adopted by the users in present days. The results obtained from the survey have been explained through visual summaries.

2 Literature Review

2.1 Cloud Computing

NIST defines cloud computing as: "Cloud computing is a model for enabling convenient, on-demand network access to a shared pool of configurable computing resources (e.g., networks, servers, storage, applications, and services) that can be rapidly provisioned and released with minimal management effort or service provider interaction. This cloud model promotes availability and is composed of five essential characteristics which are On-demand self-service, broad network access, Resource pooling, rapid elasticity and Measured Service. Three service models namely software as a service (SaaS), platform as a service (PaaS) and infrastructure as a service (IaaS) are in use. Four deployment models: Private cloud, Community cloud, Public cloud and Hybrid cloud are also popular. Key enabling technologies include: (i) fast wide-area networks, (ii) powerful, inexpensive server computers, and (iii) high-performance virtualization for commodity hardware" [2].

Many businesses—large or small—use cloud computing today either directly (e.g., Amazon, Google) or indirectly (e.g., Twitter, Facebook). There are several benefits of cloud, i.e., reduction of costs, universal access, flexibility, 24/7 supportive software etc. These benefits attract more and more people to use cloud. Cloud providers provide various facilities to users according to their needs. The main thing user do not compromise is—security of their sensitive data.

Cloud service providers have understood the importance of cloud security-related issues and are working to improve the security of it. This becomes one of the competitive issues between cloud service providers. By applying the strongest security techniques and practices, cloud security-related issues may soon be raised far above the level that IT departments achieve using their own infrastructure [3].

2.2 Cloud Computing Issues

Protecting sensitive data and information in organization is one of the critical tasks. Sometimes organization expects third-party service providers to manage cloud infrastructure. Some of the Cloud computing-related issues noticed during the literature review are described below:

(a) Security and Privacy: When you are putting your data in cloud, you don't know where your data is going to be stored. So, data theft, data loss etc. pose various threats to organization's data and software. Authorization policy should be strict for accessing data. Moreover, logs of all users should be monitored so that privacy of users does not get disturbed.

(b) Physical Security: Consumer do not know his storage location so, they may wish to specify preferred location and that requires contractual agreement between cloud service provider and the consumer that data should stay in particular location or reside in given known server.

(c) Reliability and Recovery: Provider should care that servers should not be down at any time. Downtimes will cost loss to customers. Provider must always be ready to recover data if any disaster happens. Client should aware about this feature and choose that provider who can recover their data.

(d) Legal issues and Trust: Data Location is one of the most important compliance issues faced by organizations nowadays. Cloud provider is a third-party entity; So, untrusted cloud provider should be avoided by the organization.

(e) Cloud Integrity: Publicly available data should be secured via HTTPS and SSLs so that unwanted addition, deletion, and updation could not place.

(f) Dependency and Data Segregation: Users are always dependent on provider. So, user should select that provider who is trust worthy and user's data might be never misused. Segregation means separation of data of one customer from the data of another person. If segregation solution fails at some point of time, then one customer can access data of another customer.

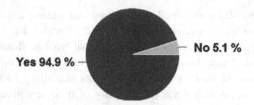

Fig. 1 Chart shows number of people thinks security is big issue for data stored in cloud

Survey Result

One of the results of our survey clearly shows that data security concern is the biggest problem considered by the users. During our survey, we found interesting result which is given in the following Pie Chart.

Figure 1 shows that among all cloud users, 94.9 % users believe that high security is important and their data should be secured in cloud. While 5.1 % people think that high security is not needed.

2.3 Multifactor Authentication

User ID and password systems are among the oldest forms of digital user authentication mechanisms. These types of authentication systems, which simply prompts a user to enter his or her ID and password to gain system access, are easy to implement and use, but they also carry some huge security risks [4]. Because of risk involved in single-factor authentication as user id and password, nowadays people move on second factor authentication. So, the term multifactor authentication is introduced for authentication. Multifactor authentication (MFA) is a method of computer access control which a user can pass by successfully presenting authentication factors from at least two of the three categories:

- Knowledge factors ("things only the user knows"), such as passwords
- Possession factors ("things only the user has"), such as ATM cards
- Inherence factors ("things only the user is"), such as biometrics [5].

There are so many companies which moved to 2 step verification. i.e. Multifactor Authentication. Unfortunately, passwords are not secure as they are used to be, and if someone gets your password, they can access your account without any problem. Even having strong password doesn't completely protect you. It means your clever password tricks are not protecting you from today's hackers. Two-factor authentications solve this problem. Two-factor authentication features is good because it asks both "Something you know" and "Something you have." Following Table shows companies which allow enabling their user to use two-factor authentications for securing their data (Table 1).

Table 1 List of companies using two-factor authentication

Company name	First factor (security)	Second factor (security)
Amazon web services (AWS)	Username and password	AWS MFA device code
Basecamp	Username and password	SMS code or phone call
BitPay	Username and password	SMS code via text
Bitstamp	Username and password	SMS code via text
Buffer	Username and password	SMS code via text or free mobile app
Dropbox	Username and password	SMS code via text or authenticator app
Facebook	Username and password	SMS code via text
Github	Username and password	SMS code via text or Authenticator app
Gmail	Username and password	SMS code via text or authenticator app
PayPal	Username and password	Small credit card size device for unique security code or SMS code via text
Twitter	Username and password	SMS code via text or via email

There are so many other companies too who except two-factor authentication. But still there are few companies who do not either trust on two-factor authentication or due to high cost of implementation not using this concept. Companies like Amazon.com, Amazon prime, Bluehost, CapitalOne, Instagram, Secret, Snapchat, Soundcloud, Stakoverflow, SurveyMonkey, Target, Wells Fargo etc. do not use two-factor authentication. They still provide one-factor authentication. Following are the various techniques which can be used for securing data.

3 Authentication Techniques in Use

There are so many techniques available to secure your data in market. Following list shows types of authentication techniques available for cloud data.

(a) *User Id and Password* User Id and password is something like a combination of strings which can be a mix-up of alphabets, numbers, symbols, and space. It is something that fits into user's memory easily and user chooses it to protect their data. The main disadvantages for adopting this mechanism is that a malicious user may hijack your account by guessing your user id and password or he can try any software which can crack your password easily. Also changing passwords regularly can be easily forgotten.

(b) *Pattern Lock System* It is used for securing your data resided in application which is running on your desktop or cloud. It is similar to locking and unlocking Android devices. You have to define your lock pattern. When you want to unlock your device, you need to redraw your pattern.

(c) *Biometric System* Biometrics is a method by which a person's identity is generated using person's physiological or behavioral characteristics. Biometric authentication verifies user's identity by comparing biometric human characteristic stored in the system. The known such mechanisms are fingerprint, IRIS, facial recognition, etc. are used in biometric system.

(d) *OTP via SMS* One-time password (OTP) tokens are also known as RSA tokens. The tokens are generally service specific, making them expensive to deploy, but a bigger problem is the added constraints to UI and experience. Your OTP tokens are sent in your registered mobile number. One disadvantage is that if you have lost your phone then that OTP token can be used by any person. Newer version of OTP token is an OTP app running on user's smartphone. Physical device generates a time based random code which the user has to enter in addition to username and password while sign in for service. An app version solves the token device distribution and deployment cost. The underlying OTP technology is based on static shared secret. This technology is awkward if the user losses token or phone or user simply upgrading their phone [6].

(e) *OTP via Email* If OTP token is sent to your registered email id then it will be more safe then getting it in your mobile devices. You will get the token only if you are going to sign in your registered email account. So, one layer of security is added. But, sometimes user feels bored and feels time consuming task to get OTP token via email.

(f) *Graphical Authentication* It is high speed data verification scheme with minimal loss probability. In this method, user needs to select images from given images as password. Now, whenever user tries to sign in, he has to select those images which he had assigned for his password. Benefit of this method is that user does not need to remember tough password. We can do complex graphical authentication, e.g., user need to choose 4 images and if all those images are matched with database then he will be asked for drawing (i.e., all points should be joint and make pattern with graphics. Here, 3D password can be used where user will select some of objects of his choice and the sequence of objects is the password of accessing the particular service) [7]. Disadvantage of this method is that the images are stored in clouds. So, it may take time for loading images.

(g) *Barcode Scanning* It is more secure than user id and password system. Here, system will send barcode image file to user. Now, user needs to import that barcode image file as second factor. Benefit of this mechanism is that barcode cannot be read or predicted by human eyes, so even actual user will not able to read or try to modify that code. While if text-based security is provided like in two-factor authentication (Google mail provides two-factor pin code authentication), then it can be read by anyone. Disadvantage of this concept is that sometimes user may feel bored to download and upload barcode image file.

(h) *QR Code Scanning* Quick response (QR) Code is the trademark for a type of matrix barcode. A barcode is a machine-readable representation of data about the object or article to which it is associated. A QR code uses four standardized encoding modes to efficiently store data [8]. One of the advantages of QR code is we do not need to write details, a simple scan captures the preferred information. QR Codes can be used to store addresses and URLs which may appear in printed/online magazines/journals, buses, business cards, etc. One of the disadvantages of QR code is that user needs a device like camera/smartphone to scan the image of QR code. Without reader, QR code is not much useful [9]. Smartphone's are technically equipped to do this task.

Through our paper we have also proposed a model which can be useful to enhance the security and data access for joint access of the cloud service [10].

4 Result Obtained and Analysis of Security Mechanisms in Use

During our survey, we have found the following important information.

(a) *Security Mechanisms Adopted by Users* Following chart shows security mechanism adopted by user for securing sensitive data (Fig. 2).
From the chart, one can observe that one-time password (OTP) via SMS in our mobile device is the best technique which can be used for securing sensitive data of users. Survey said that approximately 67 % people think that OTP via SMS in mobile device is secure methodology to access data securely. Second preference is given to user id and password mechanism. 59 % people think that user id and password can help to secure data in cloud.

(b) *Preference About Two-Factor Authentications* The following Pie Chart shows how many people prefer two-factor authentications (Fig. 3).
Result shows that 91.3 % people from survey believe that two-factor authentication is must. To secure data, simply user id and password is not sufficient. But 8.8 % people think that only single layer of security is enough to secure their data.

(c) *Technique Adopted for Two-Factor Authentication* Following Bar Chart shows that which method is best for second factor authentication for getting one-time password (OTP) (Fig. 4).

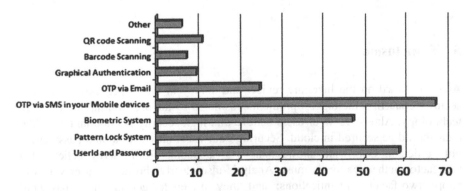

Fig. 2 Percentages of security mechanism adopted by user

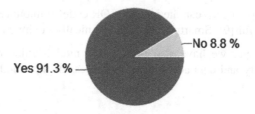

Fig. 3 Preference of two-factor authentication

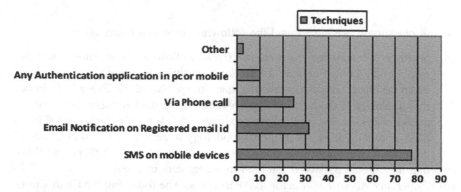

Fig. 4 Percentages of techniques adopted for two-factor authentication

Chart shows that more people preferred to get OTP via SMS in their mobile devices. Advantage is that it is very convenient to get OTP. But think for moment if you lost your mobile or if it is with other person. So, this technique is also not secure. Around 77.5 % people feel secure and get OTP via SMS now days. Email notification on registered email id is less used and only 31.3 % people prefer this technique.

5 Conclusion

Analysis based on the literature review and survey in this paper shows that data security concern is the biggest problem considered by the users during use of cloud technology. Almost 95 % of users believe that high security is important and their data should be secured in cloud. Securing data via simply user id and password is not sufficient. Our result shows that 91.3 % people from survey believe that two-factor authentication is must. Analysis also clearly shows that user wants to adopt two-factor authentications; and they prefer to get one-time password (OTP) token by SMS on their registered mobile number. This paper is one of the small steps from our side to generate awareness and provide insights regarding utilization and preferences of end users of cloud such that it can be useful to the developers of cloud-based technology.

Acknowledgments We would like to thank Mr. Raghu Khimani, Cyber Crime Expert/Advisor for his valuable support during the execution of this research work.

References

1. Retrieved March 23, 2015, from http://serverfault.com/questions/57077/what-is-the-difference-between-authentication-and-authorization
2. Retrieved March 25, 2015 http://www.nist.gov/itl/cloud/
3. Vikas, K., Swetha, M.S., Muneshwara, M.S., & Prakash, S. (July 2012). Cloud computing: towards case study of data security mechanism. *International Journal of Advanced Technology & Engineering. Research (IJATER)*, 2(4), 1–8.
4. Retrieved April 3, 2015, from http://searchsecurity.techtarget.com/tip/ID-and-password-authentication-Keeping-data-safe-with-management-and-policies
5. Retrieved November 30, 2014, from http://en.wikipedia.org/wiki/Multi-factor_authentication
6. Retrieved December 10, 2014, from http://www.secureauth.com/blog/cloud-storage-2-factor-authentication-review/
7. Rupal, R., & Sreeja, N. (2014). A novel graphical password approach for accessing cloud & data verification. *International Journal of Research in Engineering and Technology*, 3(05), 734–738.
8. Retrieved April 6, 2015, from http://en.wikipedia.org/wiki/QR_code
9. Retrieved April 6, 2015, from http://www.robabdul.com/marketing/qr-code-advantages-and-disadvantages/
10. Bansi, K., & Kuntal, P. (January–June 2015). A novel model for security and data access for jointly accessing the cloud service. *BIJIT—BVICAM's International Journal of Information Technology*, 7(1), 841–844.

Network Analysis of ICMP Ping Flood DoS Attack in WiMAX and Wireless LAN

Anu Raheja and Ajit Singh

Abstract Sharing of data over the wireless network is an important activity in today's world. A malicious user may try blocking a service or intercept data. Such attacks on network are termed as denial-of-service attack. Due to the broadcast nature of wireless communication, exploitation of this kind of attack is even easier. That is why, security is a very critical issue in e-business. It is often impossible to measure its effectiveness in real life because of the network administrators' fears or prejudice. But before measuring its effectiveness and developing mitigation methods, it is important to understand the how such attacks actually works and we should have full knowledge about their characteristics and their impacts. In this paper, we present our approach to simulate the ICMP Ping Flood attack in WiMax and wireless LAN and to analyze the effects of this attack on wireless networks using OPNET Modeler.

Keywords Wireless · Malicious · ICMP · WiMAX · Wi-Fi

1 Introduction

E-business like online shopping, bank transaction requires the exchanging of secret information. Malicious user may try attack these organization sites. Such attacks are denial-of-service attack. A denial-of-service attack (DoS attack) is an attempt to make a computer resource unavailable to its intended users. Preventing or mitigating DoS attacks is not an easy job. First, we have to understand how the attacks work. DoS attacks can be classified by many criteria. Basically, there are two methods of attacking. One method is *Vulnerability* (*Semantic*): Vulnerability

A. Raheja (✉) · A. Singh
Computer Engineering, TIT&S, Bhiwani, Haryana, India
e-mail: anuraheja40@gmail.com

A. Singh
e-mail: ajit713@gmail.com

© Springer Science+Business Media Singapore 2016   109
S.C. Satapathy et al. (eds.), *Proceedings of International Conference
on ICT for Sustainable Development*, Advances in Intelligent Systems
and Computing 409, DOI 10.1007/978-981-10-0135-2_10

attacks exploit a specific feature or an implementation bug of some protocol or of an application installed at the victim in order to consume excess amounts of its resources. The other method is *Flooding* (*Brute-force*): Flooding attacks are performed by initiating a vast amount of seemingly legitimate transactions. The common targets are web servers, DNS look up servers, and interconnecting devices.

2 Previous Work

A lot of research has been done in the field of Denial-of-service Attack.

Zaballos [1] presented his views as network security nowadays has become important for both network implementation and design. Due to this, the need of making secure communications over the network has increased at the same pace as the accessibility to services of Internet. Although security is a delicate issue in e-business, but it may be impossible to measure its effectiveness in real life because of the network administrators' fears. To find a solution to this particular problem, once more simulation opens the way to solve the problems that are difficult to fix in real life.

Elleithy [2] attack techniques vary from sending of unlimited requests to a server in an attempt to crash it, flooding a server with abundant number of packets of invalid data, to send the requests with a forged IP address. In this paper, he shows the analysis and implementation of three types of attack: Ping Attack, TCP SYN Flood, and DDOS. The Ping attack has been analyzed on a Windows 95 personal computer. The TCP SYN Flood attack will be simulated against a Microsoft Windows 2000 IIS FTP Server. DDOS has been analyzed by a zombie program that will carry the Ping attack. This paper will demonstrate the various damages from DoS attacks and analyze the mitigations of the damage.

Garantla [3] this paper evaluates firewalls, their value in securing network, and its functions such as performance, security, and efficiency. The relation between the performance efficiency and security is presented through different scenarios and the relationship between performance and security in firewalls is evaluated.

Bogdanoski [4] denial-of-service (DoS) attacks in wireless network, by sending erroneous ICMP redirect packets, a malicious host can either intercept or disrupt information from a wireless access point. He presents a technique to evaluate and analyze the effects of Ping Attack on wireless network.

3 Methodology

The step-by-step simulation of ping flood attack in a typical network is as below. For this we are designing two scenarios. Scenario 1 is to show the performance of WiMAX network under ICMP ping flood DoS attack. Scenario 2 is to show the performance of the wireless lan network under ICMP ping flood DoS attack (Table 1).

Table 1 Number of attackers and victim present in the network

Network type	Number of malicious nodes	Number of victim
WiMax	1	3
Wi-Fi	6	1

3.1 WiMax Network Under DoS Attack

Design a WiMAX network as shown in Fig. 1. Scenario 1 is depicting the WiMAX network under ping attack. Here, four base stations and one client station is linked to each base station. Hexagonal cell has been selected while designing the network. The attacker present over here is client station. The attacker is trying to attack the base stations of all the clients. Assign IP address to each station and configure the ping traffic on victim nodes. Simulate the network after setting the duration to 20 s.

3.2 Wireless LAN Under DoS Attack

Design a Wi-Fi network as shown in Fig. 2. Scenario 2 is depicting the Wi-Fi network under ping attack. Here, wireless workstations are connected to wireless router as the central node and a wireless router has been assigned the BSS Identifier. Connect the Ftp server to switch as shown in Fig. 3. Assign IP_addresses to all work stations,

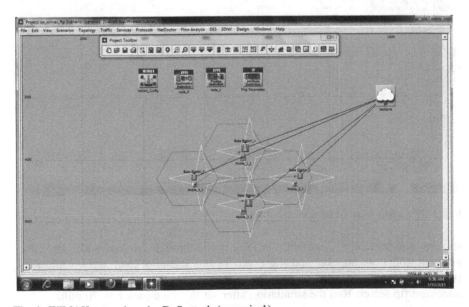

Fig. 1 WiMAX network under DoS attack (scenario 1)

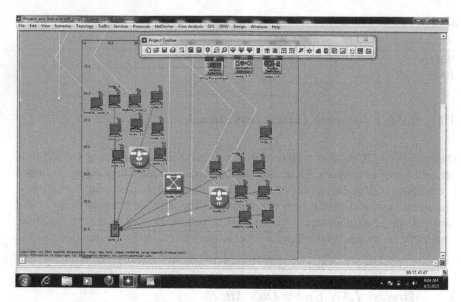

Fig. 2 Wi-Fi network under DoS attack (scenario 2)

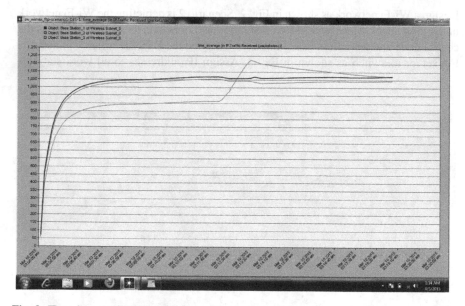

Fig. 3 IP packets received from victim nodes

servers, automatically. Configure the Ping traffic through selected nodes here; the selected nodes are attacker and fileserver. In this scenario, there are six attackers (wireless workstations) and one victim node (ftp server). Attackers are performing attack on ftp server. Run the simulation after setting the duration to 20 min.

4 Results and Discussions

This section introduces the simulation results. The purpose of using OPNET is to analyze the typical network performance under ping attack at low cost. In simulating network using OPNET, the various statistics need to be chosen. Here, we are choosing node statistics and then IP is chosen in the node statistics. This will show all IP Packets received, response, replies which are described as under with the help of graphs.

Figure 3 shows the graph obtained after the completion of simulation. It shows the IP traffic received by different victim nodes. The IP packets that are received are measured in packets per second. It can be clearly understood that it is base station 3 (victim node) which have started receiving maximum number of packets after reaching 1,050 point. Before this point, it is base station 1 which is receiving the maximum number of packets.

The ping response time denotes the delay between time a ping request was sent and the time when the first response is received. In this graph as shown in Fig. 4, blue line is indicating the overall response time from all victim base stations to attacker station point. We can easily see that the response time is nearly same of all victim nodes (Fig. 5).

Ping replies are the replies sent from the victim node to attacker. The above graph shows the response time of 3 different victim nodes that are under attack. The base station 1 was least immune to attack as it has higher response time among all. The base station 3 is highly immune to attack among all as it has the lowest response time. That's why there is more possibility that base station 3 will send IP packets safely being under attack.

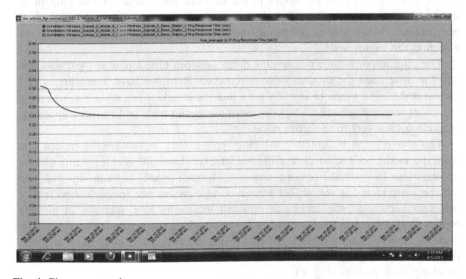

Fig. 4 Ping response time

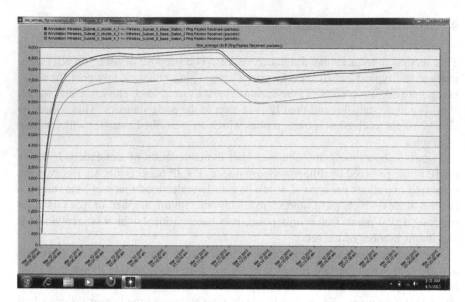

Fig. 5 IP Ping replies from victim node

Similarly, in simulating *Wireless Lan* network using OPNET, again we have to choose node statistics and further IP is chosen in the node statistics. This statistics will depicts various parameters like number of IP packets received, ping request, ping reply, ping response time, and many more. Some parameters are shown as under after completing the simulation.

Figure 6 shows the graph obtained after the completion of simulation. It shows IP traffic received by all the nodes in the network when under ICMP ping flood denial-of-service attack. The IP packets that are received are measured in packets per second. Brown line is indicating the maximum number of packets received which is the victim node.

The ping response time denotes the delay between time a ping request was sent and the time when the first response is received. Here, we have 6 attackers and 1 victim nodes. The graph in Fig. 7 shows that the attacker, i.e., node 2 is receiving the faster response among all 6 nodes from the victim node and slower response is of node 6 (attacker) from victim node.

The above graph is depicting the ping replies. Ping replies are the replies sent from the victim node to attacker. Different attackers have different reply times based on the time they started pinging request. Through graph, we can say that two attackers are receiving the replies somehow at constant rate (nearly). And rest of attackers receiving ping replies at different increasing rate. Increase in pinging replies shows that attackers are successful in attacking the victim node. The victim node is busy with ping replies and makes the network more congested. If graph degrades means ping replies are decreasing, i.e., victim node is successful in blocking such packets (Fig. 8).

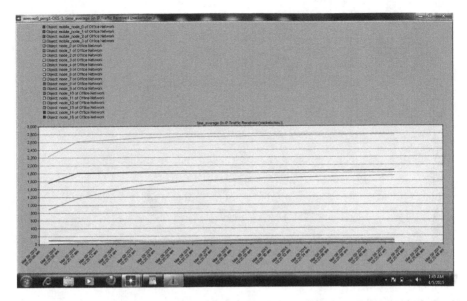

Fig. 6 IP packets received by all nodes under attack

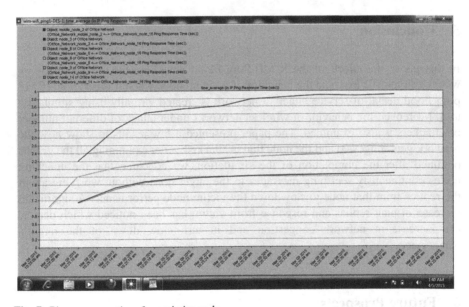

Fig. 7 Ping response time from victim node

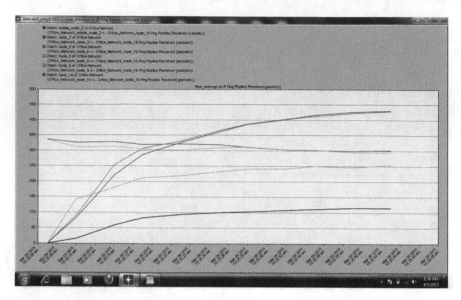

Fig. 8 IP Ping replies received from victim node

5   Conclusion

In this paper, the effects of the ICMP Ping Flood Attack on the wireless network were explored. To examine the behavior of a victim node when it is under an ICMP ping flood denial-of-service attack, a network is created virtually using simulation tool. Moreover, the behavior of wireless networks under attack of different number of attackers is also examined. The paper presented a few results to show how the network gets congested and the node that is attacked. After examining all the graphs obtained after the completion of the simulation, we conclude that the attacking nodes continuously sent ping messages to the target node without worrying about the replies from that node to slowdown the victim node performance. A significant increase in ping replies and response from victim has been noticed which depicts the increase in network congestion and in turn slow down of the target's performance.

6   Future Prospects

The concept behind the attack and its impact on the network and the network characteristics can now be very well understood. These simulations will help to build the efficient detection system using appropriate mitigation method. An efficient DoS prevention and DoS detection system can now be easily built once the concept behind the attack is clear. After examining the impact of attacks by virtually creating a network, better mechanisms can be proposed in order to prevent from these attacks. One mechanism that can be used is ScreenOS, providing screening options which set a threshold that once exceeded invokes the ICMP flood attacks [5]. Other mechanisms that can also be used is adding checks for each incoming IP fragment telling whether the packet is invalid or valid.

Acknowledgments I am really grateful to my mother for this paper. It may not be possible to complete my paper without her guidance and valuable support.

References

1. Garantla, H. *Evaluation of firewall effects on network performance.*
2. Bogdanoski, M. *Wireless network behavior under ICMP ping flood DoS attack and mitigation techniques.*
3. Elleithy, K. M. *Denial of service attack techniques: Analysis, implementation and comparison, systemics, cybernetics and informatics* (Vol. 3). ISSN:1690-4524.
4. http://arstechnica.com/security/news/2008/05/phlashing-attacks-could-render-networkhardware-useless.ars
5. Bhatti, G. (March 2013). A meliorated defense mechanism for flooding based attacks. *International Journal of Soft Computing and Engineering (IJSCE), 3*(1). ISSN:2231-2307.

Scheduling in Big Data Heterogeneous Distributed System Using Hadoop

Shraddha Thakkar and Sanjay Patel

Abstract Hadoop is Java-based programming platform which provides store and process huge amount of data of a distributed computing system. Hadoop uses HDFS for data to be stored and uses MapReduce to process those data. MapReduce used for small-scale jobs which requires low response time. Generally, Hadoop implementation predefine assumes that computing nodes in all clusters are homogeneous (i.e., having same configurations) in nature. But the fact is that, homogeneity as well as data locality assumptions are not always fulfilled in virtualized kind of data centers. Hadoop's scheduler can decrease performance in heterogeneous (i.e., different configurations) environments. We noted that longest approximate time to end (LATE), which is most suitable to heterogeneity. LATE can be improved Hadoop response times near to half of the original. In this paper, we have improved LATE scheduling policy which can decrease overall execution time.

Keywords Hadoop · HDFS · MapReduce · Scheduling algorithm · Hadoop's native scheduler · LATE · Improved LATE

1 Introduction

In cloud computing, numbers of same hardware, client, servers, and other peripherals to offer the combined capacity in demand and cost basis. The users do not know where the working servers are actually located and when we can start to work with the application. It is the primary advantage [1] of cloud which differs from

S. Thakkar · S. Patel (✉)
Department of Computer Engineering, LDRP-ITR, Gandhinagar, Gujarat, India
e-mail: Sanjay_ce@ldrp.ac.in; sanjaypatel54@gmail.com

S. Thakkar
e-mail: thakkarshradhdha@gmail.com

© Springer Science+Business Media Singapore 2016   119
S.C. Satapathy et al. (eds.), *Proceedings of International Conference on ICT for Sustainable Development*, Advances in Intelligent Systems and Computing 409, DOI 10.1007/978-981-10-0135-2_11

traditional grid computing. A main benefit of Map_Reduce is that it manages failures; do not show the time complexity of fault_tolerance from the original one. If a node destroys in any way, MapReduce sends back its tasks on another node. Like that if a node is provided still not performing as good, called as a straggler, MapReduce launch a (extra or backup) speculative copy for this type of task on other machine to complete the computation earlier. Stragglers can be created for many causes, like because of faulty hardware and mis_configuration. Google [2] has declared that speculative execution can increase job's response times almost up to 44 %.

In practical scenario, it is a complicated issue for many reasons.

- Speculated busy task—simultaneously demand for the same resources, like the network, with other task.
- Selecting the node where to run a speculative task.
- In a nonhomogeneous environment, it can be though to bifurcate between slow nodes and stragglers.

2 Scheduling Algorithm in Hadoop

Hadoop schedulers are run on scheduling algorithms. It has three basic algorithm like Fifo, Fair, and Capacity which are also called as Hadoop's native scheduling algorithms. Many scientists have improved scheduling algorithms as per the need. They are depicted as follow [1]:

2.1 Hadoop's Scheduler

The Hadoop's schedulers are used as follow

- MapReduce Scheduling system
- Hadoop's Native scheduler (Existing)
- LATE Scheduler (Improved)

3 Hadoop's Native Scheduler

Founded at 4 Sept 2007—By Apache foundation.

3.1 Hadoop's Native Scheduler (Founded at 4 Sept 2007—By Apache Foundation)

Hadoop uses FIFO [1] scheduling policy to schedule jobs from a job queue, which divides each MapReduce job into a number of tasks. Each slave speaks to the master while having empty slots. The scheduler will assign tasks. Short job is more important. Hadoop uses speculative execution for short jobs which gives quick response.

If node has empty task slot, a task for it will be chosen from any of the following:

- Failed tasks, Non-running tasks, and Speculatively executed task.

Hadoop observes task progress using a PS in between 0 and 1. For a map, the PS is the fraction of input data read. For a reduce, it is divided into three phases, each accounts for 1/3 of the score:

- The copy, Sort, and Reduce phase.

3.2 Scheduling in Hadoop

Heterogeneity impacts Hadoop's scheduler, the reason is the scheduler uses a fixed threshold for selecting tasks to speculate, too many tasks may launched. Also it does not monitor effective dynamic manner, which makes the decision a bit less accurate and can lead to delays in execution.

3.3 Speculative Execution

In speculative execution [3], following tasks has to be done

- Slow task's extra copy is created.
- Empty slot will provide that extra copy.
- Extra copy of that task will execute then the slow task will be destroyed.

  This improves job's response time.

3.4 Simulation of Hadoop Scheduling Algorithm

Each task is always scheduled using a FIFO and Hadoop concentrate on "Progress Score (PS)" (range from 0 to 1).

$$PS = \begin{cases} M/N & \text{For Map Task} \\ 1/3 \times (K + M/N) & \text{For Reduce Task} \end{cases}$$

$$PS_{avg} = \sum_{i=1}^{R} PS[i]/T \qquad (1)$$

$$\text{For task } T_i : PS[i] < PS_{avg} - 20\%$$

T_i needs a backup task.
N Number of key/value pairs required to process.
M Number of key/value pairs already processed.
K Stages of reducing.

3.4.1 Basic Classes Used in Hadoop's Native Scheduler Class Node

Class Node
Shows heterogeneous nodes in the MapReduce system

Class Map Node
Mapping Function

Class Task
Represents Heterogeneous Tasks

3.4.2 Pseudocode

```
Class Hadoop:
Public Class Hadoop{
// Reads and declares initial input parameter(n , t , SEED)
//Generate frequent Heterogeneous Tasks
//Generate non homogeneous MapNode
// allot all the Task to the Map Node & start Computing
//verify PS for every task and begin
Speculation for slow tasks
```

3.4.3 Demonstration

For Hadoop.java
   Run: JAVA Hadop <N> <T> <nR> <seed> <trials> <di>

N—No. of nodes.,	seed—random number generator
trials—No. of trial	di—Each iteration Incremented
T—No. of Tasks.	nR—No. of Reducer

3.4.4　Measurement Data

Java Hadoop 35 30 1 1234 10 5.
　See Table 1.

3.4.5　Data Plots for Hadoop's Native Scheduler

See Graph 1.

Table 1　Measured data for Hadoop's native scheduler

Serial no.	No. of nodes in system (start from 35 to end 80) (nNodes)	No. of task (T)	No. of reducer (nR)	Execution time
1	35	30	1	399.800000
2	40	30	1	399.800000
3	45	30	1	333.200000
4	50	30	1	333.200000
5	55	30	1	333.200000
6	60	30	1	333.200000
7	65	30	1	333.200000
8	70	30	1	333.200000
9	75	30	1	333.200000
10	80	30	1	333.200000

Experiment-1

T=30　nR=1 nNodes=35 to 80

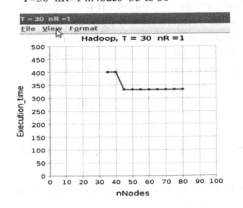

Experiment-2

T=100　nR=1 nNodes=110 to 150

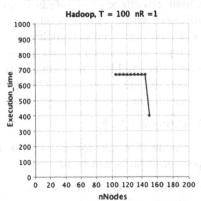

Graph 1　Data plot for Hadoop's native scheduler

3.5   Shortcomings of Hadoop's Native Scheduler

- It uses a fixed threshold for speculation.
- Number of tasks can be released, which removed the resources from important tasks.
- Hadoop release backup copy when not required and fast nodes.

3.5.1   Hadoop's [3] Assumptions

- Each Node in cluster can perform at the same execution rate.
- Progress at a constant Execution rate.
- No cost to releasing a speculative copy on a node until it has an idle slot.
- *PS* is part of its total work and has not been finished yet.
- Finish all the tasks in wave's fashion.
- Same category tasks are requiring same amount of work to be done [3].

When we have to deal with heterogeneous nodes in our cluster the above Assumption may break down.

4   Longest Approximate Time to End (LATE Scheduler)

Founded by Matei Zaharia at University of California, Berkeley in 2008.

4.1   LATE Scheduling

A main advantage of MapReduce has ability to handles failures, if nodes crash, it will again run the same tasks on a various nodes. It runs a same copy of the same task on different machine to complete the computation quick. Google has claimed that this type of concurrent or we can say speculative execution will decrease job execution times by 44 % [3]. It works only in homogeneous environment, but practically network is heterogeneous. LATE (Longest Approximate Time to End) scheduling algorithm can reduce Execution time by almost up to half of the original.

Working of LATE

If a node demands for a new task and there are fewer than Speculative Cap speculative tasks will be running:

- Ignore the request demanded by node if node's total progress is less than SlowNodeThreshold.

- Rank at presently running tasks which are not speculated by estimated time left.
- Re-Launch a copy of the top-most ranked task with PR below SlowTaskThreshold.

4.2   LATE Advantages

- Most suitable to node heterogeneity.
- Decides where to run speculative copy of tasks.
- Estimated time [4] left will be considered rather than PR.

4.3   Simulation of LATE Scheduling Algorithm

4.3.1   Parameters to Be Used

```
Process Rate of each Task = Progress Score/T
T: Time up to which  task has run
Remaining Time = (1 - Progress Score) / ProgressRate.
SlowNodeThreshold = total work has been done = sum of all PS
(In practice: 25% of the node Progress)
Speculative Cap = A number on which speculative tasks can be running at same
time.
(In practice: 10% of the available task slot.)
Slow Task Threshold = a taks's PR is compared to decide whether it is slow
enough to be speculated upon. (In practice: 25% of the task PR.)
```

4.3.2   Pseudocode [4]

```
1. Run as Hadoop, for 1 min, then begin evaluation for speculation.

2. If(node is empty, ask for a new task) &&((the Num of speculatively running

tasks)<Speculative Cap) {

if(total progress <Slow Node Threshold) { Ingore the request; }

Ranking out currently performing tasks that are not being speculated by

estimated remaining time

find ( highest priority task with PR<Slow Task Threshold) { release a same copy

of that task.}}
```

4.3.3 Demonstration

Run: java LATE <N> <T> <nR> <seed> <trials> <di>

4.3.4 Measurement Data

java LATE 35 30 1 1234 10 5
   See Table 2.

4.3.5 Data Plots for LATE Scheduler

See Graph 2.

4.4 Short Comes of LATE

- LATE statistically computes PR.
- It does not have separate calculating methods for "Map slow" and "Reduce slow".
- Uses static inputs for m1.m2.m3, r1.r2 (i.e., Map and Reduce function).

Table 2 Parameters for LATE scheduler

Serial no.	No. of nodes in system (start from 35 to end 80) (nNodes)	No. of task (T)	No. of reducer (nR)	Execution time
1	35	30	1	500.000000
2	40	30	1	500.000000
3	45	30	1	500.000000
4	50	30	1	500.000000
5	55	30	1	500.000000
6	60	30	1	500.000000
7	65	30	1	500.000000
8	70	30	1	500.000000
9	75	30	1	500.000000
10	80	30	1	500.000000

Experiment-1

T=30 nR=1 nNodes=35 to 80

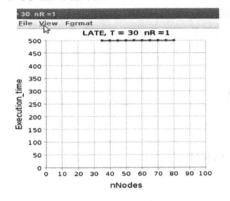

Experiment-2

T=100   nR=1 nNodes=110 to 150

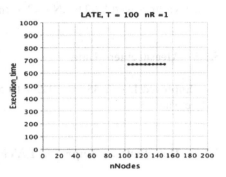

Graph 2 Data plots for LATE scheduler

5 Improved LATE

- Considers heterogeneity
- LATE's Improvements
- Dynamic calculations to improve accuracy

5.1 Features

- Past information (i.e., we can say previous history or record of node)
- Decide slow nodes not statically

5.2 Improved Late Pseudocode

1. Start: Improved LATE
2. Key_Value pairs and output will statistical results
3. Reading Past information dynamically and synchronized parameters with the use of it at each step of execution
4. Searching out slow_tasks for map and reduce as well as task tracker
5. Release backup copy of the tasks and Collecting results
6. Updating information for each node
7. end procedure

5.3   *Demonstration*

Run: java Improved LATE <N> <T> <nR> <seed> <trials> <di>

5.3.1   Measurement Data

java Improved LATE 35 30 1 1234 10 5
   See Table 3.

5.3.2   Data Plots for Improved LATE Scheduler

See Graph 3.

6   Comparative Study of Hadoop, LATE, and Improved LATE Execution Time

The compression of the Hadoop, LATE, and Improved LATE is as per Table 4 and the Graph 4.

Table 3 Parameters for improved LATE scheduler

Serial no.	No. of nodes in system (start from 35 to end 80) (nNodes)	No. of task (T)	No. of reducer (nR)	Execution time
1	35	30	1	500.000000
2	40	30	1	333.200000
3	45	30	1	334.200000
4	50	30	1	222.200000
5	55	30	1	222.200000
6	60	30	1	166.600000
7	65	30	1	166.600000
8	70	30	1	166.600000
9	75	30	1	166.600000
10	80	30	1	166.600000

Experiment-1	Experiment-2
T=30 nR=1 nNodes=35 to 80	T=100 nR=1 nNodes=110 to 150

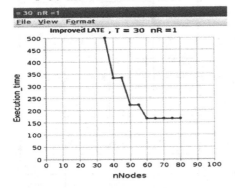

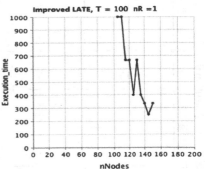

Graph 3 Data plots for improved LATE scheduler

Table 4 Comparison of execution time

Serial no.	No. of nodes in system (start from 35 to end 80) (nNodes)	HADOOP (execution time)	LATE (execution time)	Improved LATE (execution time)
1	35	399.800000	500.000000	500.000000
2	40	399.800000	500.000000	333.200000
3	45	333.200000	500.000000	334.200000
4	50	333.200000	500.000000	222.200000
5	55	333.200000	500.000000	222.200000
6	60	333.200000	500.000000	166.600000
7	65	333.200000	500.000000	166.600000
8	70	333.200000	500.000000	166.600000
9	75	333.200000	500.000000	166.600000
10	80	333.200000	500.000000	166.600000

6.1 Data Plots for Comparative Study

See Graph 4.

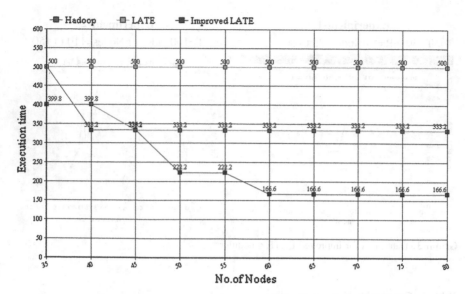

Graph 4 Data plots for comparison of execution time of different scheduling policies

7 Conclusion

It can be concluded from the study of data plot that the Longest Approximate Time to End (LATE) is most suitable for heterogeneity. The improved LATE reduces Hadoop response times nearer to half of the original which can decrease overall execution time.

8 Future Work

In future, the variable number of reducer's can be extended and results can be tested. We also would like to investigate the experimental results by assigning several tasks to the same node; in this experiment, it is considered that node can perform either map or reduce but in future we try to extend the functionality of node to run several tasks at the same time.

References

1. Thirumala Rao, B., Sridevi, N. V., KrishnaReddy, V., Reddy, L. S. S. (2011). Performance issues of heterogeneous Hadoop clusters in cloud computing. *Global Journal of Computer Science and Technology*, *11*(8), Version 1.0 May 2011.

2. Dean, J., & Ghemawat, S. (2008). MapReduce: Simplified data processing on large clusters. *Communications of theACM, 51*(1), 107–113.
3. Zaharia, M., Konwinski, A., Joseph, A., Zatz, Y. & Stoica, I. (2008). Improving map reduce performance in heterogeneous environments. In *OSDI'08: 8th USENIX Symposium on Operating Systems Design and Implementation*, October 2008.
4. Konwinski, A. Improving map reduce performance in heterogeneous environments Technical Report No. UCB/EECS-2009-183.

A New Differential Scan-Based Side-Channel Attacks Against RSA Cryptosystem

Darshna Dalvadi, Badal Kothari and Keyur Shah

Abstract By analyzing the scanned data in cryptography circuit, scan-based side-channel attacks retrieve a secret key, which are considerable as a threat into cryptosystem LSI and therefore they are not permitted and we have to restrict them. In scan-based side-channel attacks which retrieve secret keys during a cryptography, one will have to register the data simply by employing a scan path, which suggest that one can retrieve a secret key in a cryptography LSI. This can be a scan-based side-channel attack. RSA is one of the most necessary cryptography algorithms and as a result it effectively realizes a public-key cryptography system. However, typical scan-based side-channel attacks cannot be applied to it because of its complicated algorithm structure. Paper proposes a scan-based side-channel attack that permits us to retrieve a secret key in an RSA circuit. The proposed planned technique is based on identifying intermediate values calculated in an RSA circuit. We tend to specialize in a one-bit time sequence that is restricted to some intermediate values. By examining the one-bit time sequence in the scan path, we can find out the register position specific to the intermediate value and, can recognize whether the intermediate value is calculated in the target RSA circuit or not.

Keywords Scan-based side-channel attack · Side-channel · SCA · RSA · Public-key implementation · Security attack

D. Dalvadi (✉)
C. U. Shah University, Wadhwan, Surendra Nagar, Gujarat, India
e-mail: darshnadalvadi@gmail.com

B. Kothari
Department of Computer Science, Hemchandracharya North Gujarat University,
Patan, Gujarat, India
e-mail: kotbad@gmail.com

K. Shah
Department of Computer Science, L.D.R.P., Kadi Sarva Vidhyalaya, Gandhinagar,
Gujarat, India
e-mail: profkeyur@gmail.com

© Springer Science+Business Media Singapore 2016   133
S.C. Satapathy et al. (eds.), *Proceedings of International Conference
on ICT for Sustainable Development*, Advances in Intelligent Systems
and Computing 409, DOI 10.1007/978-981-10-0135-2_12

1 Introduction

RSA private keys have been retrieved through scan attacks. The attack method is based on observing the values of the intermediate register, on the scan chain for each bit of the secret key, and then correlating this value with a previous offline calculation. If the value matches with this discriminator value, a corresponding decision is taken on the key bit. Left-to-right binary exponentiation is used as the target RSA algorithm for the attack [1, 6, 7]. This is generally not implemented in hardware owing to the expensive division operation involved in modular operations.

Moreover, an inherent assumption of the attack is that there are no other exponent key bit-dependent intermediate registers which change their value after each square and multiply operation. This may not be the case in an actual hardware implementation, where multiple registers are key dependent and change their values together with the intermediate register of interest in the attack. These registers may mask the contents of the target intermediate register after XOR-tree compaction.

2 RSA Algorithm

The Rivest–Shamir–Adleman (RSA) algorithm is a widely used public-key cryptographic algorithm, employed in a wide range of key-exchange protocols and digital signature schemes. A brief description of the RSA algorithm is presented in Figs. 1 and 2.

Both the operations in Algorithm 2 are large number modular exponentiations. When RSA is implemented in hardware, there are various options and many algorithms are available. The Montgomery exponentiation method is most widely used owing to its efficient hardware implementation, as it does away with the expensive division operation required for modular multiplications involved in an

---

Algorithm 1 RSA key generation

1: Select uniformly random primes p and q
2: $N = p \cdot q$ (1024 bit)
3: $e =$ random co-prime to $\lambda(N) = lcm(p - 1, q - 1)$
4: $d = e^{-1} \bmod \lambda(N)$

Fig. 1 RSA key generation algorithm

Algorithm 2 RSA encryption and decryption

1: Ciphertext $c = m^e \bmod N$
2: Decrypted plaintext $m = c^d \bmod N$

Fig. 2 RSA encryption and decryption

Algorithm 3 Montgomery exponentiation

INPUT: Modulus N, $R = b^\ell$, exponent $e = (e_t...e_0)_2$ with $e_t = 1$, and an integer x,
  $1 \leq x < N$ (ℓ is the number of bits in the prime number, 1024 in our case, b is
  the base, which is 2 for binary)
OUTPUT: x^e mod N
1: $\tilde{x} \Leftarrow$ Mont$(x, R^2$ mod $N)$, $A \Leftarrow R$ mod N. (R mod N and R^2 mod N may be
  provided as inputs)
2: **for** i **from** t **downto** 0 **do**
3:   $A \Leftarrow$ Mont(A, A)
4:   **if** $e_i == 1$ **then**
5:     $A \Leftarrow$ Mont$(A, \tilde{x})$
6:   **end if**
7: **end for**
8: $A \Leftarrow$ Mont$(A, 1)$
9: **Return** A

Fig. 3 Montgomery exponentiation of RSA algorithm

exponentiation. Hence, we choose the Montgomery method as the target algorithm for our scan chain attack [2, 3].

The Montgomery product of two n-bit numbers A with B is denoted by Mont $(A, B) = A \cdot B \cdot R - 1$ mod N, where $A \cdot B$ denotes a modular multiplication, N is the modulus or the product of the prime numbers used in the modular multiplications, and $R = 2n$ (Fig. 3).

Mont (A, A) is known as the squaring (S) operation, while the Mont(A, ex) is known as the multiplication operation (M). Each iteration of the loop within the algorithm consists either of a square and multiply operations if the exponent bit is 1, or only a square operation if the exponent bit is 0.

In this paper for scan-based attack, we are focusing on the intermediate register, which stores the value after each Montgomery multiplication. Irrespective of how the RSA modular exponentiation is implemented, the intermediate value will always be stored in a register.

3 Differential Scan Attack Mode

One of the main advantages of the attack proposed in this paper over the previous RSA attacks is the fact that it works in the presence of industrial DfT structures. For that purpose the differential mode is used to deal with linear response compactors which are inserted by the majority of the DfT tools. In the case of parity compactors, each output bit is the XOR operation between the scan flip-flops on the same slice. It means that the actual value stored in one SFF is not directly observable. Instead, if it differs from the value expected, the parity of the whole slice also differs, and so faults may be detected. This difference is also exploited by an attacker.

Fig. 4 Design with crypto
block

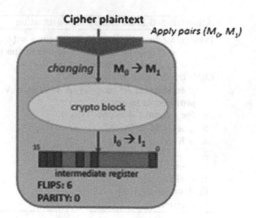

Figure 4 shows a crypto block and the intermediate register which is the target of
the scan attack. The differential mode consists of applying pairs of plaintexts, in this
example denoted by (*M*0, *M*1). The circuit is first reset and the message *M*0 is
loaded. Then after some fixed clock cycles, the circuit is halted and the intermediate
register *I*0 is shifted out. The same procedure is repeated for the message *M*1 for
which *I*1 is obtained. Let us suppose that *I*0 differs from *I*1 in 6 bit positions as
shown in Fig. 4, where a bit flip is represented by a darker box. Let us further
suppose that the intermediate register contains only 16 bits and the bits 0, 8, 10, 13,
14, and 15 are flipping [1, 4, 5]. The parity of the differences is equal to 0, since
there is an even number of bit flips.

In Fig. 5, the flip-flops of the intermediary register are inserted as an example of
a DfT scenario with response compaction. In this case there are four scan chains
divided into four slices. RX represents the test output corresponding to the slice X.
As may be seen, if only the bit 0 flips in the first slice (an odd number) this
difference is reflected into a flip of *R*1. In slice 2, no bits flip and thus *R*2 remains
the same. Two flips occur in slice 3: 8 and 10. In this case, both flips mask each
other, thus 2 flips (even) result in 0 flips at the output *R*3. In slice 4, 3 bit flips are
sensed as a bit flip in *R*4.

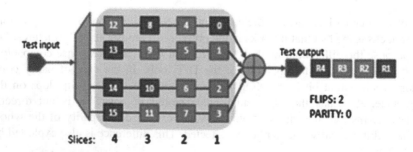

Fig. 5 DfT scheme example

The parity of flips in the intermediate register is equal to the parity of flips at the output of the response compactor. This property is valid for any possible configuration of the scan chains and slices. Additionally, it is also valid for compactors with multiple outputs. In this case, the difference measured should consider all compactor outputs. Thus using the differential mode, the attacker observes differences in the intermediate register and then retrieves the secret key.

4　Description of the Scan Attack on RSA

The Montgomery exponentiation consists of repeating the Montgomery multiplication operations several times. The first multiplication in the main loop, i.e., the squaring of A, is always performed independent of the value of the secret key bit. The second multiplication, A times ex, is performed only if the decryption key bit is 1. The main idea of the attack proposed here is to check if the second operation is executed or not, by observing the value of A afterward. If it does, then the key bit is 1, otherwise it is 0. This procedure is repeated for all the key bits.

In order to detect if the second multiplication was executed, the attacker must scan out the value of A after each loop. Additionally, as explained above, a pair of plaintexts is used to overcome the obscurity provided by the response compactor. This pair must be properly chosen so that a difference on the parity of A would lead to the decryption bit. For that, it is important that we give a pair of specific message inputs to the algorithm.

First, a pair of random 1024-bit messages is generated using a software pseudorandom number generator. We denote them here as $(M0, M1)$. Then, the corresponding output responses are computed on each of these messages assuming the key bit to be both '0' and '1'. Let $(R00, R01, R10, R11)$ be the responses for message $M0$ and $M1$ for key bit '0' and '1', respectively. Let Parity $(R00)$, Parity $(R01)$, Parity $(R10)$ and Parity $(R11)$ be the corresponding parities on these responses. Let $P0$ be equal to Parity $(R00)$ XOR Parity $(R10)$ and $P1$ be equal to Parity $(R01)$ XOR Parity $(R11)$. If $P0 ! = P1$, then the messages are taken to be useful, otherwise they are rejected and the process is repeated till a pair of 'good' messages is obtained. This is illustrated in Fig. 6.

After a good pair of messages is found, it may be applied to the actual circuit. For both pairs of elements, the application is executed in functional mode for the number of clock cycles corresponding to the targeted step (decryption key bit). For these pairs of elements, the scan contents are shifted out and the parity of the difference at the test output bitstream is measured. If the parity of differences is equal to $P0$, then the hypothesis 0 is correct and the secret key bit is 0. If it is equal to $P1$, then the secret key bit is 1. This procedure is repeated for all the bits of the decryption key.

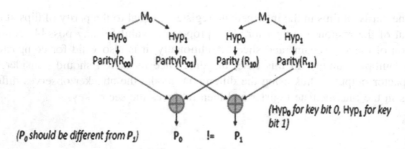

Fig. 6 Finding good pair of messages for scan attack on RSA

5   Practical Aspects of the Attack

Performing scan attacks on actual designs requires additional procedures. The two main practical issues consist of (1) dealing with the other flip-flops of the design; (2) finding out the exact time to halt the mission mode execution and to shift out the internal contents.

5.1   Leakage Analysis

The scenario of Figs. 4 and 5 is commonly taken into consideration by scan attacks, however, in real designs; other FFs of the design will be included in the scan chain. These additional FFs may complicate the attack if no workaround is taken into account. Figure 7 shows a design containing three types of FF. We define here three types of scan flip-flops (SFFs), depending on the value they store, as shown in Fig. 8. Class T1 SFFs correspond to the other IPs in the design; that is storing the data which is not dependent on the secret. T2 SFFs belong to the registers directly related to the intermediate register, which store information related to the secret key and that are usually targeted by attackers. T3 SFFs store data related to the cipher

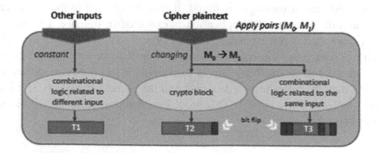

Fig. 7 Generic cryptographic design showing categories of FFs

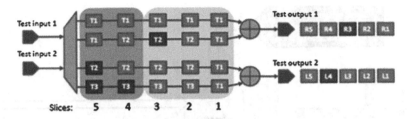

Fig. 8 Test compression with multiple scan outputs

but not the intermediate registers themselves. The leakage, if it exists, concerns the T2 type.

The goals of the leakage analysis are to find out if a particular bit of the intermediate register (T2) can be observed at the test output, and locate which output bit is related to it. Let T2N be the value stored in T2 after N clock cycles while the design is running in mission mode from the plaintext $M0$. The analysis is focused on one bit per time, looking for an eventual bit flip in T2. In order to do that, the pair $(M0, M1)$ is chosen so that the value on T2N for $M0$ differs by a single bit from the value T2N for $M1$. In Fig. 7 the darker blocks represent a bit that flips, thus the least significant bit of T2N flips. Since the attack tries to verify if it is possible to observe a flip in the LSB of T2N, it is ideal that there is no flip in T1N. To reduce the effect of the T1 flip-flops, all the inputs that are not related to the plaintext are kept constant. It means that T1N for $M0$ has the same value as T1N for $M1$. However, the same method cannot be applied to reduce the effects of T3. Since we suppose that the logic associated with T3 is unknown and since its inputs are changing, the value T3N for $M0$ may differ from T3N for $M1$. In our example, let us flip only three bits of T3.

Figure 8 shows the result of these bit flips in the scan chain and consequently in the test outputs. As an example, we suppose that the DfT insertion created four scan chains, and placed a pattern decompressed at the input and a response compactor with two outputs (R and L). As may be seen, slice 1 contains only T1 scan flip-flops, meaning that after the response compactor, the values of $R1$ and $L1$ are not supposed to flip. For slice 2, the same happens. Slice 3 contains the only flipping bit of T2N and the other flip-flops in the slice do not change. In this case, the bit flip of the LSbit of T2N is observable in $R3$. It means that an attacker could exploit the information contained in $R3$ to find the secret key. Hence, this is considered a security leakage and may be exploited by the attack.

5.2 Attack Tool

The main goal of this tool is to apply the attack method as well as the leakage analysis, to many different DfT configurations, without modifying the attack principle. The scan analysis tool is divided into three main parts: the attack methods

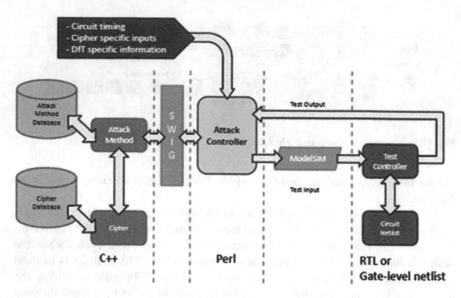

Fig. 9 Scan attack tool

and ciphers, the main controller, and the simulation part which is composed of an RTL deck and ModelSIM scripts, as shown in Fig. 9. In order to use the tool, the gate-level netlist must be provided by correctly setting the path for both the netlist and technology files for ModelSIM simulations. Then the design is linked to the RTL deck, which is used as an interface with the tool logic. This connection is automatically done by giving the list of input and output data test pins, as well as the control clock, reset and test enable pins. Additionally, other inputs such as plaintext and cipher text must be set in the configuration file.

The new RSA attack method is written in C++ for an RSA software implementation. Scan attacks on other similar cryptosystems may be conceived since the tool was built in such a way that adding a new cipher is simple. The core of the tool is implemented by the attack controller that calls the attack method through a simplified wrapper and interface generator (SWIG) interface. SWIG helps connect programs written in C/C++ with other high-level programming languages such as TCL/Perl. The attack controller ensures that the settings are initialized and then it launches both the attack and the simulation. As a secondary functionality, the controller handles some design aspects, like timing and multiple test outputs, so that the attack method itself may abstract that information. For instance, the attack method has no information on how many clock cycles it takes to execute a Montgomery multiplication. Also, it finds out the number of scan cycles that the shift operation must be enabled so that the contents of the scan chains are completely unloaded.

6 Conclusions

We have target the Montgomery Exponentiation algorithm rule, that is by far the most popular and efficient implementation of RSA in hardware, as there are not any division operations involved. Our proposed scan attack analysis takes the contents of alternative key-dependent registers present within the scan chain, and presents ways that to deal with this downside. Finally, the attack cannot be applied to secure designs having test response compaction and masking our scan attack analysis.

Our proposed scan-based attack will effectively retrieve a secret key in an RSA circuit, since we have a tendency to simply specialize in the variation of 1-bit of intermediate values named a scan signature. By observing it within the scan path, we will resolve the register position specific to intermediate values. The experimental results demonstrate that a 1,024-bit secret key may be retrieved using 29.5 messages, a 2,048-bit secret key using 32 inputs, and a 4,096-bit secret key can be retrieved using 37 messages. In the future, we are going to define a new scan-based side-channel attack against compressed scan data for RSA. In this paper, we have tendency to solely obtain RSA LSI implementation. We are going to attack these RSA implementations and with success retrieve a secret key. Developing countermeasures against the proposed scan-based side-channel attacking methodology is another future work.

References

1. Agrawal, M., Karmakar, S., Saha, D., & Mukhopadhyay, D. (2008). Scand based side channel attacks on stream ciphers and their countermeasures. *Progress in Cryptology-INDOCRYPT, 2008,* 226–238.
2. Da Rolt, J., Das, A., Ghosh, S., Di Natale, G., Flotes, M. L., Rouzeyre, B., & Verbauwhede, I. (2012). Scan attacks on side channel and fault attack resistant public key implementations. *Journal of Cryptographic Engineering (JCEN),* 2(4), 207–219.
3. Ege, B., Das, A., Batina, L., Verbauwhede, I. (2013). Security of countermeasures against state-of-the-art differential scan attacks. In *Workshop on Trustworthy Manufacturing and Utilization of Secure Devices (TRUDEVICE), Co-located with IEEE European Test Symposium (ETS),* 2013.
4. Fan, J., Verbauwhede, I. (2012). An updated survey on secure ecc implementations: Attacks, countermeasures and cost. In *Cryptography and security* (Vol. 6805, pp. 265–282), Lecture Notes in Computer Science. Springer.
5. Menezes, A., van Oorschot, P., Vanstone, S. (1997). *Handbook of applied cryptography.* CRC Press.
6. Wikipedia, the free encyclopedia. Retrieved from https://en.wikipedia.org.
7. http://www.trustedcomputinggroup.org.

Grey Wolf Optimizer (GWO) Algorithm for Minimum Weight Planer Frame Design Subjected to AISC-LRFD

Vishwesh Bhensdadia and Ghanshyam Tejani

Abstract In this paper, an optimum planer frame design is achieved using the Grey Wolf Optimizer (GWO) algorithm. The GWO algorithm is a nature involved meta-heuristic which is correlated with grey wolves' activities in social hierarchy. The objective of the GWO algorithm is to produce minimum weight planer frame considering the material strength requirements specified by American Institute for Steel Construction—Load and Resistance Factor Design (AISC-LRFD). The frame design is produced by choosing the W-shaped cross sections from AISC-LRFD steel sections for a beam and column members. A benchmark problem is investigated in the present work to monitor the success rate in a way of best solution and effectiveness of the GWO algorithm. The result of the GWO algorithm is compared with other meta-heuristics, namely GA, ACO, TLBO and EHS. The results show that the GWO algorithm gives better design solutions compared to other meta-heuristics.

Keywords Structural optimization · Meta-heuristics · Grey wolf optimizer (GWO) algorithm · Planer frame design · AISC-LRFD

1 Introduction

In structural engineering problems, the cost of structural material includes more expenses to design a structure compared to other project expenses. Hence to reduce the structural project expenses, the structure raw materials cost parameter is kept in mind during the design stage to take some cost advantages [13]. To fulfill these criteria, it is preferable to reduce the cost of structure by reducing the size (weight) of structural beam and column members up to minimum level with considering certain design constraints [12]. To achieve this goal, choosing an effective

V. Bhensdadia · G. Tejani (✉)
School of Engineering, RK University, Rajkot, Gujarat, India
e-mail: p.shyam23@gmail.com

© Springer Science+Business Media Singapore 2016
S.C. Satapathy et al. (eds.), *Proceedings of International Conference on ICT for Sustainable Development*, Advances in Intelligent Systems and Computing 409, DOI 10.1007/978-981-10-0135-2_13

optimization technique is an important task in structural engineering problems. Optimum structure design is achieved by applying efforts towards size reduction during the design stage considering their strength and stiffness parameters during optimization process.

Minimum weight of the frame structure was investigated by many researchers in view of considering the requirement of strength and displacement constraints according to AISC-LRFD [1] specifications. Many meta-heuristics such as; upper bound strategy (UBS) [2], ant colony optimization (ACO) [3], Big Bang-Big Crunch (BB-BC) [5, 10, 11], evolution strategy integrated parallel algorithm (ESIPA) [6], bat inspired algorithm (BIA) [8], adaptive harmony search (AHS) [9, 22], charged system search (CSS) [14], enhanced harmony search (EHS) [15], Design Driven Harmony Search (DDHS) [17], Genetic Algorithm (GA) [18, 20, 21] and Teaching-Learning-Based Optimization (TLBO) [23] are used in this field. Hall et al. (1989) [4] presented the combined first-order and second-order design procedure for minimum weight frame design. Hasancebi et al. (2010) [7] compared the seven different meta-heuristics for optimum design of frame structure.

This paper presents an optimum design of plane frame structure employing the GWO algorithm, which represents the skills and ability regarding leadership and hunting process of gray wolves in social atmosphere, proposed by Mirjalili et al. (2014) [16].

The rest of paper is formulated as follows: Sect. 2 formulates the optimum frame design problem, Sect. 3 describes brief of the GWO algorithm, Sect. 4 presents planer frame design problem and Sect. 5 concludes the work.

2 Formulation of the Optimum Design of Steel Frame

The objective of the design problem is to minimize the weight (Eq. 2) of the frame structure subjected to the strength constraints (Eqs. 3 and 4) specified by AISC-LRFD [1] by selecting cross-sectional area (W-Shapes) for beam and column members as a design variables as shown in Eq. (1). The design variables, i.e. cross sections, for beam members and column members are considered according to AISC-LRFD [1]. This consideration turns into the optimum structure design problem, which is given as per follows equation [23]:

$$\text{Find, } Z = [A_1, A_2, A_3, \ldots, A_{nd}] \tag{1}$$

To minimize the weight 'W' of the frame structure which is expressed as:

$$W(Z) = \sum_{i=1}^{nd} A_i \sum_{j=1}^{mt} \rho_i L_i \tag{2}$$

Subjected to, $C_k^\sigma \leq 0$, where $k = 1,...,na$

$$1 \leq A_i \leq mk, \text{ where } i = 1,\ldots,nd$$

where, 'Z' represents the design variables; 'nd' is the total number of design groups in the frame structure; 'mt' is the total number of members in group 'i' of frame structure; 'ρ_j' and 'L_j' are mass density and length of member 'j', respectively. 'A_i' is cross-sectional area of member group 'i' of frame structure. The inequalities parameter, i.e. ≤ 0 represent the strength constraints specified by the AISC-LRFD [1] specification. Since 'A_i' is the W-shaped cross-sectional area which is chosen from standard structure design manual, i.e. AISC-LRFD [1]. 'na' represents the number of beam and columns in frame structure; 'mk' shows the total number of W-shaped cross-sectional area which is considered for structure design in group 'i'.

The strength constraints, $C_k^\sigma \leq 0$, for frame members subjected to axial force and bending as per AISC-LRFD [1] specification are given as follows:

$$C_k^\sigma = \frac{P_u}{\emptyset \times p_n} + \frac{8}{9}\left(\frac{M_{ux}}{\emptyset_b \times M_{nx}} + \frac{M_{uy}}{\emptyset_b \times M_{ny}}\right) - 1 \quad, \text{if} \frac{P_u}{\emptyset \times p_n} \geq 0.2 \qquad (3)$$

$$C_k^\sigma = \frac{P_u}{2 \times \emptyset \times p_n} + \left(\frac{M_{ux}}{\emptyset_b \times M_{nx}} + \frac{M_{uy}}{\emptyset_b \times M_{ny}}\right) - 1 \quad, \text{if} \frac{P_u}{\emptyset \times p_n} \geq 0.2 \qquad (4)$$

where, 'P_u' and 'P_n' are the required and nominal axial strength (compression or tension), respectively; 'M_{ux}' and 'M_{uy}' are the required flexural strengths about the major and the minor axes, respectively; 'M_{nx}' and 'M_{ny}' are the nominal flexural strength about the major and the minor axis, respectively (for 2-D frames, 'M_{ny}' = 0); '$\emptyset$' is the resistance factor shown as '$\emptyset_c$' for compression members (equal to 0.85) and '$\emptyset_t$' for tension members (equal to 0.90), respectively; '$\emptyset_b$' is the flexural resistance factor, with a value of 0.90 [1].

The penalty function used in this study is known as the Kaveh–Zolghadr technique, which is expressed as follows [19]:

$$f(X) = (1 + \varepsilon_1 \times \upsilon)^{\varepsilon_2} \qquad (5)$$

where, 'f' represents the value of penalized function; and are taken as 2.

$$\upsilon = \sum_{i=1}^{na} s_i, \text{ where } s_i = \left|1 - \frac{c_{ki}^\sigma}{c_{ki,all}^\sigma}\right| \qquad (6)$$

where, 'na' and represents the number of beam and columns and strength constraints violation, respectively. At a design solution 'x', if the ith constraint is not violated, then the value is zero; otherwise, is as per Eq. (6) [19].

3 Grey Wolf Optimizer (GWO) Algorithm

3.1 Inspiration

Grey wolves are in the top level of the food chain in social atmosphere. Grey wolves organize the hunt activity in a pack of average 5–12 members. The social hierarchy of grey wolf consists of four levels from top to bottom, such as Alpha (α), Beta (β), Delta (δ) and Omega (ω), respectively [16]. Alpha is responsible for taking decisions about hunting, time to wake, sleeping place, to command a pack and so on. Beta provides help to alpha during the stage of decision and other activities regarding hunting. It can be consider as the best candidate to replace the alpha in case of it die. The duty of delta is to submit the activity and work regarding hunting possessed by him to alpha and beta but they dominate the omega. Omega is always responsible to submit activity and work regarding hunting to alpha, beta and delta. The grey wolf hunting activities have following main three stages [16]: (i) To track, chase and approach the prey, (ii) To pursue, encircle and harass the prey until it becomes stable, (iii) Attack in direction to the prey.

3.2 GWO Mathematical Model

The GWO mathematical models are categorized into the social hierarchy, encircling, hunting, attacking and search for prey activities, which are described as follows: [16]:

To represent the social hierarchy of grey wolves in mathematical form during designing the GWO algorithm, the Mirjalili et al. (2014) [16] considered the best solution represented by alpha candidate. The beta and delta are considered as second and third best candidates to search the prey respectively. The remaining candidates are considered as an omega.

The grey wolves encircle activity towards prey during the hunting process is proposed by Mirjalili et al. (2014) [16] in the form of equation as follows:

$$D = CX_p(t) - X(t) \tag{7}$$

$$X(t+1) = X_p(t) - AD \tag{8}$$

where, 't' shows the current iteration, 'X_p' and 'X' indicate the position vector of the prey and the grey wolf, respectively and 'A' and 'C' represent the coefficient vectors.

The vectors 'A' and 'C' are evaluated by using following equations [16]:

$$A = 2ar_1 - a \tag{9}$$

$$C = 2r_2 \qquad (10)$$

where, components of 'a' are linearly decreased from value 2 to 0 over the course of iterations, and 'r_1' and 'r_2' are random vectors in [0, 1] [16].

The hunting activity of grey wolves requires the skills and ability to locate the prey and encircle them, which is guided by the alpha. In search space initially, there is no idea regarding the optimum prey location. Now in mathematical form, we consider that the alpha is the best search agent, and beta and delta have better idea regarding the optimum prey location. So, we consider the first three search agents as best solutions (alpha, beta and delta) and remaining search agents must update their positions with respect to alpha, beta and delta. The following equations are proposed by Mirjalili et al. (2014) [16] in this regard as follows:

$$D_\alpha = C_1 X_\alpha - X, \; D_\beta = C_2 X_\beta - X, \; D_\delta = C_3 X_\delta - X \qquad (11)$$

$$X_1 = X_\alpha - A_1 D_\alpha, \; X_2 = X_\beta - A_2 D_\beta, \; X_3 = X_\delta - A_3 D_\delta \qquad (12)$$

$$X(t+1) = \frac{X_1 + X_2 + X_3}{3} \qquad (13)$$

To mathematically model the grey wolves attacking activity towards the prey, the vector 'A' (fluctuation range) decreased in range of [$-a$, a], with decreasing the vector 'a' from value 2 to 0. If condition $|A| < 1$ occurs then grey wolves attack towards the prey [16].

Grey wolves mostly search the prey by diverging their positions with respect to the alpha, beta and delta in a pack. To convert this divergence concept in mathematical form, vector 'A' utilize with random values in a range of 1 to -1 [16]. This condition permits the GWO algorithm to search the optimum prey location globally.

4   Design Problem

In present study, optimization of two-bay three-story planar steel frame is done by using the GWO algorithm. This frame consists of 15 members (6-Beams and 9-columns). Frame geometry, loading conditions and boundary conditions of two-bay three-story steel frame, are presented in Fig. 1. The frame problem was studied by the many researchers using various algorithms, namely ACO [3], EHS [15], GA [18] and TLBO [23]. The material properties are assumed as the modulus of elasticity (E) is 29000 ksi and yield stress (F_y) is 36 ksi. In frame design, 268-W shaped sections for beam members and 18-W shaped sections ($W10$ sections only) for column members are considered as per AISC-LRFD [1, 23]. The out of plane effective length factor for column and beam members are specified as 1.0 and 0.167, respectively [4].

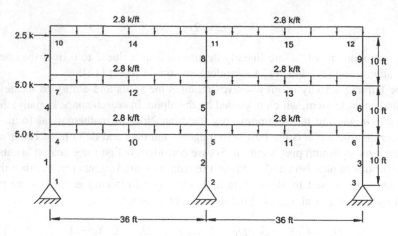

Fig. 1 Geometry and loading conditions of two-bay three-story frame

In this study, to get best tuning of algorithm parameters, population size are assumed to be 40, 20 and 10, respectively and corresponding generations are assumed to be 40, 80 and 160, respectively. Hence, in each case maximum function evolutions (FE) consumed to be 1600 . In addition, statistical results are measured by 30 independent runs and best results are displayed. Table 1 compares the results of the GWO algorithm and the best designs (AISC W-Shapes and Weight) obtained in the literature. It can be seen that a design obtained by using the GWO algorithm, W21 × 57 for beams and W10 × 49 for columns, is the best design in terms of optimum weight without violating the stated constraints. The corresponding weight achieved for this design is of 16686.5702 lb. The best frame design weight for the GWO algorithm is approximately 11.20, 11.20, 6.20 and 7.30 % less than the best design weight for the GA [18], ACO [3], TLBO [23] and EHS [15], respectively.

Table 2 represents the statistical results of the GWO algorithm for two-bay three-story frame design problem for different population and generation. Optimum weight of frame is of 16686.57 lb achieved in each set of algorithm parameter. It should be also noticed that best result is achieved 28 times out of 30 runs, and hence the GWO algorithm reported 93.333 % success rate to get best solution.

Table 1 Optimum results obtained for the two-bay three-story frame design problem

	AISC W-Shapes				
	Pezeshk et al. (2000) [18]	Camp et al. (2005) [3]	Vedat (2012) [23]	Maheri and Narimani (2014) [15]	This study
Method	GA	ACO	TLBO	EHS	GWO
Beam (10–15)	W24 × 62	W24 × 62	W24 × 62	W21 × 55	W21 × 57
Column (1–9)	W10 × 60	W10 × 60	W10 × 49	W10 × 68	W10 × 49
Weight (lb)	18792	18792	17789	18000	16686.5702

Table 2 Statistical results of the GWO algorithm

Population size	Generation	FE	Minimum (lb)	Maximum (lb)	Standard deviation	Success rate to get best solution (%)
40	40	1600	16686.57	17115.37	16686.57	90.00
20	80	1600	16686.57	17115.37	16686.57	93.333
10	160	1600	16686.57	21280.89	16686.57	93.333

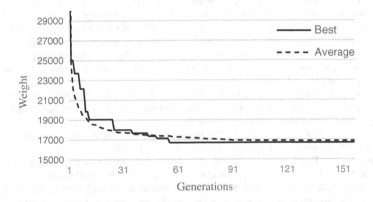

Fig. 2 Convergence history of two-bay three-story frame design using the GWO algorithm

The convergence of the two-bay three-story frame for the best weight and average weight of 30 independent runs is represented in Fig. 2. However, the GWO algorithm gives the presented result at a population size of 10, resulting in 1600 FE. This graph indicates that the optimum weight is reduced with increasing the generation, and best value of weight is achieved within 60 generations.

5   Conclusions

The present work proposed the GWO algorithm to optimize two-bay three-story frame structure according to AISC-LRFD. The GWO algorithm is inspired by leadership hierarchy of grey wolves. The obtained results are compared with results of GA, ACO, TLBO and EHS. The achieved optimum weight of frame is of 16686.57 lb in each set of algorithm parameter with considering the material and performance constraints according to AISC-LRFD. It is stated from the results that the best design weight of frame obtained using the GWO algorithm is 11.20, 11.20, 6.20 and 7.30 % less than the best design weight obtained by GA, ACO, TLBO and EHS, respectively. The best result is achieved 28 times out of 30 runs, hence the GWO algorithm reported 93.333 % success rate to get best solution. The GWO algorithm represents better computational efforts and ability over the other state-of-the-art algorithms.

References

1. American Institute of Steel Construction (AISC). (1994). *Manual of steel construction load resistance factor design* (2nd ed.). Chicago: AISC.
2. Azad, S. K., & Hasançebi, O. (2013). Upper bound strategy for metaheuristic based design optimization of steel frames. *Advances in Engineering Software, 57*, 19–32.
3. Camp, C. V., Bichon, B. J., & Stovall, S. P. (2005). Design of steel frames using ant colony optimization. *Journal of Structural Engineering, 131*(3), 369–379.
4. Hall, S. K., Cameron, G. E., & Grierson, D. E. (1989). Least-weight design of steel frameworks accounting for p-δ effects. *Journal of Structural Engineering, 115*(6), 1463–1475.
5. Hasançebi, O., & Azad, S. K. (2012). An exponential big bang-big crunch algorithm for discrete design optimization of steel frames. *Computers & Structures, 110*, 167–179.
6. Hasançebi, O., Bahçecioğlu, T., Kurç, Ö., & Saka, M. P. (2011). Optimum design of high-rise steel buildings using an evolution strategy integrated parallel algorithm. *Computers & Structures, 89*(21), 2037–2051.
7. Hasançebi, O., Çarbaş, S., Doğan, E., Erdal, F., & Saka, M. P. (2010). Comparison of non-deterministic search techniques in the optimum design of real size steel frames. *Computers & Structures, 88*(17), 1033–1048.
8. Hasançebi, O., & Carbas, S. (2014). Bat inspired algorithm for discrete size optimization of steel frames. *Advances in Engineering Software, 67*, 173–185.
9. Hasançebi, O., Erdal, F., & Saka, M. P. (2009). Adaptive harmony search method for structural optimization. *Journal of Structural Engineering, 136*(4), 419–431.
10. Hasançebi, O., & Kazemzadeh A. S. (2013). Reformulations of big bang-big crunch algorithm for discrete structural design optimization. *World Academy of Science Engineering and Technology, 74*.
11. Kaveh, A., & Abbasgholiha, H. (2011). Optimum design of steel sway frames using Big Bang-Big Crunch algorithm. *Asian Journal of Civil Engineering, 12*(3), 293–317.
12. Kaveh, A., Azar, B. F., Hadidi, A., Sorochi, F. R., & Talatahari, S. (2010). Performance-based seismic design of steel frames using ant colony optimization. *Journal of Constructional Steel Research, 66*(4), 566–574.
13. Kaveh, A., & Nasrollahi, A. (2014). Performance-based seismic design of steel frames utilizing charged system search optimization. *Applied Soft Computing, 22*, 213–221.
14. Kaveh, A., & Talatahari, S. (2012). Charged system search for optimal design of frame structures. *Applied Soft Computing, 12*(1), 382–393.
15. Maheri, M. R., & Narimani, M. M. (2014). An enhanced harmony search algorithm for optimum design of side sway steel frames. *Computers & Structures, 136*, 78–89.
16. Mirjalili, S., Mirjalili, S. M., & Lewis, A. (2014). Grey wolf optimizer. *Advances in Engineering Software, 69*, 46–61.
17. Murren, P., & Khandelwal, K. (2014). Design-driven harmony search (DDHS) in steel frame optimization. *Engineering Structures, 59*, 798–808.
18. Pezeshk, S., Camp, C. V., & Chen, D. (2000). Design of nonlinear framed structures using genetic optimization. *Journal of Structural Engineering, 126*(3), 382–388.
19. Pholdee, N., & Bureerat, S. (2014). Comparative performance of meta-heuristic algorithms for mass minimisation of trusses with dynamic constraints. *Advances in Engineering Software, 75*, 1–13.
20. Safari, D., Maheri, M. R., & Maheri, A. (2013). On the performance of a modified multiple-deme genetic algorithm in LRFD design of steel frames. *IJST, Transactions of Civil Engineering*, 169–190.
21. Safari, D., Maheri, M. R., & Maheri, A. (2011). Optimum design of steel frames using a multiple-deme GA with improved reproduction operators. *Journal of Constructional Steel Research, 67*(8), 1232–1243.

22. Serdar, Ç., İbrahim, A., & Mehmet, P. S. (2009). Optimum design of steel frames using adaptive harmony search method to LRFD-AISC. In 8th World Congress on Structural and Multidisciplinary Optimization.
23. Toğan, V. (2012). Design of planar steel frames using teaching–learning based optimization. *Engineering Structures, 34*, 225–232.

Child Growth Mentor—A Proposed Model for Effective Use of Mobile Application for Better Growth of Child

Siddhi Shah, Shefali Naik and Vinay Vachharajani

Abstract Good health of a child is a major concern for parents. Malnutrition during first 5 years of age and irregular vaccination may cause critical health-related issues. It is very difficult for a mother to remember dates of immunization. There are some existing systems which provide alerts for the next date of vaccination, but fail to manage schedule of the same. Apart from vaccination and malnutrition, proper weight and height ratio is also equally important. It will be very beneficial for a mother if these kinds of features are bundled in a single system which will be connected to the government's central database of birth. To propose this type of model for better growth of child, a survey has been conducted. On the basis of the survey, further analysis has been done to find the feasibility.

Keywords ICT in healthcare · Child growth · Vaccination · Height and weight analyzer

1 Introduction

Good health of its people plays a very important role in the country's growth as well as in one's own happiness. To avoid chances of diseases in later age, proper medication should be given at the early age. Proper medication includes regular checkups, health monitoring, and vaccination. Information and Communication Technology plays a significant role in healthcare by reducing costs and maximizing outcomes. Healthcare through ICT affects our society and the quality of our lives in

S. Shah (✉) · S. Naik · V. Vachharajani
School of Computer Studies, Ahmedabad University, Ahmedabad, Gujarat, India
e-mail: siddhi.shah@ahduni.edu.in

S. Naik
e-mail: shefali.naik@ahduni.edu.in

V. Vachharajani
e-mail: vinay.vachharajani@ahduni.edu.in

© Springer Science+Business Media Singapore 2016   153
S.C. Satapathy et al. (eds.), *Proceedings of International Conference on ICT for Sustainable Development*, Advances in Intelligent Systems and Computing 409, DOI 10.1007/978-981-10-0135-2_14

a positive way as it has become an integral part of everyone's life. Nowadays, mobile phones and applications are used widely in India. Mobile phones give easy access of information at any time and from anywhere. Indian mothers are using various child-related iPhone mobile applications such as [6] Easier Days & Nights, Baby Connect, Baby Monitor 3G, Baby Pack & Go, Baby Shusher, Baby Sleep, Best Baby Monitor, My Baby & Me, My Kids Health, Parenting Ages & Stages, Sweet Baby, etc. The model, which is proposed in this paper, will offer features like management of vaccination schedule, alerts for nutritional food, height and weight analysis, etc. The first section of the paper focuses on Literature Review, second section contains Analysis of Survey, third section includes Discussion of Analysis of Survey, and fourth section presents Proposed Model which is followed by Future Work and Conclusion.

2 Literature Review

Long-term poor health, disability, poor educational and developmental outcomes could be caused by malnutrition during early age of the child [2]. WHO report shows that by 2010, about 104 million children less than 5 years of age were underweight, 43 million were overweight and children under 2 years of age are the most affected by malnutrition [2]. Also, immunity [1] of child below 5 years of age is low which require continuous monitoring of child's growth. There are several factors which affect growth of child such as vaccination, ratio of height and weight, nutritional food, etc. Therefore, it is required to provide nutritional food, vaccinate the child as per the schedule and maintain records of height and weight. According to [4] by 2002, "failure to immunize the world's children with life saving vaccines results in more than 3 million premature deaths annually." The smartcard which stores child's photograph, name, birth year, gender, father's and mother's name, address, telephone number, location, and dates of immunization of the various vaccines is proposed as a model in [3]. According to [5], monitoring of child's growth is essential to identify any deficiencies during early age.

3 Analysis of Survey

The samples have been collected for the various age groups of mothers and it is observed that 59 % mothers have shown interest in the proposed mobile application whereas 12 % are not sure about the usage of the application. The graphical representation is given in Fig. 1.

The analysis given in Fig. 2 shows that 46 % of the mothers are working out of which 34 % are working full time, 7 % are working part time, 4 % have their own business, and 50 % mothers are housewives. Almost all the mothers are using internet and various mobile applications but it is found that despite of extensive use

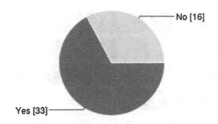

Fig. 1 Percentage of mothers interested in using proposed mobile application

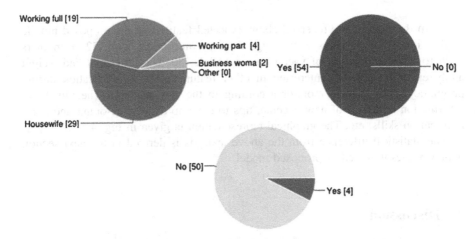

Fig. 2 Percentage of working and nonworking mothers and their internet usage

of mobile applications, they are not using any application for the better growth of their children. Because of unavailability of such type of application, they are not able to remember the vaccination schedule and specification of expected height and weight according to age of the child.

Presently, 57 % mothers are referring doctors file to find these details, 9 % are using simple phone reminders and 21 % are not using any of the system. Figure 3 shows this analysis.

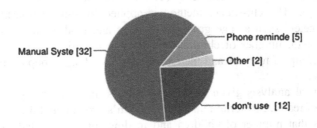

Fig. 3 Percentage of mothers using a system for child's growth

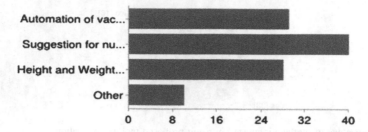

Fig. 4 Percentage of mothers who require the features in the proposed application

From the suggestions received about expected features of the proposed mobile application, 71 % mothers want suggestions for nutritional food, 52 % mothers wish to have automation of vaccination schedule, 50 % want height and weight analyzer, and 18 % are interested in other features such as medication during pregnancy, baby growth monitor according to the age, recipes of healthy food, information of arrival of new vaccine, tips to develop child's reasoning and communication skills, etc. The graphical representation is given in Fig. 4.

The statistical inference from the above analysis is derived in the next section which proves the need of proposed model.

4   Discussion

Our aim is to propose a model which could be helpful to mothers of growing children to know details about arrival of new vaccines, analyze height and weight as per the age, information of nutritional food to be given at certain age, etc. The survey is conducted to know the usefulness of this model. Random samples are drawn from the different age groups of mothers. To get variety of samples, the questionnaire was distributed online as well as offline. We have received a very good response. The survey was conducted based on working or nonworking mothers who use internet, awareness of mobile applications, willingness to read material related to children's growth, mobile application which gives vaccination schedule, analysis of height and weight, nutritional food, etc.

The statistical analysis generated by PH State tool supports the requirement of proposed model. The chi-square method is applied to find relationship between various parameters such as age group of mothers and reading material related to children's growth, number of children and reading material related to children's growth, age group of mothers and their work status, and age group of mothers and internet usage.

The statistical analysis given in Table 1 depicts that age group of mothers is independent of reading material related to children's growth, and their work status. It also shows that number of children and reading material related to children's growth are not related. Internet usage is dependent on age group of mothers.

Table 1 Statistical analysis

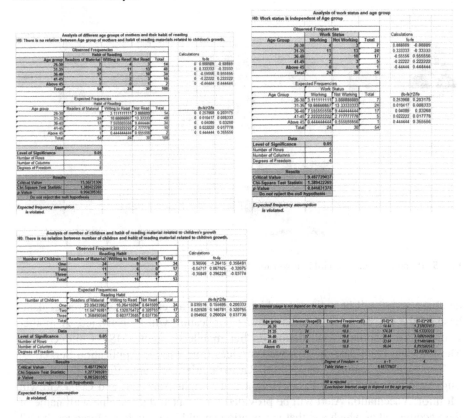

5 Proposed Model

After intensive literature review and statistical analysis of collected data, it is observed that there are very few existing systems which could be used to know vaccination dates and details about overall growth of a child. However, there is no mobile application which provides all these features together. The data which are collected state that 59 % of the mothers require a mobile application which includes most of the features related to child's growth. From this suggestion, "Child Growth Mentor" model is proposed. The detailed architecture of the proposed model is given in Fig. 5.

"Child Growth Mentor" is a mobile application which will be helpful to a mother from the birth of her child. District Repository is a database which stores details related to birth within that district. Whenever a new birth entry is registered with the "Birth and Death Department" of the district office along with birth date of the child, mother's mobile number also will be stored. With every new child's entry, a

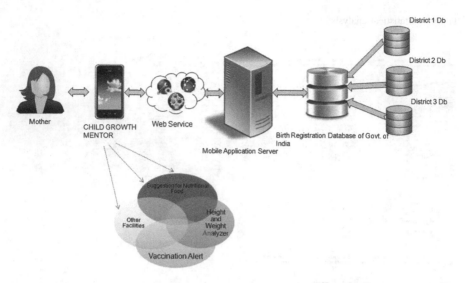

Fig. 5 Proposed model for child growth mentor

database script will be activated, which will make an entry to central server database of the Government of India and the application will be activated. A mother will get notification of registration on her mobile through SMS. "Child Growth Mentor" will fetch date through web services from Mobile Application Server.

The salient features of "Child Growth Mentor" are Vaccination Alert, Suggestion for Nutritional Food, Height and Weight Analyzer, and Child Growth Monitor. Vaccination Alert will be provided for the next due vaccine with name of the vaccine and at which age that vaccination should be provided. Moreover, it will give information of newly invented vaccines along with its importance. Additionally, the mother will be able to record history of vaccines which are already given. This information will be stored on the Mobile Application Server for future reference. According to child's age, the application will send nutritional food suggestions which will include nutritional values and its benefits. Even the mother will be able to input height and weight of the child which will be analyzed by the application and will send the appropriate response. Apart from this, the application will provide other features such as recipes which child is fond of, links for articles on child's growth, puzzles and games.

6 Future Work and Conclusion

Based on the survey, it is observed that child's growth-related applications are immensely helpful to mothers. This observation is also supported by the chi-square analysis. The features such as Vaccination Alert and Schedule, Height and Weight

Analyzer, Suggestions for Nutritional Food, etc., will be provided by the proposed model. After implementation of the proposed model, it could be extended for other features such as Speech Therapy, Growth Monitoring, IQ Test, Yoga videos for child's growth, Home Remedies, etc.

References

1. Anderson, L. M., et al. (2003). The effectiveness of early childhood development programs: A systematic review. *American journal of preventive medicine, 24*(3), 32–46.
2. Essential Nutrition Actions Improving Maternal-Newborn-Infant and Young Child Health and Nutrition Evidence for Essential Nutrition Actions. (2011). *Draft.*
3. Rwashana, A., & Ddembe, W. (2008). Enhancing healthcare delivery through ICTs: A case study of the Ugandan immunisation system. *International Journal of Education and Development using ICT* 4.2.
4. Martin, J. F., & Marshall, J. (2002). New tendencies and strategies in international immunization. *GAVI And The Vaccine Fund. Vaccine, 21,* 587–592.
5. Griffiths, M., & Rosso, J. D. (2007). Growth monitoring and the promotion of healthy young child growth.
6. http://www.ivillage.ca/parenting/stuff-we-love/10-best-baby-apps-new-parents-baby-monitors-lullabies.

Design and Development of a Rule-Based Urdu Lemmatizer

Vaishali Gupta, Nisheeth Joshi and Iti Mathur

Abstract Language is known to be one of the tools for communication in a translingual society. It is composed of many elements and the basic fundamental part of a language is the structure of words. Understanding the structure of word is not only necessary to gain the proper understanding about a language, but also an important factor for language translation. The words have numerous variant forms based on its usage; "depend" has variants as dependency, dependent, independent, etc., where depend is a root word. To drop the root from its variant form, some tools are required like Stemming or Lemmatizer. But to extract correct and meaningful root word, the mechanism of lemmatizer should be used because it is not always possible to use stemming to find the meaningful root word. Therefore, lemmatizer is an extended mechanism of stemming. In this paper, the rule-based Urdu Lemmatizer is created that works by eliminating suffix from the root word and adds some required and relevant information to extract the meaningful root.

Keywords Stemming · Lemmatizer · Root · Lemma · Suffix

V. Gupta (✉)
Department of Computer Science & Engineering, IES, IPS Academy,
Indore, Madhya Pradesh, India
e-mail: vaishali.gupta77@gmail.com

V. Gupta · N. Joshi · I. Mathur
Department of Computer Science, Apaji Institute, Banasthali University,
Banasthali Vidyapit, Rajasthan, India
e-mail: nisheeth.joshi@rediffmail.com

I. Mathur
e-mail: mathur_iti@rediffmail.com

© Springer Science+Business Media Singapore 2016   161
S.C. Satapathy et al. (eds.), *Proceedings of International Conference on ICT for Sustainable Development*, Advances in Intelligent Systems and Computing 409, DOI 10.1007/978-981-10-0135-2_15

1 Introduction

Natural Language Processing is an enormously growing research area and Machine Translation (MT) is known to be one of its applications. MT facilitates the conversion of one natural language to another; therefore, it reduces the problem of language barrier among people. To understand the development of the MT, it is required to go through various modules. The basic and first module is morphological analysis. Morphological analysis tries to study the structure of a particular word. In order to develop a morphological analyzer, it is required to get an exact root word from any source language. To find the exact root word, stemming and lemmatization techniques are widely used. Stemming works by removing the affixes and extract the root word, but it is not always possible to get the meaningful root word. So, in order to get the correct root word, we use lemmatizer. Therefore, the motivation behind this paper is to develop a lemmatizer for which some rules for suffix removal and some rules for addition of information are developed, which can provide a proper root word. Lemmatizer extracts normalized form of an input word or in more simple words it can be said that the process of obtaining the normalized form from a given word. Initially, researchers also used stemming to get the root word but unfortunately, in many occasions it returns an invalid root words. For example "create" has morphological variants as creates, created, creating, and creation. If stemming algorithm is applied on the above variant forms then "creat" is produced as a root word. This has no meaning so it is terms of higher order NLP tasks; it is unusable. We can remove this problem by applying a lemmatization algorithm on it. Through lemmatization ending of "base" lexeme is again attached and generates valid lexeme, i.e., "e" is added at the end of 'creat' giving a valid lexeme as "create." Lemmatizer discussed here is only restricted for Urdu language. Urdu is one of the constitutional languages of India. Therefore, to extract information from Urdu, an Urdu lemmatizer is developed. Here, the exact base form of any given Urdu word can be obtained. This lemmatizer is developed by using the longest suffix stripping along with the addition of various rules. It could be specially used for information retrieval.

2 Related Work and Background

Various researches are going on in this area. There are a variety of stemming and lemmatization algorithms available that have been developed in the recent past. The first discovered stemming algorithm is the suffix stripping algorithm for English language it was proposed by Porter [1] in July 1980. A lot of work has been accomplished for European and English languages but on the contrary, little work has been done in Urdu language. Paul et al. [2] proposed a work for designing of a rule-based Hindi lemmatizer. In this work, they have created some rules for suffix removal; after removal of suffix they have applied some rules for addition of suffixes and finally they obtained proper root word. Plisson et al. [3] presented some approach for finding normalized form of root word through suffix removal and addition of suffixes. They have designed algorithm on the basis of "if-then-else rules" and also designed induction algorithm on the basis of ripple down approach. Gupta et al. [4] developed an unsupervised stemming algorithm which is hybridized with partial lemmatization for Hindi Language. They have also improved the unsupervised algorithm and reduce the problem of over stemming. Later, they tackled with lemma and developed the lemmatizer. Prasenjit et al. [5] designed a clustering-based algorithm to detect equivalence categories of root words and their morphological variant forms. This clustering-based algorithm was also compared with Porter's & Lovin's stemming algorithm and they got consistent improvements in retrieval. Otair [6] has analyzed various simple and generic stemming algorithms and compared them on the basis of affix list. This algorithm was designed for improving information retrieval performance. Bhattacharya et al. [7] present a novel scheme for creation of human-mediated lemmatizers which gives lemma. They had compared accuracy of this lemmatizer with other lemmatizers and also confirmed that the combination of machine and man can easily identify the root with approximately 100 % accuracy.

3 Study of Urdu Morphology

Morphology incorporates proper understanding of word formation or simply structure of words. It provides a base to identify the formation of words as well as the class it belonged to [8]. Here, class represents different lexical categories as follows:

3.1 Urdu Noun

Noun (اسم) is a word such as the name of a person, things, place, objects, etc. Urdu noun can be inflected into number, case, and gender. Further, number can be inflected in singular/plural and cases are nominative/oblique/vocative. Gender is classified into masculine/feminine. Some examples are shown in the following Tables 1 and 2:

Table 1 Urdu noun-*number*

Singular	Plural
خیال (*khyaal*-Idea)	خیالات (*khyalaat*-Ideas)
جھرنا (*jharna*-waterfall)	جھرنے (*jharne*-waterfalls)

Table 2 Urdu noun-*gender*

Masculine	Feminine
لڑکا (*Ladka*-Boy)	لڑکی (*ladki*-Girl)
بیٹا (*beta*-Son)	بیٹی (*beti*-daughter)

Some other usual concepts of Urdu nouns are as follows:

- Singular masculine nouns end with (ا {alif}, a), (ہ {he}, h), and (ع {ain}, e) E.g., ڈاکیہ (*dakiya*-a postman).
- Plural masculine nouns end with (ان {aan}, an) and (ات {aat}) (ے {ye} y). E.g., نبان (*zahaan*-world), سوالات (*savalaat*-Questions).
- Singular feminine nouns generally end with (ی {i}, y). E.g., خاموشی (*khamoshi*-silence).
- Plural feminine nouns ending with (ا {alif}, a), (ان {aan}, an), (و {on}, on), and (ىں {ain} yen). E.g., ڈالیاں (*daliyaan*-branches).

3.2 Urdu Verb

Verb (فعل) expresses existence, an action, and occurrences in syntax. Basically, Urdu verb shows direct and indirect causative behavior. It could be transitive or intransitive. When one root form is extracted by any verb, then two other forms like direct and indirect causative forms are created. Actually, these three forms are regular verbs. For example, consider a verb: سیکہ (*seekh*-To Learn)

- Infinitive form: سیکھنا (*Seekhna*)
- Direct causative infinitive form: سکھانا (*Sikhana*)
- Indirect causative infinitive form: سخوانا (*Sikhvana*)

سیکھنا (*Seekhna*), سکھانا (*Sikhana*), and سخوانا (*Sikhvana*) are three regular verbs and these inflects in tense, mood, aspect, gender, and number.

3.3 Urdu Adjective

An adjective refers to a word that modifies the noun to make more specific. That is, حکمتی-*hikmati* (skillful), خبردار *khabardaar*-(careful). According to morphology, there are two types of adjectives. First one is only inflected on the basis of gender, number, and case. Second is inflected in degree (Positive, comparative, or superlative). For example: the singular direct مہنگا (*Mahenga*-Expensive) becomes مہنگے (*mahengey*) in all other masculine cases and مہنگی (*mahengi*) in all feminine case.

3.4 Urdu Adverb

Adverb is a part of speech which can modify the meaning of verb, adjective, and another adverb. It can be divided into following categories as mentioned below:

- Adverbs of Time:ام طور پر (*aamtaur par*-Usually), ہمیشہ (*hamesha*-Forever)
- Adverbs of Manner: مشکل سے (*mushkil se*-Hardly), تقریبں (*taqreeban*-Almost)
- Adverbs of Place: ہر جگہ (*har jagah*-Everywhere), دور (*door*-away)
- Adverbs of Degree: کم (*kam*-Less), جیادہ (*jyadah*-More), موٹا (*mota*-fatty)

4 Proposed Methodology

The proposed approach is basically designed for easy and fast retrieval of "base" form of word by which the actual meaning of word can be easily identified and can be translated into another language. Our Urdu lemmatizer is developed by using rule-based approach. In the rule-based approach, various rules for removal and addition of suffixes are created along with the database of exceptional words. These exceptional words are nothing but the complete word that means there is no need to remove any suffix part. Although, for the creation of database, large amount of memory is required. But we get fast retrieval of words in a very short time from this database. The proposed approach reduces the time complexity and extracts the accurate "lemma" or "root."

4.1 Generation of Suffix

For development of stemmer, 25 lakh words were examined from corpus of 10,000 sentences. Suffixes from all words were extracted manually and obtained 128 suffixes [9]. Some extracted suffixes are depicted in Table 3.

The derived form for every word can also be developed with the help of these suffixes. For example: if ات-'aat' is added in the given word then the following derived forms can be received as follows (Table 4).

Table 3 Some extracted suffixes

Root word	Derived word	Suffix
محتاج (*mohtaaj*)	موبتاجی (*mohtaaji*)	ی (*i*)
خیال (*khyaal*)	خیالات (*khyaalaat*)	ات (*aat*)
چمک (*chamak*)	چمکدار (*chamakdaar*)	دار (*daar*)
سیدھا (*seedha*)	سیدھاپن (*seedhapan*)	پن (*pan*)

Table 4 Example of derived words with suffix 'ات'-(aat)

Root word	Derived word
سوال (*savaal*)	سوالات (*savaalaat*)
نبات (*nabat*)	نباتات (*nabataat*)
تفصیل (*tafseel*)	تفصیلات (*tafseelaat*)

دهندهلا = ا + یں – دهندبلیں (dhundhalein - ein + a = dhundhala)
سڈک = یں – سڈکیں (sadakein - ein = sadak)

Fig. 1 Working of rule

Table 5 Words showing with suffix 'یں'-(ein) and 'یاں'-(iyan)

Input word	Apply the rule		Root/Lemma
	Extraction of suffix	Addition of rule	
مہنگیں (mahangein)	یں(ein)	ا(a)	مہنگا (mahanga)
دککتیں (dikkatein)	یں(ein)	–	دککت (dikkat)
پیڑھیاں (peedhiyan)	یاں (iyan)	ی (i)	پیڑھی (peedhi)
سیڑھیاں (seedhiyan)	یاں (iyan)	ی (i)	سیڑھی (seedhi)

4.2 Rules Generation

To find an accurate lemma, 128 rules are designed. If these rules are applied in the input word, then suffix gets removed from input word and if required, addition of lexeme takes place [10]. For example-if suffix یں -'ein' is taken then working of this is shown as follows (Fig. 1).

Some other examples are also depicted in Table 5

Sometimes, there are some exceptions and these rules are not applied on some words. These words are stored in database. For example: rule "iyan" should not apply on word "chidiyan" because if "iyan" is removed from "chidiyan" then we obtain stemmed word "chid" that does not have a meaning even if we add rule "i" then "chidi" also does not have a meaning. So this exceptional word "chidiyan" is stored in database. Although this approach requires more time, for obtaining meaningful root word, we have used this approach.

4.3 Database

Database for exceptional Urdu words is created. Exceptional words means, words which does not require any removal and addition of character. These words are a complete word themselves. Through this database, mostly the accurate root word can be extracted [11]. Some exceptions of words are shown in Fig. 2.

چڑیا - (chidiya),	پہیا - (pahiya),	کنارا - (kinara),
سریا - (sariya),	لڑکی - (ladki),	کاینات - (kaynaat),
عبادات - (ibadaat),	کسسا - (kissa),	شکریہ - (shukriya)

Fig. 2 Exceptional Urdu words

```
Step1: Take the Input word.
Step 2: Match the input word with database.
Step 3: If word found in database then display input
word as a root word.
Step 4: If word not found in database then proceed for
rules-
a)  If match found with rules then suffix extracted and
    if required addition of character takes place and
    then finally get exact root word.
b)  If match not found with rules then input word display
    as a root word.
```

Fig. 3 Lemmatizaton algorithm

4.4 *Algorithm for Lemmatization*

In this section, an algorithm is developed for a rule-based Urdu lemmatizer. This is shown in Fig. 3.

4.5 *Approach to Lemmatization*

See Fig. 4.

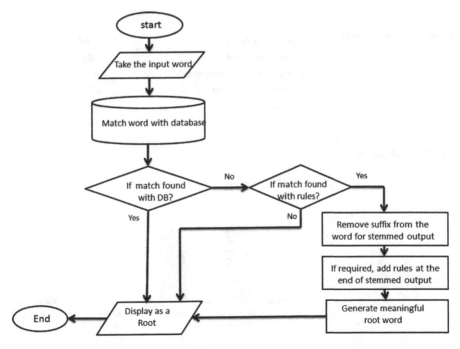

Fig. 4 Flowchart of lemmatization algorithm

5   Results and Evaluation of System

From evaluation of lemmatization algorithm, 1000 Urdu words were processed. Out of 1000 words, 903 root words were obtained accurately. Accuracy was calculated in percentage with the help of the formula given as

$$\text{Accuracy } (\%) = \frac{\text{Accurate stemmed}}{\text{Total no. of given word}} \times 100 \tag{1}$$

We achieved an accuracy of 90.30 %. Table 6 shows some results obtained from this algorithm.

Summary of 1000 words of test data is shown in Table 7 and results are shown in Fig. 5.

Table 6 Some lemmatized words

Input word	Lemma (output)
حصّے (hisse)	حصّہ (hissa)
ڈالیاں (daaliyon)	ڈالی (daali)
حوالات (havalaat)	حوالات (havalaat)-exceptional
مشرات (mushahraat)	مشراہ (mushahrah)
کویتا (kavita)	کوی (kavi)
پتا (pita)	پتا (pita)-exceptional

Table 7 Summary of test data

Features of test data	Total
Total input word	1000
Correct obtained root word	903
Wrong obtained output	97
Unique output	68

Fig. 5 Results of test dataset

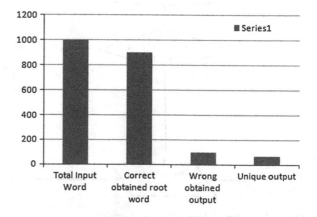

6 Conclusion

In this paper, on the basis of rule-based approach, the Urdu Lemmatizer is developed. The proposed Lemmatizer is most acceptable and efficient with respect to time. In this rule-based approach, various rules for suffix removal are created to get stemmed output and if required, some rules are also created for addition of characters at the end of stemmed output. The database is also designed for exceptional words. With the help of rules and database, an Urdu lemmatizer is developed. By which the accurate "lemma" or "root" word can easily be retrieved in short time. This approach is applied on a test data set of 1000 words and 90.30 % accuracy is obtained.

References

1. Porter, M. F. (1980). An algorithm for suffix stripping program, *14*(3), 130–137.
2. Paul, S., Joshi, N., & Mathur, I. (2013). Development of a hindi lemmatizer. *In proceeding of International journal of Computational Linguistics and Natural Language Processing, 2*(5), 380–384.
3. Plisson, J., Larc, N., & Mladenic, D. A. (2008). Rule based approach to word lemmatization. In *Proceedings of the 7th International Multiconference Information Society. IS-2004*, pp. 83–86.
4. Gupta, D., Yadav, R.K., & Sajan, N. (2012). Improving unsupervised stemming by using partial lemmatization coupled with data based heuristics for hindi. In *Proceedings of International Journal of Computer Application (0975–8887), 38*(8).
5. Majumder, P., Mitra, M., Parui, S. K., Kole, G., Mitra, P., & Datta, K. (2007). YASS: Yet another suffix stripper. *Association for Computing Machinery Transactions on Information Systems, 25*(4):18–38.
6. Qtair, M. A. (2013). Comparative analysis of arabic stemming algorithms. In *proceedings of International Journal of Managing Information Technology (IJMIT), 5*(2).
7. Bhattacharyya, P., Bahuguna, A., Talukdar, L., & Phukan, B. (2014). Facilitating multi-lingual sense annotation: human mediated lemmatizer. In *Proceedings of Global Wordnet Conference (GWC 2014), Tartu, Estonia*, January 25–29, 2014.
8. Gupta, V., Joshi, N., & Mathur, I. (2013). Rule based stemmer in Urdu. In *Proceedings of 4th International Conference on Computer and Communication Technology. Published in IEEE Xplore*. (ISBN: 978-1-4799-1572-9, pp. 1520–1525).
9. Paul, S., Joshi, N., & Mathur, I. (2013). Development of a rule based hindi lemmatizer. In *Proceedings of 3rd International Conference Artificial Intelligence, Soft Computing and Application* (pp. 67–74).
10. Ameta, J., Joshi, N., & Mathur, I. (2011). A lightweight stemmer for Gujrati. In *Proceedings of 46th Annual National Convention of Computer Society of India. Ahmedabad, India,* (2011).
11. Gupta, V., Joshi, N., Mathur, I. (2015). Design and development of rule based inflectional and derivational Urdu stemmer 'Usal'. In *Proceedings of 1st International Conference INBUSH ERA 2015. Published in IEEE Xplore*. (ISBN: 978-1-4799-8432-9).

Enhanced Microstrip Patch Antenna Using Metamaterial for DECT and Aircraft Wireless System Applications

Sunita, Gaurav Bharadwaj, Monika Kunwal and Kiran Aseri

Abstract A design and analysis of dual band rectangular microstrip patch antenna covered with the avant-garde metamaterial layer with a height of 3.2 mm from the ground plane is proposed. The antenna is resonated at two frequencies of 1.9 and 4.3 GHz, depending upon the metamaterial layer which is incorporated with double U structure between double E structures. The proposed design provides improvement in bandwidth and significant reduction in return loss at both resonating frequencies. The frequency band of 1.9 GHz has been exclusively reserved for DECT 6.0 devices. The other frequency band of 4.3 GHz covers application in Aircraft Wireless Systems. For the verification of negative permeability and negative permittivity of the structure, NRW approach is carried out and thorough presentation of the experimental results, comparison is done by simulating the design in CST-Microwave Studio.

Keywords Metamaterial · DECT · Dual band · Low range altimeter · RMPA · Cordless audio transmission

1 Introduction

Recently, the microstrip patch antenna have gained much attention because of their many advantages including ease of installation and mechanical reliability with respect to radiation property; they are versatile in polarization and resonant

Sunita (✉) · G. Bharadwaj · M. Kunwal · K. Aseri
Department of Electronics and Communication Engineering, Government Women
Engineering College, Ajmer, Rajasthan, India
e-mail: olasunita30@gmail.com

G. Bharadwaj
e-mail: gwecaexam@gmail.com

M. Kunwal
e-mail: monikakunwal@gmail.com

K. Aseri
e-mail: kiranrids18@gmail.com

© Springer Science+Business Media Singapore 2016
S.C. Satapathy et al. (eds.), *Proceedings of International Conference
on ICT for Sustainable Development*, Advances in Intelligent Systems
and Computing 409, DOI 10.1007/978-981-10-0135-2_16

Fig. 1 Geometry of RMPA

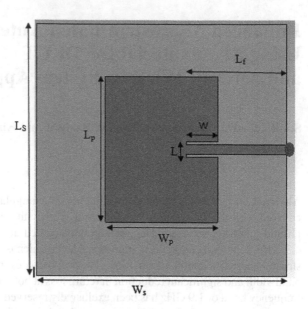

frequency. The materials which exhibit the property of negative permeability and negative permittivity at particular frequencies are Left-Handed Metamaterials.

Several multiband antennas using metamaterials have been reported in the literature [1–10]. The examination of LHM becomes interesting due to its unique properties like negative refraction and backward wave [1, 2]. The combination of thin wires (TW) and SRR is usually the basic building block of LHM, though new structures like fishnet, omega shaped, spiral multi-split, and S-Shape also exhibit the property of metamaterial [3, 4]. Since 2001, after the first prototype by Smith, LHM became a topic of interest due to the negative μ and ε which improves many antenna properties and the use in microwave circuits and antennas became very extensive [5]. Different shapes used in designing of metamaterial multiband antenna such as spiral, tapered shapes [6, 7]. A novel metamaterial-inspired technique is used [8] (Fig. 1).

In this letter, we are studying and analyzing the properties of rectangular microstrip patches and it is compared with the LHM structure of the same. The LHM design consists of U structure between E structure and sphere inside the U structure inside as illustrated in Fig. 2.

2 Antenna Design

In this work, the proposed antenna has the dimension of ground as 80 mm × 60 mm × 0.05 mm and antenna designed on FR4 substrate with loss tangent of 0.02. To enhance the return loss and Bandwidth, another substrate is

Fig. 2 Structure of
metamaterial with dimension

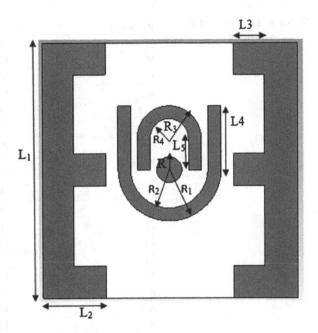

interposed between the metamaterial and antenna patch. The metamaterial is assembled using double U structure between double E structure and sphere is inside the double U structure. A slot is loaded for inset feed with the dimension of 5 mm × 10 mm to reduce the surface current at the feed point. In some cases, it is the Contact Volume Editor that checks all the pdfs. In such cases, the authors are not involved in the checking phase (Table 1 and Figs. 3 and 4).

3 Result Discussion

The design achieves S parameters in complex form. For the verification of double-negative metamaterial properties of incorporated structure, the values of S-parameter were exported to MS Excel program and Nicolson, Ross, and Weir approach are used to calculate graph of permeability and permittivity with frequency.

Equation and excel graph (Figs. 5 and 6)

$$\mu_r = \frac{2.c.(1 - v_1)}{w.d.i(1 + v_2)} \tag{1}$$

$$\varepsilon_r = \mu_r + \frac{2.s_{11}.c.i}{w.d} \tag{2}$$

Table 1 Dimension of the proposed antenna

Parameters	Values (mm)
L_g	80.00
W_g	60.00
L_s	80.00
W_s	80.00
L_p	46.07
W_p	35.84
L_f	32.00
W_f	03.00
L	05.00
W	10.00
L_1	80.00
L_2	20.00
L_3	10.00
L_4	20.00
L_5	10.00
R	04.00
R_1	16.00
R_2	12.00
R_3	10.00
R_4	06.00

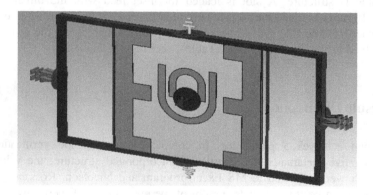

Fig. 3 Metamaterial between two waveguide ports with boundary condition

Figure 7 shows the return loss curve in which two narrow bands are observed for the resonant frequency at 1.9298 and 4.3292 GHz. We obtain the bandwidth 38.4 and 70.9 MHz, respectively. Figure 8 shows the simulated radiation pattern of far field directivity for resonating frequency at 1.9298 GHz with 4.9 dBi. Radiation pattern is unidirectional.

Fig. 4 Structure of the optimized antenna

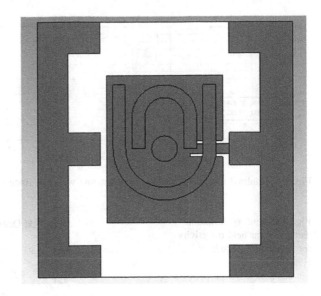

Fig. 5 Graph between frequency and permeability

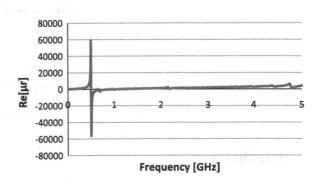

Fig. 6 Graph between frequency and permittivity

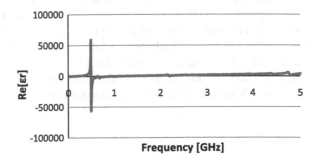

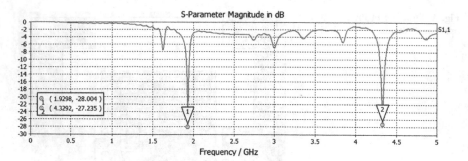

Fig. 7 Simulated return loss curve of the antenna with metamaterial

Fig. 8 Simulated radiation
pattern of far field directivity
for resonating frequency
1.92 GHz

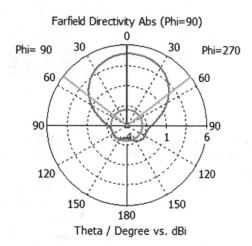

4   Conclusion

The article presented here concludes that the performance of the antenna has
meliorated by the incorporation of LHM structure. The simulation of Meta structure
with a sphere in double U shows improvements in Return Loss and Bandwidth. The
final model of double E shaped and structured antenna has return loss of −28.00 dB
on 1.9 GHz and −27.23 dB on 4.3 GHz which shows its adequacy for cordless
audio transmission and low range altimeter in aircraft systems, respectively. The
Meta structure and the antenna are designed with $\epsilon = 4.3$, $h = 3.2$ mm and $\epsilon = 4.3$
and $h = 1.6$ from the ground plane, respectively.

References

1. Aydin, A., Kaan, G., & Ekmel, O. (2006). Two-dimensional left-handed metamaterial with a negative refractive index. *Journal of Physics Conference Series, 36*(6), 11.
2. Shelby, R. A., Smith, D. R., & Shultz, S. (2001). Experimental verification of a negative index of refraction. *Science, 292*(77), 79.
3. Wu, B.-I., Wang, W., Pacheco, J., Chen, X., Grzegorczyk, T., & Kong, J. A. (2005). A study of using metamaterials as antenna substrate to enhance gain. *Progress In Electromagnetics Research, 51*(295), 328.
4. Alici, K. B., & Ozbay, E. (2008). Chareacterization and tilted response of a fishnet metamaterial operating at 100 GHz. *Journal of Physics. D. Applied Physics, 41*, 135011.
5. Smith, D. R., Padilla, W. J., Vier, D. C., Nemat-Nasser, S. C., & Schultz, S. (2000). Loop-wire medium for investigating plasmons at microwave frequency. *Physical Review Letters, 84*, 4184.
6. Rahimi, M., Ameelia Roseline, A., Malathi, K. (2012). Compact dual-band patch antenna using spiral shaped electromagnetic band gap structures for high speed wireless networks1. *International Journal of Electronics and Communications, 66*, 963–968.
7. Sadeghzadeh, R. A., Zarrabi, F. B., & Mansouri, Z. (2014). Band-notched UWB monopole antenna design with novel feed for taper rectangular radiating patch. *Progress In Electromagnetics Research C, 47*, 147–155.
8. Ouedraogo, R. O., Rothwell, E. J., Diaz, A. R., Fuchi, K., & Temme, A. (2012). Miniaturization of patch antennas using a metamaterial-inspired technique. *IEEE Transactions on Antennas and Propagation, 60*(5), 2175–2182.
9. Sulaiman, A. A., Nasaruddin, A, S. (2010). Bandwidth Enhancement in patch antenna by metamaterial substrate. *European Journal of scientific research.*
10. Mazid, H. A., Rahim, M. K. A., Masri, T. (2008). Left-handed metamaterial design for microstrip antenna application. *IEEE International RF and Microwave conference.*

An Enhanced Strategy to Minimize Makespan in Cloud Environment to Accelerate the Performance

Himanshu Sachdeva, Sakshi Kaushal and Amandeep Verma

Abstract With increase of dominance of Cloud Computing in Internet Communication Technologies, it becomes pertinent to have more number of techniques that are efficient and effective in improving system performance. Challenge here is efficient resource allocation to jobs requesting the resources in order to achieve customer satisfaction. Job Scheduling is a technique whereby the best schedule is constructed as a solution by applying various techniques and algorithms fulfilling the need of users so as they get their tasks completed in given time, cost, deadline or budget. This paper covers a new job scheduling algorithm Time Based Ant Colony Optimization Algorithm (TBACO) which is enthused from the basic Ant Colony Optimization algorithm. The objective is to minimize the makespan of given set of jobs, when they are scheduled on different datacenters which are the resource providers in the cloud. The new algorithm is modeled and simulated in Cloudsim simulator. Simulation results show the proposed TBACO algorithm outperformed basic ACO with 59 % savings in makespan.

Keywords Job scheduling algorithms · Ant colony optimization · Datacenters · Virtual machines

H. Sachdeva (✉) · S. Kaushal · A. Verma
Department of Computer Science and Engineering,
University Institute of Engineering and Technology, Panjab University,
Chandigarh, India
e-mail: 2909.himanshu@gmail.com

S. Kaushal
e-mail: sakshi@pu.ac.in

A. Verma
e-mail: verma_aman81@yahoo.com

© Springer Science+Business Media Singapore 2016
S.C. Satapathy et al. (eds.), *Proceedings of International Conference on ICT for Sustainable Development*, Advances in Intelligent Systems and Computing 409, DOI 10.1007/978-981-10-0135-2_17

1 Introduction

Cloud computing evolved from distributed computing and it provides scalable and dynamic on-demand resources. Grid computing can be part of cloud computing depending on user types. If the end users are systems managers and integrators, they install, upgrade virtualize servers and applications and overall take care of their maintenance in cloud. If the users are end customers, they need not to worry about how execution takes place cloud environment. It is a model for providing anytime, anywhere, opportune, scalable and on-demand system approach to a common pool of manageable computing resources, e.g., bandwidth, servers, storage, applications, and services that can be fastly provisioned and can also be released with least effort or service provider synergy [1]. This model consists of some important characteristics, service models, and four deployment models. The main characteristics are on-demand resource provisioning, measured service, high speed network access, resource sharing and pooling and rapid elasticity. The famous service models are Software-as-a-Service (SaaS), Platform-as-a-Service (PaaS), Infrastructure-as-a-Service (IaaS), Anything as a Service (XaaS), etc. The main deployment models are Public Cloud, Private Cloud, Community Cloud and Hybrid Cloud.

2 Job Scheduling

Job Scheduling is most basic and demanding research issues in a Cloud Computing environment other than security, scaling storage and Software licensing. A good job scheduling process plays a very crucial act in meeting user's job requirements and how to use Cloud resources proficiently. In Cloud, Job Scheduling scheme is selects the finest available and applicable reserves for user's jobs in a cloud, by taking some fixed and dynamic restrictions of user's tasks into account.

2.1 Phases and Mechanism of Job Scheduling

Basically in a Job Scheduling system, there are three phases involved. In the first phase, i.e., resource discovery, all the available resources are collected. In next phase, the report about the available resources is collected and the best applicable resource for user's task is chosen. The last phase, scheduling algorithm executes the job in the chosen system. A large number of practical network computing applications on cloud have same requirements for execution of autonomous tasks as shown in Fig. 1. In this figure, each user (1, 2, ... m) is having a computer (*client*) and flow of separate jobs is to be executed by the servers according to deadlines provided by user. The users can tolerate a small amount of failures, e.g., the

Fig. 1 One job scheduling mechanism [2]

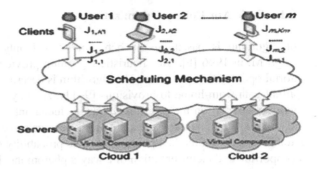

percentage of jobs failing to execute within deadlines and it should be less than 5 %. In Cloud environment, there are one or more datacenters which are also known as computational clouds Amazon EC2, etc., each offering to the users a number of computing resources, in a pay-as-you-go virtual computer form [2]. The output of execution of jobs submitted by the users should maintain a given Quality of Service (QoS) by keeping the failure rate according to SLA and hence maximizes the utilization of computing resources.

2.2 Job Scheduling Algorithms

There exist a number of job scheduling algorithms which can be static or dynamic to schedule tasks to processors or virtual machines in the Datacenter which act as resource providers [3]. In these static scheduling algorithms, the basic information needs to be learned in advance for scheduling like the sequence of the parallel tasks, the execution times of individual and separate tasks or jobs and the communication costs among tasks. Static task scheduling takes before running the parallel application, i.e., during compilation time. In case of Dynamic scheduling, once the tasks arrives, they are allocated resources accordingly and schedule plan is also made dynamically [4–6]. Many researchers have worked on the efficient dynamic job scheduling on VMs with fuzzy prediction [7] to meet the scalability of virtualization and the ambiguity of availability requirements in the scheduling strategy of virtual datacenters. Algorithms Many researchers are working on different methods for efficient job scheduling in cloud computing [5–18]. There are three mechanisms in this optimization, *namely*, Learning Mechanism, Updating Mechanism and Cooperative Mechanism. The learning mechanisms means the more trail information an edge has, the more probability of it being selected. Updating mechanisms includes that as ants pass, the intensity of trail information on the edge would be increased and thereby decreases by evaporation and in Cooperative mechanisms, the communications and cooperation between individuals by trail information enable the Ant colony algorithm to have strong capability of finding the best solutions.

2.2.1 Basic Ant Colony Optimization

Ant algorithm is based on the behavior of real ants has been introduced by Dorigo M. in 1996 [8]. This heuristic algorithm provides solution for the combinatorial optimization problems. The algorithm is described as follows: Ant finds an optimal path from home to provisions [9–11]. As they move on their ways, some pheromone is left on the position and an secluded ant senses beforehand laid trail and choose with maximum probability to follow the same path. In this case, the trail is unbreakable with the laid pheromone. The probability of ant chooses a approach is proportion to the concentration of a way's pheromone. More ants are attracted on the way that has denser pheromone. Finally, this positive feedback mechanism, helps ant to find an optimal way. At time zero, ants are located on diverse positions, the initial values τ_{ij} (0) for trail intensity are set on edge (i, j). The first element of each ant's tabu list is set to be equal to its starting position. After wards, the k-ant moves from position i to position j with a probability that is defined as [8]:

$$P_{ij}^{k}(t) = \frac{[\tau_{ij}(t)]^{\alpha}[\eta_{ij}(t)]^{\beta}}{\sum k \,\varepsilon\, \text{allowed}_{k}[\tau_{ik}(t)]^{\alpha}[\eta_{ik}(t)]^{\beta}} \quad \text{if } j \,\varepsilon\, \text{allowed}_{k}$$
$$\phantom{P_{ij}^{k}(t) =} 0 \qquad\qquad\qquad\qquad\qquad\qquad \text{otherwise}$$

where $\text{allowed}_{k} = \{N\text{-}tabuk\}$, $tabuk$ is the tabu list of kth ant, τ_{ij} (t) is the pheromone value on edge (i, j), η_{ij} is the value of the heuristic value, and $\eta_{ij}(t) = 1/d_{ij}$;

where d_{ij} is the distance between node i and node j. α, controls the relative weight of the pheromone trail and β controls the relative weight of heuristic value. At last, the most optimal and best path is selected and globally updated [12].

2.2.2 Different Variations of ACO Algorithms

Kun Li et al. presented load balancing task scheduling algorithm in cloud based on Ant Colony Optimization, i.e., LBACO algorithm [13]. The output showed minimized the makespan of a given task set. The algorithm has been simulated in Clousim simulator. Their results showed LBACO balanced the entire system load effectively with varying size of task and it was better than FCFS and ACO algorithm. Another algorithm, *namely*, Genetic Algorithm Ant Colony Optimization (GA^{2}CO) algorithm was hybrid of basic GA and ACO [14]. GA has been used to give information to distribute pheromone. Afterwards, ACO improved the accuracy of the schedule plan and optimized evaporator factor and the total pheromone information. At last, convergence of all steps takes place. The results also revealed that GA^{2}CO algorithm has more optimization efficiency and robustness. Max-Min Ant System (MMAS) which was based on the ACO algorithm has also been proposed [15]. This algorithm considered low and upper bound values and limits the pheromone range to be in between these values and that avoids ants to converge too soon in some ranges. Fast Ant System (FANT) based on ACO considered single ant to participate in each iteration search without using pheromone evaporation rule [15].

3 Proposed Work

Task placement and scheduling are studied in the aspects of resource utilization, application throughput, task execution latency and starvation. Resource allocation in Cloud computing environment should match the tasks with virtual machines of datacenter and schedule the task to the assigned virtual machines. The mapping of jobs into virtual machines of a Cloud computing environment has been an NP complete problem. To maximize the performance of the system, dynamic mapping is performed by applying Ant colony optimization as a scheduling algorithm when the arrival of task is known a priori. The goal of Time Based Ant Colony Optimization (TBACO) algorithm mapping is to reduce the value accrued of makespan of completed tasks. In abstract, this study concentrates on the time based quality of service parameter for job scheduling in cloud environment. Various gaps were there

- Basic ACO when implemented in Cloud environment used to take much time. When user submits their jobs to the virtual machines, time taken by the datacenter to execute the desired jobs was comparatively high.
- QoS parameters in basic ACO were not considered.
- On submission of cloudlets more than virtual machines, ACO was not able to produce the schedule.

The TBACO algorithm accede the concept from the basic ACO to decrease the computation time. This time is known as make-span. TBACO algorithm aims at decreasing the make-span and increasing the performance.

3.1 TBACO Implementation

The TBACO algorithm is based on the basic ACO in which aim is to decrease the overall computation time. This time is known as make-span. TBACO algorithm aims at decreasing the make-span and increasing the performance.

Following are the assumptions to conduct the experiment:

- Tasks are non pre-emptive, i.e., no other task can stop the execution of previously executing task.
- Tasks are mutually self-regulating.
- Tasks are computationally intensive.
- Tasks are fixed during their execution.
- No. of cloudlets and tasks once assigned do not change the run time environment.

3.1.1 VM Initial Pheromone Value

Ants are distributed randomly at the beginning on VMs [13] with initial equal to 1.
Value of pheromone can also be initialized by using the following equation

$$T_j(0) = \text{pe\_num}_j \times \text{pe\_mips}_j + \text{vm\_bw}_j$$

where pe_num_j is the number of vm_j processor, pe_mips_j is the Million Instructions
Per Second (MIPS) of each processor of vm_j and the parameter vm_bw_j is vm_j
communication bandwidth.

3.1.2 Selection of VM

The ith Virtual Machine for next jth task is chosen by kth ant with the help of
Roulette Wheel Selection scheme RWS. In RWS the participating items are chosen
based on the item's probability. Here the participating items are virtual machines for
RWS. And the probability is given by:

$$P_{ij}^k = \frac{T_{ij}^\alpha \eta_i^\beta}{\left(\frac{C_{ij}}{B_i}\right)^\gamma}$$

T_{ij} has the pheromone of ith virtual machine and jth cloudlet, given as:

$$T_{ij} = \text{pheromone}[i][j]$$

B_i is bandwidth of ith virtual machine and b is the control factor. And it is
calculated as follows:

$$B_i = b \times \text{vm\_bw}_i$$

C_{ij} is the jth cloudlet's expected bandwidth usage while task is in processing in
the simulator and is computed as below, here c is the control parameter:

$$C_{ij} = c \times \frac{\text{cloudlet\_filesize}_j + \text{cloudlet\_outputsize}_j}{\text{vm\_bw}_i}$$

n_i is the heuristic parameter responsible for the actual calculation of probability
of the virtual machines, under normal situation the selection of virtual machines
depends upon its capability of executing that cloudlet. And the formula is in this
case is given as follows:

$$n_i = \text{vm\_mips}_i$$

And for TBACO this heuristic parameter will be altered as discussed in Sect. 3.1.4.

3.1.3 Makespan Calculation

The make-span in TBACO algorithm is calculated using the formula as given below:

$$\text{res}[n] = \frac{A_{ij} + C_{ij}}{B_i}$$

where B_i and C_{ij} are same as discussed in Sect. 3.1.2. While A_{ij} depends upon the task total length and virtual machine computing capacity, and is computed as below:

$$A_{ij} = a \times \frac{\text{cloudlet\_total\_length}_j}{\text{vm\_mips}_i}$$

where a is controlling factor, cloudlet_total_length is the length of the task in MI, vm_mips describes the processing power of the virtual machine.

3.1.4 Heuristic Function-TimeBased (TB)

The TB heuristic prejudices the mock ants to choose the service requests with least completing time. The heuristic value is denoted by

$$n_{ij} = \text{TB}_{ij}$$

where n_{ij} denotes the heuristic function used in TBACO algorithm and TB_{ij} denotes the Time Based value for heuristic parameter for probability computation and is calculated using the expression as stated below [16]:

$$\text{TB}_{ij} = \frac{\text{max\_time}_j - \text{time}_{ij} + 1}{\text{max\_time}_j - \text{min\_time}_j + 1}$$

where max_time$_j$ is the maximum time taken by a cloudlet on the given set of virtual machines, Min_time$_j$ is the minimum time taken by a cloudlet on the given set of virtual machines And time$_{ij}$ is the time taken by *j*th cloudlet on *i*th virtual machine.

3.2 Methodology

The methodology proposed to implement TBACO algorithm is stated as follows:

Step 1: Extend the DatacenterBroker Class to DatacenterBrokerAnt

Step 2: Defining new Constructors

Step 3: Initializing the pheromone values, allocation time, number of iterations, control factors, number of virtual machines, number of Cloudlets and best so far solution

Step 4: Creating another class ANT in datacenterBroker

Step 5: For Every iteration, initializing Ant parameters

Step 6: For Every ant, goto Step 7 to Step 10

Step 7: Place every ant randomly on any virtual machine i.e., assign first cloudlet to any VM

Step 8: For each cloudlet that is not scheduled, choose VM using RWS (Roulette Wheel Scheme) and update the allocation time

Step 9: Calculate Ant makespan for current schedule, if it is better than the best so far, update it

Step 10: Release and evaporate pheromone

Step 11: If it is not a last iteration, goto Step 12 else Step 5

Step 12: Submit best so far schedule with allocation time

4   Simulation Results and Discussions

This section focuses on the implementation of proposed algorithm, simulation results and analysis.

4.1 Simulation Environment

The job scheduling optimization algorithm, i.e., TBACO algorithm is implemented in CloudSim toolkit, which schedules user defined jobs. For the experiment, one datacenter with two hosts of type both space shared and time shared are selected. Datacenter cost varies from one to fifteen units. Number of virtual machines is limited to twenty to carry out the simulation. Virtual machine's type is time shared and the MIPS of virtual machine varies from 350 to 600 MIPS. Total number of processing elements per virtual machine varies from 2 to 8 and RAM varies from 256 to 1024 MB. Number of cloudlets varies from 1 to 30 of the varying length from 5000 to 710,000.

4.1.1 Parameter Setting of Virtual Machine

To carry out the simulation, different configurations of virtual machines have been chosen. Five sets of virtual machines are created. Set 1 consists of 350 MIPS, 512 MB ram, 100 bits bandwidth and number of processing element is 1. Set 2 consists of 300 MIPS, 256 MB ram, 100 bits bandwidth and number of processing elements are 6. Set 3 consists of 450 MIPS, 512 MB ram, 1000 bits bandwidth and number of processing elements are 2. Set 4 consists of 400 MIPS, 384 MB ram, 1000 bits bandwidth and number of processing elements are 4. Set 5 consists of 600 MIPS, 1024 MB ram, 1000 bits bandwidth and number of processing elements are 3.

4.1.2 Parameter Setting of ANT

The parameters setting of ANT are: no. of tasks—1–30, no. of Ants—5, no. of iteartions—8, α—3, β—2, γ—8, Evaporation Rate—0.2

4.1.3 Parameter Setting of Cloudlets

To carry out the simulation, different configurations of cloudlets have been chosen based on length. Five sets of cloudlets are created. All the five sets vary in only length. Sets 1, 2, 3, 4, 5 have 50,000, 45,000, 710,000, 340,000 and 5000 length in Million Instructions (MI) respectively. File size, Output size and number of processing elements are same and the values are 300, 300 and 1, respectively.

4.2 Simulation Results

Based on the speed of CPU, processing power of virtual machines, amount of virtual machines, amount of cloudlets inputted into Basic ACO and TBACO algorithm, total execution time has been calculated and makespan of the schedule. Comparison has been made between Basic ACO and TBACO algorithm. Basic ACO finds the best schedule of assigning Cloudlets to Virtual Machines in a certain makespan. TBACO algorithm aims to find the best schedule of assigning Cloudlets to Virtual machines but in a lesser makespan than Basic ACO.

In the following subsections, comparison has been made between the makespan of ACO and TBACO algorithm by considering various combinations of changing cloudlets, virtual machines and iterations.

4.2.1 Fixed VMs and Varying Cloudlets

The number of virtual machines have been fixed here i.e., 15 and number of cloudlets vary from 18 to 28, number of iterations are set to 8.

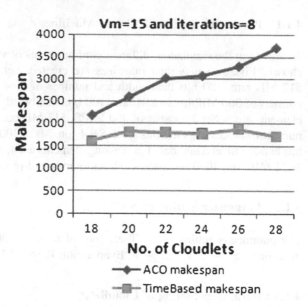

Fig. 2 Makespan versus cloudlets of basic ACO and TBACO algorithm

The resultant graph in Fig. 2 predicts that our TBACO algorithm performs as desired giving increase in performance time up to 59 % when taken all together. The reason behind this increase in performance is that TBACO algorithm focuses time in scheduling while ACO schedules are based on computational capacity of virtual machines. As virtual machines capacity does not ensure that schedule would take minimum time but in TBACO every time virtual machine is chosen which takes minimum time according to heuristic function TB explained in Sect. 3.1.4. So there is a downfall in graph of TBACO makespan when compared to ACO makespan.

4.2.2 Fixed VMs and Varying Iterations

Upon performing simulations on the same environment but with increasing number of iterations, we took average makespan of basic ACO and TBACO algorithm and plotted the graph to analyse the performance.

The graph shown below depicts that as the number of iterations increases, the average makespan of the TBACO algorithm is reduced because every time iteration is increased, the optimization is done on the previous schedules leading to decrease in makespsan. In Fig. 3, the blue line indicates the average makespan of basic Ant Colony Optimization and red line indicates the average makespan of TBACO algorithm. The decrease in the makespan is due to the change in the heuristic value that has been used in TBACO algorithm which is time constraint. The scheduling of cloudlets to virtual machines depends on the processing capability of virtual machine and the way cloudlets get submitted to virtual machine depends on a technique termed as RWS.

Fig. 3 The average makespan of basic ACO and TBACO algorithm

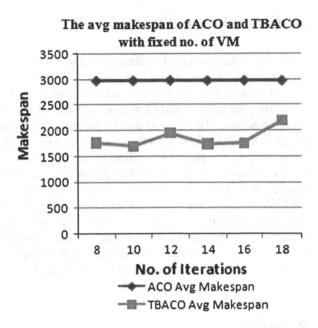

4.2.3 Fixed Iterations and Varying Cloudlets

The next simulation shows the makespan of basic ACO and TBACO algorithms upon making iterations fixed, i.e., 14 and increasing the number of submitted tasks (Fig. 4). The, TBACO algorithm minimizes the total execution time taken by the task when they are executed successfully in cloud environment.

Fig. 4 Makespan versus submitted tasks of basic ACO and TBACO algorithm

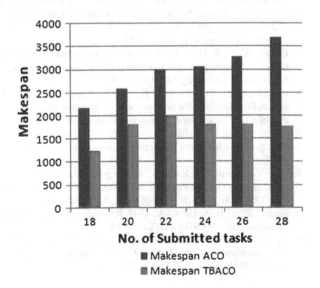

5 Conclusions and Future Scope

Time-Based Ant Colony Optimization (TBACO) algorithm's main objective was to minimize the total execution time taken by the task when they are executed successfully in cloud environment, which is ensured by considering time while scheduling the tasks on virtual machines instead of the computing capacity of those virtual machines. To be noted that it inherently checks the computing capacity and assign it with the lowest possible probabilistic value while making computations for scheduling. In this paper the considered quality of service parameter is Time. It has been experimentally evaluated that algorithm gives more than double the performance than ACO. For variable sized tasks, TBACO algorithm outperforms Basic ACO. As for future work, the focus can be made on increasing the number of cloudlets with the increase in virtual machines. The simulation is done in CloudSim, so the methodology requires some adjustments to adapt to real cloud environment which is composed of thousands of cores. To move from simulation environment to real cloud needs to be investigated.

References

1. Mell, P., & Grance, T. (2011). The NIST definition of cloud computing. National Institute of Standards and Technology, Information Technology Laboratory. Version 15, csrc.nist. gov/groups/SNS/cloud-computing/cloud-def-v15.doc.
2. Nie, L., & Zhiwei, X. (2013). Adaptive Scheduling Mechanism for Elastic Grid Computing. In *Fifth International Conference on Semantics, Knowledge and Grid*, IEEE. doi:10.1109/SKG. 2009.53.
3. Hamidzadeh, B., Kit, L. Y., & Lilja, D. J. (2000). Dynamic task scheduling using online optimization. *IEEE Transactions on Parallel Distributed Systems, 11*, 1151–1163.
4. Bansal, S., Kumar, P., & Singh, K. (2005). Dealing with heterogeneity through limited duplication for scheduling precedence constrained task graphs. *Journal of Parallel and Distributed Computing, 65*, 479–491.
5. Boyer, W. F., & Hura, G. S. (2005). Non-evolutionary algorithm for scheduling dependent tasks in distributed heterogeneous computing environments. *Journal of Parallel and Distributed Computing, 65*, 1035–1046.
6. Ilavarasan, E., Thambidurai, P., & Mahilmannan, R. (2005). Performance effective task scheduling algorithm for heterogeneous computing system. In *4th International Symposium on Parallel and Distributed Computing*, France, pp. 28–38.
7. Kong, X., Lin, C., & Jiang, Y., et al. (2010). Efficient dynamic task scheduling in virtualized data centers with fuzzy prediction. *Journal of Network and Computer Applications*, 1068–1077.
8. Hui, Y., Xueqin, S., Xing, L., & Minghui, W. (2005). An improved ant algorithm for job scheduling in Grid. In *Fourth International Conference on Machine Learning and Cybernetics* (pp. 2957–2961). doi:10.1109/ICMLC.2005.1527448.
9. Singh, M. (2010). GRAAA: Grid Resource allocation based on ant algorithm. *Academy Publisher*. doi:10.4304/jait.1.3.133-135.
10. Ajay, K., Arnesh, S., Sanchit, A., & Satish, C. (2010). An ACO approach to job scheduling in grid environment. In *SEMCCO 2010*. Berlin: Springer, LNCS 6466, (pp. 286–295). doi:10.1007/978-3-642-17563-3_35.

11. Li, L., Yi, Y., Lian, L., & Wanbin, S. (2006). Using ant colony optimization for superscheduling in computational grid. *IEEE Asia-Pacific Conference on Service Computing*. ISBN:0-7695-2751-5
12. Al Salami, N. M. A. (2009). Ant colony optimization algorithm. *UbiCC Journal, 4*(3)
13. Li, K., Xu, G., Zhao, G., Dong, Y., & Wang, D. (2011). Cloud task scheduling based on load balancing ant colony optimization. In *IEEE 2011 Sixth Annual ChinaGrid Conference*. doi:10.1109/ChinaGrid.2011.17.
14. Yan, Z., Zhang, Y., Fu, X., & Peng, S. (2009). Research of a genetic algorithm ant colony optimization based on cloud model. In *IEEE International Conference on Mechatronics and Automation*. 978-1-4244-2693-5/09.
15. Maruthanayagam, D., & UmaRani, R. (2010). Enhanced ant colony algorithm for grid scheduling. *International Journal of Computer Technology and Applications, 1*(1), 43–53.
16. Chen, W. -N., & Zhang, J. (2009). An ant colony optimization approach to a grid workflow scheduling problem with various QoS parameters. *IEEE Transactions on systems, Man and Cybernetics-Part C: Applications and Reviews, 39*(1).
17. Karthik, A. V., Ramaraj, E., & Subramanian, R. G. (2014). An efficient multi queue job scheduling for cloud computing. In *IEEE World Congress on Computing and Communication Technologies (WCCCT)* (pp. 164–166). February 27–March 1 2014.
18. Patel, S. J., & Bhoi, U. R., (2014). improved priority based job scheduling algorithm in cloud computing using iterative method. *IEEE Conference on Advances on Computing and Communication* (pp. 199–202). 27–29 August 2014.

Prefix Length-Based Disjoint Set Tries for IPv6 Lookup

Ravina Jangid, C.P. Gupta and Iti Sharma

Abstract Introduction of IPv6 with increased address length and different prefix length distribution poses new challenges to the IP lookup and forwarding algorithms. Algorithms traditionally used for IPv4 cannot be directly modified for IPv6. In this paper, we propose a new data structure named 'Disjoint Set Tries'. The aim of new design emphasis on building routing tables based on prefix length distribution in IPv6. It has lower lookup complexity compared to previous trie-based approaches and stable memory consumption. This makes it a good candidate for IPv6 routing lookup table.

Keywords Ipv6 address lookup · Trie-based address lookup

1 Introduction

With the rapid growth of traffic in the Internet, backbone links of several Gigabit/sec are commonly deployed. To handle such high traffic rates, the backbone routers must be able to forward millions of packets per second on each of their ports. *Forwarding* operation is performed by a router, in which destination address is looked up in the forwarding table or routing table to determine the forwarding direction, i.e., on which link, to forward the packet on its next step toward its destination. This lookup/forwarding mechanism became complex with the adaption of classless interdomain routing addressing scheme, as in CIDR prefixes can be of arbitrary

R. Jangid (✉) · C.P. Gupta · I. Sharma
Department of Computer Sciences and Engineering, Rajasthan Technical University,
Kota, India
e-mail: ravina.jangid@gmail.com

C.P. Gupta
e-mail: guptacp2@rediffmail.com

I. Sharma
e-mail: itisharma.uce@gmail.com

© Springer Science+Business Media Singapore 2016   193
S.C. Satapathy et al. (eds.), *Proceedings of International Conference
on ICT for Sustainable Development*, Advances in Intelligent Systems
and Computing 409, DOI 10.1007/978-981-10-0135-2_18

length due to address aggregation at several levels. However, though this proved beneficial in terms of reduction in the number of entries in the forwarding table yet gave rise to a new problem of longest prefix matching (LPM), which involves not only comparing the bit pattern itself but also to find the appropriate length.

Numbers of IPv4 lookup algorithms were suggested in order to solve the LPM problem like simple binary tries [1], Lulea Algorithm [2], multilevel index table organization [3], controlled prefix expansion [4], LC-trie [5], range-search approach [6], and hash-based binary search on length [7]. With the emergence of IPv6 as the next generation Internet protocol, these schemes could not be used directly. Due to 128-bit address length and different prefix distribution of IPv6, many refinements and modifications need to be done to the earlier lookup algorithms. Major challenges for address lookup in IPv6 include storage of longer prefixes, difficulty to accommodate larger tables sizes, to achieve 150 million, or more lookup per second needed for the new 100 Gbps interfaces. The technology and protocol for adaptation of IPv6 are already in place; yet efficient lookup, packet forwarding, and packet classification are open problems.

In this paper, we present, a new data structure, named 'Disjoint Set Tries (DST)'. Algorithms for insertion, search, and lookup operation are also presented. A new performance metric named as weighted average case complexity (WACC) is also introduced. The aim of new design emphasis on building routing tables based on prefix length distribution in IPv6. It has lower lookup complexity as compared to previous trie-based approaches, and stable memory consumption.

Rest of the paper is organized as follows: Sect. 2 presents the related work. Section 3 proposes a new data structure named the disjoint set tries. Section 4 elaborates various proposed algorithms along with a new performance metric named WACC. Section 5 gives analysis and performance of proposed algorithm. Section 6 describes the simulation results and comparison with other schemes. Section 7 concludes the paper with a summary.

2 Related Work

Binary Tries [1, 8] was proposed to solve the LPM problem in which prefix nodes contain the forwarding information. To find LPM, trie is traversed starting from the root along the path defined by the packet's destination address. A major drawback in using binary tries is long sequences of empty nodes which consumes more memory and search time.

Researchers have investigated many variations and modifications to the basic binary trie structure. Gupta et al. [3] proposed a scheme called *multilevel indexing table organization* in which reduction in memory consumption was achieved by imposing restriction on number and distribution of long prefixes. This method, however, is unsuitable with current trends of having a much higher number of long prefixes. In *Lulea algorithm* [2], entire routing was stored in the cache memory of the network processor to reduce the memory accesses. This scheme suffers from difficult insertion and deletion of the prefixes in the routing table. In *multi-bit trie* [4], a group of address bits is inspected simultaneously as opposed to a single bit. This has drastically reduced the space consumption and worst-case lookup time. Incremental update to the data structure is possible; however, it is difficult to maintain the optimal structure after the dynamic updates. Researchers investigated trie compression to reduce memory and search time. *PATRICIA* [9] used path-compressed trie. It collapses one-way branch nodes and stores additional information in the remaining nodes for efficient search operation. However, the scheme does not support LMP. Further, using path compression offers little benefit with large number of prefixes and the trie gets denser. To speed up the lookup process and to reduce the memory requirement, path compression and level compression are combined in *level compressed (LC) trie* [5]. The resulting structure has better scalability. Further improvements over LC-trie were suggested in [10]. In *priority tries* [11, 12], empty internal nodes are replaced by the longest prefix among those in the sub-trie rooted by the empty nodes. The relocated prefixes are denoted as priority prefixes. Hence, longer prefixes are compared earlier than shorter prefixes. This improved the search performance and the memory requirement of the priority trie significantly compared to the binary trie. *Flash trie* [13] is a low-cost, high-speed scalable route lookup scheme. It is a combination of the hash operation and the multi-bit Trie structure. Michel Hanna et al. [14] presented a novel packet forwarding scheme that uses multi-bit trie internode compression to reduce the total memory consumption. SRAM pipelined architecture is used in this method. Above schemes based on compressed trie are though popular due to many empty nodes, yet at certain lengths number of prefixes is very high leading to full sub-trie within the main trie. This is a performance bottleneck because these are actually most frequently looked-up prefixes.

Waldovgel et al. [7] proposed binary search on prefix length using hashing. In this method, one hash table was defined for each prefix length storing prefixes of different lengths in different hash tables. A drawback of this method is the complexity of the update procedure. Qiong et al. [15] achieved $\Theta(\log_2 W)$ (W: the address length) lookup performance in dynamic binary hash for IPv6 lookup. Key feature of this scheme was its performance guarantee of seven hash probes in the worst cast of IPv6 routing lookup and also supporting incremental update. There are limitations to the hash-based approaches also; when prefix address space is large (IPv6), it requires many tables to be managed. Collision is another drawback. Solving collision using bucket, causes performance degradation with increasing number of prefixes having the same hash value.

3 Disjoint Set Tries

In IPV6 lookup tables, large number of prefixes having length in the range from 32 to 48 is expected. Further, the received prefixes appear in disjoint range. We begin with definition of terms used in our proposal.

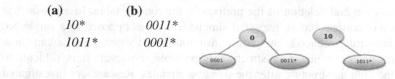

(a)   **(b)**

*10**   *0011**

*1011**   *0001**

Fig. 1 Overlapping prefixes **a** and **b** respectively

Disjoint Prefixes: Two prefixes π_1 and π_2 are said to be disjoint if they do not have any common subprefix. In an ordinary binary trie, such prefixes lie on different branches viz. 1011* and 0011.

Overlapping Prefixes: Two prefixes π_1 and π_2 are said to be overlapping if they have a common subprefix. In an ordinary binary trie, such common subprefix might be parent of π_1 and π_2, or π_1 and π_2 will have some hierarchal relationship. Following are some examples of overlapping prefixes and their corresponding tries (Fig. 1).

If a match occurs with one prefix π, then no match can occur with any of the prefixes ρ, if π and ρ are disjoint. Thus, a set of all disjoint prefixes can act as entry point for prefix matching. Performance enhancement in lookup can be achieved only if the disjoint set is large. A large disjoint set cannot be achieved if all prefixes of a lookup table are considered. Rather, very short and long prefixes should be excluded to construct an optimal disjoint set. Following is an example of sample prefix set with their corresponding Disjoint Prefix Set Tries (Figs. 2, 3 and 4).

Management of very Short and Long Prefixes: As per [13], almost all the prefixes in IPv6 have lengths between (and inclusive of) 32 and 48 bits. A linear list, if

Fig. 2 Binary tries for Table 1

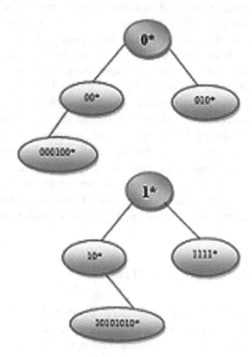

Fig. 3 Disjoint set
without 0*

Let us form the disjoint set without **0***:

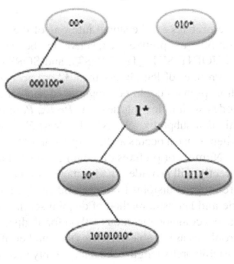

Fig. 4 Disjoint set
without 1*

Suppose we exclude **1***also:

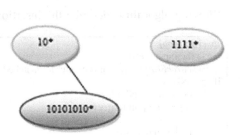

small, has the advantage of dynamic structure, easy management, and simple implementation. Hence for our proposal, we choose length less than 32 as short and length greater than 48 as long and will be implemented as linear list.

Disjoint Tries: All disjoint prefixes are maintained as a list, which act as roots of many disjoint tries. All the overlapping prefixes are inserted into a single disjoint trie with shortest prefix as root. Building of trie is similar to inserting each prefix in the trie, making it a dynamic structure. The insertion into the left sub-trie or the right sub-trie depends on the differing bit.

4 Proposed Algorithms

The prefixes can be stored into one of the three connected structures, based on the number of prefixes expected to be stored there: SORTED_LIST1 (SL1), DISJOINT_SET _TRIE (DST), and SORTED_LIST 2 (SL2).

Prefixes of length less than 32 are arranged into a sorted list called *SL1*. These short prefixes could be subprefix of another stored prefix hence the table entries are nodes with following fields as *Prefix*, *Pointer* (points to a prefix of DST for which this is a subprefix, else NULL), *Next Hop* (containing port number for forwarding when a match occurs at this prefix), and *Link* (points to the next entry in the SL1 list).

Number of prefixes of length 32–48 is large; hence any compressed trie if used directly will provide no advantage. A common observation as in [15] is that many prefixes are disjoint from each other. We combine the fast search of a compressed trie and heuristic method of disjoint set into a single structure, *Disjoint Set Trie*. To have a common insertion method for all disjoint tries, we have to deal with following problems as variable bit stride (the number of bits after which level of trie increases), variable prefix lengths and many empty nodes as per a binary trie (sparse binary trie). To overcome these problems, we arrange prefixes in nondecreasing order of length [11, 12], However, in our scheme, the shortest prefix in a trie is at the root.

SL2 contains all prefixes of length more than 32 except those disjointed from all and longer than 48 bits. Again, this list contains entries in form of nodes with fields as: *Prefix*, *Next Hop* (containing port number for forwarding when a match occurs at this prefix), and *Link* (points to the next entry in the same SL2 list).

4.1 Constructing the Forwarding Table

Following algorithms describe the insertion of prefixes in the data structures:

insert(σ, hop)	*insertDST(length,σ,hop)*
//σ is the input prefix	if DST[length-32] := NULL
p := *searchSL1* ($\sigma_{0.31}$) // p is pointer to matched prefix	//DST is an array of pointers
if (p ≠ NULL)	r := createnode(σ,hop)
if(pointer(p) ≠ NULL)	// creates a new node and returns a pointer
insertTrie(pointer(p), σ, hop)	DST[length] := r
else	else
if (length(σ)≤48)	t := DST[length-32]
r:=insertDST(length(σ), σ, hop)	while (link(t)!=NULL)
pointer(p):=r	t := link(t)
else	r := createnode(σ,hop)
insertSL2(σ, hop)	link(t) := r
else	return(r)
r: = *searchDST(σ)*	
if r ≠ NULL	
insertTrie(r, σ,hop)	
else	
if (length(σ)≤48)	
r := *insertDST*(length(σ), σ, hop)	
else	
insertSL2(σ, hop)	

Table 1 Sample disjoint prefix set

0*
1*
00*
10*
010*
1111*
000100*
10101010*

Table 2 Value of differ-bit

Mismatched bit of α	Mismatched bit of β	Differ-bit value
*	0	0
1	0	0
0	1	1
*	1	1

Differ-bit (α, β) matches the bits of α and β from beginning and stops where first mismatch occurs. Value returned by differ-bit is as follows (Table 2).

4.2 Searching Procedure

Following algorithms searches and finds longest matching prefix of any incoming address:

```
search(σ)
BMP:=NULL
p := searchSL1(σ<0....31>) //sequential search
if p ≠ NULL
    BMP := hop(p)
    if (pointer(p) ≠ NULL)
        r := searchTRIE(σ,pointer(p))
    if (r ≠ NULL)
        BMP: =hop( r)
else
    p = searchDST(σ)
    if p ≠ NULL
        p = searchTRIE(σ, p)
        BMP:=hop(p)
    else
        p = searchSL2(σ) //sequential search
    if p ≠ NULL
        BMP:=hop(p)
return (BMP)
```

```
searchDST(σ)

i := 32
match := 0
t := NULL
while (i<=48 AND match = 0)
    t := DST[i]
    while (t!= NULL AND match =0)
        if(prefix(t) = σ0...i)
            match = 1
        t := link(t)
    endwhile
endwhile
return (t)
```

Table 3 Distribution of prefix length on a sample router [17]

Prefix length	Entry count	Percentage
9–31	7	1.14
32	444	72.08
33–47	43	6.97
48	81	13.15
64	41	6.66
Total	616	100

4.3 New Performance Metric

We propose to use weighted average complexity (WACC) on the basis of expected ratio of prefixes of certain length to compare the approaches.

$$\text{Weighted Average Case Complexity} = \frac{m_1\tau_1 + m_2\tau_2 + m_3\tau_3}{m_1 + m_2 + m_3} \tag{1}$$

$$\text{If taken as percentage,} \quad \text{WACC} = p_1\tau_1 + p_2\tau_2 + p_3\tau_3 \tag{2}$$

where, p_1, p_2, p_3 are expected percentage of lookups within length range 0–31, 32–48, 49–64, respectively.

On this basis, the existing approaches can be found to have poor performance. Observations done in [15–17] can be summarized as: there are very few prefixes of length less than 16, generally prefixes are of length under 64, prefix length 32, 48, and 64 is used very frequently and maximum ratio of prefixes fall in length range 32–48 bits (Table 3).

Hence, we can safely pick $p_1 = 2$, $p_2 = 90$, and $p_3 = 8$.

5 Analysis and Performance of Proposed Algorithm

Let the total number of entries in the lookup table be N. The entries in SL1 and SL2 are n_1 and n_2, respectively. Let d be the number of disjoint sets, then average size of a trie will be $\log\left(\frac{N-n_1-n_2}{d}\right)$.

Since $n_1 \ll N$ and $n_2 \ll N$; Average Size of Trie $= \Theta\left(\log\left(\frac{N}{d}\right)\right)$.

Time Complexity of lookup can be calculated as follows. If found in SL1, linear search takes time $O(n_1)$. This may lead to a pointer in a DS Trie, followed by a trie search. $\Theta\left(\log\left(\frac{N}{d}\right)\right)$. If not found in SL1, search in DST is $O(d)$ followed by $\Theta\left(\log\left(\frac{N}{d}\right)\right)$ of trie search. If not found in DST, search in SL2 is $O(n_2)$, but is performed after a failed search in SL1 and DST Hence, $O(n_1 + d + n_2)$.

Table 4 Generated prefixes

Size of routing tables	Memory consumption (KB)		Depth of trie	
	PT	DST	PT	DST
100	8549	2950	12	1
500	37000	30030	15	2
1000	74000	60060	17	2
10000	720340	610002	22	3

$$\text{Time for lookup} = \text{Max}\left(\Theta\left(n_1 + \log\left(\frac{N}{d}\right)\right), \Theta\left(n_1 + d + \log\left(\frac{N}{d}\right)\right), \Theta(n_1 + d + n_2) \right)$$

As per Eq. (2), $\text{WACC} = p_1\tau_1 + p_2\tau_2 + p_3\tau_3$.

Hence, $\text{WACC} = p_1\left(n_1 + \log\left(\frac{N}{d}\right)\right) + p_2\left(n_1 + d + \log\left(\frac{N}{d}\right)\right) + p_3(n_1 + d + n_2)$, where, p_1 and p_3 are much less than p_2. So, $\text{WACC}_{\text{DST}} = \Theta\left(\log\left(d + \log\left(\frac{N}{d}\right)\right)\right)$ For all practical purposes magnitude of $\log(N/d)$ is much less than d.

$$\text{Hence,} \quad \text{WACC}_{\text{DST}} = \Theta(\log(d)) \tag{3}$$

In case of PT,

$$\text{WACC}_{\text{PT}} = p1 \times \tau1 + p2 \times \tau2 + p3 \times \tau3$$
$$= p1(\log\ N) + p2(\log\ N) + p3(\log\ N)$$

$$\text{So,} \quad \text{WACC}_{\text{PT}} = O(\log(N)) \tag{4}$$

6   Simulation Results and Comparison with Other Schemes

Simulations of the proposed DS Trie and priority trie [12] were conducted to compare the two based on following criteria of depth of trie and the memory consumption.

The simulation was performed on different sets of prefixes. The comparison is tabulated in Table 4.

7   Conclusion

In this paper, a new scheme for IPv6 lookup named 'Disjoint Set Tries' has been introduced. The DST scheme has time complexity = $\text{Max}(\Theta(n_1 + \log(\frac{N}{d})),$ $\Theta(n_1 + d + \log(\frac{N}{d}), \Theta(n_1 + d + n_2))$. The emphasis of this work is on considering distribution of prefix lengths to analyze performance of lookup. Hence, a new metric weighted average case complexity is suggested for IPv6 lookup. Proposed DS trie has WACC = O(d). It is believed that that this work could be applied to other packet processing domains such as packet classification.

References

1. Gupta, P. (2000). *Algorithms for routing lookups and packet classification*. Diss: Stanford University.
2. Degermark, M., et al. (1997). *Small forwarding tables for fast routing lookups, 27*(4).
3. Gupta, P., Steven, L., & Nick, M. (1998). Routing lookups in hardware at memory access speeds. In *INFOCOM '98. Seventeenth Annual Joint Conference of the IEEE Computer and Communications Societies, Proceedings, IEEE* (Vol. 3), 1998.
4. Srinivasan, V., & Varghese, G. (1999). Fast address lookups using controlled prefix expansion. *ACM Transactions on Computer Systems (TOCS), 17*(1), 1–40.
5. Nilsson, S., & Karlsson, G. (1999). IP-address lookup using LC-tries. *IEEE Journal on Selected Areas in Communications, 17*(6), 1083–1092.
6. Lampson, B., Srinivasan, V., & Varghese, G. (1999). IP lookups using multiway and multicolumn search. *IEEE/ACM Transactions on Networking, 7*(3), 324–334.
7. Waldvogel, M., et al. (1997). *Scalable high speed IP routing lookups, 27*(4).
8. Ruiz-Sánchez, M.Á., Ernst W. B., & Walid, D. (2001). Survey and taxonomy of IP address lookup algorithms. *Network, IEEE, 15*(2), 8–23.
9. Morrison, D. (1968). PATRICIA—practical algorithm to retrieve information coded in alphanumeric. *Journal of the ACM (JACM), 15*(4), 514–534.
10. Ravikumar, V. C., Rabi, M., & Liu, J. C. (2002). Modified LC-trie based efficient routing lookup. In *10th IEEE International Symposium on Modeling, Analysis and Simulation of Computer and Telecommunications Systems, IEEE, 2002. MASCOTS*.
11. Lim, H., & Ju, H. M. (2006). NXG06-1: An efficient ip address lookup algorithm using a priority trie. In *Global Telecommunications Conference, 2006. GLOBECOM '06. IEEE*.
12. Lim, H., Yim, C., & Swartzlander, E. (2010). Priority tries for IP address lookup. *IEEE Transactions on Computers, 59*(6), 784–794.
13. Bando, M., Lin, Y. -L. & Jonathan, C. H. (2012). FlashTrie: Beyond 100-Gb/s IP route lookup using hash-based prefix-compressed trie. *IEEE/ACM Transactions on 20.4 Networking*, 1262–1275.
14. Hanna, M., Sangyeun, C., & Rami, M. (2011). A novel scalable IPv6 lookup scheme using compressed pipelined tries. *NETWORKING 2011*, 406–419.
15. Sun, Q., et al. (2008). A dynamic binary hash scheme for IPv6 lookup. *Global Telecommunications Conference, 2008. IEEE GLOBECOM 2008*.
16. Huang, X., et al. (2008). A novel level-based IPv6 routing lookup algorithm. *Global Telecommunications Conference, 2008. IEEE GLOBECOM 2008*.
17. Hsiao, Y. -M, et al. (2013). A high-throughput and high-capacity IPv6 routing lookup system. *Computer Networks 57*(3): 782–794.

Implementation of FAST Clustering-Based Feature Subset Selection Algorithm for High-Dimensional Data

Smit Shilu, Kushal Sheth and Ekata Mehul

Abstract In feature selection, we are concerned with finding out those features that produces result similar to those of the original entire set of features. We concern ourselves with efficiency and effectiveness while evaluating Feature selection algorithms. Efficiency deals with the time required to find a subset of features and effectiveness, with the quality of subset of features. On these criteria, a FAST clustering-based feature selection algorithm (FAST) has been proposed and experimentally evaluated and implemented in this paper. The dimensionality reduction of data is the most important feature of FAST. First, we use graph-theoretic clustering method to divide features into clusters. Next, we form a subset of features by selecting the feature which is most representative and strongly related to the target classes. Due to features in different clusters being relatively independent; the clustering-based strategy of FAST has a high probability of providing us with a subset of features which are both useful and independent. Efficiency of FAST is ensured by using the concept of minimum spanning tree (MST) along with kruskal's algorithm.

Keywords Feature subset selection · Feature clustering · Filter method · Kruskal's algorithm · Graph-based clustering

S. Shilu (✉) · K. Sheth
eiTRA eInfochips Training, Charusat University, Changa, India
e-mail: smitshilu@gmail.com
URL: http://www.charusat.ac.in

K. Sheth
e-mail: kushalsheth28@gmail.com
URL: http://www.charusat.ac.in

E. Mehul
Research Academy, Ahmedabad, India
e-mail: ekata.mehul@eitra.org
URL: http://www.eitra.org

© Springer Science+Business Media Singapore 2016   203
S.C. Satapathy et al. (eds.), *Proceedings of International Conference on ICT for Sustainable Development*, Advances in Intelligent Systems and Computing 409, DOI 10.1007/978-981-10-0135-2_19

1   Introduction

With the aim of selecting the important and useful features, by reducing the dimensionality of the data and increasing the accuracy, we here test and develop the code for the FAST Clustering-based Subset Selection Algorithm. Generally, many feature subset selection methods have been proposed. These methods can be categorized into four different categories: Embedded, Wrapper, Filter, and Hybrid approaches. Embedded methods use the complete training set and hence have more accuracy compared to other three methods. Decision trees and artificial neural networks are examples of this embedded method. The wrapper method uses the predictive accuracy of predetermined learning algorithm and its accuracy is generally very high. However, computational complexity is on the higher side. The wrapper methods are tending to over fit on small training sets with expensive computationally. The filter methods do not require learning algorithms. Their computational complexity is low, but the accuracy of the learning algorithms is not guaranteed. It is favorable when dataset is having very large number of features. The hybrid methods are a combination of filter and wrapper methods; with the use of filter method it can reduce search space that will be considered by the subsequent wrapper. Here, in our algorithm, we use the filter method. The FAST algorithm does two main tasks, (1) Removing the irrelevant data, (2) Removing the redundant data, and works in three steps. In the first step, the features are divided into clusters using graph-theoretic methods; and in the second step, the most relevant feature from each cluster is selected and inserted into the final cluster. We have tested this algorithm on various datasets and also integrated it with WEKA for public use. The rest of the paper is organized as follows: Sect. 2 consists of the Algorithm part. Section 3 contains the working flow of the algorithm stepwise. Section 4 contains the experimental environment. Section 4 contains the results and finally, Sect. 5 contains information regarding the future enhancements, conclusions and acknowledgments.

2   Algorithm

2.1   Definitions

T-Relevance: The relevance between the individual feature which in our case is F_i and the target concept C is known as T-Relevance. This relevance value is denoted by $SU(F_i, C)$. Here, if the relevance value is greater than a certain predetermined threshold value θ, then we can say that the feature Fi is a strong feature.

F-Correlation: The relation between the pair of features is known as F-Correlation. If the two features are F_i and F_j, then the correlation value is denoted as $SU(F_i, F_j)$.

Irrelevant and Redundant Feature: Irrelevant features are those features which have no relevance to the target class or concept while redundant features are those which do not provide any new information and can be taken out of cluster.

2.2 Algorithm

FAST algorithm is having mainly three steps. In the first step, remove irrelevant feature. In the second, generate a MST. In the third, break the MST and select feature for final cluster.

---

inputs: $D(F_1, F_2, ..., F_m, C)$ - the given data set
$\quad\quad\quad\theta$ - the T-Relevance threshold.
output: S - selected feature subset .
$\quad$//==== Part 1 : Irrelevant Feature Removal ====
1 **for** $i = 1$ *to* m **do**
2 $\quad$ T-Relevance = SU (F_i, C)
3 $\quad$ **if** T-Relevance $> \theta$ **then**
4 $\quad\quad$ $S = S \cup \{F_i\}$;

$\quad$//==== Part 2 : Minimum Spanning Tree Construction ====
5 G = NULL; //G is a complete graph
6 **for** *each pair of features* $\{F'_i, F'_j\} \subset S$ **do**
7 $\quad$ F-Correlation = SU (F'_i, F'_j)
8 $\quad$ Add F'_i and/or F'_j to G with F-Correlation as the weight of
$\quad\quad$ the corresponding edge;

9 minSpanTree = Prim (G); //Using Prim Algorithm to generate the
$\quad\quad$ minimum spanning tree
$\quad$//==== Part 3 : Tree Partition and Representative Feature Selection ====
10 Forest = minSpanTree
11 **for** *each edge* $E_{ij} \in$ Forest **do**
12 $\quad$ **if** $SU(F'_i, F'_j) < SU(F'_i, C) \wedge SU(F'_i, F'_j) < SU(F'_j, C)$ **then**
13 $\quad\quad$ Forest = Forest $- E_{ij}$

14 $S = \phi$
15 **for** *each tree* $T_i \in$ Forest **do**
16 $\quad$ $F^j_R = \text{argmax}_{F'_k \in T_i} SU(F'_k, C)$
17 $\quad$ $S = S \cup \{F^j_R\}$;

18 return S

---

3 Working Flow

3.1 Flowchart

See Fig. 1.

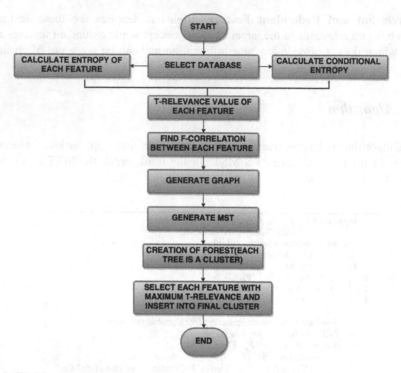

Fig. 1 Working flow of algorithm

3.2 Information Gain Calculation

The features which have a strong correlation with the target concept can be considered as the relevant features. However, the features which have strong correlation with other features are considered to be the redundant features. Hence, the concept of redundant feature and relevant feature is based on the correlation values. In this module, Information Gain is calculated to find relevance value of each attribute. Here, we use the concept of Symmetric Uncertainty (SU) which is derived from mutual information and can be used to measure the goodness of features for classification.

$$\text{Gain}(X \,|\, Y) = H(X) - H(X \,|\, Y) \tag{1}$$

$$\text{Gain}(X \,|\, Y) = H(Y) - H(Y \,|\, X) \tag{2}$$

We can compute gain value by using the values entropy and conditional entropy. The equations for that are given below

$$H(X) = -\sum_{x \in X} p(x) log_2 p(x) \tag{3}$$

$$H(X) = -\sum_{x \in X} p(y) \sum_{x \in X} p(x|y) log_2 p(x|y) \tag{4}$$

3.3 T-Relevance Calculation

T-Relevance is the relevance value of a feature with respect to the target class. This value can be calculated using the Symmetric Uncertainty which uses the concept of information gain and conditional entropy.

$$SU(X, Y) = \frac{2*\text{Gain}}{H(X) + H(Y)} \tag{5}$$

3.4 F-Correlation Calculation

F-Correlation is the correlation value of a feature with respect to other features in dataset. The Symmetric Uncertainty equation used to calculate the relevance value of features with respect to target concept is reapplied here to calculate the correlation among all the features.

3.5 MST (Minimal Spanning Tree) Generation

After the calculation of F-Correlation value, the next step is the construction of graph on basis of correlation values. This connected graph is to be converted into a minimal spanning tree to reduce the dimensionality of the dataset. Kruskal's algorithm is a greedy algorithm which is used for the construction of MST form the graph. Minimal Spanning Tree is a tree that contains all the vertices with minimum weight of edges and without any cycle.

Steps:

1. Generate a graph based on correlation values between each feature.
2. Convert graph into a MST using kruskal's algorithm.
3. At last, we get a single minimal spanning tree consisting of all the nodes.

3.6 Cluster Formation

After generating an MST, we need to reduce the tree to many smaller trees which
will form a forest. Each of this tree will be viewed as a cluster.
Steps:

1. If the correlation value between the features (weight of edge) is smaller than the
   relevance value of both the features, the edge is connecting; then remove that
   edge.
2. On removing the unnecessary edges, a forest with trees is generated, each
   representing a single cluster.
3. From each cluster (tree), the feature with the highest relevance value is selected
   and inserted into the final cluster; in our case S.

4 Results

4.1 System Specification

Required system specifications are as below
System Specification
Processor: Intel(R) Core(TM) i7-3635QM CPU @ 2.40 GHz
Memory: 8.00 GB (7.89 GB usable)
System type: 64-bit Operating System, × 64 âĂß-based processor

4.2 Platform

Java

4.3 Software—Weka Integration

WEKA 3.7

4.4 Summary of Datasets

To find the effectiveness and performance of our implemented FAST algorithm, verifying whether or not the method is fully implemented in practice 24 data sets were used which are publicly available. The numbers of features of the 24 data sets vary from 15 to 26,833. The dimensionality of the 50 % data sets is having more than 5,000, of which 20.8 % data sets have more than 10,000 features (Table 1).

Here,

F: Attributes,
I: Instances, and
C: Class distinct values

Table 1 Summary of datasets

Sr. No.	Dataset	F	I	C
1	ada-agnostic	49	4562	2
2	ada-prior	15	4562	2
3	Chess	37	3196	2
4	connect-4	43	67557	3
5	fbis.wc	2001	2463	17
6	la1 s.wc	13196	3204	6
7	la2 s.wc	12433	3075	6
8	new3 s.wc	26833	9558	44
9	oh0.wc	3183	1003	10
10	oh10.wc	3239	1050	10
11	oh15.wc	3101	913	10
12	oh5.wc	3013	918	10
13	ohscal.wc	11466	11162	10
14	re0.wc	2887	1504	13
15	re1.wc	1657	3759	25
16	sylva.wc	109	14395	2
17	tr11.wc	6430	414	9
18	tr12.wc	5805	313	8
19	tr21.wc	7903	336	6
20	tr23.wc	5833	204	6
21	tr31.wc	10129	927	7
22	tr41.wc	7455	878	10
23	tr45.wc	8262	690	10
24	wap.wc	8461	1560	20

4.5 Results Analysis

Experimental results are presented in this section. This includes selected features and the time taken to select the features. We have tested this datasets in WEKA tool on machine with the following configuration (Table 2).

Processor: 2.3 GHz Intel i7
RAM: 8 GB
Operating system: Windows 8.1

Table 2 Number of features selected after applying FAST and runtime

Sr. No.	Dataset	Runtime (ms)	Selected feature
1	ada-agnostic	959.04	3
2	ada-prior	13006.98	4
3	Chess	59.94	3
4	connect-4	3016.98	5
5	fbis.wc	42847.11	19
6	la1 s.wc	123876	17
7	la2 s.wc	399600	18
8	new3 s.wc	1210788	29
9	oh0.wc	6733.26	12
10	oh10.wc	7602.39	11
11	oh15.wc	6383.61	14
12	oh5.wc	6103.89	14
13	ohscal.wc	399600	38
14	re0.wc	9480.51	11
15	re1.wc	13186.8	10
16	sylva.wc	51648.3	7
17	tr11.wc	10989	32
18	tr12.wc	5994	10
19	tr21.wc	11288.7	8
20	tr23.wc	5304.69	8
21	tr31.wc	44455.5	23
22	tr41.wc	24245.73	14
23	tr45.wc	26473.5	5
24	wap.wc	29170.8	17

4.6 *Experimental Results*

See Figs. 2, 3, and 4.

Fig. 2 Select FAST from
cluster list

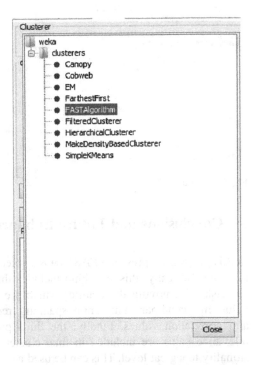

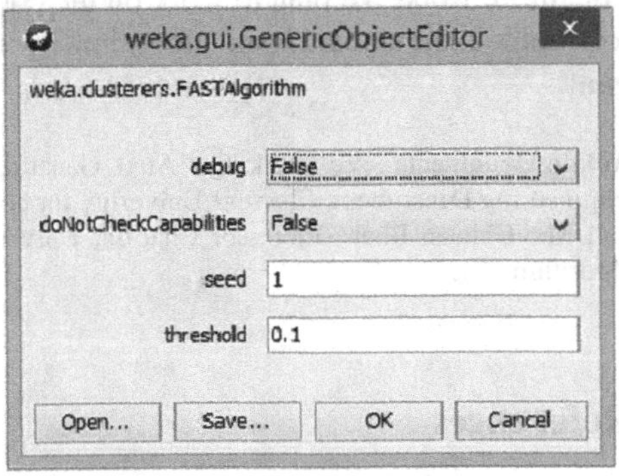

Fig. 3 Set threshold value

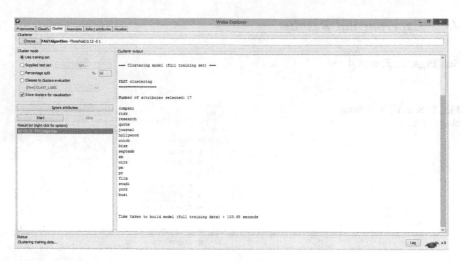

Fig. 4 Output WEKA screen

5 Conclusions and Future Enhancements

In this project, we present a FAST subset selection algorithm which can be used for big data. Basically, this algorithm includes three sub parts. The first part includes the task of removing the features which are not relevant and has low relevance value. In second part, a minimum spanning tree is constructed on basis of relevance and correlation values. Finally, the third part where the features with highest relevance value are included in final cluster. This algorithm reduces the dimensionality to a great level. This can be used as a prerequisite for the analysis purpose. For future work, we plan to work on the correlation between features and also plan to improve the accuracy of algorithm by reconsidering the logic of information gain.

Acknowledgments We thank Dr. Amit Ganatra, Dean and Head of Department Computer Engineering Department, Charusat University for comments that greatly improved the manuscript, and Mr. Chintan Bhatt, Professor Charusat University for assistance in implementation of this algorithm.

References

1. Song, Q., Ni, J., & Wang, G. (2013). A fast clustering-based feature subset selection algorithm for high - dimensional data.
2. Karthikeyan, P., Saravanan, P., & Vanitha, E. (2014). High dimensional data cluster-ing using fast cluster based feature selection. *International Journal of Engineering Research and Applications* , *4*(3), 65–71, (Version 1), ISSN: 2248-9622.

3. Yu, L., & Liu, H. (2004). Efficient feature selection via analysis of relevance and redundancy. *Journal of Machine Learning Research, 10*(5), 1205–1224.
4. Guyon, I., & Elisseeff, A. (2003). An introduction to variable and feature selection. *Journal of Machine Learning Research, 3*, 1157–1182.
5. Data used for result and analysis http://tunedit.org/repo/Data/Text-wc.
6. WEKA library documentations https://weka.wikispaces.com/.

Performance Comparison of 2D and 3D Zigbee Wireless Sensor Networks

Ranjana Thalore, Manju Khurana and M.K. Jha

Abstract Previous works on wireless sensor networks (WSNs) concentrate mainly on two-dimensional (2D) plane assuming that sensors in the network are deployed on ideal plane. In many real-life scenarios, it is required to deploy sensors in a three-dimensional (3D) plane. This paper evaluates the performance of IEEE 802.15.4, i.e., low-rate wireless personal area networks (LR-WPANs) in 2D and 3D terrains on the basis of QoS parameters like network lifetime, throughput, delay, and packets dropped. The results indicate that 3D scenarios are more appropriate for further processing in WSNs.

Keywords Wireless sensor networks (WSNs) · IEEE 802.15.4 · Two-dimensional (2D) · Three-dimensional (3D)

1 Introduction

Zigbee technology [1] is designed to fulfill the needs of low-cost and low-power WSNs for various applications like industrial automation, home control, remote monitoring, and consumer markets [2]. Many wireless monitoring and control applications require longer battery lifetime, less complexity, and lower data rates than those made available by existing standards. IEEE 802.15.4 standard defines the physical and MAC-layer protocols for many applications. Features like low-power and low-cost of IEEE 802.15.4 intend to enable dense deployment of WSNs able to work for years on provided standard batteries.

WSNs mainly consist of large number of components called sensors with limited power source. In a WSN, sensor nodes work collectively to monitor physical conditions of a geographic region. WSNs are widely studied for a range of real-life

R. Thalore (✉) · M. Khurana · M.K. Jha
College of Engineering and Technology, Mody University of Science and Technology, Lakshmangarh, Rajasthan, India
e-mail: thalorer1603@gmail.com

© Springer Science+Business Media Singapore 2016
S.C. Satapathy et al. (eds.), *Proceedings of International Conference on ICT for Sustainable Development*, Advances in Intelligent Systems and Computing 409, DOI 10.1007/978-981-10-0135-2_20

215

applications [3–8] which essentially include automatic event detection. Most of these applications cannot be analyzed properly using existing 2D networks as these applications include 3D terrains. Thus a more practical way to analyze monitoring applications of WSNs includes designing a 3D network scenario. Thus we focus on performance comparison of 2D and 3D Zigbee WSNs.

The remainder of this research paper is structured as follows. We discuss the related research on 3D wireless sensor networks in Sect. 2. We describe the simulation setups and comparison of performance parameters between IEEE 802.15.4 based 2D and 3D networks in Sect. 3 followed by conclusion of this research paper in Sect. 4.

2 Related Works

The work done so far in the field of 3D sensor networks is related to applications relating environmental monitoring.

Lin et al. [9] proposed terrain-aware beacon order adaptation (TABOA), used in 3D sensor networks. The TABOA scheme reorganizes the beacon interval and super frame duration to change the active period in the IEEE 802.15.4 MAC structure according to the in-built characteristics of different terrains and traffic loads. The work done was with 100 feedforward distribution nodes and one PAN coordinator are deployed over a 1000 m × 1000 m × 200 m terrain using ns2 simulator. Simulation results show that considering obstacles and pathways in a 3D space can affect the performance of WSNs, such as packet delivery ratio, average end-to-end delay, good put, and residual node energy of the sink node. They evaluated the performance of the IEEE 802.15.4 network with different canvas sizes via simulation setups that closely model reality and figure out the optimal beacon interval and super frame duration in the different 3D terrains.

Ghosh et al. [10] proposed a model for creation of sensor-smart highways. Cell geometries with 2D roads are implemented for 3D roads. This work examines a cell model similar to the ones used in traffic flows and also considers the different types of cells, based on the 3D characteristics of road surfaces. They justified this by computing a deployment plan given real urban geospatial data, which, in turn, leads to a simple cost estimate. This approach can be followed fairly easily by urban planners, highway engineers, and sensor network designers anywhere.

Li et al. [11] proposed a nonthreshold-based approach for the real 3D sensor monitoring environment. They employ energy-efficient methods to collect a time series of data maps from the sensor network and detect complex events through matching the gathered data to spatiotemporal data patterns. Multipath routing architectures are employed to provide robust data delivery and perform in-network aggregation on it to efficiently construct the data map. The future work includes implementing a working system in real-world environment.

Said et al. [12] proposed a model for deploying heterogeneous sensors in 3D WSNs. The model deals with two scenarios—single sensing and multiple sensing.

Sensors deployed using distributions like Gaussian, Uniform, etc., are compared for intrusion detection in 3D environment for parameters like efficiency and performance of network.

3 Simulations and Comparisons

The main objective of the simulations is to compare the performance of IEEE 802.15.4 for 2D and 3D terrains keeping same simulation parameters for both. The simulations are done using QualNet version 6.1 simulator that allows WSN simulations. The scenarios are simulated with a densely deployed network which is feasible practically.

3.1 Simulation Setup

In both simulations, we refer to a network scenario in which 500 sensor nodes are deployed randomly over a 100 m × 100 m area for 2D terrain and a 100 m × 100 m × 50 m area for 3D terrain. Going with the fact that QualNet supports only 24 nodes in a network, all the nodes are divided equally in four wireless subnets. Nodes are divided in subnets so as to have uniform distribution in the area of interest.

The simulations are done for IEEE 802.15.4 MAC protocol. It supports two types of devices, a full-function device (FFD) and a reduced-function device (RFD). An FFD is provides with full protocol stack and can communicate with RFD and other FFDs. It can operate as a PAN coordinator, a coordinator or a device. On the other hand, an RFD is provided with limited protocol stack and can communicate with similar devices only (RFDs). It operates as a primary device which senses data at primary level. Each subnet has one PAN coordinator (FFD) placed at center, rest are devices (RFDs) which either communicate to PAN coordinator or to other FFDs (if any). For the simulations TRAF-GEN application is used for data packet generation. It helps each node generate a fixed number of messages according to specified interarrival rate.

We have used IEEE 802.15.4 Zigbee MAC protocol provided in QualNet 6.1 simulator to implement 2D and 3D networks. To route data from source to sink node in network, AODV (ad hoc on demand distance vector) routing protocol [13] is used.

Figure 1a, b show scenarios in QualNet 6.1 for 2D and 3D networks, respectively, with 500 nodes divided in four subnets. Both the scenarios are simulated for 1500 s.

Table 1 shows list of parameters considered for the simulations. All the parameters are kept same for 2D and 3D in order to have proper comparison.

(a)

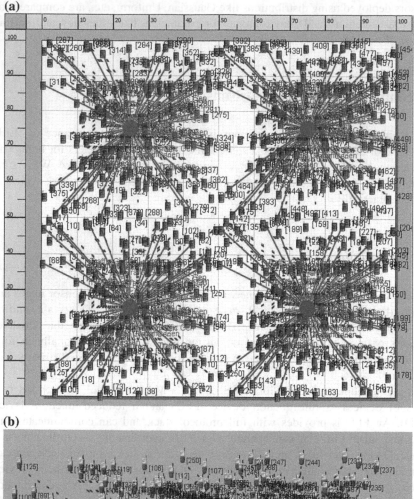

(b)

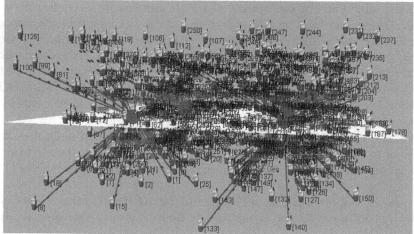

Fig. 1 **a** A two-dimensional (2D) network scenario using IEEE 802.15.4 in QualNet 6.1 Simulator. **b** A three-dimensional (3D) network scenario using IEEE 802.15.4 in QualNet 6.1 Simulator

Table 1 Simulation parameters for 2D and 3D networks

Parameter	Value (2D network)	Value (3D network)
Terrain	100 m × 100 m	100 m × 100 m × 50 m
Simulation time	1500 s	1500 s
No. of nodes	500	500
Message rate	1 packet/s	1 packet/s
Message size	38 bytes	38 bytes
Energy model	Generic	Generic
Transmit circuitry power consumption	24.75 mW	24.75 mW
Receive circuitry power consumption	13.5 mW	13.5 mW
Idle circuitry power consumption	13.5 mW	13.5 mW
Sleep circuitry power consumption	0.05 mW	0.05 mW

3.2 Performance Comparison

This subsection presents simulation results for 2D and 3D scenarios and compares the performance parameters like network lifetime, throughput, delay, and packets dropped on the basis of results obtained from QualNet 6.1 simulator.

Figure 2 shows the comparison of network lifetime (in Days) for 2D and 3D scenarios. Expiration of a node in network might let it operational or not depending upon the role played by the node in network. Thus network lifetime is an important metric. Network lifetime [14, 15] can be defined as interval of time, starting with the first transmission in the WSN and ending when number of active nodes for sensing information falls below a threshold. The calculation of Network Lifetime is done using values from simulations after running the scenario to a full battery capacity of 500 mAhr to the respective simulation time. The results indicate more practical results for a 3D scenario.

Figure 3 shows comparison of number of data packets dropped due to channel access failure for 2D and 3D scenarios. The number is defined as the data packets which failed to arrive at specified destination. The results are better for a 3D scenario.

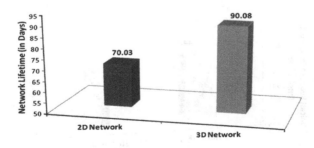

Fig. 2 Comparison of network lifetime for 2D and 3D networks

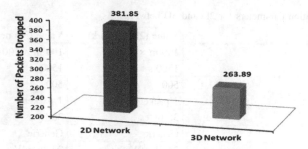

Fig. 3 Comparison of number of packets dropped for 2D and 3D networks

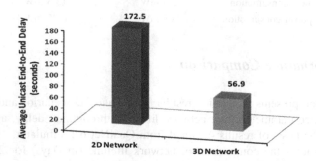

Fig. 4 Comparison of average end-to-end delay for 2D and 3D networks

Figure 4 shows comparison of average end-to-end delay for the two scenarios. It is defined as time taken by a packet to travel from source node to destination node. End-to-end delay includes the delays caused during route discovery, retransmission, propagation, processing, and querying. IEEE 802.15.4 performs better with a 3D scenario than a 2D scenario.

Figure 5 compares average throughput for 2D and 3D scenarios. The average rate of successful data packets received at destination node is referred as Average Throughput. It is measured in bits/sec or data packets/sec. The average throughput is almost same for both 2D and 3D scenarios.

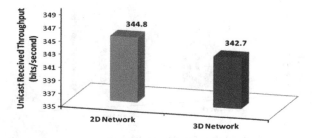

Fig. 5 Comparison of average throughput for 2D and 3D networks

4 Conclusion

The contribution of this paper is to simulate and compare two scenarios with same parameters but different architecture, i.e., 2D and 3D. We evaluated the impact of following parameters on performance of 2D and 3D networks:

- Network Lifetime
- Number of Packets Dropped due to channel access failure
- Average End-to-End Delay
- Average Throughput

Considering the fact that most of the real-life applications deal with a 3D scenario, the 2D networks are unrealistic. Thus the results for 2D networks are considered unrealistic and may result in an unrealistic performance. It is recommended to use the concept of multilayering in 3D Zigbee wireless sensor networks to improve the performance parameters of the network.

References

1. Zigbee. Retrieved from http://www.zigbee.org.
2. IEEE 802.15.4-2006: MAC and PHY Specifications for LR-WPANs. Retrieved from http://ieee802.org/15/pub/TG4.html.
3. Cannon, P. S., & Harding, C. R. (2007). Future military wireless solutions. In W. Webb (Ed.), *Wireless Communications: The Future.* Wiley.
4. Stuart, E., Moh, M., & Moh, T. -S. (2008). Privacy and security in biomedical applications of wireless sensor networks. In *First International Symposium on Applied Sciences on Biomedical and Communication Technologies, 2008. ISABEL'08, 25–28 October* (pp. 1–5).
5. Mohammed, R. A., Alex, T., Simon, C., & Stig, P. (2010). Applications of wireless sensor networks in the oil, gas and resources industries. In *24th IEEE International Conference on Advanced Information Networking and Applications 2010* (pp. 941–948).
6. Tian, H., Lin, G., Liqian, L., Ting, Y., John, A. S., & Sang, H. S. (2006). An overview of data aggregation architecture for real-time tracking with sensor networks. In *20th International Parallel and Distributed Processing Symposium, 2006. IPDPS.*
7. Mainwaring, A., Culler, D., Polastre, J., Szewczyk, R., & Anderson, J. (2002). Wireless sensor networks for habitat monitoring. In *Proceedings of the 1st ACM international workshop on Wireless sensor networks and applications (WSNA02:)* (pp. 88–97).
8. Hussain, S., Schaffner, S., & Moseychuc, D. (2009). Applications of wireless sensor networks and rfid in a smart home environment. In *Seventh Annual Communication Networks and Services Research Conference, 2009, CNSR'09,* National Center for Biotechnology Information, http://www.ncbi.nlm.nih.gov (pp. 153–157).
9. Lin, M.-S., Leu, J. -S., Li, K. –H., & Wu, C. (2013). TABOA: Terrain-aware beacon order adaptation scheme in 3D ZigBee sensor networks. *IEEE Wireless Communications, 20*(2), 122–128.
10. Ghosh, S., Rao, S., & Venkiteswaran, B. (2012). Sensor network design for smart highways. *IEEE Transactions on Systems, Man, and Cybernetics-Part A: Systems and Humans, 42*(5), 1291–1300.

11. Li, M., Liu, Y., & Chen, L. (2008). Nonthreshold-based event detection for 3D environment monitoring in sensor networks. *IEEE Transactions on Knowledge and Data Engineering, 20* (12), 1699–1711.
12. Said, O., & Elnashar, A. (2015). Scaling of wireless sensor network intrusion detection probability: 3D sensors, 3D intruders, and 3D environments. *EURASIP Journal on Wireless Communications and Networking, 2015*(1).
13. Perkins, C., Royar, E., & Das, S. (2003). Ad hoc on demand distance vector (AODV) routing. IETF RFC No. 3561, July 2003.
14. Ranjana, T., Jyoti, S., Manju, K., & Jha M. K. (2013). QoS evaluation of energy-efficient ML-MAC protocol for wireless sensor networks. *International Journal of Electronics and Communication (AEÜ)*, http://dx.doi.org/10.1016/j.aeue.2013.06.006.
15. Ranjana, T., Manju, M., & Jha, K. (2014). Optimized ML-MAC for energy-efficient wireless sensor network protocol. In *Proceedings of Confluence-2014 5th IEEE International Conference on The Next Generation Information Technology Summit, Sept 25–26, 2014*.

Enhancement of Data Security by PMK Technique

Pallavi Sharma, Mukesh Kumar and Kirti Saneja

Abstract Due to the large propagation of the Internet and multimedia technologies, data continuation from undesirable attacks has become a massive turn. One of the most profitable terms for data safety is cryptography, called 'secret coding.' It includes symmetric key cryptography and asymmetric key cryptography. To attain most expeditious, diligent, and private encryption, symmetric key algorithms are most suitably used. In symmetric key algorithms, an unrivaled key is used for both encoding and decoding schemes. This profound research throws light on encryption of small amount of data. This unique approach is beneficial for small-scale firms. The proposed PMK technique fabricates the code text that diverges from the original text. It is more suitable for impregnable conveyance of obscured propaganda over the whole network.

Keywords PMK technique · Encoding · Decoding · Code text

1 Introduction

In today's scenario, due to the rapid improvement of the Internet and network technologies, protection of data becomes essential. How can it provide comfort to fearful people? This is a perilous question in the contemporary era. Nowadays, encryption algorithms have a major disadvantage of less security of data. Within a short time, anybody can easily decrypt the data. This makes cryptography somehow endangered. So, PMK scheme for text encryption is an essential aspect of study for

P. Sharma (✉) · M. Kumar · K. Saneja
Department of Computer Engineering, The Technological Institute of Textile and Sciences,
Bhiwani, India
e-mail: pallavisharma.cp@gmail.com

M. Kumar
e-mail: drmukeshji@gmail.com

© Springer Science+Business Media Singapore 2016
S.C. Satapathy et al. (eds.), *Proceedings of International Conference
on ICT for Sustainable Development*, Advances in Intelligent Systems
and Computing 409, DOI 10.1007/978-981-10-0135-2_21

223

researchers. The main objectives are to decrease computational expenses and promote the security of data as well as reduce needless data and transmit the data in an efficient form.

1.1 Cryptography

It is the technique to attain security by converting ordinary data into a concealed format. It has basically two chief functionalities, encryption and decryption. Encryption is the procedure of altering plain text into cipher text. Decryption is the converse procedure of encryption. It is the process of reclamation of ordinary data from the cipher data. It not only protects data from illegal access but can also also be used for user verification purposes. In all cases, the ordinary data is referred to as plain text and the coded data is called cipher text. It is used generally to protect e-mail messages, credit card information, etc. Modern cryptography is totally based on mathematical and computer science computations. Encryption can be applied on images, text, videos, audios, etc.

The basic block diagram of cryptography is shown in Fig. 1.

1.2 Classification of Cryptographic Algorithms

There are different ways of classifying cryptographic algorithms which are as follows:

- **Secret Key Cryptography (SKC)**: It is also known as symmetric cryptography. In this, one key is used for both encoding and decoding operations. The sender is used for encrypting the ordinary text and the recipient is used to decrypt the encrypted text into original text again. This is a way to fulfill the needs for textual message safety, as the content of textual data cannot be read without the confidential key. It is also used to represent fairness and authenticity. The transmitter encrypts the data with the help of a secret key. The recipient then reproduces the message, decrypts what was sent, and makes a comparison

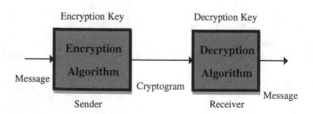

Fig. 1 Block diagram of cryptography

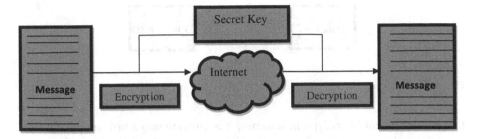

Fig. 2 Secret key cryptography

between the two keys. If both keys are identical, the message that was accepted must have been identical to that which was sent. The main problem with symmetric algorithms is that the secret key has to be taken by concerned parties (Fig. 2).

- **Public Key Cryptography (PKC)**: It is also called asymmetric cryptography. It uses two dissimilar keys for encryption and decryption. None of the keys can perform both the functions.
  Public key cryptography is stated as follows:

  (1) The private key is confidential. Only a single party knows the private key.
  (2) The public key used is not privileged. But it does not affect the security of message transmissions (Fig. 3).

- **Hash Indexing**: It explores an analytical alteration to "encode" irreversible information. Once a hash value is generated, the ordinary text is not reproduced back. The one-way hash indexing considers a flexible-length raw message and provides a fixed-length outcome. If one bit of the data is altered then a different output value is generated in case of hash indexing (Fig. 4).

Due to the popularity of computer and information technology, cryptography is the major scheme for data fortification. It assures privacy, strong user authenticity, and high encryption speed, reduces processing time, and provides more reliable secret data. It provides much benefit to modern society in terms of data secrecy. It also has supervisory control over the textual representation using coding scheme.

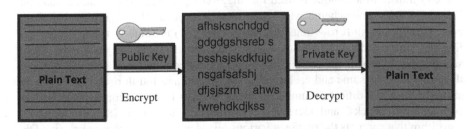

Fig. 3 Public key cryptography

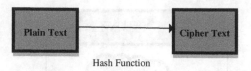

Fig. 4 Hash indexing

Due to enrichment in encryption schemes, it is growing into a brilliant prospective of never ending potential. The cryptanalysis discovers the limitations of various existent strategies. Some algorithms that can be used for strong encryption are symmetric and asymmetric key algorithms. DES and AES are symmetric type of encryption algorithms, whereas RSA is asymmetric type of encryption algorithm.

According to PMK scheme, tough encryption gets generated on the textual data that is strongly applicable for small firms, where DES and AES algorithms do not work well. This novel approach reduces the data by taking the number of 1's for occurrence of a character and the number of 0's for showing the nonexistence of text. The main benefit of this algorithm is that there is no need to show the number of times the character has occurred in the string.

2 Literature Survey

Ying et al. [1] worked on permutation transform and then performed nonlinear mapping between pixel values. Zhang et al. [2] implemented image scrambling using the T-matrix. Mainly the T-matrix is used for image encryption and image watermarking. Deng et al. [3] made a new image encryption system based on chaotic neural system and the cat map. Here, neural network is used for developing the chaos. Xiao and Zhang [4] implemented an optimized image algorithm using two methods (permutation and substitution) to enhance the concept of pseudorandom characteristics of chaotic sequences. Gu and Han [5] built a new algorithm that uses two chaotic systems. The first chaotic system fabricates a chaotic sequence, which was turned into a binary field using a threshold mechanism. The second chaotic system was used to create a permutation matrix. Sharma [6] represents data compression to reduce the need for storage and superior data transfer rate. Here, wavelet transform technique is used for image compression. Kamali and Shakerian [7] propound a new scheme with some modification in AES algorithm based on both the types of shift row transformations. Here, if the value in the first row and first column is even, the first and fourth rows are the same and each byte in the second and third rows are shifted right onto the different number, else the first and third rows are the same and each byte of the second and fourth rows of the state is shifted left on the different number of bytes. It gives better outcome, protects data from various attacks, and increases performance. Shin et al. [8] introduced an algorithm that encrypts the image at various levels using binary phase exclusive OR operation and image dividing technique. Belkhouche and Qidwai [9] suggest a scheme that mainly focuses on the encryption of binary images using several keys. The examples of keys are iterations number, intial state, etc. Bedwal and Kumar [10] suggested a new approach of hiding an RGB image behind another RGB image, based on LSB insertion mechanism. Gupta and Sharma [11] suggested a signature hiding standard. The pixels of RGB-based 24-bit image using LSB technique were eight bits show red color, eight bits show green, and the last eight bits show blue. First two bits from eight of them show the color of the next pixel using RGB color combination then the third bit will be ignored. The next two bits define the difference between current and next pixel. Again the sixth bit will be ignored and the next two bits, i.e., seventh and eighth define how much bits of signature will be hidden. The remaining portion of the paper is consolidated as follows: Sect. 3 explains the proposed methodology (PMK Scheme). Section 4 prescribes the results. Section 5 interprets the conclusion of the paper.

3 Proposed Methodology

Encryption procedure is basically the major trade-off between cost and running speed. Various encryption algorithms such as DES, AES, etc., make a good balance between all these factors. But, all these vast algorithms are not applicable for small amount of data because of increased complexity and overhead in computational time. So, there is a need for a faster encryption algorithm that is well suited for small-scale data transfer between two firms. Hence, the proposed research proposes a novel and efficient encryption algorithm named "PMK Scheme" after its authors. The benefit of this algorithm is that it also uses compression to decrease the data payload for transmission. The procedure of PMK scheme text encryption is as follows:

To provide strong encryption and compression, reduce the data by taking the number of 1's for presence of character and the number of 0's for showing the absence of text. The main benefit of this algorithm is that there is no need to show the number of times the character has occurred in the string.

3.1 Encryption procedure of PMK Technique

- Enter the original text as plain text.
- Count the dissimilar characters and store it in a database.
- Arrange the occurrence of the scanned character in ascending order.
- For every scanned character, insert binary digit '1', the same number of times it traversed in the plaintext.
- Convert the number of 1's that occur into the same number of 0's.

- Then scan the next character, insert binary digit '1' to show its presence for previously recognized character and binary digit '0' to show its absence.
- Repeat steps 5 and 6 until it traverses the whole string but the order of occurrence of the characters is maintained.
- Then all the continuous occurrence of 0's and 1's are concatenated.
- Every character has its block and has an extra bit 0 for showing the end of block. The first block contains all 1 bits and ending with 0 showing the end of the block.
- Finally, the new encrypted data is concatenated and transmitted toward the receiver (Fig. 5).

Fig. 5 Encryption procedure of PMK technique

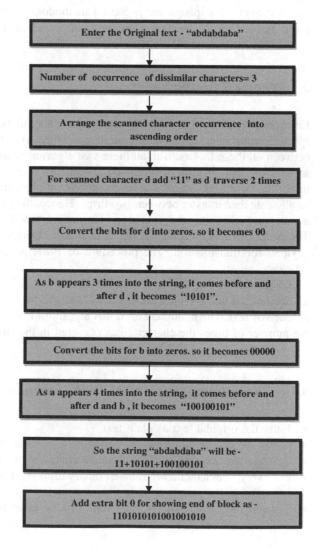

3.2 Decryption procedure of PMK Technique

The decryption procedure of the PMK scheme is exactly the reverse of the encryption procedure, because of the symmetric nature of the algorithm. So, the PMK scheme is easy and efficient to implement. However, for sending the secret key from the senders' end to the receiver's end, any well-known public algorithm can be utilized.

- In the encrypted message, first count the number of 1's before the first zero, as first zero shows the end of the first character.
- Then traverse the next block using the occurrence of the previous character. Previously defined character is represented by 0 as many times it occurs in cipher text and the next character will be shown using 1.
- Then second zero shows the end of second the block.
- In the same manner, traverse the whole string using previously defined character until no text is left behind.
- Finally it retrieves the original string (Fig. 6).

4 Result

The design and implementation of PMK scheme for text encryption are demonstrated keeping the needs of small-scale firms in mind. Hence, the PMK scheme is essentially designed for handling textual data of smaller sizes. This proposed technique is implemented in MATLAB. The following figures show:

a. The framework of PMK technique
b. Text encryption using PMK technique
c. Text decryption using PMK technique

| (a) Framework of PMK Technique | (b) Text Encryption Using PMK | (c) Text Decryption using PMK |

The performance of PMK technique can be observed with the help of Table 1.

It must be noted that the execution time (both encryption and decryption) for the proposed algorithm is calculated and presented here. The data are calculated after the encoding and decoding are done on an Intel T1600@1.66 GHz processor machine.

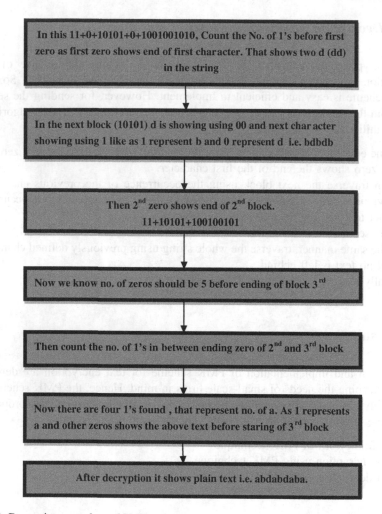

Fig. 6 Decryption procedure of PMK technique

Table 1 Execution time performance of PMK technique

S. no.	Textual data	Encryption time (s)	Decryption time (s)
1.	abdabdaba	0.01	0.01
2.	jsmjsmmpqj	0.30	0.30
3.	onssonnnnooz	0.02	0.02
4.	santoshi	1.1	1.1

5 Conclusion

The superior technical world is like a huge ocean, where tiny fish are always in danger of being taken out by big fish. Similarly, small-scale firms are always in jeopardy by big hackers. So, there is a need for a strong encryption algorithm that provides cost-effective and quick solutions. The PMK scheme for text encryption is designed by keeping all the above-mentioned things in mind. Moreover, it also does a bit of compression on the data, so that the amount of data to be transferred over the unsecure destination is relatively less. A lot of effort and time will be needed in order to break this algorithm. The performance of the proposed algorithm is brilliant for tiny-sized data and can provide superior solutions to the ever-growing security needs for smaller firms.

References

1. Ying, W., DeLing, Z., & Lei, J., et al. (2004). The spatial-domain encryption of digital images based on high-dimension chaotic system. In *Proceeding of 2004 IEEE Conference on Cybernetics and Intelligent Systems* (pp. 1172–1176). Singapore, December 2004.
2. Zhang, M. -R., Shao, G. -C., & Yi, K. –C. (2004). T-matrix and its applications in image processing. *IEEE Electronics Letters, 40*(25).
3. Deng, S., Zhang, L., & Xiao, D. (2005). Image encryption scheme based on chaotic neural system. In J. Wang, X. Liao, & Z. Yi (Eds.), LNCS 3497, (pp. 868–872), ISNN 2005.
4. Xiao, H. -P., & Zhang, G. -J (2006). An image encryption scheme based on chaotic systems. In *IEEE Proceedings of the Fifth International Conference on Machine Learning and Cybernetics*. Dalian, 13–16 August 2006.
5. Gu, G., & Han, G. (2006). An enhanced chaos based image encryption algorithm. In *IEEE Proceedings of the First International Conference on Innovative Computing, Information and Control (ICICIC'06) in 2006*.
6. Sharma, M. (2012). Image compression using enhanced haar wavelet technique. In *International Conference*, 2012.
7. Kamali, S. H., & Shakerian, R. (2010) A new modified version of advanced encryption standard based algorithm for image encryption. *1*.
8. Shin, C. -M., Seo, D. -H., Chol, K.-B., Lee, H.-W., & Kim, S. (2003). Multilevel image encryption by binary phase xor operations. In *IEEE Proceeding in the year 2003*.
9. Belkhouche, F., & Qidwai, U. (2003). Binary image encoding using 1D chaotic maps. In *IEEE Proceeding in the year 2003*.
10. Bedwal, T., & Kumar, M. (2013). An enhanced and secure image steganographic technique using RGB-box mapping. In *IET Digital Library 2013*.
11. Gupta, K., Sharma, M. (2014). Signature hiding standard: Hiding binary image into rgb based image. In *2014 International Conference on Information and Communication Technology*.

Privacy-Leveled Perturbation Model for Privacy Preserving Collaborative Data Mining

Alpa Kavin Shah and Ravi Gulati

Abstract Perturbation-based techniques are studied extensively in context of privacy preserving data mining. In this technique, random noise is added to the original distribution for privacy sensitive data. Next, they are sent to the data miner who will reconstruct the original data distribution from the perturbed sets. Perturbation approaches project a trade-off between applicability of data versus privacy achieved. Also, different entities participating in collaborative data mining have different attitudes toward privacy based on their country's customs and traditions. Contemporary-based perturbation techniques do not allow the participating entities to choose the privacy levels needed by them. This is main motivation our work. This paper presents a privacy level-based perturbation model opening new avenues for future work in this direction.

Keywords Privacy preserving · Collaborative data mining · Geometric data perturbation

1 Introduction

Computer application has seen an unprecedented growth in day-to-day business activities during past decade. Due to this, variety of areas from where data can be generated has emerged. Privacy of individuals/parties contributing to them is crucial. Privacy preserving data mining [PPDM] has been studied by research scholars

A.K. Shah (✉)
MCA Department, Sarvajanik College of Engineering and Technology, Surat, India
e-mail: alpa.shah@scet.ac.in

R. Gulati
Department of Computer Science, Veer Narmad South Gujarat University, Surat, India
e-mail: rmgulati@gmail.com

© Springer Science+Business Media Singapore 2016
S.C. Satapathy et al. (eds.), *Proceedings of International Conference on ICT for Sustainable Development*, Advances in Intelligent Systems and Computing 409, DOI 10.1007/978-981-10-0135-2_22

to open new ventures for preserving the privacy of contributors. The main aim of PPDM algorithms is to preserve the privacy of the contributors, while effective mining is carried out.

Also, multiple parties might desire to collaborate to conduct data mining without breaching privacy of each contributing party. Say for an example, contemporary hospitals might want to collaborate to find trends in diseases in certain areas, but they are unwilling to share their patient's information. Such mutual collaboration is both required and desirable. Neither party should compromise with the privacy of their data. Various organizations, both public and private, publish sensitive microdata for research and/or trend analysis. This requisite a new set of research area coined with PPDM described as privacy preserving collaborative data mining [PPCDM]. Several pioneering works by researchers in domain of PPCDM ranging from perturbation, cryptography, and secure sum computation are carried out.

We have emphasized the use of perturbation-based techniques in our model. In perturbation techniques, before making the data public, the data owner changes the information in it in a way so as to preserve the sensitive data. The data property of sensitive data is preserved so as to make it viable for data mining model. Many methods like additive, multiplicative, randomization, anonymization, shuffling, microaggregation, and swapping are applied for perturbing the original data. Perturbation model has an implicit trade-off between the privacy versus utility of information to be preserved.

Additive-based perturbation method mainly focuses on two main aspects. First being introduction of noise in the dataset and second reconstruction of original distribution [1, 2]. During addition of noise, a known distribution like Gaussian (with mean 0) is added to sensitive data. Additive data perturbation was first revisited to address PPDM problems by Agrawal and Srikant [3]. Current research work encompasses done by addition of same amount of noise to all the sensitive data. The main loophole here is that it presents a one-level privacy model for any hierarchy of sensitive data. We can term it as "one-fit" privacy model. The amount of privacy required by the contributor is solely determinant by the type of application. Say for an example, a person having certain disease may be considered sensitive attribute for hospital record but immaterial for census records. Such "one-fit" privacy model is not realistic in all applications. This is our motive for this work which focuses on developing a generic model based on privacy level which can be indicated by the contributors.

1.1 Our Contributions

The main contributions of our research in this paper are as follows:

1. Extensive literature survey on PPCDM techniques
2. Present a novel privacy-leveled perturbation model for privacy preserving multiparty data mining

1.2 Organization of the Paper

The paper has been organized as follows. In Sect. 2, concise literature surveys on techniques which are currently being used for PPCDM are presented. Based on this discussion, a clear understanding for making perturbation techniques a base for designing our model is endeavored. Section 3 describes brief the geometric data-based perturbation technique which is foundation of our model. Section 4 describes in depth the privacy-level perturbation model for PPCDM. In Sect. 5 we conclude with prospectus future work that will be carried out in this direction.

2 Literature Survey

PPDM has been studied extensively during past several years. The works on PPCDM techniques have been broadly categorized based on cryptographic principles, perturbation-based approaches, and secure sum computations. Authors' previous work [4] presents a survey on all the three techniques and their pros and cons in terms of applicability of PPDM are discussed. All the approaches are based on fundamentally different requirements. Cryptographic- and perturbation-based approaches work on distributed frameworks; whereas secure sum computations assume a centralized repository of information. The next section briefly describes each of them in a nutshell.

Encryption techniques of cryptography are considered an age old tool for preserving the confidentiality of sensitive information. Homomorphic encryption scheme [5] allows certain computations to be performed on encrypted data without any decryption operations. Zhan et al. [6] proposed a cryptographic approach to tackle collaborative association rule mining among multiple parties. Digital envelope technique allows the party to use a random number known only to it. A mathematical function is then applied between data and the random number. This makes the cryptanalysis attack almost impossible. As suggested in literature [7] by Justin Zhan, combination of Homomorphic encryption scheme with digital envelope can be used effectively for collaborative data mining without the need for sharing the private data among the collaborating parties. Zhan's work also highlights Naïve Bayesian Classification [8] with vertical collaboration. The solution as proposed by Zhan deals with any number of participants and the scalability issue for privacy preserving collaboration protocol also being addressed. With Homomorphic encryption still generating and exchanging key pairs that need to be shared between collaborative parties remains an issue. In literature [9], authors have described the use of oblivious transfer protocol for the construction of secure protocol that enhances the two-party scenarios for distributed computations.

A different approach underlying PPCDM works by perturbing the sensitive data and then using the randomized approach for protecting the sensitive data. The efficiency of perturbation-based techniques is based on the approximation of original data distribution generated after applying perturbation. The key result being the perturbed data [1] together with information on the distribution of random data used to distort the data can be used to generate the original data distribution. The original data is still not revealed. Other similar approaches with the perturbation have been proposed in [2, 10]. Reconstruction approaches are proposed by Kargupta et al. in [2]. Results of Huang et al. [10] have shown a loop hole for perturbation-based techniques for privacy preserving for specific data sets. Literature [11] and Literature [12] have proposed random rotation and multiplication-based perturbation approaches, respectively.

Yao [13] had originally proposed the groundwork for secured multiparty computation. authors in [14] have shown the possibility for using secure sum for opt-out of a computation beforehand on the basis of certain rules in statistical disclosure limitation. A secured multiparty computation framework is discussed in [15–17]. In literature [18], it has been shown that computation using secure sum computation can be done using an anonymous ID. Authors in [18] have discussed the importance of using SMC with regards to PPDM. Literature [19] proposes a technique using a commodity server as a trusted intermediate which processes the requests for data mining along with secure number product protocol. Du et al. [20] have proved that the size of protocols developed based on SMC is directly proportional to scalability with respect to number of contributors.

The main motive of our model is to allow the individual contributor determine the privacy level it wants to adhere for collaborative mining. Perturbation techniques forms the basis of our model because the privacy of the data can be preserved at the distributed node which can be controlled by the amount of noise that can be added to each data record independent to the subsequent results. Instead of traditional monolithic model of privacy, each contributor will be able to specify his privacy requirements and individually be adaptable to perturbation model. Geometric data perturbation [GDP] very strongly covers the issue of balancing data utility versus data privacy [3, 21]. Also they use a service-based framework, which enables collaboration to be scalable to high number of participants which is the most apparent disadvantage of cryptographic techniques [9, 22]. A clear applicability of cryptographic techniques for PPCDM has been described in authors' previous works [23].

3 Geometric Data Perturbation Technique: A Short Review

Perturbation-based techniques can be classified into probability distribution category and other being fixed data perturbation. In probability distribution category, the data falls under some known distribution pattern. In this scenario, the original dataset is replaced with the new values based on the distribution pattern. Thus, both the privacy of dataset and the distribution pattern are important. Latter considers perturbing the original dataset with some fixed set of values irrespective of their count in occurrence of datasets. These techniques are useful for numerical data or categorical data only.

In probability distribution-based perturbation, two methods are common. One swaps data according to some predefined matrix and the other consists of replacing the values with known distribution sample. In Literature [24], authors have described effectiveness of latter approach by experimental studies. Their works suggest that in some cases it is not even needed to perform the reconstruction steps on perturbed data. The basic probability distribution method for perturbing data consists of three main steps (1) identifying the density function of the sensitive attribute values, determine mean and standard variance of this function, (2) generate a sample series of this probability function, and (3) replace the generated data of the sensitive attributes of data set for the original data with the same rank order.

The authors in paper [25] have defined geometric data perturbation (GDP) to be a combination of random rotation perturbation, random translation perturbation, and addition of noise (if needed). This can be mathematically represented as

$$G(X) = RX + ¥ + \Delta$$

where X is the original data set containing N rows and d columns. R is a random orthonormal matrix, and ¥ is a random translation matrix. Δ denotes the amount of noise to be added to the sensitive attributes. To add this noise, values from some identically distribution values are considered. For any given set of attributes, the G (X) function can be applied for transformation, translation, rotation, and addition of noise. Addition of noise can be an independent attribute and can be from some known distribution. For such cases $G(X) = X + \Delta$. Rotation can be applied by multiplying the R random orthonormal matrix with X. Here, $G(X) = RX$ where

$$R = \begin{bmatrix} \cos\theta & \sin\theta \\ -\sin\theta & \cos\theta \end{bmatrix}$$

Here based on the values of θ, the values can be rotated clockwise for positive and anticlockwise for negative values. To scale the values to some fixed values, ¥ can be multiplied with the constant and then the function being applied to as G (X) = RX + ¥.

GDP is multidimensional data perturbation technique where all the columns are perturbed together in multidimensional way. Privacy of other columns is also implicitly achieved while perturbing a single column. Authors in literature [25] have devised a protocol based on GDP and random response technique for achieving privacy of the contributing parties.

4 Privacy-Leveled Perturbation Model for PPCDM

We now present the novel model for privacy-leveled PPCDM. Each user can provide any of the three privacy levels. The privacy settings are (1) intrinsic, (2) moderate, and (3) high. Contributors should opt for intrinsic privacy when they are not sure with what level of privacy is required. They just know that the data should be privatized. We categorize such users with a level of intrinsic privacy requirement. Contributors will specify moderate level of privacy with desired attributes for medium level privacy. Contributors will specify high privacy for sensitive data that require privacy preserving in public datasets. The categorization is based on level of privacy requirements among the contributing parties. It is necessary to provide privacy-level categorization to ensure that redundant computations for perturbing datasets are not carried. Contributing parties perform the computations required as per their privacy requirements only.

The model is two phase and also privacy-leveled. Each contributing party specifies the privacy level for their local dataset. Based on the level of privacy, GDP techniques can be applied. To the best of authors' knowledge no work is present in literature to find the optimal combinations of methods that can be applied of GDP for best-suited privacy. Based on the type of privacy level desired by the contributor, GDP transformation will be applied to local perturbed dataset. Each party then sends the data to trusted service provider. Literature only has shown its dimensions in terms of service provider for cryptography and secure sum computation. The locally perturbed data, vertically partitioned, is now used to generate the original distribution from perturbed datasets. The newly reconstructed dataset generated in former step can now be used to mine meaningful information from the model.

Figure 1 shows the model in brief. Each contributing party specifies privacy levels. GDP is used to generate locally perturbed datasets. While data being transferred to service provider, Homomorphic encryption can be applied if

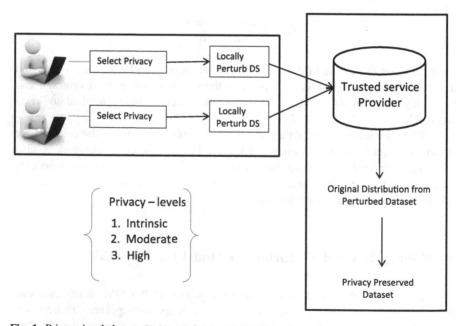

Fig. 1 Privacy-leveled perturbation model for PPCDM

sensitivity of protection desired is more. Each contributor and service provider have priory exchanged the keys for such secured communication. Service provider is responsible for further reconstruction of original data distribution from perturbed data. Service provider can now perform mining on the newly perturbed dataset. The newly proposed model both takes into consideration privacy of the user as well as the data utility of perturbed dataset. GDP based models present the same accuracy and we need only to identify one that maximizes the privacy guarantee in terms of various potential attacks to the system.

5 Conclusions and Future Work

Different contributing parties have their privacy needs. The "one-fit" approach is neither realistic nor appropriate for different types of privacy preserving mining. In order to address this, we have proposed a new perturbation model which is adaptable based on the privacy requirements of the users. We have proposed the use of GDP techniques which can be modeled in way for different privacy settings. GDP techniques have proved an edge over other perturbation techniques in terms of providing better trade-off between the privacy of sensitive data versus utility of perturbed data. Our future work encompasses of developing a model/framework for such privacy-leveled perturbation model for PPCDM.

References

1. Agrawal, D., & Agrawal, C. C. (2001). On the design and quantification of privacy preserving data mining algorithms. In *PODS, ACM*.
2. Kargupta, H., Dutta, S., Wang, Q., & Sivakumar, K. (2003). On privacy preserving properties of random data perturbation techniques. In *ICDM, IEEE Computer Society, 2003* (pp. 99–106).
3. Agrawal, R., & Srikant, R. (2000). Privacy-preserving data mining. In *Proceedings ACM SIGMOD, 2000*, (pp. 439–450).
4. Alpa, K. S., & Ravi, G. (2015). Contemporary trends in privacy preserving collaborative data mining– a survey. In *IEEE-International Conference on Electrical, Electronics, Signals, Communication and Optimization (EESCO)-2015 held on 24th and 25th January 2015*.
5. Elkan, C. (1997). *Boosting and naive bayesian learning, technical report CS97-557*. San Diego: University of California.
6. Rivest, R., Adleman, L., & Dertouzos, M. (1978). On data banks and privacy homomorphisms. In R. A. DeMillo et al. (Eds.), *Foundations of Secure Computation* (pp. 169–179). London: Academic Press.
7. Justin, Z. (2008). Privacy preserving collaborative data mining. *IEEE Computational Intelligence Magazine*.
8. Murat, K., & Chris, C. (2004). Privacy-preserving distributed mining of association rules on horizontally partitioned data. *IEEE Transactions on Knowledge and Data Engineering*, 16(9).
9. Lindell, Y., & Pinkas, B. (2000). Privacy preserving data mining. *Journal of Cryptology, 15*(3), 177–206.

10. Huang, Z., Du, W., & Chen, B. (2005). Deriving private information from randomized data. In *SIGMOD Conference, 2005* (pp. 37–48).
11. Liu, K., Kargupta, H., & Ryan, J. (2006). Random projection-based multiplicative data perturbation for privacy preserving distributed data mining. *IEEE Transactions on Knowledge and Data Engineering (TKDE), 18*(1), 92–106. doi:10.1109/TKDE.2006.14.
12. Liu, K., Giannella, C., & Kargupta, H. (2006). An attacker's view of distance preserving maps for privacy preserving data mining. In *Proceedings of the 10th European Conference on Principles and Practice of Knowledge Discovery in Databases (PKDD '06), Berlin, Germany, 2006.*
13. Yao, A. C. (1982). Protocols for secure computations. In *Proceedings of the 23rd Annual IEEE Symposium on Foundations of Computer Science, 1982.*
14. Willenborg, L., & Waal, T. (2001). Elements of statistical disclosure control. In *Lecture Notes in Statistics* (Vol. 155). New York: Springer.
15. Du, W. & Atallah, M. J. (2001). Secure multi-party computation problems and their applications: A review and open problems. In *New Security Paradigms Workshop* (pp. 11–20).
16. Vaidya, J., & Clifton, C. (2002). Privacy preserving association rule mining in vertically partitioned data. In *Eight ACM SIGKDD International conference on Knowledge Discovery and Data Mining, Edmonton, Alberta, CA July 2002.*
17. Kantaracioglu, M. & Clifton, C. (2002). Privacy preserving distributed mining of association rules on horizontally partitioned data. In *SiGMOD Workshop on DMKD, Madison, WI, June 2002.*
18. Yehuda, L. (2001). Parallel coin-tossing and constant round secure two-party computation. *Journal of Cryptology.*
19. Zhan, Z., & Chang, L. (2008). *Privacy-preserving collaborative data mining* (pp. 21–31). Computational Intelligence Magazine: IEEE Journals and Magazine.
20. Du, W. & Attalah, M. J. (2001). Privacy-preserving cooperative scientific computations. In *14th IEEE Computer Security Foundation Workshop, June 11–13, 2001.*
21. Evfimievski, A., Gehrke, J. & Srikant, R. (2003). Limiting privacy breaches in privacy preserving data mining. In *Proceedings ACM Conference Principles of Database Systems (PODS), 2003.*
22. Jagannathan, G., & Wright, R. N. (2005). Privacy-preserving distributed k-means clustering over arbitrarily partitioned data. In *Proceedings ACM SIGKDD, 2005.*
23. Alpa, K. S., & Ravi, G. (2015). Privacy, collaboration and security – imperative existence in data mining. In *VNSGU Journal of Science and Technology (ISSN 0975-5446), February 2015.*
24. Li, L., Murat, K., & Bhavani, T. (2007). The applicability of the perturbation based privacy preserving data mining for real-world data. In *Data Knowledge and Engineering.* Elsevier.
25. Keke, C., & Ling, L. (2009). Privacy-preserving multiparty collaborative mining with geometric data perturbation. *IEEE Transactions on Parallel and Distributed Systems, 20*(12).

Extended Bellman Ford Algorithm with Optimized Time of Computation

Neha and Akhil Kaushik

Abstract Large graphs having millions of vertices frequently used in many practical applications and are complicated to process. To process them, some fundamental single source shortest path (SSSP) algorithms like Dijkstra algorithm and Bellman Ford algorithm are available. Dijkstra algorithm is a competent sequential access algorithm but poorly suited for parallel architecture, whereas Bellman Ford algorithm is suited for parallel execution but this feature come at a higher cost. This paper introduces a new algorithm EBellflaging algorithm which enhances basic Bellman Ford algorithm to improve its efficiency over traditional Dijkstra algorithm and Bellman Ford algorithm and also reduces the space requirement of both the traditional approaches.

Keywords SSSP (Single source shortest Path) · Dijkstra algorithm · Bellman ford algorithm · Ebellflaging algorithm · Graphics processing unit (GPU)

1 Introduction

In a graph, finding the shortest path from a single source node to all connected nodes is a well-known and long-studied problem with many practical applications on a wide variety of graphs [1, 2]. The input to SSSP is a source node in a graph with 'v' vertices and 'e' directed edges. The conventional method for SSSP cal-

Neha (✉) · A. Kaushik
The Technological Institute of Textile & Sciences, Bhiwani, Haryana, India
e-mail: nehagarg60@gmail.com

A. Kaushik
e-mail: akhil.kaushik@yahoo.com

© Springer Science+Business Media Singapore 2016
S.C. Satapathy et al. (eds.), *Proceedings of International Conference on ICT for Sustainable Development*, Advances in Intelligent Systems and Computing 409, DOI 10.1007/978-981-10-0135-2_23

241

culation is Dijkstra's algorithm, in which only one vertex is processed at a time which means it is a sequential algorithm. While this method is an efficient serial algorithm (O (v log v + e)), it is not well suited for a parallel architectures like GPU. To expose parallelism, algorithm that can process more vertices at the same time is required. The Bellman Ford is one such algorithm that processes all vertices repeatedly; updating vertices continuously until final distance converge. However, this salient feature comes with a higher cost: O (ev) [3]. Hence, these two algorithms suffer with a parallel versus efficiency constraint. Neither is ideal: Dijkstra exposes no parallelism across edges, while Bellman Ford is expensive [4, 5]. This paper presents implementations of Dijkstra algorithm and Bellman Ford algorithm on Matlab and proposes a new EBellflaging algorithm [6]. EBellflaging algorithm is implemented on various graphs represented by sparse matrix which is space efficient than adjacency list and achieve high speedups regarding the Dijkstra algorithm and Bellman Ford algorithm [7]. Hence computation time of Dijkstra algorithm and of Bellman Ford algorithm is reduced up to 3 times and 5-12 times, respectively, improving the efficiency of both the algorithms. This paper is organized into six sections. Section I gives brief introduction about SSSP algorithms, Section II discusses the Dijkstra algorithm, Section III discusses the Bellman Ford Algorithm, Section IV discusses proposed work, In Section V results are observed and analyzed using graph implemented on MATLAB. Section VI concludes the research work.

2 Dijkstra Algorithm

Dijkstra's algorithm is a proficient sequential algorithm for SSSP calculation on directed graphs [8]. The algorithm utilizes a priority queue of vertices prioritized by its shortest distance [9]. First, it processes vertex on the top of the queue and then all edges leaving that vertex are processed. Vertices with the shortest distance from the top vertex are added into the queue if they are not visited before, or their distance value is updated if a shorter path to already visited vertex has been discovered. This method is an efficient serial algorithm (O (v log v + e)). Dijkstra's method exposes no parallelism between vertices; the only parallelism available is between edges leaving the vertex at the top of the queue. It is efficient for serial implementation, but is not well suited for parallel architectures like GPUs that require large numbers of parallel threads for efficient execution [10]. Dijkstra algorithm is explained as follows:

```
//Distance (v) store distance of each vertex from the
source vertex & Weight is the weight adjacency matrix.
 1. for each vertex v in parallel do
 2.      Distance (v) = Weight(S, v), p (v) =0;
 3. end for
 4  Distance(S) =0;    //distance of source vertex is set to zero.
 5. p(S)=1;            //put the source vertex in priority queue
 6. for i=2 to V
 7.  min=∞ ,  t=1;
 8.    for j=2 to E
 9.     if p(j)==0   && Distance(j)<min)
10.      min = Distance(j), t=j;  //find the next vertex closest
to source vertex
11.     end if
12.    end for
13.   p(t)=1;
14.   for k=1 to V
15.    if (p(k)==0)
16.     if(Distance(k)>(Distance(t)+weight(t, k)))
17.        Distance (k) = Distance (t) +weight (t, k);
18.      end if
19.     end if
20.    end for
21. end for
```

3 Bellman Ford Algorithm

Bellman Ford algorithm is a SSSP finding algorithm that calculates shortest paths from a single source vertex to all of the other vertices in a weighted directed graph [5]. It uses the relax method in which the approximate distance to each vertex is always greater than or equal to the true distance, and is replaced by the minimum of its newly calculated value and old value. In this algorithm all the edges are relaxed for $|V|-1$ times, where $|V|$ is the number of vertices in the graph [11]. In this way, each node will get its shortest distance from the source node. This algorithm usually takes a large amount of time O (ev). Bellman Ford algorithm is explained as follows:

```
//Distance (v) store distance of each vertex from the
source vertex & Weight (u, v) is the weight adjacency
matrix. Predecessor (v) stores the predecessor of each
vertex.
 1. for each vertex v in parallel do
 2.   Distance (v) = ∞;
 3.   Predecessor (v) = 0;
 4. end for
 5. Distance(S) = 0; //distance of source is set to zero.
 6. for i=2 to V
 7.    for each edge (u, v) in parallel do
 8.        if (Distance(v)>(Distance(u)+Weight(u, v)))
 9.           Distance (v) = Distance (u) + Weight (u, v);
10.       end if
11.   end for
12. end for
```

4 The Proposed Algorithm

In proposed algorithm, a flag F is used in order to find those edges which should be relaxed during each iteration [10]. To implement this algorithm, value of flag F is set to 1 for only those vertices that should be processed next and for all other it is set to zero. In each iteration, only those edges are relaxed whose distance value was updated in the last iteration, i.e., their flag value is set to 1. Each time when a vertex is processed, its flag is set to zero and it will remain the same until a shorter distance

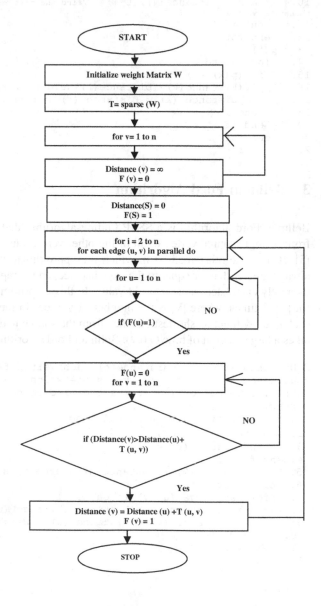

Fig. 1 Flowchart representation of the EBellflaging algorithm

to already processed vertex is found. In this way, the unwanted iterations and comparisons are prohibited. Second, to store graphs coordinate (COO) format is used, because COO is space efficient, store references to only none zero values [7]. In this way, the computation time is reduced by a large factor, because in each iteration distance value of only some of the vertices need to be updated. Steps followed by EBellFlaging algorithm are given in Fig. 1.

Algorithm EBellflaging is described as follows:

```
//Distance (v) store distance from the source vertex &
Weight (u, v) is the weight adjacency matrix. F (v) is a
flag store's value of vertices that are processed next.
 1. T=sparse(Weight);
 2. for each vertex v in parallel do
 3.    Distance (v) = ∞, F (v) =0;
 4. end for
 5  Distance(S) =0, F(S) =1; //Distance of source is set to
    zero.
 6  for i=2 to V
 7.  for each edge (u, v) in parallel do
 8.    if (F(u)==1)
 9.      F (u) =0;
10.      if (T(u, v)>0 &&Distance(v)>(distance(u)+T (u,v)))
11.        Distance (v) =Distance (u) + T (u, v);
12.          F (v) =1;
13.      end if
14.    end if
15.  end for
16. end for
```

5 Results

Table 1 represents the amount of time taken by Dijkstra algorithm, Bellman Ford algorithm, and EBellflaging algorithm when these algorithms are implemented on various graphs in Matlab.

Table 1 Represents Dijkstra algorithm, Bellman Ford algorithm, and EBellflging algorithm experimental results

No. of vertex	Time in milliseconds		
	Dijkstra algorithm	Bellman Ford algorithm	EBellFlaging algorithm
5	10	20	7
6	11	30	6
8	16	56	8
9	24	72	10
12	28	132	12

Fig. 2 Time in milliseconds versus no of vertices

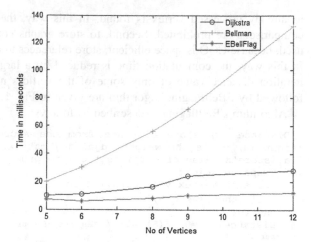

A graph, which shows the comparison of Dijkstra algorithm, Bellman Ford algorithm, and EBellflaging algorithm on a "Number of vertices versus Time" plot, is represented in Fig. 2. Graph clearly shows that EBellflaging algorithm is more efficient than of Dijkstra algorithm and Bellman Ford algorithm.

6   Conclusion

In this paper, a naive and competent EBellflaging algorithm is introduced which minimizes the number of edge relaxations in order to reduce the useless calculations. Achieved results show a considerable speed-up over corresponding serial and parallel implementations for various graph using Dijkstra algorithm and Bellman Ford algorithm, respectively. Hence this new algorithm can be used efficiently for various large graphs and networks that require parallelism as well as time efficient solution like ad hoc networks.

References

1. Shivashankar, H., Suresh, N., Varaprasad, G., & Jayanthi, G. (2014). Designing energy routing protocol with power consumption optimization in manet. *IEEE Transactions on Emerging Topics in Computing 2*(2).
2. Othman, M. A., Sulaiman, H. A., Ismail, M. M., Misran, M. H., Meor, M. A. B., & Ramlee, R. A. (2013). An analysis of least-cost routing using bellman ford and dijkstra algorithms in wireless routing network. *IJACT 5, 10*(10).
3. Patel, V., & Baggar, C. (2014). A survey paper of bellman-ford algorithm and Dijkstra algorithm for finding shortest path in gis application. *IJPTT 5*, ISSN: 2249.

4. Crauser, A., Mehlhorn, K., Meyer, U., & Sanders, P. (1998). *A parallelization of dijkstra's shortest path algorithm* (pp. 722–731). Berlin Heidelberg: Springer.
5. Thippeswamy, K., Hanumanthappa, J., & Manjaiah, D.H. (2014). A study on contrast and comparison between bellman-ford algorithm and Dijkstra's algorithm. In *National Conference on wireless Networks-09, Dec 2014*.
6. MATLAB Tutorials. http://www.tutorialspoint.com/matlab.
7. Bell, N., & Garland, M. (2009). Implementing sparse matrix-vector multiplication on throughput-oriented processors. In *Proceedings of the 2009 ACM/IEEE Conference on Supercomputing, Nov. 2009* (pp. 18:1–18:11).
8. Dijkstra, E. W. (1959). A note on two problems in connexion with graphs. *Numerische Mathematik, 1*(1), 269–271.
9. Fredman, M. L., & Tarjan, R. E. (1987). Fibonacci heaps and their uses in improved network optimization algorithms. *Journal of the ACM, 34*(3), 596–615.
10. Agarwal, P., & Dutta, M. (2015). New approach of bellman ford algorithm on gpu using compute unified design architecture. *IJCA (0975–8887) 110*(13), 11–15.
11. Horowitz, E., & Sahni, S. (1975). Fundamentals of computer algorithms.

Supervised Link Prediction Using Forecasting Models on Weighted Online Social Network

Anshul Gupta, Shalki Sharma and Hirdesh Shivhare

Abstract With the increase in size of online social network, the need to predict the future links among the nodes is enlarged. In this paper, an efficient prediction of links in the online social network is performed by considering link weights along with the temporal information. Although the existing technique is based on either weighted networks or time series based, the link prediction is based on the combination of weighted network and temporal data; and then applying supervised and unsupervised learning algorithm to predict the future link among the nodes (users) in the online social networking sites. Our task is to investigate that a weighted temporal network can be used with supervised learning to achieve a high-performance link prediction. Here research focus is to take weighted as well as unweighted network and to apply a similarity function for generating a set of connected nodes, then a time series is built for every pair of nonconnected nodes, and forecasting model is deployed on the time series. The final results obtained using supervised and unsupervised learning shown acceptable results when a weighted temporal network is used.

Keywords Link prediction · Link weights · Forecasting · Supervised learning

A. Gupta (✉)
MPSTME, NMIMS, Mumbai, India
e-mail: anshul.gupta@nmims.edu

S. Sharma
NITTTR, Bhopal, India
e-mail: shalkisharma27@gmail.com

H. Shivhare
SOIT, RGPV, Bhopal, India
e-mail: hirdeshshivhare1988@gmail.com

© Springer Science+Business Media Singapore 2016
S.C. Satapathy et al. (eds.), *Proceedings of International Conference on ICT for Sustainable Development*, Advances in Intelligent Systems and Computing 409, DOI 10.1007/978-981-10-0135-2_24

1 Introduction

As internet usage is growing at a tremendous rate, there are possibilities of more relationships and connections among the social users and various groups. A social network is formally represented as a graph, where vertices represents users, groups or organizations, and edges that connect them indicate their social relationships, shared features, and associations, where associations depends on the users' common interest. In online social networks, connections among users are open and dynamic, as new edges and vertices with time frame are added to the network.

Social network analysis (SNA) is an important field of research which deals with techniques and strategies for studying online social network [1]. Social network analysis can be subcategorized into link prediction, which focuses on links between objects rather than objects themselves. The main objective of link prediction is to solve the problem of predicting the future occurrence of links among online social network users (node) [2]. Therefore, link prediction has become interesting and different from conventional data mining which simply focuses on objects.

Evolvement of social network includes numerous variable parameters, so it has created complex problems for link prediction. But it is easy to evaluate the relationships (association) among nodes. Some of the questions that can be put forward are: In what way the association changes with respect to time? How other nodes affect the association between two users? What factors that impact relationships among users? The problem that we deal with is predicting the possibility of future association among nodes, considering that at current time, the association is not present between the two nodes. So this problem is commonly termed as the link prediction problem [3,4].

Link prediction can be applied in several fields like molecular biology, bibliographic domain, criminal investigations, and recommender systems. For tackling the problem of link prediction, numerous researches have been performed [2, 5, 6]. The well-known research formulates its results using topological patterns. Actually this research is when, at a time t in a particular network, topological similarity metrics are applied to nonconnected pair of nodes to predict that whether a link will occur at time t_0 ($t_0 > t$). So for link prediction process, the scores assigned to every pair of nodes generated by these metrics are used.

Link prediction without considering the time constraint has also shown decent results in previous researches, but they fail in exploring the network evolution as such; since they only statically analyze the network at the current moment. In our work, forecasting models are used to deal with the time series-based problem along with similarity metrics and supervised learning technique.

In Sect. 2, a brief definition of link prediction and its approaches is provided and the strategies need to deal with the link prediction problem is also defined. In Sect. 3, proposed methodology that is followed is summarized along with the similarity metrics, dataset description, and forecasting models. Section 4 contains the experiments performed with supervised and unsupervised strategies, and the result generated are shown. Finally, Sect. 5 concludes the paper.

2 Link Prediction

For predicting link among the pair of nodes, previously detected and analyzed states of networks are taken into consideration [6]. Numerous methods can deal with the link prediction problem. They are based on node features (content and/or semantics), probabilistic models (relational learning), and topological/structural patterns. Main approach among these three is topological-based approach.

The best approach with a good performance and easy implementation is topological approach [5, 7–9]. Besides topological metrics are focused on the network structure, temporal features are also considered. Therefore, our research is based on temporal metrics.

For dealing with the prediction of links, after the similarity scores are calculated, supervised and unsupervised strategies are applied. Unsupervised approach is easy to implement as it does not requires a labeled training set for link prediction; whereas in supervised approach, a labeled training set is needed. Supervised strategy is a classification approach where the nodes which are linked are assigned to class 1, i.e., positive class and nonconnected nodes are assigned to class 0, i.e., negative class. So, for an efficient link prediction, application of these two strategies is a must [10–12].

3 Proposed Methodology

The link prediction problem in social network is a major issue as it totally depends on how efficiently and exactly the "future relationships" between two nodes in a social network can be predicted.

In Fig. 1, it can be seen that in all the nodes, the nodes a and b are more efficiently dynamic through the time. For detecting these types of information, a strategy that uses temporal information for link prediction should be used.

Earlier, for overcoming this limitation some of the researchers have already worked in this field. Association rules explaining the functions of nodes and appearances has been discovered in [14] by Berlingerio et al. For computing the

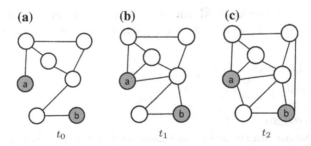

Fig. 1 Example of network states at different times [13] a) Links between nodes at time t_0 b) Links between nodes at time t_1 c) Links between nodes at time t_2

probabilities of new connections in [15] Huang et al. used an autoregressive model and merged occurrence of links with the time series. Potgeiter et al. in [14] used pair of nonconnected nodes to calculate their representative scores using different types of metrics over time periods. The methods discussed show that the use of temporal information greatly improves the link prediction which can be used for further investigation purpose in the research field.

In 2011, Hially and Ricardo, implemented "supervised learning algorithms"— Niave Bayes, J48, IBk, and SVM on "co-authorship networks datasets" to compare that link prediction on unweighted networks have less performance than weighted networks, except in some case studies where weighted graph network taken in different has less precision rate then unweighted network in Naive bayes algorithm [16].

From the previous research [16, 13], it is known that weighted network will be more reluctant for link prediction, but the research was limited to co-authorship network domain and they have not applied the forecasting model for efficient link prediction. So to enhance the efficiency of an link prediction system, some questions are need to be answered like—which network should be used (weighted or unweighted), which types of learning algorithms should be applied (supervised or unsupervised), whether the use of forecasting models increase the efficiency of an link prediction system?. In our work to check the answer of all these problems, a combination of supervised weighted temporal network is formed and its efficiency is compared with supervised unweighted temporal network and unsupervised weighted and unweighted temporal network, respectively.

In our research, a movie lens dataset is considered of both weighted and unweighted versions. Weighted version of the dataset contains the weight between the nodes and unweighted dataset does not contain the weight between the two nodes. A similarity metrics is then applied on both the dataset. Similarity metric is different for both weighted and unweighted network. Then a forecasting model is applied on the similarity scores. Finally, the supervised and unsupervised techniques are applied on the node sets produced by forecasting model.

3.1 Dataset

The detail of the Movielens1 M dataset, which is generated by the grouplens research team for the research work and, is used in our work as follows (Table 1).

Table 1 Standard movie lens dataset

User	6040
Movies	3706
Ratings	1,000,209
Timestamp	Seconds since midnight Coordinated Universal Time (UTC) of January 1, 1970

Table 2 Attributes of weighted dataset

UserID	UserID1	Weight	MovieID	Rating	Timestamp

Table 3 Attributes of unweighted dataset

UserID	UserID1	MovieID	Rating	Timestamp

In this paper, two versions of datasets, weighted and unweighted, have been obtained from the standard dataset. The weighted dataset contains a set of attributes which denotes a set of links between two nodes and their weights such as (Table 2).

In this type of dataset, 100 users are taken along with their links with weights. The nonweighted dataset contains a set of attributes such as (Tables 3).

3.2 Applying Similarity Metrics

For the prediction of connecting links on the weighted and unweighted network, similarity metrics is one of the techniques to measure the similarity between different nodes so that the similarity of different nodes can be detected. There are several similarity metrics that can be used but in our methodology the number of common neighbors metrics is used as it has shown satisfactory results in previous works. Some of the similarity metrics are mentioned below.

3.2.1 Number of Common Neighbors (CN)

For unweighted networks, it is defined as the number of nodes which are directly related with nodes p and q:

$$CN(p,q) = |\Gamma(p) \cap \Gamma(q)| \tag{1}$$

In link prediction, the CN measure is the prevalent metric adopted due to its simplicity. It is intuitive, because as the number of common neighbor increases the possibility of link between two nodes increases [13]. For weighted networks, it can be formulated as

$$CN(p,q) = \sum_{r \in \Gamma(p) \cap \Gamma(q)} w(p,r) + w(q,r) \tag{2}$$

If node p is connected to node r and node q is connected to node r, then there is a huge probability of node p connecting to node q. For collaboration networks, Newman [13] showed that at time t, a relationship exists between the number of common neighbors of p and q, with a high probability of their future collaboration.

3.3   Forecasting Models

Forecasting models are used for the future prediction based on the previous and present data analysis. There are several forecasting models, but in our research moving average is used as in previous work which showed good results.

3.3.1   Moving Average

It can be defined as the mean of all the recent values that are predicted from the dataset currently [17]. It can be given as

$$\hat{X}_t = \frac{X_{t-1} + X_{t-2} + \cdots + X_{t-n}}{n} \tag{3}$$

where, X_t is the time series forecasting

$t = 1, 2 \ldots T$ be the time series
n = Number of most recent values

3.3.2   Supervised Learning Algorithm and Unsupervised Learning Algorithms

In this paper, various supervised learning algorithms such as AD tree, ID3, SVM, Random Forest, and Simple Cart algorithms are applied on the weighted and unweighted algorithm to test the performance of the link prediction. For validating, various unsupervised learning algorithms such as k-means, Hierarchical, Expected Maximization, and Cob-web algorithms are implemented to compare the results with the supervised learning strategies.

3.4   Proposed Methodology

D Dataset
Dw_i Weighted Dataset
Duw_i Unweighted Dataset
SMW_{CN} Weighted Similarity Measure (Common Neighbor)
$SMUW_{CN}$ Unweighted Similarity Measure (Common Neighbor)
T_s Time Series
FM_{MA} Forecasting Model (Moving Average)
M_s Modified Score

1. Create a GUI environment for the Weighted Temporal Supervised Link Prediction;
2. Choose a desired Dataset D either Weighted Dw_i or Unweighted Duw_i;
3. If $D = Dw_i$
   Then $SMW_{CN}(Dw_i)$
   Else if $D = Duw_i$
   Then $SMUW_{CN}(Duw_i)$;
4. Let (x_i, y_i) be the nonconnected pair of nodes then for each pair

$$T_s = SMW_{CN}(x_i, y_i) \text{ or } T_s = SMUW_{CN}(x_i, y_i);$$

After the time series has achieved, the forecast can be find by implementing a forecasting model:

5. Apply Forecasting Model on the T_s

$$FM_{MA}(T_s);$$

6. For each T_s of (x_i, y_i)

$$M_s = FM_{MA}(T_s) + 1;$$

7. For each M_s

$$SS(M_s) \text{ or } US(M_s)$$

4 Experiments and Results

In this paper, a weighted temporal network and unweighted temporal network is taken and is passed through the supervised and unsupervised strategy, the results obtained show that weighted temporal network has high performance than the unweighted temporal network when implemented with both supervised and unsupervised algorithms.

Another scenario that was observed is that the results obtained using supervised strategy are better than that obtained from the unsupervised strategy. In our work, the similarity function used is number of common neighbors and the forecasting model used is moving average. Further elaboration of their observed results is mentioned in next subsections.

4.1 Experiments Performed with Supervised Learning Algorithms

In this research, several learning algorithms are used for the link prediction purpose of the both datasets. All the algorithms are taken from WEKA and all experiments were applied with the default parameters of WEKA [18]. For an accurate result, all the algorithms were evaluated using tenfold cross-validation. Cross-validation is used for evaluating and comparing learning algorithms.

The algorithms taken from WEKA are

    i. ADtree—used for classification and it generalizes decision trees [19];

    ii. ID3—the precursor to the C4.5 algorithm and is used to generate a decision tree [20];

    iii. CART—Decision Tree learning,Rule based and parameters do not pass;

    iv. SVM—Used for classification and for analyzing data and recognizing patterns.

    v. Random forest—Makes number of decision trees.

All these algorithms are used to enhance the performance measures for the link prediction task. Table 4 shows the precision, recall, F-measure, and accuracy obtained when unweighted dataset is taken into account along with the common neighbor similarity metrics and moving average forecasting model. It can be easily seen that CART is performing best among the five supervised algorithms with an accuracy of 88 %. The worst performance is noted from AD Tree.

In Table 5 results are obtained using supervised learning on weighted dataset are shown. These results are better than the results obtained using unweighted dataset. All the four performance measures are having higher value than the values that are present in Table 4, which concludes that when a weighted dataset is used for a link prediction work, it will be a more efficient technique than using unweighted dataset.

Precision is an important measure for measuring performance. It is also called as a positive predictive value and it is the fraction of retrieved instances that are relevant. Precision is defined as the ratio of the number of correctly classified links between the two users of the dataset to the total number of classified instances in a link prediction system.

Table 4 Results obtained using supervised learning on unweighted dataset

Unweighted dataset	Unweighted/common neighbor/moving avg.			
	Precision	Recall	F-measure	Accuracy (%)
AD Tree	0.45	0.52	0.48	47
ID3	0.67	0.74	0.71	68
CART	0.84	0.86	0.85	88
SVM	0.79	0.78	0.78	81
Random forest	0.76	0.69	0.72	78

Table 5 Results obtained using supervised learning on weighted dataset

Weighted dataset	Weighted/common neighbor/moving avg.			
	Precision	Recall	F-measure	Accuracy (%)
AD tree	0.53	0.59	0.56	55
ID3	0.69	0.78	0.61	71
CART	0.86	0.87	0.87	89
SVM	0.77	0.59	0.69	79
Random forest	0.79	0.73	0.76	81

Fig. 2 Precision obtained using supervised algorithms

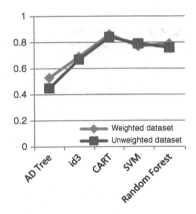

In Fig. 2 precision is shown when five supervised algorithms are implemented with the common neighbor similarity function and using moving average forecasting method on both weighted and unweighted dataset. Figure 2 shows that the precision for weighted dataset is greater than unweighted dataset. As precision denotes performance is in such a way that higher the precision higher is the performance. Therefore, weighted dataset is shows higher performance than the unweighted dataset.

The recall measure in the proposed work is calculated on the basis of the number links classified correctly and the total number of links that can be formed between the two users.

Recall is also an important measure of performance. Recall is the fraction of the relevant instances that are retrieved. From Fig. 3, it can be easily analyzed that recall is greater for weighted dataset, which shows the good performance of weighted dataset.

F-measure is the harmonic mean of precision and recall. Figure 4 shows the comparative analysis of F-measure using Ad Tree, ID3, CART, SVM, and random forest obtained on weighted and unweighted dataset. It can be easily seen that cart is performing best for both weighted and unweighted dataset.

Fig. 3 Recall obtained using supervised algorithms

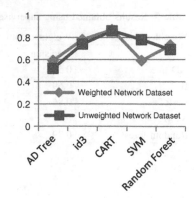

Fig. 4 F-measure obtained using supervised algorithms

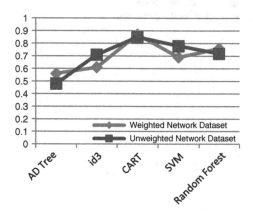

Accuracy is the best performance measure used for link prediction. Accuracy is the percentage of number of links that are classified correctly. Figure 5 shows the accuracy retrieved by supervised algorithms on weighted and unweighted dataset. As from the results, it is easily visible that whenever weighted network dataset is used it performs better than unweighted dataset in all supervised learning algorithms which are used. From the results, i.e., precision, recall, F-measure, and accuracy, cart is performing better from all.

4.2 Experiments Performed with Unsupervised Algorithms

To compare the supervised strategy results with the unsupervised strategies, four unsupervised algorithms have been implemented. They are:

i. Simple K-means—works on the principle of cluster formation
ii. EM—Used for both labeled and unlabelled datasets.
iii. Cob-Web—Used for an incremental hierarchical clustering
iv. Hierarchical—nearest neighbor clustering

Fig. 5 Accuracy obtained
using supervised algorithms

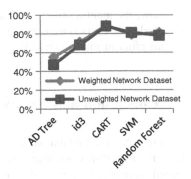

As to validate the proposed work, we have implemented unsupervised strategies both on weighted and unweighted dataset using the same similarity metrics and forecasting model, i.e., common neighbor and moving average, respectively.

Table 6 illustrates the results which are obtained from unweighted dataset using unsupervised learning. The best performance is shown by Cob-Web with the highest accuracy of 72 % which is far less than the accuracy obtained using supervised algorithms. Same is the case with precision, recall, and F-measure.

From Table 7, it is seen that Hierarchical is performing best when unsupervised algorithms are applied on weighted dataset with the highest accuracy of 79 %. Comparing Tables 6 and 7, it can be concluded that using weighted dataset is efficient than unweighted dataset when whatever algorithm is used.

Table 6 Experimental results on unweighted dataset using unsupervised algorithms

Unweighted dataset	Unweighted/common neighbor/moving avg.			
	Precision	Recall	F-measure	Accuracy (%)
k-means	0.32	0.41	0.36	40
EM	0.51	0.62	0.56	54
Cob-web	0.68	0.67	0.675	72
Hierarchical	0.62	0.64	0.63	66

Table 7 Experimental results on weighted dataset using unsupervised algorithms

Weighted dataset	Weighted/common neighbor/moving avg.			
	Precision	Recall	F-measure	Accuracy (%)
k-means	0.35	0.44	0.395	42
EM	0.54	0.63	0.585	60
Cob-web	0.73	0.71	0.72	77
Hierarchical	0.76	0.79	0.775	79

Now, the main motive is validated, from Tables 4, 5, 6, and 7, it can be easily concluded that supervised weighted temporal link prediction system should be used for an efficient link prediction.

5 Conclusion and Future Work

This research showed that supervised link prediction on weighted temporal network has greater performance than unweighted temporal network in the context of online social network. The use of forecasting model has proved to be efficient as it increases the performance of the link prediction. Alternatively, it is also observed that the results obtained using supervised link prediction revealed better results when it confronts the unsupervised link prediction for weighted and unweighted dataset taken one at a time. So to use a weighted network considering its temporal information and implementing it with the supervised strategies will result in an accurate and highly efficient link prediction.

In future, this work can be expanded using different similarity function and forecasting model on a different dataset. The dataset can be considered in a different context to make different versions of weighted and unweighted dataset.

References

1. Wasserman, S., & Faust, K. (1994). Social network analysis. In *Methods and applications*. Cambridge University press.
2. Wang, C., & Satuluri, V. (2007). Local probabilistic models for link prediction. In *ICDM 2007*.
3. Hasan, M. A., Chaoji, V., Salem, S., & Zaki, M. (2006). Link prediction using supervised learning. In *Proceedings of SDM 06 workshop on Link Analysis, Counterterrorism and Security*.
4. Ricardo, P., Soares, D.S., Ricardo, B.C.P. (2012). Time series based link prediction. In *WCCI2012 IEEE World Congress on Computional Intelligence*.
5. Xiang, E. W. (2008). A survey on link prediction models for social network data. *Science And Technology*.
6. Getoor, L., & Diehl, C. P. (2005). Link mining: A survey. *SigKDD Explorations Special Issue on Link Mining*.
7. Liben-Nowell, D., & Kleinberg, J. (2007). The link-prediction problem for social networks. *Journal of the American Society for Information Science and Technology, 58*, 1019–1031.
8. Murata, T., & Moriyasu, S. (2008). Link prediction based on structural properties of online social networks. *New Generation Computing, 26*(3), 245–257.
9. Huang, Z. (2006). Link prediction based on graph topology: The predictive value of the generalized clustering coefficient.
10. Barabasi, A. L., & Bonabeau, E. (2003). Scale-free networks. *Scientific American, 288*(5), 60–69.
11. Berlingerio, M., Bonchi, F., Bringmann, B., & Gionis, A. (2009). Mining graph evolution rules. In *Proceedings of the European Conference on Machine Learning and Knowledge Discovery in Databases: Part I, ECML PKDD'09* (pp 115–130). Springer.

12. Tan, P.-N., Steinbach, M., & Kumar, V. (2005). Introduction to data mining. Addison Wesley.
13. Newman, M. E. J. (2001). Clustering and preferential attachment in growing networks, *Physical Review Letters E, 64.*
14. Potgieter, A., April, K. A., Cooke, R. J. E., & Osunmakinde, I. O. (2007). Temporality in link prediction: Understanding social complexity.
15. Huang, Z., & Dennis, K. J. L. (2009). The time-series link prediction problem with applications in communication surveillance. *INFORMS Journal on Computing, 21,* 286–303.
16. Rodrigues, H., & Ricardo, B.C P. (2011). Supervised link prediction in weighted networks. In *Proceedings of International Joint Conference on Neural Networks, IEEE.*
17. Wheelwright, S.C., & Makridakis, S.G. (1985). Forecasting methods for management. In *Systems and controls for financial management series.* Wiley.
18. Hall, M., Frank, E., Holmes, G., Pfahringer, B., Reutemann, P., & Witten, I. H. (2009). The weka data mining software: An update. *SIGKDD Explorations, 11*(1), 10–18.
19. Pfahringer, B., Holmes, G., & Kirkby, R. (2001). Optimizing the induction of alternating decision trees. In *Proceedings of the Fifth Pacific-Asia Conference on Advances in Knowledge Discovery and Data Mining* (pp. 477–487).
20. Quinlan, J. R. (1986). Induction of decision trees. *Mach. Learn., 1*(1), 81–106.

Dual-Band Rectangular-Shaped Antenna with Sideway Extension at Top and Bottom for WLAN and WiMax Applications

Shalini Porwal, Ajay Dadhich, Sanjeev Yadav, H.S. Mewara and M.M. Sharma

Abstract A dual-band rectangular antenna with sideway extension at top and bottom having applications in WLAN and WiMAX is discussed in this paper. The designed antenna composed of a rectangular patch with wider sideway extension at bottom and smaller sideway extension at top. Antenna is designed and simulated using CST microwave studio software. The design parameters are selected to achieve a dual resonance at 5.8 and 3.30 GHz having applications in WLAN and WiMax. The first band (3.30 GHz) is controlled by the upper sideway extension of the antenna while the lower sideway extension controls the second resonating band (5.8 GHz). The simulated results show that the antenna has the bandwidths of 174 MHz (5726–5900 MHz) and 327 MHz (3127–3454 MHz) covering WLAN at the 5.8 GHz bands and WiMAX in the 3.30 GHz bands, respectively.

Keywords Dual-band antenna · Bandwidth · Radiation pattern · WLAN · WiMax

S. Porwal (✉) · A. Dadhich · H.S. Mewara · M.M. Sharma
Department of Electronics and Communication Engineering,
Government Engineering College, Ajmer, India
e-mail: shalinip49@gmail.com

A. Dadhich
e-mail: ajaydadhich13@gmail.com

H.S. Mewara
e-mail: hsmewara@gmail.com

M.M. Sharma
e-mail: mmsjpr@gmail.com

S. Yadav
Department of Electronics and Communication Engineering,
Government Women Engineering College, Ajmer, India
e-mail: sanjeev.mnit@gmail.com

© Springer Science+Business Media Singapore 2016
S.C. Satapathy et al. (eds.), *Proceedings of International Conference on ICT for Sustainable Development*, Advances in Intelligent Systems and Computing 409, DOI 10.1007/978-981-10-0135-2_25

1 Introduction

With the rapid development of wireless communication in the recently, there is huge demand for designing low-cost, small and multifrequency antennas for mobile wireless devices. For perfect transmission of information in forms of video, multimedia and data, multiband antenna has become prime consideration in wireless communication. Due to its obvious advantages like low profile, cost-effectiveness, compactness and easy to interact with circuits, microstrip patch antenna is considered to be favourite. Both WLAN and WiMAX can be integrated into one single system using these antennas.

For fulfilment of all these requirements, different designs of antenna have been reported [1–6]. The monopole antennas have various configurations. These are

T-shape [1], V-sleeve flared shaped [2] and Y-shape [3], are often taken for designing multiband antennas because of simple design, easy to implement, wide bandwidth and stable radiation patterns. But due to large size, these designs are not suitable for the mobile application which required limited space. In order to make compact multiband antenna, many slot structures [4–6] had been proposed. In [4], strip monopole was used to feed triangular-slot antenna. A dual-band antenna [5] was proposed for the 2.4 and 5.2 GHz WLAN bands. This paper is modification of design reported in [6]. In this paper, we present dual-band antenna designed for integrating WiMAX and WLAN applications. This antenna is operating at two resonating frequencies 3.3 and 5.8 GHz. FR4 is used as substrate for designing this antenna.

This paper is presented as follows. The design and geometry are explained in Sect. 2. In Sect. 3, results of designed antenna are presented with different monitoring parameters. Finally, Sect. 4 comprises of brief conclusion of this letter.

2 Antenna Design

Finite integration technique (FTT)-based CST microwave studio software is used for design and analysis of proposed antenna. The antenna designed here is modification of design described in [6]. It can be seen in Fig. 1 that antenna comprises of step slot and extension in lower and upper branch of antenna. In our study, feed line of width

1.5 mm is used with characteristic impedance of 50 Ω to obtain desired resonating frequencies. The FR4 ($\epsilon = 4.5$) is used as dielectric substrate with thickness as 50 μm and electrical loss tangent as 0.025.

The detailed dimensions of patch and ground plane can be seen in Figs. 1 and 2, respectively. Copper ground plane of 25 × 14.77 mm square is adhered on one side of substrate 27 × 36 mm square. Microstrip line and sideways extension of antenna are printed on other side of substrate. It is observed that dimension of ground plane and feed line has been carefully selected to obtain desired resonating frequencies.

Fig. 1 Front view of designed antenna

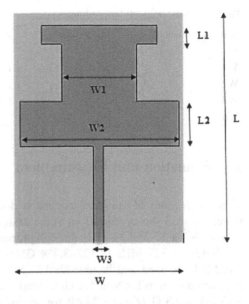

Fig. 2 Back view of designed antenna

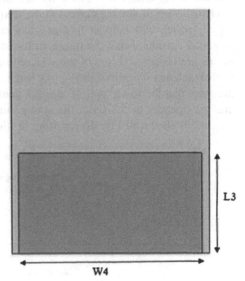

The lower part of antenna controls the lower resonating frequency, i.e. 3.3 GHz. The variation in lower resonating frequency can be obtained by changing dimension of lower branch of proposed antenna. The upper part of antenna controls the higher resonating mode at 5.8 GHz. This modification in design reported in [6] achieved the application of antenna for both WLAN and WiMAX applications and increased in gain at both resonating frequencies (Table 1).

Table 1 Dimensions of designed antenna

Antenna parameter	Value (mm)	Antenna parameter	Value (mm)
W	27	L	36
W1	11.8	L1	3
W2	25	L2	7
W3	1.5	L3	14.77
W4	25		

3 Simulation and Measurement

Simulation result of designed antenna is done using CST microwave studio software. Figure 3 shows return loss of the designed antenna. The antenna is excited at two modes at 3.3 and 5.8 GHz through proper impedance matching. The impedance bandwidth is 327 MHz (3.127–3.454 GHz), suitable for the WiMAX standard in the 3.3 GHz band and bandwidth 174 MHz (5.726–5.900 GHz) is covering the requirement for WLAN in 5.8 GHz band. The return loss for designed antenna is −23 dB at 3.3 GHz and −24 dB for second band at 5.8 GHz.

Distribution of surface current at the frequencies of 3.3 and 5.8 GHz is given in Fig. 4, which will help in further study of dual-band operation property of the proposed antenna. From the figure, different current distributions in two resonating modes are observed. Most of the surface currents are concentrated along the lower part of antenna described in Fig. 4a when the antenna operates at 3.3 GHz. This indicates that the lower part of antenna generates low-frequency resonance. When antenna operates at 5.8 GHz, the strong current flow is observed in upper part of antenna as shown in Fig. 4b resulting in higher resonance as expected.

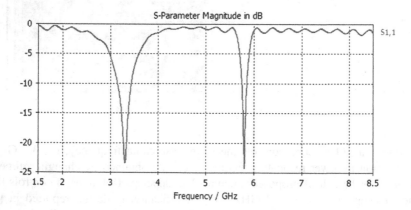

Fig. 3 Simulated return loss for dual-band designed antenna at 3.3 and 5.8 GHz

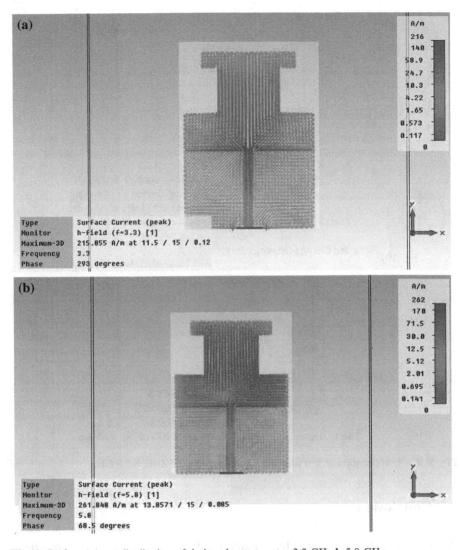

Fig. 4 Surface current distribution of designed antenna at **a** 3.3 GHz **b** 5.8 GHz

Figure 5 exhibits radiation pattern of designed antenna at both resonating frequencies. Radiation pattern obtained is unidirectional in nature and looks acceptable both at 3.3 and 5.8 GHz. Antenna have achieved gain of −10.4 dB at 3.3 GHz and of 5.1 dB at 5.8 GHz.

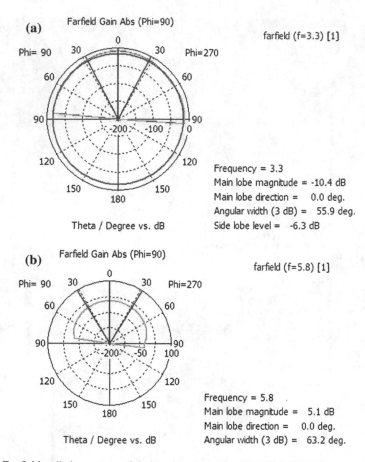

Fig. 5 Far-field radiation pattern of designed antenna at a 3.3 GHz b 5.8 GHz

4 Conclusion

A compact dual-band antenna for WLAN and WiMAX applications is presented. The designed antenna has obtained satisfactory performance, while maintaining compactness and increased in gain. Simulated results of designed antenna features stable far field radiation pattern, acceptable return loss and compact size making it suitable for WLAN and WiMAX application.

References

1. Chang, T. N. & Jiang, J. H. (2009). Meandered T-shaped monopole antenna. *IEEE Transactions Antennas Propagation, 57*(12), 3976–3978.

2. Augustin, G., Bybi, P. C., Sarin, V. P., Mohanan, P., Aanandan, C. K. & Vasudevan, K. (2008). A compact dual-band planar antenna for DCS-1900/ PCS/PHS, WCDMA/IMT-2000, and WLAN applications. *IEEE Antennas Wireless Propagation Letters, 7,* 108–111.
3. Liu, W.-C. & Hsu, C.-F. (2005). Dual-band CPW-fed Y-shaped monopole antenna for PCS/WLAN application. *Electronics Letters, 41,* 390–391.
4. Augustin, G., Shynu, S. V., Mohanan, P., Aanandan, C. K. & Vasudevan, K. (2003). Compact dual-band antenna for wireless access point. *Electronics Letters, 42,* 502–503.
5. Zhang, Z., Iskander, M. F., Langer, J.-C. & Mathews, J. (2005). Dual band WLAN dipole antenna using an internal matching circuit. *IEEE Transactions Antennas Propagation, 53*(5), 1813–1818.
6. Khaleela, H. R., Al-Rizzob, H. M., Ruckera, D. G. & Al-Naiemya, Y. (2011) Flexible Printed Monopole Antennas for WLAN Applications. In *IEEE International Symposium on Antennas and Propagation* (pp. 1334–1337). Spokane, WA.

A Framework to Rank Nodes in Social Media Graph Based on Sentiment-Related Parameters

Meghna Chaudhary and Harish Kumar

Abstract Social networks provide a platform for users to interact and engage in various activities. Information pertaining to social media can be shared, ideas can be put forward and opinions can be analysed. Sentiment analysis of user comments can be done to extract important information and to make informed decisions. This paper elucidates previous work done on sentiment analysis and different ranking techniques for utilisation in different applications. A methodology is proposed in this paper for ranking users based on parameters such as likes, shares and user comments. Two ranking techniques are proposed in the methodology. One technique is based on the cosine similarity and the other involves features such as user comments.

Keywords Social media · Facebook · Access token · Sentiment analysis · Ranking

1 Introduction

Social media usage has become an essential part of day-to-day activities of people. Graphs are used to represent social networks. Nodes represent social network users and edges are used to model relationships among them. Different social networking services such as Facebook, Twitter, YouTube, etc., allow users to view content posted by others as well as to post their own content or opinions. Opinions given by users can be used to mine important information. Text sentiment analysis or opinion

M. Chaudhary (✉) · H. Kumar
University Institute of Engineering and Technology, Panjab University,
Chandigarh, India
e-mail: meghnaofficial24@gmail.com

H. Kumar
e-mail: harishk@pu.ac.in

© Springer Science+Business Media Singapore 2016
S.C. Satapathy et al. (eds.), *Proceedings of International Conference on ICT for Sustainable Development*, Advances in Intelligent Systems and Computing 409, DOI 10.1007/978-981-10-0135-2_26

mining is used for this purpose. Ranking is a fundamental part of several information retrieval problems such as sentiment analysis, document retrieval, etc.

This paper proposes a methodology to rank users based on their likes and
preferences. There are several web pages like Facebook page of 'Panjab University,
Chandigarh' where large number of social media users write comments or show
their likeness. Data can be extracted from such a data source. Parameters including
number of likes, shares and sentiments carried by users' comments, etc., are considered for this methodology. Sentiment analysis can be carried out to extract
opinions from comments made by users. After ranking, results can be compared
with cosine similarity technique to determine performance of proposed methodology. Section 2 summarises the literature reviewed. Section 3, elucidates the proposed methodology for ranking users. Section 4, gives code snippets to obtain
identification detail, name of the user and users' comments and likes for a particular
post. The paper is concluded along with the future scope in Sect. 4.

2 Literature Review

Social media users can be put into categories such as (a) friends (b) friends of
friends (c) nonfriends at the same institute (d) nonfriends at different institutes [1].
Social media is a powerful marketing tool. Users can like the pages of various
companies or specific products. Users' comments can be examined to improve
advertising strategy and quality of products [2]. Opinion mining involves understanding of target topics and recognition of positive and negative sentiments [3].
Sentiment classification determines whether document or sentence carries positive
or negative opinion [4].

2.1 Sentiment Analysis

Sentiment analysis problem begins with opinion target or object. An object has a set
of features. The person who reveals his viewpoint is opinion holder. Opinion ori-
entations may be positive or negative. An object 'o' can be portrayed by a set of
features F = $\{f_1, f_2, ..., f_n\}$, which includes object itself. Each feature $f_i \in F$ can be
indicated with feature's synonyms which is a finite set of words or phrases $W_i = \{w_{i1},
w_{i2}, ..., w_{im}\}$. There are two types of opinions. A quintuple $(o_j, f_{jk}, oo_{ijkl}, h_i, t_l)$ is used
to express a direct opinion. Here, o_j is an object, f_{jk} is object o_j's feature, oo_{ijkl} is
orientation of opinion on object o_j's feature f_{jk}, h_i is opinion holder, and t_l is the time
when opinion is expressed by h_i. oo_{ijkl} can be positive, negative, or neutral. On the
basis of shared opinions, preference relations of two or more objects is depicted by
comparative opinion [5]. There are four approaches to sentiment analysis which are
as follows: (a) Keyword spotting: Classification is done based on the presence of
unambiguous affect words (like sad and happy); (b) Lexical affinity: Besides

identifying affect words, affinity to particular emotions is also assigned to words; (c) Statistical methods: These involve the use of soft computing techniques like Naïve Bayes and Support Vector Machines; (d) Concept-based techniques: Semantic analysis using concept-based techniques involve the use of semantic networks [3]. Main tasks involved in the examination of opinions expressed by users are: (a) Object identification: Relevant and irrelevant objects must be identified by system; (b) Feature extraction and synonym grouping: It involves identification of noun, noun phrases and verb features. Synonym features need to be grouped because same feature can be expressed by people using different words; (c) Opinion-orientation determination: It must be examined whether a sentence expresses an opinion on a feature and if expressed opinion is positive or negative; (d) Integration: In the quintuple, five chunks of information need to be integrated [5].

A linear classifier has been built to predict whether same rating is to be given to all features of a product [6]. Classification of documents has also been done on the basis of ranking scores of reviews and polarity of documents being positive or negative [7, 8]. Syntactic phrases have been also been used to classify documents [9]. In [10], a set of seed opinion words and a knowledge base (bootstrapping) have been used to classify documents. To discover subjective sentences, sentence level granularity has been used for analysis [11]. Semantic frames have also been taken into consideration [12, 13] involves the examination of a prototype system which allows sentiment analysis of data in a social network in real-time. A sentiment identification system (SES) has been developed in [2]. In [14], compositional semantics have been proposed. Experiments were carried out on movie reviews to find out overall sentiments of documents [2]. Documents were classified thereafter in [15]. In [16], an efficient and accurate algorithm on Chinese micro-blog content has been proposed. Table 1 summarizes some of the previous work done in sentiment analysis containing articles reference [2, 7, 13, 16]. Reference numbers and authors names are specified in first column. Second column specifies platform used to extract data to work with. Classifier used for analysis is stated in third column. Fourth column specifies results of analysis.

2.2 Ranking

In ranking, a document is represented by a vector $(t_1, t_2, t_3, t_4, \ldots t_n)$ with a component for each term. There are several models for ranking such as vector space model. tf − idf weighting, cosine similarity and other methods can be used to calculate scores for ranking. tf − idf weights refer to the product of term frequencies and inverse document frequencies. Term frequency refers to the number of times a term appears in document. Inverse document frequency is log of ratio of total number of documents in collection to number of documents in collection containing a particular term. In vector space model, cosine similarity is cosine of angle made by two vectors in vector space. [17] proposes an approach to check trustworthiness of social network users by ranking them. A node has a high trust score when given a

Table 1 Summary of some of the previous work done in sentiment analysis

References	Platform used	Classifier used	Results obtained
Kunpeng et al. [2]	Facebook and twitter	Decision tree, neural network, logistic regression, random forest	Random forest demonstrates greatest accuracy
Pang et al. [7]	Dataset from http://www.cs.cornell.edu/people/pabo/-movie-review-data/	Naïve bayes, maximum entropy, support vector machine	Support vector machine shows best performance and Naïve Bayes shows worst performance
Santidhanyaroj et al. [13]	Facebook and twitter	Support vector machine and naïve bayes	Support Vector Machine has highest overall accuracy. Naïve Bayes works better on negative documents
Zhao et al. [16]	Sina micro-blog	Optimized sentiment analysis method on microblog content (SAMC)	Optimised SAMC is 100.64 times more efficient than SAMC algorithm

positive vote by a highly trusted node or a negative vote by a highly distrusted node. In a directional social network namely Twitter, ranking of users is done [18]. Retweet to tweet ratio is taken as influence measure. Supervised ranking aggregation is suggested in [19]. Retweets and mentions are parameters considered to determine influence. [20] addresses the problem of search for people to follow (SPTF). An online search system has also been built named Xunren. It has four parts: tag expansion and prediction, rank, index and crawler modules. page_rank, tunk_rank, follow_rank and forward_rank algorithms were chosen to determine performance of tag expansion and ranking. [21] proposes an approach to identify close friends by ranking users in acquaintance list. "RankScore" method is used. It takes into account relationship, interaction and personal score.

A generalized algorithm is presented in [22] which examines the sentiments of entire document. An opinion mining search engine AskUs is proposed which uses two algorithms. High Adjective Count Algorithm is used to find out important features and Max Opinion Score Algorithm uses opinion scores to rank these. It can be extended to work for social media by using signals such as "Like" and "Share" in Facebook and "Retweet" in Twitter where title is missing in users' comments. This is very similar to the work proposed in this paper. The difference is that Facebook web page is used to obtain data. Also, users can be ranked using "Like" and "Share" signals as well as sentiment analysis of user comments. Table 2 summarizes some of the previous work done in ranking. It contains articles reference [17–22]. Reference numbers and authors names are specified in first column. Second column specifies parameters based on which ranking is done. Third column specifies platform used to extract data on which work is carried out. Fourth column shows algorithms to perform ranking operation.

Table 2 Summary of previous work done in ranking

References	Parameters used	Platform used	Algorithm used
Ortega et al. [17]	Graphs	Slashdot.org	Polarity rank and polarity trust
Reilly et al. [18]	Retweet to tweet ratio	Twitter	Influence ranking program
Subbian et al. [19]	Retweets and mentions	Twitter	Supervised Kemeny ranking
Liang et al. [20]	Tags of users' accounts	Twitter	Page rank
Min et al. [21]	Relationship, interaction and personal characteristics	Twitter	RankScore
Eirinaki et al. [22]	Title and body scores of reviews	Dataset from https://www.cs.uic.edu/~liub/FBS/sentiment-analysis.html	High adjective count and max opinion score

3 Proposed Methodology

Proposed methodology consists of following steps:

(a) Get access token: An access token is a string which is used for identifying a Facebook page, user or application. When a user logs into Facebook and connects with an application, access token can be obtained by application. This provides access to make graph API (Application Programming Interface) calls. Access tokens are portable. Tokens are of two types: short-lived and long lived. Short-lived tokens are those generated by web login. These tokens can be upgraded to long-term tokens which last for 60 days. There are four types of access tokens:

   (i) User access token: This access token provides permission to APIs to post, change or read data on user's behalf as a result of call to APIs by application. This token can be obtained by user login and subsequent permission to obtain it.

   (ii) Page access token: This access token is similar to user access token. However, it is required when Facebook page data is to be written, modified or read by application using APIs. To obtain this token, a user access token must be obtained followed by manage_pages permission. Using Graph API, page access token can be obtained thereafter.

   (iii) Application access token: Using server-to-server call, application access token can be obtained. It is used to change or read application settings.

   (iv) Client token: It can be placed in desktop applications to identify your application. Therefore, this is not a secret identifier. It is used to access a small subset of APIs which are application-level. There are well-defined methods to generate each type of token discussed above. User access

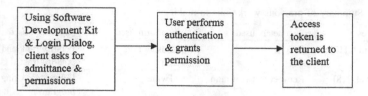

Fig. 1 Process to be followed to obtain user access token

token can be used to obtain page token. Method to obtain user access token is described in Fig. 1. Client asks for admission and permission to post, read and modify user's data using Login Dialog and Software Development Kit. Access token is returned to client after authentication by user.

(b) Retrieve number of likes, shares and user comments: Restfb is a light weight Facebook Graph API used to perform operations such as obtaining and extending access token, posting status, using Facebook Query Language, etc. It can be used to retrieve number of likes, shares and comments of users from a Facebook page. In social network, web pages are created for like-minded people to interact. These are known as social networking services [23]. Social ties can be strengthened using these services.

(c) Sentiment analysis: Dataset of positive and negative words can be used for analysis. All words which are not in dataset of positive and negative words will considered as neutral. Users' comments can be classified into three classes: positive, negative and neutral. Naïve Bayes classifier can be used for classification and tool to be used for the same is WEKA (Waikato Environment for Knowledge Analysis). Naïve Bayes classifier is very simple to use. On the basis of distribution of words in a document, posterior probability of a class is computed. It determines the label to which a set of features belong [24]. WEKA is used for data mining, classification, clustering, etc.

(d) Ranking of users: Ranking formula to rank users is stated in Eq. (1):

$$
\begin{aligned}
\text{Rank Score} = {} & \text{Log (number of Likes)} + \text{Log (number of Shares)} \\
& + \text{Log (number of Positive Comments)} \\
& - \text{Log(number of Negative Comments)}.
\end{aligned} \tag{1}
$$

(e) Computing cosine similarity: Cosine similarity of a user's comment is computed with dataset of positive and negative words. Finally, resulting cosine similarity is computed as stated in Eq. (2):

$$
\begin{aligned}
\text{Resulting cosine similarity score} = {} & \text{Cosine similarity using positive words} \\
& - \text{Cosine similarity using negative words.}
\end{aligned} \tag{2}
$$

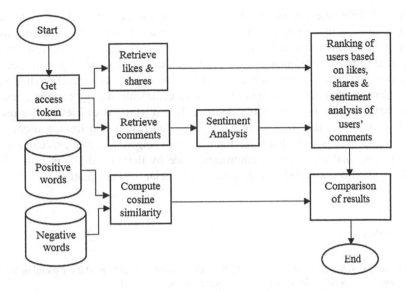

Fig. 2 Proposed methodology to be adopted for ranking of users incorporating parameters such as number of likes, shares and comments

(f) Comparing results: Rank score for each user can be compared with resulting cosine similarity score. Figure 2 gives diagrammatic representation of proposed methodology including steps from (a) to (f). It starts with obtaining access token and retrieving likes, shares and comments of users. Retrieved comments are subject to sentiment analysis using dataset of positive and negative words. Other words are considered as neutral words. Then, users can be ranked based on sentiment analysis results and number of likes and shares. Cosine similarity computation can also be done using comments and dataset of positive and negative words. These results can be compared in the last step.

4 Conclusion and Future Scope

Social networking sites have become a lifeline for communication among people. This paper proposes a methodology to rank users using Facebook parameters. Facebook pages can be used as data source. Users' comments can classified into positive, negative and neutral classes. Then, rank can be assigned to each user by adding up the logarithm of number of likes, shares and positive comments by a particular user and subtracting the logarithm of number of negative comments made by the same user for a particular Facebook page post. Also, cosine similarity can be calculated between user's comments and list of positive words. Then, cosine similarity between same user's comments and list of negative words can be calculated. Thereafter, resulting cosine similarity can be obtained by subtracting cosine similarity using negative word list from that obtained using negative word list. Finally, results obtained from ranking users by incorporating parameters are compared to results obtained using cosine similarity to determine performance of methodology put forward Ranking of users can be done to determine reputation of users. Users posting a large number of positive comments, liking or sharing several posts may be considered as highly reputed. Trustworthiness of friends in a user's profile can also be determined by utilizing ranked results and finding users with lowest ranks or most negative behaviour. Users having similar interests can also be identified by analysing similar comments made by them on different posts. This work can also be extended to data from other social network platforms.

References

1. Alkeinaya, N. Y., & Norwawi, N. M. (2014). User oriented privacy model for social networks. *Journal of Procedia: Social and Behavioral Sciences, 129*, 191–197.
2. Kunpeng, Z., Yu, C., Yusheng, X., Honbo, D., Agrawal, A., Palsetia, D., Lee, K., Wei-keng, L., & Choudhary, A. (2011). SES: Sentiment elicitation system for social media data. In *IEEE 11th International Conference on Data Mining Workshops (ICDMW), Vancouver* (pp. 129–136).
3. Cambria, E., Schuller, B., Xia, Y., & Havasi, C. (2013). New avenues in opinion mining and sentiment analysis. *IEEE Intelligent Systems, 28*(2), 15–21.
4. Chen, H., & Zimbra, D. (2010). AI and opinion mining. *IEEE Intelligent Systems, 25*(3), 74–76.
5. Liu, B. (2010). Sentiment analysis: A multifaceted problem. *IEEE Intelligent Systems, 25*(3), 76–80.
6. Snyder, B., & Barzilay, R. (2007). Multiple aspect ranking using the good grief algorithm. In *Proceedings of the Human Language Technology Conference of the North American Chapter of the Association for Computational Linguistics*, Article no. N07-1038, pp. 300–307.
7. Pang, B., Lee, L., & Vaithyanathan, S. (2002). Thumbs up? Sentiment classification using machine learning techniques. In *Proceedings of the Annual Conference of the Empirical Methods in Natural Language Processing* (Vol. 10, pp. 79–86).
8. Pang, P., & Lee, L. (2005). Seeing stars: Exploiting class relationships for sentiment categorization with respect to rating scales. In *Proceedings of the 43rd Annual Association for Computational Linguistics* (pp. 115–1240).
9. Turney, P. (2002). Thumbs up or thumbs down? Semantic orientation applied to unsupervised classification of reviews. In *Proceedings of the 40th Annual Association for Computational Linguistics* (pp. 417–424).
10. Kamps, J. (2004). Using WordNet to measure semantic orientation of adjectives. In *Proceedings of the 4th Annual International Conference of Language Resources and Evaluation, European Language Resources Association* (pp. 1115–1118).
11. Riloff, E., & Wiebe, J. (2003). Learning extraction patterns for subjective expressions. In *Proceedings of the 2003 Conference on Empirical Methods in Natural Language Processing* (pp. 105–112).
12. Kim, S., & Hovy, E. (2006). Extracting opinions, opinion holders, and topics expressed in online news media text. In *Proceedings of the Workshop on Sentiment and Subjectivity in Text* (pp. 1–8).
13. Santidhanyaroj, P., Khan, T. A.; Gelowitz, C. M., & Benedicenti, L. (2014). A sentiment analysis prototype system for social network data. In *IEEE 27th Canadian Conference on Electrical and Computer Engineering (CCECE), Toronto, Canada* (pp. 1–5).

14. Choi, Y., & Cardie, C. (2008). Learning with compositional semantics as structural inference for subsentential sentiment analysis. In *Proceedings of the Conference on Empirical Methods in Natural Language Processing* (pp. 793–801).
15. Liu, J., & Seneff, S. (2009). Review sentiment scoring via parse and-paraphrase paradigm. In *Proceedings of Conference on Empirical Methods in Natural Language Processing* (vol. 1, pp. 161–169).
16. Zhao, Y., Niu, K., He, Z., Lin, J., & Wang, X. (2013). Text sentiment analysis algorithm optimization and platform development in social network. In *Sixth International Symposium on Computational Intelligence and Design* (pp. 410–413).
17. Ortega, F. J., Troyano, J. A., Cruz, F. L., Vallejo, C. G., & Enríquez, F. (2012). Propagation of trust and distrust for the detection of trolls in a social network. *Journal of Computer Networks, 56,* 2884–2895.
18. Reilly, C. F., Salinas, D., & De Leon, D. (2014). Ranking users based on influence in a directional social network. In *International Conference on Computational Science and Computational Intelligence, Las Vegas* (Vol. 2, pp. 237–240).
19. Subbian, K., & Melville, P (2011). Supervised rank aggregation for predicting influencers in twitter. In: *IEEE International Conference on Privacy, Security, Risk, and Trust. IEEE Third International Conference on Social Computing* (pp. 661–665).
20. Liang, B., Liu, Y., Zhang, M., Ma, S., Ru, L., & Zhang, K. (2014). Searching for people to follow in social networks. *Journal of Expert Systems with Applications, 41,* 7455–7465.
21. Min, M., Choi, D., Kim. J., & Lee, J. H. (2011). The identification of intimate friends in personal social network. In *International Conference on Computational Aspects of Social Networks (CASoN), Salamanca* (pp. 233–236).
22. Eirinaki, M., Pisal, S., & Singh, J. (2012). Feature-based opinion mining and ranking. *Journal of Computer and System Sciences, 78,* 1175–1184.
23. Kwon, O., & Wen, Y. (2010). An empirical study of the factors affecting social network service use. *Journal of Computers in Human Behavior, 26*(2), 254–263.
24. Medhat, W., Hassan, A., & Korashy, H. (2014). Sentiment analysis algorithms and applications: A survey. *Ain Shams Engineering Journal, 5,* 1093–1113.

Development of Analytical Method to Determine the Deflection of Tapered Cantilever Beam with Inclined Loading Condition Using Software Simulation

Kishan H. Joshi and Chetankumar M. Patel

Abstract Deflection of a tapered cantilever beam is of very interest for many engineers, as it is used for many engineering applications like bridges, roofs, overhead cranes, collets, etc. The present research works lead to derivation of an analytical equation for finding deflection of a tapered cantilever beam with rectangular section and with inclined loading condition. Whole theory is fundamentally based on Euler beam theory. MATLAB is used for solving complex second-order differential equation. Creo Simulate software and FEA using FRAME elements in ECEL are used for the verification of analytical method.

Keywords Tapered cantilever beam · Deflection · MATLAB · Creo simulate · Euler beam theory

1 Introduction

Tapered cantilever beam is the special kind of cantilever beam in which cross section of beam is uniformly varying. This kind of non-prismatic beam is useful for various applications such as design of tapper roof, design of collet, design of bridge, etc. Analytical equation derived in this work is very helpful for finding deflection and hence to design the whole system. Uniformly varying section with uniformly distributed inclined loading condition leads to a complex problem. The presented theory can be used to find deflection which can also be extended for non-rectangular sections.

Many of researchers have utilized Euler Bernoulli concept for beam application. Malukhin et al. [1] have applied the Euler beam theory to determine the deflection of collet by considering each jaw of collet as a cantilever beam, but the theory is developed for only cantilever beam having zero tapered. Farid et al. [2] utilized the Euler beam concept to determine the fundamental natural frequency for nonuniform

K.H. Joshi (✉) · C.M. Patel
School of Engineering, RK University, Rajkot, Gujarat 360020, India
e-mail: ksnjsi@gmail.com

© Springer Science+Business Media Singapore 2016
S.C. Satapathy et al. (eds.), *Proceedings of International Conference on ICT for Sustainable Development*, Advances in Intelligent Systems and Computing 409, DOI 10.1007/978-981-10-0135-2_27

cross section or tapered cantilever beam. Frieman and Kosmatka [3] have also used Euler and FEA-based approach for nonuniform section beam. Al-Gahtani and Khan [4] have utilized generalized Euler Bernoulli equation to determine the deflection of non-prismatic beam having parabolic variation with transverse uniform loading condition, and this method has been used to determine the deflection of bridge having transverse loading and parabolic section. Shooshtari and Khajavi [5], and Reza [6] have developed the stiffness matrix and shape function for non-prismatic beam by Euler Bernoulli and Timoshenko formulation. Bhavikatti [7], Tirupathi and Ashok [8], and Daryl [9] have described the finite element method to determine the deflection of any mechanical structure or element. Jian et al. [10] have applied FEA approach for analysis of beam structure.

In this literature survey, many of researchers have utilized Euler beam concept to analyze the non-prismatic beam with transverse loading condition but there are some applications where inclined loading is considered for tapered beam, so there is a scope to develop equation to determine the deflection of tapered cantilever beam having inclined loading condition.

Euler beam theory [11] can be applied to determine the deflection of beam. Euler equation for beam is as follows:

$$\frac{d^2y}{dx^2} = \frac{M_x}{I_x E}.$$

(1)

where $y(x)$ = deflection function;
M_x Bending moment about C.G. axis at any distance x due to force F_x;
I_x Area moment of inertia of any section; and
E Modulus of Elasticity for isotropic material.

1.1 Basic Structure of Tapered Cantilever Beam

Figure 1 shows the non-prismatic cantilever having uniform inclined loading (N), length of beam (L), tapper angle (α), thickness of beam (t), variable width (b_x), longest width (b), shortest width of beam (a), and isotropic material with modulus of elasticity (E). Loading (N) applied on beam is inclined, and uniformly distributed on surface of beam.

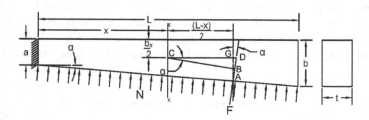

Fig. 1 Tapered cantilever beam

1.2 Boundary Conditions for Tapered Cantilever Beam

The boundary condition for tapered cantilever beam is similar to cantilever beam like

$$y(0) = 0 \text{ and } y'(0) = 0.$$

2 Analytical Method to Determine Deflection of Tapered Cantilever Beam

Euler beam theory is utilized to determine the deflection function of any kind of cantilever beam with different boundary conditions. By solving this differential Eq. (1), deflection y can be determined using boundary condition of cantilever beam. To solve Eq. (1), first we need to determine the area moment of inertia (I_x) of tapper cantilever beam and bending moment (M_x) of tapper cantilever beam. Due to variation of cross section, I_x varies at different sections.

2.1 Area Moment of Inertia (I_x)

For rectangular cross section, area moment of inertia [11] for any section at distance x about C.G. axis is

$$I_x = \frac{tb_x^3}{12}$$

From Fig. 1, $\tan(\alpha) = \frac{bx-b}{(L-x)}$

$$b_x = b - (L-x) \cdot \tan(\alpha) \text{ and } b = a + (L-x) \cdot \tan(\alpha)$$

$$I_x = \frac{t(b - (L-x) \cdot \tan(\alpha))^3}{12} \tag{2}$$

where b_x = width of beam at distance x from support and t = thickness of beam.

2.2 Bending Moment (M_x)

By solving the differential equation, deflection y can be determined using boundary condition of cantilever beam.

Force acting on the beam is N.

Uniform force along the beam is N/L.

Figure 1 shows the dimensions required to calculate the bending moment at any section from distance (x).

Force acting on section x is

$$F_x = \frac{N(L-x)}{L}.$$ (3)

From the geometry of beam, m$\angle$BCG = m$\angle$GAD = α

$$GD = \frac{b \cdot \tan(\alpha)}{2} \text{ and } CG = \frac{(L-x)}{2}.$$

$$CD = CG + GD = \frac{(L-x)}{2} + \frac{b \cdot \tan(\alpha)}{2}.$$

$$CB = CD \cdot \cos(\alpha)$$

$$CB = \left\{ \frac{(L-x)}{2} + \frac{b \cdot \tan(\alpha)}{2} \right\} \cos(\alpha).$$

$$CB = \frac{(L-x)}{2} \cos(\alpha) + \frac{b}{2} \sin(\alpha).$$

$$d_x = CB = \frac{(L-x)}{2} \cos(\alpha) + \frac{b}{2} \sin(\alpha).$$ (4)

where d_x = perpendicular distance from any force F_x.

Total bending moment about C.G. axis at any distance x is

$$M_x = \text{Force x Distance}$$

$M_x = F_x \times d_x$ (using (3) and (4))

$$M_x = \frac{N(L-x)}{L} \times \left\{ \frac{(L-x)}{2} \cos(\alpha) + \frac{b}{2} \sin(\alpha) \right\}.$$ (5)

Importing value of M_x and I_x in Euler's equation,

$$\frac{d^2y}{dx^2} = \frac{\frac{N(L-x)}{L} \times \left\{ \frac{(L-x)}{2} \cos(\alpha) + \frac{b}{2} \sin(\alpha) \right\}}{\frac{t(b-(L-x)\cdot\tan(\alpha))^3}{12} E}.$$ (6)

Second-order differential Eq. (6) gives the relation between beam deflections y at any section x. Tapered angle α, modulus of elasticity E, length L, and major width b can be considered as predefined values, which can be optimized from the solution of y.

2.3 Solution of Differential Equation Using MATLAB Software

MATLAB software is used for solving the second-order differential equation of beam deflection. MATLAB is efficient for solving higher order complexity of mathematical equation, which is difficult to solve manually.

MATLAB code for solving the differential equation is given as follows:

```
syms y(x) %symbolical representation of function
%Design parameters
syms L %Length of beam
syms E %Young's modulus of elasticity
syms t %Thickness of Beam
syms a %Minimum width of beam
syms N %Maximum width of beam
b=a+L*tan(t) %width of beam;
%Bending Momement for any section
M=0.5*N*(L-x)*(1/L)*((L-x)*cos(t)+b*sin(t));
%Area Moment of Inertia of the section
I=((b-(L-x)*tan(t))^3)*100/12;
Dy = diff(y, x);
%Solving Second order Differential equation using
boundary conditions y(0)==0, Dy(0)==0
y(x,L,E,t,a,N)=dsolve(diff(y,x,2)==M/(I*E),y(0)==0,
Dy(0)==0)
%Value assumption
%L=1000 in mm, a=100 in mm, R=400 in mm, N=1000 in N,
t=4*pi/180 in radian, E=200000.
ymax=double(y(1000,1000,200000,4*pi/180,100,1000));
```

```
Output:
y(x, L, E, t, a, N) =
(3*(N*a^2*cos(t)+N*a^2*sin(t)*tan(t)+L^2*N*cos(t)*tan(t
)^2+L^2*N*sin(t)*tan(t)^3+2*L*N*a*cos(t)*tan(t)+2*L*N*a
*sin(t)*tan(t)^2))/(tan(t)*(100*E*L*a*tan(t)^3+100*E*L*
x*tan(t)^4))-
(3*(N*a^2*cos(t)+6*N*a^2*log(a)*cos(t)+N*a^2*sin(t)*tan
(t)+L^2*N*cos(t)*tan(t)^2+L^2*N*sin(t)*tan(t)^3+2*N*a^2
*log(a)*sin(t)*tan(t)+2*L*N*a*cos(t)*tan(t)+2*L*N*a*sin
(t)*tan(t)^2+2*L*N*a*log(a)*sin(t)*tan(t)^2+4*L*N*a*log
(a)*cos(t)*tan(t)))/(100*E*L*a*tan(t)^4)+(log(a+x*tan(t
))*(9*N*a*cos(t)
+3*L*N*sin(t)*tan(t)^2+6*L*N*cos(t)*tan(t)+3*N*a*sin(t)
*tan(t)))/(50*E*L*tan(t)^4) -
(3*x*(5*N*a^2*cos(t)+2*N*a^2*log(a)*cos(t)+N*a^2*sin(t)
*tan(t) - L^2*N*cos(t)*tan(t)^2-
L^2*N*sin(t)*tan(t)^3+2*L*N*a*cos(t)*tan(t)))/(100*E*L*
a^2*tan(t)^3)+(3*N*x*cos(t)*log(a+x*tan(t)))/(50*E*L*ta
n(t)^3)

ymax =    0.0540 (maximum deflection in mm).
```

3 Verification: FEA Using Frame Elements in EXCEL

FEA is also used to determine the deflection of any structures [8]. In this method, frame element having 3 DOF is used. Four frame elements are used to describe the cantilever beam.

Jian et al. [10] suggested that the more number of elements improves accuracy of results and increases computation requirements, so four elements are found to be appropriate for this application in comparison with lesser elements.

First element stiffness matrix is defined in EXCEL using predefined value ($L = 1000$ mm, $E = 200$ Gpa, $t = 100$ mm, $\theta = 4°$, $a = 100$ mm, $N = 1000$ N), and global stiffness matrix is defined using element stiffness matrix [7] by combining their cell address in EXCEL.

This application has the total of five nodes, and for boundary condition of cantilever beam, in which first node considered as a fixed end, the values of deflection in x and y directions and angular deflection are considered as a zero. Other nodes are considered as a equally distribution of load N. Load N is angular and uniformly distributed over the length, so force at each node is also equally divided. So for $N = 1000$ N, each node is sharing $1000/5 = 200$ N of angular load. Using elimination approach [9], by considering all deflection at node 1 or fixed end is zero, will give the elimination of first three rows and columns from the global stiffness matrix. Finally, global stiffness matrixes have 9DOF or 9×9 matrix.

According to $[y] = [K]^{-1}[F]$, deflection can be determined, where $[y]$ is the deflection matrix, $[F]$ is the force/moment matrix, and $[K]$ is the global stiffness matrix. Answer obtained by FEA with one frame element is $y_{max} = 0.0537$ mm.

4 Deflection Beam Using CREO SIMULATION Software

CREO SIMULATION is a advanced software tool to determine the deflection of beam.

STEPS to determine deflection of cantilever beam using CREO are as follows:

1. Modeling of cantilever beam using CREO PARAMETRIC software: ($L = 1000$ mm, $t = 100$ mm, $\theta = 4°$, $a = 100$ mm)
2. Material assignment of model using CREO SIMULATION software: ($E = 200$ GPa)
3. Appling boundary condition in beam: ($y(0) = 0$, $y'(0) = 0$, $N = 1000$ N)
4. Solution of beam to determine the deflection of beam
5. Visualization of result: deflection along the beam with different magnitudes can be visualized as shown in Fig. 2, where intensity of red color represents higher value of deflection than intensity of blue color.

Form Fig. 2 it can be shown that maximum deflection is occurred at the free end of beam, and the value of y_{max} is 0.0534 mm.

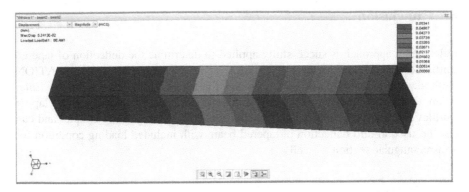

Fig. 2 FEA result for deflection over tapered cantilever beam

5 Comparison of Various Methods of Deflection

The following comparison is done to validate the scope of analytical method. All three methods have been compared based on same dimensions and loading conditions using isotropic material (Table 1).

Similarity Fig. 3 shows that analytical method shows close agrement toward the FEA and CREO SIMULATION results, so analytical method is successfully developed, and can be used to determine the deflection of tapered cantilever beam.

Table 1 Comparison of various methods of deflection

No.	Method	y_{max} (mm)	Difference (mm)	Difference percentage
1	Analytical approach	0.0540	–	–
2	CREO SIMULATE	0.0534	0.0034	1.11 %
3	FEA using FRAME elements	0.0537	0.0003	0.55 %

Fig. 3 Comparison of various methods of deflection

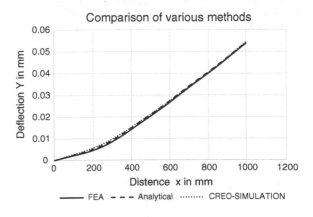

6 Conclusion

Euler beam approach is successfully applied to determine the deflection of tapered cantilever beam, and verified using FEA approach and CREO SIMULATION method. The analytical method developed for tapered cantilever beam by Euler beam approach can be used to determine the deflection and stiffness of tapper cantilever beam with inclined loading condition. This theory being simple, and can also be used to find deflection of tapered beam with included loading condition for non-rectangular section as well.

References

1. Malukhin, K., Hankyu, S., & Kornel, E. (2012). A shape memory alloy based tool clamping device. *Journal of Materials Processing Technology, 212*(4), 735–744.
2. Farid, C., Salah, D., Kamel, F., & Abderrahim, B. (2014). Tapered beam axial vibration frequency: Linear cross-area variation case. *APCBEE Procedia, 9*, 323–327.
3. Frieman, Z., & Kosmatka, J. (1992). Exact stiffness matrix of a non-uniform beam extension, torsion and bending of a Bernoulli-Euler beam. *Computers & Structures, 42*, 671–682.
4. Al-Gahtani, H., & Khan, S. (1998). Exact analysis of nonprismatic beams. *Journal of Engineering Mechanics, 124*, 1290–1293.
5. Shooshtari, A., & Khajavi, R. (2010). An efficient procedure to find shape functions and stiffness matrices of nonprismatic EulereBernoulli and Timoshenko beam elements. *European Journal of Mechanics A/Solids, 29*, 826–836.
6. Reza, A. (2010). Basic displacement functions in analysis of nonprismatic beams. *Engineering Computations: International Journal for Computer-Aided Engineering and Software, 27*(6), 733–745.
7. Bhavikatti, S. (2005). *Finite element analysis* (1st ed.). New Age International (P) Ltd., Publishers.
8. Tirupathi, C., & Ashok, B. (2009). *Introduction to finite elements in engineering*. PHI Learning Private Limited.
9. Daryl, L. (2007). *A first course in the finite element method*. Nelson, a Division of Thomson Canada Limited.
10. Jian, L., Zhou, S., Dong, M., & Yan, Y. (2012). Three-Node Euler-Bernoulli Beam Element Based on Positional FEM. *Procedia Engineering, 29*, 3703–3707.
11. Ferdinand, P., Russell, J., & John, T. (2008). Mechanics of material. The McGraw-Hill Companies.

Bio-inspired Ultralow Power Design of Comparator with Noise Compensation Using Hysteresis Technique Designed for Biomedical Engineering (Pacemaker)

Jubin Jain, Vijendra Maurya and Anu Mehra

Abstract With the emerging development of advanced trends in biomedical engineering finding its application in various biomedical electronic devices such as ECG, EEG, temperature sensing, blood pressure, and pacemaker, the biopotential signals are picked-up in small portable battery operated devices. The major concerned is about the power consumption of the electronic circuitry used in biomedical devices as well as the noise obtained from the muscular contraction and expansion, which is responsible for the interference to the signal to be measured. Hence, compensation circuitry is needed to remove noise. The comparator is a CMOS VLSI circuit which compares an analog signal with another analog signal and generates digital output due to comparison. The project is to show case the low power consumption of comparator proposed for pacemaker device having modest speed and producing less delay. The technique proposed to design the comparator in order to improve the performance is hysteresis by providing feedback. The advantage of introducing hysteresis in comparator is to compensate the noise at output signal, when operated in noisy environment. The comparator using hysteresis is designed in 0.18 μ CMOS technology operated at bias voltage of 1.8 V. The circuit is designed and simulated in TANNER EDA.

Keywords Power consumption · Hysteresis · Delay · Noise · Biologically inspired · Long battery life of implantable devices · Analog-to-digital conversion

J. Jain (✉) · V. Maurya
Geetanjali Institute of Technical Studies, Udaipur, India
e-mail: jubincb2@gmail.com

A. Mehra
ASET, Amity University, Noida, India

© Springer Science+Business Media Singapore 2016
S.C. Satapathy et al. (eds.), *Proceedings of International Conference on ICT for Sustainable Development*, Advances in Intelligent Systems and Computing 409, DOI 10.1007/978-981-10-0135-2_28

289

1 Introduction

With the day by day augmentation in the field of biomedical implantable devices that are portable and battery-driven devices, power consumption has become a major issue of research so that the battery life can be enhanced for a longer time period. The rising surge of research in the field of low power CMOS circuits for implants is supported by the rising need to extend the battery life of portable implants. In accordance to this, sensing biopotentials with various portable electronic devices there is firm requisition of ADCs with high degree of efficiency, which can done by optimizing the critical components of ADC among comparator, as proposed in this paper. Comparators find their application in analog-to-digital converters (ADCs), data transmitting applications, power regulators based on switching, and many other medical applications. With low voltage supply it has become a difficult task to design a comparator. Under such a situation it is needed to compensate the low voltage supply. The W/L ratio has to be increased, though it will let the area of chip to increase as well power consumption. To operate under low voltage condition the W/L ratios are required to be defined in order to lower down the power consumption as well at good operating speed.

There are two issues that can be improved to achieve great performance of open-loop comparator with some endeavor. These fields are regarded as input offset voltage and a single transition of comparator in noisy environment, as in the presence of noise during transition extra power consumption is committed. The first issue can be improved by using auto-zero technique and second issue by introducing hysteresis with essence of bistable circuit.

By feeding back the small portion of output voltage to the positive input, the hysteresis is introduced in comparator circuit. The feedback voltage is added to polarity-sensitive voltage which results in increased threshold voltage and proves to be fruitful on account of causing reduction in circuit sensitivity toward noise and also eradicates the multiple number of transitions when input changes slowly.

The paper is structured as follows: A conventional two-stage open-loop comparator is designed, simulated, and the concerned parameters are analyzed in 0.18 μ technology operated at 3.3 V. Section 2 is dedicated to improved version of comparator which gives the paramount parameters such as power consumption, delay, and noise eradication. The conventional and improved version of comparator parameters are compared.

2 Comparator Design

2.1 Conventional Design of Two-Stage Open-Loop Comparator

The comparator is the integral part of an ADC design and is used for converting analog-to-digital signal where first the signal is to be sampled and then compared with reference signal considered as 1-bit A/D converter. Op-amp without compensation is considered as open-loop comparator. Differential input and sufficient gain is required to achieve the desired gain. The open-loop comparator without compensation has larger bandwidth in comparison to comparator with compensation as it gives faster response. The conventional two-stage amplifier consists of three stages with the inverter connected to the final stage. The stage comprises the following stages: differential amplifier stage, common-source amplifier stage, and the inverting buffer. The bias current provided to the circuit is 1 μA. The circuit consists of current mirror which simply copies current from the reference source such that the reference current is mirrored to the first two gain stages which accounts for the total current at 3 μA. The circuit differential stage comprises of NMOS since the mobility of NMOS is considered to be greater in comparison to PMOS, whereas in circuit IN1 denotes the input analog signal and IN2 is considered as reference signal. With the need for improvement in the gain of first stage, it is required to lower the input offset voltage by increasing the width of NMOS transistor. In the presence of parasitic capacitance transistor PMOS_3, which is responsible for causing delay in circuit, the area of CS amplifier is increased and the inverter buffer stage which is responsible for adding the needed gain along with risen slew rate simply causes the comparator to operate in high speed applications.

The problems associated with the design are as follows: when the two-analog input goes to zero, even a small amount of noise overrides the signal causing fluctuation in the output of comparator. Due to fluctuation, glitches are produced causing unnecessary power consumption. Hence, output gets affected in the presence of noise in input signal.

2.2 Design of Comparator Using Hysteresis

Often it happens that comparator operating in noisy environment needs to detect transitions at the threshold points. Depending on the frequency of detected signal, if the comparator is fast enough and amplitude of noise is large, the presence of noise will result in the output of comparator. Efforts in modification of transfer characteristics are desired which can be achieved by hysteresis.

The previous design characteristics were affected with presence of noise. So as to eradicate noise the concept of hysteresis was introduced, Hysteresis is defined as the difference between the upper threshold voltage (V_{TH}) and the lower threshold voltage (V_{TL}) for which the output switches to a higher value and a lower value respectively. Circuit sensitivity toward the noise and multiple transitions are reduced at the output using this technique.

Hysteresis is considered as the degree of quality for comparator in which input threshold changes with the change in input signal. When the input crosses the threshold it results in changes in output and subsequently threshold is reduced such that input must return the previous threshold and again the output changes. The intention behind the technique is simply that output needs to follow the low frequency signal.

There are many ways by which hysteresis in the comparator can be introduced, all of which make use of positive feedback, categorized as Internal methods and External methods. In internal method internal hysteresis is implemented into comparator while in external hysteresis, hysteresis is introduced after the circuit is built up.

2.3   Working of Hysteresis-Based Comparator Circuit

To reduce the impact of noise on the circuit a small amount of hysteresis is introduced in the conventional comparator circuit design. An unbalanced differential circuit is added in the comparator circuit. The modified comparator design can be seen in Fig. 3.

The goal of achieving hysteresis can be achieved using internal positive feedback. Basically there are two paths for feedback in the differential input stage design. The first feedback is attained by NMOS_1 and NMOS_2 transistors, which is current series feedback obtained by CS configuration so that it is considered as a negative feedback. The second path is considered as a positive feedback obtained from the gate-drain connection of PMOS_2 and NMOS_6, which is simply the voltage-shunt feedback. If the positive feedback is less than the negative feedback then hysteresis is absent. But in the case the negative feedback becomes lesser than the positive feedback, hysteresis will be introduced in the circuit.

The output stage comprises of inverter plus unbalanced differential pair configured at input. A second differential pair comprises of two transistors, NMOS_5-NMOS_6, responsible for unbalancing the input differential pair. It can be seen in the figure that the gates are tied to the output signals, which is responsible for establishing positive feedback.

The hysteresis bias current for the second differential stage is provided by the current mirror composed from the transistor denoted by NMOS_8-NMOS_7. The size of second differential pair must be kept small so as to introduce the little parasitic capacitance at the input differential stage. By varying the hysteresis current the hysteresis can be programmed.

As a result it can be seen from the waveform spike removed which is mainly responsible for causing power consumption at increased rate.

2.4   Figures and Tables

2.4.1   Schematic of Two-Stage Comparator Without Hysteresis

The schematic of conventional two-stage comparator is designed using 250 nm technology powered with bias voltage of 3.3 V using S-Edit and waveform is obtained using W-Edit (Fig. 1).

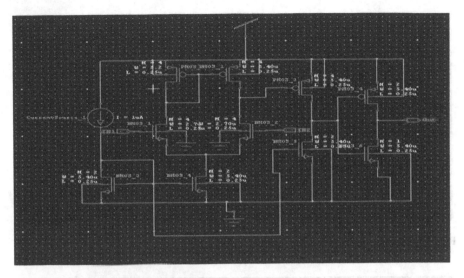

Fig. 1 Schematic of two-stage comparator without hysteresis

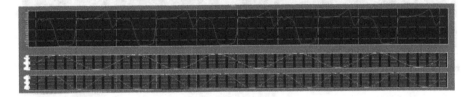

Fig. 2 Waveform of comparator without hysteresis

The waveform indicates the presence of glitch when input time reaches zero and results in increased power consumption. During zero-crossing multiple transitions take place (Fig. 2).

2.4.2 Design of Comparator Using Hysteresis

The schematic of improved design of comparator using hysteresis designed in 0.18 μ technology with bias voltage of 1.8 V (Fig. 3).

Waveform of improved design comparator using hysteresis. Hence, it can be observed the absence of glitch as it is indicated, the circuit is insensitive to the noise present in the input signal. When input IP(+) > In1(−) the output will be 1.8 V. Vice versa, if IP(+) < In1(−), the output will be 0 V (Fig. 4).

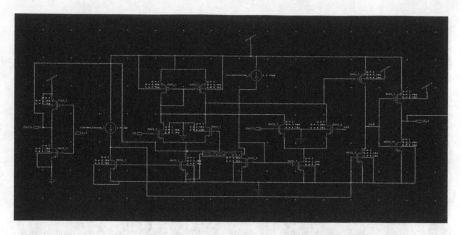

Fig. 3 Schematic of comparator using hysteresis

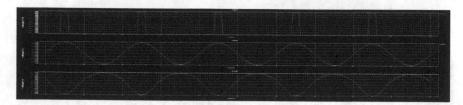

Fig. 4 Waveform of comparator using hysteresis

2.4.3 Table for W/L Ratios of Comparator Using Hysteresis

Circuit design	Transistor	W/L ratio	M
Input differential pair	PMOS_1, PMOS_2	5.40 μ/0.18 μ	4
	NMOS_1, NMOS_2	5.40 μ/0.18 μ, 2.50 μ/0.25 μ	4, 1
Differential pair stage II	NMOS_5, NMOS_6	3.60 μ/0.18 μ	2
Current mirror	NMOS_7, NMOS_8	5.40 μ/0.18μ	2
Output buffer inverter	PMOS_4, NMOS_10	5.40 μ/0.18 μ	4, 2
Inverter	PMOS_5, NMOS_11	5.40 μ/0.18 μ, 2.50 μ/0.25 μ	4, 1
Switches	NMOS_3, NMOS_4, PMOS_3, NMOS_9	5.40 μ/0.18 μ	2, 2, 4, 2

Current source	Current
Current source_1	1 μA
Current source_3	47 nA

2.4.4 Comparison and Analysis Table Between Comparators

	Comparator without hysteresis	Comparator with hysteresis
Technology	250 nm	180 nm
Voltage supply	3.3 V	1.8 V
Delay	46.55 ns	43.90533 ns
Power consumption	458 nW	411 nW
Current consumption	5 μA	3.11 μA
AC_Measure_Gain_1	−4.5749e+001	−1.2257e+002
Bandwidth	1.0000e+006	1.0000e+004
Slew rate	0.22 V/m s	0.047 V/m s
Trip point (V_{TRP+}, V_{TRP-})	+1.36 V, −1.25 V	+ 0.32 V, −0.32 V

2.4.5 Graphs

See Fig. 5.

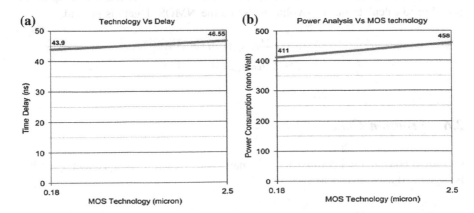

Fig. 5 a Analysis between delay and technology. **b** Analysis between power consumption and MOS technology

2.5 Formulas

It is assumed that positive and negative supplies are used such that the NMOS_1 is tied to the input signal and NMOS_2 is tied to the ground. In case input is less than zero, then NMOS_2 will be turned on and NMOS_1 will be driven to cut-off state. This is responsible for turning on PMOS_1 and PMOS_2 resulting in i_{NMOS_4} to flow through PMOS_1 and NMOS_1 causing V_{out} to go high. It is to be noted that NMOS_2 is driven in cut-off state.

$$i_{PMOS\_2} = (W/L)_{PMOS\_2} i_{NMOS\_4} / (W/L)_{PMOS\_1}$$

As the input signal crosses the threshold value some of the tail current starts to flow through NMOS_2 and it will flow till it becomes equal to the current associated with PMOS_2. As a result beyond it the comparator tends to change the state. It is mathematically represented.

$$i_{PMOS\_2} = (W/L)_{PMOS\_2} i_{PMOS\_1} / (W/L)_{PMOS\_1}$$

$$I_{NMOS\_2} = I_{PMOS\_2}$$

$$I_{NMOS\_4} = I_{NOMS\_1} + I_{NMOS\_2} (I_{NMOS\_1} = I_{PMOS\_1})$$

$$I_{PMOS\_1} = I_{NMOS\_4} / [1 + (W/L)_{PMOS\_2} / (W/L)_{PMOS\_1}] = I_{NMOS\_1}$$

$$I_{NMOS\_2} = I_{NMOS\_4} - I_{NMOS\_1}$$

When the current through the NMOS_1 and NMOS_2 is known, it becomes possible to calculate the V_{GS} voltages. Since the NMOS_1 gate is ground,

$$V_{gs1} = (2I_{nmos\_1} / \beta_1) + V_{T1}$$
$$V_{gs2} = (2I_{nmos\_2} / \beta_1) + V_{T2}$$

2.6 Program Code

Designed conventional comparator schematic is extracted in T-Spice and spice file is generated as shown below.

```
*-------- Devices: SPICE.ORDER > 0 --------

MNMOS_1 N_1 IN1 N_2 Gnd NMOS W=5.4u L=250n M=4 AS=1.6875p PS=3.95u AD=2.05875p PD=5.575u
MNMOS_2 N_3 IN2 N_2 Gnd NMOS W=5.4u L=250n M=4 AS=1.6875p PS=3.95u AD=2.05875p PD=5.575u
MNMOS_3 N_4 N_4 Gnd Gnd NMOS W=5.4u L=250n M=2 AS=3.375p PS=6.65u AD=4.86p PD=12.6u
MNMOS_4 N_2 N_4 Gnd Gnd NMOS W=5.4u L=250n M=2 AS=3.375p PS=6.65u AD=4.86p PD=12.6u
MNMOS_5 N_5 N_4 Gnd Gnd NMOS W=5.4u L=250n M=2 AS=3.375p PS=6.65u AD=4.86p PD=12.6u
MNMOS_6 Out N_5 Gnd Gnd NMOS W=5.4u L=250n AS=4.86p PS=12.6u AD=4.86p PD=12.6u

MPMOS_1 N_3 N_1 Vdd Vdd PMOS W=5.4u L=250n M=4 AS=3.375p PS=6.65u AD=4.1175p PD=9.625u
MPMOS_2 N_1 N_1 Vdd Vdd PMOS W=5.2 L=250n M=4 AS=3.25u PS=5.2000013 AD=3.965u PD=7.8000015
MPMOS_3 N_5 N_3 Vdd Vdd PMOS W=5.4u L=250n M=4 AS=3.375p PS=6.65u AD=4.1175p PD=9.625u
MPMOS_4 Out N_5 Vdd Vdd PMOS W=5.4u L=250n M=2 AS=3.375p PS=6.65u AD=4.86p PD=12.6u
********* Simulation Settings - Additional SPICE commands *********
.tran 1n 100n
.include "C:\Users\Jubin\Documents\Tanner EDA\Tanner Tools v14.1\L-Edit and LVS\LVS\SPR_Core\hp05.md"
Vdd Vdd Gnd 3.3
VIN1 IN1 Gnd dc 1.8 SIN (0 3.3 0.012 G 0)
VIN2 IN2 Gnd dc 1.8 SIN (0 3.3 0.011 G 0)
.print tran v(IN1,Gnd)  v(IN2,Gnd)  v(Out)
.measure tran delay time trig v(IN1) val=1 rise=1 targ v(Out) val=1 fall=1
.power
.end
```

Similarly improved design of comparator with hysteresis spice file is obtained using T-Spice, the code shown below.

```
*-------- Devices: SPICE.ORDER > 0 --------

MNMOS_3 N_12 N_5 3 3 NMOS W=5.4u L=180n M=2 AS=3.375p PS=6.65u AD=4.86p PD=12.6u
MNMOS_4 2 N_5 3 3 NMOS W=5.4u L=180n M=2 AS=3.375p PS=6.65u AD=4.86p PD=12.6u
MNMOS_5 N_2 Out3 N_25 Gnd NMOS W=3.6u L=180n M=2 AS=2.25p PS=4.85u AD=3.24p PD=9u
MNMOS_6 N_2 vo2 N_25 Gnd NMOS W=3.6u L=180n M=2 AS=2.25p PS=4.85u AD=3.24p PD=9u
MNMOS_7 N_25 N_7 Gnd Gnd NMOS W=5.4u L=180n M=2 AS=3.375p PS=6.65u AD=4.86p
PD=12.6u MNMOS_8 N_7 N_7 Gnd Gnd NMOS W=5.4u L=180n M=2 AS=3.375p PS=6.65u AD=4.86p
PD=12.6u MNMOS_9 vo2 N_12 Gnd Gnd NMOS W=5.4u L=180n M=2 AS=3.375p PS=6.65u AD=4.86p
PD=12.6u MNMOS_10 Out vo2 Gnd Gnd NMOS W=5.4u L=180n AS=4.86p PS=12.6u AD=4.86p
PD=12.6u MNMOS_11 Out4 In1 Gnd Gnd NMOS W=2.5u L=250n AS=2.25p PS=6.8u AD=2.25p
PD=6.8u MNMOS_1 N_2 IP 2 Gnd NMOS W=5.4u L=180n M=4 AS=3.375p PS=6.65u AD=4.1175p
PD=9.625u MNMOS_2 N_2 Out4 2 Gnd NMOS W=2.5u L=250n AS=2.25p PS=6.8u AD=2.25p PD=6.8u
MPMOS_1 N_2 N_2 Vdd Vdd PMOS W=5.4u L=180n M=4 AS=3.375p PS=6.65u AD=4.1175p PD=9.625u
MPMOS_2 N_2 N_2 Vdd Vdd PMOS W=5.4u L=180n M=4 AS=3.375p PS=6.65u AD=4.1175p PD=9.625u
MPMOS_3 vo2 N_2 Vdd Vdd PMOS W=5.4u L=180n M=4 AS=3.375p PS=6.65u AD=4.1175p PD=9.625u
MPMOS_4 Out vo2 Vdd Vdd PMOS W=5.4u L=180n M=2 AS=3.375p PS=6.65u AD=4.86p PD=12.6u
MPMOS_5 Out4 In1 Vdd Vdd PMOS W=5.4u L=180n M=4 AS=3.375p PS=6.65u AD=4.1175p PD=9.625u
```

```
********* Simulation Settings - Additional SPICE commands *********
.tran 1n 500n
.include "C:\Users\Jubin\Documents\Tanner EDA\Tanner Tools v14.1\L-Edit and LVS\LVS\SPR_Core\hp05.md"
Vdd Vdd Gnd 1.8
VIP IP Gnd dc 1.8 SIN (0 1.8 0.01G 0)
VIn1 In1 Gnd dc 1.8 SIN (0 1.8 0.01G 0)
.print tran v(IN,Gnd) v(IP,Gnd) v(Out,Gnd)
.measure tran delay time trig v(IP) val=1 rise=1 targ v(Out) val=1 fall=1
.power
.end
```

3 Conclusion

As a result of simulation and analysis done using TANNER EDA and its tools, it is observed that the noise is eradicated using hysteresis concept in comparator, though with noise compensation, the bandwidth is reduced. Power consumption is reduced in the circuit due to removal of glitches or spikes that are major factors affecting power consumption, thereby supporting longer battery life of implants. Although the interfering signal mixed with the biomedical signal to be detected does not propose any impact on circuit performance, the circuit is insensitive with respect to noise. The current consumption of comparator using hysteresis is also less. The circuit is allowed to be operated at lower voltage supply, which is paramount for implantable devices. Finally, some endeavors can be made to reduce delay of the circuit and improve bandwidth.

Acknowledgments The authors would like to thank Geetanjali Institute of Technical Studies, Udaipur for providing support to carry out the project successfully by guiding and providing the design tools.

References

1. Babayan-Mashhadi, S., & Lotfi, R. (2014). Analysis and design of a low-voltage low-power double-tail comparator. IEEE J. VLSI Syst. **22** (2014).
2. Chasta, N. K. (2012). High speed, lowpower current comparators with hysteresis. Int. J. VLSI Design Commun. Syst. 3(1).
3. Sarpeshkar, R. (2010). *Ultra low power bioelectronics: fundamentals, biomedical applications, bio-inspired signals.* Cambridge University Press.
4. Kargaran, E., Khosrowjerdi, H., & Ghaffarzadegan, K. A 1.5 V high swing ultra-low-power two stage CMOS OP-AMP in 0.18 μm technology. In *International Conference on Mechanical and Electronics Engineering (ICMEE 2010)*.
5. Mesgarani, A., Alam, M. N., Nelson, F. Z., & Ay, S. U. (2010). Supply boosting technique for designing very low-voltage mixed-signal circuits in standard CMOS. In *Proceedings of IEEE International Midwest Symposium Circuits System Digital Techniques Papers* (2010).
6. Zhang, H., Qin, Y., & Hong, Z. (2009). A 1.8-V 770-nW biopotential acquisition system for portable applications. In *IEEE Proceedings Biomedical Circuits and Systems Conference*.
7. Kulkarni, V. B. Low-Power CMOS Comparators with Programmable Hysteresis. Master Technical Report (2005).
8. Sauerbrey, J., Schmitt-Landsiedel, D., & Thewes, R. (2002). A 0.5 V, 1 μW successive approximation ADC. *IEEE Journal of Solid State Circuit.* IEEE.
9. Yan, S., & Sanchez-Sinencio, E. (2000). Low voltage analog circuit design techniques: A tutorial. *IEICE Transactions on Analog Integrated Circuits and Systems, E00-A(2)*.
10. Allen, P. E., & Holberg, D. R. *CMOS analog circuit design*, 2nd edn. Oxford University Press.
11. Louis, S. Y., & Wong, R. O. A very low power CMOS mixed-signal IC for implantable pacemaker applications.
12. Geiger, R. L., Allen, P. E., & Strader, N. R. (1990). *VLSI design techniques for analog and digital circuits.* McGraw-Hill Inc.

Comparative Analysis of Different Architectures of MCML Square Root Carry Select Adders for Low-Power Applications

Ginni Jain, Keerti Vyas, Vijendra K. Maurya and Mayank Patel

Abstract In digital electronics, adders are the most widely used circuits in order to perform fast arithmetic operations. Square root carry select adder is the fastest adder used in various digital processors. This paper presents the comparative analysis of different architectures of MCML square root carry select adders. Comparison with MCML RCA is also given. It is seen that modified MOS current mode logic (MCML) square root carry select adder (MSQ-CSA) has reduced power and increased speed. Therefore, it can be used instead of regular SQ-CSA and MCML ripple carry adder in order to perform high-speed and low-power operations. The simulation is performed in T-SPICE using 16 nm technology parameters. It is found that the proposed MCML SQ-CSA is efficient in terms of power and delay in comparison to other MCML adders.

Keywords MCML · Ripple carry adder · Square root carry select adder · Power · Delay

G. Jain (✉) · K. Vyas · V.K. Maurya
ECE Department, Geetanjali Institute of Technical Studies, Udaipur, Rajasthan, India
e-mail: jain24.ginni@gmail.com

K. Vyas
e-mail: kkvyas18@gmail.com

V.K. Maurya
e-mail: maurya.vijendra@gmail.com

M. Patel
ECE Department, College of Technology and Engineering, Udaipur, Rajasthan, India
e-mail: mayank999_udaipur@yahoo.com

© Springer Science+Business Media Singapore 2016
S.C. Satapathy et al. (eds.), *Proceedings of International Conference on ICT for Sustainable Development*, Advances in Intelligent Systems and Computing 409, DOI 10.1007/978-981-10-0135-2_29

1 Introduction

The need of high-speed integrated circuits employ the use of MOS current mode logic (MCML) technique in digital circuit design compared to conventional CMOS (complementary metal oxide semiconductor) logic technique [1]. MCML technique is exemplified by low switching noise, low-voltage swing, and the static power consumption that does not depend on frequency. These features of MCML technique make it suitable than the conventional CMOS logic technique for designing high-performance and high-speed digital circuits. Comparative analysis of static CMOS and MCML is shown in [2].

In VLSI design, adders play a vital role and are also used in various applications such as ASIC design, processors, and multipliers, in high-speed ICs and in mixed signal applications. The overall performance of the structure can be improved using efficient adders in the design. Implementation of different MCML RCA (ripple carry adder) is recommended in [3]. RCA produces worst-case delay as the carry of previous full adder stage is given as the input to the next adder stage. Every full adder is required to wait for the inward carry before generating an outgoing carry. Therefore, RCA provides lower speed among fast adders. To overcome this problem, CSA is used which consumes less power and delay. In this paper, MCML implementation of a modified SQ-CSA (square root carry select adder) with improved delay and power is proposed.

The paper first presents the brief introduction to MCML technique in Sect. 2. Then the review of different adders, i.e., RCA (Ripple Carry Adder), Regular SQ-CSA (square root carry select adder), and Modified SQ-CSA using MCML technique is presented in Sect. 3. Simulation results are discussed in Sect. 4. Simulations are performed in T-SPICE using 16 nm CMOS technology parameters. At last, the conclusions are drawn in Sect. 5.

2 MCML Technique

A MCML technique is used for high-speed and low-power digital circuits. On the whole, MCML circuit consists of three main components which incorporate pull-up load, (PDN) pull-down network, and a constant current source. The circuit of MCML inverter is depicted in Fig. 1. The pull-up load of MCML determines the output voltage swing and its PDN consists of source-coupled transistor pair M1-M2 with input 'in'. The constant current source provides steady current Iss to the MCML gate.

MCML circuits are based on the principle of current steering logic. According to this principle, depending on the input voltage the bias current is steered to one of the circuit branches. When the input voltage 'in' is low, the biasing current Iss is guided to transistor M2 and gives high voltage at output. On the other hand, when input 'in' is high, the bias current Iss is steered to M1 and results low voltage at output. Logic gates using MCML technique are shown in [5, 6].

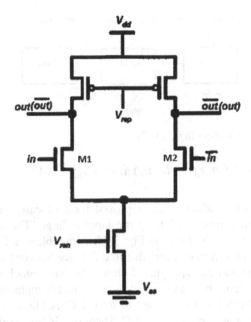

Fig. 1 MCML inverter [4]

3 MCML Adders

Different fast adders using MCML technique is presented in this section.

3.1 Ripple Carry Adder (RCA)

N-bit RCA is a combinational circuit which comprises of cascaded 'N' single bit full adders. Output carry of first full adder becomes the input carry of second full adder, and so on. Therefore, the carry of RCA traverse longest path through N full adder stages and thus provides worst-case delay. Delay of RCA increases as the value of 'N' increases. Figure 2 depicts the block diagram of 4-bit Ripple Carry Adder.

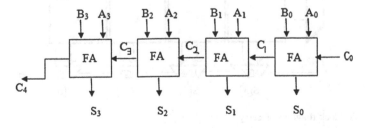

Fig. 2 4-bit ripple carry adder [3]

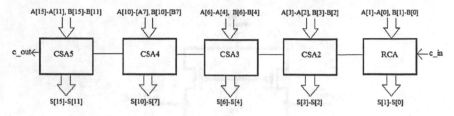

Fig. 3 Block diagram of a 16-bit SQ-CSA [7]

3.2 Square Root Carry Select Adder (SQ-CSA)

Square root carry select adder is an improved form of carry select adder. It is generally used when number of bits in the input is large. The block diagram of 16-bit square root CSA [7] is shown in Fig. 3. Here variable size CSA is considered in order to avoid mismatch that occurs due to difference between the arrival time of the signals, i.e., sum and carry. Figure 4 shows the basic block diagram of carry select adder. In this figure we can see that there are totally eight full adders used or we can say that 2 RCA blocks are used to form 1 CSA block. These RCA block consumes more power as compared to BEC. Therefore, in this work BEC (binary to excess-1 vonverter) is used instead of RCA with input carry '1' so as to lessen the power consumption. This is discussed later in the paper.

3.3 Modified Square Root Carry Select Adder (MSQ-CSA)

The modification in architecture of square root carry select adder using CMOS technology is shown in [8–10]. The modified MCML square root carry select adder is being proposed in this work. The proposed CSA uses BEC (binary to excess-1

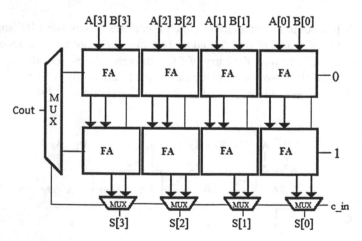

Fig. 4 Basic block diagram of carry select adder [7]

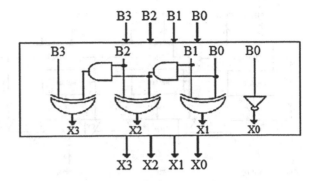

Fig. 5 4-bit binary to excess-1 converter [11]

converter) in place of ripple carry adder with C_in = 1 in regular carry select adder (Fig. 4). This concept of introducing BEC lessens the power consumption of regular CSA. Circuit of BEC is depicted in Fig. 5. This binary to excess-1 converter is also designed in MCML technique. The purpose of addition is achieved using BEC along with the multiplexer as depicted in Fig. 6. Inputs to the 8:4 mux are B0, B1, B2, B3, and the output of 4-bit BEC. Output expressions of 4-bit binary to excess-1 converter are shown below:

$$X0 = NOT\,B0 \tag{3.1}$$

$$X1 = B0\,XOR\,B1 \tag{3.2}$$

$$X2 = B2\,XOR\,(B0\,AND\,B1) \tag{3.3}$$

$$X3 = B3\,XOR\,(B0\,AND\,B1\,AND\,B2) \tag{3.4}$$

Proposed square root carry select adder is implemented by replacing N-bit RCA with (N + 1)-bit BEC. The structure of the proposed 16-bit SQ-CSA is depicted in Fig. 7. The proposed circuit of square root carry select adder consists of BEC block

Fig. 6 4-bit BEC with 8:4 multiplexer [11]

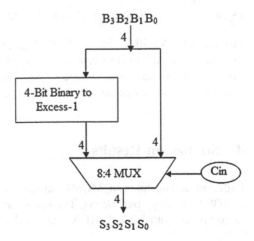

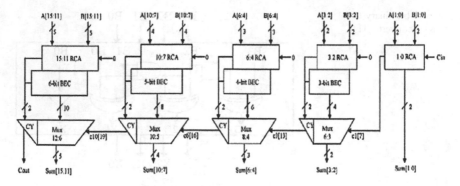

Fig. 7 Proposed 16-bit MCML square root carry select adder (MSQ-CSA)

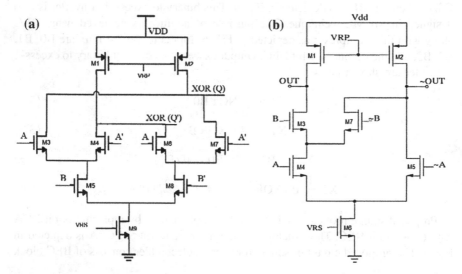

Fig. 8 **a** 2-input XOR used in BEC. **b** MCML AND circuit used in BEC

instead of RCA with C_in = 1. BEC (Fig. 5) consist of one inverter (Fig. 1), three ex-or and two AND gate circuits. The circuit of inverter using MCML is shown in Fig. 1. This provides low-voltage swing. The MCML-based circuits for XOR and AND gate implementation (used in BEC) are reported in Fig. 8a, b.

4 Simulation Results

Different architectures of MCML adders are simulated in T-SPICE using 16 nm CMOS technology parameters. The proposed MCML square root carry select adder is compared with MCML RCA and regular MCML SQ-CSA. Simulation results

Table 1 Power and delay of MCML adders

Word size	Adders	Power (mW)	Delay (ns)
8-bit	MCML RCA	0.29	30.15
	MCML Regular SQ-CSA (Dual RCA)	0.51	25.65
	MCML MSQ-CSA (with BEC)	0.45	26.94
16-bit	MCML RCA	0.54	32.33
	MCML Regular SQ-CSA (Dual RCA)	1.3	27.53
	MCML MSQ-CSA (with BEC)	0.15	28.94

Fig. 9 Comparison of adders for power (mW)

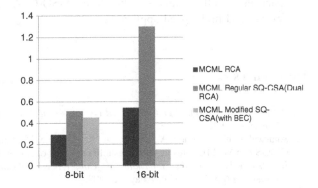

show that the performance of proposed MCML square root carry select adder (MSQ-CSA) (Fig. 7) is better as compared to other adders. From Table 1 it can be seen that the proposed square root carry select Adder reduces the power by 11.76 % in comparison to regular square root carry select adder and delay is reduced by 10.64 % in comparison to ripple carry adder.

Thus, the proposed SQ-CSA (which includes BEC instead of RCA) results in low-power and high-speed adder.

Figures 9 and 10 shows comparison of adders with respect to power and delay, respectively. From comparison, we can see that the proposed square root carry Select adder can replace the other adders in VLSI design for high-speed and low-power applications.

Fig. 10 Comparison of adders for delay (ns)

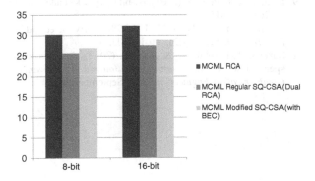

5 Conclusion

Power, delay, and area are the major parameters in VLSI design that limits the performance of any circuit. This paper presents a simple approach to reduce power and delay of carry select adders. The regular carry select adder offers the disadvantage of more power and that ripple carry adder gives more delay. A proposed MCML square root carry select adder (MSQ-CSA) overcomes the disadvantages of both RCA and regular Square root Carry Select Adder. It is found that the proposed 16-bit MCML square root carry select adder provides less delay and power in comparison to other adders. Therefore, MSQ-CSA can be used in various low-power and high-speed applications.

References

1. Rabaey, J. M. (2001). *Digtal integrated circuits—a design perspective*. Upper Saddle River, NJ: Prentice-Hall.
2. Agarwal, T. K., Sawhney, A., Kureshi, A. K., & Hasan, M.: Performance comparison of static CMOS and MCML gates in sub- threshold region of operation for 32 nm CMOS technology. In *Proceedings of the International Conference on Computer and Communication Engineering* (pp. 284–287). Malaysia, 2008.
3. Gupta, K., Pandey, N., & Gupta, M. (2010). A novel active shunt-peaked MCML-based high speed four-bit ripple-carry adder. In *Proceedings of IEEE International Conference on Computer and Communication Technology* (pp. 285–289).
4. Kim, J. B. (2009). Low-power MCML circuit with sleep-transistor. In *IEEE Proceedings 2009*.
5. Amer, S.H., Emara, A.S., Mohie El-Din, R., Fouad, M.M., Madian, A.H., Amer, H.H., Abdelhalim, M.B., & Draz, H.H. (2014). Testing current mode two- input logic gates. In *IEEE CCECE 2014*. Toronto, Canada.
6. Fouad, M., Amer, H. H., Madian, A. H., & Abdelhalim, M. B. (2013). Current mode logic testing of XOR/XNOR circuit: A case study. *Circuits and Systems, Scientific Research Publishing, 4*, 364–368.
7. Gupta, K. Radhika, Pandey, N., & Gupt, M. (2013). A novel high speed MCML square root carry select adder for mixed signal applications. In *IEEE IMPACT-2013*.
8. Ramkumar, B., Kittur, H. M., & Kannan, P. M. (2010). ASIC implementation of modified faster carry save adder. *European Journal of Scientific Research, 42*(1), 53–58.
9. Kim, Y., & Kim, L. S. (2001). 64-bit carry select adder with reduced area. *Electronics Letters, 37*(10), 614–615.
10. Ceiang, T. Y., & Hsiao, M. J. (1998). Carry–Select adder using single ripple carry adder. *Electronics Letters, 34*(2), 2101–2103.
11. Saxena, P., Purohit, U., & Joshi, P. (2013). Analysis of low power, area-efficient and high speed fast adder. *International Journal of Advanced Research in Computer and Communication Engineering, 2*(9), September 2013.

Improvement in Quality of Extractive Text Summaries Using Modified Reciprocal Ranking

Yogesh Kumar Meena and Dinesh Gopalani

Abstract Due to increasing amount of text data available in WWW, it becomes time consuming for information system users to explore every text source in detail. Automatic text summarization (ATS) is the process of generating summary by condensing text document automatically by a computer machine that can save users precious time. Major issue with most of the feature-based ATS methods is to find optimal feature weights for sentence scoring to optimize quality of text summary. This paper presents a novel voting-based approach that use modified reciprocal ranking approach which alleviates the issue of feature weighting and. Proposed approach use a specific prominent set of features for initial ranking that further boosts the performance. Experimental results on DUC 2002 dataset using ROUGE evaluation matrices show that our proposed voting approach performs better when compared to other statistical- and voting-based methods.

Keywords Statistical features · Voting priority · Extractive automatic text summarization · Feature cluster · Sentence scoring · Text mining

1 Introduction

With the increasing amount of textual information in the internet, it becomes difficult for the users to find the desired information quickly. They have to look up the whole document to get a glimpse of actual theme. Automatic text summarization solves the problem by generating summaries that could be utilized as a condensed

Y.K. Meena (✉) · D. Gopalani
Department of Computer Science and Engineering, Malaviya National Institute of
Technology, Jaipur, India
e-mail: ymeena.cse@mnit.ac.in

D. Gopalani
e-mail: dgopalani.cse@mnit.ac.in

© Springer Science+Business Media Singapore 2016
S.C. Satapathy et al. (eds.), *Proceedings of International Conference
on ICT for Sustainable Development*, Advances in Intelligent Systems
and Computing 409, DOI 10.1007/978-981-10-0135-2_30

replica of a document or a set of documents. Therefore, automatic text summarization can be defined as the process of condensing the source text document or set of text documents, while retaining main information contents using an automatic machine. Automatic text summarization could be classified mainly as extractive automatic text summation and abstractive automatic text summarization. Generic summarization condenses the overall information content available in source text. In extractive automatic text summarization, a subset of sentences from the original input set of sentences is selected as summary. In abstractive automatic text summarization, important topics in the textual unit are identified and new sentences are formed. Feature-based extractive text summarization systems in real retrieve important sentences up to an extent. However at the same time, combination of features sometimes degrades the quality of generated text summaries. Overall impact of features becomes reduced due to combination. For expert search systems, a number of voting models are proposed by various researchers. To overcome the issue of feature weighting and combination, we propose an efficient process of generating summaries using modified reciprocal ranking-based method. Rest of the paper is organized as follows: in Sect. 2 we discuss related work for extractive automatic text summarization. Section 3 presents features used. Section 4 describes our proposed summarization process. Dataset, evaluation matrices and results of the proposed approaches with existing methods are discussed in Sect. 5. Section 6 describes conclusions and future scope.

2 Related Work

Automatic text summarizations pioneered work was first started with surface-level features 1950s. Luhn [1] in 1958 proposed term frequency model for sentence scoring. Later Baxendale [2] in 1958 experimented on sentence location feature for sentence scoring. In 1969, Edmundson [3] proposed two additional features, title similarity and cue word. Rush et al. [4] 1971 used a set of rules to reject sentences that was later extended for chemical abstracts [5]. Further, other features were also proposed such as TF-IDF by Brandow et al. [6] in 1995 originally proposed by Salton [7], RIDF by Church and Gale [8] in 1995, bushy path and aggregate similarity by Salton et al. [9] in 1997, term information gain by Mori [10] in 2002, named entity by Nobata et al. [11] in 2002, Text Rank [12] by Mihalcea in 2004, Numerical data and proper noun by Fattah and Ren [13] in 2009, word co-occurrence by Liu [14] et al. in 2009. Researchers used these features along with some transformed version of these feature in genetic- and cluster-based methods as well. Most of the extractive summarization approaches use these features for sentence scoring using different methodologies. Mainly, these summarization approaches computes linear sum of feature scores. Genetic algorithms on the other hand, with additional features find the optimal weights to score sentences. Voting-based approach such as Votes, RR [15], BordaFuse [16], CombANZ, CombMED, CombMIN, CombMAX,

CombMNZ [17], expCombANZ, exCombSUM, and expCombMNZ [13] for expert search systems were proposed by researchers. In [18, 19], these voting models are compared for TREC 2005 and TEREC 2006. Voting methods were proposed for expert search to aggregate the ranks of retrieved documents. These methods basically rank retrieved information using specific standard method. Thereafter, a voting model is chosen with some similarity measure to rank the retrieved documents. For text summarization, specifically Kumar et al. [20] in 2013 proposed a cross-document relationship-based genetic approach using CombMAX voting model. Kumar et al. [21] in 2014 discussed about adaption of 12 voting models proposed for expert search for text summarization. Voting schemes are totally dependent on strength of initial ranking process and similarity measure used for finding set of voters.

3 Features Used

Sentence-level scoring methods basically use a set of features (mainly surface level) to score the sentences. These features are extracted from preprocessed source document. These features capture the important information content available in the input source text document. Features used for our proposed approaches are described as follows:

3.1 Term Frequency (F1)

It is the frequency of the term in the whole text document. According to this feature, the most frequent words in document are the most important words (other than stop words) and they convey maximum information.

3.2 Gain (F2)

Words with medium (Stop words are higher frequency words) frequency are most important, gain used this idea effectively for sentence scoring.

3.3 Word Co-occurrence (F3)

Thematic words (most frequent) if they co-occur in the sentences then higher weight is given to the respective sentences.

3.4 Sentence Location (F4)

It assigns a score to each sentence as per its location in the text document. First, sentence always got higher score in this feature.

3.5 Named Entity (F5)

Presence of named in a sentence, suggests that it contains more information and should be scored higher.

3.6 Sentence Centrality (F6)

The sentences which are more similar (Cosine, Jaccard, etc.) to other sentences are the most important ones. The similarity is measured in terms of terms overlap between the sentences.

3.7 Text Rank (F7)

It is based on one of the most popular ranking used for web link analysis and assigns the scores to sentences considering them as nodes for link analysis.

3.8 LSA (F8)

Modified latent semantic scores procedure is used for scoring sentences using this feature as proposed by Wang and Maches [22].

3.9 Bushy Path (F9)

According to this feature, the sentence that have maximum sentences related (with specific threshold value) to it, is the most important sentence.

This feature will score each sentence in the range 0 to 1. Additionally, sentence length criterium is also applied. Sentence's of length less than 4 and more than 40 are not included in summarization process.

4 Proposed Work

Our proposed summarization process completes in three steps as shown in Fig. 1. In first step, preprocessing is applied on input source document. Operations such as sentence segmentation, stop word removal, stemming and case folding are applied. We then use Stanford NLP tools for POS tagging and to find named entities in the text.

After preprocessing, sentences are scores using different features. Then we use following initial ranking process as given in Eqs. (1) and (2). We then used Jaccard Similarity measure to find S_{svoter}.

$$\text{score}_1(s) = F7(s) + F8(s) + F9(s) \tag{1}$$

$$\text{score}_2(s) = F1(s) + F2(s) + F4(s) + F5(s) + F6(s) + F8(s) + F9(s) \tag{2}$$

Proposed summarization process use modified version of reciprocal ranking (RR) [15] method that sums the reciprocal ranks of each voter of the candidate sentence. For a candidate sentence S, this can be calculated using the formula given in Eq. (3), where rank(p) is the rank of sentence v in set $S_{svoters}$ using initial ranking given in Eq. (1).

Fig. 1 Summarization process flow

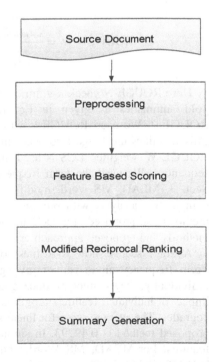

$$\text{Modified RRScore}(S) = \frac{1}{\text{score}_2} + \sum_{p \in S_{\text{voters}}} \frac{1}{\text{rank}(p)} \qquad (3)$$

After scoring the sentences using proposed modified reciprocal ranking, top-ranked sentences are selected as the summary sentences in final summary generation step. For linear sum, Eq. (4) is used to calculate the final score of sentences.

$$\text{Linear Sum}(s) = \sum_{i=1}^{9} Fi(s) \qquad (4)$$

5   Results and Analysis

We experimented our proposed scoring methods on DUC 2002 dataset. We used a subset of 10 documents for our experiments. Each document is given with a reference summary (gold summary), which we used to compare with our system-generated summary. We limited the compression rate to 100 words. We used ROUGE [23] evaluation matrices to evaluate quality of generated summaries.

$$\text{ROUGE} - N = \frac{\sum\limits_{S \in \text{Gold Summary}} \sum\limits_{\text{gram}_n \in S} \text{count}_{\text{match}}(\text{gram}_n)}{\sum\limits_{S \in \text{Gold Summary}} \sum\limits_{\text{gram}_n \in S} \text{count}(\text{gram}_n)} \qquad (5)$$

Here ROUGE-N check n-gram co-occurrence in between system generated and gold summaries as given in Eq. (5). We experimented on ROUGE-1 and ROUGE-2. We used ROUGE-L which finds the longest common subsequence. This identifies the longest co-occurring in sequence of n-grams automatically. In ROUGE-W, weighted LCS is used that favors consecutive longest common subsequences. We used the term frequency, linear sum of all features described in Sect. 3, MEAD, MS word, modified LSA, and other voting-based methods for comparative analysis with our proposed scoring techniques. Result of statistical methods and proposed approach are presented in Table 1. Results of other voting methods and proposed approach are shown in Table 2.

Average scores show robustness of our method compared to other methods. Term frequency alone cannot give good results. In real futures when applied individually, they cannot produce quality summaries. In case of linear sum, the impact of individual feature strength is reduced, so that overall quality of summary degrades. The average score for linear sum in case of ROUGE-1 is 0.45778 and for proposed method is 0.49293. In similar way, other methods used combination of features. For MEAD, MS Word, and LSA, the ROUGE-1 scores are 0.46067, 0.46315, and 0.47108, respectively. In case of ROUGE-L and ROUGE-W also the

Table 1 Average ROUGE recall scores of different statistical techniques and proposed approach

Summarization method	ROUGE metric			
	ROUGE-1	ROUGE-2	ROUGE-L	ROUGE-W
TF	0.45355	0.19496	0.37782	0.37491
Linear sum	0.45778	0.19892	0.38375	0.37491
MEAD	0.46067	0.20088	0.3818	0.38181
MS Word	0.46315	0.17541	0.36597	0.36501
LSA	0.47108	0.18972	0.38021	0.37925
Proposed method	0.49293	0.22983	0.39861	0.41298

Table 2 Average ROUGE recall scores of different statistical techniques and proposed approach

Summarization method	ROUGE metric			
	ROUGE-1	ROUGE-2	ROUGE-L	ROUGE-W
Kumar et al. [20] RR	0.45239	0.19233	0.37022	0.37168
Kumar et al. [20] RR	0.46748	0.21042	0.37334	0.37513
Linear sum + RR	0.47173	0.21115	0.3718	0.37281
Proposed method	0.49293	0.22983	0.39861	0.41298

results of our approach are higher. Similar is the case with comparison with other existing voting schemes.

Comparison of existing statistical approaches such as term frequency, linear sum, MEAD, MS Word, and LSA with proposed approach is shown in Fig. 2a. Our proposed method clearly wins over other statistical methods. ROUGE-2 specially measures 2-gram matches that are more suitable for comparing similarity in between text spans. Here also, proposed method performs better compared to LSA, MEAD, term frequency, linear sum, and MS Word.

Comparison of the existing voting-based approaches with proposed approach is shown in Fig. 2b. Here also proposed approach performs better compared to other

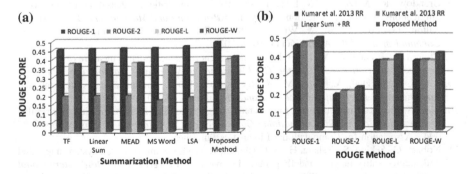

Fig. 2 a ROUGE recall comparison of existing statistical approaches and proposed approach. **b** ROUGE recall comparison of existing voting approaches and proposed approach

proposed by Kumar et al. [20, 21]. Our approach used score of features in combination with reciprocal ranking that improves the performance of summarization system.

6 Conclusion and Future Scope

This paper investigated the impact of features such as term frequency, gain, sentence location, named entity, LSA, bushy path, sentence centrality, text rank, and word co-occurrence using voting schemes. We used modified reciprocal ranking that additionally take the advantage of score of top feature combinations. Experimental results on ROUGE-1, ROUGE-2, ROUGE-1, and ROUGE-W show that our proposed scoring performs better compared to other statistical- and voting-based reciprocal ranking approaches. Additionally, our proposed approach does not require any feature weighing. In future, we will try to analyze the impact of sentence filtering approaches on the quality of text summaries using proposed voting schemes.

References

1. Luhn, H. P. (1958). The automatic creation of literature abstracts. *IBM Journal of Research and Development, 2*(2), 159–165.
2. Baxendale, P. B. (1958). Machine-made index for technical literature: An experiment. *IBM Journal of Research and Development, 2*(4), 354–361.
3. Edmundson, H. P. (1969). New methods in automatic extracting. *Journal of the ACM, 16*(2), 264–285.
4. Rush, J. E., Salvador, R., & Zamora, A. (1971). Automatic abstracting and indexing. ii. production of indicative abstracts by application of contextual inference and syntactic coherence criteria. *Journal of the American Society for Information Science, 22*(4), 260–274.
5. Pollock, J. J., & Zamora, A. (1975). Automatic abstracting research at chemical abstracts service. *Chemical Information and Computer Sciences, 15*(4), 226–232.
6. Brandow, R., Mitze, K., & Lisa, F. R. (1995). Automatic condensation of electronic publications by sentence selection. *Information Processing and Management, 31*, 675–685.
7. Salton, G., Fox, E. A., & Wu, H. (1983). Extended Boolean information retrieval. *Communications of the ACM, 26*(11), 1022–1036.
8. Church, K., & Gale, W. A. (1995). Inverse document frequency (idf): A measure of deviations from poisson. In *Proceedings of the Third Workshop on Very Large Corpora* (pp. 121–130).
9. Salton, G., Singhal, A., Mitra, M., & Buckley, C. (1997). Automatic text structuring and summarization. *Information Processing and Management, 33*(2), 193–207.
10. Mori, T. (2002). Information gain ratio as term weight: The case of summarization of ir results. In *Proceedings of the 19th International Conference on Computational Linguistics* (pp. 688–694). Association for Computational Linguistics Publisher.
11. Nobata, C., Sekine, S., Isahara, H., & Grishman, R. (2002). Summarization system integrated with named entity tagging and IE pattern discovery. In *Proceedings of Third International Conference on Language Resources and Evaluation (LREC)*. Las Palmas, Canary Islands, Spain.

12. Mihalcea, R., & Tarau, P. (2004). Textrank: Bringing order into texts. In D. Lin, & D. Wu, (Eds.), *Proceedings of EMNLP, Association for Computational Linguistics* (pp. 404–411). Barcelona, Spain.
13. Fattah, M. A., & Ren, F. (2009). Ga, mr, ann, pnn and gmm based models for automatic text summarization. *Computer Speech & Language, 23*(1), 126–144.
14. Liu, X., Jonathan, J. W., & Chunyu, K.(2009). An extractive text summarizer based on significant words. In *Proceedings of the 22nd International Conference on Computer Processing of Oriental Languages. Language Technology for the Knowledge-based Economy (ICCPOL '09)* (pp. 168–178). Heidelberg: Springer-Verlag, Berlin.
15. Zhang, M., Song, R., Lin, C., Ma, S., Jang, Z., Lin, Y., Liu, Y., & Zhao, L. (2002). Expansion-based technologies in finding relevant and new information: THU TREC2002: Novelty Track experiments. In *Proceedings of TREC*. Gaithersburg, MD.
16. Aslam, J. A., & Montague, M. (2001). Models for metasearch. In *Proceedings of ACM SIGIR 2001* (pp. 276–284). New Orleans LA.
17. Ogilvie, P., & Callan, J. (2003). Combining document representations for known item search. In *SIGIR* (pp. 143–150). New York, NY, USA.
18. Macdonald, C., & Ounis, I. (2008). Voting techniques for expert search. *Knowledge and Information Systems, 16*(3), 259–280.
19. Macdonald, C., & Ounis, I. (2006). Voting for candidates: adapting data fusion techniques for an expert search task. In *CIKM Proceedings of the 15th ACM International Conference on Information and Knowledge Management* (pp. 387–396).
20. Kumar, Y. J., Salim, N., Abuobieda, A., & Tawfik, A. (2013). Multi document summarization based on cross-document relation using voting technique. In *International Conference on Computing, Electrical and Electronics Engineering (ICCEEE)* (pp. 609–614).
21. Kumar, Y. J., Goh, O. S., Ghani, M. K., Salim, N., & Albaham, A. T. (2014). Voting models for summary extraction from text documents. In *International Conference on IT Convergence and Security (ICITCS)* (pp. 1–4).
22. Wang, Y., & Maches, J. (2013). A comprehensive method for text summarization based on latent semantic analysis. *NLPCC* (pp. 394–401). Heidelberg: Springer-Verlag Berlin.
23. Lin, C. Y. (2004). ROUGE: A package for automatic evaluation of summaries. In *Proceedings of the Workshop on Text Summarization Branches Out (WAS 2004)*. Barcelona, Spain.

A Novel Compact Monopole Multiband Antenna for WiMAX/Satellite/Military Applications

Ashu Verma, Bhupendra Singh, Sanjeev Yadav and Preeti Jain

Abstract A compact Microstrip-fed monopole multiband antenna has been designed and simulated in this paper. The design of the antenna has compact structure with size of $20 \times 18 \times 1$ mm^3. The proposed antenna has multiband characteristics which work at 4.2, 6.1, and 12.1 GHz. Additional resonances are excited by embedding two I-shaped notches in the ground plane. The bandwidth of 112 % is achieved by embedding an inverting U-shaped notch on the radiating patch. At each frequency, Return loss < -20 dB and VSWR < 2.

Keywords Monopole antenna · G-slot · Three notched bands · WiMAX · VSWR · Return loss · Radiation pattern

1 Introduction

Due to the rapid growth in wireless communication, the need of multiband frequency is raised. Thus, an antenna with multiband operations is required. Multiband antennas are developed for various wireless applications so that any equipment can employ several applications at a time. These applications can involve data transfer, video, audio, and radio. In multiband antenna, one part works for one band while another part works for different band. A multiband antenna can have lower than average gains. These are manufactured to work at high frequencies from MHz to several GHz [1–6].

A. Verma (✉) · B. Singh · P. Jain
Department of ECE, Amity University, Noida, U.P., India
e-mail: verma_ashu92@yahoo.in

B. Singh
e-mail: bsingh5@amity.edu

P. Jain
e-mail: preeti.essare@gmail.com

S. Yadav
Department of ECE, Government Women Engineering College, Ajmer, Rajasthan, India
e-mail: sanjeev.mnit@gmail.com

© Springer Science+Business Media Singapore 2016
S.C. Satapathy et al. (eds.), *Proceedings of International Conference on ICT for Sustainable Development*, Advances in Intelligent Systems and Computing 409, DOI 10.1007/978-981-10-0135-2_31

A planar monopole microstrip patch is widely used for manufacturing the multiband antenna due to its various attractive features like low profile, low cost, small size, and easy to fabricate. It has a very large antenna quality factor. This factor presents antenna's losses and a high-quality factor gives rise to narrow bandwidth and low efficiency. Quality factor can be decreased by increasing the substrate's thickness. But as the thickness increases, an increment fraction of total radiated power produced by load goes into surface wave. This surface current counts as an undesired power loss and is responsible for degradation of the characteristics of antenna. Nowadays, many researchers are working on size reduction and bandwidth enhancement techniques. Bandwidth enhancement techniques in planar antenna are obtained by E-slot patch, H-slot patch, U-shaped slot patch, shorting pin, and slit loaded. Defected ground structure is also responsible for addition resonances to enhance bandwidth. Many trade-offs are taken to optimize the geometry of an antenna [6–9].

In this paper, a monopole antenna with multiband operations is demonstrated. The defected ground structure is employed for the excitation of additional resonances to enhance the bandwidth. The proposed antenna has three resonant frequencies 4.2, 6.1, and 12.2 GHz with bandwidths of 3.98–4.54, 5.97–10.928, and 11.7–12.2 GHz, respectively. The proposed antenna also operates at 4.2 GHz frequency, the antenna is used for military applications like communication mobile/computer management vehicle (COMOB/CMOD) and small satellite earth stations applications. CMOD/COMOB is a platform for RADAR systems and a moving communication utility that can be combined with combat systems like combat-field management system (CMS) and air defense system (ADS). The one of the features of satellite communication is small earth station (Stasiun Bumi Mini) that employs parabola-type reflector. The bandwidth also covers the WiMAX (4–4.5 GHz) band. At 6.1 GHz, the antenna is employed for terrestrial microwave applications. It covers 5.9–6.425 GHz band for satellite uplink and 7.25–7.75 GHz band for satellite downlink. At 12.1 GHz, antenna is employed as satellite downlink application [2–9].

The rest of the paper is structured as follows. In Sect. 2, a detailed description of the design of proposed antenna is presented. Simulation results are presented in Sect. 3. Finally, Sect. 4 gathers the conclusion of the proposed work.

2 Antenna Design

Figure 1 shows the top and the bottom view of the multiband antenna. The radiating patch is placed on a FR4 substrate material. The substrate has the dimensions of $20 \times 18 \times 1 \ mm^3$ and dielectric constant of 4.4. For the perfect impedance matching or 50-Ω characteristics impedance, the width and length of microstrip transmission line are fixed and kept at 1.86 and 7.5 mm.

The multiband notch characteristics are introduced by inserting Γ-shaped notches and G-slot on the defected ground. Additional resonances are excited by embedding two I-shaped notches in the ground plane.

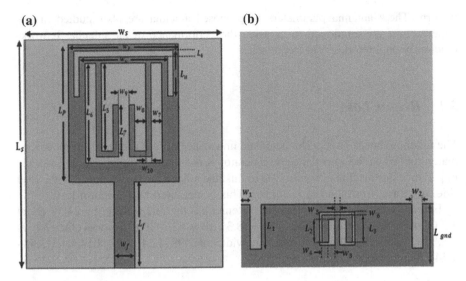

Fig. 1 Front view (**a**) and bottom view (**b**) of proposed multiband antenna

Table 1 Dimensions of proposed antenna

S. no	Name of parameter	Value (mm)
1	Length of ground plane (L_{gnd})	5
2	Length of the feed (L_f)	7.5
3	Width of the feed (w_f)	1.86
4	Width of the feed (w_f)	20
5	Width of the Substrate (w_s)	18
6	Length of the patch (L_p)	12
7	Width of the patch (w_p)	10
8	Length of Inverse U-shape (L_u)	3.5
9	Width of Inverse U-shaped (w_u)	8

Table 1 shows the parameters of the proposed antenna and some of the dimensions are as follows: $L_1 = 4$ mm, $L_2 = 1.8$ mm, $L_3 = 2.2$ mm, $w_1 = 1$ mm, $w_2 = 1$ mm, $w_3 = 0.6$ mm, $w_4 = 0.6$ mm, $w_5 = 0.4$ mm, $L_4 = 0.5$ mm, $L_5 = 0.2$ mm, $L_6 = 0.2$ mm, and $L_7 = 0.2$ mm.

3 Simulation Results

The multiband monopole antenna is designed using CST microwave simulator. It is a user-friendly software that has most accurate results. CST provides facility to study several antenna parameters like return loss, VSWR, Smith chart, and radiation pattern. These antenna parameters of proposed antenna are also studied in this paper. These are employed to measure the performance of an antenna. It works efficiently on three different frequencies.

3.1 Return Loss

The antenna should have a characteristic impedance of 50-Ω for perfect impedance matching. When the impedance at generator is not same as impedance at load, the impedance mismatching occurs. Due to this, the reflections are produced at the load side and travel from load to generator. This is measured by the return loss.

Figure 2 shows that the proposed antenna has the return loss of −21.58 dB at 4.2 GHz, −34.54 dB at 6.1 GHz, and −38.31 dB at 12.1 GHz. It works efficiently at 4.2, 6.1, and 12.1 GHz with the bandwidth of 3.98–4.54, 3.98–4.54, and 3.98–4.54 GHz, respectively.

3.2 VSWR

VSWR describes the efficiency of the antenna in terms of impedance matching. For perfect impedance matching, the VSWR should have a value of less than two.

Figure 3 shows that at each resonant frequency, the VSWR is less than 2.

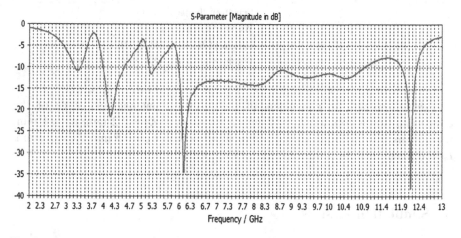

Fig. 2 Return loss of proposed multiband antenna

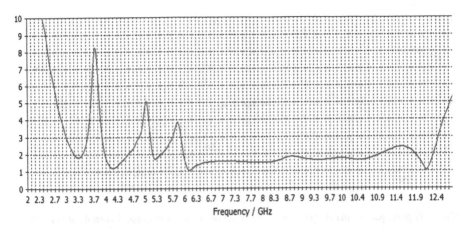

Fig. 3 VSWR of proposed multiband antenna

3.3 Radiation Pattern

The radiation pattern is the graphical representation of radiation characteristics. The radiation pattern is the combination of E-plane pattern and H-plane pattern. The direction of maximum radiation is known as major lobe and 3 dB beamwidth is calculated at this. Figures 4, 5, and 6 show the radiation pattern at 4.2, 6.1, and 12.1 GHz frequencies, respectively.

Figure 4 shows the E-plane far-field radiation pattern and H-plane far-field radiation pattern at resonant frequency of 4.2 GHz. The E-plane pattern has the main lobe magnitude of 1.29 dB. The main lobe direction is 180°. The H-pattern is omnidirectional and has main lobe magnitude of −0.246 dB.

Figure 5 shows the E-plane far-field radiation pattern and H-plane far-field radiation pattern at resonant frequency of 6.1 GHz. The E-plane pattern has the

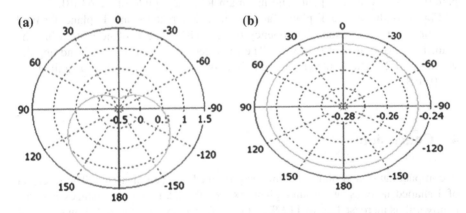

Fig. 4 E-plane pattern (**a**) and H-plane pattern (**b**) of proposed multiband antenna at 4.2 GHz

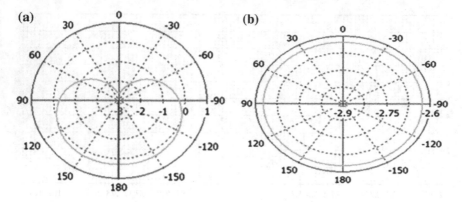

Fig. 5 E-plane pattern (**a**) and H-plane pattern (**b**) of proposed multiband antenna at 6.1 GHz

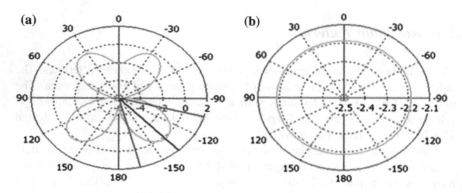

Fig. 6 E-plane pattern (**a**) and H-plane pattern (**b**) of proposed multiband antenna at 12.1 GHz

main lobe magnitude of 0.278 dB. The main lobe direction is 180°. Omnidirectional pattern is achieved at H-plane and has main lobe magnitude of −2.63 dB.

Figure 6 shows the E-plane far-field radiation pattern and H-plane far-field radiation pattern at resonant frequency of 12.1 GHz. The E-plane pattern has the main lobe magnitude of 0.143 dB. The main lobe direction is −137° and angular width of 61.2°. The H-pattern is omnidirectional and has main lobe magnitude of −2.19 dB.

4 Conclusions

A compact multiband planar antenna is presented and demonstrated. The insertion of I-shaped notches on ground plane excites the additional resonances and the bandwidth is increased up to 112 %. At each frequency, VSWR < 2 shows a better impedance matching. The presented antenna can be used for WiMAX, satellite and military applications. The radiation parameters like return loss, VSWR, and radiation pattern at 4.2, 6.1, and 12.1 GHz are also discussed.

References

1. Guha, D., & Antar, Y. M. M. (2011). *Microstrip and printed antennas new trends, techniques and applications*. John Wiley & sons Ltd.
2. Singh, N., Singh, S., Kumar, A., & Sarin, R. K. (2010). A planar multiband antenna with enhanced bandwidth and reduced size. *International Journal of Electronic Engineering Research ISSN, 2*, 341–347.
3. Iwasaki, H. (1996, October). A circularly polarized small-size microstrip antenna with a cross slots. *IEEE Transactions on Antennas and Propagation, 44*, 1399–1401.
4. Wong, K. L., & Hsu, W. H. (2000, July). A broadband patch antenna with wide slits. *IEEE Transactions on Antennas and Propagation, 3*, 1414–1417.
5. Wong, K. L. (2002). *Compact and broadband microstrip antennas*. New York: Wiley.
6. Antoniades, M. A. (2008). A compact multiband monopole antenna with a defected ground plane. *IEEE Antennas and Wireless Propagation Letters, 7*.
7. Antoniades, M. A., & Eleftheriades, G. V. (2008). A compact monopole antenna with a defected ground plane for multiband applications. In *IEEE International Symposium on Antennas and Propagation* (pp. 1–4). San Diego, CA.
8. Poorna Priya, P., Anupama, G., Pavan kumar, K., & Khan, H. (2012, June). New multiband design using chebhyshev distribution for broadband & military applications. *Journal of Emerging Trends in Computing and Information Sciences, 3*.
9. Agrawall, N. P., Kumar, G., & Ray, K. P. (1998). Wide-band planar monopole antennas. *IEEE Transactions on Antennas and Propagation, 46*, 294–295.

Critical Study and Analysis of Cyber Law Awareness Among the Netizens

Aniruddhsinh Parmar and Kuntal Patel

Abstract India is an attractive target for crackers due to high internet and technology penetration growth and limited awareness among the users. It creates moral, civil, and criminal issues in cyber space and it resulted into increase in the cyber crime. But awareness about the cyber law is an often overlooked factor among netizens. Even many stack holders of the computer science are not aware about the cyber law of the country, they are enhancing their technical skills by various means but sadly they are not serious about getting knowledge about cybercrime and cyber law. It necessitated information security awareness among the netizens. In this paper, we have conducted one survey to check cyber law awareness statistics among professionals associated with IT domains. The paper presents the result of a survey conducted and provides the recommendations for improving general awareness of cyber law in India.

Keywords Cyber security · Netizen · Cyber law · Indian IT act · Cyber law awareness · Cyber space

1 Introduction

Use of the Internet becomes more central among many of the networked-based information system in governmental agencies, corporate businesses, and among individuals. Also, due to the rapid growth of digital communication and electronic

---

The two authors contributed equally to this work.

A. Parmar (✉) · K. Patel
School of Computer Studies, Ahmedabad University, Ahmedabad, India
e-mail: aniruddhsinh.parmar@ahduni.edu.in

K. Patel
e-mail: kuntal.patel@ahduni.edu.in

© Springer Science+Business Media Singapore 2016
S.C. Satapathy et al. (eds.), *Proceedings of International Conference on ICT for Sustainable Development*, Advances in Intelligent Systems and Computing 409, DOI 10.1007/978-981-10-0135-2_32

data exchange, data and information security becomes an essential issue in businesses and administration. The requirement of information security within an organization is important today as many of the organizations are using computer-based information system. Such computerized systems are networked-based. The need of information security is even more sensitive for system that can be accessed over public telephone network, data network, or the Internet.

At present, the number of cyber crimes in India is nearly around 149,254 and is likely to cross the 300,000 by 2015 growing at compounded annual growth rate (CAGR) of about 107 percent. According to the study, every month sees 12,456 cases registered in India. During 2011, 2012, 2013, and 2014, the total numbers of cyber crimes registered were 13,301, 22,060, 71,780, and 62,189, respectively, it said [1].

Although, there exist cyber law for protecting rights of all the netizens and various tools are also available to protect the resources against the cyber attack. But in India still majority of the netizens and stack holders of information system are not aware about the cyber attack on their resources and lacked awareness and interest in the cyber crime phenomenon.

According to latest figure, 70 % of the cyber crimes are performed by insiders intentionally or unintentionally, so by making them aware about the IT Act provisions we can reduce the crimes performed by insiders (Fig. 1).

Looking to the facts observed, we have decided to conduct survey to check the awareness regarding the cyber law. This research/survey is aimed to collect responses with regards to the knowledge and awareness of respondents toward important sections of the cyber laws in India. A questionnaire containing 22 questions was designed to record the response of the participants. Such data were collected from the faculty of computer science and software professionals.

Fig. 1 Year wise registered cases related to cyber crime in India

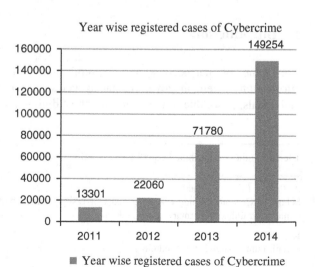

Year wise registered cases of Cybercrime

■ Year wise registered cases of Cybercrime

The main objective of the survey was to assess the awareness of the respondents. Questionnaire contains most of the questions which has been answered in the form of yes, no, or not sure. It has been designed with the objective to assess the awareness for Indian cyber law among the netizens.

2 Literature Review

According to report release by The Nation Crime Records Bureau, Ministry of Home Affairs, India there is again a rapid increase in cyber crime by 50 % on year-on-year basis from 2012 to 2013. The maximum offenders came from 18 to 30 age groups [2].

Mehta studied the awareness about cyber laws in Indian Society and revealed that Increase reliance on technology and lack of proper training has increase the incidents of cyber crime [3]. They also revealed that employed netizens (a user of the Internet) are more aware about the cyber law compare to the nonemployed netizens and requirement of trained human resources to deal with the cases of cyber crime.

Aloul felt that security awareness is an often overlooked factor in an information security program [4]. While organizations expand their use of advanced security technology and continuously train their security professionals, very little is used to increase the security awareness among the other users, making them the weakest link in any organization. The high penetration rate and limited security awareness among users is making it an attractive target for cyber criminals. Bhushan has revealed that biggest challenge for the country is to train and equip the law enforcement agencies and judiciary, especially outside the metro cities [5]. As studied by Vasant, while implementing concept of BYOD, there is a chance of security breach in the network-based resources [6].

Dalal concluded that special effort is required to make the netizens of the country aware about the cyber law [7]. Out of all the Internet users and organizations, very few are aware about the cyber law.

Saxena felt a need to educate our netizens to use the IT infrastructure properly as our nation is rapidly building its cyber infrastructure [8]. According to them, important aspects of information security are awareness, training, and education of the netizens. They also felt the need to include topics related to cyber ethics, cyber safety, and cyber security issues in educational system beginning at early age and also suggested various methods for the same. They concluded that there is a need of cyber security curriculum which will help to get more profound, securely skilled professionals in every sector.

Peng conducted the survey of the awareness about cyber law among the young Singaporeans and participants felt the need of cyber ethic in use of Internet, where problems in security are obvious [9]. Author concluded that cyber law have to be constantly monitored, revised, and updated to keep up with the changes and it should be explained and communicated regularly to every individual. Further, it was also concluded that software producer should produce reliable software. Most of the participants were not aware about the amendment in existing cyber law of Singapore.

After review of literature related to cyber law and information security, we felt the need to conduct the survey on cyber law awareness among the netizens. The survey was conducted among the people closely associated with the IT field.

3 Visual Summary of Responses Received from the Survey

From the received responses, we have prepared the visual summary, so it would be easy to find out the awareness about the cyber law among the participants. Based on this, we have recommended important points to improve awareness about cyber law. The questions asked and their responses summaries are as under:

Que.1 Are you aware about IT Act of India?

Que.2 Have you ever refer/read IT Act?

Alarming facts coming out of the summary from survey is that nearly 47 % of the participants, who are actually closely associated with the Computer Industry, are not aware about IT Act of India. Out of those who claim that they are aware about the IT Act in that also actually only 59 % participants have read the IT Act (see Figs. 2, 3).

Que. 3 Please specifies your experience in number of years.

Que. 4 Please specify per week average usage of Internet.

The summary of responses received for question 3 and 4 is given in Figs. 4 and 5.

Que.5 Have you or your organization ever become victim of Cyber Attack?

Que. 6 In case of Cyber Attack on you or your organizations are you willing to register your complaint with the authority?

Fig. 2 Awareness about IT Act

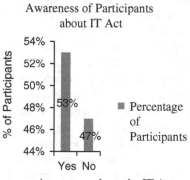

Awareness about the IT Act

Fig. 3 Percentage of participants aware and refer IT Act

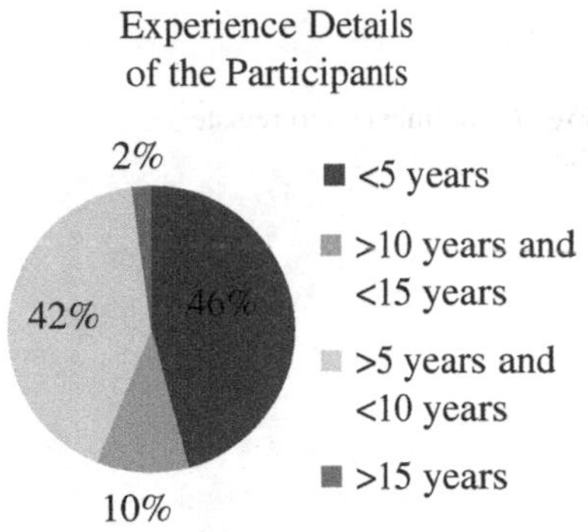

Percentage of Participants who are aware and read/refer IT Act

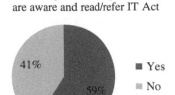

Fig. 4 Experience details of participants

Experience Details of the Participants

Fig. 5 Per week internet usage

Per week Internet Usage of the Participants

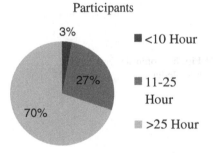

Nearly 55 % participants are not aware about the attack, 39 % were not sure about it, and only 6 % participants were aware about the cyber attack on them or their organization (see Fig. 6).

Nearly 88 % participants were willing to register their complaint with the concerned authority in case of cyber attack but only 29 % knows where to register the complaint (see Figs. 7 and 8).

Que. 7 Do you know where to register complains related to Cyber Crime?

Que. 8 Do you know that sending Offensive/Threatening E-mail/SMS to someone is an offense according to IT Act.

Fig. 6 Knowledge about
attack

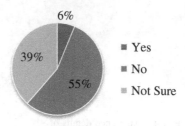

Knowledge of participants
about Cyber Attack on them or
their organization

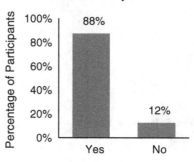

Fig. 7 Willingness to register
the complain

Willingness of the parcipants
to register the complain with
the authority

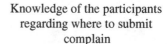

Fig. 8 Complain registration
knowledge

Knowledge of the participants
regarding where to submit
complain

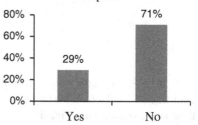

Nearly 78 % participants were aware that sending threaten message is consider offense according to IT Act (see Fig. 9.)

Que. 9 Do you know whoever dishonestly receives or retains stolen computer or communication device knowingly shall be punished according to IT Act.

Fig. 9 Threaten message as
an offense

Awareness of the participants
about sending threaten
message as an offense

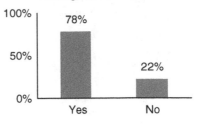

Fig. 10 Retaining stolen
device

Knoweledge about retaining
stolen communication device
is crime or not

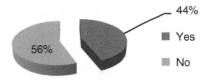

Only 44 % participants were aware that retaining stolen communication device is crime (see Fig. 10).

Que. 10 If someone will perform Cyber Crime using resources owned by you like internet connection than do you think you are liable for that crime?

Nearly 61 % participants were aware that if somebody will perform the crime using the resources own by them than they are responsible for that crime (see Fig. 11).

Que. 11 Do you know that physical damage to the computer, computer network is also an offense according to IT Act.

Only 31 % participants were aware about the provision that physical damage to the communication device own by third party is considered as crime according to IT Act (see Fig. 12).

Fig. 11 Liability of resource
owner

Liability of Owner

Fig. 12 Damage to
communication device

Knowledge about physical
damage to communication
device is crime

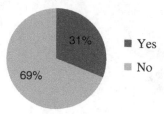

Fig. 13 Provision of
Adjudicating Officer

Do you know about
provision of Adjudicating
Officer

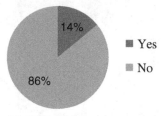

Que. 12 Do you know that according to IT Act, in case of data theft victim can claim compensation up to 5 crore from the criminal without filing a complaint with the police or other investigating agencies.

Only 14 % participants were aware about the Sect. 46 of IT Act related to power of Adjudicate using which one can claim compensation amount up to 5 crore without registering complain with the police (see Fig. 13).

4   Recommendations to Improve the Awareness of Cyber Law

- Government–public–private participatory mode should be adopted for providing training to the general public. We may take help from various local chapters and state-level societies working for IT field like Computer Society of India (CSI), Institute of Engineers, Association of Computing Machinery (ACM), Indian Society for Technical Education (ISTE), etc.
- Special cyber law awareness conferences and workshops should be planned at districts as well as at Taluka levels in India.
- One can take the help of media (television channels) for continuously posting IT security-related advices and should report IT security incidents. Such

advertisements and news should also be broadcasted on cartoon channels to generate some awareness about cyber law and security among the children.

- Basic ethics and IT applications usage etiquettes should be introduced into the regular course curriculum during the schooling.
- Law awareness should be started from the secondary educations in schools.
- Universities may advise all their constituents' colleges and departments to conducts security awareness campaigns and integrates cyber law and security-related topics into their curriculum.
- Information technology-related industries should give training to their all employees especially during their initial period of service. Training should also be imparted for all cyber laws-related amendments.
- To promote the awareness about cyber laws, special weighage should be given to the applicants having knowledge about cyber laws during recruitment process.
- Local authority should highlight the incidents related to cyber crime in regional languages.

5 Conclusions

The cyber law awareness survey summary indicates that most of the participants were not able to actively keep themselves updated with the latest information related to cyber law and computer security. These are the participants related to information technology field, and still awareness regarding the cyber law is not good. Looking to the facts of survey, we may conclude that awareness scenario may be even poorer in the people not associated with the IT field. Also, most of the participants of the survey agreed on the need for ethics in the use of the Internet, where problems in security, privacy enforcement, and threats of viruses are obvious and cannot be avoided. By following the recommendations given in the paper, we can improve the general awareness regarding the cyber law among the netizens.

Acknowledgments We thank Prof. Bipin Mehta—Director, School of Computer Studies, Ahmedabad University for his valuable support during the execution of this research work.

References

1. Retrieved January 15, 2015, from http://tech.firstpost.com/news-analysis/number-of-cyber-crimes-in-india-may-touch-300000-in-2015-248116.html.
2. National Crime Records Bureau. Retrieved February 20, 2015, from http://www.ncrb.gov.in.
3. Mehta, S., & Singh, V. (2013, January). A study of awareness about Cyber Laws in the Indian Society. *International Journal of Computing and Business Research (IJCBR)*, 4(1)

4. Aloul, F. A. (2010). Information security awareness in UAE: A survey paper. In *2010 International Conference on Internet Technology and Secured Transactions (ICITST)* (pp. 1–6), 8–11 November 2010
5. Bhushan, K. (2014). India ranks fifth among cybercrime affected country. Retrieved September 5, 2014, from http://www.thinkdigit.com/Internet/India-ranks-fifth-among-cybercrime-affected_ 9476.html.
6. Vasant, S., & Mehta, B. (2015). A case study: Embedding ICT for effective classroom teaching & learning. *Advances in Intelligent Systems and Computing, Springer International Publishing, Switzerland, 337*(1), 541–547.
7. Dalal, P. (2015). Awareness of Cyber Law in India. Retrieved February 20, 2015, from http:// cyberlawsinindia.blogspot.in/2010/05/awareness-of-cyber-law-in-india.html.
8. Saxena, P., Kotiyal, B., & Goudar, R. H. (2012). A cyber era approach for building awareness in cyber security for educational system in India. *IACSIT International Journal of Information and Education Technology, 2*(2).
9. Peng, T. K. (2007). *Bulletin of Information Technology, 27*(6), 41–53.

Information Communication Technologies for Research and Academic Development

Dinesh Kumar Saini, Lakshmi Sunil Prakash and Hemant Gaur

Abstract ICT pays a vital role in research and research quality improvement. Research quality in India is improving with ICT usage but overall quality of research is not up to mark. Efforts are made to analyze the higher education infrastructure with research institutions in India. The overall infrastructure and the process of research quality monitoring and control are discussed in this paper. The availability of information and data is addressed and how it can be used for improving the research output of the country. Overall, there is no Indian university in top 200 listed universities of the world. The accountability of the system with research quality is addressed in the paper. ICT can play important role in improved transparency and accountability in research quality improvement and research informed teaching and learning.

Keywords Information communication systems · Research quality · Process · Technologies

1 Introduction

ICT technologies used in research includes techniques used for generating data, processing data, and converting this data into information then store, retrieve, process, analyze, and transmit this information for the research and development. ICT technologies like Internet, mobile telephony, satellite communications, and

D.K. Saini (✉) · L.S. Prakash
Faculty of Computing & IT, Sohar University, Sohar, Oman
e-mail: dkssohar@gmail.com; dsaini@soharuni.edu.om

L.S. Prakash
e-mail: lakshmi@soharuni.edu.om

H. Gaur
Faculty of Engineering, Jyoti Vediyapeeth, Jaipur, India
e-mail: hgaur91@gmail.com

© Springer Science+Business Media Singapore 2016
S.C. Satapathy et al. (eds.), *Proceedings of International Conference on ICT for Sustainable Development*, Advances in Intelligent Systems and Computing 409, DOI 10.1007/978-981-10-0135-2_33

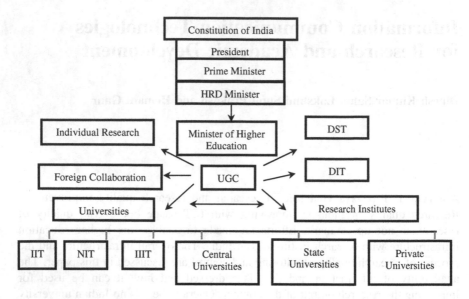

Fig. 1 Higher educational system hierarchy in India

digital television over cable are some of the classical example of ICT [1, 2]. Research is a process and it needs very specialized features in terms of information availability, resource sharing, and intellectual property generation and protection. How information is communicated in research process is just as important as how information is collected, stored, and shared with proper intellectual right protection. In this paper, we wish to describe how ICT plays vital role in the overall development of academic environment and research development in the developing economies of the world, storage area networks, and many more devices, and computing frameworks are available. Procuring and utilizing these devices are very easy for anyone who wants to use these devices and know how to use them The people are now more aware of their rights to better services from the various organizations that provide education, healthcare, and other important services that claim that they cater to the needs of the people. Moreover, these organizations (See Fig. 1) now need to be able to substantiate and justify their roles when they interact with the people and media.

ICT provides the workspace for people to actively collaborate, restructure organizations hierarchies, and promote participation of citizens. It can allow for transparency for educational institutions in all processes that include, growth of academic endeavors, attain better ranking in the world and nationally, dissemination of knowledge, and fostering teaching and research partners with both local and international partners [3, 4].

Creation and dissemination of scholarly material and media is part and parcel of the ICT frameworks for research and education, where ideas and articles are exchanged on a regular and rapid pace [5–7].

Researchers can now connect via GoogleScholar, Researchgate, and Linkedin to be able to share expertise, update and publish information about their research and other related educational activities [8].

Various journals and digital educational/research material are made available by the eminent publishers like OReilly, Springer, and EBSCO, for competitive prices on the Internet. Digital libraries allow quick dissemination of these resources at a fairly agreeable pricing [9, 10].

The cyber infrastructure, the online educational portals, and learning object repositories also online educational initiatives by various prominent educational institutions have set the stage for including every possible technology, computational forms within the easy access of the end user [11–13].

In spite of these and other initiatives, the condition that exists in the Indian Research arena is not satisfactory. It is taking quite a lot of time for India to research a fairly satisfactory ranking in the international rankings. It is quite difficult to catapult the domain of higher education and research to higher levels of achievement [14, 15].

While collaboration becoming a critical process in knowledge production, new ICTs have become the medium for long-distance collaborative work [16]. Internet access facilitates communication and the exchange of data vital to knowledge sharing in general and knowledge production in particular [13, 17].

Quality research is the need of the hour and this can be accomplished only be measuring rigorously the research output of the various tiers of the educational hierarchy [18].

1.1 Current State of Research in India

Indian researchers are actively participating with researchers of Italy, USA, Germany, UK, Japan, France, South Korea, Canada, China, and Australia. Proportion of India's research output has increased as per the report in [18, 19]; however, the quality of research has diminished to a very mediocre level as shown in Table 1 and illustrated in and Fig. 2.

These institutions featured in the Top Asian Rankings for 2015 based on certain selected performance indicators, the most important of which were teaching, research volume, and citations (carrying 30 % of overall score); only 9 universities appear in the top 100, that too the score was less than 30 from 100 in research. Tables 1 and 2 indicate that the number of institutions in the top 100 Asian universities has risen. However, the research score and citation score has slipped for the IIT institutes (IIT Kharagpur and Roorkee) as shown in Table 3 and some have even slipped below the 100 rankings (IIT Bombay).

In the Top Asian Rankings for 2015 based on certain selected performance indicators, the most important of which were teaching, research volume, citations (carrying 30 % of overall score); only 9 universities appear in the top 100, that too

Table 1 Excerpts from the Asia University rankings 2014 top 100—Year 2014

Institution	Research score	Citation score
Indian Institute of Technology, Madras	18.6	32.2
Indian Institute of Technology, Kharagpur	30	35.3
Indian Institute of Technology, Roorkee	12.3	53.6
Jadavpur University	14.9	41.8
Indian Institute of Technology, Kanpur	25.2	41.8
Aligarh Muslim University	11.3	33.8
Panjab University	14	84.7
Jawaharlal Nehru University	12.3	26.4
Indian Institute of Technology, Guwahati	11.6	53.6
Indian Institute of Technology, Delhi	23	38.5

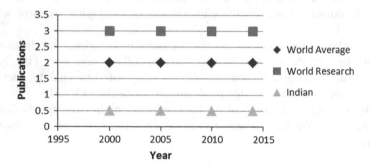

Fig. 2 Current state of research in India

Table 2 Excerpts from the Asia University Rankings top 100 2013

Institution	Research score	Citation score
Indian Institute of Technology, Kharagpur	45.3	39
Indian Institute of Technology, Roorkee	13.7	45.8
Indian Institute of Technology, Bombay	33.1	45.6

the score was less than 30 from 100 in research. Tables 1 and 2 indicate that the number of institutions in the top 100 Asian universities has risen. However, the research score and citation score has slipped for the IIT institutes (IIT Kharagpur and Roorkee) as shown in Table 3 and some have even slipped below the 100 rankings (IIT Bombay).

This can be attributed to the reasons mentioned below:

Lack of strong retention measures in universities Experienced faculties are not given enough exposure to chart out a long-term career goals based on research, innovation, and best educational practices. Academicians with a strong teaching track record must be paid according to their teaching load and assessment load.

Table 3 Growth in number of institutions across a 5-year period

Type of institutions	Number of institutions (2008–2009)	Number of institutions (2009–2010)	Number of institutions (2013–2014)
Central universities	40	42	42
State universities	231	256	310
State private universities	21	60	143
Institutions established through state legislation	5	5	5
Institutions deemed to be universities	128	130	127
Total	425	493	627
Colleges	25,951	31,324	36671

These academicians must be audited for quality of research and their students' performance. [6] Local and international collaboration must be encouraged. Senior academics must give room for younger academicians who have a vision to accelerate the process of improving the research quality and incorporating modern ICT practices into the infrastructure, methodologies, and discussions in the institutions. This must be at all levels of the hierarchy. Clarity of purpose, action, and outcomes must be documented in the institutions day-to-day activities.

Lack of strong research support Faculty members tend to leave an institution if their research aspirations or salary aspirations are not satisfactory [15]. In spite of several ICT frameworks like online research journals, Wi-Fi linked campuses, research groups and web-conferencing methods are available to collaborate within an institution or with peers from external bodies, staff usually are not motivated due to heavy teaching and commitments which are not adequately rewarded and poor research-based career planning practices within an organization.

1.2 Research Framework

It is imperative that institutions use a parameter of excellence, certain parameters for rating their staff and their research quality, as shown in Fig. 3. Most of the institutions are not very transparent about the quality of their faculty and the research that they support in their academic schedules.

Research is taken for granted and in some cases as a personal activity/achievement which is rarely appreciated or encouraged. All major research institutions enjoy substantial government support in the form of subsidies and grants, as shown in Fig. 4.

These government institutes are no able to attract serious researchers because of several reasons as mentioned in the report submitted by The Council of Scientific AND Industrial Research (CSIR), India, a premier national R&D

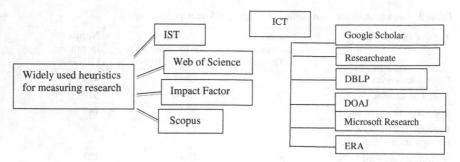

Fig. 3 Research impact made available by ICT

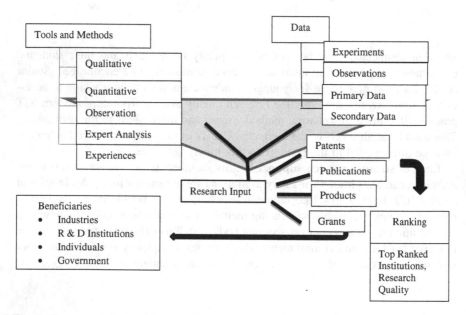

Fig. 4 The research framework

organization, is among the world's largest publicly funded R&D organization. CSIR's pioneering sustained contribution to S&T human resource development is acclaimed nationally. It consists of 29 labs. Many scholars would get a chance to include and enhance their research through their involvement in teaching young and enthusiastic graduates also that would attract the attention of the world to the research activities in this institution. Human resource development group has been contributing significantly toward producing an inquiring society and fast-growing knowledge economy.

However, the HRD website itself is very poorly designed offering very little useful information to researchers, academics, or scholars about the innovation in the Indian tertiary education arena, opportunities or grants easy access pathways.

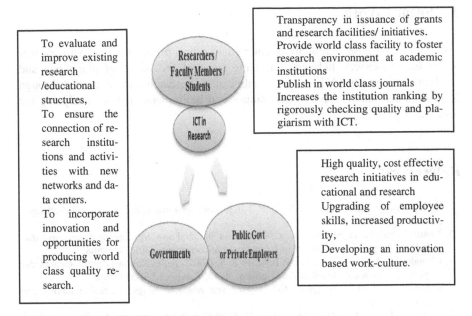

Fig. 5 Benefits of ICT to the main stakeholders of research domain

The ranking of institutions, volume of research per institutions, citations, teaching excellence track records, domain of excellence must be the integral part of the website. Excellence should not be compromised for social inclusion and the gimmicks of bureaucracy.

This is where ICT frameworks, as illustrated in Fig. 5, can help in improving the way the bureaucracy can leverage the projects, grants and programs to accelerate the pace of progress and award excellence, and bring the much needed transparency to a system which is slowly and surely racing towards mediocrity.

2 Conclusion

In the paper, we discuss the growing need of ICT to improve the quality of the education system and research outcome of the country's research organizations. Indian academicians and researchers need to be better informed about the composite ranking system based on scientometric indicators, H-index, and other similar work. H-index metric, is also congruent to the energy-based quality-proxy approach. The accountability and assessment system [20–22] that incorporates the qualitative aspects of research needs to be automated in the county as proposed in the paper. This is evident from the fact that higher output producing institutions are not necessarily highly placed on qualitative parameters. Therefore, a quantity–quality composite ranking system is highly appropriate and desirable.

3 Future Work

The authors propose that analysis coupled with text processing and network theoretic techniques can help in addressing some of the issues of plagiarism and academic dishonesty [23] as well. Quality of the research can be audited through ICT tools and soft computing techniques can be implemented for analyzing the results.

References

1. Mondal, A., & Mete, Jayanta. (2012). ICT in higher education: opportunities and challenges. *Institutions, 21*(60), 4.
2. Bhattacharya, I., & Sharma, K. (2007). India in the knowledge economy-an electronic paradigm. *International Journal of Educational Management, 21*(6), 543–568.
3. Choudhury, M. A., Zaman S. I., & Harahap S. S. (2007). An evolutionary topological theory of participatory socioeconomic development. *World Futures* 63.8: 584–598.
4. Creswell, J. W. (2012). Qualitative inquiry and research design: Choosing among five approaches. Sage.
5. Creswell, J. W., & Brown, M. L. (1992). How chairpersons enhance faculty research: A grounded theory study. *Review of Higher Education, 16*(1), 41–62.
6. Danziger, J. N. (1977). Computers and the frustrated chief executive. *MIS Quarterly* 43–53.
7. Heeks, R. (2006). Using competitive advantage theory to analyze IT sectors in developing countries: a software industry case analysis. *Information Technologies and International Development, 3*(3), 5.
8. Hsieh, J. J. P.-A., Rai, A., & Keil, M. (2008). Understanding digital inequality: Comparing continued use behavioral models of the socio-economically advantaged and disadvantaged. *MIS quarterly* 97–126.
9. Joseph, D., Kok-Yee, N., Koh, C., & Soon, A. (2007). Information technology professionals: a narrative review, meta-analytic structural equation modeling, and model development. *MIS Quarterly, 31*(3), 547–577.
10. Kleine, D. (2009). The ideology behind the technology–Chilean microentrepreneurs and public ICT policies. *Geoforum, 40*(2), 171–183.
11. Mistry, J. J. (2005). A conceptual framework for the role of government in bridging the digital divide. *Journal of Global Information Technology Management, 8*(3), 28–46.
12. Qureshi, S. (2003). Movement in the information technology for development debate: How can it meet the challenges of global competition? pp. 147–149.
13. Saini, D. K., & Prakash, L. S. (2012). Plagiarism detection in web based learning management systems and intellectual property rights in the academic environment. *International Journal of Computer Applications* 57.14.
14. Bhattacharya, I., & Sharma, K. (2007). India in the knowledge economy-an electronic paradigm. *International Journal of Educational Management, 21*(6), 543–568.
15. Olson, G. M., & Olson, J. S. (2000). Distance matters. *Human-computer interaction, 15*(2), 139–178.
16. Vasileiadou, E., & Vliegenthart, R. (2009). Research productivity in the era of the internet revisited. *Research Policy, 38*(8), 1260–1268.
17. Prakash, L. S., & Saini, D. K. (2012). E-assessment for e-learning. In *2012 IEEE International Conference on Engineering Education: Innovative Practices and Future Trends (AICERA)*, IEEE.

18. Castells, M. (2004). Informationalism, networks, and the network society: a theoretical blueprint. In Castells, I. M. (red) *The network society. A cross-cultural perspective.*
19. Prakash, L. S., Saini D. K., & Kutti, N. S. (2009). Integrating EduLearn learning content management system (LCMS) with cooperating learning object repositories (LORs) in a peer to peer (P2P) architectural framework. In *ACM SIGSOFT Software Engineering Notes* 34.3: 1–7.
20. Kostoff, R. N., Boylan, R., & Simons, G. R. (2004). Disruptive technology roadmaps. *Technological Forecasting and Social Change, 71*(1), 141–159.
21. Heimeriks, G., Van den Besselaar, P., & Frenken, K. (2008). Digital disciplinary differences: an analysis of computer-mediated science and 'Mode 2'knowledge production. *Research Policy* 37.9: 1602–1615.
22. Prakash, S., Saini, D. K., & Sunil, L. (2013). Factors influencing Progression Rate in Higher Education in Oman-Data Engineering and Statistical Approach. In Proceedings of the World Congress on Engineering (Vol. 1).

An Insider Cyber Threat Prediction Mechanism Based on Behavioral Analysis

Kaushal Bhavsar and Bhushan H. Trivedi

Abstract Detection of insider cyber threats is a challenging problem. With traditional security systems like firewalls, intrusion detection and prevention systems, etc., [1] rendered completely ineffective where there is a need for a newer mechanism that approaches insider threat as a new kind of cyber threat and helps to prevent it. In this paper, we propose a mechanism that can prevent insider attacks by predicting the possibility of an insider threat using behavioral analysis of people in an organization.

Keywords Insider cyber threats · Threat detection · Cyber threat prediction

1 Introduction

An insider cyber threat is a person or process with malicious intention with an access (authorized or non-authorized) to an organization's network, system, or data storage devices containing information in any form. Such an access has a potential capability to negatively affect the confidentiality, integrity, or availability of the organization's information or information systems. Traditional network security systems like Intrusion Detection and Prevention Systems protect the network from external attackers by limiting network connectivity between the extranet and intranet, and closely monitoring the network stream.

Since an insider attack is "inside" the organization, his activities go undetected by such systems which are typically located outside the LAN as a network gateway—whereas the insider is able to access the LAN systems from behind the

K. Bhavsar (✉)
Research Scholar, GLS University, Ahmedabad, Gujarat, India
e-mail: kaushal@pratikar.com

B.H. Trivedi
Faculty of Computer Technology, GLS University,
Ahmedabad, Gujarat, India

© Springer Science+Business Media Singapore 2016
S.C. Satapathy et al. (eds.), *Proceedings of International Conference on ICT for Sustainable Development*, Advances in Intelligent Systems and Computing 409, DOI 10.1007/978-981-10-0135-2_34

gateway. Also, an insider is aware of the structure of the network systems and the organization in general which help him plan the attack quickly without being noticed.

Before executing an attack, an insider (like an outsider in a case of an outsider attack) exhibits several changes in the activities–known as *precursors* [2]. The precursors that are a resultant of the unmet expectations, disgruntlements, and loss of trust are known as behavioral precursors. Since the insider is aware of the structure of the network systems and the organization, he starts playing around with the systems with an attempt to masquerade or break the systems. These activities known as technical precursors are prologs of possible security attacks.

We propose a system that keeps a track of activities a user performs on a host and in a network via any static or mobile devices connected to the network. The activity log of a user can be then analyzed and this analysis can be used to predict the forthcoming actions of the user, based on which the user can be assigned a "threat-rank" on a scale of 1 and 10. Users with frequent deviations from their threat rank can be treated as insider threats and organization can take relevant action against them. The following paper describes the necessity and working of the proposed system.

2 Related Work

The recent techniques for detection of insider threats have been shown as follows.

2.1 NLP Analysis of Text Communications

In the paper Semantic Analysis for Monitoring Insider Threats [3], the authors have described semantic analysis using Natural Language Processing (NLP) system, of the insider's text-based communications produces conceptual representations that are clustered and compared on the expected versus observed scope. The determined risk level produces an input to a risk analysis algorithm that is merged with outputs from the system's social network analysis and role-based monitoring modules. Finally, the system defines a "threat level" for the person of interest.

The drawback of this method is that the only source of information is text-based communication between an insider and a perpetrator outside the organization.

2.2 Computer Usage Activity Tracking

In the paper Detecting Insider Threats in a Real Corporate Database of Computer Usage Activity [4], the authors have developed a model called PRODIGAL

(PROactive Detection of Insider threats with Graph Analysis and Learning) that applied and evaluated multiple AD algorithms and supporting technologies based on models of different aspects of user behavior; over 100 semantic (i.e., domain-knowledge-based) and structural (graph-based) features; a schema representation for comparing results of different AD algorithms; a visual AD language; data extraction, loading, and transformation components; and an integrating software framework for experimentation.

Their model relies on insider's interaction with the computer file system, i.e., upload/download of files, copying files to removable media as well as sending in email attachments. This method is good for data protection but it ignores activities like communication via text chatting, internet browsing, etc.

2.3 Mouse Pointer Movement Tracking for Detection of Insider Threats

A unique technique of identifying insider threats from a large dataset of suspects is discussed in the paper, Identifying Insider Threats through Monitoring Mouse Movements in Concealed Information Tests [5]. In this paper, the authors describe a mechanism that measures the deviation in patterns of mouse pointer usage of a person to identify if that person has been a part of an insider attack. The observations are made when the persons are made to use a specially developed application that asks multiple choice questions relevant to the security threat and records the mouse pointer movements of the person.

This technique is very easy to implement, but just like any other polygraph test it cannot be guaranteed. However, it can be used along with other techniques to reduce chances of false positives as well as false negatives.

In Analysis and Detection of Malicious Insiders [6], the authors explain the various observable actions that an insider may exhibit as anomalous. These actions can be classified into Behavioral Actions as well as Technical Actions. Collection of technical action data is possible but without correlating that with behavioral profile of a person, there would be many false positives or false negatives.

2.4 Behavioral Profiling for Insider Threat Detection

Remote assessment of insiders and content analysis of activities done by them are important methods described in the paper, The Role of Behavioral Research and Profiling in Malicious Cyber Insider Investigations [7]. Remote assessment means working with surveillance teams, review of archived records including personnel records, call records, attendance records, etc. Content analysis builds up the psychological profile of the person by lexical analysis of the textual content involved.

Specific markers like spelling and grammar mistake, frequent occurrence of words, abbreviations, tone, etc., are used as parameters for identifying the original author of the text data by correlation with the writing behaviors of all personnel in a network.

2.5 Cyber Behavior Analysis and Detection Method—System and Architecture [8]

This US patent has been published on May 6th, 2014. The description of the patent is given as

"A scalable cyber-security system, method and architecture for the identification of malware and malicious behavior in a computer network. Host flow, host port usage, host information and network data at the application, transport and network layers are aggregated from within the network and correlated to identify a network behavior such as the presence of malicious code."

However, Insider Threat Detection is more difficult than many other anomaly detection (AD) problems [4] not only because insiders are knowledgeable about an organization's computer systems and procedures are authorized to use these systems, but, and more important, because malicious activity by insiders is a small but critical portion of their overall activity on such systems.

2.6 Proactive or Predictive Insider Threat Detection

In the paper Modeling Human Behavior to Anticipate Insider Attacks [9], the authors have described about a system that collects data from various sources like SEIM systems, IDS systems, DLP systems, packet tracking systems, HR systems, etc. Each of the data source has an ontology defined which identifies the datatype for that particular domain. This comprehensive threat assessment framework promises to automate the detection of high-risk, concerning behaviors ("precursors" or "triggers") on which to focus the attention and inform the analysis of cyber-security personnel, who would otherwise be required to analyze and correlate an overwhelming amount of data. Incorporating psychosocial data along with cyber data into the analysis offers an additional dimension upon which to assess potential threats within a comprehensive, integrated threat analysis framework.

2.7 Comparison of Techniques

Preliminary analysis of the above techniques gives us the following observations.

Name	Advantage	Drawback	Approach
NLP analysis of text communication	Fast	Limited to text communication	Proactive
Computer activity usage and tracking	Accurate	Limited to computer activities	Proactive
Mouse pointer movement tracking	Cost-effective	Not proactive not reliable	Reactive
Cyber behavior analysis	Accurate	Network traffic only	Proactive
Predictive insider threat detection	Predict behavior	Experimental	Proactive

Based on the above criteria, we have identified that while current systems have advancements in behavioral threat detection and ranking, they lack in user-based threat detection.

However, for complete evaluation, we devised a few evaluation criteria which are mentioned as below

A. Host Audit

The ability of the system to collect usage information from the system logs, application logs, and other various logs for investigation purpose.

B. Host Monitoring

The ability of the system to monitor the activity that is happening currently on the host. This may include processes running, files accessed, applications opened, network connections, input devices like mice, keyboard, etc.

C. LAN Audit

The ability of the system to collect information of all the devices that are connected or removed from the local area network along with specifics like MAC address, host OS, IP address, etc.

D. LAN Monitoring

The ability of the system to capture network packets in real time and inspect them for anomalous activity.

E. User Detection

The ability of the system to identify activity by an individual user from various hosts on a network based on the activity logs collected from hosts or network.

F. Behavior Detection

The ability of the system to identify the type of behavior based on actions carried out by a specific host or a user.

G. Threat Detection

The ability of the system to identify and predict current or forthcoming threats based on the actions carried out by a specific host or a user.

H. Threat Ranking

The ability of the system to allocate a threat rank which may be a number between 1 and 100 based on the actions carried out by the specific host or a user.

We decided to give a score of one for every criterion which was successfully satisfied. Hence, we got this table

No.	Name	A	B	C	D	E	F	G	H	Score
1	NLP analysis of text communication	N	Y	N	N	Y	Y	N	Y	4
2	Computer activity usage and tracking	Y	N	N	N	N	Y	Y	N	3
3	Mouse pointer movement tracking	N	Y	N	N	N	Y	N	Y	3
4	Cyber behavior analysis	N	N	Y	Y	N	Y	Y	Y	5
5	Predictive insider threat detection	N	Y	N	Y	N	Y	Y	N	4

3   Proposed System

Based on the mechanisms that we have reviewed till now, we have come up with a proposed solution which we call "Scalable Automated Technology for Analysis and Ranking of Known threats" known as SATARK (Fig. 1).

We propose addition of a few components in a local area network as follows:

3.1   Host Unit

The host unit is a software package installed on each host belonging to a network which contains a Host OS, a Host Collector that identifies key information from the logs of the host operating system and a Host Monitor that keeps a track on events happening on the host operating system like file access, program launch, network connectivity, etc.

3.2   LAN Unit

The LAN unit tracks network packets. It is necessary for hosts which do not have the host unit software installed, i.e., mobile hosts. Additionally, it injects a unique ID in the network packet in order to associate the data packet with the unique identity of the user that has transmitted the packet.

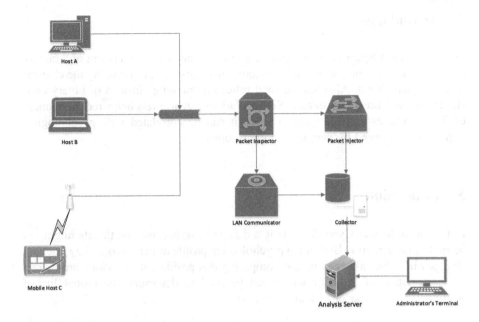

Fig. 1 Arrangement for SATARK system in a network

3.3 Central Detection Unit

It collects log data from the host unit and LAN unit, storing it into log database for further analysis by reading the log data stored into log database and tries to define possible anomalous events. It then provides a threat rank between 1 and 10 based on the factors like severity of the threat detected and frequency of anomalous behavior of a user or a host.

SATARK will initially collect forensic data from the computer and it will use that data as a training data as well as it will calculate a threat rank. This will be done for all persons in the computer network. After that, SATARK will keep monitoring applications, networks, text input, etc. At the end of the day, it will create another threat rank for that person. There will be a deviation in threat rank of person if the type of usage has changed from regular usage pattern.

Each daily rank will be collected and deviations will be recorded to build a "threat-profile" of the person. This will help in the detection of insider threat before they perform any threatfull activity.

4 Advantages

Our method is a Reactive approach and it does not need a large amount of "training data" to get it working; so it can be effective from first day, minimizing the chances of a zero-day threat. Also, our method relies on "ranking" instead of binary classification like "threat/non-threat." Setting various threat levels helps reduce chances of false positives and false negatives as it can be correlated with psychological parameters observed by people of organizations.

5 Conclusion

Detection of Insider Cyber Threats is a difficult task because the threats might not be malicious in nature. Building a psychological profile of the personnel by tracking changes in technical behavior and comparing this profile with previous profile can show deviation of behavior which can be used to determine the probability of being a threat in near or distant future.

6 Future Work

We have proposed a mechanism for detection and prevention of insider threats. We are currently testing this mechanism over a real organization and our future work would be in the direction of using this data to develop an algorithm that can predict insider threats before they occur.

References

1. Ginter, A. (2012). DuQu, stuxnet, APT and other failures of ICS security. In *AFPM Q&A and Technology Forum*.
2. Stolfo, S. J., & Bellovin, M. S. (2008). Insider attack and cyber security: Beyond the hacker, Springer.
3. Symonenko, S., & Liddy, E. D. (2004). Semantic analysis for monitoring insider threats. *Lecture Notes in Computer Science, 3073*, 492–500.
4. Senator, T., & Bader, D. (2013). Detecting insider threats in a real corporate database. In *19th ACM SIGKDD Conference on Knowledge Discovery and Data Mining (KDD), Chicago, IL*.
5. Valacich, J. S., & Jenkins, J. L. (2013). Identifying insider threats through monitoring mouse movements in concealed information tests. In *Hawaii International Conference on System Sciences. Deception Detection Symposium*.
6. Maybury, M., Chase, P., & Cheikes, B. (2005). Analysis and detection of malicious insiders. In *International Conference on Intelligence Analysis, McLean, VA*.

7. Shaw, E. (2006). The role of behavioral research and profiling in malicious. *Digital Investigation* pp. 20–31.
8. Joll, B., & Ross, K. (2014). Cyber behavior analysis and detection method, system and architecture. USA Patent 20140157405.
9. Greitzer, F. L., & Hohimer, R. E. (2011). Modeling human behavior to anticipate insider attacks. *Journal of Strategic Security, 4*, 24–47.

Enhancing Amplifier Characteristics Using Quantum Dots

Parnika De, Jeetesh Giri Goswami and Murtaza Abbas Rizvi

Abstract Wavelength division multiplexing (WDM) is getting popularity because it is using optical fiber technology, which allows thousands of channels with various wavelengths to be transmitted at the same time. Practically, the transmission capacity of WDM systems strongly depends on the gain bandwidth of a fiber amplifier. Optical fiber amplifiers that are doped with rare earth ions are the most worked upon fiber amplifiers over few decades. In recent years, quantum dots are parts of semiconductor nanocrystals being studied extensively, because they have unique optical properties and electronic properties compared to the bulk semiconductors [1]. This is because they have low band gap due to their tiny particle size. Due to this, QDs can provide near-infrared emission covering the important wavelengths. Researchers have doped the optical fiber core by quantum dots (QDs) to integrate the emission characteristics of quantum dots with the propagation characteristics of optical fiber [2]. The promising feature for all-wave optical amplifiers is that the PbS nanocrystals could provide emission for silica fibers over the whole transmission window (1200–1700). Simulation results show that it is possible to design an optical amplifier with low noise figure, moderate optical signal-to-noise ratio with minimum gain of 10 dB.

Keywords Quantum dot · Optical fiber · Excitons · Amplifier noise · OSNR

P. De (✉) · M.A. Rizvi
National Institute of Technical Teachers' Training and Research, Bhopal, India
e-mail: parnikade@gmail.com

M.A. Rizvi
e-mail: marizvi@nitttrbpl.ac.in

J.G. Goswami
Distance Education Council, Sikkim Manipal University, Gangtok, India
e-mail: goswami.jeet@gmail.com

© Springer Science+Business Media Singapore 2016
S.C. Satapathy et al. (eds.), *Proceedings of International Conference on ICT for Sustainable Development*, Advances in Intelligent Systems and Computing 409, DOI 10.1007/978-981-10-0135-2_35

1 Introduction

Instant access to large amount of data has led to demand for its huge transmission capacity in order to address the increasing demand for data traffic. As per today and future requirements of transmission bandwidth and data rate, optical fibers promise enormous transmission bandwidths and high data rate. The wavelength of the coarsest optical fiber ranges from 1.3 to 1.55 μm [3]. In this range, a single-mode optical fiber has the lowest attenuation of 0.2 dB/km. The ever-increasing data traffic along with the positivities of fiber optics for the transmission of data encourages the development of optical components. The increasing use of optical amplifiers in fiber communication is because of the losses that occur in the optical fiber and the signal power differences in the network points. The optical amplifiers help in amplification and regeneration of the optical signals. The ITU-T has defined several spectral bands which are described in Table 1.

The amplifying range of erbium-doped fiber amplifier is the wavelength range of C and L bands. They amplify signals with very good gain and noise performance. The optical fiber amplifiers from S to L bands are yet to be designed in order to meet the growing demands for high speed and large bandwidth. This study shows that quantum dots have remarkable optical and electronic properties compared to bulk semiconductors. An important property of the quantum dots is near-infrared emission covering all important wavelengths, which is achieved by controlling the particle size. We can control the particle size by tuning the band gap. The energy level of the quantum dots is discrete and not continuous so addition or subtraction of atoms can change the boundaries of the band gap. If the geometry of the surface is changed the band gap energy is also changed, because of the minute structure of the quantum dots (QDs). It is not difficult to control the output of a quantum dot because the emission frequency of the quantum dot is dependent on its band gap. Quantum confinement can be achieved over a wide range due to high bulk exciton of PbS. The PbS QDs can provide emission over 1200–1700 nm transmission window, as a result an optical amplifier with flattened gain characteristics over S, C, and L bands is possible to design.

For systems which occupy large area, the losses were traditionally eliminated by the use of optoelectronic repeaters. But the use of such repeaters for regeneration of signals became complex and very expensive for WDM light wave systems. As an alternative, we use optical amplifiers for loss management, it amplifies the optical signal directly. Various kinds of optical amplifiers were developed to meet the

Spectral bands	Operating frequency (nm)
O band	1260–1360
E band	1360–1460
S band	1460–1530
C band	1530–1565
L band	1565–1625

Table 1 The operating regions of most commonly used optical fiber amplifiers

system requirements, but they are limited to a range of wavelengths. The best advantage of quantum dot-doped fiber amplifier is tuneable capability that means the operation wavelength depends on the size of quantum dot.

In order to achieve the requirements of today and coming future of high channel capacity, it is very important to design an optical amplifier with flattened gain characteristics over S, C, and L bands. The objective of this project work is to study a quantum dot-doped fiber amplifier and their characteristics over S, C, and L bands. We aim to accomplish aforementioned amplification characteristics by changing the parameters of the quantum dot-doped fiber amplifiers.

2 Literature Review

2.1 Quantum Dot

In a quantum dot-doped semiconductor, the excitons are confined in all the spatial dimensions. Because of this reason, QDs have properties in-between bulk semiconductors and discrete molecules. The QDs were discovered by Alexei Ekimov in a glass matrix and by Louis E. Brus in colloidal solutions. Quantum dot, the name was coined by Mark Reed [4]. These quantum dots are also called nanocrystals and these are composed of materials from the periodic table groups of II–VI, III–V, or IV–VI. The QDs are a special class of semiconductors because of their minute size ranging from 2 to 100 nm in diameter. Because of this minute size these materials behave differently, giving the QDs very good tunability and giving an application that was never seen before in science and technology [5].

If one is working with semiconductors, it is important to clarify in which dimension they are existent. Semiconductors with quantum confinement in zero to three dimensions are shown in Fig. 1. The simplest form of a semiconductor is the bulk semiconductor which is limited in no spatial direction and is therefore three-dimensional. If the extent is prevented to one dimension one gets a semiconductor film, namely a quantum well. Decreasing the structure to one dimension one gets a semiconductor line, a quantum wire. The smallest existing nanostructure

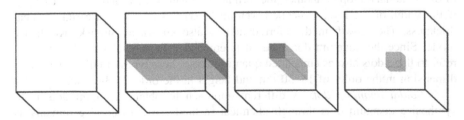

Fig. 1 Different semiconductor nanostructures: bulk material, quantum well, quantum wire, and quantum dot [5]

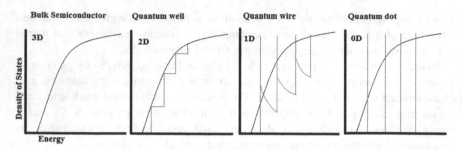

Fig. 2 Density of states for 3D, 2D, 1D, and 0D systems [5]

is the one used in this work, the zero-dimensional quantum dot whose extent is limited in all three dimensions.

The different nanostructures can be described through a so-called confinement potential. Because of the restriction of the dimensions of extension, there are energy edges between the single materials that build the potential. Thereby, the movement of the carriers is restricted. This potential has an influence on the density of states. In Fig. 2, the relation between the energy and the density of states is shown. The density of states of an unrestricted bulk semiconductor (three-dimensional) goes with $\sqrt{E}$. A steplike density of states is given for a restriction in one dimension (quantum well). The density of states of the relevant quantum dots has discrete energy levels. Because of this characteristic, quantum dots are often referred to as artificial atoms [5].

The properties of quantum dots and their possible applications are largely dependent on the method they have been obtained with, which can therefore be used as a criterion for classification of different types of quantum dots:

Electrostatic quantum dots One can fabricate quantum dots by restricting the two-dimensional electron gas by electrostatic gates laterally and by etching vertically. These types of QDs are sometimes called as electrostatic quantum dot, this can be done by changing the potential gates and by changing the geometry of the gates or by applying external magnetic field. These types of quantum dots typically range in the order of 100 nm.

Self-assembled quantum dots Self-assembled quantum dots are obtained in heteroepitaxial systems with different lattice constants. During the growth of a layer of one material on top of another, the formation of nanoscale islands takes place [3], if the width of the layer (so-called wetting layer) is larger than a certain critical thickness. The growth mode referred here is also known as Stranski–Krastanov mode. Since the quantum dot material is embedded in another material, we will refer to these dots also as embedded quantum dots. These types of QDs have lateral dimension in the order of 15–30 nm and height in the order of 3–7 nm.

Colloidal quantum dots A different approach to obtain quantum dots is to synthesize quantum dots through chemical methods so that the size remains as small as possible. The dots obtained this way are called nanocrystals or colloidal quantum dots. The sizes and shapes are controlled by duration, temperature, and ligand molecules used in the synthesis [6]. These types of quantum dots are normally of spherical shape. They are often smaller than embedded quantum dots and the diameter range from 2 to 4 nm.

2.2 Excitons

For having a semiconductor emitting light, one has to shift electrons from the valence band to the conduction band so that their subsequent recombination creates a photon. There are two possible ways of describing the new situation. First, there is the two-particle picture where the electron now situated in the conduction band is the one particle, and the hole which it leaves in the valence band is considered as a second particle. The charge of the hole is the negative equivalent of the electron charge. This charge is essential to the implementation of the one particle picture, which is the second possibility to describe the excitation. Because of the charges and the Coulomb exchange interaction there is an attractive connection between the electron and the hole. For the purpose of simplification, the electron–hole pair is considered as a quasiparticle which is named as exciton. In Fig. 3, the potentials of both the pictures are shown schematically. To assure the validity of the approximation made in this work with the introduction of the effective mass, it has to be clarified that the excitons are considered to be Wannier excitons. That is, the electron-hole pair, which represents the exciton, extends through the distance of some lattice constants. This definition is contrary to the so-called Frenkel excitons, where an electron and a hole are located within one lattice constant.

Fig. 3 Schematics of the two-particle picture (electron and hole) on the *left* and of the one-particle picture (exciton) on the *right* [7]

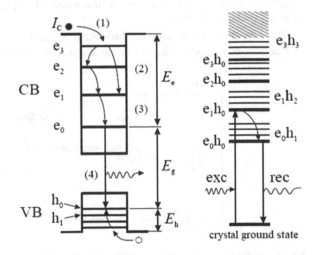

2.3 Creation of Quantum Dots

There are three major methods known to build up quantum dots:

1. Etching, where the dots are literally cut out of quantum wells.
2. Colloidal quantum dots that are created in liquids by chemical processes.
3. Self-assembling, where the dots grow by themselves because of a sufficient mixture of different materials having suitable properties.

The latter is how the quantum dots used in this work are created. More concrete dots were made using molecular beam epitaxy (MBE) that is explained in the following. A schematic drawing of a MBE chamber is shown in Fig. 4. First, the material for application is evaporated in the effusion chambers, which is in our case indium, arsenic, and gallium. Second, the molecular beam is aligned to the substrate (GaAs). The atoms of the molecular beam settle on its surface. With the temperature of the substrate and the timing of applying material, one can finally control the growth. Usually, some layers of the substrate material are grown in advance of the nanostructures to overcome substrate irregularities. There are two kinds of phenomena corresponding to the self-organized growth of layers, and island growth. If the lattice constant of the substrate and the applied material are similar smooth layers are formed. On the other hand, a significant difference between the lattice constants strain is created which can prevent the growth of closed layers and lead to the appearance of islands [8].

In most cases, which is true also for the current, first a closed coating of few monolayers is formed which is called wetting layer. Only when the strain is big enough islands grow on top of it, see Fig. 5a, top. In Fig. 5b an atomic force microscopy (AFM) picture of an ensemble of such self-assembled quantum dots can be seen. Furthermore, chosen the right environmental conditions, i.e., giving the material not enough time to react to the stress, it is possible also to grow highly stressed quantum wells [6].

After creation of the quantum dots either a spacing layer is applied to the sample that acts as an obstacle, like in our case, a well is grown on top of the dots shifting

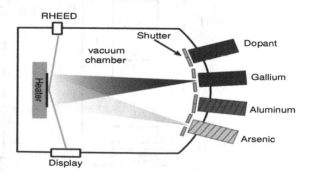

Fig. 4 Schematic presentation of a MBE chamber which can be used to produce self-assembled quantum dots [8]

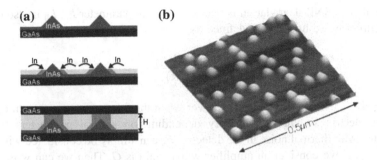

Fig. 5 **a** Scheme of the growth of quantum dots. *Top* Wetting layer with quantum dots. *Middle* Application of a well meant to shift the emission wavelength. *Bottom* Application of a spacer. **b** AFM picture of an ensemble of self-assembled quantum dots [9]

the emission wavelength to more desired ones followed by the spacer (as can be seen in Fig. 5a, middle). Such a nanostructure is called QDs in a well. After that another layer of QDs can be applied following the same methods. In our case, 15 layers of quantum dots in a well were grown, the nominal density of the dots is n_{QD} 2×10^{10} cm^{-2} and the thickness of the spacer layer is 33–35 nm [8].

3 Problem Statement

It is a necessity to undo the attenuation losses in the optical fiber if the transmission distance is very high (>100 km). Earlier, this recovery of loss was accomplished by the use of optoelectronic amplifier. The optoelectronic amplifier consists of optical receivers, regeneration and equalization system, and an optical transmitter. In this arrangement, we can convert optical to electrical and electrical signals back to optical signals.

There were various optical amplifiers suggested to replace this conversion and regeneration system. The optical amplifiers do not convert the signal-to-electronic signals rather it amplifies and regenerates the optical signals. This is the main reason why the optical amplifiers are so successful in today's communication system.

4 Methodology

4.1 Amplifier Noise and OSNR

Generally, most of the amplifiers downgrade the SNR (signal-to-noise ratio) of the signals. The reason behind this is the spontaneous emission which results in noise in the signal. The SNR degradation is measured by the parameter F_n. F_n is also called the amplifier noise figure. It is defined as

$$F_n = \frac{(\text{SNR})_{\text{in}}}{(\text{SNR})_{\text{out}}} \tag{1}$$

where SNR is the generated electric power when there is a conversion from optical signal-to-electric signal. F_n can vary depending on several parameters that is associated with thermal noise in the detector. F_n can simply be considered with shot noise only. If we consider an amplifier whose gain is G. Then we can write

$$P_{\text{out}} = GP_{\text{in}} \tag{2}$$

Therefore, the SNR is given by

$$(\text{SNR})_{\text{in}} = \frac{P_{\text{in}}}{2hv\Delta f} \tag{3}$$

where $<l> = RP_{\text{in}}$, the average photocurrent,
$R = q/h$ is the responsivity of a photodetector with unit quantum efficiency

$$\sigma_s^2 = 2qRP_{\text{in}}\Delta f \tag{4}$$

The amplifier noise figure is

$$F_n = \frac{(\text{SNR})_{\text{in}}}{(\text{SNR})_{\text{out}}} = \frac{1 + 2n_{\text{sp}}(G-1)}{G} \tag{5}$$

The parameter n_{sp} is the spontaneous emission factor
Along with the amplified signal, there is ASE power, which is given by the following equation [10]

$$P_{\text{ASE}} \approx 2n_{\text{sp}}(G-1)hv\Delta f \tag{6}$$

Then the amplifier noise figure can be given by

$$F_n = \frac{P_{\text{ASE}}}{hv\Delta fG} + \frac{1}{G} \tag{7}$$

We define the optical signal-to-noise ratio (OSNR) as the ratio of the output of the optical signal power to the ASE power which is shown by the following formula

$$\text{OSNR} = \frac{P_{\text{out}}}{P_{\text{ASE}}} = \frac{GP_{\text{in}}}{2n_{\text{sp}}(G-1)hv\Delta f} \tag{8}$$

5 Simulation Models and Result

The calculated noise figure and OSNR for QDs-doped fiber amplifiers are shown in Figs. 6 and 7. The minimum NF we have achieved is 3.3 dB. For the wavelengths (λ) 1100–1150 nm, NF is much high (>10 dB). Noise figure value for S and C bands are lying between 3.3 and 6 dB, and for L band the NF value varies from 6 to 8 dB. The maximum calculated value for OSNR is 14.5 dB, shown in Fig. 7.

In the above diagram, we can see that as the wavelength increases the noise figure decreases. This decreasing trend is followed till a certain limit after that limit the noise figure starts increasing which is not desirable. So the most preferable wavelength for the working of the quantum dots is between 1200 and 1700 nm approximately.

In this diagram, we will evaluate the results for OSNR(optical signal-to-noise ratio). Here we see that the OSNR increases after a certain bandwidth and stays almost constant till a certain bandwidth, and then starts decreasing. The trend followed in this diagram is same as the trend followed in the Fig. 6. The OSNR

Fig. 6 Noise figure variation of QDs-doped fiber amplifiers (1100–1700 nm)

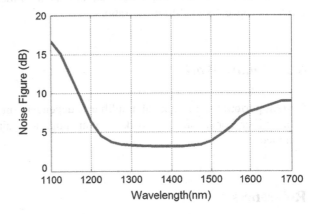

Fig. 7 Variation of OSNR for QDs-doped fiber amplifiers (1100–1700 nm)

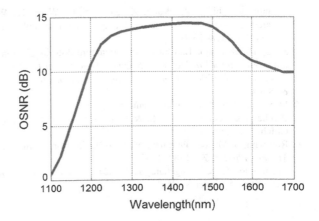

stays maximum for the wavelength between 1200 and 1700 nm. So here through the graphs we have found out that the most suitable range of working of QD-doped fiber amplifiers are between 1200 and 1700 nm.

6 Conclusion and Future Work

6.1 Conclusion

Here we have reported a thorough study of quantum dot fiber amplifiers, and have demonstrated that they gain amplification capability in a wide range of wavelengths, i.e., from 1200 to 1700 nm. The simulation is done using MATLAB and calculated the noise figure and the OSNR value. Quantum dot-doped fiber amplifiers have high value of loss coefficient, in the range of 0.3 dB/m. So the fiber length is an important parameter in the amplification of the signals, for the maximum amplification the fiber length needs to be optimized. Simulation shows that it is possible to design and implement an optical amplifier with low noise figure, moderate optical signal-to-noise ratio.

6.2 Future Work

System performance of optical amplifier is dependent on the gain characteristics of an amplifier. For satisfactory working of an amplifier, gain characteristics should be flattened.

References

1. Huang, W., Chi, Y.-Z., Wang, X., Zhou, S.-F., Wang, L., Wu, E., et al. (2008). Tunable infrared luminescence and optical amplification in PbS-doped glasses. *Chinese Physics Letters, 25*, 2518–2520.
2. Jong, H., & Chao, L. (2007). Pbs quantum-dots in glassmatrix for universal fiber optic amplifier. *Journal of Materials Science: Materials in Electronics, 18*, S135–S139.
3. Agrawal, G. P. (2002). *Fiber-optic communication systems* (3rd ed.). New York: John Wiley & Sons Inc.
4. http://en.wikipedia.org/wiki/Quantum_dot.
5. Bimberg, D., Grundmann, M., & Ledentsov, N. N. (1999). *Quantum dot heterostructures*. Chichester: John Wiley.
6. Reimann, S. M., & Manninen, M. (2002). Electronic structure of quantum dots. *Reviews of Modern Physics, 74*, 1283–1342.
7. Masumoto, Y., & Takagahara, T. (2002). *Semiconductor quantum dots*. Berlin, Heidelberg, New York: Springer Verlag.

8. Zhukov, A. E., Kovsh, A. R., Maleev, N. A., Mikhrin, S. S., Ustinov, V. M., Tsatsul'nikov, A. F., et al. (1999). Long wavelength lasing from multiply stacked InAs/InGaAs quantum dots on GaAs substrates. *Applied Physics Letters, 75*, 1926–1934.
9. Michalet, X., Pinaud, F. F., Bentolila, L. A., Tsay, J. M., Doose, S., Li, J. J., et al. (2005). Quantum dots for live cells, in vivo imaging and diagnostics. *Science, 307*, 538–544.
10. Giles, C. R., & Emmanuel, D. (1991). Modeling erbium-doped fiber amplifiers. *The Journal of Lightwave Technology, 9*(2), 271–283.

An Approach to Secure Internet of Things Against DDoS

Krushang Sonar and Hardik Upadhyay

Abstract Internet of Things is an interconnected network where physical things become digital objects with the capability of communication via internet. World is moving speedily toward the era of IoT with increasing use of digital things, from smart home to smart city, smart street to smart industry, where all human-required information is either under surveillance or monitored through it via internet medium. By such a large-scale application of IoT, it becomes essential and important to secure the network, prevent it form unwanted attack. IoT is still evolving, but there are certain issues related to security like confidentiality, integrity, and availability. Here, we try to solve Distributed Denial of Service issue against IoT network. DDoS is the attack penetrated from compromised systems that result in poor network performance, bandwidth consumptions, and resource consumptions; as IoT have small processing unit, we must provide solution to restrict such attacks. We introduce solution based on an agent to protect DDoS attack on IoT.

Keywords Denial of service · Device-to-device · Distributed denial of service · Internet of Things

1 Introduction

We humans live in between real world and virtual world; it also need human activity implemented through virtual services. So, to solve this problem new technology is required to be implemented between real world and virtual world, called Internet of Things. Based on a large number of low-cost sensors for

K. Sonar (✉)
GTU PG School, Ahmedabad, Gujarat, India
e-mail: krushang.sonar@gmail.com

H. Upadhyay
GPERI, Mehsana, Gujarat, India
e-mail: hardik31385@gmail.com

© Springer Science+Business Media Singapore 2016
S.C. Satapathy et al. (eds.), *Proceedings of International Conference on ICT for Sustainable Development*, Advances in Intelligent Systems and Computing 409, DOI 10.1007/978-981-10-0135-2_36

surveillance, monitoring, and wireless communication for data sharing takes internet technology to a new dimension. This change of human life and business models works with benefits in future. Internet of Things include various application areas like smart home, smart street, smart city, e-Hospital, e-Agriculture, etc., where sensors sense data on demand and send to internet for further process as well as they also communicate with each other for collective work. According to Cisco, by the end of 2020 almost 50 million devices connected to internet; for which it obviously needs the of use IPv6 [1]. Apart from this, there are some privacy issues and security concerns at different layers of IoT. Here, in this paper, security toward availability of resources, i.e., Distributed Denial of Service on IoTs by defining challenges and our solution to protect it in real world.

There are main three security policies for IoT as follows [2].

(i) **Confidentiality** Message should be hidden from all relay nodes—means message securely passing end to end is required in IoT.

(ii) **Integrity** Message passing from source to destination should not alter; it should be received at receiver side same as it is sent at sender side.

(iii) **Availability** For continuous working of IoT and access to the data whenever necessary, it is also important that services that are offered by devices should always be available and continuous in working mode.

IoT architecture is mainly composed of three layers, i.e., application layer, network layer, and perception layer, as shown in Fig. 1. These all three layers are loosely coupled and differentiate the layer from each other on the basis of services they provide, i.e., data capturing/monitoring, routing, and presentation. Data flow from lower layer to upper layer, i.e., from perception layer to application layer via network layer.

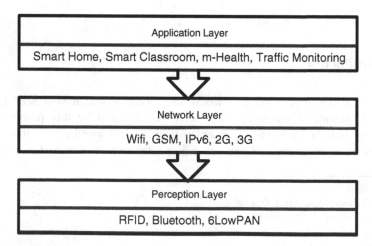

Fig. 1 Architecture of Internet of Things [3]

(1) **Perception Layer** Perception layer is also called data collection layer as its function is capturing data from the environment such as temperature, pressure, light, humidity, etc. It is nothing but collection of sensor; actuators which forms Wireless Sensor Network. In this layer, sensors mainly collect data on user request or on event-driven basis. The main problem with this layer is capturing accurate and sensitive data in respect to low energy consume and processing capability.

(2) **Network Layer** Network layer is the middle layer to take control of processing data/information, broadcasting data, aggregates data, etc. It is the middleware between perception layer and presentation layer, provide path or direction to data on proper destination. The main problem with this layer is that transmitting data in efficient way in heterogeneity network without losing any data in original form. Transport layer is placed between application layer and network layer which take care of routing, end-to-end delivery based on either TCP or UDP as per requirement.

(3) **Application Layer** Application layer is the top most layer which contains business logic, formulas, and UI to user end. Application layer is accessible via CoAP [4] specialized lightweight protocol equivalent to http, designed by IETF. Constrained Application Protocol is a specialized protocol made by IETF for low processing and low-powered nodes (low power, lossy) network. As HTML is not good for low processing and powered constrain node, as it is a heavy weight protocol, they made new protocol CoAP based on request–response model. It is made as it can easily communicate via HTTP through web with very low overhead.

DDoS is a traditional attack and the oldest attack but most common and frequent attack found on internet nowadays, as it eats up network bandwidth or resource capacity from genuine users and made access denial to resources. DDoS attacker compromised some system that make it as handler, which further compromised another system called agent; this agent send out packets to destination. So it is hard to identify the attack nature and destination becomes compromised due to overhead. In IoT, ddos attack is on small sensor-based device; so range of attacker are not in range of high load capable of servers. Various attacks classified as flooding attacks like UDP and TCP where number of packets are bombarded toward network, Amplification attack like smurf attack where source ip spoofed with ICMP request, malformed IP where source and destination IP remain same, and logical or software-based attack like ping of death where ICMP hello message flooded with large number of data [5–7].

2   Related Work

As IoT is a future concept and we are about to enter new world of it, there are few researches done on this previously, but scope of our work is good in spite of limitations. According to solution given in paper [8], which is based on RSSI value. Each node calculate Residual Energy, then it is compared with predefine Residual Energy. If it is less then max Residual Energy, then node is inactive; else node is active and is selected as monitoring node. Then based on received signal strength (RSSI), Packet Deliver Ratio (PDR) values from all other node, weight function applied on it to find DoS attack that cause jamming on node. It periodically checks RSSI received signal strength of node which is good but not suitable for IoT as it continuously ask for RSSI.

SVELTE [9] is first IDS system for IoT, in which system is implemented on Contiki. They keep track of path by 6LoWPAN mapper which reconstructs RPL DODAG (Directed Acyclic Graph) for Border Router and all parent information. The system itself capable of identify internal spoofing but cannot secure outsider attacks.

One of the methods given in the paper is based on learning automata [10]. Where it behaves as a middleware between IoT gateway and end devices, it takes some random sampling rate at different time and check according response to it, when rate of incoming traffic exceeds threshold DoS attack occurs. One alert is sending out alert message to all neighbor nodes about attack. This method is totally based on automata sampling rates and behavior of system.

3   The Proposed Solution

The motivation for the proposed solution is to identify ddos attacks in IoTs network before network state drastically alter or destroy and provoke proper steps to countermeasures to avail services to legit users and block unwanted traffics that may slow down our services. We putting agents are nothing but software-based managers that placed between our network and gateway or border router which identify attack and take appropriate operation to operate our network under such situation.

We also maintain traditional GreyList and BlackList, which are special access control list to give access either temporary or parentally and revoke access toward IoT network.

```
Algorithm:    Attack Recover Algorithm [ARA]
Initialize:   Alert = true / false;      // Attack identification
              A_victim =Alert generated IP address;
              Recover Time t_r = 20/40s; //for which remain in
                                             Alert mode
              State flow Table T = [];   //Incoming source
                                             address list
if alert then do
for recover time t_r not expired do
        for each packet  do
                if incoming destination IP == A_victim then
                        go to : state_table();
                end if
                else
                        forward packet();
                end else
        end for
end for
for each entry in state table do
        if(trust_level < trust_sample);
                PUSH->GreyList;
        end if
end for
for fix filter time t_f not expired do        // filter time
        if IP in BlackList then
                        drop();                //Drop Packet
        end if
end for
end if
else
        forward_packet();
end if
```
```
state_table( )
if new_entry then
        PUSH() -> T;
end if
else
        T->counter ++;
        trust_factor = counter * Thresh_n / tfactor_l;
end else
```
```
if (Detected Again) then
        add to BlackList
end if
else
        false positive alert
        remove from GreyList
end else
        reset state_table();
        Alert = false;
```

We maintain Graylist which update every 40 s so any false identification can easily remove from temporary block state and can access resource again. Blacklist we update in every 300 s as well.

4 Simulation and Result Analysis

The simulation program is written in C language with Contiki OS and Cooja Simulation. Cooja is used for simulation motes in case of absent of real physical motes and we want to test our code in simulation [11]. The simulation is done with first 20 s with normal traffic, called Learning Period, during which it calculates threshold values. The attack simulation is started for next 20 s and end with next 20 s to check recovery of system. Following cases are considered (Fig. 2).

4.1 Simulation Parameters

For simulation, we have choosen parameters shown in following Table 1.

4.2 Performance Metric and Results

1. **Packet Delivery Ratio** It is proportion of packet conveyed to destination to those created by the source (Figs. 3 and 4).

Fig. 2 Contiki programing scenarios

Table 1 Simulation parameters

Parameter	Value
Simulation time	60 s
Number of legal client L(n)	5/15/30
Number of attacking client A(n)	5/15/30
Transmission range	50 m
Routing protocol	RPL + UDP
Learning period N(t)	10/20 s
Attack traffic period A(t)	10/20 s
Recover period R(t)	20/40 s

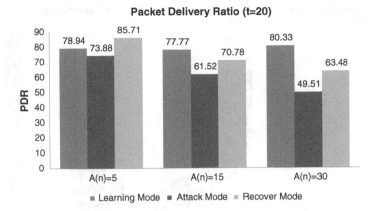

Fig. 3 Packet delivery ratio for time period 20 s

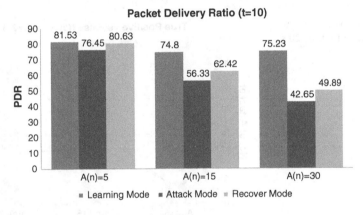

Fig. 4 Packet delivery ratio for time period 10 s

Fig. 5 Dropped packet for time period 20 s

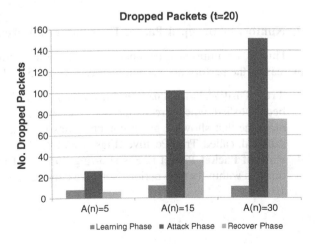

Fig. 6 Dropped packet for
time period 10 s

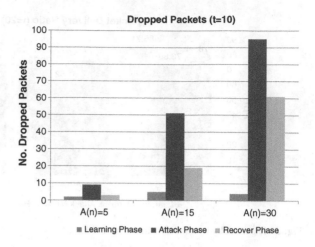

Fig. 7 True positive versus
false negative for time 20 s

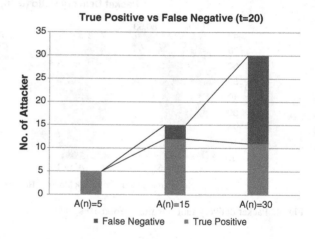

2. **Number of Dropped Packet** The number of packets dropped at given node.

This is an important parameter because if the number of dropped packets
increases, the performance would decrease (Figs. 5 and 6).

3. **True Positive/False Positive** An outcome that shows a given condition has
   been satisfied, when it really has not been satisfied, called False Positive. And an
   outcome that shows a given condition has been satisfied, when it really been
   satisfied, called True Positive (Figs. 7 and 8).
4. **Rate of Packet** Packet rate is showing number of packet coming toward destination within fix time period. Here, we consider time period $t = 5$ s (Figs. 9 and
   10).

Fig. 8 True positive versus false negative for time 10 s

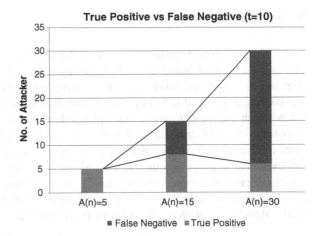

Fig. 9 Packet rate for time 20 s

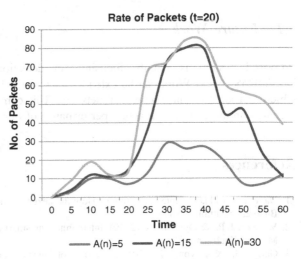

Fig. 10 Packet rate for time 10 s

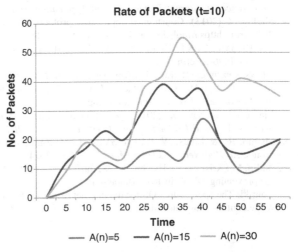

5   Conclusion and Future Work

In this paper, a mechanism is presented for detection and prevention of DDoS attacks on an agent based at border/gateway node. We found so many different approaches in related work with each have some limitation like middleware approach need extra effort to implement, only able to detect physical level with RSS value which energy consumed. Our proposed mechanism will be applied to either Network Side or Distributed on Agent at Border Router which can prevent attacks from outside to deform its basic requirement and usage and protect IoT network from volumetric flooding attack at network layer. Bases on Result Analysis we can say our approach is more suitable where numbers of user are not in large number, i.e., applicable to Smart Home, Smart Apartment, Smart Building, etc., so it can easily identify and protect IoT network from attackers.

5.1   Future Work

Proposed system is mainly focusing on detection and prevention against DoS/DDoS attack. Work can be extended to make it Intrusion Prevention System which can identify and secure IoT network. This can also be tested for real-time scenario on motes to check actual performance of our work.

References

1. Dave, E. (2011). The internet of things: How the next evolution of the internet. Cisco Internet Business Solutions Group.
2. Vasseur, J. P., & Dunkels, A. (2010). Interconnecting smart objects with IP the next internet. Morgan Kaufmann.
3. Gang, G., & Zeyong, L. (2011). Internet of things security analysis. In *International Conference on Internet Technology and Applications (iTAP), Wuhan.*
4. Shelby, Z. (2013). Constrained application protocol (CoAP), June 2013. Retrieved October 2014 from https://tools.ietf.org/html/draft-ietf-core-18.
5. CA-1996-01, CERT. Retrieved November 2014 from http://www.cert.org/historical/advisories/CA-1996-01.cfm.
6. DDoS Resources. Retrieved November 2014 from http://anml.iu.edu/ddos/types.html.
7. Albert, F. (2014). ICMP Attacks, INFOSEC Institute. Retrieved November 2014 from http://resources.infosecinstitute.com/icmp-attacks/.
8. Manju, V., & Sasi, K. (2012). Detection of jamming style DoS attack in wireless sensor network. In *2nd IEEE International Conference on Parallel, Distributed and Grid Computing.*
9. Shahid, R., & Linus, W. (2013). SVELTE: Real-time intrusion detection in the internet of things. *Ad Hoc Networks (Elsevier) 11*(8) 2661–2674.
10. Sudip, M., Krishna, V., Harshit, A., & Antriksh, S. (2011). A learning automata based solution for preventing DDoS in IoT, Kharagpur.
11. Contiki: The open source OS for the internet of things. Retrieved November 2014 from http://www.contiki-os.org/index.html.

Issues in Quantitative Association Rule Mining: A Big Data Perspective

Dhrubajit Adhikary and Swarup Roy

Abstract In recent decades, different Quantitative Association Rule Mining (QARM) techniques evolved for mining significant association rules in real-world quantitative databases. Unlike the classical AR mining techniques, these techniques are more effective in revealing hidden associations in quantitative databases and hence they are explicitly applied to understand patterns, learn behavior, predict events, and make decisions. But, with the rapid change in real-world databases in terms of volume, nature, and speed of data generation, the QARM techniques appear to be ineffective because of certain issues pertaining to them. In this paper, we try to discuss the concepts and issues pertaining to QARM in the real-world knowledge discovery scenario, including Big Data Analytics. We also highlight how QARM may contribute towards analyzing Big Data.

Keywords Association rules · Quantitative association rules · Accuracy measure · Big data · Stream-Data

1 Introduction

Association Rule Mining (ARM) [1] helps in learning behavior, predicting events and making decisions from an abundance of data. It derives hidden associations within frequent patterns inherent in large databases. Such associations, represented as implications of the form $X \Rightarrow Y$ (where X and Y are any nonempty frequent item sets in a database) are known as Association Rules (AR). To find the interestingness of AR, measures like Support and Confidence are also considered while mining

D. Adhikary · S. Roy (✉)
Department of Information Technology, North-Eastern Hill University, Shillong 793022, Meghalaya, India
e-mail: swarup@nehu.ac.in

D. Adhikary
e-mail: dhrubajit.adhikary@gmail.com

© Springer Science+Business Media Singapore 2016
S.C. Satapathy et al. (eds.), *Proceedings of International Conference on ICT for Sustainable Development*, Advances in Intelligent Systems and Computing 409, DOI 10.1007/978-981-10-0135-2_37

rules. But, unlike the conventional techniques which are limited to market basket data, the modern AR mining techniques had to satisfy the need of mining rules in databases that mostly cover quantitative data. To deal with this facet, a newer concept called QARM was coined in [2]. Since then, QARM became one of the well-researched techniques in Data Mining.

The QARM techniques initially dealt with smaller quantitative databases. But, with the passage of time and advances in technology the nature and volume of data started changing remarkably; resulting into high-dimensional databases containing both qualitative and quantitative[1] data. Such change in the real-world database scenario brought in fresh challenges for the QARM research community; following which, numerous techniques using different approaches and ideas; eventually, came into the picture. Nevertheless, potential issues still remain in most of the QARM techniques.

In this paper, we highlight some of the trending issues in QARM and discuss them for further comprehension.

2 Definition of Quantitative AR

Like a conventional AR, a Quantitative Association Rule (QAR) is an improvised implication of the form $X \Rightarrow Y$. The left hand side of the implication, i.e., X (called *antecedent*) and the right hand side, i.e., Y (called *succedent* or *consequent*) are nonempty attribute sets in a database. (A *cedent* with one attribute is termed *trivial cedent* else it is termed *nontrivial cedent*).

Contrasting a conventional AR, in a QAR both quantitative and qualitative/categorical attributes may participate as any of the cedents. Moreover, unlike the conventional ARs, *negative* associations may also be highlighted using QARs. Such associations relate negative dependencies among attributes in a database and expose how the absence of certain attributes may drive the presence or absence of other attributes in the database. Hence, they are termed *negative QARs* and they may have negated items within antecedent or succedent or both [3]. Here, the negation ($\neg$) symbolizes absence. An example of a QA Rule is given below:

$$(Age : [30 \cdots 39]) \ \& \ (Married : Yes) \Rightarrow (NumCars : 2)$$

In this QAR, *Age* and *NumCars* are quantitative attributes and *Married* is a categorical attribute (with categories Yes & No). This is a positive QAR as it shows

---

[1]Quantitative data is expressed in terms of numbers but not in terms of language descriptors unlike Qualitative or Categorical data which is expressed in terms of language descriptors but not in numbers. Categorical data may be Ordinal—having natural ordering like *small, medium, large* or Nominal—having no natural ordering like *gender, religion, color*.

a *positive* association. A negative QAR with negation within antecedent is shown below:

$$(Age \; : \; \neg[20 \cdots 29]) \; \& \; (Married \; : \; Yes) \Rightarrow (NumCars \; : \; 2)$$

To determine the interestingness of any QAR, the two common rule interestingness measures, viz., Support and Confidence may be used. Support of a QAR actually quantifies the presence of the implication given by the QAR in the entire space of the database. Greater support implies better quality of the QAR in terms of quantity. Next, Confidence is used to express the correctness of the implication shown in a QAR. Hence, greater Confidence of a QAR implies better quality of the QAR in terms of correctness. For further and better assessment of quality of the discovered QARs, other available rule evaluation measures available are Lift, Conviction, Gain, Certainty-Factor, and Leverage which are well discussed in [4].

3   QARM in Big Data Analysis

With databases growing in volume, variety and velocity due to numerous information sensing and information gathering devices and techniques; analysis of data is turning equally complex. Such complexities impose new challenges to the established data mining techniques to analyze data in Big Data perspective.

In [5] authors proposed a three tier framework for Big Data processing with various research challenges systematically integrated into these tiers, such that each tier conforms a specific data processing paradigm. As suggested in tier III of this framework a big data mining algorithm specially has to handle the following:

1. Data at local sites
2. Complex and Dynamic Data
3. Sparse, Uncertain and Incomplete data

and thus the objective of global mining from multiple information sources may be achieved by featuring local mining and global correlation at data, model and knowledge levels respectively. The mining results (data statistics, pattern and knowledge) of each local site at these three levels may be aggregated later to obtain the final effective global results.

Therefore, Tier III is the appropriate stage where QARM can play a significant role to contribute towards Big Data analysis by discovering interesting associations and patterns from quantitative databases at local sites. In Big Data, data types include structured, unstructured and semi-structured data and so on. Hence, QARM can be well utilized in finding associations in structured quantitative databases mostly in finance and business informatics, genomic and other biological researches.

However, efficient application of QARM techniques in Big Data analysis is possible in part provided the current issues pertaining to it get nullified. Below we discuss some issues associated to current QARM techniques.

4 Issues Concerning QARM

In recent decades, different QARM techniques evolved from approaches viz., partitioning [2], clustering [6], statistical [7], evolutionary [3], etc. that found applications in various domains [8] but some of the issues yet remain untreated, unsolved or are partially solved. In this section, we discuss the issues concerning QARM in general and in the perspective of Big Data analysis.

4.1 Information Loss

The information loss issue was first highlighted in 1996 by Srikant and Agrawal in [2]. This issue lies predominantly in most of the QARM techniques under partitioning approach. The Support-Confidence conflict and the partitioning paradigm itself are the reasons behind it. The Equi-depth and Equi-width partitioning methods are highly vulnerable to information loss. Therefore, in [9] the authors introduced a concept that discretizes partitions in a self-adaptive way in order to maximize both support and Confidence, thus minimizing information loss. Clustering techniques were also used to enhance partitioning approach. In [10] the authors suggested to cluster all attributes together and project the clusters into the domains of the quantitative attributes finding overlapped intervals. But, such clustering techniques seem to have scalability issues in return.

4.2 Useless Rule Generation

Irrespective of the approach used, some QARM techniques are susceptible to the generation of numerous useless rules. By useless rules we mean *redundant, uninteresting and misleading rules*. When QARM techniques use methods that may lead to combinatorial explosion of item sets or intervals, similar kind of implications repeatedly get discovered in the form of rules. For example, Rule 1 and Rule 2 below are conceptually *redundant*.

$$\text{Rule1}: \ A \in [10 \cdots 20] \& \ B \in [15 \cdots 30] \Rightarrow C \in [5 \cdots 15]$$
$$\text{Rule2}: \ B \in [15 \cdots 30] \& \ A \in [10 \cdots 20] \Rightarrow C \in [5 \cdots 15]$$

Again when the number of attributes (or dimensions) in a database is quite large, a QARM technique may continue yielding—rules with low scores for the rule evaluation measures; or rules comprising attributes of not much importance to the analyst/user. Such rules are considered *uninteresting*.

Misleading rules are however, theoretically interesting (because they comply with the evaluation measures) but practically they imply an impractical, rather illogical association. Such rules are well discussed in [7]. Here, the authors explained how the use of a range for describing a distribution of quantitative values can be limited and misleading too.

4.3 Mining Negative QARs

As stated earlier, QARs can expose *negative* associations that highlight how the absence of certain attributes may drive the presence (or absence as well) of other attributes in a database. Hence, negative QARs are as important as the positive ones for knowledge discovery in many real-world databases.

Negative QAR mining considers the same set of attributes, but finding such negative implications may require a separate test. Hence, most of the QARM techniques developed so far paid lesser attention to it. But the importance of negative QARs cannot be ignored. For example, a negative QAR somewhat like the one shown below may prove interesting.

$$Age \in [25 \cdots 35] \; \& \neg BloodSugar \in [High] \Rightarrow BP \in [Normal]$$

However, after analyzing a good number of available QARM techniques theoretically, it can be asserted that techniques other than those from the evolutionary algorithmic approach; have this issue in common. The evolutionary algorithmic approach however seemed to find both positive and negative rules but the utilization of techniques from this approach might turn computationally expensive in larger databases having numerous dimensions and instances.

4.4 Scalability, Scans and Execution Time of QARM Techniques

Discussion in one of the above sections concluded leaving behind the scalability issue of QARM techniques w.r.t high-dimensional databases. This issue often referred as the *curse of dimensionality* hovers over most of the QARM techniques because the real-world databases from different domains (like business, healthcare and time-series) use to have several dimensions containing quantitative data. Moreover, Big Data Analytics also have concern over the dimensionality of databases generated by various autonomous, distributed and decentralized databases.

Analysis reveals that the techniques from partitioning and statistical approaches are quite unsuccessful in handling high-dimensional databases. In majority cases, rules generated by these approaches are single-dimensional that associate only two dimensions (attributes) per rule. On the other hand, if rule mining considers all the dimensions together then it result in many-rules problem, higher execution time and larger database scans. But contrasting them, the clustering techniques showed credibility towards handling multidimensional databases. In [6] the authors derived a notion that QAR mining can be transformed to the problem of finding regions with enough density by projecting a database to a multidimensional space and finally mapping the dense regions to QA rules. Their method finds positive multidimensional rules and because of the *density* measure it is capable of getting rid of the trivial and redundant rules. Further contributions using clustering approach include the works in [11, 12] that can deal with higher dimensional databases with scalable performance. However, disadvantages still remain as the techniques were unable to mine negative rules and sometimes require the users to specify many thresholds.

Dimensionality of a database induces the number of database scans and transitively affects the execution time of any QARM technique. Therefore, an efficient QARM technique must try to enhance its scalability by mining QARs with reduced number of database scans so that a reasonable trade-off can be achieved between higher-dimensions of a quantitative database and lower execution time.

4.5   Handling Stream-Data (in Terms of Big Data Analytics)

Considering analysis of modern databases, we may extend our discussion towards Big Data Analytics where analysts from different corners of the world meet difficulties with large data sets in areas including Internet search, finance, business informatics, meteorology, genomic, scientific simulations, biological and environmental research etc. Some of these areas generate stream-data and hence precision of knowledge discovered using traditional techniques, happen to have a short span. In case of stream-data, the patterns may change rapidly with the entry of newer items and hence, interpretation of knowledge discovered just a few moments earlier to an entry; may result erroneous the next moment. Therefore, sophisticated technology is required to handle such stream-data.

Now, if we consider QARM as one of the tools of big data analytics then QARM techniques must also have the ability to handle stream-data; which at present time might be identified as an issue. None of the QARM techniques evolved so far had to handle such stream-data hence they are not sophisticated enough to do so. But in near future, if QARM has to contribute toward Big Data Analysis, presence of methods to handle stream-data; is preferred in QARM techniques.

4.6 Absence of Accuracy Evaluation Measures in QARM Techniques

In [13] the authors stated after analysis that there is no uniformity on the selection of measures to evaluate the rules generated by any ARM technique. Though the combination of the two basic rule interestingness measures viz., Support and Confidence are used extensively in all approaches this itself does not guarantee that the mined rules are free from all sort of inconsistencies. Hence, newer evaluation measures discussed in [4, 13] find utilization in a few modern QARM techniques. But such measures can only deduce *how good a particular QAR is* comparing to the other discovered QARs. And most of the time these are the thresholds taken as user inputs that ultimately decide the strength and goodness of each such rule. Hence, the bottom line is—rule evaluation measures can only provide a degree of reliance to the user but can no way find the actual accuracy of the implications revealed in the QARs.

As such, there originate a need of accuracy evaluation measure of the QARM techniques. But determining the accuracy of discovered rules post-mining in a subject database may not sound reasonable. Therefore, every technique (whatever be the approach) should go for a pre-mining accuracy test where the technique would be given a test database to mine QARs. Next, the discovered QARs would be compared to some predetermined correct associations (conforming to the same test database) to generate an accuracy score for the technique. This score would be calculated upon the precision with which the discovered QARs resemble the predetermined correct associations. Later, when need arises this accuracy score can help analyst to make a correct choice of a QARM technique for different mining objectives, under different mining situations. As the rule interestingness measures determine the reliability of the discovered rule thus an accuracy evaluation measure would determine the reliability and effectiveness of a QARM technique.

To summarize the above discussion, a comparison is drawn in Table 1 among different QARM approaches showing their relative merits and demerits in terms of the issues discussed. A (✓) represents relative *presence* and a (✗) represents relative *absence* of an issue in each of the approaches listed.

Table 1 QARM approaches with relative merits and demerits while handling issues

Sl. no	Issues	Partitioning	Clustering	Statistical	Evolutionary
1	Information loss	✓	✗	✓	✗
2	Useless rules generation	✓	✗	✗	✗
3	Mining negative QARs	✓	✓	✓	✗
4	Scalability	✓	✗	✓	✗
5	Larger database scans	✓	✓	✓	✓
6	Higher execution time	✓	✓	✓	✓
7	Absence of accuracy measure	✓	✓	✓	✓
8	Handling stream-data	✓	✓	✓	✓

5   Conclusion

In this paper, we discuss several issues related to QARM techniques for generating effective association rules from real-world databases containing quantitative data. We compare the relative merits and weaknesses of the existing QARM approaches in light of the above issues. We highlight certain areas where the QARM research community still need to dig in to find advanced strategies of handling modern databases so that quality rule generation can be achieved. Towards the end, we also make an attempt to see QARM as a tool for Big Data Analysis and find how the inherent issues may hurdle such utilization.

To conclude, we may state that an ideal QARM technique is one that results quality (not quantity) rule generation without information loss and is scalable for high-dimensional databases with optimal execution time. Moreover, if such a technique can be equipped with functionalities for handling stream-data it can be utilized intensely for Big Data Analysis also.

References

1. Agrawal, R., Mannila, H., Srikant, R., Toivonen, H., & Verkamo, A. I., et al. (1996). Fast discovery of association rules. In *Advances in knowledge discovery and data mining* (Vol. 12 (1), pp. 307–328).
2. Srikant, R., & Agrawal, R. (1996). Mining quantitative association rules in large relational tables. In *ACM SIGMOD Record* (Vol. 25, pp. 1–12). ACM.
3. Alatas, B., & Akin, E. (2006). An effcient genetic algorithm for automated mining of both positive and negative quantitative association rules. *Soft Computing, 10*(3), 230–237.
4. Martinez-Ballesteros, M., & Riquelme, J. (2011). Analysis of measures of quantitative association rules. In *Hybrid Artificial Intelligent Systems* (pp. 319–326). Springer.
5. Wu, X., Zhu, X., Wu, G. Q., & Ding, W. (2014). Data mining with big data. *IEEE Transactions on Knowledge and Data Engineering, 26*(1), 97–107.
6. Lian, W., Cheung, D. W., & Yiu, S. (2005). An efficient algorithm for finding dense regions for mining quantitative association rules. *Computers & Mathematics with Applications, 50*(3), 471–490.
7. Aumann, Y., & Lindell, Y. (2003). A statistical theory for quantitative association rules. *Journal of Intelligent Information Systems, 20*(3), 255–283.
8. Adhikary, D., & Roy, S. (2015). Mining quantitative association rules in real-world databases: A review. In *2015 1st International Conference on Computing and Communication Systems (I3CS)* (Vol. 1, pp. 87–92). IGI Global.
9. Dancheng, L., Ming, Z., Shuangshuang, Z., & Chen, Z. (2012). A new approach of self-adaptive discretization to enhance the apriori quantitative association rule mining. In *2012 Second International Conference on Intelligent System Design and Engineering Application (ISDEA)* (pp. 44–47), IEEE.
10. Tong, Q., Yan, B., & Zhou, Y. (2005). Mining quantitative association rules on overlapped intervals. In *Advanced data mining and applications* (pp. 43–50). Springer.

11. Guo, Y., Yang, J., & Huang, Y. (2008). An effective algorithm for mining quantitative association rules based on high dimension cluster. In *4th International Conference on Wireless Communications, Networking and Mobile Computing, WiCOM'08* (pp. 1–4). IEEE.

12. Junrui, Y., & Feng, Z.: An effective algorithm for mining quantitative associations based on subspace clustering. In *2010 International Conference on Networking and Digital Society (ICNDS)* (Vol. 1, (pp. 175–178)). IEEE.

13. Martinez-Ballesteros, M., Martinez-Alvarez, F., Troncoso, A., & Riquelme, J. C. (2014). Selecting the best measures to discover quantitative association rules. *Neurocomputing, 126,* 3–14.

A Framework for Temporal Information Search and Exploration

Parul Patel and S.V. Patel

Abstract Volume of digitized Information is growing drastically on web, digital libraries and other archives. Demand for searching a relevant document or data of specific time period over large amount of data has also increased. Therefore, Time dimension has its own importance in any information domain. Despite of the importance of temporal data available in the document, current search engines and searching techniques provide limited search facilities using date of timestamp or document publication date. Existing retrieval models do not take advantage of *temporal expressions* embedded into a document. This paper describes our framework to exploit temporal expressions in documents in order to add value to the existing information retrieval systems by providing searches like "before elections 2014," "after Diwali," etc., and retrieve relevant documents satisfying temporal expression search criteria.

Keywords Temporal information retrieval · Temporal search time-based clustering

1 Introduction

Web is growing with digitized document where search is an important activity to get required information from large amount of data. Search engine is one of the biggest tools to be used by everyone around the world. Search engine is a kind of information retrieval system that asks user for a specific query and return a list of ranked URL, or documents with their titles and summary of web page or document.

P. Patel (✉)
M.Sc (I.T) Programme, VNSGU, Surat, Gujarat, India
e-mail: parul.patelns@gmail.com

S.V. Patel
Department of Computer Science, VNSGU, Surat, Gujarat, India
e-mail: patelsv@gmail.com

© Springer Science+Business Media Singapore 2016
S.C. Satapathy et al. (eds.), *Proceedings of International Conference on ICT for Sustainable Development*, Advances in Intelligent Systems and Computing 409, DOI 10.1007/978-981-10-0135-2_38

387

In some search engine, facility is provided to search between specific time period by allowing user to enter start and end date into input box and then sorting a retrieved results as per user specified chronological order. But queries like "Elections in India before 2000" requires proper treatment of temporal expressions embedded into a user's query. In above example, user is interested into a document stating information about election before year 2000. So as a result, all documents containing information related to election before the year 2000 must be returned. Another Example, someone who is new to India wanted to know about Indian politics and moreover interested in knowing about "Anna Hazare". In this example, user is interested in knowing details of "Anna Hazare" in chronological order like Anna in 1990, Anna in 1991, etc. A simple query like "Anna Hazare" will not satisfy that requirement. User has to give query like "Anna Hazare from 1960 to 2015." Existing Search engine are not able to handle such queries where temporal expression is leveraged. Moreover, existing retrieval model do not take benefit of temporal expressions contained into the documents.

This paper presents a framework to overcome with above limitations by adding new functionalities to use temporal expression embedded into the documents to utilize them into retrieval. It also handles temporal expression into user's query.

The paper is organized as follows: Sect. 2 presents literature survey on temporal information processing and time based retrieval models. In Sect. 3, Research methodology that includes framework of temporal information retrieval with components such as our temporal tagger, process to retrieve document based on time and an algorithm to represent the retrieved documents on timeline is described in Sect. 3. In Sect. 4, Results and Evaluation of system is presented. Section 5 concludes the paper and gives direction for the future work.

2 Related Work

Developing Framework for temporal information retrieval focus on two different area: (1) Temporal Information Extraction and Processing (2) Use of Such expression in Exploration of search results. Our Literature survey focuses on research that has been done in both of this area. First, we have described research that has been done in development of temporal tagger in various languages. Second phrase is a literature survey about work that has been done in temporal information retrieval.

The Message Understanding Conferences (MUCs) in 1996 and 1998 have played a significant role, but their evaluations covered only recognition of TEs, while a novel contribution towards the normalization of TEs was made in 2000 [1]. GUTime was a rule based system which was developed an extension of TempEx tagger. It was based on TimeML TIMEX3 format, which allows a functional style of encoding offsets in time expressions. It was evaluated on TERN 2004 corpus and achieved 85 % of F-measure [2]. Llorens has developed temporal information extraction system based on CRF for Spanish documents with F-measure of 91 % [3]. KUL is a machine learning-based system for recognition and normalization of temporal expression with 0.85 % precision and recall of 0.84 % [4]. Negri and Merseglia has developed a rule based system which involves tokenization, part-of-speech tagging based on a list of 5000 entries retrieved from WordNet. Then, the recognized text is processed by a set of approximately 1000 basic rules. Recognized temporal expressions and information around that is used for normalization. Then composition rules are used to resolve ambiguities wherever multiple tag placements are possible. The results in terms of F-measure on ACE 2004 data are 92.6, 83.9 and 87.2 % for detection, recognition and determining the VAL attribute value, respectively [5]. Heideltime is high quality rule based tagger for temporal expression recognition and normalization with 0.90 % precision and 0.82 % recall [6]. The Yamcha is machine learning based tagger which uses SVM and FOIL for chunking and classification of chunks. They got precision of 80.05 %, recall of 73.71 % and F-measure of 76.75 %. They have concluded that use of SVM leads to overfitting [7]. Jelena has developed a system for temporal information extraction and interpretation for serebian language with precision of 0.93 %, recall of 0.96 % and F-score or 0.94 % [8]. SUtime is the library for recognizing and normalizing temporal expressions developed by Stanford University. It is rule-based system developed in java [9].

Research has been done in extracting and processing temporal information from document in various languages like English, Hindi, Spanish, Chinese, etc., but less efforts are made in using that processed data for retrieval and presentation of the document. Research paper on the special issue on temporal information processing by Mani gives road map in this domain. It also focuses on challenges and opportunities in this domain [10]. Google has also added a prototype view:timeline() to display search result on timeline [11]. Xiaoyan Li and Croft has proposed Time bases language models which incorporate time into both query likelihood language models and relevance based language models [12]. Temporal mining of blogs is presented in [13]. J. Allen and R. Gupta and Khandelwal has proposed methods to construct temporal summaries of news stories [14]. Ricardo Baeza Yates has developed an algorithm to obtain future possible events and then searching those events for future information needs [15]. SNAKET is a system developed by paolo and Antonio for unifying hierarchical web snippet clustering with a web interface for web search, books, news and blog domains [16]. Rosie Jones and Diaz have focused on constructing query specific temporal profiles based on publication time of relevant document [17].

Various temporal taggers have been developed to extract and normalize temporal expressions from the document. However, these taggers mainly focus on Explicit temporal expressions hence they extract very few implicit temporal expressions. It may be observed that some documents, we may have large number of implicit temporal expressions like "last diwali," "next holi," etc. In such cases our objective is to develop a temporal tagger which extract all Indian festivals as well as of other temporal expressions from document and normalize it into a specific value. By developing such tagger, we have used it into development of our framework for temporal information retrieval and presenting retrieved document into time lined manner.

3 Research Methodology

3.1 Time, Temporal Expression and Temporal Tagger

Time is very important dimension in any information retrieval system. Temporal information is present into the form of temporal expression in any document. Processing such temporal expression from raw text is fundamental requirement for application like text summarization, question answering. A temporal expression also known as Timex also refers to every natural language phrase that denotes a temporal entity like interval or an instant. For example, "Prime Minister Narendra Modi will visit China tomorrow," "India won the test match on last Friday."

Temporal expressions can be classified into following categories according to Schilder and Habel [18].

Explicit Date Expressions such as "13/08/2013", "15th August" refer explicitly to entries of a calendar system and can be mapped directly to temporal Chronons in a timeline.

Implicit All temporal expressions that can be evaluated via a given time ontology and capability of the named entity extraction approach such as name of holiday (last chritmas), next valentine day, etc.

Relative Some temporal expressions express vague temporal information and it is rather difficult to precisely place the information expressed on a time line. Such temporal expressions can be only anchored in a timeline in reference to another explicit or implicit already anchored temporal expression. For example, "on Monday," "Before June and After March," etc. If the document has creation date, then they can be easily anchored. Such reference date can be used to map with chronon and can be used during normalization.

We have developed our own rule based temporal tagger to extract temporal expression from document and normalize in into some standard format. First we have extracted all temporal expressions from the document, then all temporal expressions are normalized into standard values based on offset and reference date. Our tagger has one important characteristics compared to other temporal tagger that it supports normalization of Indian festivals which do not occur on some fixed days. It can handle temporal expression like "last diwali" and can translate into specific date based on selected reference time. First we have extracted temporal reference date and then tried to normalize all temporal expression by considering this reference date. We have stored data of 50 years of Indian festivals into dataset because all Indian festivals do not occur on fixed date. Our tagger is generalized to incorporate new festivals, and with new values of coming year for existing festivals. It also allows incorporating some special events like "tsunami," "attack on taj," etc.

3.2 Temporal Outline of Document

Based on the extracted temporal expressions and their respective normalized values, temporal outline of the document is generated. Temporal Outline can be defined as:

$$TOD : D \rightarrow [t \times n \times d \times m \times y \times p]$$

where t is a set of temporal expressions extracted from documents.

n is a respective normalized value of temporal expression

m is month chronon,

y is year chronon,

d is date chronon, and

p is a position of the temporal expression into the document.

We can have much temporal expression in the document. So D can be a collection of

$$\{(t_1 \times n_1 \times d_1 \times m_1 \times y_1 \times p_1)\,(t_2 \times n_2 \times d_2 \times m_2 \times y_2 \times p_2)\ldots\ldots\ldots(t_r \times n_r \times d_r \times m_r \times y_r \times p_r)\}$$

where r is number of temporal expressions into the document.

Temporal outline of the document makes all temporal expressions from the document explicit for the further processing.

3.3 Exploring Search Result on Timeline

In the following section, we describe our algorithm to explore search result on timeline.

```
Input : User Query
Output: List of Documents arranged in Timeline Manner

Begin
Step 1:      Parse User query to Temporal Tagger
Step 2:      If Query contains Temporal Expressions
                 search based on the keyword + Temporal
                 Expression (e.g Query is :election on
                 last  Christmas then search applied on
                 keyword Diwali+ 25/12/XXXX+christmas)
             else
                 Search based on query (e.g elections)
             end if
             End
```

Let R is collection of retrieved document on specific user query. We assume that each document has unique id. Following algorithm is used to generate timeline.

```
Begin
Step 1 : Select Smallest and Largest Temporal Chronon
         form selected document's temporal
         outline(tod)
     Chmin(R)= Chminimum(chmin(d1), chmin(d2), chmin(d3)
         ..........chmin(dn))
     Chmax(R)= Chmaximum(chmax(d1), chmax(d2), chmax(d3)
         ..........chmax(dn))
Step 2:  Based on chmax and chmin upper bound and
         lower bound of timeline is decided
Step 3:  If   IssameGranularity(getgranularity(Chmax),
              getgranularity(Chmin)) is same
                   granularity= getgranularity(chmax)
         else
              granularity=getgranularity
                        (coarsegranule(chmax, chmin))
         end if
Step 4:  Initialialize clusters based on granularity
         seleceted.
Step 5:  If issameyear(chmax,chmin)
              Generate level i of Timeline for 12
              months
         else
              if issamemonth(chmax, chmin)
                   Generate Level i of Timeline for
                   weeks
              Else
                   if issameweek(chmax, chmin)
                        Generate Level i of Timeline
                        for days
                   end if
              end if
         end if
Step 6:  Repeat step 5 till documents are there with
         finer granule available into collection R

End
```

Once the upper and lower bound of timeline is fixed, it classification of each document based on their temporal values stored into TDO needs to be done. Each Cluster in timeline contains documents belonging to that chronon. Each document may contain more than one temporal expression, so their TDO may contain more than one value. So it is obvious that that document may belongs to more than one cluster. It may be possible that some clusters do not find any document belonging to that chronon. We have finally revised timeline by removing such clusters from timeline. Once all clusters are initialized with their corresponding links, it is sent to user interface. Each Cluster can be refined into smaller chronon by user if documents have finer granules available into temporal document outline.

4 Evaluation

The initial step was to annotate document by time. From The Times of India archive of different time period, we extracted 100 news documents based on key word "Elections." All these documents were processed using our temporal tagger. The extracted temporal expressions were stored into database with their normalized values and position into a document. Through web interface we queried like

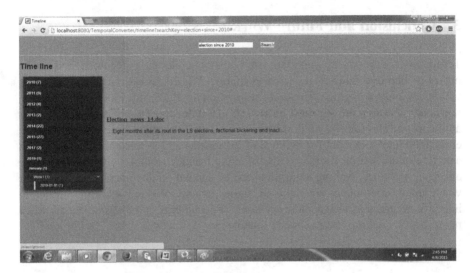

Fig. 1 TimeLine for user query "election since 2010"

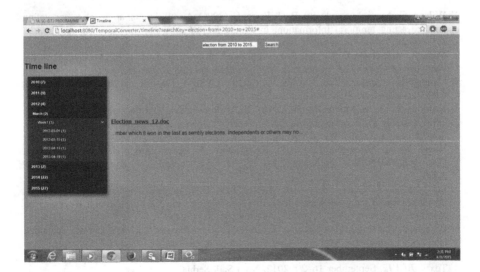

Fig. 2 Search results based on query "election from 2010 to 2015"

"Election from 1990 to 2000," "Election before this diwali," "election after this diwali," "election," "election since 2000," etc. Each document in the respective cluster was checked manually and compared with the respective values. There were 90 % relevant documents into each cluster. Following snapshots show the output of above queries (Figs 1 and 2).

The result is quite satisfactory to use the system for temporal information retrieval supporting temporal expressions (Fig 2).

5 Conclusion and Future Work

Temporal expressions are important structures available into a document and can be useful to improve traditional search technique. We discussed our temporal tagger which not only recognize temporal information available into document, but also normalize it into some standard form such that it becomes explicit for use in other applications. The framework developed can be used to utilize temporal information embedded into document for retrieval of documents and to make time based search and to explore search results on the timeline manner to make visualization more effective. In future, ranking algorithms can be applied on documents in each cluster when many documents are there of same granule. We are working further to improve accuracy as well as doing ranking of documents in individual cluster when many documents are there of same granule.

References

1. Wilson, G., Mani, I., Sundheim, B., & Ferro, L. (2001). A multilingual approach to annotating and extracting temporal information. In *Proceeding of workshop on temporal and spatial Information Processing* (Vol.13, pp. 1–7).
2. Mani, I., & Wilson, G. (2000). Robust temporal processing of news. In *Proceedings of the 38th Annual Meeting on Association for Computational Linguistics (Hong Kong)* (pp. 69–76).
3. Llorens, H., Saquete, E., & Navarro, B. (2010). TIPSEM (English and Spanish): Evaluating CRFs and semantic roles in TempEval-2.
4. Kolomiyets, O., & Moens, M.-F. (2010). KUL: Recognition and normalisation of temporal expressions In *Proceedings of the 5th International Workshop on Semantic Evaluation, ACL 2010 Uppsala, Sweden* (pp. 325–328).
5. Negri, M., & Marseglia, L. (2005). Recognition and normalization of time expressions: ITC-irst at TERN 2004. Technical Report WP3.7, Information Society Technologies, February 2005.
6. Strotgen, J., & Gertz, M. (2010). HeidelTime: High quality rule-based extraction and normalization of temporal expressions. In *Proceedings of the 5th International Workshop on Semantic Evaluation, ACL, Uppsala, Sweden* (pp. 321–324).
7. Poveda, J., Surdeanu, M., & Turmo, J. (2007). A comparison of statistical and rule induction learners for automatic tagging of time expressions in english.
8. Jacimovic, J. (2012). Recognition and Normalization of Temporal Expressions in Serbian Texts: *BCI'12*, September 16–20, 2012, Novi Sad, Serbia.

9. Chang, X., & Manning, C. D. (2012). SUTime: A library for recognizing and normalizing time expressions: Angel. In *Eighth International Conference on Language Resources and Evaluation (LREC)*.
10. Mani, I., Pustejovsky, J., & Sundheim, B. (2004) Introduction to the special issue on temporal information processing. *ACM Transactions on Asian Language Information Processing 3*(1), 1–10.
11. http://www.google.com/experimental/.
12. Li, X., & Croft, W. B. (2003). Time-based language models. In *CIKM '03: Proceedings of the Twelfth International Conference on Information and Knowledge Management, New York, ACM* (pp. 469–475).
13. Qamra, A., Tseng, B., & Chang, E. (2006). Mining blog stories using community-based and temporal clustering. In *Proceeding of 15th ACM International Conference on Information and Knowledge Management, ACM* (pp. 58–67).
14. Allan, J., Gupta, R., & Khandelwal, V. (2001). Temporal summaries of news topics. In *Proceedings of the 24th International ACM SIGIR Conference, ACM* (pp. 10–18).
15. Baeza-Yates, R. A. (2005). Searching the future. In *Proceedings of ACM SIGIR Workshop MF/IR*.
16. Ferragina, P., & Gulli, A. (2005). A personalized search engine based on web-snippet hierarchical clustering. In *14th International Conference on World Wide Web (Special Interest Tracks and Posters)* (pp. 801–810).
17. Jones, R., & Diaz, F. (2007). Temporal profiles of queries. *ACM Transactions. Information System., 25*(3), 14.
18. Schilder, F., & Habel, C. (2001). From temporal expression to temporal information: Semantic tagging of news messages. In *Proceeding of the ACL 2001 Workshop on Temporal and Spatial Information Processing*.

Item Amalgamation Approach for Serendipity-Oriented Recommender System

Ravi Shah, Ashishkumar Patel and Kiran Amin

Abstract Nowadays, Recommender System is quite a useful system which helps people to navigate through complex items. There are many different recommender systems proposed and many business solutions have been found. But, because of the high complexity and uncertainty of the problem there is no best approach found. Recent research in the stream not just limited to the accuracy of the system. There are many another factors such as serendipity means as surprise, is defined as the finding the unexpected as well as useful items for the user. In our system, we are providing serendipity by the intrinsic accidents and user will find the value by applying their knowledge on it which says sagacity. We considered this mechanism as serendipity-oriented recommender system. Our idea is to give serendipity-oriented recommender system by Item Amalgamation Approach. The core logic of this technique is to find the items which have common features of the given input items by the user. We are considering benchmark and well known dataset MovieLens dataset for our Approach.

Keywords Recommendation system · Serendipity · Amalgamation · Sagacity

R. Shah (✉) · A. Patel
Department of Computer Engineering, LDRP-ITR, Gandhinagar, Gujarat, India
e-mail: rvshah1992@gmail.com

A. Patel
e-mail: ashish_ce@ldrp.ac.in

A. Patel
C U Shah University, Wadhwan, Gujarat, India

K. Amin
Department of Computer Engineering, UVPCE, Kherva, Gujarat, India
e-mail: kiran.amin@ganpatuniversity.com

© Springer Science+Business Media Singapore 2016
S.C. Satapathy et al. (eds.), *Proceedings of International Conference on ICT for Sustainable Development*, Advances in Intelligent Systems and Computing 409, DOI 10.1007/978-981-10-0135-2_39

1 Introduction

In modern years, many studies going on the development of the recommender system that not only consider accuracy measure of the system, other measures like novelty, diversity, and serendipity [1, 2] also comes in the frame. Many studies found that users are not every time satisfied with the high accuracy in recommender systems. Other various factors or viewpoints are also makes their marks in this new era of the recommender system.

In attempt to satisfy the need of users with new factors, in our study we are focusing on the serendipity. Serendipity means "the ability to make unexpected and valuable discoveries by accident." [3] We thus define unexpected items are the serendipitous items, valuable and user thinks that he/she can't ever find it by them self, and we think that such an item can varied users' interest without their experience in it, thus making their standard of living rich and high [3].

The terms serendipity originated from the story called "The Three Princes of Serendip" [4], which describes the journey of the three princes. Because of the unexpected events of their journey princes invented a series of unique things, which they credited to their luck. After reading this story Horace Walpole, said that "princes were always making discoveries, by accident and sagacity," to describe which he stated the term "serendipity," which means "the ability to make unexpected delivery by accidents and sagacity" [5]. So, with Horace Walpole's definition we trust that a serendipity-oriented recommendation should have obtain an interface that has system that take input as "accidental events" and generate "unexpected discoveries" based on users sagacity and experience.

Furthermore, Shigekazu et al. states that there are two types of accidents: "extrinsic" and "intrinsic" [5]. For example, a serendipitous discovery everyone knows is the invention of rules of gravity Newton. [6] Newton got the idea of the gravitation force when an apple fell on his head from the tree. [6] In this story, apple dropping from the tree can be considered as an "extrinsic event," means an event that occurs in which person do not have played any role. One more example of serendipitous discovery found by Koichi Tanaka, which help him to won the Nobel Prize in Chemistry in 2002 [3]. He admitted that he accidentally added glycerine instead of acetone in his experiment, but he do not stop his experiments and continued it to see the results. This lead to him finding some unknown phenomenon can be said as "intrinsic accident," that is cause by the action of the human with the positive expectation [3].

So, from the above examples we can conclude that a serendipity-oriented recommender system must have faces consisting below facts. (1) The System should create extrinsic accidents. (2) The System should create intrinsic accidents. (3) The User can find the result from accidental events and through their sagacity.

In this paper, we have proposed an Item Amalgamation Approach for Serendipity-Oriented Recommender System which tries to fulfill above requirements. We can call the below items falls into the category of serendipity. (1) The User thinks that he/she cannot ever find the items by themselves, but the item has excited user interest when it sees the item very first time. (2) The User thinks that he/she is not interested in the items, but the item has excited user interest when it sees the items very first time. (3) After displaying the items, user may think that he/she is interested in it.

2 Related Work

Many researchers have already started their research on serendipity in the surrounding of recommendation. Zigler et al. suggested that to improve user satisfaction we need to diversify recommendation lists. They used an intra-list similarity metric to proposed topic diversification [4, 7]. Sarwar et al. suggested that by removing obvious items from the recommended list we can improve serendipity [8]. Berkovsky et al. stated recipe recommendation for the group. They told that we can recommend recipes to others which liked by a member of the group, which may increase serendipity [9].

To provide novelty or unexpectedness Hijikata et al. and Murakami et al. proposed recommendation methods. The former study [1] uses known/unknown profiles to predict items which are not known for the target user using proposed collaborative filtering and said that novelty can be improved with unknown items when providing to the user. The latter study [10] project a method that uses action history of the user to implicitly predict unexpectedness. They give model which predict items that user likes which called as a preference model and a model which predicts items selected by the user depend on their habit. By considering the difference between models method will estimate the unexpectedness given by the system. To obtain models for the single user, this method is very useful. Our projected system allows the user to select items and depend upon the selected items generate the serendipitous items.

For evaluating the unexpectedness and serendipity of RS Murakami et al. and Mouzhi et al. stated different measures [10, 11].

Measures of Unexpectedness

To measure serendipity, we use an approach proposed by Murakami et al. [10] and Mouzhi et al. [11]. In particular, they define an unexpected set of recommendations (UNEXP) as

$$UNEXP = RS \setminus PM \, [8] \tag{1}$$

where, PM is a recommendation set generated by a prediction model, such as items are predicted based on user's likely categories or ratings of items and RS denotes the recommendations created by a recommender algorithm. When there is no element of PM in the list of the RS, they consider this element to be unexpected.

As the authors suggest, based on their definition of unexpectedness, unexpected recommendations may not be always useful and, thus, they also introduce serendipity measure as

$$\text{SRDP} = \frac{|\text{UNEXP} \cap \text{USEFUL}|}{|N|} \tag{2}$$

where, USEFUL denotes the set of "useful" items and N is the size of the recommendation list.

3 Experimental Setup

Dataset
We decided to carry our research with MovieLens Dataset. GroupLens Research Project has collected MovieLens data sets at the University of Minnesota [12]. This data set consists of (1) 943 users and 1682 movies over 100,000 ratings (2) Every single user has given rate at least 20 movies. (3) Simple users-related information like (age, gender, occupation, and zip).

From the above list of tables, we have taken genres_movies and rating for our purpose. We are creating more tables from these two tables to implement amalgamation approach. We are creating three more tables named recommended_items, items_for_rs and movie_mean_total_rating for different phases of the approach for the operations like a recommendation, prediction, etc.

4 Our Approach: An Item Amalgamation Approach

In our approach, first we are finding Useful items. So, the approach is, a user selects the two input items from the set of base items. The system takes these two items as an input and finds the features of those items. Then from the common features of those found features list, the system finds the new items which have these common features. At this point, we have some set of result which we call as a "Useful item" (UL) set. To improve the accuracy of result we will remove the items reviewed by the user from the UL set. To find the unexpectedness we have to find other two values RS and PM. RS means the recommended set generated by the Recommendation algorithm and PM means the recommender set generated by the prediction. Then, we find the unexpected set, from the Eq. (1), it says that unexpected set is equal to the set generated by RS relatively compliment to the set generated by prediction. The relatively compliments means remove the items generated by PM from the items generate by the RS.

Our algorithm

Step 1   User selects two movies from the base list.

Step 2   Find the genres of input movies.

> list_1 = Find the genres list of movie1;
> list_2 = Find the genres list of movie2;
> User gives the two movies as input and system find the list of the movies.

Step 3   Find the common genres.

> common_genres = list_1 ∩ list_2;
> The system finds the common genres by intersecting from the list of genres.

Step 4   Find the movies which satisfy the founded common genres.

> useful_movies = movie list which contains common genres;
> By using the genres found in step 2, system finds the useful movies which contain the common genres.

Step 5   Remove the movies which reviewed by the user from the list of movies.

> useful_movies = useful_movies.remove (movies reviewed by the user);
> To improve the accuracy of the resulting system removes the movies review by the user. So, our useful item set gets updated.

Step 6   Find the set generated by the recommendation algorithm (RS).

> rs_items = item list generated with User-based Pearson Correlation Similarity;
> We are using user-based Pearson Correlation Similarity to find the recommender set using apache mahout toolkit. For that, we are using table items_for_rs.

Step 7   Find the set generated by the prediction model (PM).

> ppm_item = top 100 items based on mean rating ∪ top 100 item based on average rating;
> Table movie_mean_total_rating which stores the mean and total value of rating for each individual movie. For mean rating, we are calculating total rating and divided that with number of you give the rating to that movie and for the total rating we are just calculating total amount of rating for the movie given by the user.

Step 8   Find the unexpectedness.

> unexpted_set = rs_items \ ppm_items;
> Unexpectedness equals to items which are therein set generated by the recommender system but not there in set generated by prediction.

Step 9 Finally, find the serendipitous items by

$$\text{SRDP} = \frac{|\text{UNEXP} \cap \text{USEFUL}|}{|\text{N}|}$$

Amalgamation Method: Genres–genres amalgamation approach

In this approach, when any user selects the two movies from the list of movies system will find the genres of the movies and find the common genres from those list of genres. After that, using those common genres system will find the movies which contains those genres and to improve accuracy system remove the movies which are reviewed by the user. Now, system finds the unexpected set and uses the equations mentioned above to generate unexpected item set and to provide serendipity.

5 Results

Assume that we have three genres in list one and two genres in list two. Then we find the two common genres by intersecting two lists of genres. After that, we find around 61 movies which contain these two genres. To improve accuracy we have removed the movies reviewed by the user. So, up to this we have 62 movies as useful movies. Now we are finding the set generated by recommender system using recommendation algorithm. We have taken top 100 items from the list generated by recommendation system. We also find the list generated by the prediction model which contains 171 movies. By using recommended item set and predicted item set, we find the unexpected set which contains 52 movies in the list. Now, we have both the useful items and unexpected item to find serendipity. We find four items as the serendipity items and our serendipity measure is 0.25514.

Figure 1 shows the comparison between the existing approach and our approach. In this graphical representation the serendipity is high for the existing approaches

Fig. 1 The comparative study with the existing system

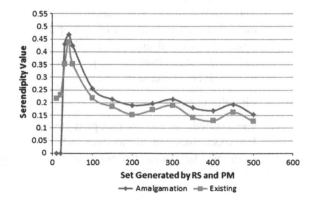

when the set size generated by recommender system and the prediction model is low.

So, they are focusing on the small set of values. Against this, our approach gives good amount of serendipity when the set of recommender system and the set of predicted model is big.

6 Conclusion

In this study, we shown an item amalgamation approach for serendipity-oriented recommender system based on the idea of serendipity. This system possesses mechanisms that cause an intrinsic accident and enables the user to find new values from the sagacity. The key idea behind the approach is to combine the items attributes and find the list of items which contain those attributes. For our experiments, we have used the benchmark dataset MovieLens. We have generated the results which shown the live example of the system with the serendipity value.

7 Future Work

In this paper, we have considered only two user input. In future, we can mix multiple user inputs to check the serendipity measure and the accuracy of the system. We can also find the complex relation from the dataset and mix them to find the serendipitous items. We can combine more than two attributes of the items and find the more stable combinations which give better amount of serendipity. We can also try this technique on different data sets and compare and measure the results. We can also find the serendipity-oriented recommendation for the group of people. We can also develop some mechanism which possess interface where we can recommend items for the group of peoples. Groups may be based on occupation, region, age, etc. We have done some analysis on the groups of people to see the behavior of the serendipity value. Here is the chart for the same (Fig. 2).

Fig. 2 The behavior of serendipity value for the groups of people

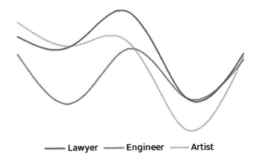

References

1. Hijikata, Y., Shimizu, T., & Nishida, S. (2009). Discovery-oriented collaborative filtering for improving user satisfaction. In *Proceedings of the 13th International Conference on Intelligent User Interfaces* (pp. 67–76). ACM, 2009.
2. Herlocker, J. L., Konstan, J. A., Terveen, L. G., & Riedl, J. T. (2004). Evaluating collaborative Filtering recommender systems. *ACM Transactions on Information Systems (TOIS), 22*(1), 553.
3. Oku, K. & Hattori, F. College of Information Science and Engineering, Ritsumeikan University 1-1-1 Nojihigashi, Kusatsu City Shiga, Japan oku@fc.ritsumei.ac.jp fhattori@is. ritsumei.ac.jp. *User Evaluation of Fusion-based Approach for Serendipity-oriented Recommender System.*
4. Hodges, E. J. (1964). *Three Princes of Serendip.* New York: Atheneum.
5. Sawaizumi, Shigekazu, Katai, Osamu, Kawakami, Hiroshi, & Shiose, Takayuki. (2009). Use of serendipity power for discoveries and inventions. *Intelligent and Evolutionary Systems, Studies in Computational Intelligence, 187,* 163–169.
6. Roberts, R. M. (1989). *Serendipity: Accidental discoveries in science.* Wiley.
7. Ziegler, C. N., McNee, S. M., Konstan, J. A., & Lausen, G. (2005). Improving recommendation lists through topic diversification. In *Proceedings of the 14th International Conference on World Wide Web* (pp. 22–32). New York, New York, USA: ACM.
8. Sarwar, B., Karypis, G., Konstan, J. & Reidl, J. (2001). Item-based collaborative filtering recommendation algorithms. In *Proceedings of the 10th International Conference on World Wide Web* (pp. 285–295). New York, New York, USA: ACM.
9. Berkovsky, S., & Freyne, J. (2010). Group-based recipe recommendations: analysis of data aggregation strategies. In *Proceedings of the Fourth ACM Conference on Recommender Systems* (pp. 111–118). ACM, 2010.
10. Murakami, T., Mori, K., & Orihara, R. (2008). Metrics for evaluating the serendipity of recommendation lists. *New frontiers in artificial intelligence,* pp. 40–46.
11. Ge, M., Delgado-Battenfeld, C., & Jannach, D. (2010). Beyond accuracy: evaluating recommender systems by coverage and serendipity. In *Proceedings of the Fourth ACM Conference on Recommender Systems* (pp. 257–260). ACM, 2010.
12. http://movielens.umn.edu.

A Two-Stage Integrated Approach of DNA Cryptography

Neha Nandal and Suman Panghal

Abstract Cryptography is an approach known for the authentication, security, and intruder preventive communication. The work presented here is an improvement over the traditional symmetric cryptography mechanism with the inclusion of deoxyribonucleic acid (DNA) encoding. The work is divided into two main stages. First a DNA encoding based substitution is used for cryptography where a data sequence is taken as an Input key, and second is databits transformation and addition. The work is applied on Images. MSE and PSNR values are used to perform result analysis.

Keywords Cryptography · DNA · Authentication · MSE · PSNR · Robustness

1 Introduction

Cryptography is an encoding approach used to convert the raw information in encoded form to improve the integrity over the network. Cryptography actually modifies the information itself in some encoded format that can be decoded back to original form. The mechanism basically requires two main components. First Cryptographic algorithm to encode the information and Second, key which is the actual password information to encode the information (Fig. 1).Basically Cryptography approaches are mainly divided into two categories: Symmetric and Asymmetric Key Cryptography.

N. Nandal (✉)
Department of Computer Sciences, Manav Rachna University,
Faridabad, Haryana, India
e-mail: nehanandal.mrce@mrei.ac.in

S. Panghal
Department of Computer Sciences, TIT&S College, Bhiwani, Haryana, India
e-mail: srcutesuman18@gmail.com

© Springer Science+Business Media Singapore 2016
S.C. Satapathy et al. (eds.), *Proceedings of International Conference on ICT for Sustainable Development*, Advances in Intelligent Systems and Computing 409, DOI 10.1007/978-981-10-0135-2_40

405

SECURING DATA THROUGH A CRYPTOGRAPIC PROCESS

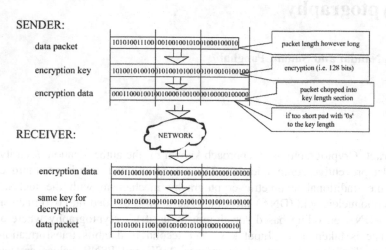

Fig. 1 Cryptography process

1.1 Symmetric Key Cryptography

This Cryptography uses the same key to perform data encryption and to retrieve the data back from cipher text because of which it is also known as Private Key Cryptography.

Symmetric Key Cryptography is the most traditional type of cryptography, where common key information is used for both sender and receiver. In such a system, the sharing mechanism of key requires some effective approach. Single key is defined here to perform data encoding and decoding. To perform the cryptography, the approach requires some algorithm called encryptor and the key. As the cryptography algorithm is applied, the information is encoded to the cipher data form or called encoded information. The receiver receives the information in encoded form. The decryptor uses the decoding algorithm and the same symmetric key to get the information data back. High level security is provided by them.

1.2 Asymmetric-Key Cryptography

This cryptography approach uses different keys to enable the communication over the network and is also called Public Key cryptography approach. According to this approach, encryption process starts with the generation of two keys, a Public key and a Private Key. The generator A keeps the private key with him and distributes the public key to all users that can send information to it. Now, if some user B wants to send information to the user A, user B will use the public key of User A to perform the encoding process.

Here, the cryptography will be performed using public key of receiver. Now after the encoding process, the cipher information is transferred to the receiver A. As receiver receives this information, the decoding process is performed using private key of User A. The security of this algorithm depends on the algorithm type and the key size.

1.3 DNA

The main objective of bioinformatics is to identify the relationship between large dataset group and its sequences. This dataset groups are available in the form of protein, acid sequences, structures, etc. This structural information can be presented in different forms. Some of these forms include DNA, RNA, Protein, Genetic codes, etc. In each cell, number of processes that resides are controlled by protein. The presented work is focused on same concept of bioinformatics sequence to perform a pattern search over the DNA sequence. The work is divided in two main stages, the first stage is about to generate the pattern sequence itself by performing the study on DNA sequence and the second stage is transformation of databits.

1.4 DNA Cryptography

Cryptography is the most significant component of the infrastructure of communication security and computer security. However, there are several latent defects in a number of classical cryptography technologies of recent cryptography—such as RSA and DES algorithms—which are broken by some attack programs. DNA cryptography and knowledge science was born after analysis within the field of DNA computing field by Adleman. It has become the forefront of international research on cryptography.

Cryptography relies on biological problems. In this theory, a DNA system not only has constant computing power as a contemporary system, however, it has a efficiency and function traditional ancient computers cannot match. First, deoxyribonucleic acid chains have a really large scale of parallelism, and its computing speed may reach 1 billion times per second; second, the deoxyribonucleic acid molecule—as a carrier of information—encompasses a huge capacity. It appears that one trillion bits of binary information may be stored in one cubic decimeter of a deoxyribonucleic acid solution; third, a DNA molecular system has low power consumption, solely up to billionth of a traditional system.

2   Existing Work

Information security is the fundamental problem of computer science defined with various applications as its fundamental part. Lot of work is already done by different researchers in the area of cryptography and DNA sequencing which is discussed in this section.

Wang [1] presented a work on pattern search using Data Mining approach as well as using three-dimensional (3D) Graph. Author defined the effective search mechanism on 3D graph. To perform the search, pattern is represented in the form of nodes and edges.

The pattern elements can be modified by inserting or deleting the nodes over the graph. Author defined the clustering improved mechanism to perform the pattern-based classification and recognition [1]. Rao [2] has presented a clustering approach to identify the gene pattern data using wavelet-based decomposition. Author defined the data mining approach to perform the data computation and to perform the pattern search. Author defined a functional group-based clustering approach to separate the gene expression. Author discovered the valuable information over DNA by performing the hybridization of data. The pattern-based discovery over gene was performed using cell cycle-based biological process. Author also defined a theoretical view to analyze the gene behavior and to identify the relationship between genes. Based on this relationship, the clustering is performed under the regulatory behavior [2]. Pei [3] has presented a fast algorithm to perform the clustering over DNA sequence. This clustering approach is analytical and taken the DNA microarray data as the input dataset. Author defined the effective and efficient mining approach to perform clustering over large DNA sequence. Author resolves the problem of maximal pattern identification and based on the same analysis, the clustering process is performed. Author combined the scalable search and pruning method to generate the clusters and the distance-based matching was performed using distance-based matching [3].

Wang [4] has presented a pattern similarity identification approach using subspace clustering. Author worked on traditional clustering methods to generate the group on similar data elements and to identify the pattern similarity. Author defined the pattern distance identification based on rise- and fall-based subspace approach. The work is applied on large dataset and large sequencing. The algorithm presented in this work was capable to handle the real-time dataset effectively [4]. Zhang [5] has presented a dataset capturing and coherence-based approach to perform the subset generation under different conditions. Author defined deterministic biclustering approach to identify the frequency patterns over the sequence. Author defined the mining approach to regulate and identify the genes under defined rules and condition. Author defined the work in two phases. In the first phase, clustering is performed under frequent pattern analysis and in the second phase, the members of these clusters perform condition-based and distance-based matching [5]. Jiang [6] has presented a cluster based analysis approach for gene expression classification. Author presented a survey on existing approaches. Author defined the gene expression analysis on biological processes so that the data samples are generated effectively. Author presented a distance-based analysis on gene expression data so that functional genomics based understanding is defined here. Based on this analysis, the feature groups are generated and the group is based on specific features under the data points. Author presented the work on gene expression data elements so that the gene group and samples are defined. Author defined microarray technology under clustering approach. The work presented the clustering with higher quality and reliability [6]. Patra [7] has presented a neural network-based approach for expression generation and selection based on DNA microarray data. Author defined a neural network-based approach for expression analysis. This classification approach also removed the redundant genes and thus the expression patterns are defined. Author eliminates the data dimensions so that the search process will be effective. As the data size was reduced, more effective results were derived by the author [7]. Pan [8] has defined an effective algorithm to perform the sequence search over the biological dataset. Author defined the characteristic analysis-based approach so that the work can be performed on large datasets. Author defined the pattern search based on frequency analysis over the sequence. Author presented the dataset sequence pose analysis to identify frequency of specific pattern over the dataset. The use of prefix span improves the search criteria and projection growth was also improved. Author presented two novel algorithms to control the sequence search and improve the search results. Author presented the sequence exploration under different algorithmic approaches [8].

Hirsh [9] has presented a work on the learning approach for DNA sequences. Author provides the inductive learning techniques to train large data under different regularities over the system. Author discussed the system domain and molecular biology and provided the analysis on different suitable learning approach. Author explored the background knowledge of different assumptions associated with DNA sequences. Author also classifies the DNA sequences in two main classes under different inductive methods such as decision tree approach and neural network approach [9]. Wu [10] has defined a determination of minimum sample size discovery approach for temporal gene expression pattern analysis. DNA microarray analysis under gene monitoring is defined to reveal the information and expression. Author defined the classification approach so that the pattern will be divided to subtype. The gene expression is presented under the same tissue-based time point analysis. The biological process was defined for the analysis. Author has defined a method to perform the sample size-based determination that is temporal gene expression analysis in time frame was implemented. The clustering is also performed to categorize these patterns. Author performed the similarity analysis under clustering approach. Author defined gene expression dataset under the hierarchical clustering so that effective pattern group identification was performed [10]. Ma [11] has presented a noisy gene expression datamining using coexpression analysis oriented iterative approach. Author defined the clustering to generate the group similar data partitions. Author generated non-overlapped clusters and keeps the data under different functional class and performs the same biological role in same group. Author defined the external gene analysis and performs the classification in different coexpressed genes. Author defined a clustering approach for discovery of overlapping clusters and to reduce the noise over the expression. Author defined mining approach in two phases. In phase 1, the clustering is applied to divide data in clusters and in second phase, the pattern discovery was performed. Author tested the work under different algorithmic approaches [11]. Yan [12] has defined structural pattern analysis approach to perform the Motif analysis over the sequence. The structural analysis includes the gap analysis based on component analysis. The mining of structural pattern is performed by eliminating the redundant patterns. The work is defined under pruning approach so that the pattern discovery and the space usage will be improved. Author defined an effective algorithm and thus the composite check and generation of patterns as well as the pruning was performed. Author defined the structural pattern analysis under the evaluation of synthetic data biological data. Author defined an effective structural pattern analysis approach to perform knowledge discovery [12].

3 Proposed Model

The presented work is about to define a DNA approach to perform the encryption on text. The work is divided into two layers to achieve the efficiency as well as the reliability. In first layer, the generation of the dynamic key based on DNA sequence will be done. In the second layer, the actual DNA dictionary based encryption will be done so that encoded text will be obtained. The work will improve the reliability and the security of encoding process.

In this work, the DNA concept will be used for the key generation as well to encode the text. At the earlier stage, the dynamic DNA pattern will be identified over the sequence to generate the key to perform the encoding. Later on, the DNA code dictionary will be defined to perform the cryptography. The model of the presented work is shown in Fig. 2.

3.1 DNA Sequencing

The main concept of the work is the DNA sequence pattern generation. The DNA sequence is taken as input and a DNA pattern is identified over it. This DNA pattern works as the key to the system. Now this key is combined with image information to encode the image data.

Here, DNA sequence mining is use to get the large sequence of pattern over the DNA. This sequence key is used as the actual DNA key based on which the DNA transformed image is generated.

In the end, DNA Cryptography is applied on an encoded image. To do this, two bit Binary codes are assigned to DNA Characters as Binary Code 00 to DNA Character 'A', 01 to 'G', 10 to 'T', and 11 to 'C'. Now, the DNA encoded image is

Fig. 2 Proposed model

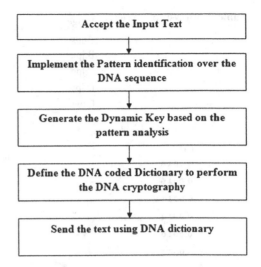

Table 1 DNA key generation algorithm

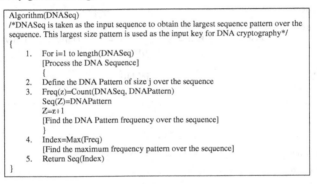

transformed to binary codes. These codes are grouped into two bit codes. Then the final cryptographic DNA encoded object is generated based on the substitution of binary codes. The result will be an encoded object image which is obtained by the transformation of the DNA sequence. To obtain this pattern sequence, an algorithmic approach is used which is shown in Table 1.

4 Results

The work is implemented in matlab environment. The results here are shown in the form of input image, and encoded image. The quality of work is analyzed here in terms of MSE and PSNR values.

Table 2 Analysis parameters

Image	PSNR	MSE
A.jpg	75.8787	0.0017
B.jpg	79.9379	0.0007
C.jpg	78.5497	0.0009
D.jpg	77.5613	0.0011
E.jpg	81.5256	0.0005

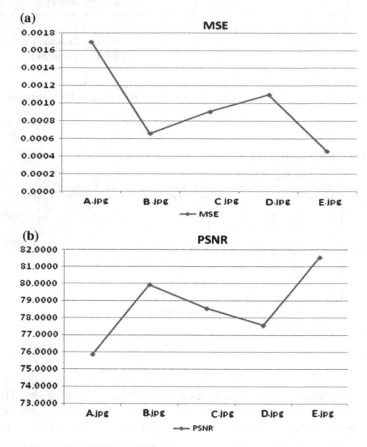

Fig. 3 Analysis results **a** MSE. **b** PSNR

The work is tested on multiple input images. The results obtained from the work under different parameters are shown in Table 2.

The graphical representation of results is shown in Fig. 3.

The obtained results shows, the presented work is effective in terms of obtained PSNR and MSE values.

5   Conclusion

In this paper, a reliable image Cryptography approach is defined using DNA encoding and transformation. In this work, a two-stage cryptography work is defined for images. In first stage, the image encoding is performed under DNA component analysis where a data sequence is taken as an input key using substitution approach. The second and final stage of work is to transform the databits and addition. To perform this transformation, bit shifting and switching approach is defined. This approach is implemented under block level analysis and processing. The obtained result shows that the work has provided effective MSE and PSNR values for the work and a cryptographic image with improved reliability and robustness.

References

1. Wang, X. (2002). Finding patterns in three-dimensional graphs: Algorithms and applications to scientific data mining. *IEEE Transactions on Knowledge and Data Engineering.* 1041-4347/02@2002 IEEE.
2. Rao, A. (2002). *A clustering algorithm for gene expression data using wavelet packet decomposition.* 0-7803-7576-9/02@2002 IEEE.
3. Pei, J. (2003). MaPle: A fast algorithm for maximal pattern-based clustering. In *Proceedings of the Third IEEE International Conference on Data Mining (ICDM'03).* 0-7695-1978-4/03 © 2003 IEEE.
4. Wang, H. (2004). A fast algorithm for subspace clustering by pattern similarity. In *Proceedings of the 16th International Conference on Scientific and Statistical Database Management (SSDBM'04).* 1099-3371/04 © 2004 IEEE.
5. Zhang, Z. (2004). Mining deterministic biclusters in gene expression data. In *Proceedings of the Fourth IEEE Symposium on Bioinformatics and Bioengineering (BIBE'04).* 0-7695-2173-8/04 © 2004 IEEE.
6. Jiang, D. (2004). Cluster analysis for gene expression data: A survey. *IEEE Transactions on Knowledge and Data Engineering.* 1041-4347/04@2004 IEEE.
7. Patra, J. C. (2005). Neural networks for gene expression analysis and gene selection from DNA microarray. In *Proceedings of International Joint Conference on Neural Networks.* 0-7803-9048-2/05©2005 IEEE.
8. Pan, J. (2005). Efficient algorithms for mining maximal frequent concatenate sequences in biological datasets. In *Proceedings of the 2005 The Fifth International Conference on Computer and Information Technology (CIT'05).* 0-7695-2432-X/05 © 2005 IEEE.
9. Hirsh, H. (1994). *Using background knowledge to improve inductive learning of DNA sequences.* 1043-0989/94@ 1994 IEEE.
10. Wu, F. X. (2006). On determination of minimum sample size for discovery of temporal gene expression patterns. In *Proceedings of the First International Multi-Symposiums on Computer and Computational Sciences (IMSCCS'06).* 0-7695-2581-4/06 © 2006 IEEE.
11. Ma, P. C. H. (2009). An iterative data mining approach for mining overlapping co expression patterns in noisy gene expression data. *IEEE Transactions on Nano Bioscience.* 1536-1241 © 2009 IEEE.
12. Yan, L. (2009). *Closed structured patterns and motifs mining without candidate maintenance.* 978-0-7695-3880-8/09 © 2009 IEEE.

Advanced Irrigation Systems Impacting Sustainability and Reducing Water Needs—Role of ICT in Irrigation

S.M. Gopikrishnaa

Abstract Water is essential for sustaining life and it is one of the most important resources that we have. According to the experts, recent climatic changes and drought conditions have decreased surface water flows in many parts of the world. The Governments face these issues by constructing dams, canals, and pipelines for better irrigation in various parts of their country. Approximately, 70 % of the water withdrawn from various fresh water sources is used for Agricultural activities. The global population is increasing at rapid phase. But, the current water resources and the way in which we spend the water for various activities indicate that the available water resources will not satisfy the demands of the future generations. So, better irrigation practices need to be followed using latest in-available information and communication technologies (ICT) using sensor controlled solar powered drip and sprinkler irrigation methods to optimize the water usage for agricultural practices.

Keywords Information and communication technologies · Solar powered drip irrigation · Sprinkler irrigation · Sensors

1 Introduction

The demand for water is intensifying in the world. Over the past 100 years, global population has tripled and water consumption has increased sixfold, but the total global water supply remain unchanged. This exponential increase in the water consumption is due to growing middle class population in emerging countries. As the income level of the middle class population rises, there will be a considerable change in their eating practices. A total of 1300 L of water is required to produce 1 kg of wheat, 3400 L of water is required for 1 kg of rice, 15,500 L of water is

S.M. Gopikrishnaa (✉)
Department of Management Studies, Indian Institute of Science,
Bangalore 560012, India
e-mail: gopikrishnaas@mgmt.iisc.ernet.in

© Springer Science+Business Media Singapore 2016
S.C. Satapathy et al. (eds.), *Proceedings of International Conference on ICT for Sustainable Development*, Advances in Intelligent Systems and Computing 409, DOI 10.1007/978-981-10-0135-2_41

required to produce 1 kg of beef and with the continuous increase in population, meat consumption is expected to double by 2050. At this phase, the global demand of water will exceed the global supply by 40 %.

Urbanization and Industrialization puts pressure on the global fresh water resources. Industrial activity accounts for about 20 % of global water consumption [1]. Every activity from cloth manufacturing to electricity generation requires lot of water. Agriculture accounts for total 70 % of total consumption of water resource. By adopting technologies such as micro drip irrigation, farmers can reduce the ground water usage for their crops up to 70–80 % [2]. Most people feel that the smart irrigation only saves water as saving the water is so important which is susceptible in many countries. But many people do not know that the smart irrigation also improves quality and quantity of the crops.

Currently, 80 % of the world farmers have no control on irrigation practices in their farm lands. But soon, they will be forced to follow better and efficient ways of irrigation in their farm lands due to water scarcity. So ways to improve the water efficiency in farms using water conserving technologies such as solar pumps, drip irrigation systems, sprinkler irrigation systems, sensors to monitor the water usage by the crops at the crop level, leaf level, and at the stem level, and the sensors to monitor environmental changes to water the crops in the farm lands are being developed and practiced respectively. Precision farming helps the farmers to have a greater control over their operation on crops and to achieve quick results.

2 Water Scarcity

The Water Scarcity is defined as an imbalance of supply and demand if the supply potential is difficult to tap. In other words it is excess of water demand over available supply. Of the total available water in earth, only 2.5 % constitute fresh water. Only a third of the fresh water is available economically for the humans to use. The volume of water that a person 'drinks' is much less than the water that a person 'eats' everyday contained in food products which comes through agricultural practices [3].

The reason for the above fact is Agriculture being the biggest use of fresh water resources. Agriculture consumes on average around 70 % of all fresh water available for human use, while the Industrial and Household uses accounts for an average of around 20 and 10 % respectively. Furthermore, it is expected that the water requirements for irrigation activities in agriculture practices will increase by 14 % by 2030 [3]. Almost 85 countries suffer from shortage of water which poses a question to the health and economies, while more than 2.5 billion populations in the world exist without proper access to clean water and sanitation.

People usually think of water scarcity as the lack of drinking water. But the real problem is the impact of water scarcity on food security. Water is the main linking factor between food, climate, energy, economic growth, and human security challenges and main limiting factor in the ability of mother earth in feeding the

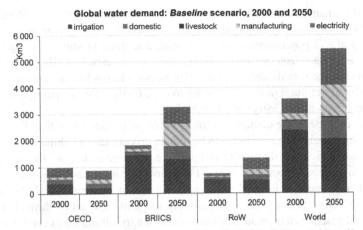

Fig. 1 Future prediction on increase in water usage in irrigation, domestic, livestock, manufacturing, and electricity in OECD, BRIICS, RoW countries [4]

world population. It is estimated that the global population count will reach 9 billion by 2050.

As per the Organization of Economic Co-Operation and Development report "Environmental Outlook to 2050: The consequences of inaction," the amount of water required for human domestic use, electricity and manufacturing in the global context is expected to increase by 126, 144, and 406 % respectively, by 2050 [4]. When the economies of the global countries expand, the need for food, infrastructure, and energy associated with water required for well-being of humans also expand. The following chart from the above-mentioned report on water demand in OECD, BRIICS, and Rest of World countries is the clear evidence for the above-mentioned fact (Fig. 1).

Hence, it is clear that it is the right time to take necessary actions and management strategies to follow better water management practices in agriculture, infrastructure, energy, manufacturing, and miscellaneous activities to avoid world heading toward a water crisis which affects human existence on the planet earth.

2.1 Why Do We Need Efficient Irrigation Method for Agriculture Practices?

An efficient agricultural practice should be designed in such a way that it should reduce or minimize the water losses from evaporation, deep percolation, and runoff. To irrigate effectively, the right amount of water has to reach the right place at the right time. Approximately, a liter of water is required for producing 1 cal of energy.

A normal human consumes more than 2000 cal of energy per day. Hence, more than 2000 L of water is required to produce food for one person per day. The increasing global population, climatic change, and mass production in agriculture are other important factors which further strain water resources. The current water management practices if continue, by 2050 we need to double the amount of water required for agricultural practices in order to cope up the growing population, which of course brings biodiversity into a task [5].

Steady increase in the demand for the agricultural products to satisfy the need for the growing population contributes to be a main driving factor behind the exorbitant water usage. Efficient irrigation techniques are required to irrigate the agricultural lands to save large amounts of water. Field flooding is an unsustainable irrigation method being practiced in 80 % of the agricultural land accounts for 40 % of water loss. By effective delivery of water directly to plants and crops through modern agricultural practices the amount of water used in agricultural lands can be reduced. Almost 30–70 % of water loss through evaporation can be avoided based on crop and weather conditions if effective irrigation methods are followed.

3 Micro Irrigation Methods

3.1 Drips Irrigation System

Drip irrigation is the incredibly efficient watering method to the plants at garden or to the crops at agricultural plot that slowly delivers water directly to the plants' roots system. This eliminates the water loss due to evaporation which is common with overhead or surface watering methods. University studies show that the plants grown with the help of drip irrigation which has very good yield due to consistent watering cycle and reduction in plant stress. Drip irrigation helps the farmers to save 30–50 % of the water compared to conventional surface irrigation systems [6]. Following are some of the merits of the drip irrigation system [7].

3.1.1 Advantages of Drip Irrigation System

1. Increased water use efficiency
2. Better crop yield
3. Uniform and better quality of the produce
4. Efficient and economic use of fertilizer through Fertigation
5. Less weed growth
6. Minimum damage to the soil structure
7. Avoidance of leaf burn due to saline soil
8. Usage in undulating areas and slow permeable soil
9. Low energy requirement (i.e.) labor saving
10. High uniformity suitable for atomization

Not only the water usage but also the electricity required for lifting water from wells is less in drip irrigation technique when compared with the conventional surface irrigation method. A field-based study done by Narayanamoorthy [8] shows clearly that the electricity consumption is reduced drastically when drip irrigation is followed instead of conventional surface irrigation.

3.2 Sprinkler Irrigation System

In the sprinkler method of irrigation, water is sprayed into the space and allowed to fall on the ground similar to that of rainfall. The water is distributed to various sprinkler pole pipes at various parts of the agricultural or garden plot, and it is expelled out of the pipe through nozzle under pressure. Operating conditions such as pump supply system, pressure level, nozzle pore level, and sprinkler types should be specified clearly for uniform application of water.

3.2.1 Advantages of Sprinkler Irrigation System

1. Suitable to all types of soil except heavy clay
2. Suitable for irrigating crops, where the plant population per area is very high. It is most suitable for oil seeds and other cereal and vegetable crops
3. Closer control of water application convenient for giving light and frequent irrigation and higher water application efficiency
4. Increase in yield
5. Mobility of system
6. May also be used for undulating area
7. Saves land as no bunds, etc., are required
8. Influences greater conducive micro-climate
9. Areas located at a higher elevation than the source can be irrigated
10. Possibility of using soluble fertilizers and chemicals
11. Less problem of clogging of sprinkler nozzles due to sediment laden water

The trials conducted in different parts of the country revealed water saving due to sprinkler system varies from 16 to 70 % over the traditional method with yield increase from 3 to 57 % in different crops and agro climatic conditions.

4 Role of ICT in Efficient Irrigation Technique: Innovation Methods

4.1 Solar Powered Drip/Sprinkler Irrigation Method

Solar Pumps are increasingly replacing the traditional diesel and electric pumps in most of the farms in India. As solar water pumps saves electricity, reduces costs associated with watering, and neglects the usual problems of conventional diesel pumps, it is found to be a promising technology by millions of farmers and governmental organizations across the nation. Solar or photo voltaic (PV) powered drip irrigation system possesses the efficiency of solar powered water pump and reliability of drip irrigation system. The photo voltaic array converts the solar power to electric power and operates the pump (either be a surface pump or submersible pump) which pours into the nearby tank or reservoir. The water from the reservoir is distributed to crops or plants in the field through a low pressure drip irrigation system [6].

4.2 Wireless Plant Monitor: Sensors for Optimal Irrigation

Battery powered sensors fixed near the root of the crop which measures the Light, Soil Moisture, Temperature, and Humidity of the environment and determines whether the crop needed water or not. The information on the water need can then be transmitted to the farmer or the agriculturist (via Mobile SMS) or sent to the computer controlled irrigation system which in turn trips the solar powered drip or sprinkler irrigation to turn ON or OFF according to the crop's thirst for water. With the information on Light, Soil Moisture, Temperature, and Humidity of the environment, the sensors can not only informs the system or the users about the water need of the crops, but also suggests the kind of crop better for the prevailing environment and the parameters to grow and water them sustainably [9].

The sensor system can have the provision to connect either to drip irrigation systems or to sprinkler irrigation systems to avoid over or under watering the crops. Using this sensor, the water usage can be reduced by 50 % compared to the traditional surface irrigation systems thereby saving the resources for the future. The sensor system can also connect the nearest weather reporting station through the internet, forecast the weather patterns and waters the crops in accordance to the weather report through the solar powered smart drip or sprinkler irrigation system.

4.3 Leaf Shrink Status: Sensors for Optimal Irrigation

A new leaf lever sensor which is almost an inch by a quarter of an inch and powered by a small solar panel at its top, can easily fit on almost any leaves and measures the water need of a crop. When the plants start drying out, its leaves contract and the sensor which is present on the leaves identifies the level of liquid pressure, tracks the contract change, and converts it into an electrical voltage. The voltage change is then transmitted to the information system software in the computer. This information can then be communicated to the farmers appropriately to water the crops at farms. Moving a step ahead, the output from the sensor is fed to the solar powered relay which in turn makes a trip on the drip or sprinkler irrigation system connected to the solar pump in precise time and precise quantity [10].

Through this method, the farmers' intervention can be avoided and crops in the field can be watered in an automatic manner by making the irrigation system operated by the plants themselves according to their real-time water need. At the same time, the costly resources of water and fertilizer on improving the quantity and quality of the yield can be reduced. Studies have proven that, one such device per 15–20 ha of agricultural land is precise enough to identify the water need of plants [10].

4.4 Stem Water Potential: Sensors for Optimal Irrigation

If the water movement from root to leaves is followed in a tree, a potential gradient can be observed across the tree. Hence, there exist an opportunity to measure the water potential in the stem by embedding a sensor in the stem of the tree. This method of measuring the water potential in the stem is considered a best indicator for water status measurement [11]. A sensor embedded in the stem of the tree can have direct contact with the water transporting tissues in the stem. The information on water intake by the tree at different time period is observed/tracked and can be utilized by the agricultural scientist on the specific tree/crop to advice the farmers about optimum watering to the crops. Since there use be identical crop pattern in a minimum of 1–2 ha of agricultural land, a maximum of 1 or 2 sensors can be embedded for an entire 1–2 ha of land [12].

With such sensors, the farmers will be able to irrigate the exact amount of water that the crops need. This results in better yield of the crops in both quantitative and qualitative way, higher income, less risks and losses, and water savings to the farmers. Vines, Citrus, Deciduous Fruits, Nuts, Olives, Bananas, and even in cotton crops this type of sensors can be embedded.

4.5   Variable Rate Irrigation (VRI): Sensors for Optimal Irrigation

Currently, single irrigation system is being applied to 99 % of farm lands in the world. If the land is split into many segments and multiple crops are cultivated or if the field is filled with obstacles (many crests and troughs), variable soil types, and variable terrain there will be the probability of some regions being over watered and some regions may be under watered. In such cases, precision variable rate of irrigation can be used using advanced Wi-Fi controlled sprinkler systems. With this innovative technology, farmers can manage the variability in the field which allows them to save 15–20 % of water and cuts the input cost resulting in optimum irrigation and variable yield [13]. Cite-specific agronomics and GPS coordinates of the farm plan form the foundation of this technology. The farm areas of variable irrigation need can be specified in the software system in the form of precision water application zonal plan. Then the plan containing precision application zones can be loaded into the precision variable rate irrigation controller.

The precision variable rate irrigation controller is placed in the movable sprinkler system with many pivot points in the farm. The VRI controller transmits water release signal as per the zonal plan to the sprinklers at various Wi-Fi enabled pivot points. This method of irrigating the crops let the farmers to water the crop as per the farm terrain and crop segmentation, achieve higher yield, achieve increased efficiency of energy and chemicals, improve tract maintenance, reduce runoff and leeching, and avoids over or under watering in specific regions [14].

5   Case Studies of ICT in Irrigation—Implemented Projects

5.1   Solar Water Pumps and Drip Irrigation Technology—Rajasthan, India

Rajasthan is an Indian State where 60 % of total population depends on agriculture. Sorghum, Millets, Maize, Mustard, and Cotton are the main crops of cultivation. Oranges, Pomegranate, Perry, Guava, new crops of Olive, Dates, and Colored capsicum. Horticulture crops play a main part in increasing farmers' income in sustainable way. Entire country knows about the shortage of water prevailing in Rajasthan. Rajasthan possess 10 % of countries land, 5 % of countries population, and 1 % of fresh water source. Yet farmers of Rajasthan made the State as one of the top ranking states in terms of agriculture. Only 35 % of agricultural land could be bought under irrigation in the state. Other parts of agricultural land gets underground water pumped out through electric or diesel motors. Providing electricity to all the farm lands throughout the state is a challenge. In most villages only 4–6 h of electricity is being supplied either day or at night [15].

The farmers believe that Diesel-based electric pumps are costly to buy as well as to maintain due to fan belt failure, clamp failure, etc. Realizing the problems faced by the farmers, the Government of Rajasthan, Department of Horticulture in 2007 came up with a practical solution of Solar Pumps. Out of 365 days in a year for almost 325 days Rajasthan get excellent, bright sunny days. Hence, solar rays have excellent energy values in the state. As a pilot project in the years 2008 and 2009, the government implemented solar pumps in 35 farm lands and the results were successful in the year 2010 and 2011. Encouraged by the success, the Government of Rajasthan implemented the same project in 14 districts by installing 1675 solar pumps. Soon, everyone started realizing the benefits of solar pumps. Following this, the state has helped farmers to install 4500 solar pumps in all 33 districts. Realizing the benefits and importance of solar pumps the government has made an ambitious target of installing 10,000 solar pumps in fiscal year of 2013–2014 [15].

The department of Horticulture, Government of Rajasthan is in the plan of creating a call center to monitor all the 17,000 solar pumps in the field throughout Rajasthan. The call center would provide assistance to the farmers on how to operate, how to maintain, how to monitor the solar pump systems incase if they have any doubts. Also an Management Information System (MIS) is being developed which will have information about the farmers, fields, solar system, the pump system, the pumps discharge values, the water delivery rate, and the maintenance schedule and the controlling of the MIS system will be handled by the computer experts. Currently 86 % subsidy is given to farmers from central and state government to purchase/install the solar pump system in their farms. For collecting water in canal area, Reservoirs called 'Diggies' are constructed. Water points are constructed along the areas where wells/tube wells are used. In Hot surface areas, farm points are created. A large number of such Diggies/Water points/Farm points are being constructed by the state government.

To check the water wastage and its judicious use, **drip irrigation is made compulsory** after the installation of solar pumps. Drip irrigation has helped to reduce the water use up to 95 %. Besides saving water drip irrigation has helped to increase the productivity, product quality, and boosted farmers' income. Making drip irrigation compulsory the farmers save 43 million cubic liters of water which in turn helped to irrigate additional 12,000 ha of land in the state. The government helps farmers in cultivating more cash rich horticulture crops so that farmers with small land can also generate more revenue. Solar pumps have also helped to serve 24 million liters of diesel which is again a direct financial benefit to farmers. Besides, it also helped them in getting relieved from electricity supply and allied headaches. The Rajasthan government has also the plan of installing another 1,00,000 solar pumps in the next 5 years [15].

The entire energy generated through solar panels in a full day is not completely being used for irrigation purposes. The government plans to install a 3 way switch in the system through which the excess solar energy after utilization for irrigation can be diverted to household activities for the powering of electric bulb and to small-scale industry activities for powering sewing machines to help women empowerment. The benefit of solar powered drip irrigation is clearly visible to entire Rajasthan. In a dry state like Rajasthan, it is so important to save both electricity and water and simultaneously increase the farm yield. The only solution for the above claim is to install solar water pump and drip irrigation system which helps in saving electricity and water parallel increasing the farm yield. Rajasthan has entered the 'Limca book of world Records' for installing highest number of solar pumps with drip irrigation in the world. Indeed, Rajasthan's solar powered drip irrigation's success is an exemplary story for the entire nation.

5.2 Success Story: Efficient Irrigation cum Power Generation—Gujarat, India

The Government of Gujarat along with the country's Ministry of Renewable Energy has setup a solar power plant at a stretch of 750 m above one of the canals transporting water from Narmada Dam in Vadodara District, Gujarat, India. As India invests heavily in solar power, it explores all innovative ways to fit in solar panels with another process, which paves the way for mutual benefit. The new solar plant is setup on top of Narmada River Irrigation Canals by considering two main advantages:

1. Reduce water evaporation and increase in the irrigation area to farm lands
2. Efficient and Cleaner Energy, and Cheaper land use for the power plant

The solar plant which has the maximum capacity to produce 10 MW power is setup on top of canals between Baroda's Sama and Chhani locations. If the same plant is setup on land it would cover an area of around 20 acres. Currently, the solar plant is stretch across 3.5 km on the canal and has the potential to generate 16.2 units of power every year [16].

The entire program was commissioned for implementation within 1000 days of conception and it is estimated to be around 90, 00, 000 L of canal water prevented from evaporation process. Unlike other solar panels, the power output of this kind of solar panel installation will be higher because of the reason that water running in the canal keeps the panels cool which in turn yields around 15 % extra power. Considering the success of the pilot project in terms of efficient irrigation and innovative power generation, the Government of Gujarat along with Ministry of Renewable Energy is planning to implement this project across 19,000 km of canal length in the state of Gujarat. Considering the irrigation and power benefits that the Gujarat enjoys, other Indian States such as Maharashtra and Kerala plans to implement 'Canal-Top' solar power plant on their lands.

6 Conclusion

Even with the today's decision to improve the efficiency of water use, it would be critical for future generations to improve the policies surrounding the management and conservation of one of our planets most precious natural resource—Water. Millions of world's poorest people subsist on fewer than five gallons of water per day. Nearly, one billion people lack access to a clean and safe water supply. It is believed that in future wars will be fought over water and not the politics. Implementing a better solution to avoid the noble problem of running out of water is indispensable in the current scenario. Due to over pumping, the underground water in several countries is almost gone. Depleted aquifers lead to cut breaks in grain harvests which lead to more food shortages and higher prices in India. The water problem is fast becoming a hunger problem. High consumption and lack of water conservation leads to 'No More Water,' which in turn means 'No More Life.' Hence, it is time to give water a second thought by giving importance to efficient ways of water usage and conservation.

References

1. *Coping with water scarcity—An action framework for agriculture and food security*, Technical Report. (2012). Rome: United Nations.
2. Varshney, R. S. (1995). Modem Methods of Irrigation. *GeoJournal, 35*, 59–63.
3. Rijsberman, F. R. (2006). Water scarcity: Fact or fiction? *Agricultural Water Management, 80*, 5–22.
4. *OECD Environmental Outlook to 2050: The Consequences of Inaction*, Technical Report. (2012). Paris: OECD Publishing.
5. *The United Nations World Water Development Report 3: Water in a Changing World*, Technical Report. (2009). Paris and London: UNESCO and Earthscan.
6. Jennifer Burney, P. (2010). Solar-powered drip irrigation enhances food security in the Sudano-Sahel. *Proceedings of the National Academy of Sciences, 107*, 1848–1853.
7. Tamil Nadu Agricultural University. Retrieved from http://agritech.tnau.ac.in/.
8. Narayanamoorthy, A. (2007). Microirrigation and electricity consumption linkages in Indian agriculture: A field based study. In *International Conference on Linkages Between Energy and Water Management for Agriculture in Developing Countries* (pp. 29–30). Hyderabad, India.
9. Ning Wang, W. (2006). Wireless sensors in agriculture and food industry—Recent development and future perspective. *Computers and Electronics in Agriculture, 1*, 1–14.
10. *New Device Lets Plants Talk—Smart sensors let crops text-message growers for more water.* Retrieved from http://spectrum.ieee.org/.
11. McCutchan, S. (1992). Stem-water potential as a sensitive indicator of water stress in prune trees (Prunus domestica L. cv. French). *American Society for Horticultural Science, 117*, 607–611.
12. Naor, A. (1999). Midday stem water potential as a plant water stress indicator for irrigation scheduling in fruit trees. In *IIIrd International Symposium on Irrigation of Horticultural Crops* (pp. 447–454).
13. Yule, I. J., Hedley, C. B., & Bradbury, S. (2008). Variable-rate irrigation. In *12th Annual Symposium on Precision Agriculture Research & Application in Australasia*. Sydney.
14. King, L. (1995). Variable rate water application through sprinkler irrigation. *American Society of Agronomy, 485*, 485–493.

15. Department of Horticulture, Gov. of Rajastan. Retrieved from http://horticulture.rajasthan.gov.in/ContentDetail.aspx?pagename=Aboutus_Introdution.aspx.
16. Gujarath Energy Development Agency, Gov. of Gujarat. Retrieved from http://geda.gujarat.gov.in/.
17. Sivanappan, R. K. (1994). Prospects of micro irrigation in India. *Irrigation and Drainage System.*, *8*, 49–58.
18. Evans, T. F., LaRue, T., Stone, K. C., & King, B. A. (2013). Adoption of site-specific variable rate sprinkler irrigation systems. *Irrigation Science*, *31*, 871–887.
19. McCarthy, A. C., Hancock, N. H., & Raine, S. R.: Advanced process control of irrigation: the current state and an analysis to aid future development. *Irrigation Science*, *31*(3), 183–192.

Parallelization of Load Flow Analysis

Chayan Bhatt, Rahul Saxena, D.P. Sharma and R. Jaya Krishna

Abstract This paper has been proposed to present a simple approach for load flow analysis of a radial distribution network using parallel programming in Computationally Unified Device Architecture (CUDA). The proposed approach applies Breadth First Search to evaluate the nodes in the network and Kirchhoff's current law (KCL) as well as Kirchhoff's Voltage Law (KVL) for evaluating the current and voltages at each of the network nodes. The procedure is repeated till the convergence criterion is achieved. The paper demonstrates the working of Breadth First Search using CUDA. The efficiency of load flow algorithm has been enhanced by utilizing parallel computational power of Graphics Processing Unit (GPU). This approach has been tested for 33-nodes as well as for 69-nodes radial distribution systems and comparison has been done between the performances of sequential approach over CPU and parallel approach on GPU. The results show that introducing CUDA to load flow analysis speeds up the performance of the system by faster executions and gives accurate desired results as compared to sequential approach.

Keywords Load flow analysis · Radial distribution network · Parallel programming · Performance

C. Bhatt (✉) · R. Saxena · D.P. Sharma · R. Jaya Krishna
School of Computing and Information Technology, Manipal University Jaipur,
Jaipur, India
e-mail: chayan.bhatt53@gmail.com

R. Saxena
e-mail: rahulsaxena0812@gmail.com

D.P. Sharma
e-mail: dps158@gmail.com

R. Jaya Krishna
e-mail: jayakrishnaa.r@gmail.com

© Springer Science+Business Media Singapore 2016
S.C. Satapathy et al. (eds.), *Proceedings of International Conference on ICT for Sustainable Development*, Advances in Intelligent Systems and Computing 409, DOI 10.1007/978-981-10-0135-2_42

427

1 Introduction

The electrical power system performs three major tasks that consist of generation, transmission, and distribution. The emphasis has been always very high for the generation and transmission. But the distribution system maintains an important link between the bulk power system and the consumers therefore the activity of these distribution system requires an important analysis.

With increasing demand of domestic, industrial, and commercial load, an efficient planned distribution network is required. An effective, reliable, and good converging load flow of distribution system provides voltage stability and avoids voltage collapse. It determines power loss of the network and accurate selection of branch conductor and effective planning of load transfers.

Many researchers have proposed various load flow algorithms to deal with load flow analysis. Ghosh and Sherpa [1] presented a load flow solution for radial distribution networks which required minimum data preparation. Many load centers could be handled by this method, but it requires a lot of programming. The concept of ladder network theory was applied by many researchers for load flow analysis of a radial network [2, 3]. Kumar and Arvindhababu [4] presented a simpler way, similar to Newton-Raphson (NR) technique. To perform analysis of Load flow, Baran and Wu [5] used three nonlinear equations for each branch in the network regarding branch power flows and bus voltages. A number of equations were reduced by using certain terminal conditions. Sharma et al. [6] utilized linear data structure with algorithmic complexity of $O(n)$ to build an efficient load flow analysis system for radial network. Das et al. [7] proposed a methodology in which a unique numbering procedure was done for nodes and branches. Moreover, simple algebraic equations were used for solving the radial distribution system. Haque [8] applied the concept of backward and forward sweep technique which was used for radial as well as mesh power distribution network. Sparse technique was applied by Nagaraju et al. [9]. The approach works well for sequentially numbered networks but for nonsequentially numbered network, manual work is required.

In this paper, the modeling of radial distribution network which is used for load flow analysis, is presented in Sect. 2. Then the methodology is provided in Sect. 3 along with the calculation of current, voltage, impedance, and power. The parallel implementation of Load flow analysis is given in Sect. 4. And then finally the results and conclusion are shown.

2 Radial Distribution Network

The radial distribution network is used for load flow analysis. The network is more preferable because of its simpler design and low cost. It is represented by single line diagram depicting generators, loads, and transmission lines present in the network.

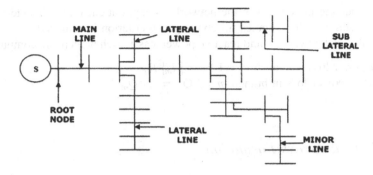

Fig. 1 Radial distribution network

It consists of source node, a main line, nodes, lateral lines, and its sublateral lines. The source node is considered to be the substation and nodes are the destinations where power is to be supplied.

The transmission line emerging out of the source node is main line and the line emerging out of main line is lateral line along with sublateral lines.

The radial network methods have many advantages. They are less sensitive to high R/X ratio and they provide simple formulation. Figure 1 in [10] depicts the radial distribution network.

3   Load Flow Analysis Methodology

Load flow analysis is also known to be power flow study. This study is a numerical analysis of the power flow in a network. The analysis focuses parameter of power such as voltages, reactive power, and real power.

The Fig. 2 in [11] depicts the electrical equivalent of the radial distribution network, the voltage magnitudes, $V1$ and $V2$, are present at node 1 and node 2. Let the current flowing from one node to another is I. The impedance factor (Z) is $R + jX$ and the power factor (P) is $P2 + jQ2$.

For analyzing the network, the branch current at each node and at each branch of the network is calculated. This approach starts from the end nodes of sublateral line, then lateral line and main line, and then finally moves toward the source node during branch current computation.

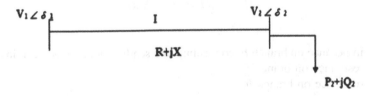

Fig. 2 Electrical equivalent of radial distribution network

After updating the current in the network, voltages at each node is determined. This procedure which continues till convergence criterion is achieved.

After that real power loss and reactive power loss at each branch, are computed as

- Real power loss in branch $m = LP_m = |I_m|^2 R_m$
- Reactive power loss in branch $m = LQ_m = |I_m|^2 Q_m$

3.1 Lateral Arrays Formation

For the load flow analysis solution of radial distribution network, an input file is taken in which details of the network are provided. The details are the information about sending node, receiving node, branch number, resistance, reactance, and power of the distribution network.

From the input file, two-dimensional arrays are formed

List []—contains columns of sending node, receiving node, and the branch number by which the two nodes are connected.
Child []—contains columns of sending node and its respective child nodes.
Level []—provides levels of each nodes in the network.

3.2 Determining the Order of the Network Through BFS

Breadth first search (BFS) is a mechanism to traverse or to search a tree or graph data structures. The searching starts from the source node and ends till the leaf nodes are explored. The searching occurs level-wise, i.e., the neighbor nodes of the same level are explored first, before exploring the next level nodes.

3.3 Calculation of Impedance and Power

The impedance (Z) is calculated on each branch present in the network

$$Z(b) = \sqrt{R1(n)^2 + R2(n)^2} \tag{1}$$

where
$Z(b)$ impedance on branch b, connecting and sending node to its receiving node.
$R1(b)$ resistance on branch b
$R2(b)$ reactance on branch b.

The power (P) is calculated on each node of the distribution network

$$P(n) = \sqrt{p(n)^2 + q(n)^2} \qquad (2)$$

where
P (n)   power on node n
p (n) and q (n)   load power on node n.

3.4 Branch Current Calculation

For branch current calculation, the order of the nodes is accessed in reverse order:
The voltage at each node is defined as 1 V.
First, load current calculation on each node is done by

$$IL\ (n) = P\ (n)/V\ (n) \qquad (3)$$

where
IL (n)   load current on node n
P (n)   power on node n
V (n)   voltage on node n.

For calculating branch current connected with leaf nodes:

$$IB\ (b) = IL\ (n) \qquad (4)$$

where
IB (b)   branch current on branch b
IL (n)   load current on leaf node to which the branch b is connected.

Similarly, total current in branches connected with branch nodes and junction nodes will be the sum of branch currents coming from their receiving nodes by the respective branches that are connecting them and the load current present in the node itself, i.e.,

$$IB\ (b) = sum + IL\ (n) \qquad (5)$$

where
IB (*b*)   branch current in branch node
Sum   sum of the branch current coming from receiving nodes
IL (*n*)   current on node *n*.

3.5 Voltage Calculation

After calculating the current in each node, voltage is calculated for each node.

$$V\ (n) = V\ (n - 1) - IB\ (b) * Z\ (b) \tag{6}$$

where
$V\ (n)$ voltage at node *n*
IB (*b*)   current in branch *b* which is connecting node *n* to its receiving nodes
Z (*b*)   impedance on branch b which is connecting node *n* to its receiving node.

Voltage calculation is done for some iteration until the convergence of load flow solution occurs. The convergence occurs when there is less than 0.00001 V of difference of the voltage calculated for any node in two successive iterations.

4 Parallel Implementation Using CUDA

4.1 Overview of CUDA

CUDA is a parallel programming model that has been invented by NVIDIA. Parallel programming is a concept that describes a system in which instruction threads are executed in parallel over a partitioned data source or shared memory resources. This processing uses the graphics processing unit (GPU) and thereby dramatically increases the computing performance. GPU is low at cost and has high computation power. Thus by using CUDA, the GPUs are utilized for general purpose processing and so the approach is known to be GPGPU.

4.2 Programming Model of CUDA

CUDA API provides a set of library functions as mentioned in [12] that can be coded as an extension of the C language. CUDA program is organized into a host program. The program has a host in which of one or more threads are running sequentially on the CPU and a device in which threads are running parallel in GPU. In CUDA, functions are defined which are known as kernels. These kernels are executed on the GPU. The hardware architecture of the GPU is not seen by the programmer. It deals only with the number of threads that are present in their respective blocks.

4.3 CUDA Implementation of Load Flow Analysis

This paper demonstrates certain procedures of the load flow analysis that has been implemented in parallel. The Breadth first approach, to find the order of the network, has been made parallel. In this approach, threads are executed concurrently to generate adjacency list of every node in the network. This list is represented as CHILD array. From the CHILD array, levels of all the nodes are determined and stored in LEVEL array.

Similarly, threads are generated to perform parallel search on LEVEL array and thereby order of the network is determined by exploring the level of nodes.

The procedures for evaluating branch impedances and power load at each node has been made parallel. Details regarding the impedances and power are taken from the input file and threads are executed in parallel to perform the calculation.

4.3.1 CUDA Block for BFS Approach

```
Search_Childnode(A, item)
{
id ← getThreadId for each thread
if(item =A(id,0))
   Child[id]=A(id,1)      //Searching and mapping the child
                           node into Child array
}

Level_search(l,index)
{
id← getThreadId for each thread

if(index =l(id,0))
   Level[id]=l(id,0)      //Searching and mapping the levels
                           Of all nodes into Level array
}
```

4.3.2 CUDA Block for Impedance and Power Evaluation

```
Cal_powerimpedance ()
{
id ← getThreadId for each thread

P[id] ←Resultant sum of reactive and real power of node
present at 'id' position.
Z[id]←Resultant sum of resistance and reactance of branch
present at 'id' position

}
```

5 Experimental Results

The analysis of load flow has been done on two network configurations, i.e., 33-nodes radial network and a 69-nodes radial network. Evaluation has been done as per CUDA profiling in [13] on NVIDIA Quadro-600 consisting of 16 multi-processors in which 8 processors have CUDA 6.0 Runtime environment. The result has been presented in Table 1 and Table 2.

Table 1 33-nodes radial distribution

Function	CPU execution time (μs)	GPU execution time (μs)	No. of times kernel execute	Speedup factor
Search_Childnode()	420.75	82.58	33	5.095
Level_search()	352.65	63.26	18	5.574
Cal_powerimpedance()	81.115	7.88	1	10.29

Table 2 69-nodes radial distribution

Function	CPU execution time (μs)	GPU execution time (μs)	No. of times kernels execute	Speedup factor
Search_Childnode()	756.43	158.34	69	4.777
Level_search()	685.83	112.7	27	6.0854
Cal_powerimpedance()	150.542	9.260	1	18.225

6 Conclusion

A simple methodology for analyzing the load flow solution of radial distribution network has been proposed. This method involves simple formulation of current and voltage in the network. The effectiveness of the system has been tested with 33 and 69 bus radial distribution systems. By introducing parallel programming approach using CUDA, certain amount of saving has been done in number of steps execution as compared to sequential approach. Thereby, increasing the throughput and performance of the analysis this method also helps to reduce the time for reconfiguration of the network.

References

1. Ghosh, S., & Sherpa, K. (2008). An efficient method for load—Flow solution of radial distribution networks. *Proceedings International Journal of Electrical Power and Energy Systems Engineering*.
2. Kersting, W. H., Mendive, D. L. (1976). An application of ladder network theory to the solution of three phase radial load flow problem. In *IEEE PES Winter Meeting*. New York.
3. Kersting, W. H. (1984). A method to teach the design and operation of a distribution system. *IEEE Transactions on Power apparatus and Systems, 103*(7), 1945–1952.
4. Aravindhababu, P., Ganapathy, S., & Nayar, K.R. (2001). A novel technique for the analysis of radial distribution systems. *International Journal of Electrical Power and Energy Systems, 3,* 167–171.
5. Baran, M. E., & Wu, F. F. (1989). Optimal sizing of capacitors placed on a radial distribution system. *IEEE Transactions on Power Delivery, 1,* 735–743.
6. Sharma, D. P., Chaturvedi, A., Purohit, G., & Shivarudaswamy, R. (2011). Distributed load flow analysis. *Proceedings International Journal of Electrical Power and Energy Systems Engineering,* 203–206.
7. Das, D., Nagi, H. S., & Kothari, D. P. (1994). Novel method for solving radial distribution networks. *IEEE Proceedings on Generation Transmission and Distribution, 141*(4), 291–298.
8. Haque, M. H. (1996). Load flow-solution of distribution systems with voltage dependent load models. *Power System Research, 36*(3), 151–156.
9. Nagaraju, K., Sivanagaraju, S., Ramana, T. and Prasad, P. V., A Novel Load Flow Method for Radial Distribution Systems for Realistic Loads, *Electric Power Components and Systems, 2,* 128–141.
10. Dinesh, M. S. Dr. Singh, A. K. (1997). Voltage stability analysis of radial distribution networks. *IEEE Transactions on Power Systems* (Impact Factor: 3.53), *12*(3), 1121–1128. doi:10.1109/59.630451.
11. Vinoth Kumar, K., & Selvan, M. P. (2012). A simplified approach for load flow analysis of radial distribution network with embedded generation. *IEEE, 1*(10), 2278–0181.
12. CUDA Programming Guide. Retrieved from http://docs.nvidia.com/cuda/cuda-c-programming-Guide.
13. Cuda programs profiling. Retrieved from https://developer.nvidia.com/cuda-zone.

Hierarchical Role-Based Access Control with Homomorphic Encryption for Database as a Service

Kamlesh Kumar Hingwe and S. Mary Saira Bhanu

Abstract Database as a service provides services for accessing and managing customers data which provides ease of access, and the cost is less for these services. There is a possibility that the DBaaS service provider may not be trusted, and data may be stored on untrusted server. The access control mechanism can restrict users from unauthorized access, but in cloud environment access control policies are more flexible. However, an attacker can gather sensitive information for a malicious purpose by abusing the privileges as another user and so database security is compromised. The other problems associated with the DBaaS are to manage role hierarchy and secure session management for query transaction in the database. In this paper, a role-based access control for the multitenant database with role hierarchy is proposed. The query is granted with least access privileges, and a session key is used for session management. The proposed work protects data from privilege escalation and SQL injection. It uses the partial homomorphic encryption (Paillier Encryption) for the encrypting the sensitive data. If a query is to perform any operation on sensitive data, then extra permissions are required for accessing sensitive data. Data confidentiality and integrity are achieved using the role-based access control with partial homomorphic encryption.

Keywords Cloud computing · Access control · Multitenant database · DBaaS · Database security

K.K. Hingwe (✉) · S. Mary Saira Bhanu
Department of Computer Science and Engineering, National Institute
of Technology, Tiruchirappalli, India
e-mail: kkhingwe@gmail.com

S. Mary Saira Bhanu
e-mail: msb@nitt.edu

© Springer Science+Business Media Singapore 2016   437
S.C. Satapathy et al. (eds.), *Proceedings of International Conference
on ICT for Sustainable Development*, Advances in Intelligent Systems
and Computing 409, DOI 10.1007/978-981-10-0135-2_43

1 Introduction

The databases used in the cloud can be of NoSQL type (Amazon, SimpleDB, Yahoo PNUT, CouchDB) or SQL type (Oracle and MySQL). In cloud, a service called database as a service (DBaaS) is provided for database installation and maintenance. The service provides features such as on-demand independent service for managing the data, instant access to the ubiquitous service, etc.

The DBaaS provides the cost reduction, easy database maintenance, performance tuning, and it also supports multitenancy. The use of the multitenant database in cloud computing leads to security challenges, due to resource sharing [11]. The cloud users compromise the security of their data and computing application for cheaper service because the data management for the large number of users is not easy, and the database configurations are creating the vulnerabilities.

The DBaaS security issue is due to the absence of user authentication mechanism, data authorization, lack of session management, and unsecured key management system. The DBaaS threats [1] are as follows:

1. **Confidentiality Threats** The information is stored on the database server. The authorized user should get the access to the database. If data access is through DBaaS and if encryption mechanism is weak, then data will be compromised with confidentiality. The attacks related to confidentiality are

    (a) **Insider attack** The database administrator has all the privileges to access the database for the maintenance purpose. If the privilege is misused, then it leads to big confidentiality threat.
    (b) **Outsider Attack** The outsider attacks in DBaaS are related to the exploitation of the software vulnerability. The attacker can also do the spoofing, side channeling, and man-in-middle attacks. Intrusion is also a problem of the DBaaS in which the attacker accesses the login credentials.
    (c) **Access Control Issues** Policies of access control are managed by the DBaaS provider not by the data owner. So due to lack of the monitoring system, the access control policies cannot be customized.

2. **Integrity Threats** The data integrity refers to protecting the data from unauthorized modification or deletion. The data tempering in DBaaS can happen at any level of storage.

The access control mechanism plays an important role to provide DBaaS security such as data confidentiality and integrity [1]. It validates the rights of users against the set of the authorization rules and states to perform the operation on the database. The authorization states are dependent on the access control policies of the database owner or organization. The confidentiality of the database is improved by encrypting the database and the data integrity is provided by the access control mechanism. The user's database access requests are properly authorized by enforcing the access control polices.

The access control mechanisms commonly used are mandatory access control (MAC), discretionary access control (DAC) [1], and role-based access control (RBAC). The RBAC is used for the traditional databases and it assigns permissions according to the role of the user in the organization. The three primary rules of RBAC are role assignment, role authorization, and permission authorization. RBAC is followed in this paper.

The use of access control provides security to DBaaS but still there are some challenges [2] such as Integration of DBaaS access control with efficient role hierarchy management, and session management. This paper proposes an access control mechanism that performs the user authentication using roles, and group authentication using group key. The proposed work also maintains secure session for the query transactions, maintains the role hierarchy, and secures data using Paillier encryption.

2 Related Work

Jia et al. [8] proposed a privacy-preserving access control that is based on secret sharing and ElGamal homomorphic properties. It provides security to the data owner, but also provides protection for the data requester using the access control policies. Their model did not consider the multitenant database architecture.

Calero et al. [4] proposed a model for authorization that supports multitenancy role-based access control. The path back object hierarchy is used. Hu et al. [7] proposed a work that is based on distributed role-based control for web technology. Echeveria et al. [5] proposed a solution for the decoupling access control using attribute encryption.

The Siebel systems [3] used a role-based access control mechanism that allows multiple tenants, in which each tenant is the owner of his separate virtual database. This mechanism supports an access control subsystem for multi-user database access, where the each user has access of at least one organizational database attribute. They divide the database into files, files into the records, and record into the fields. This mechanism is based on separation of individual database files, which is based on attribute ownership or granted access control.

Yaish et al. [13, 14] have proposed a multitenant database access control mechanism, called elastic extension table access control (EETAC) that allows each tenant with different types of access grants to access data in multitenant database. The mechanism of data retrieving in multitenant database is different from single-tenant database. The data of users is subdivided by partitioning between particular tenants data and by access rows and columns granted to users, which is based on group and role assignment. The EETAC has role back access control for multitenant database but does not maintain the role hierarchy in the system.

Wu et al. [12] proposed access control as a service (ACaaS) for providing supports for the multiple access control model. They implemented role-based access control which is configured for the amazon web services. The role hierarchy is maintained within the access control mechanism. The drawbacks of this method are it is designed only for amazon web services, and also it does not support multi-level access control policies and efficient session management for the user.

The existing works do not provide all solution at one place like secure session management, maintenance of role hierarchy, multi-level access control, and data encryption. Some of the existing [8, 12] work does not support the multitenant database architecture.

3 Proposed Work

The proposed work uses role-based access control mechanism that will perform on the user's query. The proposed access control mechanism provides the confidentiality as well as integrity. The shared database and shared schema type isolation are used for the multitenant database.

The proposed work has two main modules: (i) authentication and (ii) access control. The authentication module is responsible for the user authentication and generation of the session key. It validates user's credentials by checking the user name and its password. After validating, a session key is issued to the user. This key is used for the data encryption that provides the secure communication between user and database owner. Session key is generated using the Secure Hash Algorithm (SHA-2). The input for SHA-2 is a pseudo random number, which is generated by the most efficient random number generator called Mersenne Twister [10]. It generates integer in the range between 0 and $2^k - 2$ for k-bit word length. Queries are validated by the access control module and are redirected to the database for further processing. The access control module takes encrypted query, group key (if any group is assigned), and optional requests from users as well as it takes user id and session key as input from authentication module. The administrator is responsible for maintenance of the role hierarchy.

The access control mechanism contains eight essential sub-modules as shown in Fig. 1. The modules are

1. Org: It is responsible for registration, deletion, and listing of users in the DBaaS within a tenant.
2. User: It is responsible for managing all information of the user.

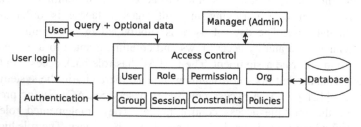

Fig. 1 Block diagram of architecture

3. Group: It is responsible for managing the group in a single organization. An organization can have many groups. Moreover, each group has its own set of roles.
4. Role: Role module is responsible for creating and deleting the roles. It manages the role information in database and also responsible for activation and deactivation of the role.
5. Permission: It contains all the set of rules for a role. The permission can be modified by Admin.
6. Session: It is responsible for maintaining the session for a complete query transaction.
7. Constraints: It contains set of rules to restrict some operations.
8. Policies: It contains a set of rules for providing access to the user's query.

The proposed work provides data security for the tenants and their customers by deploying the access control model in DBaaS. The authentication module at the server side generates a session key which is used by the client to encrypt the query. The access control module at the server decrypts the query using the same session key. The data sent by the client can be sensitive as well as non-sensitive. To ensure security, sensitive data is encrypted using a private key generated by server. The server processes the query and the result is sent to the client in the encrypted form. The result of the query is decrypted using the server public key at client machine.

The user's query needs right privileges for accessing database. For providing the secured resource access, a role has to be allotted to the user. These roles are binded with the permissions and constraints. If the user is part of a group, then a group key is also provided for accessing databases.

Figure 2 represents the data flow diagram of access control module. The query handler takes user id, query, group key, and optional requests as a single string of input; it parses users input and separates various attributes from the user input. First, the role of the user is checked. The user may be allotted individual roles, or group roles or both. Once the role is identified, the assigned role is verified with the policies and constraints and the information is added in a set of roles. If user belongs to any group, then perform group authentication using group key. After the successful authentication, add the group roles in the set of roles. The set of roles is given input to activate role for the role activation, which is responsible for the activating the roles by adding the permissions to access the resource. If the set of roles has more than one role, then this module searches for the parent role in the given set and activates the parent role. However, if the parent role is not present in the given set, then add permissions for the role activation. After the role activation, get the set of columns in the query that is accessible to the user using the activated roles. If all queried columns are belonged to the accessible set of columns, then regenerate query according to the policies and constraints. The regenerated query takes input as the set of the accessible column for the user and the set of columns in the query. Then encrypt the sensitive data in the query using a Paillier encryption

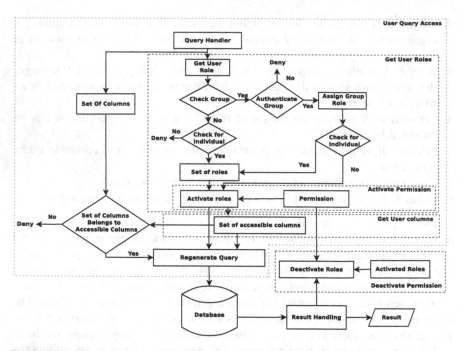

Fig. 2 Flow diagram of access control module

algorithm. The regenerated query is executed on the database, and the result of the query is sent to the result handler which is responsible for checking whether the query execution is successful. If successful, the result is sent to the user, otherwise if any error occurs, generate an error message. In both of the cases after the query execution, it triggers the deactivate role module which deactivates the user's role that is activated by the activate role module.

The access control module performs the user query access function which is responsible for database query execution and encrypted query regeneration. The three functions that are performing user query access function are as follows:

1. Get user roles: It adds the assigned individual or group roles in the set of roles after the verification and validation of the roles.
2. Activate permission: It is part of the get user role. It activates appropriate role to provide least access for the query from the set of roles.
3. Get user column: Get the accessible columns from the activated roles.

The tables that are used to provide database access control are as follows:

1. Tenant Table: It stores the information about the tenants.
2. User Table: It can be more than one for a tenant in the database.
3. Group Table: It contains information of groups and associated user for the tenant.

4. Role table: It contains information about the roles.
5. Permission Table: It is used for the permission to the user that whether he is capable of performing a particular operation or not.

The access to the table depends on the access control policies and constraints because every table has their own access policies and constraints.

3.1 User Query Access Function

The sensitive data of the query is encrypted using Paillier encryption algorithm [6]. QA_{ret} is obtained by passing all the set of policies and constraints associated with the users, group, and role that is related to the requested query. The encryption is performed using private key for sensitive data in the query. The sensitive columns in the database are defined by the database owner. To access the sensitive data, extra permission is required to users all the time for all roles (except admin role). The users have the public key that is known to the user that belongs to the role (role having permission to access sensitive data). The decryption takes place at user machine using the public key.

The key generation steps for the Paillier encryption are as follows:

1. Select two independent large prime numbers P_1 and P_2 randomly such that $\gcd(P_1 P_2, (P_1 - 1)(P_2 - 1) = 1)$ (if prime numbers of equal length).
2. Compute $n = P_1 P_2$ and $\gamma = \mathrm{lcm}(P_1 - 1, P_2 - 1)$.
3. A random integer g is generated where $g \in \mathbb{Z}_n^*$.
4. Ensure n divides the order of g by checking the existence of the following modular multiplicative inverse: $\mu = (T(g^\gamma \bmod n^2))^{-1} \bmod n$ where T is defined as $T(u) = \frac{u-1}{n}$.
5. The private (encryption) key is (n, g).
6. The public (decryption) key is (γ, μ).

3.2 Get User Roles Function

This function is responsible for assigning the user's role and activating the assigned role for which the user belongs. If user belongs to any group role, then validate the group authentication and assign to user.

Algorithm 1 User_ Query_Access($T_{id}, U_{id}, O, Q, G_{key}$)

```
1:  O_col ← Set of column of Tenant(T) and Table(O) using query filter
2:  Q_type ← Parse query and get its behavior
3:  Rol_ret ← Get_User_Role(T_id, U_id, O, G_key)
4:  Col_ret ← Get_User_Columns(T_id, U_id, O, Rol_ret, Q_type)
5:  if size of O_col=size of Col_ret0,0 then
6:      if Q_sel = ∅ then
7:          QA_sel ← ∅
8:      else
9:          QA_sel ← Q_sel
10:     end if
11: else
12:     if Q_sel = ∅ then
13:         QA_sel ← ∅
14:     else
15:         QA_sel ← Q_sel ∩ Col_ret.0.0
16:     end if
17: end if
18: if Col_ret ≠ ∅ then
19:     if Q_where ∈ Col_ret,0,1 then
20:         QA_where ← Q_where
21:     else
22:         QA_where ← ∅
23:     end if
24: end if
25: if Col_ret ≠ ∅ then
26:     if Q_write ∈ Col_ret,0,2 then
27:         QA_write ← Q_write
28:     else
29:         QA_write ← ∅
30:     end if
31: end if
32: Sen_col ← set of sensitive column
33: if (QA_sel ∪ QA_where ∪ QA_write) ∩ Sen_col then
34:     if U_id ∈ XU_permission ∨ Rol_ret ∈ XROL_permission
35:         Encrypt(Q, Key_private)
36:     else
37:         Deny
38:     endif
39: end if
40: QA_ret,0,0 ← QA_sel
41: QA_ret,0,1 ← QA_where
42: QA_ret,0,2 ← QA_write
43: return QA_ret
```

Algorithm 2 Get_ User_Roles($T_{id}, U_{id}, O, G_{key}$)

```
1:  Rol_table ← Roles assigned to a table from role_info table
    by using tenant and Table query filter policies.
2:  if U_id ∈ G and G_pwd === G_key then
3:      Rol_group ← Roles assigned to user from group using
        the query filter policies.
4:  end if
5:  if G_pwd ! = ∅ then
6:      Rol_group ← ∅
7:  else
8:      deny
9:  end if
10: Rol_user ← Roles assignesd to User from userrole table
    by using tenant and User query filter policies.
11: Rol_ret ← ∅
12: i ← 0
13: for all Rol_table do
14:     Rol_id ← Rol_table,i
15:     if R_id ∈ Rol_group ∨ Rol_id ∈ Rol_user then
16:         Rol_flag ← true
17:         exit loop
18:     end if
19:     i ← i + 1
20: end for
21: if Rol_flag ≠ true then
22:     Rol_ret ← Rol_group
23:     j ← j + 1
24:     for all Rol_user do
25:         Rol_id ← Rol_user,j
26:         if Rol_id ∉ Rol_ret then
27:             Rol_ret ← Rol_ret ∪ Rol_id
28:         end if
29:         j ← j + 1
30:     end for
31: end if
32: Activate_Permissions(U_id, Rol_ret)
33: return Rol_ret
```

3.3 Activate Permission and Deactivate Permission

The activation and deactivation functions are based on [12]. The user's role access permission is included in proposed work. Usually, the user is assigned with more than one role, to provide the query access to the user so that the least privilege is met to complete the task to the user. The nested set model [9] with the use of tree data structure is used for maintaining the role hierarchy in the access control mechanism. The main advantage of using this model is that it requires a single entry for each role to manage the role hierarchy. The security policies enforce the role hierarchy like a regular role that has the least privilege and least access to the database.

If a user U_{id} has an immediate senior role in role hierarchy, then that role is assigned to role Rol_a which needs to be activated, and an empty permission set is returned because the immediate senior role has default permission by policies and constraints to access database (like admin role). If the user U_{id} does not have immediate senior, then for each junior and siblings the permission sets are calculated to activate the Rol_a. If multiple queries with the same roles are processed, then the roles overlap and the deactivation function will not affect the other queries having the same roles.

Algorithm 3 Activate_Permission(U_{id}, Rol_a)

1: $per, Per_{all} \leftarrow \emptyset$
2: $Rol_{is} \leftarrow Get\_Immediate\_senior\_Role(Rol_a)$
3: **if** $hasRole(U_{id}, Rol_{is} = TRUE$ AND $active(U_{id}, Rol_{is})$ **then**
4:     **return** $\emptyset$
5: **else**
6:     $ComputeP(U_{id}, Rol_a)$
7:     **for all** $per \in Permissions(Rol_a)$ **do**
8:       **if** $per \notin Per_{all}$ **then**
9:        add per into Per
10:       **end if**
11:     **end for**
12:     **return** Per;
13: **end if**
14: $ComputeP(User\ U_{id}, Role\ Role_a)$
15: $Rol \leftarrow Siblingroles(Rol_a) \bigcup juniorroles(Rol_a)$
16: **if** $Rol = \emptyset$ **then**
17:     **return**
18: **else**
19:     **for all** $Rol_{id} \in Rol$ **do**
20:       **if** $active(U_{id}, Rol_{id}) = TRUE$ **then**
21:        **for all** $per \in Permissions(Rol_{id})$ **do**
22:         **if** $per \in P_{all}$ **then**
23:          *add per into* Per_{all}
24:         **end if**
25:        **end for**
26:       **else**
27:        $ComputeP(U_{id}, Rol_{id})$
28:       **end if**
29:     **end for**
30: **end if**

Algorithm 4 Deact._Per.(U_{id}, Rol_d) $\rightarrow Per$

1: $per, Per_{all} \leftarrow \emptyset$
2: $Rol_{senior} \leftarrow getseniorrole(Rol_d)$
3: **if** $Rol_{senior} \neq \emptyset$ **then**
4:     **for all** $r \in Rol_{senior}$ **do**
5:       **if** $active(U_{id}, Rol_i d) = TRUE$ **then**
6:        **return** $\emptyset$
7:       **end if**
8:     **end for**
9: **end if**
10: $Rol_{sibling} \leftarrow getAvtivatedSiblingRoles(Rol_d)$
11: **if** $Rol_{sibling} = \emptyset$ **then**
12:     **return** $Permissions(Rol_d)$
13: **else**
14:     **for all** $Rol_{id} \in R_{sibling}$ **do**
15:       **if** $active(U_{id}, Rol_{id}) = TRUE$ **then**
16:        **for all** $per \in Permissions(Rol_{id})$ **do**
17:         **if** $per \neq Per_{all}$ **then**
18:          add per into Per_{all}
19:         **end if**
20:        **end for**
21:       **end if**
22:     **end for**
23:     **for** $per \in Permissions(Rol_d)$ **do**
24:       **if** $per \neq Per_{all}$ **then**
25:        add per into Per_{all}
26:       **end if**
27:     **end for**
28: **end if**
29: **return** Per

The role deactivation algorithm is shown in Algorithm 4 and during deactivation an empty set of permission is returned any senior role to a role Rol_d, which required to deactivate for the user. Otherwise, if any role is needed to deactivate, for which the user who does not have any activated siblings roles, and then Per_{all} is permission set containing all permission that has associated with activated sibling's role for the user. Moreover, with Rol_d each permission is associated, and if it does not belong to Per_{all} then it adds to returned permission set.

3.4 Get User Columns

The get user columns function is responsible for returning the set of accessible list of columns (Col_{ret}) which exist in different types of clauses (like select and where) in user's query.

Algorithm 5 Get_User_columns($T_{id}, U_{id}, O, Rol_{ret}, Q_{type}$)

1: $Col_{user} \leftarrow$ Get col and column rules for U_{id} belongs to Rol_{ret}
2: $i \leftarrow 0$
3: **for all** Col_{user} **do**
4:     $Col_{sel} \leftarrow Col_{user,i,0}$
5:     $Col_{where} \leftarrow Col_{where} \bigcup Col_{user,i,1}$
6:     **if** $Q_{type} == write$ and $U_{id} \in writepermission$ **then**
7:       $C_{write} \leftarrow col_{write}$
8:     **end if**
9:     $i \leftarrow i + 1$
10: **end for**
11: $Col\_ret, 0, 0 \leftarrow Col_{sel}$
12: $Col\_ret, 0, 1 \leftarrow Col_{where}$
13: $Col\_ret, 0, 2 \leftarrow Col_{write}$
14: **return** Col_{ret}

4   Implementation and Analysis

A client server architecture is considered for the implementation of proposed work. The server is a centralized one, but the database storage nodes are distributed by default distribution of MYSQL Cluster database. The implementation of RBAC work is at the server side. The cryptographic access control is created using python, C++, and Crypto library.

The access control is a secure authentication mechanism that generates the session key using SHA-2 to encrypt the query at the client system. The session key is valid until the completion of the transaction. The server also encrypts the result (after successful execution of the query) using the same session key. Hence, query and the result are secured during the communication. The proposed approach performs the group validation using the group key stored at the server. If the user belongs to the group, it has to provide the group key with the query. The group validation reduces the privilege escalation attacks because if the user escalates the role, and if that role belongs to any group, without group key the access control will deny the query.

The proposed work manages the role hierarchy using the nested set model. The attacks related to privileges are reduced due to the role hierarchy management with least privilege grant by adding minimum permissions for query execution. The activation and deactivation functions play a major role to protect from the escalation attack because by default roles are considered as deactivated roles and both functions need a user id to activate the role. The Paillier encryption algorithm is used to encrypt the sensitive data. So the sensitive data is secured during the execution of the query as well as in a database. Since the Paillier encryption has the properties of homomorphic encryption and works on the public key cryptosystem, it protects the sensitive data from the cryptographic attacks such as chosen plaintext attacks (IND-CPA) and adaptive chosen cipher text attacks (IND-CCA2).

Experiments are conducted using twenty five different roles and eight groups are created for the tenant's database user. For the analysis, three types of queries are tested: (i) sensitive and non-sensitive data in query, (ii) only sensitive data in query, and (iii) non-sensitive data in the query. The database has the four sensitive data columns. Figure 3 shows number of queries versus query access time and it is observed that there is little difference between query access time of sensitive data and non-sensitive data. This difference is due to extra computation time needed for sensitive data encryption. However, this overhead provides the data confidentiality for the database owner. The role activation and deactivation times are represented in Fig. 4. The role activation function and deactivation are responsible for providing integrity feature for proposed work. The role activation time is calculated by considering a maximum of eight roles of the users and three groups of users. The queries contain sensitive attributes which need some extra permission that is required for the role activation.

Fig. 3 Access time versus number of query

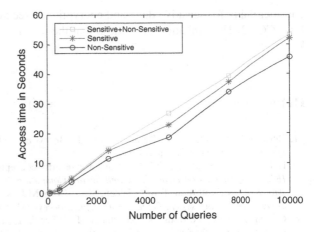

Fig. 4 Activation and deactivation times versus number of query

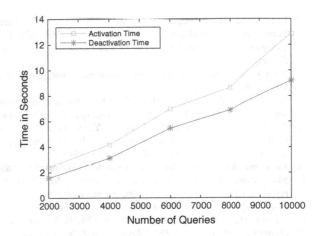

5 Conclusion

In this paper, a role-based access control for the DBaaS with data encryption using Paillier (partial homomorphic) public key encryption is proposed. The approach is secure from the privilege escalation because of the role hierarchy management with least privilege grants. It protects from the SQL injection attacks since the role is to be activated to perform any query on database. The proposed approach works for the application as a service to provide secure query access control. The session key is used for securing the user query and on another side the group keys are used for checking whether the user belongs to groups. The role activation and deactivation functions help to maintain the role hierarchy. It adds the permission in the permission set. So to perform any query access it adds minimum permission to execute the query and provide the least privilege for the task. At the server end data stored is in encrypted form. The partial homomorphic encryption is used to provide confidentiality for sensitive data, and encryption is secured from the IND-CPA and IND-CCA2. The limitation of work is that the user has to remember two or more keys.

References

1. Bertino, E., Ghinita, G., & Kamra, A. (2011). *Access control for databases: Concepts and systems*, vol. 8. Now Publishers Inc.
2. Bertino, E., & Sandhu, R. (2005). Database security-concepts, approaches, and challenges. *IEEE Transactions on Dependable and Secure Computing, 2*(1), 2–19.
3. Brodersen, K., Rothwein, T. M., Malden, M. S., Chen, M.J., & Annadata, A. (2004). *Database access method and system for user role defined access* (May 4 2004), US Patent 6,732,100.
4. Calero, J. M. A., Edwards, N., Kirschnick, J., Wilcock, L., & Wray, M. (2010). Toward a multi-tenancy authorization system for cloud services. *IEEE Security and Privacy, 8*(6), 48–55.
5. Echeverria, V., Liebrock, L.M., & Shin, D. (2010). Permission management system: Permission as a service in cloud computing. In *Proceedings of the 2010 IEEE 34th Annual Computer Software and Applications Conference Workshops* (pp. 371–375). IEEE Computer Society.
6. Gentry, C. (2009). A fully homomorphic encryption scheme. Ph.D. thesis, Stanford University.
7. Hu, L., Ying, S., Jia, X., & Zhao, K. (2009). Towards an approach of semantic access control for cloud computing. In *Cloud Computing* (pp. 145–156). Springer.
8. Jia, Z., Pang, L., Luo, S. S., Zhang, J. Y., & Xin, Y. (2012). A privacy-preserving access control protocol for database as a service. In *2012 International Conference on Computer Science & Service System (CSSS)* (pp. 849–854). IEEE.
9. Kamfonas, M. J. (1992). Recursive hierarchies: The relational taboo. *The Relational Journal, 27*.
10. Matsumoto, M., & Nishimura, T. (1998). Mersenne twister: A 623-dimensionally equidistributed uniform pseudo-random number generator. *ACM Transactions on Modeling and Computer Simulation (TOMACS), 8*(1), 3–30.
11. Takabi, H., Joshi, J. B., & Ahn, G. J. (2010). Security and privacy challenges in cloud computing environments. *IEEE Security and Privacy, 8*(6), 24–31.
12. Wu, R., Zhang, X., Ahn, G.J., Sharifi, H., & Xie, H. (2013). Acaas: Access control as a service for iaas cloud. In *2013 International Conference on Social Computing (SocialCom)* (pp. 423–428). IEEE.
13. Yaish, H., & Goyal, M. (2013). Multi-tenant database access control. In *2013 IEEE 16th International Conference on Computational Science and Engineering (CSE)* (pp. 870–877). IEEE.
14. Yaish, H., Goyal, M., & Feuerlicht, G. (2011). An elastic multi-tenant database schema for software as a service. In *IEEE Ninth International Conference on Dependable, Autonomic and Secure Computing (Dasc), 2011* (pp. 737–743). IEEE.

Hybrid Miner Tracking System at 2.4 GHz for Underground Mines

Amber Haidery and Kanchan Bakade

Abstract The need for improving mining communications technology has become apparent over the past several years. Miners continue to lose their lives in mine disasters pertaining to challenging environmental conditions. There is loss in productivity due to manual tracking. As Global Positioning System (GPS) signals cannot penetrate into the ground, they cannot be used inside the mines. Employing Radio Frequency Identification (RFID) network further increases deployment and installation overhead along with a separate network for tracking. Hence, a cost-effective hybrid Wi-Fi location tracking network is proposed which can seamlessly integrate with the existing 802.11 communication infrastructure. The proposed system employs Wi-Fi technology to estimate the location of miners by Received Signal Strength Indicator (RSSI) method with higher accuracy and coverage area than conventional RFID method of tracking. It can also be used for asset tracking and increasing productivity, thereby overcoming the constraints of proprietary network solutions.

Keywords Location-based services · Node-based tracking · Active RFID · RSSI · Wi-Fi

1 Introduction

802.11 wireless standard has truly blossomed in the past decade. With the integration of Location Based Services (LBS), the Wireless Local Area Networks (WLANs) have become more popular in all the sectors including business enterprise, industries, warehouses, healthcare, and emergency services. It not only helps them with asset management but also improves productivity through effective

A. Haidery (✉) · K. Bakade
Mukesh Patel School of Technology, Management and Engineering, NMIMS University, Mumbai, India
e-mail: haidery.amber@gmail.com

K. Bakade
e-mail: kanchan.bakade@nmims.edu

© Springer Science+Business Media Singapore 2016
S.C. Satapathy et al. (eds.), *Proceedings of International Conference on ICT for Sustainable Development*, Advances in Intelligent Systems and Computing 409, DOI 10.1007/978-981-10-0135-2_44

scanning of asset, improves customer satisfaction, and coordinates Wi-Fi device location with security policy enforcement.

Mining, by its inherent nature, is a hazardous activity. Explosive gases such as carbon monoxide and methane present inside the mine pose a threat to the potential miners. High humidity and corrosive dust make maintenance of equipment a challenge. Mineral content of the earth also alter radio signals propagation [2]. In such cases, when two-way interaction becomes necessary, ensuring safety and coverage to all areas inside the mine is a huge concern.

To underscore the importance of mining communications, one needs only to look some of the recent mine disasters around the world. On April 5, 2010, a disaster occurred at the Upper Big Branch mine in Montcoal, West Virginia (Twenty nine miners were killed) [3]. In January of 2006, an explosion occurred at the Sago mine in Buckhannon, West Virginia. The rescue team had no way to communicate with the trapped miners, and did not know where they were located (Twelve miners died in this disaster) [4]. Following these disasters, the Mine Improvement and New Emergency Response (MINER) Act was signed into law on June 15, 2006. It requires the mine owners to submit an emergency response plan (ERP) for a redundant means of communication with the surface for underground workers, such as a two-way telephone or equivalent two-way communication for miner safety [5].

Study and analysis of LBS systems show that RFID technology is used and implemented using traditional tag and reader methods for location tracking [6]. Active RFID systems over ZigBee and P2P network have been implemented where dual-mode mobile phone and video camera connect to the BS use Wi-Fi technology, while wireless sensor and ID card use ZigBee technology [7, 8]. Systems employing the tracking methods such as RSSI method, Time Of Arrival (TOA), and Time Difference Of Arrival (TDOA) have been implemented [9]. Systems have also been developed using Wi-Fi location-based services in citywide areas [10] and Wi-Fi mesh technology in underground mines [11].

The tracking systems mainly are reader-based and node-based methods. Reader-based methods are RFID and reverse RFID employ active RFID tags which have internal battery. In RFID technology, an active RFID tag is placed on the person or asset to be tracked and the tag readers are placed at fixed locations. Owing to the high expense of the readers and cheap tags, in reverse RFID technology, many active RFID tags are placed at fixed locations in the area whereas the readers are placed on people to be tracked. Due to high density of tags deployed at various locations, the expandability of the network is easier and the range of coverage area is higher. Also, the battery life of the overall network is higher due to fixed tag infrastructure [5].

Node-based tracking systems use the same physical components as the node-based communications systems. Each tag has a unique identifier which is assigned to it. A fixed node with a known location is linked to a radio with a unique ID and assigned to a specific miner, and hence the location of the miner is known. Integrating this method with RSSI technique of location tracking, the distance of the miner with respect to the position of nodes can be determined.

Taking mine topologies and environment into consideration, a complete wired or wireless network has its own advantages and disadvantages. While wired systems have a disadvantage of cable cuts during mine cave-ins and limited mobility of users, they have an added advantage of higher data rate and better coverage. On the contrary, wireless networks result in lower data and comparatively poor coverage, but have no mobility issues and no instances of cable cuts [12].

In this paper, combining the advantages and disadvantages of both wired and wireless, a hybrid node-based miner tracking system at 2.4 GHz has been proposed to address the above issues. The system will thereby provide visibility and redundancy to the existing communication system.

This paper is organized as follows. Section 2 describes the system overview of the tracking network. Section 3 discusses the methodology and technique used for tracking, followed by Sect. 4 which shows experimental results.

2 System Requirements

A miner tracking system must be able to send the location information of the miners in real time to allow efficient tracking and monitoring. Considering the mine environment, the following features are essential in the system:

1. Productivity monitoring related to work shifts of miners.
2. Providing redundancy to the existing communication network.
3. Authentication of location information provided by miners.
4. Reduced labor search time.
5. Increased visibility of assets to prevent spoilage and thefts.
6. Timely rescue during emergency.
7. System efficiency in terms of time and money.

3 System Overview

The proposed tracking system, as shown in Fig. 1, is based on 802.11 standard and utilizes Wi-Fi-based active RFID tags. Wi-Fi-based active RFID (Wi-Fi) tags are active RFID tags that work on 802.11 communication protocol. The system is mainly composed of two parts—(1) Wi-Fi tags at client side, and (2) Windows application developed at server side.

The system utilizes 802.11 standard as a communications protocol, enabling customers to use WLAN access points as active RFID "readers." The communication backbone of this system is a well-planned WLAN infrastructure consisting of very reliable low latency Wi-Fi access points (WAPs) across the underground mine tunnels. This WLAN network is interfaced with server. The Wi-Fi tag sends the location tracking parameters, which are signal strength level, Medium Access

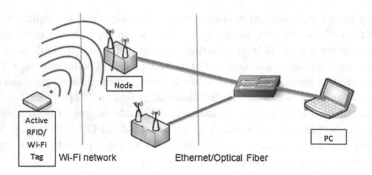

Fig. 1 Proposed tracking system

Control (MAC) address, and Service Set Identifier (SSID) name of the selected WAP. The windows application at the server processes this information received to produce reliable location data for assets and people tagged with Wi-Fi tags.

As indicated in Fig. 1, the proposed system can be easily integrated with the existing communication network in mines. Hence, the installation and deployment of the network become faster and easier.

3.1 System Specifications

The system specifications are provided in Table 1 which includes the programming environment and the programming language.

The Wi-Fi tag used here is a Raspberry pi B+. The function of this Wi-Fi tag is to scan for the nearby WAPs and find out their signal strengths. Each Wi-Fi tag scans across many WAPs within its footprint. The corresponding parameters of location tracking for all WAPs are displayed (Signal strength level, MAC address, and SSID name). Out of all the scanned WAPs, the one with maximum signal strength value is found out. The location parameters for this WAP are sent to the server through socket programming.

Table 1 Technical specifications of the system

Parameters	At server	At Wi-Fi tag
Programming environment	Microsoft Visual Studio 2013 Express Edition	Fedora 21 (Linux)
Programming language	Visual basic with .NET framework 3.5	Shell scripting
Socket programming language	Visual basic with .NET framework 3.5	

3.2 Data Collection

Before setting up the network, the Wireless Network Interface Card (WNIC) of the tag is identified. This identifier is used for scanning the nearby networks in its range using the scan command. This command displays the information of all the nearby WAP along with its MAC address, SSID name, signal strength level, mode and encryption and security parameters. Thus each WAP is referred to as a single cell, and the information of all the nearby WAPs are subsequently displayed as under cell 01, cell 02, and so on. The location parameters which are required for the estimation of tag's location are fetched.

After fetching the location parameters, out of the scanned WAPs, the tag then selects and connects to the corresponding WAP with the maximum signal strength. The location parameters of connected WAP are sent to the server. This process is set to take place after every 't' seconds and the location information that is sent to the server gets updated periodically. This timing can be set manually pertaining to the accuracy of the tracking system and battery issues of the tag.

3.3 Implementation

The various location tracking techniques include RSSI, TOA, TDOA, and finger-printing techniques. Considering the mine environment and the feasibilities, it is very rare that a Wi-Fi tag will be read simultaneously by three WAPs. TOA and TDOA methods require input from three WAPs for distance calculation, and this method is called as trilateration. But the trilateration method is difficult for implementation in mines. Also, taking simplicity in operation and cost-effective system deployment, RSSI technique is used for location tracking.

For a fixed transmitter power, the total power received RSSI decreases with distance. The relationship between RSSI and 10log10 of the distance is given by [13]

$$10 \log 10 \left[\mathrm{RSSI}(d) \right] = 10 \log 10 \left[A \right] - 10n \log 10 \left[d \right] \tag{1}$$

where n is the path loss exponent, d is the distance of separation between transmitter and receiver, and A is the constant set by the transmitted power and the measurement system gain during calibration. Using (1), if we substitute the value of A, for cable and connector losses on the transmitter (TX) side and the receiver (RX) side as $\mathrm{Loss_{TX}}$ and $\mathrm{Loss_{RX}}$, respectively, in dB, the corresponding antenna gain for the same as $\mathrm{Gain_{TX}}$ and $\mathrm{Gain_{RX}}$ in dBi, the transmitter output power as $\mathrm{Tx_{PWR}}$ and standard deviation associated with the degree of shadow fading present in the environment as s, in (1) and rearranging, we get

$10n \log 10 \, [d] = 10 \log 10 \, [\text{TX}_{\text{PWR}} + \text{Gain}_{\text{TX}} + \text{Gain}_{\text{RX}} - \text{Loss}_{\text{TX}} - \text{Loss}_{\text{RX}} + s]$
$- 10 \log 10 \, [\text{RSSI} \, (d)].$

$$(2)$$

In addition, if we take into account a reference path loss $\text{PL}_{1 \text{ M}}$ in dB for a desired frequency when the distance between the transmitter and receiver is 1 m, the resultant value of d meters is

$$d = 10^{(\text{TXPWR} + \text{PL1Meter} + \text{GainTX} + \text{GainRX} - \text{LossTX} - \text{LossRX} + s - \text{RSSI}\,(d))/(10n))}. \quad (3)$$

Canadian center has computed the value of n for Minerals and Energy Technology (CANMET) at 115 measurement locations with four different transmitter locations (taking measurements situated at both sides of the transmitter). These four sets of measurement data were processed using linear regression and path loss exponent values have been found to be equal to 2.13, 2.33, 2.15, and 2.17, respectively. Finally, the value of the path loss exponent $n = 2.16$ is determined for the above data and the value of standard deviation $s = 6.13$ [13]. The procedure of data collection and calculation of distance is summarized in Fig. 2.

4 Experimental Results

The experimental environment chosen here is a closed room. As shown in Table 2, the nearby WAPs are scanned and the ESSID name, MAC address, and signal strength, is fetched.

Out of all the signal strengths displayed, the maximum is found out to be −51. The data in the row containing '−51' in the above table is sent to the server for location tracking. Using the value of maximum signal strength, already found path loss exponent value n and standard deviation s, the location of the Wi-Fi tag can be found out at the server using (3).

As shown in Fig. 3, the relationship between RSSI value and distance is given. The experiment is performed in a long hallway with walls on all sides. The maximum coverage area of the Wi-Fi tag is found out to be 35 m after which the signal weakens considerably as shown in the above figure. It is observed that as the distance increases the received signal strength decreases.

As shown in Table 3, the distance is measured considering the values of n and s taken according to the mine environments. It is observed that the accuracy of distance measurements drastically decreases for low transmit power. So a high value of transmit power is preferred for better accuracy. However, pertaining to battery issues in mine environments, the transmit power level is usually kept low. Also, for a particular transmit power, the accuracy distance measurement worsens. As shown in Eq. (1), and also verified by Table 3, the relationship between distance and RSSI value is not linear.

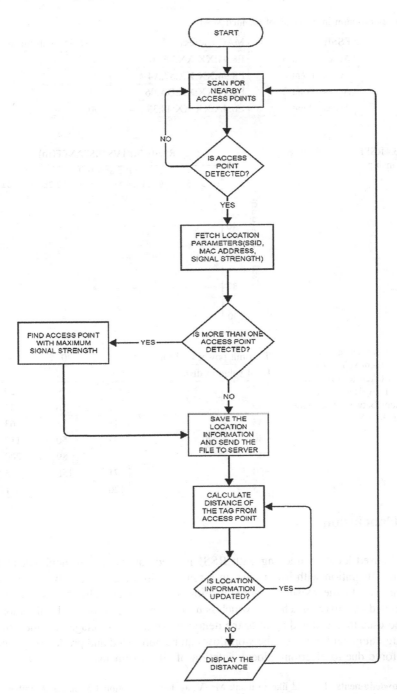

Fig. 2 Flowchart showing the data collection and implementation process

Table 2 Location information of scanned WAPs

S. no.	ESSID name	MAC address	Signal Strength (dBm)
1	Access Point 3	E8:94:XX:XX:7F:70	−87
2	Access Point 1	E8:94:XX:XX:57:A4	−93
3	Access Point 2	E8:94:XX:XX:DA:06	−51
4	Access Point 4	C0:4A:XX:XX:48:38	−90

Fig. 3 RSSI versus distance relationship

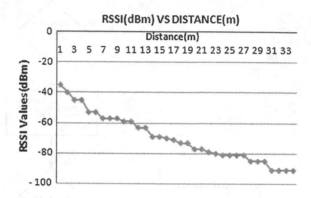

Table 3 Distance measurement values (in meters) taken for different transmit levels at fixed distances between transmitter and receiver

Transmit power in dBm	27	20	13
RSSI value in dBm			
−25	4	9	20
−30	7	16	35
−35	13	28	63
−40	22	50	112
−45	40	89	200
−50	71	158	355
−55	126	228	631

5 Conclusion

Wi-Fi-based location tracking with RSSI is used for its ease in deployment and system integration with lower cost, in a mine environment. The network provides redundancy to the existing communication system. It can also be used to track assets and expensive machinery which is used for mining purposes. Furthermore, it can be used to detect and monitor the delays in workflow, spoilage, and theft of the mining equipment. Overall, the workflow can be optimized and productivity can be monitored due to electronic documentation of all movements.

Acknowledgments I would like to thank Mr. Vijay Jethani (Regional Manager, Mumbai) in a leading IT company of India for his kind efforts in the perusal of my project. I would also like to extend my gratitude to Mr. Abir Bhowmick (Technical Lead) and Mr. Prosun Chakraborty for helping me and guiding me whenever required.

References

1. *Wi-Fi location-based services 4.1 design guide.* (2008). San Jose, CA, USA: Cisco Systems, Inc.
2. Bandyopadhyay, L. K., Chaulya, S. K., & Mishra, P. K. (2009). Wireless communication in underground mines. In *RFID-based Sensor Networking*. New York: Springer Science + Business Media (2009).
3. *Poor maintenance cited in West Virginia mine blast that killed 29.* (2011). The Associated Press, January 19, 2011.
4. *After 44 Hours, Hope Showed Its Cruel Side.* (2006). The Washington Post, January 5, 2006.
5. *NIOSH.* (2009). Advanced Tutorial on Wireless Communication and Electronic Tracking, 2009.
6. Ni, L. M., Zhang, D., & Souryal, M. R. (2011). Rfid-based localization and tracking technologies. *IEEE Wireless Communications, 18*, 45–51.
7. Tao, P., & Xiaoyang, L. (2011). Hybrid wireless communication system using ZigBee and WiFi technology in the coalmine tunnels. In *Proceedings of the International Conference on Measuring Technology and Mechatronics Automation (ICMTMA)*, 2011.
8. Hui, F. C. P., Chan, H. C. B., & Fung, S. H. (2014). RFID-based location tracking system using a peer-to-peer network architecture. In *Proceedings of the International MultiConference of Engineers and Computer Scientists (IMECS)*, vol. I. Hong Kong, 2014.
9. Cho, H., Jung, Y., Choi, H., Jang, H., Son, S., & Baek, Y. (2008). Precise location tracking system based on time difference of arrival over LR-WPAN. In *Proceedings of the ACM International Workshop on Mobile Entity Localisation and Tracking in GPS-less Environments*. San Francisco, California, USA, September 19, 2008.
10. Moen, H. L. (2007). *A study of Wi-Fi RFID tags in citywide wireless networks.* Norwegian University of Science and Technology, June 2007.
11. Wen, S., Fei, W., & Jianbo, D. (2010). A emergency communication system based on WMN in underground mine. In *Proceedings of the International Conference on Computer Application and System Modeling (ICCASM)*, 2010.
12. Garkan, S., Guzelgos, S., Arslan, H., & Murphy, R. (2009). Underground mine communications: A survey. *IEEE Communications Surveys and Tutorials, 11*(3), 125–142.
13. Nerguizian, C., Despins, C. L., Affès, S., & Djadel, M. (2005). Radio-channel characterization of an underground mine at 2.4 GHz. *IEEE Transactions on Wireless Communications, 4*(5), September 2005.

Partition-Based Frequent Closed Pattern Miner

Anu Soni, Mukta Goel and Rohit Goel

Abstract Frequent closed pattern (FCP) mining has been an important step in data mining research. This paper introduces an algorithm to deal with the problem of finding out (FCP) from a given set of transactions. The miner works on a parallel approach based on compact matrix division to partition the data set. To filter these subtasks two methods are adopted (1) transaction set redundancy removal method and (2) itemset redundancy removal method. Mining of filtered subtasks are done separately. Consolidated result obtained from mining of these filtered independent partitions show all FCPs present in transactions.

Keywords Frequent closed pattern · Mining algorithm · Parallel mining

1 Introduction

Frequent patterns (FP) are itemsets, substructures, or subsequences that appear in a data set with occurrence more than or equal to a user-specified threshold. Frequent patterns play a necessary role in showing interesting relationships among data such associations, correlations, causality as well as it has its own importance in data indexing, clustering, association-based classification, and other data mining tasks as well [1, 2, 3]. However, the number of frequent patterns can be too large to handle and if data is dense or low threshold frequency is used then this complication become vanquish. To overcome this problem, a new term is introduced which is

A. Soni (✉) · M. Goel · R. Goel
The Technological Institute of Textile and Sciences, Bhiwani, India
e-mail: anusunalia@gmail.com

M. Goel
e-mail: rishu.muk@gmail.com

R. Goel
e-mail: rohit_160@rediffmail.com

© Springer Science+Business Media Singapore 2016
S.C. Satapathy et al. (eds.), *Proceedings of International Conference on ICT for Sustainable Development*, Advances in Intelligent Systems and Computing 409, DOI 10.1007/978-981-10-0135-2_45

459

known as frequent closed patterns (FCP) [1, 4]. FCP is a pattern for which no superset exists which has occurrence more than or equal to that pattern [1– 3, 5]. Some notable FCP mining schemes include APRIORI [1], PATTERN–GROWTH APPROACH FOR FCP MINING [1], CLOSET+ [6], C-MINER [4], D-miner [7], and SLIDING WINDOW BASED ALGORITHM. Despite the fact that these algorithm work for small amount of data set well but when it comes to handle large data set, either they work very inefficiently or they do not work. Here a partition-based FCP miner is introduced that mine FCP from dense data effectively and increasingly. This algorithm is different from previous ones because of the following benefits: (1) it handles duplicacy in starting and does not let data go duplicate in further processing, (2) it compresses and divides data based upon compact matrix division strategy, and (3) it divide partitions mined independently thus impose parallelism.

2 Related Work

There are a number of previous proposed actions which deals with FP mining. But numbers of FPs are very large and difficult to handle. Thus procedures for FCP mining came into existence because number of FCPs are less and easy to handle. Few important algorithms proposed so far are PRIORI [1], PATTERN–GROWTH APPROACH FOR FCP MINING [1], and CLOSET+ [6]. These algorithms are good and able to find all FCPs, but these methods cannot work for dense data set. FCP mining algorithm CARPENTER is designed to work with large columns and small rows. CARPENTER combines the depth first with row enumeration strategy with some efficient search techniques, which results in a scheme that performs traditional closed pattern (CP) mining. Another algorithm B-MINER [4] is designed to divide the data with the help of base row projections technique and then mined independently each divided pattern. C-MINER [4] also used same strategy, but division is based upon compact matrix division method. Although these two algorithms are quite good even in case of dense data, they do not handle row duplicacy in starting, thus inefficient. D-miner [7] works for dense data set. However, the efficiency of D-miner highly depends on the minimum number of the data set's rows/columns containing "0." More the zero less is the efficiency. Thus, when the data set has a relatively large number of rows and columns, D-miner loses its beneficiation. Computational cost of data mining is very high, so a lot of attempts are made to design parallel and distributed algorithms. A lot of extensions are made of algorithms like APRIORI, ParEclet, etc., to convert them into parallel algorithm but these are still very costly. Till now attempts to find a good parallel algorithm for FCP mining is going on.

3 Definitions

Key concepts used in frequent pattern mining are:-

Transaction database — If there are n number of transactions and m are number of items available then $T = \{t_1, t_2. \,. \,.t_n\}$ be a transaction database, here each $t_j \in T, \forall j = \{1 \,\ldots. \, n\}$

Itemset — Each transaction consists of a set of items, say $t_j = \{i_1, i_2, i_3 \ldots . \, i_m\}$.

Pattern — A set $P \subseteq t_j$ is called a pattern.

Pattern length — Number of items contained in a pattern is called Pattern length.

Support — Number of transactions in which a pattern appears is known as support of pattern.

Frequent pattern — A pattern P is defined as frequent pattern if its support is at least equal to the minimum threshold.

4 Proposed Work

Here an algorithm is introduced which not only mine frequent pattern on the basis of threshold will support, but also on basis of threshold pattern length. This algorithm first takes transaction in which frequent pattern mining is performed. This input is then converted into binary matrix such that transactions are represented by rows, and items are represented by columns. Suppose if a transaction t_j contains item i_k then cell c_{jk} of matrix contains value "1" else it contains "0." All rows of matrix are scanned properly to find out identical rows in matrix; if there are any identical rows present in matrix then they are collectively treated as a single row rather than multiple rows. Now data of this binary matrix is compressed using clustering. This compressed data is divided into various tasks using zero removal principle. Now these divided tasks are scanned properly to check if there is any duplicate subtasks exist, if exist then only one of them is taken. These subtasks are mined independently. Result obtained from mining of every subtask is collected together to produce overall result. Control of flow throughout the process in Flow charts 1 and 2.

Working of algorithm

Suppose 9 transactions and 5 items are given in Table 1 and we have to find number of FCPs to decide a market strategy for it.

Various steps involved in finding FCPs

Step 1 Conversion into binary matrix

First of all whole data is converted into a Boolean context. Binary conversion of Table 1 is shown in Table 2.

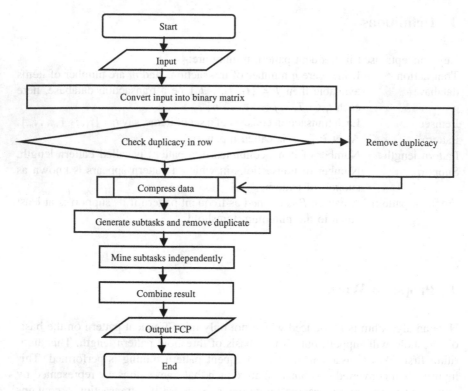

Flowchart 1 Partitioned-based FCP-miners

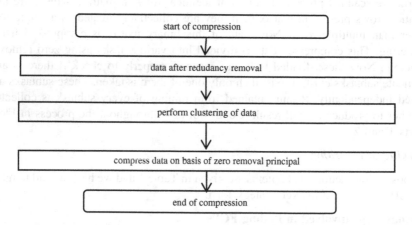

Flowchart 2 Compression technique used

Table 1 Sample data set

TID	List of items
t_1	i_1, i_2, i_5
t_2	i_2, i_4
t_3	i_2, i_3
t_4	i_1, i_2, i_4
t_5	i_1, i_3
t_6	i_2, i_3
t_7	i_1, i_3
t_8	i_1, i_2, i_3, i_5
t_9	i_1, i_2, i_3

Table 2 Binary data set

r/c	i_1	i_2	i_3	i_4	i_5
t_1	1	1	0	0	1
t_2	0	1	0	1	0
t_3	0	1	1	0	0
t_4	1	1	0	1	0
t_5	1	0	1	0	0
t_6	0	1	1	0	0
t_7	1	0	1	0	0
t_8	1	1	1	0	1
t_9	1	1	1	0	0

Table 3 Removal of duplicate rows

C	i_1	i_2	i_3	i_4	i_5
t_1	1	1	0	0	1
t_2	0	1	0	1	0
t_4	1	1	0	1	0
t_8	1	1	1	0	1
t_9	1	1	1	0	0
t_3, t_6	0	1	1	0	0
t_5, t_7	1	0	1	0	0

Step 2 combine identical rows together

Rows which are exactly same are combined, i.e., multiple rows are considered as one, so there is no need to process them differently throughout the process. Data set after removal of duplicate rows is shown in Table 3.

Step 3 Perform rowwise clustering

Now rowwise clustering is performed. Any of the clustering techniques [8] can applied, here those rows are clustered together in which at least half the number of total items are similar. To represent a cluster, item wise ORing of all rows in a

Table 4 Clustering

r/c	i_1	i_2	i_3	i_4	i_5
$c_1(t_1)$	1	1	0	0	1
$c_2(t_2, t_4)$	1	1	0	1	0
$c_3(t_3, t_5, t_6, t_7)$	1	1	1	0	0
$c_4(t_8, t_9)$	1	1	1	0	1

Table 5 Generators

$G(A, B)$
$G_1(c_1, i_3i_4)$
$G_2(c_2, i_3i_5)$
$G_3(c_3, i_4i_5)$
$G_4(c_4, i_4)$

cluster is taken, i.e., $c(t_a, t_b, ...t_z) = t_a \vee t_b \vee ...t_z$. After clustering of transactions in Tables 3 and Table 4 is obtained.

Step 4 Generation of generators

If G represents generator, A indicates clusters, and B indicates itemset then $G(A,B)$ is said to be a generator. $G(A,B)$ will take only those values for which A has 0 in Bth column. For Table 3 generators are given by Table 5.

Sorting of generators on the basis of number of items

As generators are used to divide given task by removing useless zeros, we take generator which has largest number of items, by which we are able to remove more zeros in the starting. So sorting of generators is performed in descending order of number of items, generators after sorting is completed.

Step 5 Partition into subtasks

With the help of generators, a binary tree is made. A node is represented by (cluster set, itemset). Root node contains all clusters and items. Now generators are applied one by one to generate left and right child. A left child derived from a node contains all clusters and itemset which are in node except the clusters present in generator. A right child derived from a node contains all clusters and itemset which are in node except the items present in generator. Child having support or pattern length less than threshold support or threshold pattern length are dropped. Minimum threshold support is 2 and minimum pattern length threshold is 2. Tree generated using Tables 4 and 6 is shown in Fig. 1. Here leaf nodes are represented by double

Table 6 Sorted generators

$G(A, B)$
$G_1(c_1, i_3i_4)$
$G_2(c_2, i_3i_5)$
$G_3(c_3, i_4i_5)$
$G_4(c_4, i_4)$

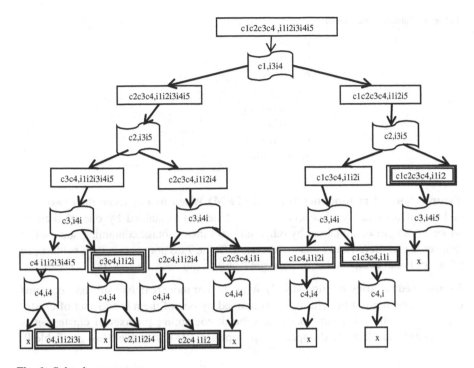

Fig. 1 Subtasks generators

Table 7 Subtasks

Cluster, itemset
$c_4,\ i_1i_2i_3i_5$
$c_3c_4,\ i_1i_2i_3$
$c_2,\ i_1i_2i_4$
$c_2c_4,\ i_1i_2$
$c_2c_3c_4,\ i_1i_2$
$c_1c_4,\ i_1i_2i_5$
$c_1c_3c_4,\ i_1i_2$
$c_1c_2c_3c_4,\ i_1i_2$

boundary rectangles. Subtasks obtained by this process are given in Table 7. Sometimes, more than one subtasks contain the same clusters, but items contained by them can be a superset of other and vice versa. This duplicacy need to be handled in subtasks, otherwise they move through all process and make algorithm inefficient. To make algorithm efficient, two strategies are used, and these are **(1) Transaction set redundancy removal method and (2) Itemset redundancy removal method.**

Table 8 Subtasks after TRM

Cluster, itemset
$c_4,\ i_1i_2i_3i_5$
$c_3c_4,\ i_1i_2i_3$
$c_2,\ i_1i_2i_4$
$c_2c_4,\ i_1i_2$
$c_2c_3c_4,\ i_1i_2$
$c_1c_4,\ i_1i_2i_5$
$c_1c_3c_4,\ i_1i_2$
$c_1c_2c_3c_4,\ i_1i_2$

Transaction set redundancy method (TRM) When two or more than two sub-tasks contains exactly same cluster set but itemset contained by one of them is superset of itemset contained by other subtasks then subtask containing superset of itemset is considered and other are dropped. Table 7 do not contain such subtask, so after applying TRM on Table 7 we get Table 8.

Itemset redundancy method (IRM) When two or more than two subtasks contains exactly same itemset but cluster set contained by one of them is superset of cluster set contained by other subtasks then subtask containing superset of cluster set is considered and other are dropped. After applying IRM on Table 8 we get Table 9.

Table 9 Subtasks considered

Subtasks	Cluster involve	Column set	Item set	Support	No. of items involve
s_1	c_4	$i_1i_2i_3i_5$	t_8t_9	2	4
s_2	c_3c_4	$i_1i_2i_3$	$t_3t_5t_6t_7t_8t_9$	6	3
s_3	c_2	$i_1i_2i_4$	t_2t_4	2	3
s_4	$c_1c_2c_3c_4$	i_1i_2	$t_1t_2t_3t_4t_5t_6t_7t_8t_9$	9	2
s_5	c_1c_4	$i_1i_2i_5$	$t_1t_8t_9$	3	3

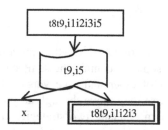

Fig. 2 Mined tree of subtask s_1

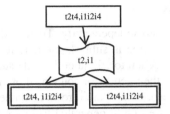

Fig. 3 Mined tree of s_3

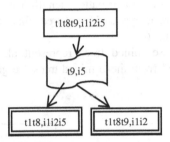

Fig. 4 Mined tree of subtask s_5

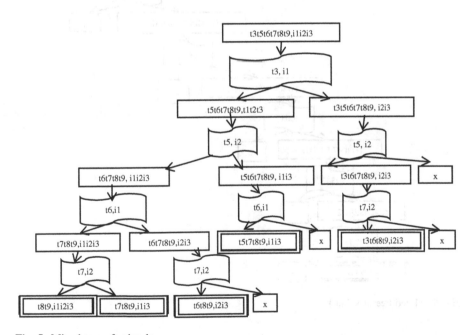

Fig. 5 Mined tree of subtask s_2

Step 6 mining of subtasks

Now these subtasks are mined independently. To mined subtask a binary tree is created. Root node of binary tree is subtask itself. Left and right node of tree is generated with the help of generator. If node is (T,I) such that T is set of transactions and I is set of items, then generator contains those rows and items for which row contain 0 value at corresponding item if rows contained in node has variance in value at that item position. Left child generated from a node contains all rows and items which are in node except row contained in generator. Right child generates from a node contains all rows and items which are in node except items contained in generator. Child having support or pattern length less than threshold support or threshold pattern length are dropped. Mined tree obtained from all subtasks are given by Figs. 2, 3, 4, 5 and 6.

Here leaf nodes of these mined trees represent all FCPs in corresponding transactions. FCPs obtained from these mined trees are given in Table 10.

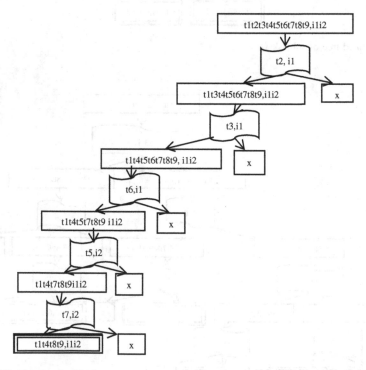

Fig. 6 Mined tree of subtask s_4

Table 10 FCPs generated

Row set	FCP
$t_1t_4t_8t_9$	i_1, i_2
t_8t_9	$i_1i_2i_3$
$t_7t_8t_9$	i_1i_3
$t_6t_8t_9$	i_2i_3
$t_5t_7t_8t_9$	i_1i_3
$t_6t_8t_9$	i_2i_3
t_2t_4	i_2i_4
t_1t_8	$i_1i_2i_5$
$t_1t_8t_9$	i_1i_2
t_8t_9	$i_1i_2i_3$

Table 11 Results

Resultant row set	FCP
t_8t_9	$i_1i_2i_3$
$t_1t_4t_8t_9$	i_1i_2
$t_5t_7t_8t_9$	i_1i_3
$t_6t_8t_9$	i_2i_3
t_2t_4	i_2i_4
t_1t_8	$i_1i_2i_5$

5 Results

Result can be obtained from Table 10 by removing duplicate FCPs. FCPs obtained after removal of duplicate FCPs are given in Table 11.

6 Conclusion

In this paper, partition-based FCP miner is proposed which handle identical rows as one row in the beginning. The key idea is to compress data and partition it into various subtasks. These subtasks are filtered using TRM and IRM. Mining of filtered subtasks is done independently and parallely. This algorithm facilitates parallel mining even in case of dense data set with high efficiency. Transaction wise results are obtained which use efficiently in market strategy designing.

References

1. Han, J., & Kamber, M. *Data mining concept and techniques*, 3rd edition.
2. Mannila, H., Toivonen, H., & Verkamo, A. I. (1994). Efficient algorithms for discovering association rules. In *Proceedings of the 12th National Conference on Artificial Intelligence (AAAI '94) Workshop Knowledge Discovery in Databases (KDD '94)* (pp. 181–192), 1994.
3. Zaki, M., Parthasarathy, S., Ogihara, M., & Li, W. (1997). New algorithms for fast discovery of association rules. In *Proceedings of the Third International Conference on Knowledge Discovery and Data Mining (KDD '97)* (pp. 283–286), 1997.
4. Ji, L., Tan, K. L. Member, IEEE Computer Society, & Tung, A. K. H. (2007). Compressed hierarchical mining of frequent closed patterns from dense data sets. *IEEE Transactions on Knowledge and Data Engineering, 19*(9), September 2007.
5. Han, J., Cheng, H., Xin, D., & Yan, X. (2007). Frequent pattern mining: Current status and future directions. Received: 22 June 2006/ Accepted: 8 November 2006/ Published online: 27 January 2007, Springer Science + Business Media, LLC 2007.
6. Wang, J., Han, J., & Pei, J. (2003). CLOSET+: Searching for the best strategies for mining frequent closed itemsets. In *Proceedings of the Ninth ACM SIGKDD International Conference on Knowledge Discovery and Data Mining (KDD '03)* (pp. 236–245), 2003.
7. Besson, J., Robardet, C., & Boulicaut, J.-F. (2004). Constraint-based mining of formal concepts in transactional data. In *Proceedings of the Eighth Pacific-Asia Conference on Knowledge Discovery and Data Mining (PAKDD'04)* (pp. 615–624), 2004.
8. Soni, A., Goel, M., & Goel, R. (2015). Comparative study of various clustering techniques. In *Proceedings of the National Conference on Innovative Trends in Computer Science Engineering (KDD '94)* (pp. 148–150), 2015.

A Study of Working of Ad Auctioning by Google AdWords

Farhat Jahan, Pranav Fruitwala and Tarjni Vyas

Abstract The globe is migrating toward World Wide Web (WWW). Any task which is required to be performed manually is slowly moving toward web application. The web applications have emerged from simple static client side HTML pages to the complex word processors. Hence, the advertisers are also slowly transforming from their offline advertising to online advertising. Online advertising is helpful to the advertisers as it is behavioral advertising, i.e., tailored to the likely interest of the users. There are various services that offer online advertising, but here we will be focusing on Google's online advertising which is AdWords. AdWords have become the prime source of revenue for Google as the total advertising revenue from AdWords were $43.7 billion in 2012. AdWords uses specific organization to help the advertisers, and second prize algorithm which is beneficial for the advertisers as well as the users.

Keywords AdWords · AdRank · CTR · Ad position · Keyword match

1 Introduction

Google, Yahoo, and MSN have revolutionized the use of the WWW along with their way to advertise to the consumers [8]. The advantage of these search engines are that their search queries are short but still reveals a great deal of information. Due to this, it makes them able to display targeted ads to user.

F. Jahan (✉) · P. Fruitwala
Institute of Technology, Nirma University, Ahmedabad, India
e-mail: alfarhat.786@gmail.com

P. Fruitwala
e-mail: fpranav@gmail.com

T. Vyas
Computer Science & Engineering Department, Nirma University,
Ahmedabad, India
e-mail: tarjni.vyas@nirmauni.ac.in

© Springer Science+Business Media Singapore 2016
S.C. Satapathy et al. (eds.), *Proceedings of International Conference on ICT for Sustainable Development*, Advances in Intelligent Systems and Computing 409, DOI 10.1007/978-981-10-0135-2_46

471

Mechanisms used in online advertising are basically auctions, where individual businesses can place their bids on keywords and also specify their maximum daily budget. If the user clicks on the ad which is displayed in relevance to the search query, the search engine earns revenue. Unlike the conventional advertisers, search engine companies are able to cater to advertisers with lower budgets. In Google AdWords, advertisers participate in auctions to show their advertisements to users who come to Google and search for information [10].

AdWords is typically based on Pay-per-Click (PPC). It also offers Cost per Click, Cost per Thousand Impressions, or Cost per Acquisition advertising. It also allows local, national, and international distribution. The primary advantage of AdWords is the ads are short with a headline of 25 characters followed by two additional text lines of 35 characters each and display URL of 35 characters. Image ads are based on Interactive Advertising Bureau (IAB) standards.

2 Basics

In PPC advertising is effective because it mirrors the search process. The search process may seem to be simple; A searcher visits search engine, enters a search query, and receives results [3]. The key to long-term success on AdWords—and keeping your bid prices down—is always split testing two ads at the same time, then deleting the inferior one, and trying to beat the best one [7].

A. Google Search Network

It consists of group of search related websites where ads can appear. Group of website includes the Google search sites and other search partners I.E. non-Google search sites like AOL. When we choose this network for advertising, ads will be shown next to the search results. The bids you pay–per-click are lower than revenue per visitor you get. We use display network only, misspelled or negative keywords [6].

B. Google Display Network

It is a collection of websites including Google sites like Blogger, Finance, Gmail, and YouTube which display AdWords ads. This network gives a broader reach as it includes application and mobile sites. Wide range of users can be targeted by choosing specific sites and pages to appear on.

C. Click Through Rate

It is calculated as the ratio of numbers of clicks on the ad to number of times the ad has been displayed.

$$\text{Click/Expressions} = \text{CTR} \tag{1}$$

D. Cost Per Click

In this bidding, you pay for each click on your ads. You can set the highest amount that you are willing to pay for the click. This is also known as PPC.

E. Cost Per Thousand Impressions

In this type of bidding, you need to pay for each set of unique thousand views of your ad. This is highly suited for the advertisers who are focused on brand awareness. This bidding is not useful if your goal is sales or web traffic.

F. Cost Per Acquisition

In this bidding, you only pay for a conversion that is only when actions are likely to be taken on your website. It is also a part of Conversion Optimizer. It will focus on maximum number of conversions rather than clicks. You would still be paying for clicks, but AdWords will automatically set bid in such a manner that will help you get more conversions. Two types of CPA are:

(1) Target CPA: This is the average amount you are willing to pay for the conversion. Some bids may be above and some may be lower but altogether, conversion will target to the average target.
(2) Maximum CPA: This is the maximum amount you are willing to pay for the conversion but if you are using Conversion Optimizer, most of the bids will be below the maximum.

G. Automatic CPC

This bidding is like autopilot, where you allow AdWords to decide the bid automatically with the goal to get maximum possible clicks. Bid limit can also be set to see if the cost per click is not exceeding void.

3 AdWords Organization

AdWords typically follows layered organization. These layers are account, campaigns, ad groups, and ads (Fig. 1).

(1) Accounts are primarily associated with email id, password, and billing information. You can also give a backup credit card to continue your ads running if the primary payment options go out.
(2) Every campaign will have its own budget and settings to determine the appearance of your ads.
(3) Each ad group will have a set of similar ads and keywords, which triggers your ad to show.

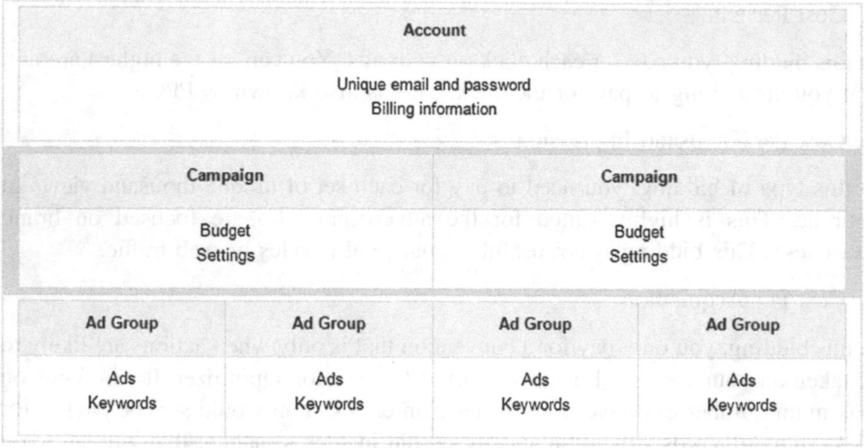

| Account |
| Unique email and password
Billing information |

| Campaign | | Campaign | |
| Budget
Settings | | Budget
Settings | |

| Ad Group | Ad Group | Ad Group | Ad Group |
| Ads
Keywords | Ads
Keywords | Ads
Keywords | Ads
Keywords |

Fig. 1 AdWords organization [1]

To reach out the maximum number of users, put related ads with related keywords in an ad group. Collection of ad groups will form a Campaign which is the master control for all ad groups. Campaigns allow you to control how much you want to pay for clicks or conversions, geographical locations where you want to display your ads, and other settings which can affect all the ad groups.

4 Keyword Matching in AdWords

To generate nonobvious and common keywords, TermsNet can be used which leverages search engines to determine relevance between terms and captures their semantic relationships as a directed graph [5]. Keyword match is used to control which search the trigger of the ad should be performed. Depending on the requirement, various match type can be selected as given in the table below. The narrower the keyword matching option is used, the more relevant ads will be displayed. Choosing the right keyword match can help you improve the investment. Each match type is specified by a special symbol (Fig. 2).

Some points to consider are:

(1) Keywords are not case-sensitive.
(2) The keyword match types can only be used in search network as display network only uses broad match.

Match type	Special symbol	Example keyword	Ads may show on searches that	Example searches
Broad match	none	women's hats	include misspellings, synonyms, related searches, and other relevant variations	buy ladies hats
Broad match modifier	+keyword	+women's +hats	contain the modified term (or close variations, but not synonyms), in any order	hats for women
Phrase match	"keyword"	"women's hats"	are a phrase, and close variations of that phrase	buy women's hats
Exact match	[keyword]	[women's hats]	are an exact term and close variations of that exact term	women's hats
Negative match	-keyword	-women	are searches without the term	baseball hats

Fig. 2 Types of keyword matching [1]

5 Auction in AdWords

Auction is the process that happens every time you do a search on Google to decide where ads will appear and its order. AdWords auction mechanism makes targeted, low-cost advertising available to almost everyone, and means that there is no need to hire specialized advertising agency [2].

- Everytime an ad becomes eligible to appear, it goes through the auction. Auction will decide whether to display ad or not and if yes then which position ads will be displayed.
- Here's how the auction works:
  (1) When you start a search, AdWords system will find all the ads related to keyword match.
  (2) From all the retrieved ads, nonrelevant ads will be ignored and the ads which are targeted for a specific geographical location are ignored.
  (3) From the remaining ads, the ads with higher AdRanks may be shown.
- The most important thing to remember is that even if your competition bids higher than you, you can still win a higher position—at a lower price—with highly relevant keywords and ads.
- Since the auction process is repeated for every search on Google, each auction can have potentially different results depending on the competition at that moment. Therefore it's normal for you to see some fluctuation in your ad's position on the page and in whether or not your ad shows at all.

A. Ad Position and AdRank

Ad position determines in which order your ad will be shown on a page. It can be shown on top of a search result, on the side or bottom of a page. The higher the ad position, the more customers will see the ad.

AdRank in the auction plays a vital role in determining the position of the ad. AdRank can be considered as a score which is calculated on the basic on your bid, ad format, expected impact, and the components of quality score. Quality score is determined using the expected CTR, ad relevance, and landing page experience. Quality of your ad text and user relevant landing page determines the quality components of AdRank. If there are two ads with same bid and quality, AdWords will display the ad with better expected impact from extensions.

B. Quality Score

Quality score determined for each keyword represents the quality of ads and landing pages that are triggered by that keyword. High quality score determines more relevance. To know the quality score of each keyword, AdWords provide keyword diagnosis.

Running a keyword diagnosis:

(1) Go to campaigns tab.
(2) Select keywords tab.
(3) Now you need to hover the speech bubble which is located next to the status of the keyword. You will see the complete quality score including the keyword relevance, landing page loading time, and landing page experience.

Quality score is basically assigned on scale of 1–10 where 1 is lowest and 10 indicating the highest. Quality score is just meant to let the advertiser know the quality of ads. It does not consider any auction time factors. You can consider quality score as descriptive estimate. When in auction, AdWords considers real-time measurements and computes AdRank and this determines where your ad will appear.

(1) How components of Quality Score affect AdRank?
    Now here, we will be considering some of the factors which on improving can help you improve quality components of AdRank.

  (1) Your ad's expected CTR: This is determined by ad's history like how many clicks it got or number of impressions. It does not take into consideration about the ad position, extensions, and other ad formats.
  (2) Your display URL's past CTR: The number of impressions and clicks your display URL has received.
  (3) The quality of your landing page: What is the relevance, transparency, and the ease of navigation of the page.
  (4) Your ad/search relevance: How much is the relevance of the ad text to the search.
  (5) Geographic performance: How successful is the campaign in a particular geographical region you are targeting.
  (6) Your targeted devices: How well the ads are performing on different devices.

(2) How ad quality affects advertiser?: Quality components can affect various things in your account such as:

    (1) Ad auction eligibility: Ad quality can determine whether ad will qualify to appear or not. Also it makes it easy and cheap for a good quality ad to enter in auction.

    (2) Your actual cost-per-click (CPC): The more the ad quality the lesser you pay per click.

    (3) Your keyword's first page bid estimate: It is easy to display the ads on the first page of search results as they are typically associated with lower first page bid estimates.

    (4) Your keyword's top of page bid estimate: It is easy to display the ads on the first page of search results as they are typically associated with lower first page bid estimates.

    (5) Ad position: Higher quality ads can result in better ad positions.

    (6) Eligibility for ad extensions and other ad formats: There is possibility that some ad formats require minimum ad quality threshold. Also AdRank determines whether the ad is eligible with extensions and other ad formats.

Higher quality ads will lead to lower costs and better ad positions. The AdWords system works best for advertisers, customers, publishers, and Google. More success can be achieved by relevant ads as they will earn more clicks and higher ad position.

C. Landing Page Experience

Landing page experience can simply be referred as the webpage the users land after clicking on the ad. Some factors to consider when improving landing page experience:

- Relevance and original content,
- Transparency and trustworthy,
- Ease of navigation, and
- Attractiveness and quick page loading encouraging customers to spend more time.

Better landing page can not only increase your quality score but also has an impact on AdRank and advertising costs. The landing page should be such that it is easy for the visitors to sign up or purchase.

(1) Improving Landing Page Experience: AdWords uses combination of auto-mated systems and human evaluation to determine landing experience. If your ad is pointing to a website which can result in poor user experience it can result in the number of times your ad will be shown. A tune up is required to improve the landing page experience.

    (1) Relevant, useful, and original content

        - Relevance between the ad text and keyword.
        - Landing page should contain useful information about the advertisement.
        - Useful features or content determining the uniqueness of the site.

(2) Transparency and trustworthiness

- Contact page should be easy to find.
- Make the customers clear about why you need the personal information and what will you do with it.
- Site content and sponsored ads should be distinguished.
- Share information about the business.

(3) Ease of navigation

- Does not make people jump from one page to another for the information.
- Product ordering should be quick and easy.
- Less interference with the navigation of the site by pop ups or other features.
- Information on advertised product should be easily available.

    Suppose, your landing page takes long time to load and the user clicks on the ad and gives up the website due to long waiting time and this can indicate Google about the poor landing page experience leading to negative impact.

(2) Landing Page Experience versus Site Policies: When Google reviews the landing pages, sometimes it finds pages which do not follow the advertising policies. This can include pages like malware infected pages or virus resulting in a very bad landing page experience and hence AdWords will give "Not Applicable" as the landing page experience status. Website will be suspended and would not be allowed to advertise with AdWords.

In order to advertise on AdWords, you need to refer to policies which must be followed on landing pages and website. These policies are referred as Site Policies. If the advertiser does not follow the site policies, AdWords might suspend the site for policy violations.

6   AdWords Versus Adsense

Google search engine makes no money on its own or directly. Google's service like AdWords helps it to make all the money. Google's AdSense service helps to distribute ads of campaigns to online publishers. AdSense is available on mobiles, tablets, and YouTube.

A. Google AdWords

At the most basic level, Google AdWords manipulates search results to artificially prioritize an advertiser's website over other possible results [9]. AdWords is a service provided by Google to create ads. There are various tools available for this. Also it allows to open free accounts. Tool helps in choosing relevant keywords and with relevance keywords the advertisement can be displayed alongside Google search results. As AdWords cover the search as well as the display network, it reaches huge number of users seeking information. The whole AdWords business runs on the PPC (Pay Per Click) basis. It is also simple and efficient allowing businesses to track the results from their campaigns.

B. Google AdSense

Hundreds of thousands of websites show AdWords ads on their pages as part of the AdSense program, which pays website owners who show AdWords ads on their sites [4]. AdSense can be considered as a distributor for the ads produced by AdWords. It helps to place ads at the most relevant locations. AdSense is freely available for online publishers. The publishers can sign up with Google. Once sign up is completed, Google evaluates the site overall. Once the publisher becomes approved it gets the code which will allow them to display Google ads.

Think of Google's AdWords and AdSense as two complementary parts of Google's advertising program:

- AdWords allow business to sign up and create ads to be displayed across the Google network.
- AdSense lets web publishers to partner with Google to help in spreading of the advertisement for a share of profit.

7 Conclusion

In this paper, we have discussed the basic terminologies used by Google AdWords and how it calculates the click through rate of the advertisements. We also saw list of other services which provides services like AdWords. AdWords organization was discussed in detail. We saw how Google uses different types of keyword matching during the bidding. We took a deep insight on the working of the auction of AdWords and how ad position and AdRanks are allocated to the ads. We also considered the quality score, the landing page experience, and running a keyword diagnosis. Detailed difference is also discussed between AdWords and AdSense to understand both the terms clearly and how they complement each other.

References

1. https://support.google.com/adwords/#topic=3119071.
2. Davis, H. (2006). *Google advertising tools: Cashing in with AdSense*. AdWords, and the Google APIs, O'Reilly Media, Inc.
3. Geddes, B. (2014). *Advanced google AdWords*. Wiley.
4. Jacobson, H., McDonald, J., & McDonald, K. (2011). *Google AdWords for dummies*. Wiley.
5. Joshi, A., & Motwani, R. (2006). *Keyword generation for search engine advertising*.

6. www.ppchero.com/10-alternatives-to-google-adword/.
7. Marshall, P. (2004). *Playing to win in google AdWords: How to structure your campaigns for maximum results from the very beginning.*
8. Mehta, A., Saberi, A., & Vazirani, V. (2007, Auguest). AdWords and generalized on-line matching. *ACM Transactions on Computational Logic, V.*
9. Tan, A. (2010). Google AdWords: Trademark infringer or trade liberalizer. *Michigan Telecommunications and Technology Law Review, 16*(2).
10. Yoon, S., Koehler, J., & Ghobarah, A. (2010). Prediction of advertiser churn for Google AdWords. *JSM Proceedings.*

A Novel Approach for Polarity Determination Using Emoticons: Emoticon-Graph

Manalee Datar and Pranali Kosamkar

Abstract Owing to the rising popularity of social networking sites and chat-based applications, visual sentiment clues such as emoticons are increasingly being used in blogs, tweets, games, and product reviews. The existing sentiment analysis tools mainly focus on predicting the polarity based on textual content, and displaying the results in the form of graphs or charts. In this paper, we propose a system to account for emoticons and exclamation marks along with words while performing sentiment analysis of the input text. The output of this analysis is represented on a unique figure, which we define as an 'emoticon-graph'. An online survey was conducted to collect product and news reviews to analyze the sentiment and also to evaluate the acceptance of the 'emoticon-graph'. The findings of this survey indicate that dynamically plotted emoticon-graphs could play a major role in simplifying the results of polarity determination methods.

Keywords Emoticons · Sentiment analysis · Polarity determination · Emoticon-graph

1 Introduction

The volume, variety, and velocity of electronic communication have increased by leaps and bounds in the past few years. The modes of expressing feelings and opinions range from messages on chat applications and online forums to emails, blogs, tweets, etc. Thus, any social, political or religious event, new product, sports tournament, or even climate change is analyzed and discussed on the internet, by people from every corner of the world. This generates an immensely large volume of unstructured data. Proper sorting and processing of this data yields rich infor-

M. Datar · P. Kosamkar (✉)
Department of Computer Engineering, Maharashtra Institute
of Technology, Pune, India
e-mail: Pranali.kk@gmail.com

© Springer Science+Business Media Singapore 2016
S.C. Satapathy et al. (eds.), *Proceedings of International Conference
on ICT for Sustainable Development*, Advances in Intelligent Systems
and Computing 409, DOI 10.1007/978-981-10-0135-2_47

mation, which is useful for scientists, policy makers and many companies. This requirement gives rise to various sentiment analysis methods.

Sentiment analysis involves a systematic method of understanding and analyzing views or opinions on specific topics. By developing tools to perform this study, we save a lot of time and efforts, otherwise required to manually analyze the entire data. The past few years have witnessed an ever-increasing usage of symbols like emoticons, stickers, or hand gestures in electronic communication. Technically, an emoticon is a string of keyboard characters, which seem to suggest a facial expression. Emoticons are often used to compensate the lack of facial expressions in text messages [1]. Hence, it is important for sentiment analysis algorithms to take into account these graphical clues. Studies suggest that emoticons affect viewers in ways similar to facial expressions, while triggering other unique effects too [2]. They impact message interpretation in computer-mediated communication [3]. In order to determine the exact emotions that are conveyed, emoticon samples extracted from the web using various methods have been annotated automatically [4, 5]. By mapping 95 emoticons into 4 categories of sentiments and processing them further, an online real-time sentiment monitoring system called MoodLens was developed. Previous research has also shown that the whenever emoticons are used, their associated sentiment dominates the sentiment conveyed by textual cues and forms a good proxy for intended sentiment [7]. Linguistic analysis of student chat conversations done by Maness proved emoticons as an important means of online communication [8].

2 Framework

While developing an algorithm for sentiment analysis it is important to take into consideration the role played by emoticons. On these lines, our framework has been developed to process the document and determine the sentiment that it conveys. The input would be a text file containing chat messages, tweets or product reviews, with or without emoticons. Before processing the input, a sentiment database containing commonly used positive and negative words and emoticons is defined. In future, this database could be expanded to include more words and emoticons, by applying specific machine learning algorithms on the unmatched tokens from the input document.

After defining the sentiment database, the input file is accepted for processing. Initially, it is split into a number of tokens depending upon its length. The tokens are obtained on the basis of delimiters like blank spaces, punctuation marks, and new lines. Whenever a punctuation mark is encountered, the characters following that mark are checked. Consecutive presence of more than one different punctuation mark indicates the presence of an emoticon. For example, if ":" is immediately followed by ")", then this character sequence could be a possible emoticon. Hence, such a set of punctuation marks is separated as one token. After the entire input is separated into tokens, each token is compared with the contents of the sentiment database. Tokens containing alphabets are compared with words and those containing a series of punctuation marks are compared with emoticons. Initially, the positive and negative score (denoted by pos_score and neg_score) is set to zero. Whenever a token is matched with a positive word or emoticon from the sentiment database, pos_score is incremented by 1. Similarly, a token matched with a negative word or emoticon would increment neg_score by 1.

To enhance the accuracy of this process, another addition is the consideration of repetitive usage. It is observed that multiple similar emoticons or exclamation marks are used consecutively to stress on the sentiment being conveyed. For example, the statement—'the test was bad!!!!!' indicates a greater degree of negativity than the statement—'the test was bad!'. Similarly, the statement—'the dress

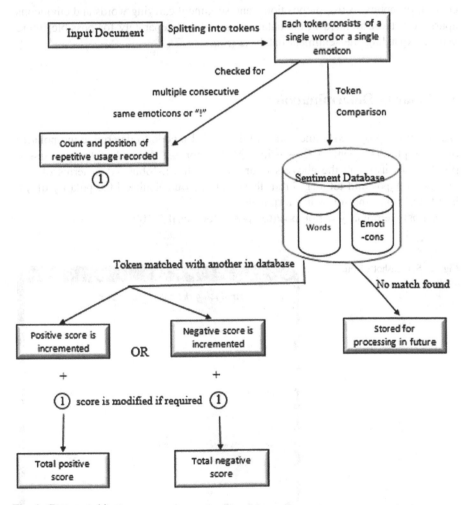

Fig. 1 System architecture

is beautiful! ☺ ☺ ☺' indicates a higher positive intensity than the statement—'the dress is beautiful! ☺'. For a particular statement containing more than one consecutive exclamation marks or same emoticons, the score is incremented as follows:

If pos_score > neg_score,

Then, pos_score = pos_score + [(count of repetitive emoticons or exclamation marks)/2]

If neg_score > pos_score,

Then, neg_score = neg_score + [(count of repetitive emoticons or exclamation marks)/2]

This feature ensures that while determining the polarity, the sentiment which is emphasized in the input text is taken into account. Thus, all tokens are compared with those in the sentiment database and the total positive and negative score (denoted by tot_pos and tot_neg) is calculated. The unmatched tokens which could contain pronouns, verbs, prepositions, and sentiment carrying words and emoticons apart from those defined in the database, are stored separately for possible future use in expanding the sentiment database (Fig. 1).

3 Polarity Determination

Based on the proposed framework, we developed a code to determine the polarity of the input document in C++ using QT Creator. At the end of the processing pipeline discussed in the above section, the result was obtained in terms of two values—tot_pos and tot_neg. From these values, we calculated the polarity of the input text using the following formulae:

% positive polarity = [tot_pos/(tot_pos + tot_neg)] * 100

Fig. 2 Screenshot of our application

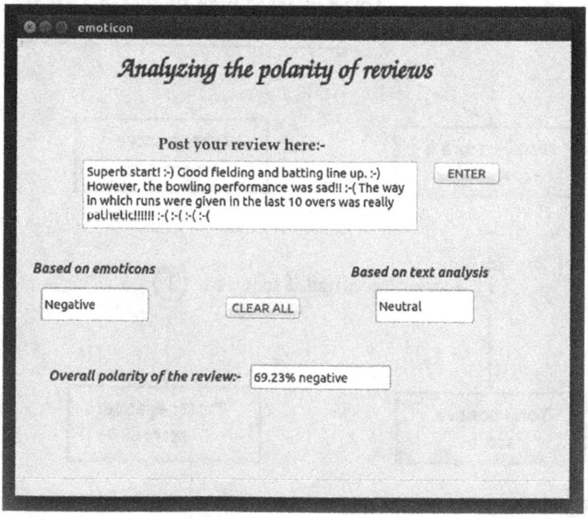

% negative polarity = [tot_neg/(tot_pos + tot_neg)] * 100

The final polarity was set as the greater value of the above two percentages. For example, if % positive polarity = 72 and % negative polarity = 28, then the final polarity of the document was said to be 72 % positive (Fig. 2).

4 Result Analysis

This code, including the formula for polarity determination was tested on a dataset containing 200 reviews. These reviews were collected from an online survey designed by us, in which the participants were asked to share their opinions regarding the results of a sports tournament and the popularity of two online applications. Initially, the reviews were manually analyzed by 3 people and the polarity for each review was given on a scale of 1–10. The average polarity for every review was calculated and converted into a percentage form. Then, the reviews were individually tested on our QT application and the polarity of each review was recorded. The second time, all the reviews were tested individually for determining the polarity, excluding the emoticons. For this testing, the sentiment database was modified to contain only positive and negative words and no emoticons. Thus, the polarity of all the reviews was calculated only on the basis of textual sentiment clues.

On comparing the polarities calculated by these two methods, it was found that, when emoticons were included in the sentiment database, the values obtained were closer to the manually assigned polarities. The difference between the results obtained by the two methods is evident from the following two graphs. For the ease of understanding, these graphs have been plotted only for the first 50 reviews from the dataset. However, a similar trend is observed for the entire dataset.

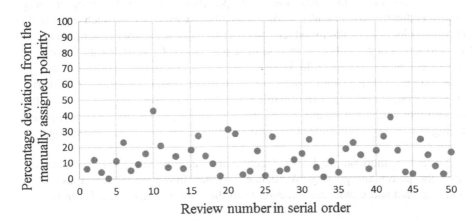

Graph 1 Including emoticons in polarity determination

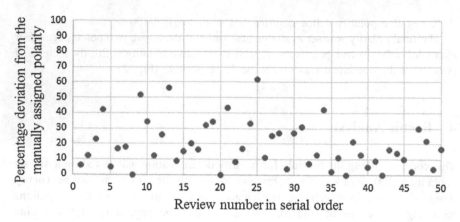

Graph 2 Excluding emoticons in polarity determination

As seen in Graphs 1 and 2, the reviews had a polarity deviation of more than 20 % when compared with the manually assigned polarities. Also the average polarity deviation for the first 50 reviews was 13.16 %. The second graph was plotted for the method in which emoticons were not considered while calculating the polarity. Here, nearly 20 reviews had a polarity deviation of more than 20 %. For this method, the average polarity deviation for the first 50 reviews was 19.1 %. Thus it is evident from the above results that, consideration of emoticons while determining the polarity is crucial for accuracy of the method.

5 Analysis Using Emoticon-Graph

The result obtained by the polarity determination method can be projected in various ways, on a bar graph, line graph, pie chart, etc. The drawback of using graphs is that the ease of understanding depends on various factors such as the scale chosen, color combination used, etc. In order to make the output easier to analyze, we propose a new method of representing the results. Considering the increasing use of emoticons to denote the intended sentiment, the polarity percentage is represented on a figure which we define as an emoticon-graph. This figure is primarily an emoticon, suggesting a face with eyes and a nose. The changing factor is the curve representing the mouth. By normal convention, in an emoticon, an upward facing curve suggests a smile or a positive feeling and a downturned curve suggests a sad feeling.

So in the emoticon-graph, the direction and angle of this curve is determined from the percentage polarity. We define the outer limits for this curve as 45° in both, upward and downward direction from the central horizontal axis, on the left and right sides. The possible values of polarity range from 0 to 100 % and the range of angles for the curve is from 0 to 90° (taking the lowest angle below the horizontal axis as 0° and highest angle above the horizontal axis as 90°). Based on these ranges, the formula for mapping the polarity on the curve is defined as follows:

Angle of the upward curve for positive polarity = (% polarity * 9)/10

Angle of the downward curve for negative polarity = 90 − [(% polarity * 9)/10]

So, according to this formula, the emoticon-graph for a few sample positive polarities can be drawn as shown (Fig. 3).

To find out whether such an emoticon-graph is actually easier to analyze as compared to the conventional graphs, we carried out an online survey in which 200 people participated. In the survey form, four graphs were displayed—bar graph, line graph, pie chart, and an emoticon-graph. The participants were asked to rate all the four graphs on the basis of ease of understanding and then select one graph out of the four which they would prefer to use. The results of the survey show that the proposed emoticon-graph was easier and faster to analyze as compared to the conventional graphs (Fig. 4).

50%   68%   84%

Fig. 3 Emoticon-graphs for positive polarities

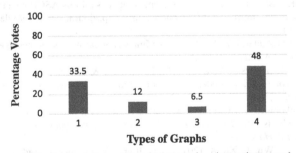

1: pie chart   2: bar graph   3: line graph   4: emoticon-graph

Fig. 4 Result of our online survey

6 Limitations

One of the limitations of the proposed framework is its inability to evaluate those words and emoticons which are not defined in the sentiment database. The total positive and negative scores are calculated only on the basis of matching tokens. Another drawback is that the emoticon-graph can only be used to represent outputs which have only two parameters. When the result contains multiple parameters to be plotted on a figure, the emoticon-graph cannot be used.

7 Conclusion

The findings of this survey indicate that dynamically plotted emoticon-graphs could play a major role in simplifying the results of polarity determination methods. The unique feature of our proposed system is the evaluation of emoticons and exclamation marks, along with words, for performing sentiment analysis of the input text. Also from the results of our survey, it is evident that emoticon-graphs are easier to analyze and preferred over the conventional graphs for studying the results of polarity determination methods. A full-proof method with proper validations, designed to generate these emoticon-graphs would prove to be an important step in the study of huge datasets.

References

1. Riva, G. (2002). The sociocognitive psychology of computer-mediated communication: The present and future of technology-based interactions. *CyberPsychology and Behavior 5*, 581–598.
2. O'Neill, B. (2013). Mirror, mirror on the screen, what does all this ASCII mean? A pilot study of spontaneous facial mirroring of emotions. url: http://journals.uvic.ca/index.php/arbutus/article/view/12681.
3. Walther, J. B., & D'Addario, K. P. (2001). The Impacts of emoticons on message interpretation in computer-mediated communication.
4. Ptaszynski, M., Maciejewski, J., Dybala, P., Rzepka R., & Araki, K. (2010). CAO: A fully automatic emoticon analysis system based on theory of kinesics. *IEEE Transactions on Affective Computing, 1*(1) 46–59.
5. Tanakay, Y., Takamura, H., Okumura, M. (2005). Extraction and classification of facemarks with Kernel methods. In *IUI '05 Proceedings of the 10th International Conference on Intelligent User Interfaces*.
6. Zhao, J., Dong, L., Wu, J., Xu, K. (2012). MoodLens: An emoticon-based sentiment analysis system for chinese tweets in weibo. In *Proceedings of the 18th Acm Sigkdd International Conference on Knowledge Discovery and Data Mining*.

7. Hogenboom, A., Bal, D., Frasincar, F., Bal, M., de Jong, F., Kaymak, U. (2013). Exploiting emoticons in sentiment analysis. In *Proceedings of the 28th Annual ACM Symposium on Applied Computing*.
8. Maness, J. M (2008). A linguistic analysis of chat reference conversations with 18–24 year- old college students. *The Journal of Academic Librarianship '08, 34*(1), 31–38.

Scheduling for Distributed Applications in Mobile Cloud Computing

Hitesh A. Bheda and Chirag S. Thaker

Abstract Mobile networks processing and Cloud Computing Approach can integrated as a unit called as Mobile Cloud Computing (MCC). Recent trends for ubiquitous device technology have resultant in smart mobile devices as future computing device and service accessible devices. Subscribers are intended to execute computational intensive tasks on Smart Mobile Devices (SMDs) as like capable standalone computer. Although SMDs are having less computing capacity as having limited CPU power, certain storage capacity, memory constraints, and limited battery life. To come out from these problems, MCC provides latest practical solution to improve limitation of capacity by spreading services as well resources of clouds to SMDs based on requirements. Existing algorithms upload computational intensive applications to distinct data centers using various cloud models. The problem belongs with such algorithms is the scheduling of distributed applications with often needs on demand resources on SMDs. This paper describes Scheduling approach for distributed intensive applications for SMDs in MCC Environment. The aim of this paper is to describe problems and challenges with an existing algorithm in creating, executing, and testing computational concentrated applications in MCC. This paper highlights the hierarchy of existing scheduling approach and analysis of consequences as well as current framework for critical aspects has been proposed.

Keywords Mobile cloud computing · Scheduling · Distributed applications · Intensive applications · Smart mobile device (SMD)

H.A. Bheda (✉)
School of Engineering, RK University, Rajkot, Gujarat, India
e-mail: hitesh.bheda@rku.ac.in

C.S. Thaker
Shantilal Shah Engineering College, Bhavnagar, Gujarat, India
e-mail: chiragthaker@yahoo.com

© Springer Science+Business Media Singapore 2016
S.C. Satapathy et al. (eds.), *Proceedings of International Conference on ICT for Sustainable Development*, Advances in Intelligent Systems and Computing 409, DOI 10.1007/978-981-10-0135-2_48

1 Introduction

Smart mobile devices (SMDs), PDAs, and cloud computing are touching in the latest, a quickly rising area of Mobile Cloud Computing (MCC) [1]. Within a span of time, there will be 1 trillion cloud-ready gadgets. MCC is the concept in which few levels of services are offered by a cloud and retrieved by mobility platforms [1]. Cloud computing allows suitable, on-demand network requirement to a shared pool of configurable computing resources, such as networks, servers, storage, applications, and services, that can be easily and quickly provisioned and released with minimum management effort or service provider's interaction [2, 3]. Cloud offers three service models: (i) Software as a Service (SaaS) [4], (ii) Platform as a Service (PaaS) [4], and (iii) Infrastructure as a Service (IaaS) [4]. MCC can be termed as [1] "the availability of cloud computing services in a mobile ecosystem. This incorporates many elements, including consumer, enterprise, femtocells (small cellular base stations), transcoding, end-to-end security, home gateways, and mobile broadband-enabled services."

This paper proposed scheduling approach for distributed applications in MCC. Section 2 describes the idea about Cloud Computing [4] model and MCC [4] paradigm. It also gives constraints to Mobile Cloud's SMDs. Section 3 demonstrates Scheduling policy for distributed applications in SMDs. At the end, Sect. 4 concludes Scheduling policy for intensive distributed applications.

2 Overview of Mobile Cloud Computing

MCC [4] can be considered as an integration of Mobile Computing and Cloud Computing functionalities.

2.1 What Is Cloud Computing?

Cloud Computing offers various companies to use computing power and other resources as a utility as like electricity—instead of generating it we use it. Same way no need to worry about production of computing power just uses it.

Cloud computing provides various characteristics for business organization and to end users [5]. As shown in Fig. 1, few important benefits of cloud computing includes:

- **On-Demand Self-service** [5]: User can exchange computing resources or devices for all categories of dynamic workload on-demand.
- **Resource Pooling**: Organizations or cloud subscribers can easily take rentbase resource advantages by resource pooling.

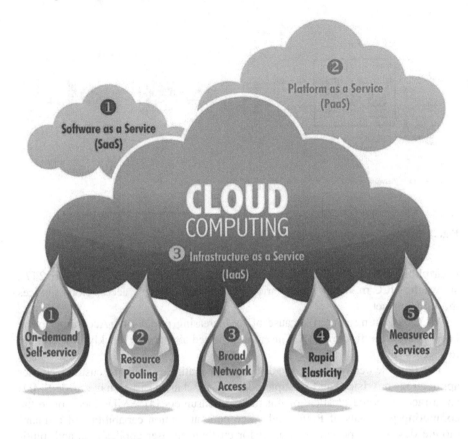

Fig. 1 Cloud computing [2] model

- **Broad Network Access**: Large amount of network can be accessed which is offered by cloud service providers.
- **Rapid Elasticity**: Organizations can scale up if requirements increase and it can be scale down if requirements decrease [5].
- **Measured Services**: Computing resources are captured at a level, permitting users to pay for the resources what they have used [5]. Its pay-as-you-go service.

2.2 What Is Mobile Cloud Computing (MCC)? [6]

"Mobile Cloud Computing at its simplest refers to an infrastructure where both the data storage and the data processing happen outside of the mobile device. Mobile cloud applications move the computing power and data storage away from mobile phones and into the cloud, bringing applications and mobile computing to not just

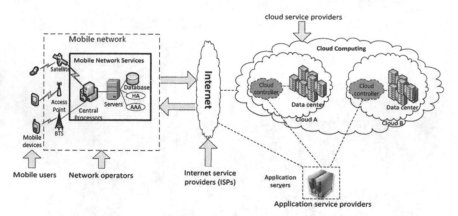

Fig. 2 Mobile cloud computing [6] model

smartphone users but a much broader range of mobile subscribers" [6]. Figure 2 [7], shows the MCC model in which various mobile users directly access cloud services through Internet.

MCC is gaining stream because of its increasing popularity. According to the latest survey, the figure of MCC users is expected to increase quickly in upcoming few years [8].

The portable behavior, flexible design, high quality resolutions, customized user applications provision, and multiple connectivity characteristics have made SMDs an attractive choice of attention for mobile consumers [4]. SMDs incorporate the computing potentials of PDAs and voice communication capabilities of ordinary mobile devices by providing support for customized user applications and multi-modal connectivity for accessing both cellular and data networks [4]. SMDs are controlled by their limited processing capacity, limited battery age, and limited storage. As we know that, cloud computing always offers unlimited resources and computing power capacity. New paradigm called MCC has been introduced which combines mobile devices and cloud computing in order to build a new infras-tructure [9], where cloud executes highly loaded computing intensive tasks [9] and store bulk data. Processing and Storage of data normally occur at outside of mobile instrument in MCC.

SMD applications influence this IT benefits to create below mentioned rewards [7]:

- Lengthy battery life
- Enhancement in computing and data storage capacity
- Data management improvement because of "store at central place, access from anywhere" [10] policy
- Consistency improvement and stability
- Access of incorporation.

Below benefits are forcing to adopt MCC approach:

- **On-demands**: users assume the suitability of using corporations' websites or application at any time and from any place. Mobile instruments can offer this suitability [9].
- **Enhanced broadband network**: Latest technologies like 3G, 4G, Wi-Fi, femto-cells, etc., offers best connectivity for SMDs [10].
- **Supporting technologies**: Recent technologies like HTML5, CSS3, virtualizations for smart phones, cloudlets, and Intelligent Web will ride acceptance of MCC [10].

Nowadays, according to increasing popularity of SMDs, MCC innovation focus on application user interface by constructing new software and service solutions. Various cloud-based storage services are present on cloud server for supplementing storage abilities of user devices [4]; like Amazon S3 [11], Google Docs [12], MobileMe [13], and DropBox [14]. Likewise, Amazon EC2 is the service offering of Amazon as a cloud service provider. The purpose behind MCC is to improve resources boundaries of SMDs by reducing services and computing resources of cloud datacenters [4].

3   Scheduling for Distributed Applications in SMDs

For distributed mobile application uploading intensive applications are uploaded to remote servers. Existing uploading process provides varied schemes for the distribution of execution time distributed application processing platform on SMDs [4]. The biggest problem in existing Scheduling Policy is the extra computing requirement on SMDs in placement and control of runtime distributed application finishing.

MCC employs cloud storage services [11–14] by offering cloud-based storage and cloud execution services to increase dispensation capacity of SMDs [15]. Large amount of online file storing applications are available on cloud data centers which improves the storing capacities by offering outside device storing facility. Amazon S3 [11] and DropBox [14] are the suitable products who offer cloud-based storage service to their users.

The current Scheduling Policy for intensive distributed applications for SMDs provides a variety of strategies for the creation of execution time distributed application execution platform. Here, we provide approach for Scheduling policy and examinations of the traditional approach on the basis of framework attributes [8]. Framework for existing approach again divided into VM Migration and Entire Application Migration policy.

Figure 3 shows Application Processing Approach and classification of intensive application uploading policy by their attributes. Here, we determine existing application uploading policy and inspects the inferences and dangerous approaches of existing scheduling of Distributed Application policy.

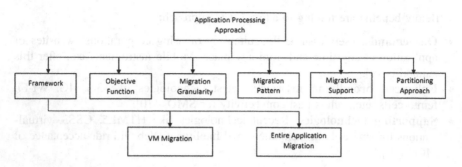

Fig. 3 Scheduling policy for distributed applications

3.1 VM Migration

For SMDs, uses of computational resources for computing devices are associated with Cyber framework [16]. The purpose of this framework is to create client/server model. On-demand services like process uploading and communicating with server are also going to be provided by this framework. To connect with multiple servers by its configurations and creation of Virtual Machines for remote application execution is also supported by this framework. An individual server is able to execute vast amount of individual virtual servers with separation, elasticity, resource management, and cleaning functionality. Isolated server can execute all uploaded applications. For the sake of security during communication between SMD and server, this framework normally uses cryptographic technique. This framework also provides best features like very small delay, locally accessibility, and easier interface with higher privacy and security standard. The challenge for this framework is to deploy template-based virtualized approach which acquire hire time consumption and also demand for higher amount of resources for deployment of VMs [17]. The limitation of this framework is that it restricts the availability of services as well as resource on local servers. Figure 4 shows the mapping of execution time for VM Migration versus Normal scenario. As we increase the number of applications, it requires comparatively lower execution time than normal scenario.

3.2 Entire Application Migration

Virtual Server Manager (VSM) is created by Lightweight secure cyber foraging infrastructure [15]. URL-based request can be directed from SMD to VSM to execute on server. URL can download entire program and execute it remotely. Hidden expansion technique for replica cloud [18] deploys complete application migration on remote host. Migration processes occur at remote local server and outcomes are available on Mobile device returned from background process. Antivirus and file indexing [4] for quick retrieval are the best example of this kind

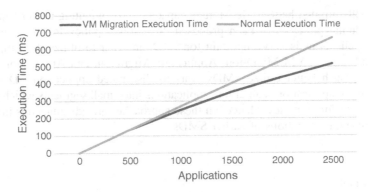

Fig. 4 Mapping of execution time for VM Migration versus normal scenario

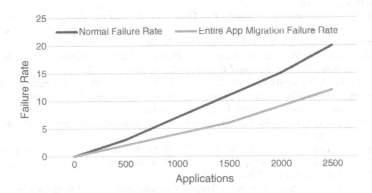

Fig. 5 Mapping of failure rate for entire app migration versus normal scenario

of application. The virtual cloud computing offering resolution for mobile devices [19] is an ad hoc cloud framework emphasis on the formation of virtual cloud of SMDs [4]. Architecture is build-up from various distinct components. Uploading main component is dedicated to send and receive complete application, control of execution time scattered atmosphere and identifying failure and failure administration. Figure 5 shows the mapping of failure rate for Entire App Migration versus Normal scenario. As we increase the amount of applications, the failure rate will be decreased compared to normal scenario.

4 Conclusion

Clear conception has been summarized for cloud computing platform, MCC platform as well as SMDs qualified portability and utility. In this paper, analysis of the current approach for distributed applications has been described. Also to resolve the problems like limited battery life, storage capacity and computing power capacity, and Scheduling policy have been proposed. Scheduling policy for intensive distributed applications is very important for SMDs in order to utilize its computing power and storage. VM Migration, Application Migration, and Application partitioning approach better utilize SMDs' various distributed applications. Dynamic partitioning of applications can divide applications into small segments which result in proper scheduling policy. Hence, all these approaches are advantageous in order to overcome the limitations of earlier SMDs.

References

1. Mobile Cloud Computing. http://public.dhe.ibm.com/software/dw/cloud/library/cl-mobileclo-udcomputing-pdf.pdf.
2. Abolfazli, S., Sanaei, Z., Ahmed, E., Gani, A., & Buyya, R. (2014). Cloud-based augmentation for mobile devices: Motivation, taxonomies and open challenges. *IEEE Communications Surveys & Tutorials, 16*(1), 337–368.
3. Whaiduzzaman, M., Sookhak, M., Gani, A., & Buyya, R. (2014). A survey on vehicular cloud computing. *Journal of Network and Computer Applications, 40*, 325–344.
4. Shiraz, M., Gani, A., Khokhar, R. H., & Buyya, R. (2013). A review on distributed application processing frameworks in smart mobile devices for mobile cloud computing. *IEEE Communications Surveys & Tutorials, 15*(3), 1294–1313.
5. Cloud Computing Fueling Startup Businesses. http://theavinashmishra.com/cloudcomputing-fueling-startup-businesses.
6. Hoang, T. D., Lee, C., Niyato, D., & Wang, P. (2011). A survey of mobile cloud computing: Architecture, applications and approaches. In *Wireless communications and mobile computing* (pp. 1–27). Wiley. doi:10.1002/wcm.1203.
7. Mobile Cloud Computing. http://www.freeinfoblog.com/mobile-cloud-virtualization.
8. Jia, W., Zhu, H., Cao, Z., Wei, L., & Lin, X. (2011). SDSM: A secure data service mechanism in mobile cloud computing. In *2011 IEEE Conference on Computer Communications Workshops (INFOCOM WKSHPS)*.
9. Kaur, K., & Walia, N. K. (2014). Survey on mobile cloud computing. *International Journal of Science and Research (IJSR), 3*(6), 2536–2540.
10. Smart Mobile Device Applications. http://thoughtsoncloud.com.
11. Amazon s3. http://status.aws.amazon.com/s3-20080720.html.
12. Google docs, http://docs.google.com.
13. Mobileme. http://en.wikipedia.org/wiki/MobileMe.
14. Dropbox. http://www.dropbox.com.
15. Zhang, X., Kunjithapatham, A., Jeong, S., & Gibbs, S. (2011). Towards an elastic application model for augmenting the computing capabilities of mobile devices with cloud computing. *Mobile Networks and Applications, 16*(3), 270–284.
16. Goyal, S., & Carter, J. (2004). A lightweight secure cyber foraging infrastructure for resource-constrained devices in Mobile Computing Systems and Applications. In *WMCSA 2004—Sixth IEEE Workshop* (pp. 186–195). IEEE.
17. Wang, K., Rao, J., & Xu, C. (2011). Rethink the virtual machine template. ACM SIGPLAN *Notices, 46*(7), 39–50.

18. Chun, B., & Maniatis, P. (2009). Augmented smartphone applications through clone cloud execution. In *Proceeding of 8th Workshop on Hot Topics in Operating Systems (HotOS)*, Monte Verita, Switzerland.
19. Huerta-Canepa, G., & Lee, D. (2010). A virtual cloud computing provider for mobile devices. In *Proceeding of 1st ACM Workshop on Mobile Cloud Computing & Services, Social Networks and Beyond* (p. 6). ACM.

High Availability of Databases for Cloud

Yogesh Kr. Sharma and Ajay Shanker Singh

Abstract In current cyber age, almost all the services are being provided to users over the cloud. Many of these services need to be highly available. Since these services require databases, the databases themselves must be made highly available. Redundancy is the technique of doing this. For this purpose Remus and its adaptation RemusDB use complete virtual machine migration to a backup host which is completely transparent to DBMS. This approach incurs a lot of overhead as the amount of data transferred to the backup host is large and this transfer is done very frequently. Another system Postgres-R works only with PostgreSQL databases. This system replicates data without taking into account the number of requests for a particular table and the load on the servers. In this paper, we proposed a solution which is based on another existing system Threshold-Based File Replication (TBFR) and uses the current system load to achieve load distribution.

Keywords Remus · RemusDB · Posrgres-R · PostgreSQL

1 Introduction

Nowadays, a large number of services are being provided to the users over the cloud. Some such services are banking, social networking, video streaming, etc. These services need to be up and running all the time. High uptime of a system is critical to the success of the service providers. Downtime results in financial losses

Y.Kr. Sharma (✉) · A.S. Singh
Galgotias University, Greater Noida, India
e-mail: yogesh.sgi1992@gmail.com

A.S. Singh
e-mail: ajay.shanker@galgotiauniversity.edu.in

© Springer Science+Business Media Singapore 2016
S.C. Satapathy et al. (eds.), *Proceedings of International Conference on ICT for Sustainable Development*, Advances in Intelligent Systems and Computing 409, DOI 10.1007/978-981-10-0135-2_49

and customer dissatisfaction. So, the uptime must be very high. In other words, such systems must be made highly available. High availability of systems implies that the databases at their backend must also be highly available. A user would want a service being available to him at all times, be it during the day or the middle of the night. Failure to provide access results in downtime and the system is said to be unavailable. High availability is a system design approach and associated service implementation that ensures that the systems are available for a certain amount of time governed by the contract or Service Level Agreement (SLA). Adding redundant components would increase the availability of services. But adding more components means that the number of points where failures can occur also increases. This can lead to fairly complex systems which can be extremely difficult to implement and maintain. Despite this inconsistency, most highly available systems use a simple architecture in which one high quality physical system with redundant hardware is used. The downside with such systems is that they need to be brought offline for maintenance (upgrading, patching, etc.). Newer systems eliminate this drawback by allowing patching and maintenance upgrade without any downtime. Such systems use load balancing and failover techniques.

The data replication approaches [5] vary with the types of nodes and their characteristics. A nonvolunteer node does not replicate or store anything; it just uses the system, whereas a volunteer node always replicates on demand and while quitting submits all at site updations to the hierarchical parent node or nearest neighbor node. The persistent nodes always replicate to increase availability maintaining data consistency.

Resources provisioning [9] like CPU, Memory through virtual machines versus provisioning through physical machines and evaluated the effect of different parameters on data transfer between Virtual Machines (VMs).

To handle multitenancy [4], a three tier data tables are used to increase sharing and reduce redundancy [8]. As far as replication is concerned a persistent data-server at the major area of operation. Failure transparency is achieved by mirroring itself. High availability is increased by replication. A complete replica is first stationed at the ad hoc site. Future updates are received at this node depending upon the bandwidth and availability.

Collaborative Trust Enhanced Security (CTES) model [7] is used in the process of node authentication and authorization for distributed cloud services. CTES model is more efficient than Kerberos despite of increase number of messages. Secure and Efficient Multitenant Database [6] is also used for high availability.

2 Related Work

A lot of work has been done to make systems highly available. The techniques used for doing this can also be used for databases. Here, we are discussing four such techniques.

2.1   Remus

Remus [1] is a software system that provides transparent high availability to ordinary VMs running on Xenon. It does this by continuously live migrating a copy of a running VM to a backup server which automatically activates if the primary server fails.

Its key features are:

(i)   The backupVM is an exact copy of the primaryVM (disk/memory/network). When a failure occurs, the VM continues running on the backup host as if the failure had never occurred.
(ii) The backup is completely up-to-date; even active TCP sessions are maintained without interruption.
(iii) Protection is transparent; existing guests can be protected without modifying them in any way.

2.2   RemusDB

Remus works well as a general purpose high availability solution. But it suffers a noticeable performance hit when it comes to database systems. RemusDB [2] is an improvement over Remus for databases. There are two reasons for the performance overhead caused by Remus and other similar VM check pointing systems.

(i)   Database systems make heavy use of memory. In normal check pointing, the complete memory state is transferred to the backup from the primary system. This amount of data is too large.
(ii) Database workloads can be sensitive to network latency. Any mechanism used to ensure that client-server communication survives failure adds latency.

The following observations help to adapt Remus to database workloads:

(i)   Not all changes to memory need to be sent to the backup. Remus transfers all the pages that have changed between epochs (time period between two consecutive checkpoints). Many page updates can be reconstructed or thrown away altogether in the case of working memory that can be recomputed or safely lost.
(ii) Not all transmitted messages need output commit. Network buffering of messages prevents the clients from seeing execution state that may be rolled back in case of a failure. But this intermediate state is already protected by transaction boundaries in a DBMS.
(iii) While changes to memory are frequent, they are often small. Remus uses hardware page protection to identify the pages that have changed in a given checkpoint and then transfers those pages to the backup at page granularity. But such changes to pages in database workloads are often smaller than page size and thus can be compressed.

2.3 Postgres-R

Postgres-R [3] is an extension to PostgreSQL database which provides efficient database replication for clusters while preserving the consistency. It only works with PostgreSQL databases. It is designed to be as transparent as possible to the client, stable and secure. It is primarily used for load balancing and high availability of database systems. The stretchy architecture of Postgres-R enables to scale the replication process. Further, compared to a centralized system it is more reliable and flexible. It can replicate large objects and uses a store and forward asynchronous replica engine. The crashed nodes are detected and removed automatically without affecting the operations of database system. It uses two-phase locking for concurrency control with locking at relation level.

Transaction execution in Postgres-R uses read-one-write-all approach and the transaction execution is divided into four phases. In local phase, the transaction is executed at local replica. In send phase, the updates to data are propagated to replicas. In synchronization phase, serializability of the transactions is preserved. In write phase, remote replicas execute the writes and respective replicas execute the transactions.

2.4 Threshold-Based File Replication (TBFR)

The TBFR [10] provides a file replication model for cloud, a client node requests a file from a file server. The file server replicates the file on other servers on the basis of the number of requests it receives for a particular file. A group of file replication servers works in peer-to-peer manner to provide the most updated version of files to clients and to make the replication process smooth and noncomplicated.

3 Proposed Solution

The existing systems do not take the load on the servers into account while replicating data. The proposed approach is based on the TBFR model and considers the current CPU load to intelligently replicate data and route requests on lightly loaded servers. The overall design of the system can be summarized as:

(i)   There is one manager program handling several database servers.
(ii) The clients send their requests to the manager which determines where to route the request.
(iii) The manager maintains a lookup table storing (key, value) pairs. The key is the pair (database, table) and the value is the list of nodes where this table is stored. Along with this, the current CPU load of each system running a database server is also stored.

(iv) The strategy for routing requests is read-one-write-all.

 (v) A read query is routed to one lightly loaded server. The clients directly query the database server whose address is returned by the manager.

(vi) A write query is propagated to all the replicas of the table in the query either asynchronously or synchronously. The manager executes writes on the database servers and the success/failure of the query is routed to the clients through the manager.

3.1 Design and Implementation

The system consists of three major modules:

 (i) Backend—For every node having an RDBMS, there is a Backend module running on the node. This module is responsible for sending metadata about the databases in the RDMBS to the Manager. The metadata includes the list of (database, table, version no.) triples. After connection with the Manager is established, it sends this metadata. Additionally, it periodically (every second) sends the CPU load of the node to the Manager. This load information is useful for routing requests to lightly loaded nodes.

 (ii) Client—This component is used for issuing queries to the databases present through the help of Manager and RDBMS systems. It supplies the Manager with the name of the databases and the tables to query. It also supplies the query to be executed if it is a write query. It is aware of the schema of the databases and thus, knows exactly what is to be queried.

(iii) Manager—This is the central coordinator of the system. All the Backend and Client instances communicate with this component to carry out their tasks. The Manager implements the routing logic and is responsible for maintaining consistency of the replicas. After it receives a request to execute a query from a Client instance, it finds out which Backend to route the requests to depending on the type of query and CPU load.

To handle multiple Clients and Backends simultaneously, the Manager makes extensive use of threads. It listens on two ports for incoming connections; one for Clients and the other for Backends. Once a connection is established with a Client or a Backend, the Manager spawns a new thread and handles the connection in that thread only. This allows it to be free to listen for other incoming connections (Fig. 1 and Table 1).

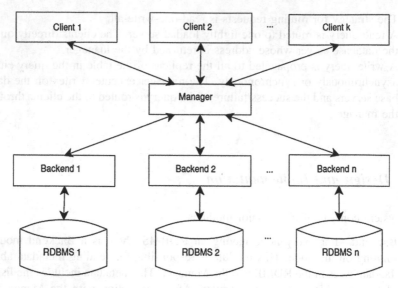

Fig. 1 System architecture

Table 1 addrToLoad—hash table for storing CPU load

IP	Load
192.168.56.100	0.53
192.168.56.101	1.51
192.168.56.102	0.79

3.2 Data Structures

The Manager maintains the following three crucial data structures for its functioning (Table 2):

(i) addrToLoad—This hash table is used to store the CPU load of the Backends. The keys are the IP addresses of the nodes and the values are the corresponding CPU load values which are updated periodically. This data structure is used while looking for the most lightly loaded node.

(ii) addrToDb—This hash table stores IP addresses as keys and the list of (database, table, version number) triples as values. This is to quickly find out which node has what tables.

Table 2 addrToDb—hash table for storing the list of tables on nodes

IP	List of triples
192.168.56.100	[(d1, t1, 1), (d1, t2, 2)]
192.168.56.101	[(d1, t1, 1), (d2, t1, 1)]
192.168.56.102	[(d1, t2, 2), (d2, t1, 1)]

Table 3 dbToAddr—
inverted index

(Database, table)	Version number and list of nodes
(d1, t1)	1–[192.168.56.100, 192.168.56.101]
(d1, t2)	2–[192.168.56.100, 192.168.56.102]
(d2, t1)	1–[192.168.56.101, 192.168.56.102]

(iii) dbToAddr—This hash table is used as an inverted index for (database, table) pairs. These pairs serve as keys, and the values are binary search trees with version numbers as the keys and the list of IP addresses of nodes as values. This data structure allows to very quickly fetch all nodes with the most recent version of (database, table) pairs and carry out read/write operation (Table 3).

4 Experimental Setup and Results

4.1 Hardware and Software Used

The system requires several nodes to work, i.e., one Manager, several Backends, and several Clients. To act as nodes, VMs are used and the system has been deployed on these VMs. The configurations of the systems used are as follows:

(i) Manager—64-bit Kali Linux running on Intel Core i3 @2.2 GHz with 3 GB RAM.
(ii) Backend—3 instances of 64-bit Ubuntu Linux 12.04 running in Oracle VM VirtualBox on a single core virtual processor with 512 MB RAM.
(iii) Client—Client instances have been run on both the host and guest operating systems.

4.2 Results

The system has been run on the above-mentioned configuration and the query operations have been timed (response time to clients) under heavy and light load situations. The heavy load situations are simulated by running one or more copies of a program that executes an infinite loop and does nothing. The light load situations are simulated by killing off processes and leaving the system idle. The results show that asynchronous write operations have better response times (0.97 %) than synchronous write operations but the difference becomes smaller as CPU load gets higher.

The CPU load metric shown in the graph is a measure of the average number of processes waiting for execution in a given time duration. In Linux, load averages for the last 1, 5, and 15 min can be found by reading the/proc/loadavg or executing

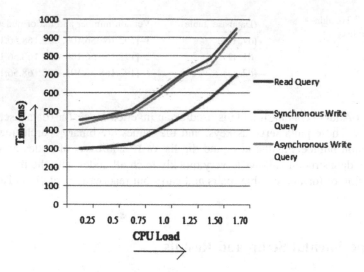

Fig. 2 Timing results

uptime command. A load average of more than the number of cores means the system is overloaded and less than the number of cores means the system is underloaded. This means that for high load, query execution should take more time. The results shown in the graph affirm this. So, queries should be routed to lightly loaded nodes for better response time (Fig. 2).

5 Conclusion and Future Work

High availability for databases has become critical to the success of the services provided to users over the cloud. Providing this is a complex task and it requires considerable cost and engineering effort. High availability systems provide automatic failover which has become easier with the emergence of virtualization. The primary technique for providing it is replication. The existing systems blindly replicate data without taking into account the number of requests and load on the database servers. Remus and its adaptation RemusDB use a VM-based approach and continuously live migrate a running VM to a backup physical host. Postgres-R works only with PostgreSQL databases. The proposed approach is based on the TBFR model and considers the load on servers into account to intelligently replicate data and route requests to lightly loaded servers and thus avoids the extra overhead. Asynchronous writes has a better response time than synchronous write by about 0.97 % and thus should be preferred.

In future, we may work on fault tolerance for backend servers, single point failure of manager, and system can be made transparent to clients.

References

1. Cully, B., Lefebvre, G., Meyer, D., Feeley, M., Hutchinson, N., & Warfield, A. (2008). Remus: High availability via asynchronous virtual machine replication. In *Symposium Networked Systems Design and Implementation*.
2. Minhas, U., Rajagopalan, S., Cully, B., Aboulnaga, A., Salem, K., & Warfield, A. (2013). RemusDB: Transparent high availability for database systems. *The VLDB Journal, 22*(1), 29–45.
3. Moiz, S. A., Sailaja, P., Venkataswamy, G., & Pal, S. N. (2011) Database replication: A survey of open source and commercial tools. *Database, 13*(6).
4. Pippal, S., & Kushwaha, D. S. (2012) Architectural design of education cloud framework extendible to ad hoc clouds. In *1st IEEE International Conference on Recent Advances in Information Technology (RAIT)*, 16–17 March 2012.
5. Pippal, S., & Kushwaha, D. S. (2013). A simple, adaptable and efficient heterogeneous multi-tenant database architecture for ad hoc cloud. In *Springer Journal of Cloud Computing: Advances, Systems and Applications (JoCCASA), 2*(5).
6. Pippal, S., Sharma, V., Mishra, S., & Kushwaha, D. S. (2011). Secure and efficient multitenant database for an ad hoc cloud. In *1st International Workshop on Securing Services on the Cloud (IWSSC), IEEE, 6–8 Sept., 2011 in Conjunction with 5th International conference on Network and System Security (NSS)*, Milan. doi:10.1109/IWSSCloud.2011.6049010.
7. Pippal, S., Sharma, V., Kumari, A., & Kushwaha, D. S. (2011). CTES Based Secure Approach for Authentication and Authorization of Resource and Service in Clouds. In *2nd IEEE International Conference Computer and Communication Technology, ICCCT 2011*, 15–17 Sept 2011. doi:10.1109/ICCCT.2011.6075140.
8. Pippal, S., Mishra, S., & Kushwaha, D. S. (2012) Architectural design and issues for ad-hoc clouds. In *3rd Springer International Conference on Advances in Communication, Network, and Computing (CNC—2012)*, 24–25 Feb 2012.
9. Pippal, S. K., Dubey, R. K., Malik, A, Singh, N., Jain, P., Bharti, R. K. et al. (2014). Performance analysis of resource provisioning for cloud computing frameworks. In *Fifth International Conference on Advances in Communication, Network, and Computing—CNC 2014*, 21–22 Feb 2014. Elsevier, Chennai.
10. Vardhan, M., Jain, N., Mishra, S., & Kushwaha, D. S. (2012) A demand based fault tolerant file replication model for clouds. In *Proceedings of the CUBE International Information Technology Conference*.

Customized Parameter Configuration Framework for Performance Tuning in Apache Hadoop

Bhavin J. Mathiya and Vinodkumar L. Desai

Abstract When Hadoop is deployed, it provides more than 200 default configuration parameters. These parameters are common for all the applications. But in reality, each and every application have different characteristics and require proper configuration parameter setting with different tuning options for better utilization of available resources like CPU, I/O, Memory, Network to decrease job execution time, increase throughput, reduce I/O, and minimize network transmission cost. Hadoop parameter configuration is still a black art and requires knowledge of hardware as well as Hadoop workload characteristics like CPU Intensive, I/O Intensive, etc. Misconfiguration of hadoop configuration might lead to inefficient execution and underutilization of resources. This research paper focuses on unresolved issue of Hadoop parameter configuration for performance tuning and proposes Customized Parameter Configuration Framework for Performance Tuning in Apache Hadoop.

Keywords Hadoop · Hadoop yarn · HDFS · Mapreduce · Hadoop parameter configuration

1 Introduction

Hadoop is an open source framework for distributed storage and parallel processing. Hadoop provides platform for Big Data deployment. Big Data has attributes like variety, velocity, and volume. Big Data can be in various forms like structure,

B.J. Mathiya (✉)
C.U. Shah University, Wadhwan City, Gujarat, India
e-mail: bhavinmath@gmail.com

V.L. Desai
Department of Computer Science, Government Science College Chikhli,
Navsari, Gujarat, India
e-mail: vinodl_desai@yahoo.com

© Springer Science+Business Media Singapore 2016
S.C. Satapathy et al. (eds.), *Proceedings of International Conference on ICT for Sustainable Development*, Advances in Intelligent Systems and Computing 409, DOI 10.1007/978-981-10-0135-2_50

semistructure, and unstructured data. Big Data generates through various kinds of Sensor devices, scientific instruments, web sites, social media, mobiles phones, etc., and it can be in text, audio, video, image, etc. Hadoop is a platform which provides big data deployment and it is still difficult to understand how the different layers of the hardware and software influence the overall performance.

This research paper focused on unresolved issue of Hadoop parameter configuration for performance tuning and proposes Customized Parameter Configuration Framework for Performance Tuning in Apache Hadoop.

This paper is organized as follows. Section 1 Introduction, Sect. 2 Related work, Sect. 3 Apache Hadoop Yarn architecture. Section 4 Problem Statements, Sect. 5 Propose Customized Parameter Configuration Framework for Performance Tuning in Apache Hadoop. Section 6 Conclusion and future work.

2   Related Work

Poggi et al. [1] focus on issues like hardware, software, and performance profiling. Yang et al. [2] identify relationships between workload characteristics and hadoop parameter configuration and propose a statistic analysis approach. Wang et al. [3] focus on parameter configuration issues and introduce Predator. Predator is an experience guided configuration parameter optimizer based on experience learnt from Hadoop parameter configuration settings practice. Li et al. [4] identify Hadoop parameter configuration issues and propose a mathematical model an adaptive automatic configuration tool (AACT). Joshi [5] discussed hardware as well as software tuning techniques including BIOS, OS, JVM, and Hadoop configuration parameters tuning. Garvit et al. [6] attempted to analyze the effect of various configuration parameters on Hadoop Map-Reduce performance under various conditions, to achieve maximum throughput. Zhang et al. [7] offer a novel performance evaluation framework for easing the user efforts of tuning the reduce task settings while achieving performance objectives. Bonifacio et al. [8] proposed an ontology based semantic approach to tuning parameters to improve Hadoop application performance.

3   Apache Hadoop Yarn Architecture

Apache Hadoop Yarn is an open source framework for distributed storage and parallel processing. Yarn Means Yet another Resource Negotiator. Apache Hadoop Yarn provides facilities to execute multiple jobs at the same time. All Resource provided through Resource Manager based on request. Client submit job to the resource manager. Resource manager send job to multiple node managers. Node manager execute job and send response back to resource manager. Resource manager send response back to client. Apache Hadoop Yarn provides job scheduler

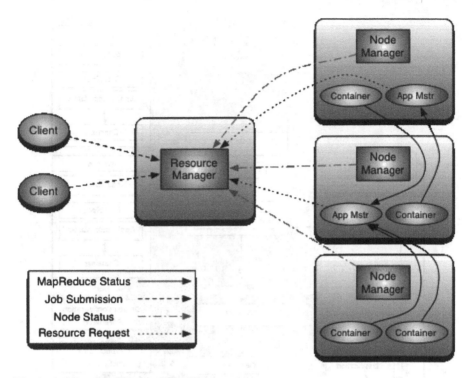

Fig. 1 Architecture of Hadoop Yarn [9]

and task scheduler for scheduling and executing submitted job. Apache Hadoop Yarn provides two main components HDFS and MapReduce. HDFDS means Hadoop Distributed File System use to store data locally as well as distributed with features like scalability and failure recovery. MapReduce is a programming model-based on key value pair (Figs. 1, 2, 3, 4 and 5).

4 Problem Statements

When Hadoop is deployed, Hadoop provides more than 200 default configuration parameter when user deploy it. It is common for all applications. But in real different application have different characteristics and require proper configuration parameter setting with different tuning options for better utilization of available resources like CPU, I/O, Memory, Network to decrease job execution time, increase throughput, reduce I/O, and minimize network transmission cost. Hadoop proper parameter configuration is still a black art and requires knowledge of hardware as well as Hadoop workload characteristics like CPU Intensive, I/O Intensive, etc. Misconfiguration of hadoop configuration might lead to inefficient execution and underutilization of resources.

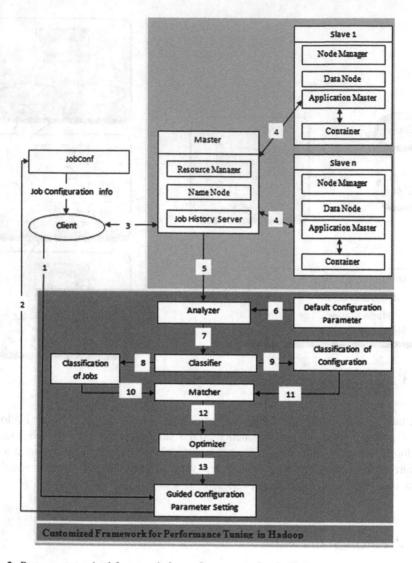

Fig. 2 Propose customized framework for performance tuning in Hadoop

5 Propose Customized Parameter Configuration Framework for Performance Tuning in Apache Hadoop

Based on literature review, Customized Parameter Configuration Framework for Performance Tuning in Apache Hadoop is proposed.

1. Before submitting the job, client requests and check Guided Configuration Parameter Setting according to job.

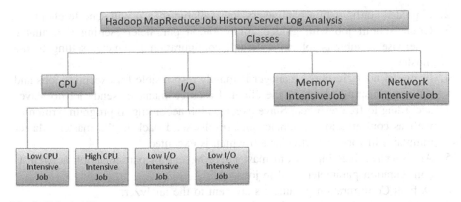

Fig. 3 Job classifier

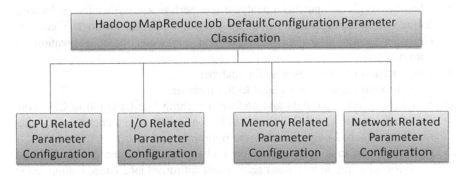

Fig. 4 Hadoop mapreduce job configuration parameter classifications

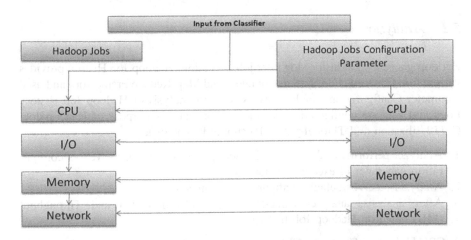

Fig. 5 Matcher

2. If guided configuration parameters are available then it will send to client.
3. Client submit job with guided configuration parameters setting if available otherwise it submits job with default configuration parameter setting to the master.
4. In master node, resource manager is mainly responsible for executing jobs and returning response back to the client. Resource manager sends job to slaves according to free resource. Slave executes job according to program written as well as configuration parameter and results send back to the master. Master maintains history of particular job which is executed.
5. Analyzer receives input from master like history of particular job as well as configuration parameter used in jobs.
6. Default Configuration parameters are sent to the analyzer.
7. Analyzer will do analyses of Configuration parameter as well as hadoop history job counter then send processed data to the classifier.
8. Classifier receives input from analyzer and performs classification of Hadoop Job as well as Configuration parameter. Classified jobs are sent to the Classifier.
9. Classifier sends Classified Configuration parameter to Classification of parameter.
10. Classification of jobs is sent to the matcher.
11. Classification parameters are sent to the matcher.
12. Matcher process input data and perform matching like CPU job to CPU configuration parameter, I/O job to I/O Configuration parameter, etc., after matching matched output send to the optimizer.
13. Optimizer performs optimization on hadoop job by tuning job and setting various configuration parameter setting and optimized job. Tuned configuration parameters are sent to Guided Configuration parameter.

5.1 Analyzer

Hadoop generates job history log after job execution. Hadoop Job History provides various Job Counters, File System Counters, and Map-Reduce Framework and used parameter Configuration. Analyzer is used to do analysis of Hadoop Job History Logs and Hadoop configuration parameter. For analysis purpose of Hadoop Job, CPU Utilization and Throughput (MB) should be calculated.

1. Analyzer performs analysis of both hadoop job history log as well as configuration parameter of executed hadoop jobs.
2. Analyzer receives default configuration parameter.
3. After analysis, analyzer calculate CPU Utilization (%) and Throughput (MB) based on Hadoop Job history log

CPU Utilization % = (Total CPU times in Second/Execution time (Seconds)) * 100
Throughput (MB) = (Input Bytes/Execution time (Seconds))/1024/102.

5.2 Classifier

Classifier is used for classification of Hadoop job configuration parameter as well as Hadoop Job (Workload) based on CPU Utilizaton (%) and Throughput (MB). Hadoop Job can be classified into various classes like CPU Intensive, IO Intensive, etc.

1. Classifier receives input from analyzer like CPU Utilization (%), I/O Throughput, and Configuration Parameter.
2. Classifier uses Data mining Clustering Method Partitioning Method for classifying hadoop job as well as hadoop configuration parameters.
3. In this classes are already predefined. Based on classes value will be set.
4. For Job Classification, Classes are Low CPU Intensive Job, High CPU Intensive Job, Low I/O Intensive Job, High I/O Intensive Job, Low CPU and I/O Intensive Job, High CPU and I/O Intensive Job, Low CPU and High I/O Intensive Job, High CPU and Low I/O Intensive Job.
5. Hadoop Job Configuration Parameter can be classified into various classes likes CPU related, Input/output related, Memory related, and Network related.

5.2.1 Hadoop MapReduce Job Classifier

Hadoop MapReduce job can be classified into one of the Low CPU Intensive job, High CPU Intensive job, Low I/O Intensive job, High I/O Intensive job, Memory Intensive, and Network Intensive job based on Hadoop MapReduce Job History Server Log Analysis.

5.2.2 Hadoop MapReduce Job Configuration Parameter Classifier

Hadoop provides default job parameter configuration common for all kind of jobs with customization facility. Hadoop job parameter configuration can be classified into various classes like CPU Related Parameter Configuration, I/O Related Parameter Configuration, Memory Related Parameter Configuration, and Network Related Parameter Configuration based on Hadoop MapReduce Job History Server Log Analysis.

5.2.3 Classification of Hadoop Job Parameter Configuration

Hadoop provides more than 200 default job parameter configuration with customization facility. Hadoop job parameter configuration can be classified into various classes like CPU, I/O, Memory, and Network related classes. Table 1 shows various classification of Hadoop Job parameter configuration.

Table 1 Classification of configuration parameter

CPU	I/O	Memory	Network
mapred.tasktracker. map.tasks.maximum	dfs.block.size	io.sort.mb	mapred.compress.map. output
mapred.tasktracker. reduce.tasks.maximum	dfs.replication	io.sort.factor	mapred.map. output.compression.codec
	mapred.compress.map. output	io.sort.spill. percent	mapred.output.compress
	mapred.compress.map. output	io.sort.factor	mapred. output.compression.type
	mapred.map. output.compression.codec	mapred. child.java. opts	mapred. output.compression.codec
	dfs.heartbeat.interval		

5.3 Matcher

Matcher provides Matchmaking functionality. Matcher Match Hadoop Job (Workload) with Hadoop Job Configuration Parameter setting.

5.4 Optimizer

Optimizer is main component which optimize overall performance of Hadoop Job based on best Hadoop Job Configuration Settings. Optimizer optimizes Hadoop Job based on various kinds of combination based on Hadoop Job (Workload) and Hadoop Job Parameter Configuration. Figure 6 shows Flow Chart of Optimizer.

Algorithm

1. Execute and analyze Hadoop MapReduce jobs performance using default configuration parameter values.
2. Store results like job completion time, CPU utilization, I/O Throughput, etc., as default configuration.
3. Customize Hadoop Configuration Parameter and change the value and again execute and analyze Hadoop MapReduce jobs performance and store the result.
4. First time Comparison is done with Hadoop Default configuration results, but second time comparison is done with Customize Hadoop Configuration results and analyzed that performance is tune or not?
5. If performance is tuned then repeat step 3 till results are improved, otherwise go to step 6.
6. Stop and exit.

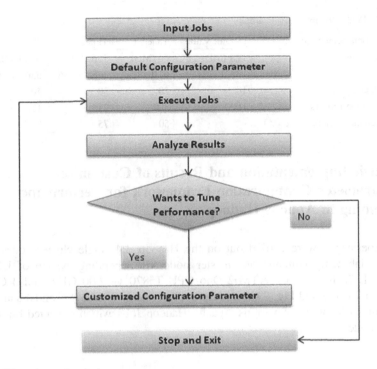

Fig. 6 Flow chart of optimizer

5.5 Guided Configuration Parameter Setting

Guided Configuration Parameter is used to store Hadoop Job Parameter Configuration Setting value. Guided Configuration Parameter contains combination of parameter configurations based on Optimizer as per job (Workload) type. Guided configuration parameter is useful for whom who have no detail knowledge about Hadoop Hardware, Software, and Hadoop Job Parameter Configuration setting and tune performance.

5.6 Predicted Optimizer Example

Predicted Optimizer Example contains list of combination of various kind of Hadoop Job Parameter configuration and different types of tune level. Table 2 contains Predicted Optimizer Example.

Table 2 Predicted optimizer example

Hadoop parameter name	Default value	Tuned 1	Tuned 2	Tune up to n
dfs.block.size	128 (MB)	64 (MB)	256 (MB)	512 (MB)
	134217728	67108864	268435456	536870912
io.sort.factor	10	20	30	50
Job execution time (s)	1000	500	250	175
Improvement over baseline (%)	–	50	75	82.5

6 Basic Implementation and Results of Customized Parameter Configuration Framework for Performance Tuning in Apache Hadoop

The experiments were carried out on the Hadoop 2.4 single cluster nodes. The Hadoop lab setup contains one master node with operating system of Ubuntu 14.04.1 LTS, Intel(R) Core(TM)2 Duo CPU T5870 @ 2.00 GHz, and 3 GB of RAM. In Table 3 and Fig. 7 shows results like Execution time (Seconds) and Total Cpu times (Seconds) of various Apache Hadoop Jobs which executed on single cluster node.

Table 3 Execution time (seconds) and total cpu times (seconds) of various hadoop jobs

No of node	Pi	Teragen	Terasort	Tera validate	Test DFSIO	Test DFSIO	Word count
		(1 GB data)	(1 GB data)	(1 GB data)	(Read)	(Write)	(1 GB data)
Execution time (s)							
1	16	63	2144	45	43	53	1285
Total cpu times (s)							
1	1.95	38.61	443.25	21.66	8.81	14.67	257.63

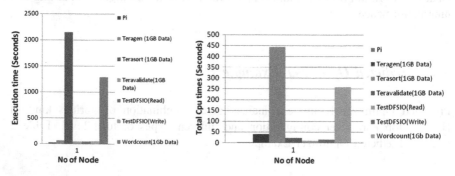

Fig. 7 Execution time (seconds) and total cpu times (seconds) of various hadoop jobs

7 Conclusion and Future Work

In this paper, Hadoop Job Parameter Configuration Open Issues are identified. Study of various research paper related to Hadoop Job Parameter Configuration to find out current Hadoop Job Parameter configuration issue and solutions is done. Based on Literature Review, Customized Parameter Configuration Framework for Performance Tuning in Apache Hadoop is proposed. Future work can be done in implementing the proposed framework and evaluate Hadoop Performance and tune the Hadoop Job performance through Hadoop Job Parameter Configuration setting.

References

1. Poggi, N., Carrera, D., Call, A., Mendoza, S., Becerra, Y., Torres, J., Ayguade, E., Gagliardi, F., Labarta, J., Reinauer, R., Vujic, N., Green, D., & Blakeley, J. (2014). ALOJA: A systematic study of Hadoop deployment variables to enable automated characterization of cost-effectiveness. In *2014 IEEE International Conference on Big Data (Big Data)* (pp. 905, 913, 27–30) October 2014.
2. Yang, H., Luan, Z., Li, W., Qian, D., & Guan, G. (2012). Statistics-based workload modeling for mapreduce. In *2012 IEEE 26th International Parallel and Distributed Processing Symposium Workshops & PhD Forum (IPDPSW)* (pp. 2043, 2051), 21–25 May 2012.
3. Wang, K., Lin, X., & Tang, W. (2012). Predator—An experience guided configuration optimizer for Hadoop MapReduce. In 2012 IEEE 4th International Conference on Cloud Computing Technology and Science (CloudCom) (pp. 419, 426) 3–6 December 2012.
4. Li, C., Zhuang, H., Lu, K., Sun, M., Zhou, J., Dai, D., & Zhou, X.: An adaptive auto-configuration tool for hadoop. In *2014 19th international conference on engineering of complex computer systems (ICECCS)* (pp. 69, 72) 4–7 August 2014.
5. Joshi, S. B. (2012). Apache hadoop performance-tuning methodologies and best practices. In *Proceedings of the 3rd ACM/SPEC International Conference on Performance Engineering (ICPE '12)* (pp. 241–242). ACM, New York, NY, USA. http://doi.acm.org/10.1145/2188286. 2188323
6. Garvit, B., et al. (2014). A framework for performance analysis and tuning in hadoop based clusters. In *Smarter Planet and Big Data Analytics Workshop (SPBDA 2014), held in conjuction with International Conference on Distributed Computing and Networking (ICDCN 2014)*, Coimbatore, India.
7. Zhang, Z., Cherkasova, L., & Thau Loo, B.: Getting more for less in optimized MapReduce workflows. In *2013 IFIP/IEEE International Symposium on Integrated Network Management (IM 2013)*. IEEE, 2013.
8. Bonifacio, A., Menolli, A., & Silva, F. (2014). Towards an ontology-based semantic approach to tuning parameters to improve hadoop application performance. *Information Technology in Industry, 2*(2), 56–61.
9. http://hadoop.apache.org/

Hand Skin Classification from Other Skin Objects Using Multi-direction 3D Color-Texture Feature and Cascaded Neural Network Classifier

Sonal Gupta, Munesh C. Trivedi and Suraj kamya

Abstract Hand Segmentation from skin color objects is an open problem in number of applications including hand gesture recognition, classification of hand gestures when other skin color objects like wrist, face, arm, and background are also exposed to camera. A novel approach in this direction is proposed in which multi-direction three-dimensional (3D) color-texture feature (CTF) are extracted and then classification of hand skin is done using neural network cascade classifier. It results 95 % true detection on a standard NUS hand gesture database consisting of variety of skin colors.

Keywords Hand classifier · Multi-Direction 3D feature · GLCM · CLCM · CTF features

1 Introduction

The first step in hand verification, classification, recognition systems is image acquisition. The acquiesced image is preprocessed, segmented, followed by extraction of features, and finally classified or recognized using classifiers. However, an important observation made is that researchers make various assumptions while developing such systems as only hand is exposed to the acquisition device (camera or other devices), background should be black, white, or

S. Gupta (✉) · M.C. Trivedi
Computer Science and Engineering Department, ABES Engineering College,
Ghaziabad, India
e-mail: sonal.gupta@abes.ac.in

M.C. Trivedi
e-mail: munesh.trivedi@abes.ac.in

S. kamya
IIMT College of Engineering, Greater Noida, India
e-mail: kamyasuraj@yahoo.com

© Springer Science+Business Media Singapore 2016   523
S.C. Satapathy et al. (eds.), *Proceedings of International Conference
on ICT for Sustainable Development*, Advances in Intelligent Systems
and Computing 409, DOI 10.1007/978-981-10-0135-2_51

must not contain any skin color object like wood, leather, sand, etc. In this paper, we address the issue of hand skin detection from other skin color objects (face, arm, neck, background) without considering the assumptions mentioned above. Segmenting hand directly from an image containing skin and non-skin objects involves extensive calculations and high complexity. Several hand segmentation techniques segment hand by dividing them as skin and non-skin components. The skin components includes all skin color objects (hand, face, background objects-leather, wood etc.) whether desired or not, unless the environment is controlled and rest all is included in non-skin component. But less effort is done in segmenting hand from other skin components which is the main desired component whose features are extracted. To this end, a different approach is proposed to segment hand in two stages (i) Separating skin and non-skin components using color information as most researchers proposed. It gives all skin data from the image acquiesced. (ii) Classification of hand region such as palm and fingers from the skin component (face, arm, and background objects like wood, leather) obtained in stage (i) using CTF and cascaded neural network classifier. Color feature, alone is notable to distinguish hand skin regions from other skin color object in stage (ii). However, texture of hand and other skin components (face, arm) varies and can be used to classify them but texture alone does not give accurate results. Therefore, color-texture features (CTF) are extracted to separate hand skin regions. The features extracted in stage (ii) are then feed into cascaded neural network classifier which classifies hand from other skin objects (face, arm, background) etc.

Color detector: Color-based detection is simple and invariant to rotation and geometry of hand. RGB is the simplest color model but the pixel values are correlated and varies as intensity changes while other models such as YCbCr accurately detects color as color values are decoupled from intensity values. A threshold value is set for different color planes and is the most efficient method for color-based detection.

Texture detector: Texture is the contextual property that is widely used in variety of classification-based applications. It depends on how pixels are spatially related to each other. It can be structured or statistic method of arrangement. In former method, the variation in intensity results in repetitive patterns which contribute to visual texture such as rough, smooth, silky, etc. Range, standard deviation, and entropy (degree of randomness) are the basic statistics that characterize the texture. Texture classification creates a classification map of an image where regions of similar texture are grouped into classes. A statistical approach of finding texture in an image is gray level co-occurrence matrix (GLCM) that calculates how often a pair of pixel values (i, j) occurs with some spatial relationship, i.e., direction (0, 45, 90, 135). This creates gray level co-occurrence matrix and hence statistical features are collected and used as criteria for segmentation and classification.

Shape detector: Shape descriptors are used to represent the image content. Various shape extraction techniques (one dimensional function, polygonal approximation, moments) are used to describe image content, For example Hand centroid, area, eccentricity, finger length, etc., are some of the properties used to describe hand features. However, these shape features varies to a greater extent due to large variation in human hands. Thus, shape feature alone cannot solve the problem. Therefore, in this paper, multi-direction CTFs are used.

The final phase of skin modeling and classification involves variety of classifiers such as Bayesian network classifiers, Gaussian classifiers, self-organizing classifiers, neural network classifier, multilayer perceptron classifier entropy based classifiers, etc. The selection of these classifiers is an important factor in attaining good results and depends on application-type, size of training and test dataset, high true positive results (TPR), and low false positive results (FPR). Proposed method uses pattern recognition multilayer back propagation neural network.

2 Literature Survey

2.1 Data Acquisition

Not much focus has been made in current problem domain of separating skin hand region from other skin components as researchers prefer making preassumptions and use of sensing devices/tools to extract the hand region [1]. Magnetic field trackers, body suits, data gloves, color markers, stereo, or depth cameras are few of them. This reduces the ease of naturalness in user's interaction with the computer. To avoid this, vision-based approaches were used in which researchers use camera with certain assumptions like light conditions, background, speed, etc. Vision-based approaches [2] are further divided into appearance-based (color, geometric and motion based models) and three-dimensional (3D) model-based approaches (3d geometrical and 3d skeleton features). Gupta and Ma [3] assume a uniform background with florescent lights in the laboratory prior to segmentation. Kang [4] used disparity map collected from stereo camera and skin color prior to segmentation. Some challenges involved in vision-based approaches are speed and number of camera, structuring environment, low-level features involved (edges, regions, silhouettes, moments, histograms), dynamic or static, and type of application.

2.2 Feature Extraction Methods

After the hand data is acquired, feature extraction and feature reduction techniques are applied so that further processing can be done with less space and time complexity. Color, texture, shape are the most effective features extracted depending on the type of application. In case of color, the selection of correct color model is to be done. The color models [5] are broadly classified into basic color models (RGB, normalized RGB), perceptual color spaces (HSI, HSV, HSL), Orthogonal color spaces (YCbCr, YIQ, YUV). RGB is the most simple and effective color model choice for skin detection and is by Bergasa et al. [6]. The HSV model used by Brown et al. [7] is invariant to high intensity at white and ambient light and hence, can be a good choice for skin detection methods. Hsu et al. [8] used orthogonal color space model. It reduces the redundancy present in RGB color channels and represents the color with statistically independent components. There are statistical methods, geometric methods (Voronoi tessellation), model-based methods (Fractals), and signal processing methods (Gabor and Wavelets) to define the textural properties of an image [9]. Uniformity, density, frequency, phase, Entropy, directionality, correlation, homogeneity, coarseness, energy, are common texture features obtained from first- and second-order statistics. Landeweerd and Gelsema [10] extracted various first-order statistics to classify different types of white blood cells.

Researchers use shape of the hand as vital feature for detection of hand. The contour of the hand independent of light, viewpoint represents the shape of the hand. Fingertip points, four points in the valley of fingers, four finger length and width, palm width, palm length, hand area can be obtained from contour analysis. Doublet [11] used active shape model as the basis of feature extraction. Thus, a hand shape can be represented by a vector of these features.

2.3 Skin Classifiers

One of the most efficient methods is to set threshold levels or decision boundaries for the chosen color space model. Then, the image pixel values that fall within these predefined range(s) are defined as skin pixels for each color component. Dai and Nakano [12] set a fixed range on RI = [0, 50] component in YIQ space for detecting skin. Sobottka and Pitas [13] set fixed range values RH = [0, 50] and RS = [0.23, 0.68] on the HS color space. Wang and Yuan [14] combined RGB Rr = [0.36, 0.465], Rg = [0.28, 0.363] and HSV, RH = [0, 50], RS = [0.20, 0.68], and RV = [0.35, 1.0] space for discriminating pixels. Zarit et al. [15], Yoo used a histogram-based approach. He computed the probability distribution and defined a threshold value for classification. Lee [9] used a statistical approach (Gaussian mixture model) to classify pixels as skin and non-skin components.

3 The Proposed System

The overall design of the proposed system is shown in Fig. 1. The input to the system is an image consisting of skin and non-skin part against complex background as shown in Fig. 2 and the resultant image contains segmented hand area from other skin objects, it uses a marker to represent skin and non-skin areas as shown in Fig. 4. The process from input to output involves following phases: skin segmentation as shown in Fig. 3, multi-direction 3D CTF extraction, neural network back propagation hand classifier, hand object detection, postprocessing, and marking. The description of each of the phase is explained in Part IV.

Fig. 1 Design of the
proposed system

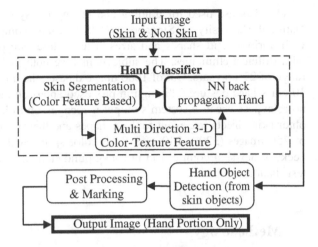

Input Image
(Skin & Non Skin

Hand Classifier

Skin Segmentation
(Color Feature Based)

NN back
propagation Hand

Multi Direction 3-D
Color-Texture Feature

Post Processing
& Marking

Hand Object
Detection (from
skin objects)

Output Image (Hand Portion Only)

Fig. 2 Shows input image

Fig. 3 Shows skin detection
image

Fig. 4 Shows result image

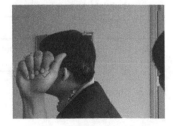

The database used for training and testing the system has shot in and around National University of Singapore (NUS), against complex natural backgrounds, with various hand shapes and sizes. The postures are performed by 40 subjects, with different ethnicities. The subjects include both males and females in the age range of 22–56 years. Out of 1000 image dataset, the training database contains the 10 class hand posture (although in proposed approach meaningful postures having no relevance because system's output is recognition of hand area in comparison to other skin objects irrelevant to their shapes and their meaning.) images with a total of 750 images (320 × 240 size, RGB color space) with noises (human face, arm, neck, or any skin color object in background etc.) and the 250 images are taken in test database.

4   Methodology

The detailed flow design is shown in Fig. 5. Part 4.1, 4.2, and 4.3 shows detailed explanation of the proposed system.

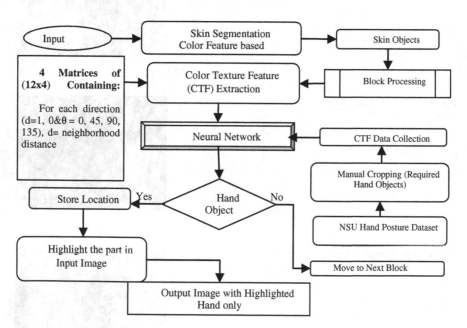

Fig. 5 Shows detailed flow chart

4.1 Color-Based Skin Segmentation

The first step of the proposed approach is image acquisition containing hand portion (remaining human skin part is noise). The goal of this step is to extract all skin information from the image. As HSV model separates the luminance component from the color components, they are more effective in discrimination skin and non-skin pixels. Therefore, our approach uses Hue information (H) along with rgb color model for effective skin segmentation. To segment skin components, bounding rules are constructed for rgb and H components. The bounding rules are decided from the training images. The training dataset includes images under daylight and flashlight and were analyzed to set the threshold values.

In RGB color space, rules are slightly modified and given by Kovac model [16]. The bounding rules varies depending on the training dataset, color model, light conditions, and camera.

Rule 1: R > 98 AND G > 42 AND B > 25 AND

Rule 2: Max {R,G,B}-Min {R,G,B} > 15 AND

Rule 3: |R-G| > 15 &

Rule 4: R > G and R > B

Rule 1, 2, 3, and 4 are combined using logical AND to form Rule A. The bounding rules for H color component color are:

Rule 5: H > 25 & Rule 6: H < 230

Rule 5 and 6 are combined using logical AND to form Rule B. A pixel is classified as skin pixel if it satisfies Rule C stated as: Rule A AND Rule B

Morphological operators dilation and flood fill is used further to improve the segmentation result as postprocessing that helps to fill holes and gaps and join fragmented parts. The result of this step contains all skin pixels which act as input to CTF extraction phase.

4.2 CTF Extraction

This step involves extraction of CTF for feeding an input into neural network which helps in classification of hand skin data from human noise. In this direction, first training data is divided into positive and negative dataset using manual cropping. The cropped hand skin region of each image is collected as positive data and cropped all other skin data like arm, neck, face (only skin objects) as negative data. Four Texture properties like Contrast, Correlation, Energy, and Homogeneity are extracted using gray level co-occurrence matrix GLCM [17]. This matrix calculates how often a pixel with gray level value i occurs to adjacent pixels with value j and is based on distance d (between pixel of interest and adjacent pixel) and angular spatial relationship theta (Θ = 0, 90, 45 and 135) of an image. Here, simultaneously color component is also added while calculating GLCM, and hence the matrix is called CLCM. In color image representation, a pixel on position (x, y) is shown by a vector involving three values I$(x, y, p1)$, I$(x, y, p2)$, and I$(x, y, p3)$. These three values create a 3D representation of the pixel.

Contrast: $\displaystyle\sum_{i=1}^{m}\sum_{j=1}^{n}(i-j)2\,\text{GLCM}(i,j)$ Energy: $\displaystyle\sum_{i=1}^{m}\sum_{j=1}^{n}(\text{GLCM}(i,j))2$

Homogeneity: $\displaystyle\sum_{i=1}^{m}\sum_{j=1}^{n}\frac{\text{GLCM}(i,j)}{1+|i-j|}$ Correlation: $\displaystyle\sum_{i=1}^{m}\sum_{j=1}^{n}\frac{\{i*j\}*\text{GLCM}(I,j)-\{\mu x-\mu y\}}{\sigma x-\sigma y}$

For each of the four properties described above, a matrix of 12 features for different plane combination, distance value, and theta is extracted for both positive and negative data set as shown in Fig. 6. Here value of theta is 0. Similar matrix is calculated for theta = 90, 45, and 135. The value of distance is 0 when neighborhood is in same position or in different planes (RG, RB and BG). For distance = 1, there are three neighborhoods for each pixel in red plane (RR, RG, RB). Similarly for green (GG, GR, GB) and blue planes (BB, BR, BG). The analysis for CTFs for positive and negative data is shown in Figs. 7 and 8.

In Figs. 7 and 8 values of all four major properties (clockwise contrast, homogeneity, correlation, Energy) for each NSU image dataset of all 12 planes are shown in form of 3D surface plots for both positive and negative dataset, variation in features is analyzed in detail to set a distinction, and importance of particular feature. As in contrast feature of positive data the values varies from 0 to 4 only but in negative data the same feature value varies largely from 0 to 20 and it can be easily concluded that any value greater than 4 belongs to negative data and similarly for ambiguous values between 0 and 4 the rules formed by analyzing other features. Although only these simple rules from these analysis cannot solve the whole

d, Θ	0,0	0,0	0,0	1,0	1,0	1,0
Plane	RG0	RB0	BG0	RR	BB	GG
Image1	1.26	2.83	0.54	0.21	0.22	1.40
Image2	1.45	2.68	0.44	0.17	0.11	1.49
d, Θ	1,0	1,0	1,0	1,0	1,0	1,0
Plane	RG	RB	GR	GB	BR	BG
Image1	2.50	1.39	1.39	0.61	2.91	0.62
Image2	2.37	1.96	1.96	0.47	2.85	0.52

Fig. 6 Color texture feature for theta = 0

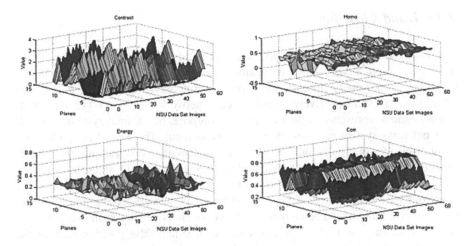

Fig. 7 Color-texture feature variation for positive data

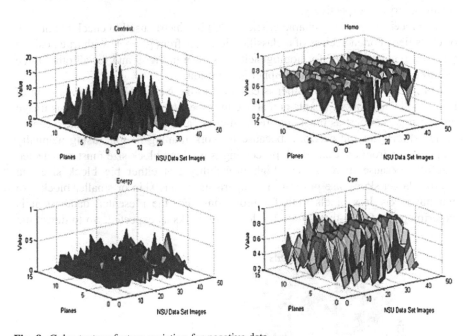

Fig. 8 Color-texture feature variation for negative data

problem, but can make it easier to solve. Further these rules set are combined and inducted in hand classifier to set a threshold in final result for marking of only hand area among human skin noise.

4.3 Hand Classifier

A two-layer feed-forward network, with sigmoid hidden and soft-max output neurons is used. Four pattern recognition neural networks are used in parallel. Contrast, Homogeneity, Energy, and Correlation networks having 10, 20, 10, and 10 hidden layers respectively. Input to each network is 12 × 4 (12 represents features and 4 represents angles) for training purpose, but in final system to use all four networks system requires 48 × 4 matrix as input. The Scaled conjugate gradient back propagation is used as the training function. For training and performance derivative back propagation scaled conjugate gradient algorithm is used. This method can train any network as long as its weight, net input, and transfer functions have derivative functions. It can train any network having its parameters as derivative functions. The confusion matrix for Homogeneity is shown in Fig. 9, which represents the performance in terms of true and false positive rates of the network used and its output class is plotted against the target class. Contrast, Homogeneity, Energy, and Correlation are 92.4, 98.3, 99.2, and 99.2 % for confusion matrices, respectively.

The receiver operating characteristic (ROC) is a metric used to check the quality of classifiers. For each class of a classifier, it ranges from [0 → 1] with true positive and negative ratio. ROC for homogeneity is shown in Fig. 9 and for all other three features it also lays in top most upper left portion.

Output from the skin classifier is cascaded to the Neural Network consisting of four parallel networks as explained above in respect to each feature. But this image having non-skin part as black and remaining as same in the original image cannot be fed directly to the network, because network training is done using manually cropped part from dataset. Block processing is used but block size must be selected carefully because there is very high probability that either big block size can overlap larger skin noise portion in comparison to hand skin or smaller block size can have very less pixels unfit for processing. For the presented database it is experimentally found that 20 by 20 block size works as expected. So to detect the

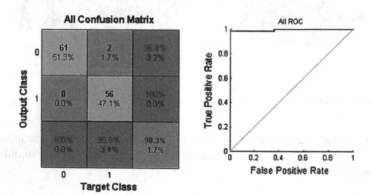

Fig. 9 Confusion matrix and ROC

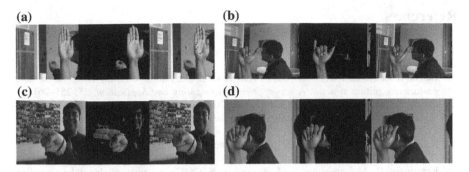

Fig. 10 **a**, **b**, **c**, and **d** shows input, intermediary, and final image

hand part using network, skin image from skin classifier is fed in block by block. Resultant value ranges between 0 and 1 corresponding to each block. 1 represents the block is perfectly a hand part and 0 represents certainly a non-hand part or it is a skin noise. From the feature analysis, the threshold value is experimentally set to 0.7, any block having value 0.7 or above is hand part. Location for each positive block is stored. To mark the hand portion in original image these locations are used and required part is highlighted.

5 Results

A total of 250 test images were tested from standard NUS hand posture dataset. Figure 10 shows the result for different hand postures. Figure 10a shows the input image to the designed system, Fig. 10b shows the image after segmenting all skin objects, and Fig. 10c shows the final image that classify hand skin region using red markers from other skin objects. Out of 250 test images, 237 images showed positive result and hence 95 % accuracy is achieved.

6 Conclusion and Future Work

In this paper, the objective to classify hand from other skin color objects is achieved. It shows 95 % true detection on NSU dataset and is efficient for images. I would like to extend my work by optimizing this technique for real-time applications and using this for developing hand verification applications. Due to high computational complexity, proposed method cannot be used for hand detection in real-time videos. Therefore, further area of improvisation can be used of integral image methods to reduce computational complexity and time.

References

1. Mitra, S., & Acharya, T. (2007). Gesture recognition: A survey. *IEEE Transactions on Systems, Man and Cybernetics, 37*(3), 1–14.
2. Hasan, H., & Abdul-Kareem, S. (2012). Human–computer interaction using vision-based hand gesture recognition systems: A survey. *Neural Computing and Application, 25*, 251–261.
3. Gupta, L., & Ma, S. (2001). Gesture-based interaction and communication: Automated classification of hand gesture contours. *IEEE Transactions on Systems, Man, and Cybernetics, 31*(1), 114–120.
4. Kang, S., Roh, A., & Hong, H. (2011). Depth and skin color for hand gesture classification. In *IEEE International Conference on Consumer Electronics (ICCE)* (pp. 155–156).
5. Kakumanu, P., Makrogiannis, S., & Bourbakis, N. (2007). A survey of skin-color modeling and detection methods. *Pattern Recognition, 40*, 1106–1122.
6. Bergasa, L. M., Mazo, M., Gardel, A., Sotelo, M. A., & Boquete, L. (2000). Unsupervised and adaptive Gaussian skin-color model. *Image Vision Computing, 18*(12), 987–1003.
7. Brown, D., Craw, I., & Lewthwaite, J. (2001). A SOM based approach to skin detection with application in real time systems. BMVC01.
8. Hsu, R. L., Abdel-Mottaleb, M., & Jain, A. K. (2002). Face detection in color images. *IEEE Transactions on Pattern Analysis and Machine Intelligence, 24*(5), 696–706.
9. Tuceryan, M., & Jain, A. K. (1998). The handbook of pattern recognition and computer vision (pp. 207–248). World Scientific Publishing Co.
10. Landeweerd, G. H., & Gelsema, E. S. (1978). The use of nuclear texture parameters in the automatic analysis of Leukocytes. *Pattern Recognition, 10*, 57–61.
11. Doublet, J., Lepetit, O., & Revenu, M. (2006). Contact less hand recognition using shape and texture features. In *International Conference on Signal Processing, China*.
12. Dai, Y., & Nakano, Y. (1996). Face-texture model based on SGLD and its application in face detection in a color scene. *Pattern Recognition, 29*(6), 1007–1017.
13. Sobottka, K., & Pitas, I. (1998). A novel method for automatic facesegmentation, facial feature extraction and tracking. *Signal Processing Image Communication, 12*, 263–281.
14. Wang, Y., & Yuan, B. (2001). A novel approach for human face detection from color images under complex background. *Pattern Recognition, 34*(10), 1983–1992.
15. Zarit, B. D., Super, J. B., & Quek, F. K. H. (1999). Comparison of five color models in skin pixel classification. ICCV99.
16. Julesz, B. (1981). a theory of preattentive texture discrimination based on first-order statistics of Textons. *Biological Cybernetics, 41*, 131–138.
17. Bencol, M., Hudecl, R., Kamencay1, P., Zachariasova, M., & Matuska, S. (2014). An advanced approach to extraction of color texture features based on GLCM. *International Journal of Advanced Robotic Systems*, 1–8.

Texture Features for the Detection of Acute Lymphoblastic Leukemia

Vanika Singhal and Preety Singh

Abstract Acute Lymphoblastic Leukemia (ALL) is a cancer of the blood or bone marrow. Detection of ALL is usually done by skilled pathologists, automatic detection of leukemia will reduce the diagnosis time and will also be independent of the skills of the pathologist. In this paper, we propose using texture descriptors extracted from the nucleus image for detection of ALL. The disease causes change in the chromatin distribution of the nucleus, which can be observed in the form of texture. We have used two texture features, namely Local Binary pattern and Gray Level Co-occurrence Matrix for automatic detection of ALL. A comparative analysis of both the features is presented. It is seen that LBP features perform better than GLCM features.

Keywords Blast · Texture · Leukemia

1 Introduction

Leukemia is a cancer of blood or bone marrow which is caused due to increase in number of immature white blood cells (WBC). WBC form the immune system of the human body and disturbance in the population of these cells causes many health problems [1]. Leukemia can be classified into four categories: Acute lymphoblastic Leukemia (ALL), Chronic Lymphoblastic Leukemia (CLL), Acute Myelogenous Leukemia (AML) and Chronic Myelogenous Leukemia (CML). The classification (acute or chronic) is based on the time span in which the disease progresses and the type of WBC affected by the disease (lymphocyte or myeloid) [2].

V. Singhal (✉)
Manipal University, Jaipur, India
e-mail: vanikas31@gmail.com

P. Singh
The LNM Institute of Information Technology, Jaipur, India
e-mail: prtysingh@gmail.com

© Springer Science+Business Media Singapore 2016
S.C. Satapathy et al. (eds.), *Proceedings of International Conference on ICT for Sustainable Development*, Advances in Intelligent Systems and Computing 409, DOI 10.1007/978-981-10-0135-2_52

ALL is caused due to rapid increase in the number of immature lymphocytes called blasts. ALL accounts for 80 % of childhood leukemia and is mostly found in the age group of 2–5 years [3]. The diagnosis of the disease is difficult as the symptoms of ALL are common to other health disorders like fever, anemia, weakness, joint pain, etc. The manual method for detection of ALL includes the inspection of the blood or bone marrow sample under a microscope by a skilled pathologist [1]. This method of diagnosis is time-consuming and subjective as it depends on the skills of the pathologist. Automation of this process can help in reducing the detection time and also be beneficial for remote diagnosis.

The basic difference between normal and blast cells is based on the changes in shape, size and changes in the chromatin pattern in the nucleus [4]. The normal lymphocytes are regular in shape and smaller in size as compared to blast cells. Changes in chromatin distribution can be visualized as texture of nucleus. Thus, texture of nucleus can be used for discrimination between normal and blast cells. Many methods have been proposed in literature for automatic detection of ALL. Asadi et al. [2] use zernike moments as features. Two classification methods: k-nearest neighbor (k-NN) and minimum distance mean are used and best accuracy of 93 % is reported using k-NN. They have considered all four types of leukemia for experiments. Madhloom et al. [5] have used a combination of shape and texture features for classification. k-NN is used for classification and 92.5 % accuracy is reported. In [4], shadow c-mean clustering (SCM) technique is used for nucleus segmentation. Three types of texture descriptors: wavelet, Haralick and Fourier, in combination with shape and color features, are used to train the classifier. Classification accuracy of 94.73 % is reported using an ensemble of classifiers.

In this paper, we have used two types of texture feature descriptors: Local Binary Pattern (LBP) and Gray Level Co-occurrence Matrix (GLCM) for the detection of ALL. We have used LBP features in an earlier work [6]. Since chromatin changes occur in the nucleus, these texture features are extracted from images of lymphocyte nucleus only. We present a comparative analysis of the performance of the two features for ALL detection. Our paper is structured as follows: Sect. 1.1 describes the proposed methodology. The results are analyzed in Sect. 2. Section 3 includes the concluding remarks.

1.1 Proposed Methodology

The microscopic blood images consist of three components: red blood cells (RBC), white blood cells (WBC), and platelets. The first step in the automation of leukemia detection is to extract WBC from the other blood components. As ALL is concerned with lymphocytes only, the next task is to separate lymphocytes from other types of WBC.

The nucleus is then segmented from the lymphocyte cells. In order to determine the texture variation in the nucleus of lymphocyte, features are extracted from the nucleus of the lymphocyte. These features are then used for classifying the

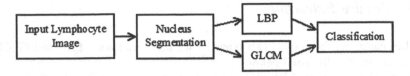

Fig. 1 Proposed methodology

lymphocyte as normal or blast. The database we have used contains single cell images of lymphocytes, so we have skipped the lymphocyte segmentation step. Our proposed methodology is shown in Fig. 1.

1.2 Segmentation

We have used HSI color model for nucleus segmentation, since it performs better than RGB color-based segmentation [7]. The process used for segmentation can be explained by using the following steps:

- Convert the input RGB blood image (refer Fig. 2a) into HSI color image.
- Apply thresholding on the saturation component of the image for nucleus segmentation. The threshold is selected manually.
- Apply median filter of size 5 × 5 on the resultant image. With this, small pixel groups of noise are removed from the image.
- Gray scale image of nucleus is now obtained by mapping obtained binary image of nucleus to the gray scale image of the input RGB image (refer Fig. 2b).

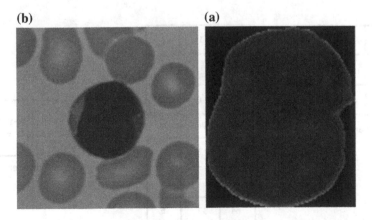

Fig. 2 Nucleus segmentation. **a** Nucleus. **b** Original image

1.3   Feature Extraction

In this paper, we have used two types of texture descriptors: LBP and GLCM. These are briefly discussed below.

Local Binary Pattern: LBP [8] is a texture descriptor which is very effective and robust to illumination changes [9]. LBP is computed by first dividing the segmented nucleus image into 16 subimages. For each pixel in a subimage, an 8-bit pattern is computed by comparing its value with its 3×3 neighboring pixels. When the center pixel's value is less than the neighboring pixel's value 0 is generated, otherwise, a 1 is generated.

A label is generated by multiplying each s value with the weight assigned to the neighborhood. Labels are computed for each pixel in the subimage and a histogram is formed using these labels. An example of label generation is shown in Fig. 3.

Gray Level Co-occurrence Matrix: A co-occurrence matrix [10] over an image is defined as the distribution of co-occurring gray level values at a given offset. GLCM is a very effective technique for texture computation of an image. For GLCM calculation, the image is first mapped to smaller number of gray level values say n. The size of the co-occurrence matrix G will then be $n \times n$. The entry (i, j) in the GLCM denoted by $G(i, j)$ will give the number of times the gray level values i and j co-occur at distance d and at angle a in the image. The GLCM computation with angle $a = 0$ and distance $d = 1$ is shown in Fig. 4. The GLCM thus obtained is used to extract four features (Fig. 4).

- Contrast is the measure of intensity distribution between a pixel and its neighborhood over the whole image, defined as:

$$\text{Contrast} = \Sigma |i - j|^2 G(i,j) \tag{1}$$

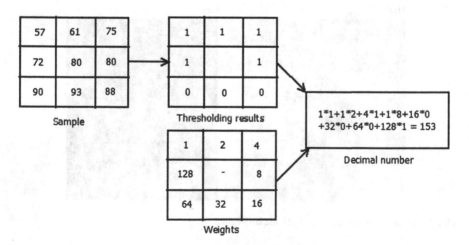

Fig. 3   Computation of label for a pixel

(a)   **(b)**

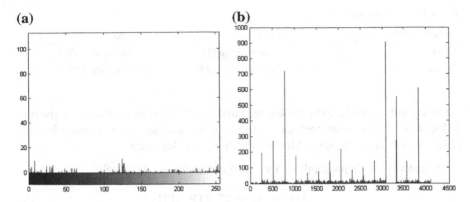

Fig. 4 LBP of a nucleus. **a** Histogram of a subimage. **b** LBP obtained by concatenating histograms of all subimages

- Correlation provides the correlation of a pixel to its neighborhood over the whole image, defined as:

$$\text{Correlation} = \Sigma_i \Sigma_j (i - \mu_x)\,(j - \mu_y)\,G(i,j)/_{\sigma_x \sigma_y} \qquad (2)$$

where, $i = 1$ to n and $j = 1$ to n, and μ_x, μ_y, σ_x, and σ_y are the mean and variances of row and column sums, respectively.

- Energy is defined as the sum of the squared elements in the GLCM given by:

$$\text{Energy} = \Sigma G(i,j)^2 \qquad (3)$$

- Homogeneity is the measure of how much the distribution of gray level intensities in an image are close to the diagonal. It is defined as:

$$\text{Homogeneity} = \Sigma_{i,j} G(i,j)/(1 + |i - j|) \qquad (4)$$

We have divided the nucleus image into 16 subimages and for each subimage, four features are computed. Features obtained from each subimage are then concatenated to form a feature vector of 64 values. We have computed GLCM for distance $d = 1$ and angles $a = [0°, 45°, 90°, 135°]$ on our dataset images. GLCM is computed for four values of levels $n = [10, 20, 40, 60]$.

1.4 Classification

We have employed tenfold cross validation [11] method for classification of our dataset [12]. Sequential Minimal Optimization algorithm from WEKA [13] is used. Polynomial kernel function has been used for training the SVM classifier.

Table 1 Confusion matrix

Actual class/predicted class	Blast	Normal
Blast	True positive (TP)	False negative (FN)
Normal	False positive (FP)	True negative (TN)

To analyze the classification results, we have used the confusion matrix as given in Table 1. Four evaluation metrics are used for the analysis of the results obtained [14]: Sensitivity, Specificity, Misclassification, and Accuracy.

- Sensitivity is the probability of correctly classifying a blast cell:

$$Sensitivity = TP/(TP + FN) \tag{5}$$

- Accuracy

$$Accuracy = (TP + TN)/(TP + TN + FP + FN) \tag{6}$$

- Specificity is the probability of correctly classifying a normal cell:

$$Specificity = TN/(TN + FP) \tag{7}$$

- Misclassification is the number of cells classified incorrectly:

$$Misclassification = FP + FN \tag{8}$$

Evaluation metrics are computed for each type of texture feature and the results are analyzed.

2 Experiments and Result Analysis

We have used the ALL-IDB2 database obtained from Universit degli Studi di Milano, Italy [12]. The database contains a total of 260 images, out of which 130 are blast and 130 are normal images. For each image, we segment the nucleus. LBP and GLCM features are computed over each nucleus image, as explained in Sect. 1.1. Computation of LBP gives us a feature vector of length 4096. While application of GLCM gives a feature vector of 64 features for each level n and angle a. The classification results obtained using these two types of texture features are discussed in the following subsections.

2.1 Local Binary Pattern

The confusion matrix obtained for LBP features is given in Table 2. As can be seen, there are eight False Positives. It can also be observed that eight cells are classified falsely as normal. The overall accuracy using LBP texture descriptors is 93.84 %.

2.2 GLCM

Table 3 shows the results obtained by using different combination of directions and levels. Best results are obtained using number of levels $n = 60$ and direction $a = 0°$. This gives us a maximum classification accuracy of 87.30 %. The confusion matrix for $n = 60$ and direction $a = 0°$ is shown in Table 4. As can be seen, 18 blast lymphocytes are falsely classified as normal. There are 15 False Positives.

2.3 Comparative Analysis

Table 5 shows the evaluation metrics of LBP and GLCM texture features ($n = 60$, $a = 0°$). It can be seen that LBP features perform better than GLCM features. Accuracy obtained with LBP features is 93.84 % as compared to 87.30 % accuracy of GLCM features.

Table 2 Confusion matrix for local binary pattern features

Actual class/predicted class	Blast	Normal
Blast	122	8
Normal	8	122

Table 3 Accuracy in (%) using GLCM for different directions and number of gray levels

Direction/number of levels	10	20	40	60
0°	85.38	86.15	86.53	87.30
45°	86.53	85	86.15	86.15
90°	84.23	86.15	86.53	86.92
135°	83.31	82.30	85	85

Table 4 Confusion matrix for GLCM features with $a = 0°$ and $n = 60$

Actual class/predicted class	Blast	Normal
Blast	112	18
Normal	15	115

Table 5 Comparative
analysis of LBP and GLCM
features

Evaluation metrics	LBP	GLCM
Misclassification	16	33
Sensitivity (%)	93.84	86.15
Specificity (%)	93.84	88.46
Accuracy (%)	93.84	87.30

Sensitivity is more using LBP features which signifies that number of blast cell recognized correctly is more using LBP features. LBP features show more specificity than GLCM features. It can also be observed that number of misclassified cells is more using GLCM features than LBP features.

2.4 Comparison with Existing State-of-the-Art

Comparison of our results with existing state-of-the-art is difficult since different databases have been used. Mohapatra et al. [4] have used a database of 270 images and shape and texture features. An accuracy of 94.73 % is reported using an ensemble of three classifiers, which is computationally cumbersome.

They also mention a classification accuracy of 91.43 % with SVM classifier. The authors have made an assumption that all the WBC in the images of blood are lymphocytes, which may not be the case always because there are five types of WBC.

Asadi et al. [2] reported an accuracy of 93 % with k-NN classifier while working with zernike moments applied on 800 images. However, results are for classification of all four types of leukemia. Madhloom et al. [5] use shape and texture features extracted from 260 images and show an accuracy of 92.5 %. In [15], an error rate of 0.0133 is reported. However, the database contains only 150 images and the results need to be validated on a larger database. Our proposed LBP feature set able to give a classification accuracy of 93.84 %. Compared to these results, we see that our texture features perform reasonably well.

3 Conclusion

In this paper we have used two types of texture features, LBP and GLCM for automation of ALL detection process. LBP feature is able to give classification accuracy of 93.84 %. Classification accuracy of 87.30 % is obtained using GLCM features. The results show that LBP performs better than GLCM texture features. As future work, more texture descriptors can be explored to achieve better classification accuracy.

References

1. Haworth, C., Hepplestone, A., Jones, P. M., Campbell, R., Evans, D., & Palmer, M. P. (1981). Routine bone marrow examination in the management of acute Lymphoblastic Leukaemia of childhood. *Journal of Clinical Pathology, 34*, 483–485.
2. Asadi, M., Vahedi, A., & Amindavar, H. (2006). Leukemia cell recognition with Zernike moments of holographic images. In *Proceedings of the 7th Nordic Signal Processing Symposium (NORSIG)* (pp. 214–217).
3. Sawyers, C. L., Denny, C. T., & Witte, O. N. (1991). Leukemia and the disruption of normal hematopoiesis. *Cell, 64*, 337–350.
4. Mohapatra, S., Patra, D., & Satpathy, S. (2013). An ensemble classifier system for early diagnosis of acute lymphoblastic leukemia in blood microscopic images. In *Neural Computing and Applications* (pp. 1–18).
5. Madhloom, H., Kareem, S., & Ariffin, H. (2012). A robust feature extraction and selection method for the recognition of Lymphocytes versus acute Lymphoblastic Leukemia. In *International Conference on Advanced Computer Science Applications and Technologies* (pp. 330—335).
6. Singhal, V., & Singh, P. (2014). Local binary pattern for detection of Acute Lymphoblastic Leukemia. In *National Conference on Communication (NCC)* (pp. 1–5).
7. Nor Hazlyna, H., Mashor, M., Mokhtar, N. R., Aimi Salihah, A., Hassan, R., Raof, R. A. A., & Osman, M. (2010). Comparison of acute leukemia Image segmentation using HSI and RGB color space. In *10th International Conference on Information Sciences Signal Processing and their Applications (ISSPA)* (pp. 749–752).
8. Ojala, T., Pietikäinen, M., & Mäenpää, T. (2002). Multiresolution gray-scale and rotation invariant texture classi_cation with local binary patterns. *IEEE Transactions on Pattern Analysis and Machine Intelligence, 24*, 971–987.
9. Nanni, L., Lumini, A., & Brahnam, S. (2010). Local binary patterns variants as texture descriptors for medical image analysis. In *US National Library of Medicine National Institutes of Health* (pp. 117–125).
10. Haralick, R., Shanmugam, K., & Dinstein, I. (1973). Textural features for image classification. *IEEE Transactions on Systems, Man and Cybernetics*, 610—621.
11. Kohavi, R. (1995). A study of cross-validation and bootstrap for accuracy estimation and model selection. In *Proceedings of the Fourteenth International Joint Conference on Artificial Intelligence* (pp. 1137–1143).
12. Labati, R., Piuri, V., & Scotti, F. (2011). All-IDB: The acute lymphoblastic leukemia image database for image processing. In *18th IEEE International Conference on Image Processing (ICIP)* (pp. 2045–2048).
13. Hall, M., Frank, E., Holmes, G., Pfahringer, B., Reutemann, P., & Witten, I. H. (2009). The WEKA data mining software: An update. *SIGKDD Explorations Newsletter, 11*, 10–18.
14. ALL-IDB. Acute Lymphoblastic Leukemia Image Database for Image Processing. http://www.dti.unimi.it/fscotti/all/results.php.
15. Scotti, F. (2005). Automatic morphological analysis for acute leukemia identification in peripheral blood microscope images. In *IEEE International Conference on Computational Intelligence for Measurement Systems and Applications, (CIMSA)* (pp. 96–101).

Design and Implementation of Non Touch Enabled Password System

Monica Varia and Hardik Modi

Abstract In the field of virtual environment applications we are using mouse, keyboards, and so forth are the common controlling and directing devices. In the current age of technology, touch and non touch enabled technologies has prevailed over it. This paper presents a system where red color detection technology has been used which provides more a natural way of feeling of interacting with the devices. This work is an attempt to replace earliest devices to enter the input with the natural finger wrapped with red color tape by non-touching the screen. It displays the keypad on detection of red color. Keypad contains fundamental keys such as 0–9 digits, Delete, and All Clear key to enter the password. The system can be used in real-time applications for password security systems in the areas such as ATM, Jewelers Shop, Home Security, etc. This proposed system gain advantages of cost-effectiveness, replacement of keyboard, and more preferable where space is scarce. It provides accuracy of 92 %.

Keywords Human machine interaction · Non touch enable technology · Red color detection · Centroid · ATM · Jewelers shop · Home security

1 Introduction

Since earliest times, keyboards are commonly used to enter the password in all the human machine interaction devices. It begins a new era to see over the existing technologies which deal to interact with the digital devices. In our system, we have proposed the concept of virtual password for ATMs. We assume that the camera for virtual password is focused in front line direction and its camera scans the area of

M. Varia (✉) · H. Modi
Electronics and Communication Engineering Department,
Charotar University of Science and Technology, Changa, India
e-mail: varia.monica19@gmail.com

H. Modi
e-mail: modi8584@yahoo.com

© Springer Science+Business Media Singapore 2016
S.C. Satapathy et al. (eds.), *Proceedings of International Conference on ICT for Sustainable Development*, Advances in Intelligent Systems and Computing 409, DOI 10.1007/978-981-10-0135-2_53

the user standing near the machine. Here, software processes the scanned picture taken through the captured area and detects the red color object or finger wrapped with red color tape.

A key step in the whole concept of non touch enable password is the detection of red color and locating its centroid to enter the password. Finally, it displays the keypad having 0–9 digits along with other keys like Delete and All Clear on the screen. We have proposed the concept of red color detection technology. The focus is on to enter the numbers for password by non-touching any device or screen [1]. While on entering the correct password, the message box appears on the screen which shows "Password Accepted," whereas it is unresponsive on entering the wrong password.

2 Non Touch Enabled Technology

It is advancement to the touch enabled technologies that have been implemented so far. The strong tracking of hand has been a lively area of research in the applications, where finger movements or hand geometry kind of system is needed [1]. Figure 1 shows a picture of touchless technology.

Recently, many companies have introduced touchless technology in their products which lets one to control the smart phone or tablet without actually touching the display. Using it, one can swipe, drag, and prod at the touch screen device [2]. It has also a different way where touchless control lets one to control the phone by speaking commands. For that one has to train the phone to recognize a user's voice. Thereafter, it is ready to launch command, execute voice searches and unique device commands [3].

In current scenario, non touch screens are available in mobile phones, laptops, and such digital devices. Yet, it has not been used extensively due to lack of some features and high accuracy. Mostly, bare index finger is used to provide the input. But when it comes to non touch, current research is probably limited to any color over the skin in some areas.

Another technology is Gesture Recognition where human gestures are inferred via mathematical algorithms. Gesture can originate from any bodily motion or state, but mainly originate from face or hand. Gesture recognition can be seen as a way

Fig. 1 Touchless technology [2]

for computers to begin to understand human body language [4]. Hence, current focus is on emotion recognition and hand gesture recognition.

In the system of non touch technology, it provides input without touching the screen. In this system, it works on the principle of comparing the centroid of red color part and the pixels inside the circle of any particular number to be entered. As the finger moves on the locations of the different numbers, that particular number is detected [4]. Eventually, one can enter the defined password. So, basically it is similar to natural way of dealing with the device.

3 System Overview

In this study, we implement a system that allows the user to enter the password without need of keyboard. The entire system configuration of the proposed algorithm is shown in Fig. 2 [5].

Fig. 2 Flow chart of algorithm

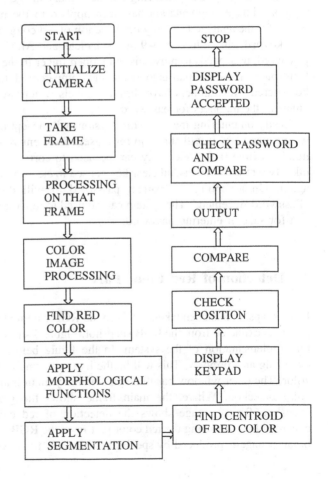

4 System Description

In this study, the system provides privilege to user to enter password input without the aid of keyboard. This system uses a webcam either inbuilt in system or plugged [1]. Figure 2 shows the flow chart of Algorithm of the proposed non touch enabled password system. The system is implemented in MATLAB considering real-time constraints [1]. In this proposed technique, the camera initialization will be done foremost. This will be done by clicking on the PLAY button which will start the camera and also start live capturing of the particular area. Now, while capturing, it will take a frame of the focused area including the display of the device. Frame will be in RGB color space.

Further, the captured frame is to be processed so that red color part can be extracted from the RGB color frame as here we have considered particular red color for the system. Moreover, for proper detection of red color part, morphological functions have been used to remove all connected components from a binary image that have fewer pixels producing another binary image [6, 7].

Also, image segmentation has been applied to the resulted image to make it easier for the analyze [8]. Only on detection of red color, it will display the keypad. The keypad will be having 0–9 digits, Delete, and All Clear keys. For entering the password, user needs to move his red tapped finger in the direction of the numbers. Centroid of red color part is to locate and compare with the pixels of the number to be entered. All numbers have different pixels which are used for comparing and entering the numbers for password.

Lastly on entering the password, system will accept the right password and on wrong password it will show no response. While entering the password of having numbers from 0–9, Delete key can be used to correct a single digit entered mistakenly wrong. Whereas, all clear key is used to clear the whole password to enter it again. On accepting the correct password, it will display a message box of "Password Accepted." The system can be used to replace keyboards where they are just for sake of entering password.

5 Detection of Red Color Part

RGB snapshot has been taken out from the RGB captured video preview. Red color part gets extracted from the RGB snapshot. Figure 3 shows the output resulted from the implementation of the system. In the figure below, first window shows the capturing area preview. This will be the live capturing of the directed area in RGB color. The other window has three parts namely main frame, binary image, and red color detection. Where, the main frame shows the gray scale image of RGB snapshot. Binary image shows the detection of red color part which has been executed by subtracting the red color part from the RGB color space snapshot. This binary image is produced by specifying threshold to convert all the pixels above it

Fig. 3 *Red color* detection of a *red color* tape wrapped index finger

as 1(white) and rest of the pixels with the value 0(black). This binary image goes under processing to reduce "salt and pepper" noise.

Finally, in the red color detection window, part image is shown after the application of morphological functions to remove small objects and get a fine image.

6 Locating Centroid

Foremost, the procedure is executed to detect the red color part. Thereafter, Centroid is located in x and y coordinates which specifies the center of mass of the region. The first element of centroid shows the horizontal coordinate (x coordinate)

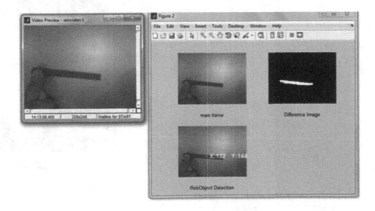

Fig. 4 Centroid of a *red colored* pen

of the center of mass, and the second element shows the vertical coordinate (or y coordinate) [9, 24].

Figure 4 shows the centroid of red color pen with x and y coordinates in yellow color in the third window of Fig. 2. It shows the x coordinate as 132 and y coordinate as 144.

7 Implementation Results

The proposed system has been implemented and the following pictures will depict the experimental results. Figure 5 shows the index finger wrapped with red color tape. Now, the system window has a PLAY button and Enter your password box on startup. The PLAY button will become blue on moving hand cursor to it. On clicking PLAY button, it will start capturing the specified area for taking a snapshot.

Figure 6 shows the window, where capturing of the area has been started. It also shows system window along with display of keypad. The keypad will be displayed with keys 0–9, Delete, and All Clear keys. The different colors are used to show specified key.

Delete key will be used to delete a single number entered wrong mistakenly, whereas All Clear key will be used to clear all the data entered to enter a fresh password.

Now, Fig. 7 shows the system window displaying the password entered along with the message box "Password Accepted." The password stored in the database of coding here is 123. Thus, on entering the correct password, the following message box appears.

Fig. 5 Index finger wrapped
with *red color* tape

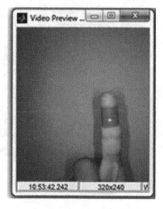

Fig. 6 System window
displays keypad on detection
of *red color*

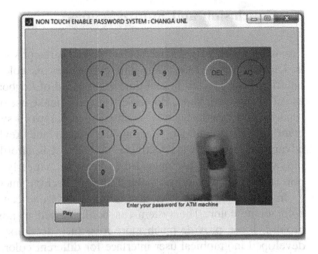

Fig. 7 System window
displays message box
'password accepted'

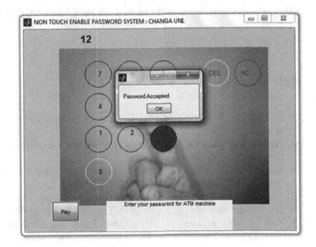

8 Applications

Design of Non Touch Enable Technology can be used in Real-Time Applications
for commercial purposes such as ATMs, Jewelers shop, and non commercial
purposes such as Home security, and so forth. The system can be helpful to replace
keyboards to provide input with red color tape wrapped finger by non-touching
the screen. It can also be useful to reduce the cost of the overall system and at the
systems where there is scarcity of space [4].

9 Conclusion and Future Scopes

Password is being used since ancient times for the privacy of the valuable resources and to keep them safe. Thus, this paper presents color detection technology for entering the password in real time without aid of keyboard. Existing systems such as ATM, Jewelers Shop, Home Security, etc., make use of keyboards while entering security codes, whereas non touch enabled password system provides privilege to enter password without touching the screen and keyboard. This would be an advantage to reduce the hardware cost and it is effortless to use. The touchless password entry can be controlled from as far as nearly 2–3 inches. Moreover, the non touch system supply a natural human machine interaction.

In this system, red color tape is used while one can make a system using any color or no color. The system can be developed in noisy as well as plain background. It can provide much more robustness to the system. Moreover, it can be developed in graphical user interface for different colors for different persons.

Acknowledgments We would like to thank the Charotar University of Science and Technology for its constant support all the way through our work.

References

1. Chaudhary, A. (2014). Natural Computing: Finger-Stylus for Non Touch-Enable Systems. arXiv:1409.3554.
2. Non Touch Enabled Technology. http://www.cnet.com/news/touchless-touch-screen-gives-you-control-without-contact-video/.
3. Touchless Control Technology. https://motorola-global-portal.custhelp.com/app/answers/prod_answer_detail/a_id/94881/p/30,6720,8696.
4. Monica, V., & Modi, H. (2014). Comprehensive study of non touch enable password system. Int. J. Adv. Res. Comput. Commun. Eng. *3*(12), 8793–8796.
5. Kim, J. -M., & Lee, W. -K. (2008). Hand shape recognition using fingertips. In *Fifth International Conference on Fuzzy Systems and Knowledge Discovery, 2008. FSKD '08*, vol. 4, pp. 44,48, October 18–20, 2008.
6. Morphological Functions. https://www.cs.auckland.ac.nz/courses/compsci773s1c/lectures/ImageProcessing-html/topic4.htm.
7. Morphological Functions. http://www.phon.ucl.ac.uk/home/dick/enc2010/articles/morphological-function.htm.
8. Image Segmentation. http://en.wikipedia.org/wiki/Image_segmentation.
9. Gonzalez, R. C., Woods, R. E., & Eddins, S. L. (2004). *Digital image processing using MATLAB*. Upper Saddle River: Pearson Prentice Hall.
10. Hagara, M., & Pucik, J. (2013). Fingertip detection for virtual keyboard based on camera. In *23rd International Conference Radioelektronika (RADIOELEKTRONIKA)*, pp. 356,360, April 16–17, 2013.
11. Raheja, J.L., Chaudhary, A., & Singal, K., (2011). Tracking of Fingertips and Centers of Palm Using KINECT. In *Third International Conference on Computational Intelligence, Modelling and Simulation (CIMSiM), 2011* pp. 248, 252, September 20–22, 2011.

12. Bragatto, T.A.C., Ruas, G.I.S., & Lamar, M.V. (2006). Real-time video based finger spelling recognition system using low computational complexity Artificial Neural Networks. *Telecommunications Symposium, 2006 International*, pp. 393, 397, September 3–6, 2006.
13. Sudderth, E.B., Mandel, M.I., Freeman, W.T., Willsky, A.S., Visual Hand Tracking Using Nonparametric Belief Propagation," *Computer Vision and Pattern Recognition Workshop, 2004. CVPRW'04. Conference on*, vol., no., pp.189,189, 27–02 June 2004.
14. Tu, J., Huang, T., Hai Tao, "Face as mouse through visual face tracking," *Computer and Robot Vision, 2005. Proceedings. The 2nd Canadian Conference on*, vol., no., pp.339,346, 9–11 May 2005.
15. Chaudhary, A., Gupta, A., "Automated switching system for skin pixel segmentation in varied lighting," *Mechatronics and Machine Vision in Practice (M2VIP), 2012 19th International Conference*, vol., no., pp.26,31, 28–30 Nov. 2012.
16. Hsieh, C.-C. Tsai, M.-R., Su, M.-C. (2008). A fingertip extraction method and its application to handwritten alphanumeric characters recognition. In *IEEE International Conference on Signal Image Technology and Internet Based Systems, 2008. SITIS '08*. pp. 293, 300, November 30–December 3, 2008.
17. Oka, K., Sato, Y., & Koike, H. (2002). Real-time fingertip tracking and gesture recognition. *Computer Graphics and Applications, IEEE, 22*(6), 64, 71.
18. Oka, K., Sato, Y., & Koike, H. (2002). Real-time tracking of multiple fingertips and gesture recognition for augmented desk interface systems. In *Proceedings of the Fifth IEEE International Conference on Automatic Face and Gesture Recognition, 2002*. pp. 429, 434, May 21–21, 2002.
19. Wu, Y., & Huang, T.S. (2001). Hand modeling, analysis and recognition. *Signal Processing MagazineIEEE 18*(3), 51, 60.
20. Abe, K., Saito, H., & Ozawa, S. (2000). 3-D drawing system via hand motion recognition from two cameras. *IEEE International Conference on Systems, Man, and Cybernetics 2*, 840,845.
21. Iwai, Y., Watanabe, K., Yagi, Y., & Yachida, M. (1996). Gesture recognition using colored gloves. In *Proceedings of the 13th International Conference on Pattern Recognition 1*, 662, 666, Auguest 25–29, 1996.
22. Sato, Y., Kobayashi, Y., & Koike, H. (2000). Fast tracking of hands and fingertips in infrared images for augmented desk interface. In *Proceedings of the Fourth IEEE International Conference on Automatic Face and Gesture Recognition*, pp. 462, 467, 2000.
23. Password. http://en.wikipedia.org/wiki/password.
24. Jain, A.K. (1989). *Fundamentals of digital image processing*. Prentice-Hall, New Jersey.

Intelligent Web Security Testing with Threat Assessment and Client Server Penetration

Hardik Gohel and Priyanka Sharma

Abstract The web today is a rising universe of interlinked web pages and web apps, crawling with videos, photos and interactive content. Web is very interactive nowadays to which we are calling web intelligence. The security standards we are providing with the web are not benchmark enough, it requires more security. It leads us to learn and develop intelligent web security testing with threat assessment and client server penetration testing. It results about security of any website you are testing. In this paper, we have implemented threat assessment and attacks which can be possible on web by using burp suite. We have also demonstrated about procedure of threat and attack testing and client server penetration using burp suite. The last paper has concluded corrective action to protect your web from various implemented as well as tested threats and attacks.

Keywords Web security · Cyber security · Web intelligence · Penetration testing · Threat · Attack assessment

1 Introduction

As a branch area of information communication security, security for web application deals with website as well as web security [11, 12]. At advance level, the principle of security application by using concept of security web application aspects especially internet and web systems [9, 15]. Classically, web applications are getting developed by using various programming languages such as Java, PHP, Python, ASP.NET, C#, VB.NET, HTML with other aspects. Whenever we are talking about web security immediately website attacks, credit card information

H. Gohel (✉)
Gujarat Technological University, Ahmedabad, Gujarat, India
e-mail: hagohel@gmail.com

P. Sharma
RSU, Ahmedabad, India
e-mail: pspriyanka@yahoo.com

© Springer Science+Business Media Singapore 2016
S.C. Satapathy et al. (eds.), *Proceedings of International Conference on ICT for Sustainable Development*, Advances in Intelligent Systems and Computing 409, DOI 10.1007/978-981-10-0135-2_54

stealing, denial of services and these many types of examples comes in our mind. Apart from these attacks worms, Trojan horses, a virus also comes in our thoughts but these are only few problems. Other significant problems, including internal threats by administrator or employees across data pose significant and risks [10]. The major problem would be ignorance. The learning of technology is easy but providing security to web applications is very difficult task. It is fragmentary process concerning practice and people.

2 Web Security Threat Assessment

The treat assessment is a controlled process in group to assess the risk masqueraded by any person, characteristically as a reply to a definite or alleged threat with reference to performance. Threat assessment as a procedure was created by the secret service as a reaction to occurrence of violent behaviour (OSPI [1]).

A threat is any probable happening, malicious or otherwise, which would harm an asset. In short, a threat is any awful object which appears to your asset. Threat is interconnected with attacks and vulnerabilities. Vulnerability is a one kind of weakness which makes possibility of threats. It is because of mistakes in configuration and poor design or improper coding. An attack is the one kind of exploitation with vulnerability or ratifies a threat. For example, an attacker can send multiple inputs to the particular application and trying to attempt denial of services [2].

In short, a threat is a probable occurrence which can adversely have an effect on an asset, where a victorious attack exploits vulnerabilities towards your system [16].

In terms of web application security, let us deliberate and assess the threat. In the beginning of web, there were no any kinds of attacks but with emergence of web generation 2.0 sharing of information has increased and with the concept of social networking the adaptation of web with delivering service and businesses [3]. With the view of sharing much information, business and personal, online may be attacked directly. By compromising network of corporate, company or accessing website by downloading through drive subjective hacker can seek to compromise [4].

Nowaday, corporate world is doing lot of expenses to give attention towards security of web applications apart from operating systems and computer networks. The major websites and web services can be attacks by using either SQL injection attack or cross site scripting that is XSS which are flawing result from coding and failure to web applications' which disinfect input to output (Microsoft [5]. The web application requires security from attacks which comes from vulnerabilities for that point it is having potential attacks from various aspects to vulnerabilities. In the statistics given by Cenzic, a vendor of security, the following attacks comes more through vulnerabilities to websites [6] (Table 1).

In the terms of threat assessment, the first question is suppose to ask that when we are thinking about threat is how that threat can reach to me and how is it easy for it.

Table 1 Top threat vulnerability assessment	Sr. no	Vulnerabilities	% of vulnerabilities attack
	1	Cross site scripting (XSS)	37
	2	SQL injection	16
	3	Other attacks includes PHP injection, JavaScript injection, etc.	15
	4	Denial of services	5
	5	Disclosure of path	5
	6	Request forgery of cross site	4
	7	Corruption of memory	4
	8	Execution of code	4
	9	Information disclosure	3
	10	Arbitrary file	3
	11	Including local file	2
	12	Including remote file	1
	13	Buffering overflow	1

The person is able to coming from any street or parking and directly without any intervention. If that answers are easy and yes then there is a reason to be a concern. The sharing of information regarding potential threats is very critical to survive. Threat can be undeveloped or controlled at outer level. Individual should know the motivation and intended target of the threats. Individual should never assume that by targeting threat the only person is in danger that has victim [5].

Furthermore related to threat assessment, individual should be aware and also able to recognise potential threats. The potential threats can include disgruntled employee who are having recent termination, domestic relationships, clients or customers who are angry on your organisation, motivated criminals planning to robbery, assault or sexual assault or it can be any random or opportunistic incidents. After anyone found the occurrence of threat, immediately he has to inform or warn others as well as provide safety to own first.

After having study of threat assessment related to web application security let us also discuss the number of tools which we are going to implement by using burp suite, the great tool for security testing of web applications [7].

2.1 Proxy

In web services, proxy is a bypass or server which acts as an interface request from client who is looking for resources from other server. As a part of web security, client can bypass original way and get banned services from other server. The banned files, connection, web pages and other resources client can access by proxy.

2.2 Spider

Spider is a process or program which involuntarily obtains web pages. To feed pages to search engines spiders are used. Because of it crawls over the web so it's known as spider (Beal [8]).

2.3 Scanner

Web scanner is a process or program in which web application communicating through web front end to identify vulnerabilities of potential security in website and weaknesses of architectural.

2.4 Intruder

To find out and exploit vulnerabilities, intruder can perform very powerful as well as customised attack. It is also for unauthorised access, damage the system and disturb the data.

2.5 Repeater

It is for resending individual request with some manipulations. It is modifying manually and issuing again individual request of client.

2.6 Sequencer

The sequencer is for identifying and testing the tokens of session.

3 System (Server) Penetration Using Burp Suite

Now, in this part we are going to demonstrate web application penetration by using website of www.jeremyellman.com. The website is related to sports and also known as Hale Sports Club (HSC). It offers a different facility which includes swimming pool, gym, racket, tennis, badminton and squash. Individual must be a member of the club to have auspicious facilities. The swimming pool and gym are only facilities that any member can enjoy it without booking. There is also booking time policy which identifies with minimum and maximum in which individual booking facility can done. It is minimum with 30 min and maximum with 120 min.

Here, we are documenting how penetration was achieved and corrective actions as well. Through very powerful tool we are going to perform web services penetration testing. For example, login method provided by web services and when are you going to bypass login method it requires to repeat the authentication request with many times to the credentials of brute force and it is very easy to implement with Burp Suite.

Burp suite is used by many security professionals. To perform web penetration testing this tool is very useful and popular as well. It is a platform with integration of security testing of web application and in most cases we can use it for testing web services with mobile applications as well. It gives full control to enhance and automate the process of testing. The key components of burp are the same that we have discussed in threat assessment component in previous part.

Now, let us get setup with burp suite. For that following step we are going to implement.

This demo focuses on setup burp suite and browser to test web penetration. As per our lab exercise we are going to perform using Ubuntu Linux system which is very secure operating system.

1. Login to Windows
2. Start VMWare player 6
3. If you can see OWASP_LTE on the menu start. We can see the Fig. 1.
4. Login as OWASPWTE.
5. Mouse over the icon on the top left to see the system menu.
6. There is a mac-like action bar that will appear when you mouse over the bottom middle of the screen.

After performing above we need to cancel upgrades of system. So by cancelling many upgrades we can save several hours which requires installing them. So decline upgrading from 'Trusty Tahir' and it is not necessary to upgrade VMWare.

Fig. 1 Screen of VMWare player

Now the next task is to upgrade burp suite. If there is updated version f burp suite is available we can update it by using various commands which we are not going to discuss over here. And now next process is starting process with Burp Suite. For starting testing web penetration with burp suite we require to perform following commands. Generally, we can start burp suite by double clicking

(1) At a command prompt type:
    cd/opt/owasp/Burp Suite
(2) Now we start burp suite[1], with enhanced memory by typing:
    Java -jar -Xmx1024m Burp Suite _free_v1.6.jar
    Where, 1024 is the amount of memory (in Mb) that you want to assign to Burp.
(3) If this is the first time, please accept the licence.
(4) Leave the command prompt open. If you kill it, Burp Suite will die.

Now, the next step is to configure browser. Generally there are various browsers we can use but we are going to use Firefox only as we have done in our lab exercise.

The following steps are there for Configuring Firefox.

(1) Select Firefox options (grid icon on top right)
(2) Choose Preferences
(3) Open the advanced tab
(4) Select network and settings
(5) Choose manual proxy
(6) We will be proxying all ports through 8080
(7) Delete 'No proxy for localhost, 127.0.0.1' We will be proxying through the localhost

Try opening any page after you have accepted. The proxy is not running, so you should get an error message. (No error message means either you have not set the proxy up, or one is already running) (Figs. 2 and 3).

The following step is for configuring Burp Proxy:

1. Start Burp Suite if not running as above
2. Select proxy and then options
3. Remove the proxy port for 8080
4. Add a new proxy for port 8007

Now we are ready for testing because Burp Suite is available between our browser Firefox and web server which we are going to access. We must be able to look at the interrupt or edit any request as well as responses.

---

[1]<-!Burp Suite: Video Tutorials - Portswigger.net at https://portswigger.net/burp/tutorials/Burp Suite - Portswigger.net at https://portswigger.net/burp/ !->

Fig. 2 Refusing connections while accessing browser

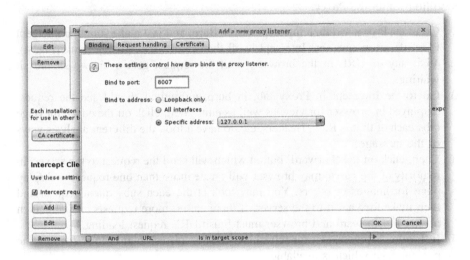

Fig. 3 Add a new proxy listener to browser

1. Ensure the proxy 'intercept' is turned OFF
2. Open any web page. If Firefox say 'proxy in not responding' check carefully that the port number correspond between Firefox and burp.

Now, we are going to examine with interaction with client and server and we going to perform server penetration.

The first is proxy which lies workflow of users and gives direct view into targeted application works 'under the hood' which operates proxy server of web and takes availability as a man in the middle between our browser and the server which is our destination. It allows intercept with modification of raw traffic which is passing in two ways or we can say in both direction. Burp is breaking the Secure Socket Layer (SSL) connection between browser and server if our web application employs with HTTPS.

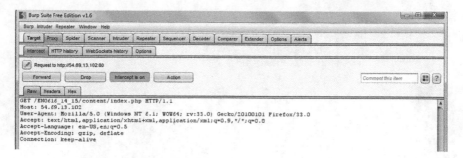

Fig. 4 Proxy with intercept on

If the application employs HTTPS, Burp breaks the SSL connection between your browser and the server, so that even encrypted data can be viewed and modified within the Proxy.

1. Go to the Proxy and then intercept tab, In Burp, and just make sure that intercept is on if button says that Intercept is off then click t the intercept rank (Fig. 4).
2. Visit any of URL in the browser, until the request gets over, we should sit waiting.
3. Go to the Intercept in Proxy tab, in burp, individual should see the request displayed in browser for view as well as edit. Then, click on the editor message tabs each of that is Raw, Headers, etc. to have a look the different analysis ways of the message.
4. Then, click on the 'Forward' button which will send the request to the server. In majority of the cases, may browser will create more than one request to display page for images or others. You may look at the each subsequent request and then make forward it to the server. If there are no more requests available then no need to forward and browser must finish URL request loading.
5. In Firefox browser, just for refreshing click on refresh button for reloading the present page which is available.

In proxy there is an optional button in which proxy listener is there where local HTTP proxy listens for incoming connections from your browser which allows intercept and monitor with all request as well as responses. As we have configured our browser with 127.0.0.1: 8080 as a proxy server. This is a default listener and we can change it according to our requirements. It allows us to create multiple listeners and provides configuration options with its behaviour.

4 Attack on Other Users (Client) Penetration Using Burp Suite

Now we are going to implement different types of attack through Burp Suite (Fig. 5 and 6).

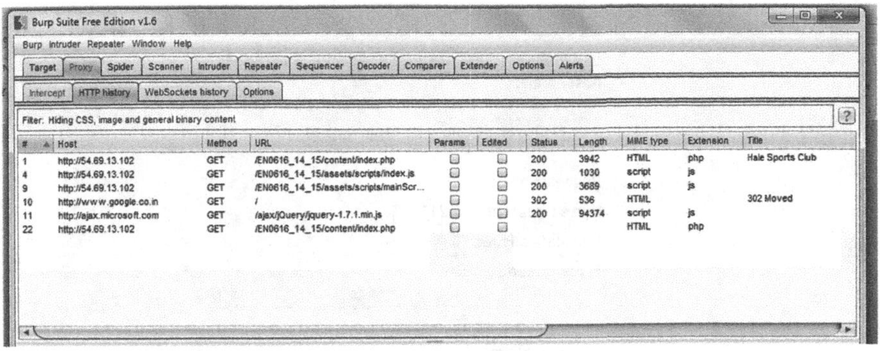

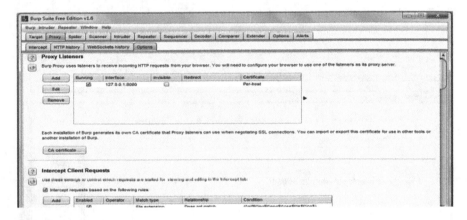

Fig. 5 Proxy with HTTP history status

Fig. 6 Proxy with listener Proxy4

4.1 Spider by Burp Suite

As now, we are having all setup with proxy and have server penetration so now it's beneficial to go for next testing that is spider the host. It is very easy with Burp Suite by simply just clicking on the target's root branch in the sitemap and selecting 'Spider this host' (Fig. 7).

Once, we are completing spider attack we can check in our sitemap and can pick up new pages also. We are having other pages also with our browser to which we can apply the spider attack. If there are new login prompts as well as input boxes which we can make it happen. Furthermore, just by having right click on the root branch and from the engagement tool, which is not available in our free version of Burp Suite, we can select the Discover Content. In most of the sites this will run for long time. This is the way we can check web penetration by applying spider tool available on Burp Suite.

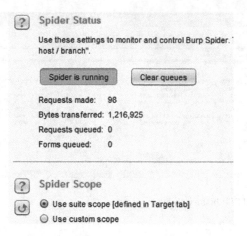

Fig. 7 Spider status after spider on host

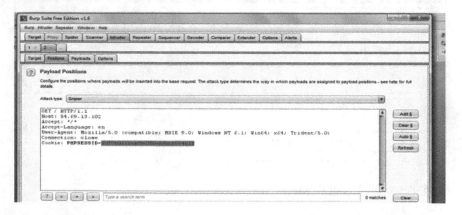

Fig. 8 Burp suite with intruder testing

4.2 Intruder by Using Burp Suite

With the limited time and of course with multiple so many request with individual parameters through test is possible manually. For semi-targeted fussing and automated performance burp suite intruder is really powerful and great way. I used it against multiple parameters with request of HTTP. Just by right clicking on what we are going to do for other testing also and select 'Send to Intruder'. Now select the tab Intruder available on main menu and click on sub tab positions. It will display window which has been shown in Fig. 10.

I specially recommend using Clear button to remove selection that is PHPSESSID. The default behaviour is to with '=' sign everything. Highlight the particular parameter which we do not want to fuzz and click on Add with simply.

Fig. 9 Burp suite with repeater

Then after, we need to go to Payloads with sub tab and tell the burp to test it to perform to run fuzzy. We can select 'Fuzzing—full', this is not available in our free burp suite but it is very useful to change content from various options but with limitation to highlight in intruder.

4.3 Repeater by Using Burp Suite

The repeater is the most useful feature available on burp suite. Individual can use it thousand times on every web applications when they go for web penetration testing. It is also very easy to use and simple as well (Figs. 8 and 9).

Just by giving right click within the Target tab or proxy tab and just selecting 'Send to Repeater'. Then click over the tab of Repeater and just hit on Go. It will give below given window which appears with Request and Response as well.

Herewith, we can also manipulate any portion related to HTTP request headers and can see response that is available in above window. I have really spend good amount of time with repeater by playing various HTTP request with the parameters of GET and POST which are really nice experience along with request whichever I have sent with many parameters.

4.4 Sequencer by Using Burp Suite

When we would like to check the random extent with to the session and its tokens which are generated by its web application, it is a tool, also known as tailor made tool to carry out such kind of tests. When we are trying every possible combination of breaking authentication is known as brute force search which breaks web application by applying every possible attack. It creates very serious concern in

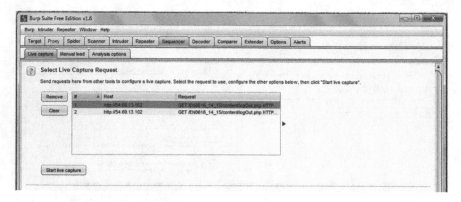

Fig. 10 Sequencer with burp suite

session ID token with high randomness of degree. The session token with sending request is explained below.

In Fig. 10 we can see the token with request of the site with IP http://54.69.13. 102. In the screen right side starting and ending token expression is present. Individual can either specify a session with an expression of web, in given IP, or even offset setting from where token should start. With the token end panel, the same thing holds and where we can set the delimiters as well or fixed length for the start capture.

5 Conclusion

Security for web applications and its implementation with burp suite is really interesting and innovative study. In above study, we have carried out document of threat assessment in which we came across all types of threats and attacks which can take place as a part of web security [13, 14]. Then after, we have demonstrated web application penetration by applying gold membership of HSC and we have set proxy to apply all types of attack on web. We have also suggested corrective actions that developer should take to secure from web penetration on server. At last, we have implemented penetration achievement on individual user by applying different types of attack on them and also mentioned corrective action for that. Following the conclusion points we can carry out the actions (Fig. 11).

- Server penetration is more risky than user penetration.
- If legitimate user has been attacked by any attack then it is not limited to that user, it can also affect other users as well.
- Sometimes legitimate users are also harmful for web applications for what we have to specify some different ways to secure.

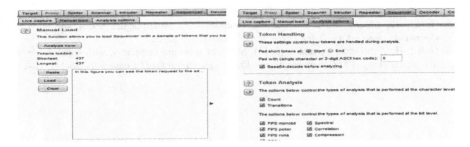

Fig. 11 Manual load and token handling with sequencer

- All threats and attacks we have learnt are come from the vulnerability of the web application, so we should find out vulnerability and have to fix it up.
- The best corrective action is timely auditing of the web application transaction. Sometimes it should be surprise audit as well.

The above corrective actions are useful to secure out web applications from different attacks which we have discussed above.

References

1. OSPI Threat Assessment (2013). http://www.k12.wa.us/.
2. Meier, J. D., Mackman A., Dunner, M., & Vasireddy S. (2010). Ray escamilla and anandha murukan improving web application security: threats and countermeasures. http://msdn.microsoft.com.
3. Gohel, H. A. (2014). Looking back at the evolution of the internet. *CSI Communications—Knowledge Digest for IT Community 38*(6), 23–26. http://www.csi-india.org/.
4. Fonseca, J. (2011). CISUC—Polithecnic Institute of Guarda, Guarda; Vieira, M.; Madeira, H. Testing and Comparing Web Vulnerability Scanning Tools for SQL Injection and XSS Attacks, Available at: http://ieeexplore.ieee.org/.
5. Microsoft Improving Web Application Security: Threats and Countermeasures. (2013). http://msdn.microsoft.com/.
6. Trustwave. (2014). Application Vulnerability Trends Report. https://www2.trustwave.com (2014).
7. PortSwigger "PortSwigger Web Security Blog".(2014). http://blog.portswigger.net/.
8. Vangie Beal Spider. (2014). http://www.webopedia.com/.
9. Antonyms Open Web Application Security Project (OWASP). (2013). https://www.owasp.org.
10. Hardik, G. (2015). Design and development of combined algorithm computing technique to enhance web security. *International Journal of Innovative and Emerging Research in Engineering (IJIERE), 2*(1), 76–79.
11. Hardik, G. (2015). Design of intelligent web based social media for data personalization. *International Journal of Innovative and Emerging Research in Engineering(IJIERE)* 2.1: 42–45.
12. Hardik, G., & Upadhyay, A. (2012). Reinforcement of knowledge grid multi-agent model for e-governance inventiveness in India. *Academic Journal* 53.3: 232.
13. Gohel, H., & Gondalia, V. (2013). Executive information advancement of knowledge based decision support system for organization of United Kingdom.

14. Jenniferc. (2014). A burp suite tutorial: learn the basics. https://www.udemy.com.
15. Gohel, H. (2015). Role of machine translation for multilingual social media. *CSI Communications—Knowledge Digest for IT Community* 35–38.
16. Gohel, H., & Sharma, Priyanka. (2015). Study of quantum computing with significance of machine learning. *CSI Communications—Knowledge Digest for IT Community, 38*(11), 21–23.

QoS-aware Autonomic Cloud Computing for ICT

Sukhpal Singh and Inderveer Chana

Abstract Emergence of Information and Communication Technologies (ICT) plays an important role in networking sector by providing services through cloud-based systems. Based on application requirements of cloud users, discovery and allocation of best workload-resource pair is an optimization problem. Acceptable Quality of Service (QoS) cannot be provided to the cloud users until provisioning of resources is offered as a crucial ability. QoS parameters based resource provisioning technique is therefore required for efficient scheduling of resources. In this paper, QoS-aware autonomic resource provisioning and scheduling for cloud computing technique has been proposed. The proposed technique caters to provisioned resource distribution and scheduling of resources. The performance of the proposed technique has been evaluated through Cloud environment. The experimental results show that the proposed technique gives better results in terms of execution cost and execution time of different Cloud workloads.

Keywords Resource provisioning · Resource scheduling · Quality of service · Autonomic cloud · Information and communication technologies

1 Introduction

Cloud Computing enables resources (Infrastructure, Platform or Software) to be offered as services for Information and Communication Technologies (ICT). These resources are provided using a pay-as-you-use pricing plan [1]. To satisfy the request of customers, ICT-based service must be provided in accordance with required level of QoS. However, providing dedicated ICT-based Cloud services that

S. Singh (✉) · I. Chana
Computer Science and Engineering Department, Thapar University,
Patiala 147004, Punjab, India
e-mail: ssgill@thapar.edu

I. Chana
e-mail: inderveer@thapar.edu

© Springer Science+Business Media Singapore 2016 569
S.C. Satapathy et al. (eds.), *Proceedings of International Conference on ICT for Sustainable Development*, Advances in Intelligent Systems and Computing 409, DOI 10.1007/978-981-10-0135-2_55

ensure user's dynamic QoS requirements and avoid Service Level Agreement (SLA) violations, a big challenge in Cloud Computing. Currently, Cloud services are provisioned and scheduled according to resources' availability without ensuring the expected performances [2]. To realize this, there is a need to consider important aspect of ICT-based service which reflects the complexity introduced by the Cloud management: QoS-aware autonomic management of ICT-based Cloud services [3]. QoS-aware aspect involves the capacity of the ICT-based service to be aware of its behavior to ensure the minimum execution time and cost.

Other reason of increase in execution cost is resources are running in idle or underutilization state. Efficient resource scheduling in Cloud is a challenging job and the scheduling of appropriate resources to Cloud workloads depends on the QoS requirements of Cloud applications [3]. Execution Time and execution cost in case of heterogeneous cloud workloads is very difficult to improve. Therefore, there is need of Cloud-based framework which schedules computing resources automatically by considering execution time and execution cost as a QoS parameter to provide efficient ICT services. Autonomic resource provisioning and scheduling is an ability to reduce cost and time in ICT-based autonomic systems which are self-optimizing. This research work focuses on one of the important aspects (QoS parameters) of self-optimization, i.e., execution time and execution cost.

The motivation of this paper is to design a cloud-based QoS-aware autonomic resource provisioning and scheduling technique for effective scheduling of resources for ICT-based services which considers execution time and cost as important QoS parameters. The main aim of this research work is: (i) to propose an autonomic resource provisioning and scheduling technique for execution of heterogeneous workloads for effective ICT services, (ii) to optimize the QoS parameters such as execution time and cost, and (iii) to implement and perform evaluation with existing work. Paper is structured as follows: Sect. 2 presents related work and contributions. Proposed technique is presented in Sect. 3. Section 4 describes the experimental setup used for performance evaluation and results. Section 5 presents conclusions and future directions.

2 Related Work

This section is presenting the related work of resource provisioning and scheduling in brief.

2.1 Resource Provisioning

Kuan et al. [4] proposed QoS-based autonomous SLA model of violation-filtering for IaaS and PaaS applying a SLA appraising many ways and penalty architecture and presenting a resource provisioning mechanism to manage resource efficiently without specifying the QoS parameters. Linlin et al. [5] proposed SLA-based provisioning technique to reduce resource price and SLA deviations. The management of customer requests, and mapping them with resources is defined along with the supervision of different types of workloads by considering QoS such as execution time. Qiang et al. [6] presented a virtual environment-based framework for better supervision of infrastructure which offers separation among workloads running concurrently with similar resources and sanctions dynamic horizontal and vertical scalability to realize Service Level Objectives. Trieuet et al. [7] proposed a framework for dynamic workloads based on threshold number of dynamic periods for dynamically assigning and quickly provisioning of virtual resources to users based on their QoS requirements. Nikolas et al. [8] described self-adaptive resource provisioning approach to find the appropriate predicting ways for a given perspective through the use of decision tree. This approach considers QoS parameters like relative error and SLA violation, and minimizes both the parameters but does not consider execution time and execution cost.

2.2 Resource Scheduling

Pandey et al. [9] presented a Particle Swarm Optimization-based heuristic technique to schedule the applications to Cloud resources that proceeds both computation and data transmission cost. Topcuoglu et al. [10] presented the HEFT algorithm to discover the average execution time of each workload and also the average communication time among the resources of two workloads. Wu et al. [11] suggested a Market Oriented Hierarchical Scheduling approach which contains of both service level scheduling and workload level scheduling. The service level scheduling deals with the Task to Service assignment and the workload level scheduling deals with the optimization of the Task to Virtual Machine assignment in local Cloud data centers. Yu et al. [12] proposed a Cost-Based Workflow Scheduling algorithm that reduces the execution cost, however, meeting the deadline for delivering results. Varalakshmi et al. [13] described an Optimal Workflow-based Scheduling framework to discover a solution that tries to meet the user-desired QoS constraints, i.e. execution time. QoS-aware autonomic resource provisioning and scheduling technique needs to consider the basic features of Cloud computing for ICT in order to execute the heterogeneous Cloud workloads automatically with minimum execution time and execution cost, which is not considered in above discussed existing work.

3 QoS-aware Autonomic Resource Provisioning and Scheduling Technique for ICT-Based Services

Provisioning and scheduling of resources in cloud is an important part of resource management system. Mapping of cloud workloads to appropriate resources is mandatory to improve QoS parameters like execution time and execution cost etc.

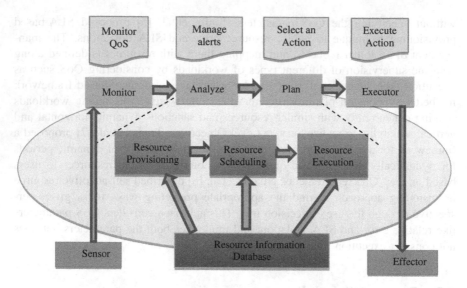

Fig. 1 Architecture of QoS-aware autonomic resource provisioning and scheduling technique

[14]. Based on QoS requirements, scheduling finds and maps the resources and workloads. Resource provisioning and scheduling in Cloud is done in the following steps [2, 3]: (i) understand the expectations and requirements of Cloud user, (ii) analyze and cluster the workloads through machine learning algorithm, i.e., K-Means based Clustering Algorithm, (iii) find the required number of resources, (iv) map the resources and workloads, and (v) schedule and execute the workloads on appropriate resources with minimum time and cost. This scheduling framework executes the workloads without self-optimization. But in the present scenario, there is need of Cloud-based technique for ICT which provisions and schedules computing resources automatically by considering execution time and execution cost as a QoS parameter. In this research paper, we focused on these two parameters and automated the existing framework [2, 3]. In this paper, we have extended the existing work by considering two important QoS parameters through automation for ICT-based service. Architecture of QoS-aware autonomic resource provisioning and scheduling technique is shown in Fig. 1. This technique is based on IBM's autonomic model [15] that considers four steps of autonomic system: (1) Monitor, (2) Analyze, (3) Plan, and (4) Execute.

3.1 Monitor [M]

Initially, *Monitor* is used to collect the information from sensors (*Sensors* (Wireless Sensor Network) get the information about execution time and cost of all the systems working under ICT based Cloud environment and update the information time to time) for monitoring continuously the value of execution time and execution cost and transfer this information to next module for further analysis.

3.2 Analysis and Plan [AP]

Analyze and Plan module start analyzing the information received from monitoring module and make a plan for adequate actions for corresponding alert. In this step, based on QoS requirements of workload(s), resources are provisioned, scheduled, and executed.

3.2.1 Resource Provisioning

Monitor continually checks the status of resources provisioned, workloads queued, and SLA deviation. The objective of resource provisionor is to provision the resources to Cloud consumer without violation of SLA. The workloads submitted should be executed within their budget and deadline. Proposed ICT-based technique provisions and schedules the resources based on time and cost to the workloads automatically is shown in Fig. 2. Workload submitted by user to resource provisionor is stored into bulk of workloads for their execution. All the submitted workloads are analyzed based on their QoS requirements described in terms of SLA. Workload patterns are identified for better classification of workloads, then pattern-based clustering of workloads is done. QoS metrics for every QoS requirement of each workload are identified [2]. Based on importance of the attribute, weights for every cloud workload are calculated. After that, workloads are re-clustered based on K-Means based clustering algorithm for better execution. Calculate the value of

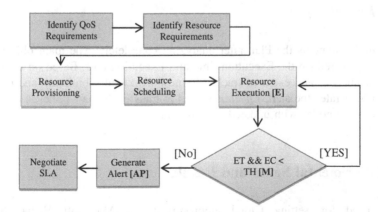

Fig. 2 Automatic execution of QoS-aware autonomic resource provisioning and scheduling technique

Execution time and Execution cost. If the value of workloads executes within deadline and budget [Execution Time (ET) and Execution Cost (EC) is lesser than Threshold Value (TH)] then it will provision resources otherwise generate alert for analyzing the workload again after resubmission of SLA by Cloud consumer.

3.2.2 Resource Scheduling

After successful provisioning of resources, Resource Scheduler (RS) takes the information from the appropriate workload after analyzing the various workload details which Cloud consumer demanded [3]. Decision tree is used to select the particular scheduling policy based on consumer workload details [3]. RS then collect the information available resources from Resource Information Database (RID). RID contains details of all the resources available in resource pool and reserve resource pool. Based on Cloud consumer details RS assigns resources and executes Cloud workloads.

3.2.3 Resource Execution

During execution of a particular Cloud workload, the Resource Executor (RE) will check the current workload. If the resources are sufficient for execution then it will continue with execution otherwise request for more resources. RE will check policy conditions and cost and time. If the Execution time and Execution cost is lesser than threshold value then RE will execute workloads, otherwise RE will generate alert. After successful execution of Cloud workloads, RE releases the free resources to resource pool and RE is ready for execution of new Cloud workloads.

3.3 Executor [E]

Executor implements the Plan after analyzing completely. The main objective of *executor* is to reduce the Execution time and Execution cost. Based on the output given by analysis and executor tracks, the new workload submission and resource addition generates the alert. *Effector* is used to transfer the new policies, rules, and alerts to other nodes with updated information.

4 Experimental Setup and Results

Tools used for setting Cloud environment are Microsoft Visual Studio, NetBeans IDE 7.1.2, CloudSim, IntegratedNETJavaWeb, and SQL Server. Microsoft Visual Studio 2010 is an Integrated Development Environment from

Fig. 3 Number of workloads
versus cost

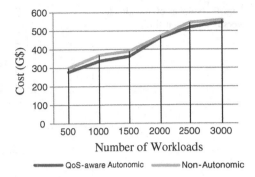

Microsoft. Cloud user interacts with ICT-based autonomic framework through Cloud Workload Management Portal (CWMP) to submit the workload details. User information, workload detail, and resource detail are stored in database through SQL Server. Cloud workload management portal is implemented in .NET framework and framework is running in Microsoft Visual Studio. We have explained the description of simulation environment in our previous work [3].

Figure 3 shows the cost of different number of workloads (500–3000) with QoS-aware autonomic resource provisioning and scheduling technique (QoS-aware Autonomic) and non-autonomic technique. Non-QoS based resource scheduling technique used for experimental evaluation in this paper has been designed by combining two traditional resource scheduling algorithms (First Come First Serve FCFS and Round Robin), in which resources are scheduled without considering QoS parameters. Cost is increasing with increase in number of workloads but QoS-aware autonomic resource provisioning and scheduling technique performs better. Cost of different number of resources (50–250) of QoS-aware autonomic resource provisioning and scheduling technique (QoS-aware Autonomic) is compared with non-autonomic technique as shown in Fig. 4. Cost is decreasing with increase in number of resources and result shows the QoS-aware autonomic technique executes the same number of Cloud workloads at a lesser cost.

Figure 5 shows the execution time of different number of workloads with QoS-aware autonomic resource provisioning and scheduling technique (QoS-aware

Fig. 4 Number of resources
versus cost

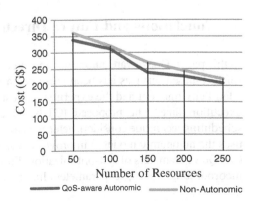

Fig. 5 Number of workloads
versus execution time

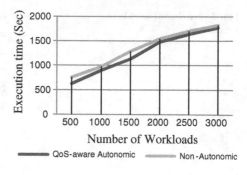

Fig. 6 Number of resources
versus execution time

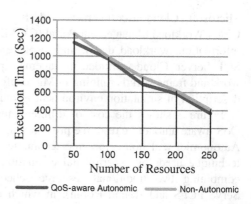

Autonomic) and non-autonomic technique. Execution Time is increasing with
increase in number of workloads, but QoS-aware autonomic resource provisioning
and scheduling technique performs better. Execution Time of different number of
resources of QoS-aware autonomic resource provisioning and scheduling technique
(QoS-aware Autonomic) is compared with non-autonomic technique as shown in
Fig. 6. Cost is decreasing with increase in number of resources and result shows the
QoS-aware autonomic technique that executes the same number of Cloud workloads at a lesser Execution Time.

5   Conclusions and Future Directions

In this paper, QoS-aware autonomic resource provisioning and scheduling technique
for ICT-based services has been presented and this technique has been validated in
Cloud environment and the experimental results perform better in terms of cost and
execution time. The proposed ICT-based autonomic resource provisioning and
scheduling technique considers heterogeneous workload for resource scheduling and
uses the autonomic model to improve cost and time. This framework considers only
two QoS parameters of self-optimization. Further, this technique can be extended by
incorporating other QoS parameters like reliability, availability, energy, etc.

Acknowledgments One of the authors, Sukhpal Singh (SRF-Professional), gratefully acknowledges the Department of Science and Technology (DST), Government of India, for awarding him the INSPIRE (Innovation in Science Pursuit for Inspired Research) Fellowship (Registration/IVR Number: 201400000761 [DST/INSPIRE/03/2014/000359]) to carry out this research work. We would like to thank Dr. Maninder Singh for his valuable suggestions.

References

1. Singh, S., & Chana, I. (2012). Cloud based development issues: A methodical analysis. *International Journal of Cloud Computing and Services Science (IJ-CLOSER), 2*(1), 73–84.
2. Singh, S., & Chana, I. (2015). Q-aware: Quality of service based cloud resource provisioning. *Computers and Electrical Engineering—Journal—Elsevier.* (http://dx.doi.org/10.1016/j.compeleceng.2015.02.003).
3. Singh, S., & Chana, I. (2015). QRSF: QoS-aware resource scheduling framework in cloud computing. *The Journal of Supercomputing, 71*(1), 241–292.
4. Lua, K., Yahyapoura, R., Wiedera, P., Yaquba, E., & Jehangiria, A. I. (2013). QoS-based resource allocation framework for multidomain SLA management in clouds. *International Journal of Cloud Computing 1*,(1). (ISSN 2326-7550).
5. Wu, L., Garg, S. K., & Buyya, R. (2011). Sla-based resource allocation for software as a service provider (saas) in cloud computing environments. In *IEEE/ACM International Symposium on Cluster, Cloud and Grid Computing (CCGrid)* (pp. 195–204).
6. Li, Q., Hao, Q., Xiao, L., & Li, Z. (2009) Adaptive management of virtualized resources in cloud computing using feedback control. In *1st International Conference on Information Science and Engineering (ICISE)* (pp. 99–102).
7. Chieu, T. C., Mohindra, A., Karve, A. A., & Segal, A.(2009). Dynamic scaling of web applications in a virtualized cloud computing environment. In *IEEE International Conference on e-Business Engineering, ICEBE'09* (pp. 281–286).
8. Herbst, N. R., Huber, N., Kounev, S., & Amrehn, E. (2014). Self-adaptive workload classification and forecasting for proactive resource provisioning. *Concurrency and Computation: Practice and Experience 26*(12), 2053–2078.
9. Pandey, S., Wu, L., Guru, S., & Buyya, R. (2010). A particle swarm optimization-based heuristic for scheduling workflow applications in cloud computing environments. In *24th IEEE International Conference on Advanced Information Networking and Applications (AINA).*
10. Topcuoglu, H., Hariri, S., & Wu, M.-Y. (1999). Task scheduling algorithms for heterogeneous processors. In *Heterogeneous Computing Workshop, (HCW'99).*
11. Wu, Z., Liu, X., Ni, Z., Yuan, D., & Yang, Y. (2013). A market-oriented hierarchical scheduling strategy in cloud workflow systems. *The Journal of Supercomputing, 63*(1), 256–293.
12. Yu, J., Buyya, R., & Tham, C. K. (2005). Cost-based scheduling of scientific workflow applications on utility grids. In *Proceeding of IEEE e-Science and Grid Computing.*
13. Varalakshmi, P., Ramaswamy, A., Balasubramanian, A., & Vijaykumar, P. (2011). An optimal workflow based scheduling and resource allocation in Cloud. In *Advances in Computing and Communications* (pp. 411–420). Berlin: Springer.
14. Chana, I., & Singh, S. (2014). Quality of service and service level agreements for cloud environments: Issues and challenges. In *Cloud Computing* (pp. 51–72). New York: Springer.
15. Kephart, J. O., & Walsh, W. E. (2003). An architectural blueprint for autonomic computing. Technical Report, IBM Corporation (2003), 1–29, IBM. Retrieved December 25, 2014 from http://www-03.ibm.com/autonomic/pdfs/AC%20Blueprint%20White%20Paper%20V7.pdf.

Emerging Green ICT: Heart Disease Prediction Model in Cloud Environment

Anju Bala, Shikhar Malhotra, Nishant Gupta and Naman Ahuja

Abstract In the past 25 years, ICT has fundamentally changed practices and procedures in all aspects of life. With the world moving toward digitization, Cloud computing provides an ideal solution to manage and analyze the colossal data through big data analytics and machine learning techniques. Cloud computing, the delivery of on-demand computing resources, has applications in fields such as Education, Governance, Health care, etc. But the benefit of cloud for medical purposes, especially for heart disease prediction, is seamless. Therefore, we propose an emerging green ICT-based prognosis model for medical experts to predict heart disease status based on the historical data of patients. Naïve Bayes has been selected as an effective model among various data mining algorithms applied on the heart disease dataset as it provides the highest accuracy of 86.42 %. The experimental results are further validated using Hadoop on a cloud platform which yields an accuracy of 88.89 %.

Keywords Cloud computing · Heart disease · Big data · Hadoop · Machine learning

1 Introduction

Information Communication and Technology (ICT) has made global, social and cultural interaction very easy. We live in an interdependent global society, where people need to interact and communicate swiftly. With the increase in use of ICT

A. Bala (✉) · S. Malhotra · N. Gupta · N. Ahuja
Computer Science and Engineering Department, Thapar University, Patiala, India
e-mail: anjubala@thapar.edu; anjubala@gmail.com

S. Malhotra
e-mail: shikharmalhotra1@gmail.com

N. Gupta
e-mail: nishu94@outlook.com

N. Ahuja
e-mail: naman@live.in

© Springer Science+Business Media Singapore 2016
S.C. Satapathy et al. (eds.), *Proceedings of International Conference on ICT for Sustainable Development*, Advances in Intelligent Systems and Computing 409, DOI 10.1007/978-981-10-0135-2_56

579

devices, there is a concurrent need to create sustainable environment by reducing the rate of emissions and conserving energy. Through this research paper, effort has been made to shift to green ICT which can be achieved by the use of cloud computing.

Cloud computing following a pay as you go pricing is a service providing on-demand delivery of IT resources and applications via the Internet. Cloud promises to transform the future of service delivery and provide a flexible way to meet the technology needs of industries, which is the reason for its increasing use in various fields of business, education, entertainment, banking, and health care.

Cloud computing has been used for various medical applications such as diabetes, breast cancer, and cardiovascular diseases in the recent past. Of these various maladies, heart disease is the primary reason for deaths in several countries. The World Health Organization estimated that in 2012 around 31 % of the deaths around the world were due to cardiovascular diseases [1]. There is an urgent need for an intelligent model that can predict whether a patient is suffering from any kind of cardiovascular disease and take necessary measures to save precious lives.

Our motivation to carry out the research is that many of the heart disease prediction models report accuracies that they get by training and testing on the same dataset. This often leads to misleading results. To rectify this error, we split the dataset into training and testing records for the model built. Also, various existing prediction models do not take into account the vast amount of data and information explosion in today's world. The model based on such huge data cannot perform accurately if simulated on a standalone machine as it necessitates extensive computing resources and processing speed. Hence the cloud platform can be effectively used to store and process this data.

Cloud also uses virtualization technology which reduces the number of physical systems required compared to traditional ICT devices, thus moving toward Green ICT.

2 Related Work

In this section we discuss some notable research work in the field of heart disease prediction. These research studies employ a variety of machine learning algorithms for prediction and have achieved high classification accuracies.

Patil proposed a novel hybrid method employing the MAFIA and the K-means clustering algorithm. Neural network (NN) is trained with the selected substantial patterns to predict heart disease [2]. The Gennari's CLASSIT conceptual clustering system achieved a 78.9 % accuracy on the Cleveland heart disease dataset [3]. Das introduced a methodology that uses SAS base software for diagnosing heart disease. The core of the system is based on Artificial NN [4]. A prototype Intelligent Heart Disease Prediction System (IHDPS) developed by Sellappan employs techniques such as Decision Tree, NN, and Naïve Bayes. The system is implemented on .NET platform and can answer intricate queries that are not supported by decision support systems [5]. Chowdhury shows the use of Artificial NN in predicting neonatal disease diagnosis. The study exhibits ANN with a back propagation learning algorithm-based prediction of neonatal disease yielding diagnosis accuracy of 75 % [6]. Avci and Turkoglu study an intelligent diagnosis system based on principal component analysis and ANFIS for heart valve diseases [7].

All of the existing systems discuss prediction of cardiovascular diseases on a Machine Learning tool deployed on standalone machine. The massive boom of data in coming years will significantly reduce the accuracy of standalone machine-based models, thus paving the way for an intelligent safety critical system, reaping benefits of cloud storage and processing.

3 Methodology

Our research methodology as shown in Fig. 1 is divided into two modules. In the first module, we explore the accuracy of various machine learning algorithms using WEKA (Waikato Environment for Knowledge Analysis) on standalone machine [8]. Data preprocessing is first applied, followed by the application of different data mining approaches to predict the occurrence of heart disease on the cleaned dataset. Different evaluation measures are used to examine and compare the accuracy of proposed models. The results are then visualized with the help of various bar charts.

In the second module, we assess the accuracy of heart disease prediction model using Mahout, a machine learning API built on the top of Hadoop. The machine learning approach giving the highest accuracy on standalone machine environment is used for the prediction model in this module. The whole model has been deployed on Amazon EC2 (Platform as a Service) and is configured with Maven and Eclipse. The recommended heart disease prediction results are compared with the standalone machine results to measure the accuracy.

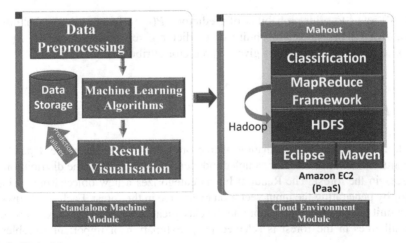

Fig. 1 Methodology

4 Machine Learning Approaches Applied in Implementation

4.1 Decision Tree (J48)

J48 is a classification algorithm that uses the concept of information entropy to build decision trees from a set of training data. Information Gain acts as splitting criteria to split the samples into subsets enriched in a class. The attributes are ordered by Information Gains, and then the potential attributes to be used in the classifier are chosen. The Information Gain for every attribute is calculated according to the formula [9] shown in Eq. (1).

$$\sum_{i=1}^{n} Pi \log_2 Pi \tag{1}$$

where n signifies the number of classes of the target attributes and Pi corresponds to the number of occurrences of class i divided by the total number of instances.

4.2 Naïve Bayes

The Naive Bayesian classifier, built on Bayes' theorem, assumes independence between the input attributes. It represents a supervised learning method as well as a statistical method for classification. The model is useful for very large datasets because it does not employ complicated iterative parameter estimation. Bayes theorem is stated mathematically [10] in the form of Eq. (2).

$$P(C|X) = (P(X|C)P(C))/(P(X)) \tag{2}$$

$P(X)$ refers to prior probability of predictors; $P(C)$ refers to prior probability of class; $P(X|C)$ measures probability of predictor given a class attribute; $P(C|X)$ refers to probability of a class given a predictor attribute.

4.3 Random Forest

Random Forests are a combination of tree predictors where each tree depends on the values of a random vector sampled independently with the same distribution for all trees in the forest. The Random Forest categorizes a new object from an input vector by penetrating the input vector on every tree in the forest. Each tree is used to cast a unit vote at the input vector and the classification that has the maximum votes over all trees in the forest is selected [11]. Estimation of important variables in classification and an experimental method for detecting variable interactions is given by Random Forest.

4.4 Multilayer Perceptron

Multilayer Perceptron (MLP) is an information processing paradigm composed of a large number of highly interconnected processing elements (neurons) working in unison to solve specific problems [12]. A typical MLP consists of an input layer, hidden layer(s), as well as an output layer. Each layer contains nodes. The network is first initialized by setting up all its weights to be small random numbers. The input patterns are applied and the output is calculated. Then the error of each neuron is measured. This error is then used to change the weights in such a way that the accuracy improves. The process is iteratively repeated until the error is minimized.

In our research we use the Back Propagation Algorithm of MLP with a training rate of 0.7. The input layer consists of 13 nodes and the hidden layer has 7 nodes. The output layer consists of 2 nodes signifying the absence or presence of heart disease.

5 Experimental Results

To measure the performance of the prediction model, all the machine learning approaches mentioned in Sect. 4 are applied. On our standalone machine, WEKA has been used for applying these approaches on our preprocessed dataset. The machine has Intel Core i3 processor @ 2.40 GHz with RAM of 4.00. The best machine learning approach performing on our machine is then implemented on Hadoop as an application deployed on Amazon EC2 cloud platform. We have used m3.medium on cloud which has 3.75 GiB Memory, 1 vCPU, 1 × 4 SSD storage (GB) and high frequency Intel Xeon E5-2670 v2 Processors. Our experimental setup has been divided as follows:

5.1 Data Collection and Preprocessing

The Cleveland dataset for heart disease prediction [13] contains a total of 76 raw attributes with the class attribute indicating a presence or absence of heart disease. Data preprocessing is applied to reduce the set of attributes to a meaningful set of 14 attributes. Dimensionality reduction and principal component analysis has been applied to reduce the set of attributes. Dataset is extensively cleaned, removing all noisy data. Data are then transformed by changing some numeric attributes to ordinal values. If the diameter narrowing is greater than 50 % then the patient is predicted to be having a potential heart disease and is recommended to consult a medical officer immediately.

5.2 Measuring Performance Using WEKA on Standalone Machine

Table 1 summarizes the results of percentage split of various algorithms using WEKA. The model has been built using 70 % of data for training and 30 % of data for testing. The models have been compared based on their area under curves (ROC), root mean squared error (RMSE), and mean absolute error (MAE) [14].

Based on classification accuracy, Fig. 2a, Naïve Bayes gives the best accuracy of 86.42 % and J48 performs the worst in predicting patients with heart disease. Figure 2b shows that Naïve Bayes performs the best, giving the highest values for ROC (0.930). Figure 2b also shows that though MAE of Naïve Bayes (0.169) is slightly greater than that of MLP (0.165), RMSE of Naïve Bayes (0.341) is the least which contributes to better prediction results. Hence from the results of comparison of various evaluation criteria, we have found that model based on Naïve Bayes

Table 1 Evaluation criteria

Evaluation metric	Random forest	J48	MLP	Naïve Bayes
Classification accuracy (%)	81.48	77.78	83.95	86.42
ROC	0.922	0.789	0.925	0.930
RMSE	0.348	0.427	0.347	0.341
MAE	0.267	0.253	0.165	0.169

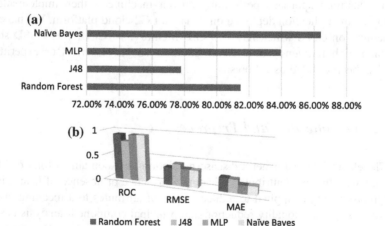

Fig. 2 Evaluation metrics using percentage split; **a** Classification accuracy; **b** ROC, RMSE, and MAE

gives the highest prediction accuracy on percentage split followed by MLP, Random Forest and J48.

5.3 Measuring Performance of the Best Algorithm Selected Using Hadoop on Amazon EC2 Cloud Environment

After comparing the performance of various data mining algorithms implemented in WEKA on standalone machine and choosing the algorithm with the highest accuracy, our work presents the performance of Naïve Bayes using Mahout (Hadoop) on cloud for the prediction of heart disease. 70 % of data was used for training while 30 % was used for testing. Figure 3 shows the screenshot of Mahout Naïve Bayes classifier results on the test dataset of 81 instances. It correctly classified 68 of the instances yielding an accuracy of 83.95 %. Figure 3 also shows the confusion matrix generated by Mahout giving the number of instances classified in respective classes.

5.4 Comparison of Results on Standalone Machine and Cloud Platforms

As illustrated in Fig. 4, the classification accuracy of standalone machine model is 86.42 % and that of cloud model is 88.89 %. Since the cloud model is backed by fast processing speed and large memory resources, it performs better in terms of accuracy.

```
Summary
-----------------------------------------------------------------
Correctly Classified Instances        :      72        88.8889%
Incorrectly Classified Instances       :       9        11.1111%
Total Classified Instances            :      81


=================================================================
Confusion Matrix
-----------------------------------------------------------------
a       b      <-- classified as
38      2      |   40          a = absent
7       34     |   41          b = present


=================================================================
Statistics
-----------------------------------------------------------------
Kappa                                      0.7781
Accuracy                                  88.8889%
Reliability(Standard Deviation)           0.3333
```

Fig. 3 Experimental results on cloud environment

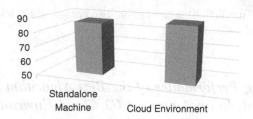

Fig. 4 Comparison of experimental classification accuracy

6 Conclusion

In this paper, various data mining classification algorithms have been implemented on Cleveland Dataset for heart disease. First, the algorithms have been applied using WEKA on standalone machine. Naïve Bayes yields the highest accuracy of 86.42 % and enhances the performance on various evaluation criteria. Further, this selected model has been implemented using Hadoop on Amazon EC2 cloud platform giving an accuracy of 88.89 %.

With data constantly increasing due to information explosion, in the near future, healthcare dataset will be much larger than the current dataset. In such a scenario, the cloud model will give much better accuracy compared to standalone machine model. WEKA would not work on big data due to scalability limitations, whereas Hadoop has the ability to horizontally scale its resources according to the size of data by implementing algorithms over its Map-Reduce Framework. The proposed cloud model would be expected to reduce the number of deaths from heart disease and can be implemented in smart cities supporting green ICT.

6.1 Future Work

In our research, we have implemented few data mining approaches, but in the future other algorithms, such as Association Rule Mining and FP Growth, can be applied to make better decisions and provide proper treatment to patients vulnerable to heart diseases. More important attributes can be added in the current dataset to increase the efficiency of the proposed model. Also other Machine Learning tools like R tool and Spark can be used. The prediction model can further be used for other medical problems and utilize real-time clinical data of patients present in the cloud.

References

1. CVD Factsheet http://www.who.int/mediacentre/factsheets/fs317/en/.
2. Patil, S. B., & Kumaraswamy, Y. S. (2009). Intelligent and effective heart attack prediction system using data mining and artificial neural network. *European Journal of Scientific Research* 642–656.
3. Gennari, J. (1989). Models of incremental concept formation. *Journal of Artificial Intelligence* 11–61.
4. Das, R., & Abdulkadir, S. (2009). Effective diagnosis of heart disease through neural networks ensembles. *Expert Systems With Applications* 7675–7680 (2009).
5. Palaniappan, S., & Awang, R. (2008). Intelligent heart disease prediction system using data mining technique. 978-1-4244-1968-5/08 IEEE.
6. Chowdhury, D. R., Chatterjee, M., & Samanta, R. K. (2011). An artificial neural network model for neonatal disease diagnosis. *International Journal of Artificial Intelligence and Expert Systems* 96–106.
7. Avci, E., & Turkoglu, I. (2009). An intelligent diagnosis system based on principle component analysis and ANFIS for the heart valve diseases. *Journal of Expert Systems With Applications* 2873–2878.
8. Weka 3 http://www.cs.waikato.ac.nz/ml/WEKA/.
9. Han, J., & Kamber, M. (2006). *Data mining concepts and techniques*. San Francisco: Morgan Kaufmann.
10. Naive Bayesian Classifier http://www.saedsayad.com/naive_bayesian.htm.
11. Guo, L., Ma, Y., Cukic, B., & Singh, H. (2004). Robust prediction of fault-proneness by Random Forests. *15th International Symposium on Software Reliability Engineering* 417–428 (2004).
12. Neural Network doc.ic.ac.uk/ ~ nd/surprise_96/journal/vol4/cs11/report.html.
13. U.C.I. Heart Disease Database https://archive.ics.uci.edu/ml/machine-learning-databases/heart-disease/.
14. Bala, A., & Chana, I. (2014). Intelligent failure prediction models for scientific workflows. *Expert Systems With Applications* 980–989 (2014).

Energy Conscious Allocation and Scheduling of Tasks in ICT Cloud Paradigm

Tarandeep Kaur and Inderveer Chana

Abstract Energy-aware allocation and scheduling are major concerns for the ICT industry. Today, cloud computing has emerged as an assurance to curb the energy consumption problem with the support of virtualization and multicore processors. This paper proposes an Energy-aware Scheduling Model (ESM) that allocates and schedules the deadline-constrained heterogeneous tasks to energy conscious nodes exploiting the capability of virtualized cloud environment. The energy-conscious task allocation decisions are taken dynamically and thereby, high performance and desired QoS in terms of reduced overall system execution time are achieved. The proposed model was evaluated and experimentally compared with two other techniques by setting up a cloud environment. The results indicate that ESM achieves 69 % of energy savings and high performance in terms of deadline fulfillment.

Keywords Cloud computing · Energy-aware scheduling · Information and communication technology · Scheduling · Virtualization

1 Introduction

Energy efficiency has emerged as the biggest challenge for the ICT sector today. Currently, the IT industry is troubled by growing energy crisis and associated higher energy costs [1]. Several ICT firms and researchers have attempted to overcome the rising energy problem by adopting certain hardware and software-based energy management measures. However, being restricted within monetary constraints and the high costs of hardware optimizations, greater stress is

T. Kaur (✉) · I. Chana
Thapar University, Patiala, India
e-mail: tarandeep.kaur@thapar.edu

I. Chana
e-mail: inderveer@thapar.edu

© Springer Science+Business Media Singapore 2016
S.C. Satapathy et al. (eds.), *Proceedings of International Conference on ICT for Sustainable Development*, Advances in Intelligent Systems and Computing 409, DOI 10.1007/978-981-10-0135-2_57

given to software-based ICT energy optimizations. This includes development of energy-aware resource allocation techniques; scheduling algorithms; resource management systems, etc. It is felt that the software level energy optimization measures are more forceful in minimizing the energy demands.

Additionally, for a successful and effective accomplishment of energy-conscious resource provisioning and scheduling algorithms, the support of the underlying ICT technology or ICT platform is significant. Eventually, cloud computing paradigm has emerged as a promise to beat the energy wastage concerns through the extensive implementation of virtualization and support extended by the multicore architectures [2–4]. The realization of energy awareness through cloud-based task scheduling can be termed as Green Cloud Task Scheduling.

Problem and Motivation for the Work

A survey by [5] had predicted, "The energy consumption throughout the world will grow by 56 percent between 2010 and 2040 and ICT industry will be the major culprit." Being driven by the growing concerns for rising global warming and energy demand posed by the ICT sector, the world community is busy in devising phenomena to handle it.

As one of the software-oriented solutions to this problem, the energy-aware scheduling model (ESM) offers energy-aware allocation of cloud tasks to the heterogeneous resources without degrading the performance and in a time-bound manner. It implements a heterogeneous computing scheduling technique that is vital in the current era of distributed computing systems and with the growth of heterogeneous clusters and grid systems. ESM implements an energy-aware scheduler (EAS) unit that runs a scheduling algorithm for allocation of the tasks to only energy-aware resources as per the deadline constraints specified by the users. It has been designed to dynamically allocate any new tasks entering the system to only energy efficient nodes without compromising the desired QoS in terms of execution time and deadline.

The ESM helps in benefitting both the user and providers of the ICT sector. The reduction in energy tends to improve the performance and resource utility levels that benefit the ICT service providers, while the attempts to meet the task deadlines specified by the users helps to fasten the task execution process thereby benefiting the ICT users.

2 Related Work

A detailed survey and comparative analysis of the existing energy efficiency techniques in cloud computing was presented in our previous work given in [6]. It is important to analyze the existing resource scheduling techniques and be aware of their impact on energy management before proceeding toward developing more techniques. The research community has proposed several scheduling techniques as listed in Table 1.

Table 1 Existing resource scheduling techniques in cloud computing

S. no.	Related work	References
1.	EnaCloud approach	[7]
2.	Energy-efficient application-aware online provisioning scheme	[8]
3.	An energy-efficient scheduling approach based on private cloud	[9]
4.	vGreen system	[10]
5.	T-Alloc: Energy efficient resource allocation algorithm	[11]
6.	Energy-efficient resource provisioning scheme	[12]
7.	Optimal online deterministic algorithms and adaptive heuristics	[13]
8.	Energy-conscious task consolidation heuristics	[14]
9.	Environment-conscious scheduling	[15]
10.	Energy efficient resource allocation strategy	[11, 16]
11.	Energy-aware scheduling for infrastructure clouds	[17]
12.	Memory-aware scheduling	[18]
13.	Workload scheduling in high-performance multicore Processors	[19]
14.	Power efficient resource allocation for clouds	[20]

From the analysis of the above techniques, it can be observed that no technique focuses on reducing the energy consumption as well as minimizing the task execution time as ESM. The ESM technique as compared to [9] focuses on reducing energy and overall response time of system, while all other techniques either exploit heterogeneity and energy efficiency (Technique presented in [13]) or cost-energy efficiency optimization (Technique presented in [15]) or energy consumption-workload balancing both (in Technique [11, 16]).

3 Proposed System Model and Mathematical Explication

The energy-aware scheduling model offers a heterogeneous computing scheduling technique vital in the current era of distributed and heterogeneous clusters and grid systems. It enables energy-aware management of the system resources and servers and aims to lower the energy consumption in the cloud system without degrading the system performance. The tasks are allocated to the energy-aware nodes as per the deadline constraints. Consequently, it attains maximum resource utilization preventing further energy wastage and performance degradation that can otherwise occur with inefficient resource utilization. The EAS unit of ESM schedules the tasks to nodes that are energy conscious and also as per the deadline specified by the users thereby offering faster execution in addition to energy awareness. Figure 1 shows the proposed energy-aware scheduling model (ESM).

In particular, it monitors the energy consumed by each node in the cloud. However, the power consumed by each node is taken in terms of the power consumption of individual computing units available on a node. The computing units

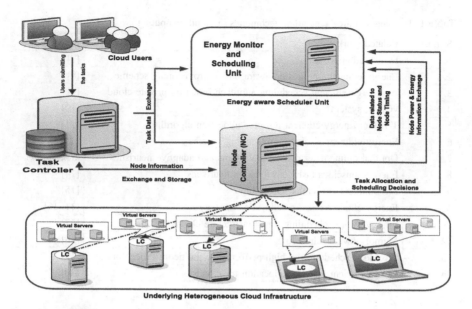

Fig. 1 Proposed energy-aware scheduling model (ESM)

considered here correspond to the CPU and memory. The ESM is composed of the following components:

- Users/Clients: The users submitting their tasks for execution to the ESM system.
- Underlying heterogeneous cloud infrastructure: It comprises the actual cloud infrastructure involving heterogeneous and virtualized cloud servers.
- Task Controller (TC): This unit controls the tasks entering the cloud system. It analyzes the resources required by the tasks and the deadlines pertaining to each task and stores this information in its database.
- Node Controller (NC): The nodes operating in the cloud infrastructure are monitored and supervised by the node controller (NC) unit that employs local controllers (LCs) sitting on each node. The NC unit keeps track of the status of the nodes and the number of resources with each node based on the information provided by the LCs. The LCs examine the node capabilities related to available resources and the number of VMs running on them.
- Energy-Aware Scheduler Unit (EAS): The EAS is a primary functional unit of ESM that is responsible for scheduling the tasks. It tends to keep up with the performance of the system. It consists of an energy monitor unit to compute the power consumption on each node. The ECS performs the scheduling of the tasks on the nodes identified as the most energy efficient and deadline fulfilling nodes using the information given by the NC unit and energy monitor unit.

3.1 Mathematical Formulation

Analytically, the optimization algorithm tries to locate the best node with least energy function (EF) that is computed based on the power consumption values measured by the Joule meter running in the energy monitor unit of the EAS [21, 22]. The ESM aims to minimize EF along with satisfaction of task deadlines. The proposed ESM follows a non pre-emptive task execution behavior and also assumes that the tasks are autonomous units that have predefined deadlines and are indivisible units of workload. It tends to optimize the energy consumption done by the CPU and memory, whereas the power consumed by the network and storage units is considered as negligible.

Mathematically, the problem formulation comprises variable constituents. The cloud infrastructure is composed of a set $\{node_1, node_2, node_3, \ldots \ldots ., node_N\}$ of N system nodes such that Nodes $= \{node_i | 1 \leq i \leq N\}$ is the collection of N multicore nodes; a set $V = \{v_1, v_2, v_3, \ldots \ldots ., v_M\}$ is the collection of M VMs subject to constraints, $V = \{v_j | 1 \leq j \leq M\}$; and a set Tasks $= \{task_1, task_2, task_3, \ldots \ldots ., task_L\}$ of tasks such that Tasks $= \{task_k | 1 \leq k \leq L\}$ is the collection of L tasks to be run on VMs operating on N nodes. The set $U = \{a_1, a_2, a_3, \ldots \ldots ., a_u\}$ forms the total number of computing units operating on each node.

The energy monitor unit measures the power consumption $Power_{used}$ of each node i. The EF_i is the energy consumed by a node given by the product of $Power_{used}$ during t time instant. On each node, the power consumed by a node can be divided into active power and idle power given by, $Power_{active}$ and $Power_{nonactive}$ respectively. Some idle power is consumed by each node during its inactivity period, that is, the period when a node although being active, is sitting with a fixed screen image while no user interaction or application is being run. The $Power_{nonactive}$ is assumed to be constant when a task executes and power consumption of computing units $Power(U_a, t)$, $1 \leq a \leq u$, at time instant t if active. At a given time instant, $Power_{used}$ for the ith node running M VMs is given as:

$$Power_{used} = \sum_{k=1}^{L} \sum_{j=1}^{M} \sum_{a=1}^{u} Power_{jk}(U_a, t) + Power_{nonactive} \qquad (1)$$

where M is the number of VMs running on ith node and L is the number of tasks assigned to M VMs. The used power during activity period of a node is calculated by obtaining the difference between $Power_{used}$ and $Power_{nonactive}$ and is represented as

$$Power_{active} = Power_{used} - Power_{nonactive} \qquad (2)$$

The proposed system also considers the energy optimization of the memory and thus takes into account the multiple cores in the nodes. Thus, $Power_{used}$ needs to be optimized with the available number of cores during the task execution. For this purpose, the computed Power$_{active}$ value is then multiplied with the number of cores used in the operation divided by the total number of cores in the node.

$$\text{Power}_{multicore} = \text{Power}_{active} \times \frac{\text{Used}_{cores}}{\text{nmc}} \tag{3}$$

where Used$_{cores}$ is the number of cores used in the operation of the node in running state and nmc is the number of cores in the node. The actual Power$_{actual}$ is thereby given as

$$\text{Power}_{used} = \text{Power}_{multicore} + \text{Power}_{nonactive} \tag{4}$$

The energy function (EF) for ith node gives the energy consumed by a node.

$$\text{EF}_i = \text{Power}_{used} \times t \tag{5}$$

In order to satisfy the deadline constraint, the total node execution time has to be computed. The execution time (ET) for ith node is equal to the time taken by the node to execute all the tasks running on it.

$$\text{ET}_i = \sum_{k=1}^{L} \sum_{j=1}^{M} \text{ET}_{ijk} \tag{6}$$

where ET$_{ijk}$ is the time taken by j VMs to execute k tasks on ith node.

The main goal is to optimize the energy and satisfaction of the task deadlines. Thus, it is important to compute the fitness function for the same. It is given as

$$\text{fit}_N = \theta(\text{EF}) + \delta\delta(\text{ET}) \tag{7}$$

where $0 \le \theta < 1$ are the weights to prioritize the components of fitness function. $\text{EF}(\text{sn}_i, \text{task}_k)$ is the energy consumed by task k on node i. The energy function (EF$_i$) of the ith node should not exceed the threshold value energy function (EF$_{th}$) set for the node i. The EF$_{th}$ value depends on the node utility level and is computed by obtaining the total number of instructions running on a node per unit of time.

3.2   Operation of Energy-Aware Scheduling Model

The ESM aims to optimize the energy consumed by the memory and the processor. The cloud users submit the tasks to the cloud system through the task controller unit. The users also specify the resource requirements, type, and deadline of the tasks. The TC database stores this information and also holds the existing executing tasks data pertaining to their resource utilizations and energy consumption values.

In case no initial task information is available, the required resources are allocated to the tasks and after the tasks complete execution their information is stored in the database. This stored task information is used by the scheduler to make future scheduling decisions. Based on the check on task data availability in its database, the TC can easily classify the task into its type, i.e., whether CPU-bound or memory-bound based on the task resource utilization and energy consumption data held in its database.

The NC unit maintains the node and the VM information. The VMs that are being utilized are powered on and have been highlighted as shown in Fig. 1 while the VMs that are sitting idle are in sleep mode to save energy. The NC unit is regularly updated about the node utilization levels by the LCs. The LCs gather information regarding the total number of active and nonactive VMs on each node, the resources currently running, and the number of still available resources for future task allocations. The NC unit keeps track of the node status by checking a *Sleep* variable associated with the nodes. The value of *Sleep* if 0 indicates the node is in sleep or in energy saving mode while a value of 1 indicates the node is in running state. In order to bring a node back to running state, another Boolean variable *Power On* can be set to 1, else it is 0. All the information pertaining to the nodes and tasks are sent to the EAS unit. Using the node information, the energy monitor unit of EAS computes their power and energy consumption and then forwards the computed values to the core EAS.

The EAS unit after obtaining the node and task information performs energy efficient scheduling of the tasks on most appropriate nodes without violating the deadlines for each task. The scheduling decisions taken by the EAS unit are based on the comparison of the energy consumed by each node with the energy threshold value. Based on the comparative analysis, the nodes are classified as LessEnergy or MoreEnergy nodes and are stored into separate lists. The LessEnergy (energy efficient) nodes are the primary candidates for the task allocation subject to the availability of resources with them and check on their deadline fulfillment capability. In case none of them can satisfy the deadline constraint, a new idle node can be turned on for processing the task. This process will be repeated for every unassigned task entering into the system.

4 Experimental Evaluations and Results

In order to validate our proposed system, a prototype heterogeneous cloud data center environment consisting of different virtualized servers has been set up. Table 2 shows the configuration of the cloud data center set up for the evaluation of the proposed ESM model. For estimating the energy consumption, a time period t was defined and was set to on a single day execution. Table 3 shows data center parameters used. The total power consumption of the system peaks at about 103 W during the experiment. The average power consumed by the computing units in idle state has been observed to be 43 W with all the components attached.

Table 2 Configuration of the cloud environment

Processor used	CPU frequency (GHz)	Total cores	Cores used in operation	Power consumption (Watt)	PC$_{nonactive}$ (Watt)	Optimized PC$_{used}$	EF$_i$ (Joules)	ET$_i$ (min)
Node 1	2.67	4	3	34.0	10.1	28.025	84.075	2.2
Node 2	3.07	2	2	101.4	43.1	101.40	304.01	1.44
Node 3	2.53	2	1	26.76	14.30	17.530	52.59	12.3
Node 4	2.01	4	4	42.31	10.0	42.310	126.93	3.60
Node 5	2.60	6	5	50.46	5.30	42.933	128.79	4.6
Node 6	1.86	2	1	55.4	12.44	33.920	30.92	1.51
Node 7	1.90	12	10	64.10	15.56	56.01	168.03	2.12
Node 8	2.66	2	2	67.6	29.01	67.60	202.80	2.31
Node 9	2.40	4	3	78.32	22.34	64.325	192.96	1.12
Node 10	2.01	4	3	91.56	20.30	73.745	221.24	1.15
Node 11	2.5	4	2	93.25	15.11	54.18	164.4	5.30
Node 12	2.13	4	4	87.02	13.57	87.02	84.02	2.56
Node 13	2.2	4	2	70.87	18.76	44.815	134.45	4.32

Table 3 Prototype cloud data center parameters

Parameter	Value
Number of virtual machines	20–40
Number of cloud nodes	5–20
Average energy consumed	283 Joules
Average energy spent for computing job placement	50 Joules
Average power rate of nodes	103 W

Figure 2 depicts the comparative analysis of the power and energy consumption done by the system nodes over a period of time. It can be observed that overall energy consumption done by the nodes remains minimal, thereby achieving energy efficient operation. Moreover, the execution time for the processing remains low satisfying the overall response time of the system and this helps to enhance the system performance in terms of the earlier completion of the tasks within the deadline imposed by the users. Figure 3 shows the energy consumption graph obtained from the running of the cloud setup. It can be analyzed from the graph that the overall energy consumption done by the system is minimized. Figure 4 depicts the percentage of deadline as per the tasks fulfilled by ESM. Approximately 76 % of tasks complete within the deadline specified by the users.

The proposed ESM had been experimentally compared with two other techniques proposed in [23, 24]. The experimental results are shown in Figs. 5 and 6. It can be inferred that ESM attains lower energy consumption than the other two scheduling techniques and achieves lesser execution time. Overall, ESM achieves 69 % of energy savings compared to 65 and 63 % of the two other techniques, that is, SLA-based resource constraint VM scheduling and priority-based scheduling scheme respectively.

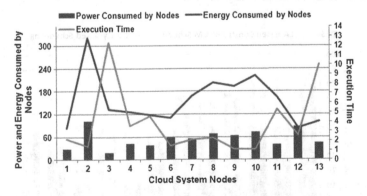

Fig. 2 Power, energy consumption and execution time monitoring result of the system nodes

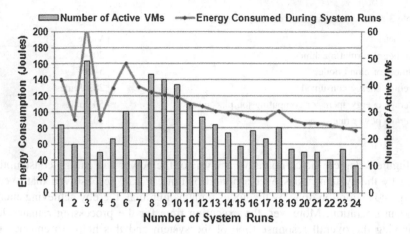

Fig. 3 Overall system energy consumption during different system runs

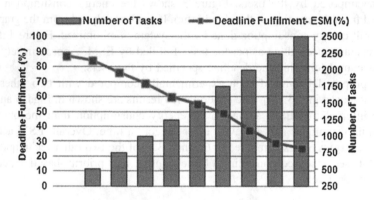

Fig. 4 Deadline satisfaction percentage of ESM

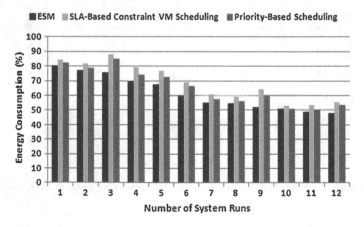

Fig. 5 Energy consumption comparison during different system runs

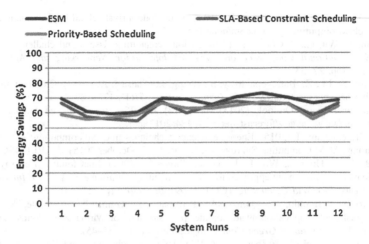

Fig. 6 Comparative representation of percentage of energy savings achieved

5   Conclusion and Future Work

Energy efficiency has become a major issue for the ICT. The present ICT industry has adopted cloud computing as the most beneficial computing approach to realize energy efficiency. Several ICT Cloud data centers have been set up that extensively implement virtualization for offering cloud services. This paper proposes an energy-aware scheduling model (ESM) that makes task allocation and scheduling decisions considering the energy-aware capability of the heterogeneous cloud nodes and also considers the nodes that can fulfill the task completion time limits. In other words, the ESM system not only achieves energy efficiency but also tends to offer desired QoS to the ICT users in terms of the tasks deadline metric. ESM performs fast and autonomic energy-aware task allocation and scheduling. The experimental results predict that the proposed ESM achieves energy savings up to 69 % and almost 76 % tasks are completed within the deadline constraints pertaining to each task. The future work can be optimization of the proposed model for yielding economic benefits, delivering the desired QoS to the users.

Acknowledgments This research was supported by the University Grants Commission (UGC) sponsored major research project "Energy Aware Resource Scheduling for Cloud Computing" under F. No. 41-629/2012(SR).

References

1. Kaur, T., & Chana, I. (2014). Energy efficient cloud: Trends, challenges and future directions. In *International Conference on Next Generation Computing and Communication Technologies (ICNGCCT '14), Dubai, UAE.*

2. Hille, E. (2014). Cloudcommons. Top 10 apps for cloud, private cloud implementation issues. http://cloudcomputing.sys-con.com/node/1653265.
3. Dillon, T., Wu, C., & Chang, E. (2010). Cloud computing: Issues and challenges. In *24th IEEE International Conference on Advanced Information Networking and Applications, Australia* (pp. 27–33).
4. Marston, S., Li., Z., Bandyopadhyay, S., Zhang, J., Ghalsasi, A. (2011). Cloud computing— The business perspective. *Decision Support Systems, 51*(1), 176–189.
5. International Energy Outlook. (2013). (IEO2013), July 25, 2013. Retrieved August 7, 2013, from http://www.eia.gov/forecasts/ieo/pdf/0484(2013).pdf.
6. Kaur, T., & Chana, I. (2015). Energy efficiency techniques in cloud computing: A survey and taxonomy. ACM Computing Surveys, 48(2), Article 22 (October 2015), doi:10.1145/2742488
7. Li, B., Li, J., Huai, J., Wo, T., Li, Q., & Zhong, L. (2009). EnaCloud: An energy-saving application live placement approach for cloud computing environments. In *IEEE International Conference on Cloud Computing. (CLOUD'09), Bangalore* (pp. 17–24).
8. Rodero, I., Jaramillo, J., Quiroz, A., Parashar, M., Guim, F., & Poole, S. (2010). Energy-efficient application-aware online provisioning for virtualized clouds and data centers. In *International Green Computing Conference* (pp. 31–45).
9. Li, J., Peng, J., Lei, Z., & Zhang, W. (2011). An energy-efficient scheduling approach based on private clouds. *Journal of Information and Computational Science, 8*(4), 716–724.
10. Dhiman, G., Marchetti, G., & Rosing, T. (2009). vGreen: A system for energy efficient computing in virtualized environments. In *Proceedings of the 14th ACM/IEEE International Symposium on Low Power Electronics and Design, ACM* (pp. 243–248).
11. Quan, D. M., Mezza, F., Sannenli, D., & Giafreda, R. (2012). T-Alloc: A practical energy efficient resource allocation algorithm for traditional data centers. *Future Generation Computer Systems, 28*(5), 791–800.
12. Liao, J. S., Chang, C., Hsu, Y. L., Zhang, X. W., Lai, K. C., Hsu, C. H. (2012). Energy-efficient resource provisioning with SLA consideration on cloud computing. In *41st International Conference on Parallel Processing Workshops (ICPPW), Pittsburgh* (pp. 206–211).
13. Beloglazov, A., & Buyya, R. (2012). Optimal online deterministic algorithms and adaptive heuristics for energy and performance efficient dynamic consolidation of virtual machines in cloud data centers. *Concurrency and Computation: Practice and Experience, 24*(13), 1397–1420.
14. Lee, Y. C., & Zomaya, A. Y. (2012). Energy efficient utilization of resources in cloud computing systems. *Journal of Supercomputing, 60*(2), 268–280.
15. Garg, S. K., Yeo, C. S., Anandasivam, A., & Buyya, R. (2011). Environment-conscious scheduling of HPC applications on distributed cloud-oriented data centers. *Journal of Parallel and Distributed Computing 71*(6), 732–749.
16. Quan, D. M., Basmadjian, R., Meer, H. D., Lent, R., Mahmoodi, T., Sannelli, D., Mezza, F., Telesca, L., & Dupont, C. (2012). Energy efficient resource allocation strategy for cloud data centres. In *Computer and Information Sciences II, Springer London* (pp. 133–141).
17. Knauth, T., & Fetzer, C. (2012). Energy-aware scheduling for infrastructure clouds. In *4th IEEE International Conference on Cloud Computing Technology and Science* (pp. 58–65).
18. Merkel, A., & Bellosa, F. (2008) Memory-aware scheduling for energy efficiency on multicore processors. In *Proceedings of Conference on Power Aware Computing and Systems (HotPower'08), USA.*
19. Coskun, A. K., & Rosing, T. S. Improving energy efficiency and reliability through workload scheduling in high-performance multicore processors.
20. Chimakurthi, L., & Madhukumar S. D. (2011). Power efficient resource allocation for clouds using ant colony framework. arXiv:1102.2608.
21. Kansal, A., Zhao, F., Liu, J., Kothari, N., & Bhattacharya, A. A. (2010). Virtual machine power metering and provisioning. In *Proceedings of the 1st ACM symposium on Cloud Computing, ACM, USA* (pp. 39–50).

22. Hernandez, P. (2010). Microsoft joulemeter: Using software to green the data center. http://gigaom.com/2010/04/25/green-software-qa-microsoft-research-joulemeter/.
23. Liao, J. S., Chang, C., Hsu, Y. L., Zhang, X. W., Lai, K. C., & Hsu, C. H. (2012). Energy-efficient resource provisioning with consideration on cloud computing. In *41st International Conference on Parallel Processing Workshops (ICPPW), Pittsburgh* (pp. 206–211).
24. Hussin, M., Lee, Y. C., & Zomaya, A. Y. (2011). Priority-based scheduling for large-scale distribute systems with energy awareness. In *9th IEEE International Conference on Dependable, Autonomic and Secure Computing, Australia* (pp. 503–509).

Controlling of FPGA-Based Optical Polarimeter Using LabVIEW

Binal Baraiya, Amish Shah and Hiren Mewada

Abstract LabVIEW is an interactive program development and execution system in which one creates programs using a graphical notation. This paper gives an idea about development of a graphical user interface for digital collection, and how one can control an instrument with the use of LabVIEW. It proposed the use of LabVIEW for controlling an optical polarimeter, which is based on Spartan 3E FPGA system. Optical Polarimeter works on the principle of rapid modulation of light, and measures the angle of rotation caused by passing polarized light through an optically active substance. A GUI is developed in LabVIEW to communicate with optical polarimeter in accordance with user's requirement. Serial connection takes place between FPGA board and host PC through LabVIEW. At a time, one data bit is send during serial communication and a complete byte is being sent with a start bit, stop bit, and parity bit. Entire system consists of two parts: Spartan 3E FPGA programming device and NI LabVIEW software.

Keywords LabVIEW · GUI · Optical polarimeter · Spartan 3E FPGA board · Front panel · Vis · VISA port

1 Introduction

Optical Polarimeter captures light from astronomical object and works on that light and gives information about that light. The instrument can be developed on general purpose hardware like embedded board or FPGA board and code can be written in

B. Baraiya (✉) · H. Mewada
Department of Electronics and Communication Engineering,
Charotar University of Science and Technology,
Changa, Anand (Gujarat), India
e-mail: bins.baraiya@gmail.com

H. Mewada
e-mail: hirenmewada.ec@charusat.ac.in

A. Shah
Astronomy and Astrophysics Division, Physical Research Laboratory,
Ahmedabad (Gujarat), India
e-mail: abshah@prl.res.in

© Springer Science+Business Media Singapore 2016   603
S.C. Satapathy et al. (eds.), *Proceedings of International Conference on ICT for Sustainable Development*, Advances in Intelligent Systems and Computing 409, DOI 10.1007/978-981-10-0135-2_58

either Xilinx or Libero. This instrument can be controlled by many programming language softwares like C, C++, JAVA, VB, VB.net, or LabVIEW. Hardware and software used for this instrument are FPGA and LabVIEW respectively. FPGA Code is written using Xilinx tool.

The optical Polarimeter has been in use as one of the backend instrument at telescope [1]. The Polarimeter works on the principle of rapid modulation of light and measures the angle of rotation caused by passing polarized light through optically active substance. Light beam from object is captured by telescope and passed through optical Polarimeter. Control and acquisition system of the instrument has been designed on FPGA system, and FPGA is from Spartan 3E family. Polarimeter consists of a Glan prism, filter controller, aperture controller, flip mirror, counter array, stepper motor, half-wave plate, Wollaston prism, and two cameras. Controlling of the instrument is done from the host computer. For the controlling purpose, serial connection has been established between instrument and host computer via USB.

1.1 Need for Software Controlled Hardware

Graphical User Interface is basic interface for human/user with the machine/ instrument interaction. GUI is presented on any digital screen. GUI is used to connect user with instrument with the help of any programming or designing software. GUI provides easy access of instrument for user, as well as fast data transfer, or communication between device and user. In this system, GUI is used to control the Polarimeter by giving commands from user and to take feedback from FPGA development board. Various alternatives, i.e., programming software are available to develop the GUI.

Any GUI must have satisfied some dialog principles, which are: Suitability for the task, Self-descriptiveness, Controllability, Conformity with user expectations, Error tolerance, Suitability for individualization, and Suitability for learning [2]. As per this principles and requirements of our system, some programming/Graphical developing software supports to develop GUI for Polarimeter. Those programming softwares are C, C++, JAVA, VB, VB.net, or LabVIEW. From all these software, LabVIEW is perfect to develop GUI for this system.

1.2 Reason for the Selection of LabVIEW and FPGA

LabVIEW stands for Laboratory Virtual Instrument Engineering Workbench, a graphical programming language to develop test, control, and measurement applications. Other programming software mentioned in previous section needs complex coding to develop GUI. In comparison with all those, LabVIEW provides flexibility of powerful programming language without complex coding. In addition with this LabVIEW it is easy to learn and use, it provides completer functionality and it has integrated I/O capabilities [3].

FPGA is short form of Field Programmable Gate Array. Polarimeter can be implemented using embedded development board like micro-processor and micro-controller or using FPGA development board. To implement this type of huge system, more number of embedded development boards is utilized and it requires wide area. Whereas using FPGA development board, less number of board as well area will be utilized.

2 Block Diagram of System

Entire system consists of graphical programming software LabVIEW and programming FPGA development board. Block diagram for the system is shown in Fig. 1.

Entire system works as follows:

VHDL code is written in Xilinx software to control the instrument and this code is used to program Papilio One FPGA development board using Papilio loader. Graphical programming has been done in LabVIEW for user interface purpose. Serial communication has been established between FPGA development board and LabVIEW using USB cable. Command given by user through LabVIEW will be received and executed in FPGA board. It also provides feedback of received command to the LabVIEW such that user can check whether command written in FPGA board is correct or not.

2.1 Software and Hardware Used for This System

Entire system works on Graphical programming software LabVIEW and Spartan 3E programmable FPGA development board. Program developed in LabVIEW are

Fig. 1 Block diagram of system

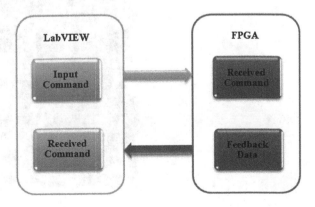

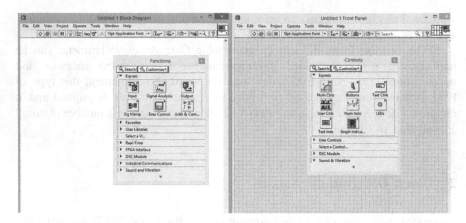

Fig. 2 Block diagram window (*left*) and front panel window (*right*) of LabVIEW

called Virtual Instruments (VI). Figure 2 indicates two windows of LabVIEW. Left part of Fig. 2 indicates block diagram window of LabVIEW in which we can prepare our VI using functions and right part of Fig. 2 indicates front panel of LabVIEW, which stands for user interface [4]. LabVIEW has graphical, floating palettes which helps user to create and run VIs. The three palettes are tools, controls, and functions palettes.

The Papilio is an open source FPGA development board on the Xilinx Spartan 3E FPGA. In this system, Spartan 3E FPGA is being used for data acquisition to collect data from LabVIEW and to send data to the LabVIEW. Figure 3 shows the Papilio development board for this system [5]. UART code has been dumped into the FPGA board such that serial communication can be possible between computer and FPGA.

Fig. 3 Spartan 3E FPGA board

3   Overview of LabVIEW Functions to Implement GUI

As mentioned in section II, serial communication is needed to transfer data from computer to FPGA or vice versa. LabVIEW provides some functions to communicate between external device and computer [6], it also facilitates to configure external device with your PC.

VISA Configure Serial Port VISA is short for Virtual Instrument Software Architecture. Object of using VISA in this system is to configure serial interface with external device. VISA provides programming interface between FPGA and LabVIEW. Initialization of serial port has been done using VISA resource name (Fig. 4).

VISA Write/Read VISA write function (Fig. 5 left), writes data from write buffer to the external device which is configured by VISA resource name. Data/Command written in write buffer has been transmitted asynchronously to the external device.

VISA Read VISA read function (Fig. 5 right), reads the particular number of bytes from external device which is interfaced and returns the data in read buffer. Byte count indicates number of byte to be read during serial communication.

VISA Close VISA close (Fig. 6 Left), closes an external device session specified by VISA resource name.

Write to Spreadsheet File Write to Spreadsheet file (shown in Fig. 6 right), takes data from array and write into the spreadsheet file specified by file path. In this

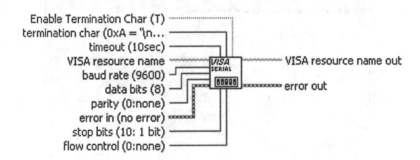

Fig. 4 VISA configure port of LabVIEW

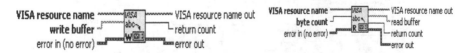

Fig. 5 VISA write/read function of LabVIEW (*left*) write function (*right*) read function

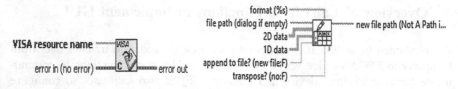

Fig. 6 *Left* VISA close function of LabVIEW. *Right* Function to write data to spreadsheet

system, input command, received data, and photon counts are being stored in specified file.

All the functions mentioned above are main functions which are used to build this system in LabVIEW. In addition to this some other functions and structures are also included in developing the system.

4 Results

VHDL program which is written in Xilinx is loaded into Spartan 3E FPGA board through which Polarimeter is to be operated, and controlling of this is done by connecting a serial interface between FPGA and PC. Figure 7 shows front panel of GUI developed in LabVIEW. Using this GUI, user can give input data for

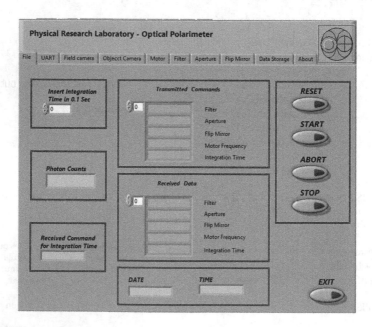

Fig. 7 GUI main window

integration time to count population of photons. As well as it indicates photon counts from FPGA, transmitted commands from LabVIEW to FPGA in "transmitted commands" window, received command from FPGA in "received data" window, and current date and time. With this it provides functionality to reset, start, stop, or abort system and/or quit LabVIEW. Figure 8 (left) provides functionality to interface/configure with external device. Figure 8 (right) shows tab for motor, which allows user to set speed of motor and indicates command received at FPGA according to it. Figure 9 (left) shows input path for the files to store data of transmitted/received commands and photon counts. In addition to this other tabs like field and object camera, filter, aperture, flip mirror provides user to set appropriate position. Finally, last tab gives information of it. Command will be sent to FPGA board from LabVIEW is indicated in Fig. 9 (right).

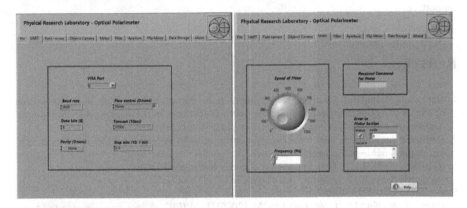

Fig. 8 *Left* VISA configuration property to interface with external device. *Right* Selection for speed of motor and it's received command

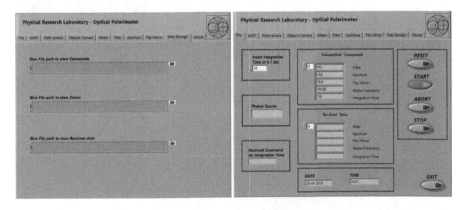

Fig. 9 *Left* Data storage path. *Right* Command sent to FPGA

5 Summary

Polarimeter is backend instrument mounted in telescope to observe astronomical objects. The acquisition and control system of the optical Polarimeter has been designed on FPGA system. Graphical User Interface of the system is developed through National Instruments LabVIEW Software. LabVIEW is easy to access as well as it has some inbuilt functions which helps you to make your design less complex and more comfortable. LabVIEW provides a bridge between human and machine interaction.

Acknowledgments I would like to thank Department of Electronics and Communication Technology at CHARUSAT University, Changa for helping us. I also want to extend my heartiest thanks to Physical Research Laboratory, Ahmedabad. I am also thankful to Mr Jay Patel, Mr Nirmalsinh Parmar, Mr Viral Rathod, and my family for their continuous encouragement and support.

References

1. Ganesh, S., Joshi, U. C., Baliyan, K. S., Mathur, S. N., Patwal, P. S., & Shah, R. R. Automation of PRL's astronomical optical polarimeter with a GNU/Linux based distributed control system. *Astronomy & Astrophysics Division, Physical Research Laboratory.*
2. Retrieved April, 2015, from www.jiscdigitalmedia.ac.uk/guide/graphical-user-interface-design-developing-usable-and-accesible-collection.
3. Retrieved April, 2015, from http://www.ni.com/white-paper/8536/en/.
4. Retrieved Sept, 2015, from http://cnx.org/content/col11408/1.1/.
5. Retrieved Oct, 2015, from http://papilio.cc/index.php?n=Papilio.GettingStartedISE.
6. Bitter, R., Mohiuddin, T., & Nawrocki, M. (2006). *LabVIEW advance programming technique* (2nd ed.). CRC Press LLC.

Automatic Intelligent Traffic Controlling for Emergency Vehicle Rescuing

Megha Tank, Hardik Mewada, Viraj Choksi and M.B. Potdar

Abstract As we all know, the number of vehicles are increasing day by day and there is traffic jam because of that. Therefore, we have to think of a different method than what is existing. This helps emergency vehicles to reach their destination without any delay. It would be helpful for all other EMERGENCY Vehicles and not limited to an ambulance, police van, VIP vehicles, fire brigade. Due to delay in arrival of ambulance to the hospital, people lose their lives and nothing is important in the world than the life of a human. So there is a need to change the traffic system rules. It can help to save human life. The main use of this modified traffic system is to minimize the delay that is caused by traffic congestion.

Keywords Traffic management · LCD display · Traffic signal controlling · Ambulance unit · Traffic junction unit and RF module

1 Introduction

The ambulance for emergency was started to bring the patient to hospital in a comfortable manner and as fast as possible from the year 1988. It was introduced by Y.S. Rajasekhara Reddy for the first time in India, who was the chief minister of Andhra Pradesh at that time [7]. He has done wonderful work after implementing

M. Tank (✉) · H. Mewada
Parul Institute of Engineering and Technology, Gujarat, India
e-mail: tankmegha21@gmail.com

H. Mewada
e-mail: sjbv.hardik@gmail.com

V. Choksi · M.B. Potdar
Bhaskaracharya Institute for Space Applications and Geo-Informatics,
Gujarat, India
e-mail: vmchoksi@gmail.com

M.B. Potdar
e-mail: mbpotdar11@gmail.com

© Springer Science+Business Media Singapore 2016
S.C. Satapathy et al. (eds.), *Proceedings of International Conference on ICT for Sustainable Development*, Advances in Intelligent Systems and Computing 409, DOI 10.1007/978-981-10-0135-2_59

the 108 service for INDIA. GVK EMRI operates their services from Hyderabad. It is a public–private partnership with the state governments [6].

Last month I visited the 108 ambulance service in Naroda, Ahmedabad, from where I collected data about the total number of emergencies that came around to 5 lakhs. Of that the total number of lives saved was only 3.5 lakhs [1]. This is very much less. Therefore after implementing this system more lives can be saved. Unless the government spends lakhs and crores, more number of lives cannot be saved. Here, our goal is to give a clear route to Emergency vehicles with minimum interruption to regular traffic flow.

Because of traffic jams, there is a possibility of fuel consumption and ambulances getting stuck. Such incidences can be decreased by implementing the modified traffic system. In foreign countries, they successfully save human life, because whenever an ambulance comes they move aside to clear out the route till the ambulance passes through. On the other hand in INDIA, whenever an ambulance comes it is controlled manually at the traffic junction by a traffic officer. Nowadays all systems are working automatically. So why do we depend on manual control at the traffic junction in an emergency. After implementing this system it will rely totally on intelligent automatic control and guarantee a clear route for emergency vehicles.

The idea behind this paper is to implement the traffic system, which can help the ambulance to reach the hospital quickly and save the life of a human. It will also work for the fire brigade to save the life of multiple humans. And of course the police van to catch the thief.

Let us see how the ambulance passes through the traffic junction in the below instance (Fig. 1):

As seen, there are two cars moving ahead of the ambulance. They do not give way for an ambulance to pass through the junction. Here in this case, the ambulance cannot reach the hospital as fast as it can, and because of that people are dying.

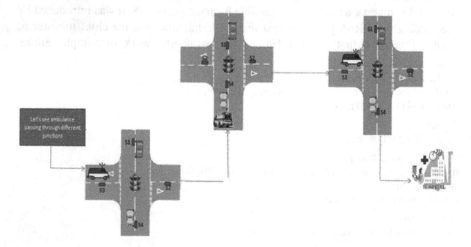

Fig. 1 Ambulance passes through traffic junction

Fig. 2 Ambulance running in a Foreign

Next, see the same scenario in a developed country. Here you can see how the people allow an ambulance to pass (Fig. 2).

This is what motivated me to change the traffic system, so that the ambulance passes easily through the traffic junction and does not have to stay in the middle of traffic. This is not only helpful for the ambulance but can also be helpful for other emergency vehicles [3]. Like the fire brigade which saves the life of humans, police vans to catch criminals, the ambulance can reach hospital safely and save the life of a patient. Last but not least, VIP vehicles can reach their destination without affecting the routine traffic (Fig. 3).

The above illustration shows the Intelligent Automatic traffic control system for an ambulance. Whenever an emergency vehicle come near to the traffic junction, then a traffic system automatically display the green signal to that lane and display red signal to all other lanes [2]. In this way, the system gives first priority to the ambulance over all other vehicles.

Fig. 3 One intelligent ambulance with automatic traffic control system

2 Architecture

The system contains two units. One of them is Emergency vehicle Unit situated in ambulance and other one is Traffic Junction Unit situated at Traffic junction. The Emergency unit will give its indication via wireless module to the Traffic junction unit. And then after transmitting this signal the Traffic junction unit will display the upcoming emergency vehicles and accordingly change the traffic signal. In accordance with this, the traffic junction also displays a blinking message continuously on traffic signal till the emergency vehicle passes by its route. By this way, the Emergency vehicle can easily reach to their destination without delay. And patient gets their best care.

2.1 Emergency Vehicle Unit

The Emergency vehicle unit consists of RF transmitter, Controller, Encoder, and LCD Display. From that RF Transmitter is used to send the signal to the traffic junction unit for the upcoming of emergency vehicle. Controller is used to control all other parts, Encoder is for generating a code. And last LCD is used here to display the route toward destination which helps the driver of an ambulance to reach hospital fast and in comfort manner (Fig. 4).

Whenever an Emergency vehicle comes near to the traffic junction then the RF transmitter which is situated in ambulance sends its indication to the RF receiver which is situated near to the traffic junction. But before this, the code is generated by using encoder and sends this code to the controller for processing. Controller passes this information via RF module to the traffic junction.

2.2 Traffic Junction Unit

The Traffic junction unit consists of RF receiver, Controller, LCD Display, and Decoder. Among that LCD Display is used here to display the upcoming

Fig. 4 Block diagram of emergency vehicle unit

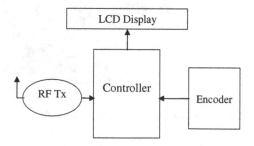

Fig. 5 Block diagram of
traffic junction unit

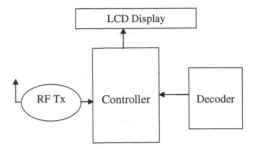

emergency vehicles on the screen of traffic junction. Controller is controlling the
other parts. Decoder mainly decodes the transmitted signal (Fig. 5).

The RF receiver which is situated at traffic junction catches the transmitted
signal by emergency vehicle. The decoder will decode this cached data and send it
to the controller for changing the traffic signal. The green and Red light will blink
continuously for indicating the Emergency vehicle on the lane from which it is
coming. And LCD will display "Ambulance is coming. Please give side." on the
screen of traffic junction. By this way, the ambulance can easily cross the traffic
junction without lag of time.

When more than two ambulances come to traffic junction for proceeding then we
have to give priority. By assigned priority, the Emergency vehicle easily crosses
that junction without delay (Fig. 6).

Now see more than two ambulances reaches to particular traffic junction, and
then the working of traffic junction is as shown in Fig. 7:

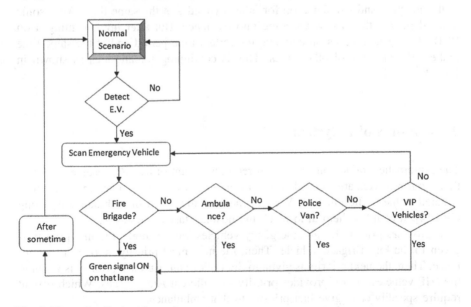

Fig. 6 Flow of traffic junction unit

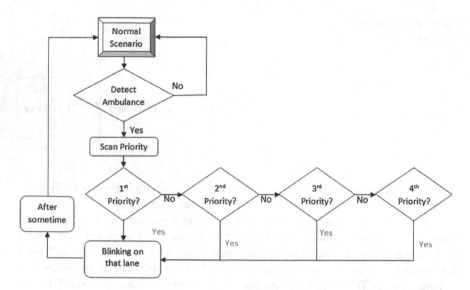

Fig. 7 Flow of traffic junction unit while multiple ambulances

3 Simulation Results

First of all I am simulating the current traffic system which is working nowadays. I simulate it on proteus (version 8.00) simulator (Fig. 8).

As you seen in the above figure, there are green signal on for the two side of traffic junction and red signal on for other two sides at the same time. After some defined period, the vice versa come into existence. But after implementing it on PCB, the green signal is on one side for certain time period and at the same time make red signal on all other sides. This is continuing for all sides as shown in Figs. 9 and 10.

4 Features of a System

The Automatic Traffic control system requires a total of five RF receivers. Out of them four receivers are situated at four different sides of traffic junction. And one is situated at the traffic junction. We can measure the speed of ambulance by using GPS [4]. It could be helpful to reach the hospital fastly and easily.

It provides priority for all emergency vehicles. For example, the first priority is given to the Fire Brigade vehicle. Then, the next most priority is given to ambulance. Then, the next priority is given to the Police van. And last priority is given to the VIP vehicles. It also provides priority for different Ambulances. Which patient require speedily care, give first priority to that ambulance.

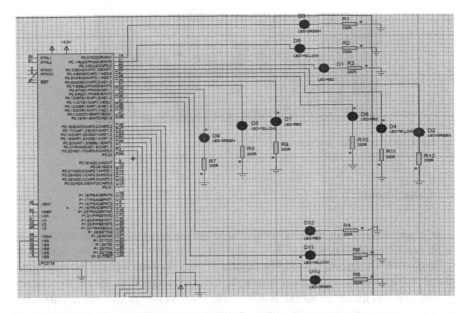

Fig. 8 Simulation result of proteus

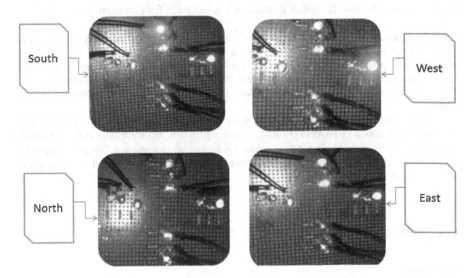

Fig. 9 Implementing on PCB

The route toward hospital is displayed in ambulance. So that it would be helpful for the driver of an ambulance. It will release a flag after the emergency vehicle passes by its route. Therefore, the normal scenario of traffic junction has comes into existence.

Fig. 10 Display on traffic junction

5 Conclusion

After implementing the traffic system, the ambulance would be able to cross all
traffic junctions without waiting. It would relay completely on automatic intelligent
traffic control. Therefore, it would be helpful for reducing the waiting time of traffic
officer to stay over there. While crossing the route of emergency vehicle, the system
gets an alert and gives red signal to other lanes till the emergency vehicle passes by
its route. Along with that traffic junction display the message of upcoming ambulance [5]. It would be of great use to the emergency vehicle if the traffic in path of
the destination is less. It would guarantee a clear path for emergency vehicles.

Acknowledgments This report is based on the Emergency Medical Services (EMS). I express my
profound gratitude and deep regards to my guide Professor Hardik Mewada for his exemplary
guidance, monitoring, and constant encouragement. The blessing, help, and guidance given by him
time to time have carried my way to implement this work. And I express my sincere thanks to
Director of BISAG (Bhaskaracharya Institute for Space Application and Geo-informatics), Gandhi
nagar.

The preparation of writing this paper faced many challenges. I am very grateful for the level of
cooperation and assistance provided virtually by every person whom the inquiry staff I consulted.

I must especially acknowledge Mr. Amritlal Tank, Retired Government Officer for the willingness of search and he provided numerous documents and generally provided whatever information I requested.

The References Section

Appendix

There are several glossaries of some words which are listed as below:

Sensor	A sensor is a mechanical device which detects and responds to some type of input from physical environment
Controller	One that controls all other components. A controller is a mechanism that controls the operation of a machine
LCD	It stands for Liquid Crystal Display. It is a method of displaying readings continuously, as on digital watches, portable computers, etc.

| Traffic | A road signal for directing vehicular traffic by means of colored lights, |
| signal | typically red to stop, green for go, and yellow for proceed with caution |

There are several Abbreviation and Acronyms which are listed as below:

GPS   Global Positioning System

LCD   Liquid Crystal Display

LED   Light Emitting Diode

VIP   Very Important Person

There are several Supplementary resources particularly websites as listed below:

Emergency Response Service (www.emri.in)—This site gives information about the total emergency came last year and out of that how many people's were saved.

All Datasheet (www.datasheetdirect.com)—This site provide datasheet of all components.

References

1. Kennedy, J., & Sexton, B. (2009, November). *Literature review of road safety at traffic signals and signalized crossings.*
2. Rosli, M. A. A., Wahab, M. H. A., Sanudin, R., & Sahdan, M. Z. (2008, August). A hardware based approach in designing infrared traffic light system. *International Symposium, 4*(ITSim), 1–5.
3. Athavan, K., Balasubramanian, G., Jagadeeshwaran, S., & Dinesh, N. (January 2012). Automatic ambulance rescue system. *IEEE Advanced Computing and Communication Technologies (ACCT) (2nd International Conference)* (pp. 190–195).
4. Sangeetha, K., Archana, P., Ramya, M., & Ramya, P. (2014). Automatic Ambulance Rescue With Intelligent Traffic Light System. *IOSR Journal of Engineering (IOSRJEN), 04*(02), 53–57.
5. Djahel, S., & Salehie, M. (2013, March). Adaptive traffic management for secure and efficient emergency services in smart cities. *Pervasive Computing and Communications Workshops (PERCOM Workshops)* (pp. 340–343).
6. Emergency Response Service. www.emri.in.
7. Total number of emergency arrived and total number of life saved. (2014, July). www.deshgujarat.com.

A Capacity Constraint Distributed Data Dissemination Protocol for Ad Hoc Cognitive Radio Networks

Dipjyoti Deka, Sanjib Kumar Deka and Nityananda Sarma

Abstract Cognitive radio (CR) has emerged as a proven technique to overcome the spectrum scarcity problem in wireless communication. Data dissemination in CR networks (CRNs) is an important activity for successful deployment of CRN. In the presence of challenges like (i) opportunity detection and (ii) requirement for strict primary user (PU) protection, modeling a technique for efficient data dissemination in CRNs is an interesting problem. Motivated with this problem, in this paper we propose a capacity rate constraint distributed data dissemination protocol (DDDP), which includes a weighted channel selection strategy and a technique to prepare distributed data dissemination schedule based on adopting a neighbor discovery method for a multi-hop ad hoc CRN. The simulation results demonstrate the efficacy of the proposed model in terms of improving packet delivery ratio, minimizing interference to the primary user (PU), and reducing the number of redundant messages in the network, which eventually improves the channel utilization.

Keywords Cognitive radio (CR) · Data dissemination · Opportunity detection · primary user (PU)

1 Introduction

In today's world of communication, the necessity for wireless services is proliferating which leads to an ever-increasing demand for radio spectrum. As a result, the spectrum is becoming congested. Cognitive radio (CR) networks are innovative

D. Deka (✉) · S.K. Deka · N. Sarma
Department of Computer Science & Engineering, Tezpur University, Tezpur 784028, India
e-mail: ddeka@tezu.ernet.in

S.K. Deka
e-mail: sdeka@tezu.ernet.in

N. Sarma
e-mail: nitya@tezu.ernet.in

© Springer Science+Business Media Singapore 2016   621
S.C. Satapathy et al. (eds.), *Proceedings of International Conference on ICT for Sustainable Development*, Advances in Intelligent Systems and Computing 409, DOI 10.1007/978-981-10-0135-2_60

and intelligent approach to tackle the spectrum scarcity problems in wireless communication by enabling secondary users or unlicensed users to utilize unused licensed spectrum in opportunistic manner without interfering with primary users or licensed users. This new network paradigm is also known as NeXt Generation (xG) Networks as well as dynamic spectrum access (DSA) [1]. The concept of cognitive radio was first introduced by Joseph Mitola in the late 1990s [2].

Data dissemination is an important function in wireless ad hoc network. It is defined as the distribution of information from a single source to multiple destinations. The main objective of data dissemination is the highest message reachability, i.e., every sent information should be reached to maximum number of destinations. In CR networks, data dissemination has come across different challenges like (i) detection of available spectrum and (ii) primary users' (PU) protection, i.e., utilization of licensed band by secondary users or unlicensed users should not interfere with primary users. In the literature, a lot of works have been carried out for data dissemination in CR networks. Some of the related approaches are Selective Broadcasting (SB) [3], SURF [4], and DTMDD [5]. Motivated with the challenges faced by dissemination of data in CR networks, in this paper we present a Distributed Data Dissemination Protocol (DDDP) for efficient data dissemination. The contributions of our work are as follows: (i) a channel selection scheme by which a secondary user (SU) is able to select the best channel for data dissemination and (ii) a Distributed Data Dissemination Schedule that can accomplish message reachability as high as possible and minimize broadcast redundancy and collision among CR nodes.

The rest of the paper is organized as follows: In Sect. 2, we present the system model and assumptions. The proposed model, DDDP, is explained in Sect. 3 in detail. We discuss the simulation methods and analyze the results in Sect. 4. Finally, conclusion and future works are presented in Sect. 5.

2   System Model and Assumptions

2.1   Network Model

We consider N number of secondary users (SUs) that form a multi-hop cognitive radio ad hoc network (MHACRN) [6] and M number of channels which can be used for data dissemination. However, each SU can operate on a subset of these channels depending on the channel availability at that node. We assume that bandwidths of channels are different and each SU maintains a minimum SNR [7]. Each SU knows about its neighbors and the list of their available channels from the process of neighbor discovery. We assume out-of-band common control channel (CCC) [8]. The neighbor discovery process can be done in MHACRN with the help of CCC. We assume that each SU is equipped with one wireless transceiver (transmitter and receiver) [9]. Therefore, a SU is capable of either transmitting or receiving (but not both) at any given moment.

2.2 Spectrum Sensing Activity

In cognitive radio ad hoc network, CR nodes or SUs work independently and make their decisions based on information they have acquired locally. In order to detect ideal spectrum, i.e., the spectrum that is not being used by primary user, each CR node has to perform spectrum sensing. We assume that the spectrum sensing is carried out by every CR node at regular intervals of time. The spectrum sensing block is responsible for spectrum sensing [10]. We assume that each CR node contains a spectrum sensing module which is not included within the scope of this paper. In the proposed model, the channel selection strategy will only work on the list of available channels. These available channels are the outcome of the spectrum sensing by the CR node.

2.3 Primary Radio Activity Model

For the PR activity model we use continuous-time, alternating ON/OFF Markov renewal process (MRP) [11–13] to detect the presence or absence of primary radio (PR) signal. According to the ON/OFF PR activity model, it captures the time period in which the channel can be utilized by CRs without causing any harmful interference to PR nodes [14]. This model defines two states of PR nodes: ON state which indicates that the channel is currently used by PR nodes, i.e., the channel is busy while OFF state indicates that the channel is not used by PR nodes, i.e., the channel is idle. Figure 1 illustrates the PR activity model. In the model T_{ON}^i

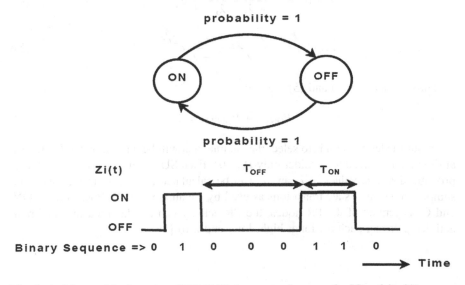

Fig. 1 Activity model: alternating ON/OFF Markov renewal process for PR activity [4]

represents the duration of ON state and T_{OFF}^i represents the duration of OFF state of channel i. The renewal period of a channel consists of one consecutive ON and OFF period. Figure 1 shows $Z_i(t)$, the renewal period of channel i at time t as $Z_i(t) = T_{ON}^i + T_{OFF}^i$ [11, 13–15].

For ON state

$$fx(t) = \lambda_x \times e^{-\lambda}x(t) \tag{1}$$

For OFF state

$$fy(t) = \lambda_y \times e^{-\lambda}y(t) \tag{2}$$

According to the authors in [11, 15] the length of ON and OFF periods is exponentially distributed. In this paper, we use the same formulation as in [11, 13–15] that ON and OFF periods can be expressed by (1) and (2) using Poisson distribution function (p.d.f.). In [14] the author defined channel utilization as u^i,

$$u^i = \frac{E\left[T_{OFF}^i\right]}{E\left[T_{ON}^i\right] + E\left[T_{OFF}^i\right]} = \frac{\lambda_y}{\lambda_x + \lambda_y} \tag{3}$$

Here, λ_x and λ_y are the rate parameters for exponential distribution where $E\left[T_{ON}^i\right] = \frac{1}{\lambda_x}$ and $E\left[T_{OFF}^i\right] = \frac{1}{\lambda_y}$. Let $P_{ON}(t)$ be the probability of channel i in ON state at time t and $P_{OFF}(t)$ be the probability of channel i in OFF state at time t. These probabilities can be calculated as:

$$P_{ON}(t) = \frac{\lambda_y}{\lambda_x + \lambda_y} - \frac{\lambda_y}{\lambda_x + \lambda_y} e^{-(\lambda_x + \lambda_y)t} \tag{4}$$

$$P_{OFF}(t) = \frac{\lambda_y}{\lambda_x + \lambda_y} - \frac{\lambda_y}{\lambda_x + \lambda_y} e^{-(\lambda_x + \lambda_y)t} \tag{5}$$

Thus, by adding (4) and (5) we get:

$$P_{ON}(t) + P_{OFF}(t) = 1 \tag{6}$$

In our model, the aim is to select the channel that will be unused by the PR nodes at time t, so we need to consider only $P_{OFF}(t)$. Each SU locally can determine these probabilities. The values of λ_x and λ_y can be calculated by SUs from the historical samples of channel state transitions as used by the author in [14]. Based on the ON and OFF periods of the PR nodes, the PR activity can be classified into different activity patterns, such as: long, high, low, and zero [16].

3 Proposed Model

In this section, we introduce the proposed model DDDP for data dissemination in multi-hop ad hoc CRN. The design of DDDP is comprised of two schemes: *a weight-based channel selection strategy* based on which CR nodes can select the best available channel for data dissemination and *Distributed Data Dissemination Schedule* by which each SU is able to allocate the best selected channel to disseminate a message.

3.1 Channel Usability

In the CR network, a channel can be used opportunistically when the channel is not being used by a primary user. But even though a channel is free for opportunistic use, it may or may not be usable from the application point of view. It is because, the usability of a channel depends on the possible data rate that the channel can offer, which might or might not be sufficient for a SU transmission. Therefore, depending on the capacity rate that a channel can offer, a SU can decide to use it for its volume of data to be transmitted for certain duration, which may eventually enhance the overall data dissemination activity.

3.2 Channel Selection Scheme of DDDP

Inspired by the work in [4], the weight-based channel selection strategy has been developed in order to select the most preferable channel for data dissemination. The strategy takes into consideration three important aspects that signify a channel's quality. They are PR unoccupancy [4], CR occupancy [4], and data rate factor of a channel. Using these parameters of channel's quality, a formulation has been derived to compute the channel's weight, which allows a SU to select the best available channel. The parameter called PR unoccupancy decides the channel availability which is represented by η. We consider CR occupancy to achieve maximum connectivity and is represented by μ. The last important component of the channel selection scheme is the data rate factor of a channel which is represented by α.

PR unoccupancy (η) of a channel can be calculated in terms of probability of a channel's OFF state [4], i.e., a channel is free from PR node's activity. η_i means the probability of channel i in terms of OFF state at time t.

CR occupancy (μ) is defined as the number of neighbors that can utilize a channel which can be obtained as in [4]:

$$\mu_i = \text{nCR}_i, \tag{7}$$

where μ_i is the CR occupancy and $n\,\text{CR}_i$ the number of neighbors using channel i.

As it is assumed that the bandwidth of the channels is different, therefore each of these channels will offer different data rates that can be attainable by SUs, which can be calculated from channel's capacity (using Shannon's channel capacity theorem [17]). Let R_i be the data rate that is offered by channel i. The data rate factor (α) of channel i can be given as follows:

$$\alpha_i = \frac{R_i}{\beta}, \tag{8}$$

where α_i is the data rate factor of channel i and β is the series of multiplication of data rates of the available channels. Mathematically β can defined as:

$$\beta = \prod_{i=1}^{n} R_i, \ i \text{ is the channel index ranges from 1 to } n$$

From (6), (7), and (8), the channel weight can be formulated as follows:

$$\forall i \in C : P_w^i = \eta_i \times \mu_i \times \alpha_i \tag{9}$$

where C is the available channel set of a SU and P_w^i is the weight of channel i.

3.3 Ranking of Channel

From (9) it can be observed that if the value of α is increased then P_w also increases. So we can say that data rate of a channel has an impact on the channel's weight. Using (9) each SU can calculate the weight of their list of available channels. Depending on the weights, channels are prioritized and the channel with the highest P_w will be selected as the best channel. Finally, it can be concluded that, by using the channel selection scheme each SU is able to choose a best channel for data dissemination which provides the (i) highest PR unoccupancy, (ii) maximum number of CR neighbors, and (iii) highest data rate.

3.4 Distributed Data Dissemination Schedule of DDDP

Using the rank list of channels the proposed model prepares the Distributed Data Dissemination Schedule which is utilized by the MAC policy during data dissemination. The schedule allows the SUs to operate in synchronous manner to disseminate data in MHACRN. The schedule is prepared by the SUs, utilizing node's neighbor lists and their available channel lists. In this schedule, every SU creates a preferable list of forwarding nodes before disseminating a message. The forwarding nodes are the neighbors of SUs. The list is created in decreasing order of forwarding node's neighbor size. Then the SU selects the best candidate node from the preferable list for next hop level dissemination whose neighbor size is maximum, provided the best selected channel for both the SU and the candidate node is same. After selecting the candidate node, the SU starts disseminating the message to its neighbors on the best selected channel. Upon receiving the message, only one node from the neighbors, i.e., the selected candidate node becomes the sender and is allowed to transmit the message for the next hop level dissemination. The candidate node repeats the same operation as done by the sender SU. So, in this manner the message is disseminated from hop to hop in a distributed way and dissemination process is continued until there exists a forwarding node or a receiver in the network.

To elaborate the preparation of the schedule, an example is prepared as shown in Fig. 2. In the figure, it is assumed that MHACRN consists of SUs denoted by (A, B, C, D, E, F, G, H, Z) and R be the transmission range of SUs. The available channel lists are recorded with associated indices (shown within curly braces) against the SUs. These available channel lists are prioritized by SUs based on the channel selection strategy as discussed in Sect. 3.2. Let us assume that A be the sender and B, C, D, E, and Z are its neighbors. Now A will create a preferable list of forwarding nodes based on their neighbor's size. Let A's preferable list of forwarding nodes be (B, C, D, E, Z). Let B have the maximum neighbor size and its selected channel for dissemination be {2} which is same as A. So, B is selected as the candidate node for next hop level dissemination. Figure 3 shows that SU A disseminates a message on its selected channel {2} (shown in red arrow) to its neighbors B, C, and D. However, E and Z do not receive the message since their selected channels are not same as A. Since B is the selected as the candidate node therefore it is allowed to perform the next hop level dissemination. In order to perform dissemination in the next hop level B becomes the sender and performs the

Fig. 2 SUs in MHACRN and sender A's neighbors in transmission range R

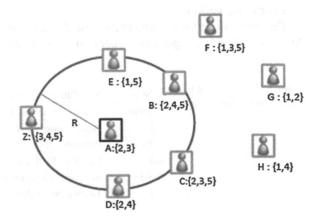

Fig. 3 SU A disseminates the
message on its selected
channel {2}

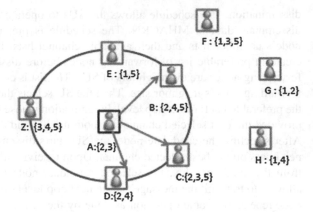

Fig. 4 SU B performs the
next hop level dissemination
on its selected channel {1}

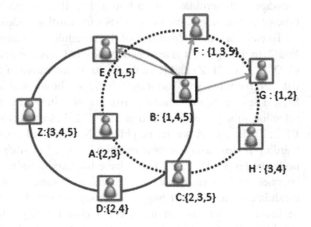

same operation as A does to disseminate the message. Figure 4 shows that B
disseminates the message on channel {1} (shown in green arrow). So, in this
manner the message is disseminated from hop to hop in a distributed way and
dissemination process is continued as long as there exists a forwarding node or a
receiver in the network.

The pseudocode for construction of the data dissemination schedule is given in
Algorithms 1 and 2. Algorithm 1 states how does a SU select a candidate node for

Table 1 Notation used in the
data dissemination schedule

N(s)	Set of the neighbors of node s
W(u)	Size of the neighbor of node u
Fn	Node responsible for next hop level dissemination
Plist	Preferable list of Fn nodes
Rx	Set of nodes that receives a message from node s
Sch(u)	Best selected channel for dissemination by node u
k	1st element of Plist

next hop level dissemination and disseminate the message. Algorithm 2 states how the next hop level dissemination is performed by the selected candidate node. The steps of the algorithms are given in Algorithms 1 and 2. The notations used in our proposed data dissemination schedule are listed in Table 1.

Algorithm 1: Selection of a node for next hop level dissemination and starts disseminating a message.

Input: s, N(s)
Output: select a node for next hop level dissemination, disseminating a message
Step 1: for each u ∈ N(s) do
Step 2:   calculate w(u) /*from neighbor list of s */
Step 3: End for
Step 4: create a Plist //list is created in decreasing order of w(u)
Step 5:   for each k ∈ Plist do
Step 6:   if { Sch(s) ∩ Sch(k) != Ø }
Step 7:   Fn ← k
Step 8:   go to step 14
Step 9:   End if
Step 10:   else
Step 11:   pop element k from Plist
Step 12:   End else
Step 13: End for
Step 14: Disseminate the message to its neighbors

Algorithm 2: Dissemination of data for next hop level by the forwarding node

---

Input: Rx, Fn
Output: disseminate a message for next level
Step 1: for each v ∈ Rx do
Step 2:   if (Rx(v) = = Fn)
Step 3:   s ← Fn // the Fn node becomes the sender s
Step 4:   End if
Step 5: End for
Step 6: s repeat the algorithm 1

---

4 Simulation Results and Observations

NS-2 based simulation has been performed to study the efficacy of the proposed model. Using CRCN patch [18] in NS-2, the simulation of the model has been carried out to verify the working of the proposed technique. To perform simulation the PR node activity model is incorporated in CRCN patch. For simulation a multi-hop ad hoc CRN with 100 SUs is deployed randomly in a square at grid area of size $700 * 700$ m^2. The transmission range of SUs is set to 250 m. We run the simulation for 1000 s where in every second a message of size 512 bytes is disseminated in the network by randomly selected SU (sender). The message or data packet in the network is generated using constant bit rate (CBR) traffic. We consider four different simulation scenarios by varying the number of available channels of SUs as 3, 5, 8, and 10 out of 15 number of total channels. We consider the different bandwidths of these channels.

Figure 5 shows the performance of the proposed model in comparison to SURF [4], in terms of percentage of message received by SUs in the network. It shows that the percentage of message received by SUs in the proposed method DDDP is higher than in SURF [4]. With increase in number of available channels, message received by the SUs also increases. In DDDP the maximum percentage of disseminated message received by SUs is 20, 60, 75, and 90 % with available channels 3, 5, 8, and 10, respectively, as compared to 15, 40, 50, and 65 % in SURF [4].

Figure 6 shows the result of produced interference by the SUs during data dissemination in terms of PR harmful interference ratio (HIR) [4] of the proposed technique in comparison to SURF [4]. It shows that with varying the available channels, i.e., 3, 5, and 8 during the experiment, the HIR values recorded against

Fig. 5 Comparison of percentage of message received by SUs in DDDP and SURF

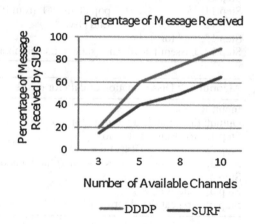

Fig. 6 Comparison of HIR for DDDP and SURF

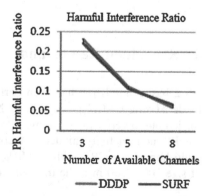

the proposed DDDP technique are as per the SURF [4]. It can also be seen from the figure that with increase in number of available channels the interference to the primary user gets reduced significantly.

In Fig. 7, the performance of the proposed DDDP technique in terms of average packet delivery ratio is shown. The experiment is conducted to study the packet delivery behavior of the proposed DDDP technique considering the PR activity pattern as in [16]. The packet delivery behavior is analyzed allowing 1000 packets those which are broadcasted in the network during the simulation and the average delivery ratio achieved for long term, low term, normal, and zero term PR activity is 290, 380, 341, and 420, respectively.

Figure 8 shows the impacts of broadcast redundancy while the total number of SUs is increasing. It shows that when the number of SUs is increased from 20 to 50 and then to 100 during the experiment, the proposed DDDP technique reduces the redundant broadcast messages drastically, which indirectly improves the packet drop probability during data dissemination. This happens, because the distributed data dissemination schedule used by DDDP technique selects only one node in the network to perform the next hop level dissemination in synchronous manner, which in turn impacts with no or less collision alongside the possibility of the chances for receiving less redundant message by the receivers.

Fig. 7 Average delivery ratio under different PR activities

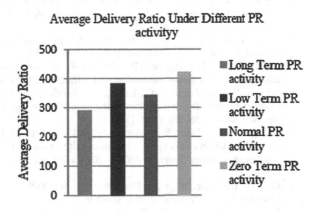

Fig. 8 Increase in reduction of broadcast redundancy with increasing number of SUs

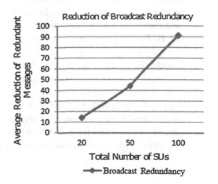

5 Conclusion and Future Works

In this paper, we have presented a distributed data dissemination protocol for efficient data dissemination in ad hoc cognitive radio networks. The proposed model enables a SU to disseminate a message using the best selected channel by minimizing interference to the PU and reducing the number of redundant messages in the network. The simulation and performance study shows that the proposed model achieves improved message delivery. Although the channel selection strategy has improved the performance of the proposed model, the optimization of channel selection technique with consideration of channel's utilization time is interesting. In such situation, improving message reachability while reducing the interference to PUs is more interesting which is left for our future work.

Acknowledgments The work has been supported by the project "MAC Protocols Design for Cognitive Radio Networks" (Ref. No. 14(2)/2012-CC&BT) of DeitY, Govt. of India.

References

1. Akyildiz, I. F., Lee, W. Y., Vuran, M. C., & Mohanty, S. (2006). NeXt genera-tion/dynamic spectrum access/cognitive radio wireless networks: A survey. *Computer Networks, 50*(13), 2127–2159.
2. Mitola, J., & Maguire, G. Q, Jr. (1999). Cognitive radio: Making software radios more personal. *Personal Communications, IEEE, 6*(4), 13–18.
3. Kondareddy, Y. R., & Agrawal, P. (2008, April). Selective broadcasting in multi hop cognitive radio networks. In *Sarno Symposium, 2008 IEEE* (pp. 1–5). IEEE.
4. Rehmani, M. H., Viana, A. C., Khalife, H., & Fdida, S. (2013). Surf: A distributed channel selection strategy for data dissemination in multi-hop cognitive radio networks. *Computer Communications, 36*(10), 1172–1185.
5. Yarnagula, H. K., Deka, S. K., Sarma, N. (2013, December). Distributed TDMA based MAC protocol for data dissemination in ad-hoc cognitive radio networks. In *Advanced Networks and Telecommunications Systems (ANTS), 2013 IEEE International Conference on* (pp. 1–6). IEEE.
6. Akyildiz, I. F., Lee, W. Y., & Chowdhury, K. R. (2009). CRAHNs: Cognitive radio ad hoc networks. *Ad Hoc Networks, 7*(5), 810–836.
7. Haenggi, M., Andrews, J. G., Baccelli, F., Dousse, O., & Franceschetti, M. (2009). Stochastic geometry and random graphs for the analysis and design of wireless networks. *IEEE Journal on Selected Areas in Communications, 27*(7), 1029–1046.
8. Lo, B. F. (2011). A survey of common control channel design in cognitive radio networks. *Physical Communication, 4*(1), 26–39.
9. Harada, H. (2008, September). A small-size software defined cognitive radio prototype. In *Personal, Indoor and Mobile Radio Communications, 2008. PIMRC 2008. IEEE 19th International Symposium on* (pp. 1–5). IEEE.
10. Yucek, T., & Arslan, H. (2009). A survey of spectrum sensing algorithms for cognitive radio applications. *Communications Surveys & Tutorials, IEEE, 11*(1), 116–130.
11. Lee, W. Y., & Akyildiz, I. F. (2008). Optimal spectrum sensing framework for cognitive radio networks. *Wireless Communications, IEEE Transactions on, 7*(10), 3845–3857.

12. Yuan, G., Grammenos, R. C., Yang, Y., & Wang, W. (2010). Performance analysis of selective opportunistic spectrum access with traffic prediction. *IEEE Transactions on Vehicular Technology, 59*(4), 1949–1959.
13. Min, A. W., & Shin, K. G. (2008, April). Exploiting multi-channel diversity in spectrum-agile networks. In *INFOCOM 2008. The 27th Conference on Computer Communications*. IEEE.
14. Kim, H., & Shin, K. G. (2008). Efficient discovery of spectrum opportunities with MAC-layer sensing in cognitive radio networks. *IEEE Transactions on Mobile Computing, 7*(5), 533–545.
15. Sriram, K., & Whitt, W. (1986). Characterizing superposition arrival processes in packet multiplexers for voice and data. *IEEE Journal on Selected Areas in Communications, 4*(6), 833–846.
16. Rehmani, M. H., Viana, A. C., Khalife, H., & Fdida, S. (2011, October). Activity pattern impact of primary radio nodes on channel selection strategies. In *Proceedings of the 4th International Conference on Cognitive Radio and Advanced Spectrum Management* (p. 36). ACM.
17. Forouzan, A. B. (2006). *Data communications & networking (sie)*. Tata McGrawHill Education.
18. http://stuweb.ee.mtu.edu/~ljialian/..

Enhancing Performance of Security Log Analysis Using Correlation-Prediction Technique

Kanchanmala Bharamu Naukudkar, Dayanand D. Ambawade
and J.W. Bakal

Abstract Today's computer network architecture generates massive amounts of security log data. The analysis of such huge security log data is very difficult. In addition to correlation of security alerts, we require valid and proper predictive log analysis to track the future attacking possibilities. The existing techniques for prediction take input as some preprocessed or mined data. That's why, the predictive system becomes time consuming and it affects accuracy rate. So in order to enhance the performance of predictive analysis, the proposed system replaces the data processing phase with event correlation technique. It is based on rule-based approach for processing real-time events and produces attack classes as output for multistage attack detection. It reduces processing overhead and leads to low utilization of memory. The hidden Markov model (HMM) makes use of such highly processed data for future attack prediction which makes the system more efficient. In a direct comparison, we concluded that the inclusion of correlative analysis results improves the prediction performance.

Keywords Hidden markov model · Event correlation · Log data · Multistage attack detection · Prediction analysis · Attack class

K.B. Naukudkar (✉)
Department of Computer Engineering, Sardar Patel Institute of Technology,
Mumbai, India
e-mail: kbnaukudkar1103@gmail.com

D.D. Ambawade
Department of Electronics and Telecommunication Engineering,
Sardar Patel Institute of Technology, Mumbai, India
e-mail: dd_ambawade@spit.ac.in

J.W. Bakal
Department of Computer Engineering, Shivajirao S. Jondhale College
of Engineering, Mumbai, India
e-mail: bakaljw@gmail.com

© Springer Science+Business Media Singapore 2016
S.C. Satapathy et al. (eds.), *Proceedings of International Conference
on ICT for Sustainable Development*, Advances in Intelligent Systems
and Computing 409, DOI 10.1007/978-981-10-0135-2_61

1 Introduction

The rapid deployment of network technology is moving toward the wide network security threats. This has led toward numerous network attack methods. The issues of network security have become more serious thus, acquiring wide attention. In order to offer the security-IDS, vulnerability scanning system, firewall, and many more safety devices are usually used in the network. Each network device is responsible for generating huge amount of security event information every day, every minute. These devices work independently. Logs generated by these contain a large number of the repeated or fake warnings [1]. Tremendous increase and diversity in network architecture results in huge amount of alarm data. It will be very difficult for administrator to process such vast amount of data in real time and identify the attack intention from hidden information. In fact, most of the security incidents are not isolated; they are related to each other in some way.

Therefore, it is mandatory requirement to have proper analysis of such huge data which is important for security measures. Such huge data can be handled by applying filters in terms of particular attributes. We can discard the duplicate data, retain the true values, explore the real causal relations that are hidden, and provide more reliable, more valuable information for network administrator [2]. In order to deal with all such serious problems, there is a requirement of firm and valid solution which easily handles and analyzes real-time data. That will also reduce redundancy and duplication problems using intelligent, smart, and corrective actions.

Event correlation is the technique through which the analysis of the effective causal relation between security events, security incidents, and operating environment is possible [3]. It is useful for processing network security event data. The vulnerability detection and expectation of attack is given by effective event correlation method. If any attack is detected within defined timestamp, an alert is generated. Correlation is better than normal data mining process as it retrieves data on the basis of some causal relationship among the data. So it gives better solution over normal data mining [4].

Event correlation is the process of grouping sets of events detected at the end of log analysis process and applying intelligence to check their inter-relation. If so, find out in what way they are related and up to what degree [5]. This information can be achieved by comparing the available observations obtained from various parameters like source and destination IP address, network topology, techniques used by attacker, and duration of activity. There are number of event correlation types like patter-based, rule-based, statistical correlation, etc. Each method has its own features. So, the results obtained at the end of alert correlation can help the administrative staff to retrieve correct events from random log data, take useful decisions regarding attack detection, extract attack strategies using correlative rules, and finally give the correct prediction for future attacks [6].

2 Literature Review

For the analysis of the massive amount of log data generated by networking activities, there are a number of correlation and aggregation techniques. Also, in parallel with analysis of existing system, we should be aware of future attack prediction.

Network security event correlation analysis based on similar degree of the attributes is proposed by Zhang et al. [7]. This method mentioned the classification and merge of network security events according to similar degree of the attributes like IP address, protocol used, etc. It is used to remove redundant alerts and compress number of events. But this solution is only feasible for attribute similarity scenario. It is based on previously acquired knowledge of attributes, requiring network topology and system configuration information. Attack scenario extraction algorithm (ASEA) is proposed by Farhadi et al. which is further followed by hidden Markov model (HMM) model for future attack prediction [8]. It uses ASEA, a mining approach for attack pattern extraction. But the system is not able to track all log data and is not able to adapt new attack patterns.

Vaarandi and Pihelgas [1] proposed a system which describes log analysis methods for collecting security metrics from available log data. It describes a framework for collecting and reporting such metrics for big data. Vaarandi [9] proposed a technique to monitor and correlate events from security logs using specified rules and presented a platform-independent technique for rule-based event correlation. SEC (simple event correlator) is open-source and lightweight solution [10]. This is one of the best approaches for correlation as it leads to low memory consumption and reduces processing overhead.

HMM is used to detect the intrusion based on available data. For detection of multistage attacks, correlation engines are used by specifying particular attack signature [11]. Signature database is developed after analyzing every stage of HMM. This literature survey leads to the proposal of a new system which will be a combination of Simple Event Correlation (SEC) for correlation followed by HMM for future attack prediction [12].

3 Simple Event Correlation

Sec is an event correlation engine based on rule specification. Logs generated by the number of networking devices are input to the *Sec* and produce the final output by executing user-defined rules in terms of regular expressions. It will handle different formats of regular expression. *Sec* is a platform-independent technique as it is written in *perl*. Along with that, there is in-built regular expression support available with Perl. *Sec* provides correlation engine for handling more critical correlation operations with parameterized user predefined correlation rules [9, 10].

There are nine different rules associated with SEC. Each rule has its own definition and meaning. They are explained as follows [9, 10].

- **Single**—It checks input logs and on matching executes an action.
- **SingleWithScript**—Depending on script result, it matches input events and executes an action.
- **SingleWithSuppress**—It matches input event and executes an action and for next t seconds ignores the particular matching events.
- **Pair**—It works like *SingleWithSupress* and then arrival of second event executes another action.
- **PairWithWindow**—It matches input event and for next t seconds waits for other input event. Unavailability of event within the given time slot, executes the same action or executes another action.
- **SingleWithThreshold**—It counts matching input events for t seconds and as it reaches threshold value n, executes an action.
- **SingleWith2Thresholds**—It works like *SingleWithThreshold* for first t time interval and then continues the process for next t time interval and executes another action.
- **Suppress**—It is used to prevent matching input event.
- **Calendar**—It specifies time constraints for execution of action.

By using the above rules, the execution of scripts is performed in terms of actions. Also it is possible to create and delete contexts which will activate or deactivate rules. Along with that, Boolean expressions and Boolean operators (AND, OR, NOT) can be used for rule specification. The rule application depends on the final truth value of the expression. By specifying *Sec* rules including various actions, Boolean and regular expressions, complex event correlation can be performed [9, 10].

4   Hidden Markov Model

The hidden Markov model is presented as state model of finite states. Probabilities associated with each state define transitions among states. The observations associated with each state are specified in terms of probability distribution associated with the state [8]. In this model, next state decisions depend only on the previous state. The HMM can be used to determine the nature of attack of a specific type using necessary variables associated with it. For this, the observables are the set of alerts. So the basic goal for the HMM is to determine the type of attack corresponding to a sequence of alerts [11].

Several properties of alerts are associated with multistage attacks that match with the HMM scenario. Each stage of multistage Internet attack is dependent on the output of the previous stage. HMM calculates probability thus, each step is dependent on the previous step in *probabilistic* manner. This probability depends on the frequency of transaction with which the attack has appeared in the attacking sequence [8]. There are a number of ways to track the existence of the host at a given ip address in the network. They are initiating a telnet connection with the host, consulting with DNS server of network, establishing a FTP connection, and many more. Among these various possible ways, only one is selected, which gives observation results for that particular step [11].

The frequency of particular alert type in attacking sequence gives the probability value of each alert type [12]. The confusion matrix is the representation of assigning the possibility of an input of a particular alert class to a particular output category. The precision, recall, and F-measure are defined as follows [11]:

(1) **Precision** is defined as $P = \{tp/(tp + fp)\}$, where tp is the number of positive examples in the input which are correctly identified and fp is the number of negative examples that are incorrectly identified as positive.

(2) **Recall** is defined as $R = \{tp/(tp + fn)\}$, where tp is the number of positive examples in the input which are correctly identified and fn is the number of positive examples that are incorrectly identified as negative.

(3) **F-measure** is defined as $F = 1/\{(\alpha/P) + ((1 - \alpha)/R)\}$, where α is a parameter assigning weightage of the importance to precision P or recall R. For equal weighting of precision and recall, α is set to 0.5.

5 Proposed System

The proposed system is a combination of SEC and hidden Markov model (HMM) which is used to enhance the performance of HMM for correct prediction. HMM model predicts on the basis of alerts generated from the available log data which are input to it. As the secure system, there is requirement of accurate predictive results. So instead of using any mining and filtering techniques, the proposed system uses *Sec*.

Sec receives input events in terms of log data and by executing rules specified in configuration files produces output events. Execution of *Sec* is based on regular expression language and displays them in specified formats by integrating with mysql. The *Sec* will analyze in terms of number of rules per file, number of records per file, and total processing time. The performance of *Sec* also depends on hardware platform, rule file size, perl regular expression complexity, *Sec* actions, processing speed of input data, processor load, storage system, and network conditions.

Figure 1 describes, the result of *Sec* gives alert classes which will be given as input for HMM. The different alert classes will be *ip scan, port probe, root login, login failures, ip sweeps*, etc. It is useful for future attack prediction depending on the probability of individual events, precision and recall values. Before passing the log data to the *Sec* module, it is necessary to convert into some standard format as the log format of each file is different one. Such formatted data is input to the *Sec* module. Figure 2 shows, *Sec* works on two parts, signature-based and anomaly-based IDS detection. For signature-based IDS, all rules are by default written in *Sec*

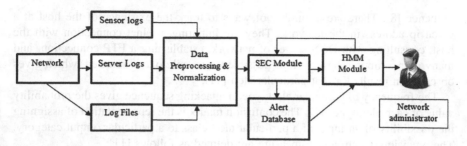

Fig. 1 System architecture

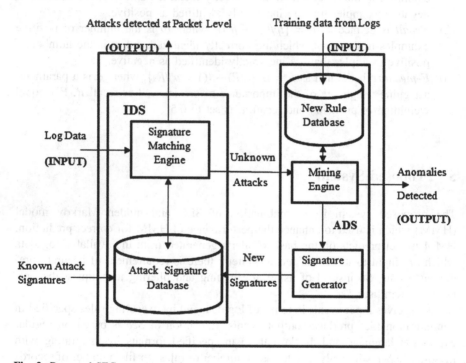

Fig. 2 Proposed SEC system module

configuration files and for new anomaly, anything other than system normal behavior will detect as threat. As soon as threat is detected, it will become new alert class. At the end of analysis of log records, visualization tools are used to show the analysis of results in terms of pie charts and line charts which improves user interaction with system results.

6 Result and Simulations

The proposed system, i.e., SEC+HMM environment is compared with the existing system, i.e., HMM predictive environment. Using the scripts for attack scenario and rules, numerous tests were performed. Table 1 shows the averaged result of multiple tests on input log data. The testing platform for result is Core i5-4200 M CPU, 2.50 GHz, 6 GB RAM, internal 1 TB IDE disk, with KDE desktop. All logs are local and tested on single machine.

Figure 3 shows the comparative results of the log analysis in terms of number of rules per file, number of logs per file, and total processing time. The predictive analysis results of HMM are calculated as precision, recall, and F-measures that give performance rate of each model using definitions (1), (2), and (3). Here for equal weighting the importance parameter corresponding to precision and recall is considered as 0.5.

The comparative result of multiple tests performed on different file sizes in terms of processing time and predictive parameters is shown in Table 2 and Fig. 4. Due to the complexity of rules and actions of *Sec*, inclusion of *Sec* to already existing prediction module processing time is increased. But because of better correlative analysis the final prediction results are improved by 6–7 %. This is considerable improvement in the proposed system. Therefore the combination of SEC+HMM is preferred over the normal data preprocessing and machine learning correlating strategies.

Table 1 Comparative performance of HMM and SEC+HMM environment

No. of rules per file	No. of logs per file (K)	Total processing time (data preprocessing+HMM) (s)	Total processing time (SEC+HMM) (s)
1	50	3.16	3.57
	100	6.68	7.14
	500	27.64	35.7
50	50	9.48	13.38
	100	22.77	26.76
	500	125.70	133.8
100	50	18.65	21.74
	100	38.60	43.4
	500	210.47	217.39

Fig. 3 Processing time analysis for 100 K log file

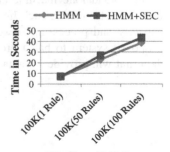

Table 2 Comparative predictive analysis of HMM and SEC+HMM environment

	Data preprocessing+HMM	SEC+HMM
Precision	0.88	0.94
Recall	0.84	0.90
F-measure	0.85	0.93

Fig. 4 Predictive analysis results

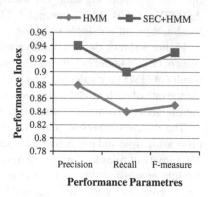

7 Conclusion

In this paper, we demonstrated a system which extracts, correlates different alerts, and predicts the future attacker action. We solved the problem of event correlation using SEC technique and used the HMM to detect multistage attacks and predict next attack class. We performed multiple tests on different log sets collected from standalone systems, servers, log files, etc. The results showed that the system can extract the attack scenarios efficiently and predict the attacker's future action. In general, the proposed system is advantageous over the existing system in a number of ways. The SEC is able to process real-time data, its configuration results in low memory utilization and reduces computational overhead. *Sec* provides platform-independent and lightweight solution. Absence of network and system information does not affect HMM's performance. Thus the combination of *Sec* and HMM results in high-level efficient prediction model.

As the data size increases, due to tremendous amount of log generation, the normal standalone machine environment with certain processing powers is quite inefficient to operate such huge data. There will be problems in terms of storage capacity and processing power. In order to deal with it, we need to switch the proposed system to batch processing systems like Hadoop to process such huge data that will provide advantages of distributed storage and distributed computing.

References

1. Vaarandi, R., & Pihelgas, M. (2014). Using security logs for collecting and reporting technical security metrics. In *Proceedings of the 2014 IEEE MILCOM Conference* (pp. 294–299).
2. Smith, R., Japkowicz, N., Dondo, M., & Mason, P. (2008). Using unsupervised learning for network alert correlation. In *Advances in Artificial Intelligence* (pp. 308–319).
3. Valeur, F., Vigna, G., Kruegel, C., & Kemmerer, R. A. (2004). A comprehensive approach to intrusion detection alert correlation. *IEEE Transactions on Dependable and Secure Computing, 1*(3), 146–169.
4. Pietraszek, T. (2004). Using adaptive alert classification to reduce false positives in intrusion detection. In *Recent Advances in Intrusion Detection* (pp. 102, 124).
5. Morin, B., Mie, L., Debar, H., & Ducasse, M. (2002). M2D2: A formal data model for IDS alert correlation. In *Proceedings of the 5th International Symposium on Recent Advances in Intrusion Detection, RAID '02*.
6. Fischer, F., Mansmann, F., & Keim, D. A. (2012). A cross platform intrusion detection system using inter server communication technique: real-time visual analytics for event data streams (pp. 26–30).
7. Zhang, S., Gao, Y., & Ge, J. (2013). The study of network event correlation analysis based on similar degree of attributes. In *2013 Fourth International Conference on Digital Manufacturing Automation*.
8. Farhadi, H., AmirHaeri, M., & Khansari, M. (2011). *Alert correlation and prediction using data mining and HMM* (Vol. 3/(2), pp. 77–101).
9. Vaarandi, R. (2006). Simple event correlator for real-time security log monitoring. Haking Magazine, *1*(6), 28–39.
10. Vaarandi, R. (2002). SEC—a lightweight event correlation tool. In *Proceedings of the 2002 IEEE Workshop on IP Operations and Management* (pp. 111–115).
11. Ourston, D., Matzner, S., Stump, W., & Hopkins, B. (2003). Applications of hidden Markov models to detecting multi-stage network attacks. In *Proceedings of the 36th Annual Hawaii International Conference on System Sciences, HICSS '03*.
12. Lee, D., Kim, D., & Jung, J. (2008). Multi stage intrusion detection system using hidden Markov model algorithm. In *Proceedings of the International Conference on Information Science and Security, ICISS '08* (pp. 72–77).

Differential Weight Based Hybrid Approach to Detect Software Plagiarism

Nrupesh Shah, Sandip Modha and Dhruv Dave

Abstract In this paper we propose different representations of a source code, which attempt to highlight different aspects of a code; particularly: (i) lexical, (ii) structural, and (iii) stylistics. For the lexical view, we used levenshtein distance without considering all reserved words of the programming language. For the structural view, we proposed a similarity metric that takes into account the function's signatures and variable declaration within a source code. The third view consists of several stylistic features, such as the number of white spaces, lines of code, upper case letters, etc. At the end, we combine these different representations in several ways. Obtained results indicate that proposed representations provide some information that allows to detect particular cases of source code re-use.

Keywords Software plagiarism detection · Source code re-use · Plagiarism detection · Software cloning

1 Introduction

Identification of source code re-use is an interesting topic from two points of view. Firstly, the industry that produces software is always looking for protecting their developments, thus they usually search for any sign of unauthorized use of their own blocks of source code. Secondly, in the academic field, it is well known that the habit of copying programs is a common practice among students. Such phenomena is also motivated due to all the facilities that web forums, blogs,

N. Shah (✉) · S. Modha · D. Dave
Department of Computer Engineering, LDRP – ITR, Gandhinagar, India
e-mail: shahnrupesh007@live.com

S. Modha
e-mail: sjmodha@gmail.com

D. Dave
e-mail: dhruvdave.ce@gmail.com

© Springer Science+Business Media Singapore 2016
S.C. Satapathy et al. (eds.), *Proceedings of International Conference on ICT for Sustainable Development*, Advances in Intelligent Systems and Computing 409, DOI 10.1007/978-981-10-0135-2_62

repositories, etc., offer to share source codes which most of the times have been already debugged and tested. Consequently, source code re-use detection has become an important research topic, motivating different groups to define the problem more formally in order to build automatic systems to identify such problem.

As an example, in 1987 Faidhi and Robinson [1] proposed a seven level hierarchy that aimed at representing most of the program's modifications used by students when they plagiarize source code. As a consequence, many approaches that try to identify plagiarized code are based on these levels of complexity. However, it is important to notice that programmers who re-use a source code usually apply not one, but several obfuscation techniques when re-using sections from a program. Therefore, even though there are several proposed techniques to detect different types of source code re-uses, it is very difficult for a single automatic system to detect all these different types of obfuscation practices.

In this work we propose different representations of a source code, namely: character n-grams, function prototypes, identifiers' names, and stylistics features. Our intuitive idea is that by means of considering different aspects from a source code, it will be possible to capture some of the most common practices performed by programmers when they are re-using a source code.

2   Related Work

Lately, developed automated systems to identify source code re-use are applying natural language processing (NLP) techniques that are being adapted to this specific context. One example of those systems is one that takes into account a remanence trace left after a copy of source code, such as, white space patterns [2]. The intuitive idea behind this approach indicates that a plagiarist camouflages almost everything when copying a source code but the white spaces. Accordingly, it computes similarities between source codes taking into account the use of letters (all represented as X) and white spaces (represented as S).

As another example of automatic systems that employ NLP techniques, are those based on word n-grams [1, 3]. These works consider several features of source code, such as, identifiers, number of lines, number of hapax, etc. Their obtained results were very promising.

Some other works employed transformation techniques based on LSA, for example the work presented in [4]. In this work, authors focused on three components: preprocessing (keeping or removing comments, keywords or program skeleton), weighting (combining diverse local or global weights), and the dimensionality of LSA.

As can be observed, a common characteristic of previous works is that they attempt to capture several aspects from source codes into one single/mixed representation (i.e., a single view) in order to detect source code re-use. Contrary to these previous works, our hypothesis states that each aspect (i.e., either structural or superficial elements) provides its own important information and cannot be mixed with other aspects when representing source codes.

3 Problem Description

The basic idea of this problem is that there are two program codes to compare, a plaintiff program p and suspicious program s, and we have to measure the similarity between them. We calculate the function

$$\text{Sim}(P, S) \in [0, 1].$$

We can define $T \in [0, 1]$ such that if

$$\text{Sim}(P, S) \geq T \text{ then there is plagiarism.}$$

$$\text{Sim}(P, S) < T \text{ then no plagiarism exists.}$$

4 Proposed Solution

In this section we describe our proposed representations for source code in order to find several aspects of the code that help to detect source code re-use. We divided these representations into three views: i.e., lexical, structural, and stylistics.

4.1 Lexical Representation

This is the basic representation of the source code. Here we compare two source codes without considering their internal structure. We just compare them as we are comparing two strings for similarities.

First of all we remove all the reserved words from the java source because that reduces the false positive similarity in this particular representation.

Now we are using the levenshtein distance for finding the approximate similarity between the given pair of source codes.

Levenshtein distance is a measure of similarity between two strings. It is also called as edit distance and is the minimum number of edits required to convert one string to another. It is calculated as follows [5]:

$$\text{lev}(i,j) = \begin{cases} \max(i,j) & \text{if } \min(i,j) = 0 \\ \min\begin{cases} \text{lev}(i-1,j)+1 \\ \text{lev}(i,j-1)+1 \\ \text{lev}(i-1,j-1)+1(ai \neq bj) \end{cases} & \text{otherwise} \end{cases} \tag{1}$$

4.2 Structural Representation

In this given representation we try to measure how similar the code pair is from structural aspect. We are trying to find the similarities in the attributes only related to coding.

Here we have used java parser [6] available from Google code under a GNU license to extract method signatures and variable declarations into a string. After we have both of these extracted they are compared to find the similarity.

We have extracted method signature in a specific way. First we extract name of the method preceding its parameter type list and return type. If the method has a throws statement it is appended to the string.

For example: if the method signature is *void finalize() throws Throwable* then the extracted string will be *finalize voidvoid Throwable*.

In a similar manner we are extracting the fields of the source code. Here we are extracting the declaration statements of these objects into a string. Now both the methods and fields extracted from the single source code are concatenated into a single string. These concatenated strings are now the final structural representation of the given source code. These strings are now compared using char n-gram distance with the value of n being 3.

4.3 Stylistic Representation

This representation aims at finding unique properties from the original author such as his/her programming style. In this sense, we compute nine stylistic features to represent each source code. Then, we found the similarities between two source codes.

The features are: number of white spaces, number of tabulations, number of empty lines, number of functions, average word length, number of upper case letters, number of lower case letters, number of underscores, and total number of words in a source code. We have tested stylistic similarity on two different metrics. One is the n-gram distance and the other is cosine similarity. Here n-gram distance with $n = 3$ provides better results than cosine similarity. Hence results shown below use n-gram distance instead of cosine similarity for stylistic similarity.

4.4 Final Score

The final similarity score can be calculated by calculating the weighted average of the similarities calculated from all above representations. The threshold we have decided after multiple experiments is 60 % because that provides best *F*-measure results.

The final similarity can be calculated according to the below equation. This equation calculates the weights of the similarity obtained from various aspects or views (representation) of the source code.

$$\text{sim} = (\alpha * \text{LexSim}) + (\beta * \text{StructureSim}) + (\gamma * \text{StyleSim}) \tag{2}$$

where α is the weight of the lexical similarity, β is the weight of the structural similarity, and γ is the weight of the stylistic similarity.

Here we are finding values of α, β, and γ empirically, i.e., with the use of various experiments. The best results we have obtained are for $\alpha = 0.45$, $\beta = 0.35$, and $\gamma = 0.20$.

5 Results

We carried out a series of experiments using single views in order to find the amount of relevant information given by each representation.

For each experiment we compute the similarity values of each source code file with other source code files in the training set. Then, we measure the performance of each proposed representation by means of establishing a manual threshold for considering when two codes are plagiarized (re-used). Here we have taken *F*-measure as the ultimate evaluation metric.

The results obtained are given in Table 1. We also tested another popular software plagiarism detection tool Sherlock [7] on our dataset which was provided by FIRE 2014, SOCO track [8] and the results are shown in the table below.

The results of this evaluation are given in Figs. 1, 2, 3 and 4. Figure 1 presents the performance of the lexical representation. The figure below shows the effect of changing lexical weight according to *x*-axis on the precision. We can see that increase in lexical weight α clearly increases the precision up to some threshold value. Then it starts to stabilize.

Table 1 Results obtained

	Precision	Recall	F-measure
Our approach	0.881	0.619	0.727
Sherlock	0.882	0.535	0.667

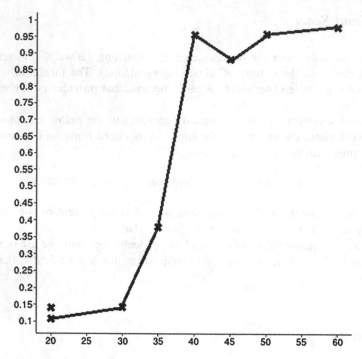

Fig. 1 Lexical weight versus precision

Figure 2 presents the performance of the structural representation. The figure below shows the effect of changing structural weight according to x-axis on the precision.

We can see that increase in structural weight β clearly decreases the precision up to some threshold value. Then it starts to stabilize. But that means that increase in β also increases recall.

Figure 3 presents the performance of the stylistic representation. The figure below shows the effect of changing stylistic weight according to x-axis on the precision. We can see that increase in structural weight γ does not clearly decrease or increase the precision value.

Figure 4 presents the effect of changing threshold weight according to x-axis on the precision. Which obviously decreases recall means we have to determine the value of threshold that maximizes both precision and recall. And that value for threshold is 60 % in our experiments.

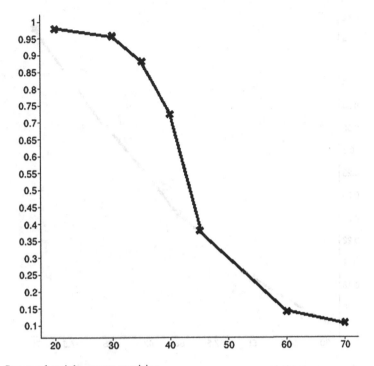

Fig. 2 Structural weight versus precision

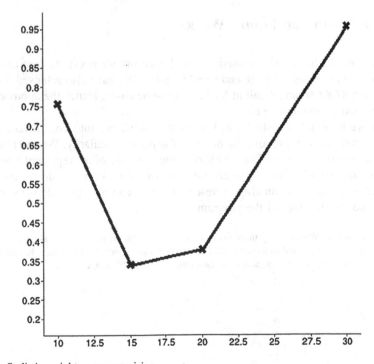

Fig. 3 Stylistic weight versus precision

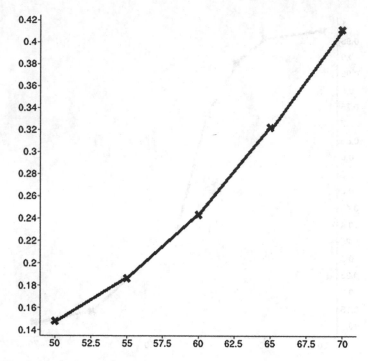

Fig. 4 Threshold versus precision

6 Conclusion and Future Work

So far, the results have been promising. The F-measure we got in the best case was 72.72 % with precision 88.13 % and recall 61.90 %. We have also achieved the best precision at 97.87 % and recall at 84.52 % in some cases. Hence the approach we proposed gives sufficient results.

Here we have taken only limited amount of structure into consideration and hence in future we can improve the quality of structural similarity. We can also add more parameters to the stylistic similarity and can add other representations for consideration. To add other representations we can, for example, add the program dependence graph [9] as another representation that can also provide some useful insight into the structure of the program.

Acknowledgments We are truly thankful to Prof. Prasenjit Majumder for his valuable time and advice. Initially he motivated us to work with this problem and given right direction to address the problem. We are inspired by international conference FIRE 2014 SOCO track.

References

1. Faidhi, J. A. W., & Robinson, S. K. (1987). An empirical approach for detecting program similarity and plagiarism within a university programming environment. *Computers and Education, 11.1*, 11–19.
2. Baer, N., & Zeidman, R. (2012). Measuring whitespace pattern sequences as an indication of Plagiarism. *Journal of Software Engineering and Applications, 5*(4), 249–254.
3. Narayanan, S., & Simi, S. (2012). Source code plagiarism detection and performance analysis using fingerprint based distance measure method. In *2012 7th International Conference on Computer Science and Education (ICCSE)*. IEEE.
4. Cosma, G., & Mike, J. (2012). Evaluating the performance of lsa for source-code plagiarism detection. *Informatica, 36.4*.
5. Lavenshtien Distance. http://rosettacode.org/wiki/Levenshtein_distance.
6. Java Parser. https://code.google.com/p/javaparser.
7. Sherlock: Plagiarism Detector. http://sydney.edu.au/engineering/it/ ∼ scilect/sherlock/.
8. Flores, E. et al. (2014). Pan@ fire: Overview of soco track on the detection of source code re-use. In *Sixth Forum for Information Retrieval Evaluation (FIRE 2014), Bangalore, India*.
9. Liu, C. et al. (2006). GPLAG: Detection of software plagiarism by program dependence graph analysis. In *Proceedings of the 12th ACM SIGKDD International Conference on Knowledge Discovery and Data Mining*. ACM.

References

Selecting Favorable Reference Nodes to Aid Localization in Wireless Sensor Networks

Gaurav Dhaka and Nileshkumar R. Patel

Abstract The wireless sensor network is ad hoc network, which consists of small light weighted wireless nodes called sensor nodes. These nodes are deployed to measure physical parameters such as sound, pressure, temperature, and humidity. Wireless sensor network is resource constraint in terms of energy, computation, memory, and limited communication capabilities. All sensor nodes in the wireless sensor network interact with each other directly or via intermediate sensor nodes. The main purpose of the sensor node is to transmit sensed data to the base station or a central server which processes received data. It is better for efficient processing to have location of the sensor node, which senses that data. In many of the sensor applications, nodes need to find their locations. Manual configuration of location is not feasible for large-scale networks or networks where sensors may move from one position to other frequently. Manual configuration of location may also increase the hardware requirements of the device which will increase overall cost of the system. This paper introduces an approach based on selecting favorable reference nodes, which can contribute toward accurate localization. In the proposed approach, a node replies to a request packet if its error is less than the error of the node broadcasting the request packet. The error is calculated as the sum of difference between Euclidian distance from reference node and RSSI distance from reference nodes. Several checks are implemented to ensure accuracy, security, and energy efficiency.

Keywords Wireless sensor networks · WSN · Localization

G. Dhaka (✉) · N.R. Patel
Department of Computer Science and Engineering, Jaypee University of Engineering and Technology, Raghogarh, Guna 473226, India
e-mail: dhaka.gaurav@yahoo.in

N.R. Patel
e-mail: nayan.spce@gmail.com

© Springer Science+Business Media Singapore 2016
S.C. Satapathy et al. (eds.), *Proceedings of International Conference on ICT for Sustainable Development*, Advances in Intelligent Systems and Computing 409, DOI 10.1007/978-981-10-0135-2_63

1 Introduction

Sensor network is an infrastructure comprised of sensing, computing, and communication elements. Sensing refers to the phenomenon of detecting something, computing refers to the process of doing some processing on the data that has been sensed, and communication refers to the process of transferring data and processing results over a communication medium, i.e., network. Sensor networks provide the ability of instrumenting, observing, and reacting to events and phenomena in a specified environment for which the sensor nodes are deployed. The first major Implementation of wireless sensor networks was done during cold war by United States for the purpose of submarine surveillance. Some of these sensors are still being used by the National Oceanic and Atmospheric Administration (NOAA) to monitor seismic activity in the ocean [1].

Application areas of WSNs vary from critical, i.e., military operations, disaster relief operations, traffic management, medical operations, to the most generous once, i.e., intelligent buildings, logistics. WSNs have some issues related to them, which vary from the type of service provided, i.e., quality of service, fault tolerance, energy efficiency to the implementation of the strategies, i.e., auto configuration, collaboration, and in-network processing and localization [2].

1.1 Localization

Localization is one of the major issues in WSNs in situations where a fixed deployment of sensor nodes is not possible, i.e., war areas, fire affected areas, unreachable terrains. In these situations, random deployment of sensor nodes is done either by an aircraft or any other manner. In such situations, location of the sensor, which is sending data, must be known to process data efficiently. Without location of sensor, processing cannot be done. Localization is the process of estimating the location of randomly deployed sensor nodes [3]. Localization has an important role to play in geographical routing to forward packet to the next node.

1.2 Components of Localization System

Localization system can be considered as consisting of three components, i.e., distance/angle measurement, position estimation, and localization algorithm. Methods available for distance and angle measurement are time of arrival (ToA), angle of arrival (AoA), received signal strength indicator (RSSI), and time difference of arrival (TDoA). ToA is based on measuring distance using the time of arrived signal. AoA is based on measuring angle of the arrived signal with respect to the global axis. RSSI is based on measuring distance based on signal strength received by the device. TDoA is based on difference in arrival times of two different signals. Distance and angle provided by above methods are used to estimate the position of nodes. Methods for position estimation are trilateration, multilateration, triangulation, and bounding box. Triangulation uses angles to find location and other three use distances to find location. Finally, the localization algorithm deals with the task of propagating location information among all the nodes in the system. Localization system consists of different types of nodes. Based on the node's location information, a node can be classified as one of the three available classes of nodes, i.e., beacon nodes, settled nodes, and unknown nodes [2].

(1) Beacon Nodes: These nodes do not require any localization system to obtain their position. They have their fixed location information provided to them either by manual deployment or by any other external method, i.e., GPS. These nodes can also be referred to as anchor nodes and landmark nodes.

(2) Settled Nodes: These nodes were initially unknown nodes but using any localization scheme, they have obtained their position now and became settled nodes. These nodes can now serve as reference point for other unknown nodes.

(3) Unknown Nodes: Unknown nodes are those nodes which do not know their position information and the localization process tries to find the location of these nodes. Many times instead of unknown nodes, it may be referred to as dumb nodes or free nodes [3].

Localization system deals with the task of providing location information to unknown nodes using the data provided by beacon nodes and settled nodes, converting unknown nodes into settled nodes, which will take part in location estimation of other unknown nodes.

1.3 Design Objectives of Localization System

Sensor nodes are battery-powered, low capacity devices and the environment is also dynamic. Thus, sensor networks create some difficult challenges for the developers. Every localization system has some common objectives that could lead to an efficient system.

(1) Independence from Anchor Node Placement: Different applications have different requirements and different arrangements of anchor nodes. In all applications, anchor nodes are required to calculate the location of unknown nodes. Thus, localization scheme should not cover only a specific arrangement of beacon nodes.

(2) Energy Efficiency: All sensor nodes are battery powered, which gets drained with time and processing, it is essential that localization scheme must be designed keeping energy efficiency constraint in mind. The complexity of a localization approach increases with the increase in number of references used [4]. Increased complexity results in increased energy consumption.

(3) Security: Wireless networks are vulnerable to many security issues and attacks. Similarly WSNs can also be attacked. So the localization scheme should deal with security issues present in environment.

(4) Accuracy: WSNs are used in critical operations like military operations and security services. These operations require highly accurate position estimation. On the other hand, many applications can accept data with some amount of errors. Technique should be designed considering different situations in mind [5].

1.4 Categories of Localization Algorithm

Table 1 describes the different categories of localization algorithms.

2 Existing Approaches

Many researchers are working in the field of localization for WSNs. The earliest implementations of localization include SerLoc [6], HirLoc [7], and Monte Carlo localization [8].

Table 1 Different categories of localization algorithms

Base of categorization	Categories	Advantages	Disadvantages
Process distribution	Centralized	Accurate	High data transfer between nodes
	Distributed	Requires less resources and is scalable	Less accurate
Number of iterations	Single iteration	Fast estimation and consumes less energy	Less accurate
	Multiple refinements	Highly accurate and robust	Error propagation
Number of references	All references	Accurate and easy to implement	Complex computation and require more resources
	Subset of references	Works in error prone environment and simple computation	Less accurate if wrong subset is selected

In SerLoc, beacon nodes are equipped with omni-directional high power sec-tored antennas. These nodes transmit their location and the two angles which are together used to estimate range of its signal. This scheme does not require nodes to interact with each other but it has a limitation in areas where transmission of antenna signals is jammed.

In HIRLoc, to determine their location, nodes calculate the intersection of the areas covered by the beacons of multiple reference points. Some security measures were added to make it efficient.

Monte Carlo localization introduced the concept of anchor box created at the intersection of different beacon signals.

All the above strategies used actual distance for calculations. Then some tech-niques based on distance considered as hop counts, emerged. DV-Loc [9] is one of those approaches. It used the DV-Hop method for distance measurement in which number of hops were multiplied by hop distance. This approach reduced the computational overhead but calculating average distance is not accurate all the time. In randomly deployed sensor environment, average hop distance will not give the actual distance between two nodes and the error will propagate from one node to another making whole system unbalanced.

So far, the major effort was put in calculating the best approximate location based on the available nodes. ALWadHA [10] introduced the concept of selecting a subset of available reference nodes for estimating the location. They have intro-duced the approach as smart reference selection. References are selected based on their accuracy level and error values.

The complexity of approach in ALWadHA increases as multiple checks were implemented to achieve better accuracy, security, and reduced beacon messages. High complexity of algorithm results in large amount of processing thus increasing energy consumption. High level of accuracy can be compromised with the energy consumption in most of the cases.

The number of references in ALWadHA varies according to the accuracy of estimation. References will increase if the desired level of accuracy is not achieved which also increases the processing.

This leads to the development of an energy-saving approach using a subset of nodes.

3 Proposed Approach

The proposed method is based on selecting the fittest three reference nodes for estimating the nodes' position. As the complexity increases when the number of reference nodes increases, the reduced number of nodes will reduce the

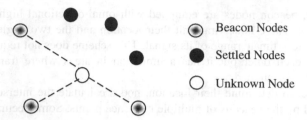

Fig. 1 Fittest reference selection

computation overhead. Reference nodes are selected in each iteration based on predefined error level decided by the unknown node.

Figure 1 shows that the method will select three beacon nodes from a set of three beacons nodes, 3 Settled nodes that is available to an Unknown node.

The process concludes in four phases.

Phase I: Initialization

- Unknown node and settled node send a location request message containing its current error level. Settled node will send request to get an improved location.
- All the beacon nodes will reply to the message and each settled node that has error level less than the error level of the requesting node will reply.

Phase 2: Subset Creation

- Based on received messages, the node will arrange the queue according to error level.
- Three nodes with least error will be selected for trilateration.

Phase 3: Location Estimation

- Trilateration is performed using three selected nodes.
- Then the error is calculated by subtracting the distance between two nodes and available RSSI distance between those nodes and is stored. This error will be stored by the node for further activities.

Phase 4: Termination

- Accept the location if new error level is better than previous.
- Terminate the process if error level reaches a certain threshold which depends on application to application.

The termination condition can be varied according to the requirement of the application. If the implemented system has some critical application like military operation then error threshold can be taken as low and for less critical operations, error threshold can be taken a bit higher than the one taken for critical applications thus resulting in lesser iterations for obtaining stable location information.

4 Analysis

The core feature of the proposed approach is to select the best three reference nodes from all the available nodes. The analysis of the approach is provided in this Section.

(1) **Energy Efficiency** Energy efficiency of an algorithm in WSNs depends on many aspects like the complexity of calculations, computation overhead, and many more. The proposed approach is using only three reference nodes for calculating position. So, the reduced number of nodes will reduce the computation overhead. Another contribution toward energy efficiency is that when a node estimates its position using three beacon nodes, that position will be final for that node until a better estimation is introduced, so less updation is required.

(2) **Security** Security is also a major issue in wireless sensor networks. The error mechanism is providing the security from introduction of malicious response message. The error will increase in case of malicious response and that distance estimation will then be ignored.

(3) **Accuracy** In the proposed approach, only those nodes are sending the response message, those which have the error level less than the value required by the unknown node. This value depends on the error in previous estimation. Then the second check is introduced to make the estimation more accurate by keeping malicious responses away from the estimation by calculating the error.

(4) **Independence from anchor node placement** The proposed approach is fully independent from the specific arrangement of anchor nodes. If a node does not have an anchor node then it can estimate its position using settled nodes as reference.

5 Simulation

The algorithm is being implemented in Network Simulator-2 which was modified to simulate WSN by Abu-Mahfouz and Hancke [11]. Transmission range of 50 m is set for each node. To measure the distance between nodes RSS was used. For initial measurements, a total of 19 nodes were taken. Three nodes are beacon and the rest are unknown nodes.

Figure 2 represents the placement of nodes in the topology in which blue nodes are beacon nodes and orange nodes are unknown nodes.

IP Header was modified to contain the field for error which a node will send either in request packet or in response packet. Response IP Header is generated only if the error in request packet is greater than the processing node.

Fig. 2 Topology

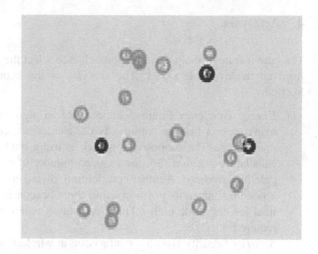

6 Conclusion and Future Work

Different localization algorithms available focus on different issues of localization such as errors, number of beacons, number of settled nodes, GPS usage, or energy consumption or based on combination of different issues.

For sensor networks, energy consumption is a major issue as battery is limited in those sensor devices. The major requirement for reducing battery consumption is to reduce the computational complexity of the localization strategy. Number of nodes used as reference in the process also contributes to the computational complexity of the system. Lesser references will lead to simplified calculations.

The proposed approach may lead to an accurate, energy-efficient approach for localization in wireless sensor networks.

To simulate complete algorithm is the future plan to evaluate the overall performance of the system in comparison with the existing approaches.

References

1. Sohraby, K., Minoli, D., & Znati, T. (2007). *Wireless sensor networks-technology, protocols, and applications*. Publication: Wiley.
2. Holger, K., & Andreas, W. (2005). Protocols and architectures for wireless sensor networks. Wiley.
3. B, A., HABF, O., EF, N., & AF, A. (2007). Localization systems for wireless sensor networks. *IEEE Wireless Communications, 14*(6), 6–12.
4. Lieckfeldt, D., You, J., & Timmermann, D. (2008). An algorithm for distributed beacon selection. In *Proceedings of the Sixth Annual IEEE International Conference on Pervasive Computing and Communication* (pp. 318–323). Hong Kong, China.

5. Ziaur Rahman, M., & Kleeman, L. (2009). Paired measurement localization: A robust approach for wireless localization. *IEEE Transactions on Mobile Computing, 8*(8), 1087–1102.
6. Lazos, L., & Poovendran, R. (2005). SeRLoc: Robust localization for wireless sensor networks. *ACM Transactions on Sensor Networks (TOSN), 1*(1), 73–100.
7. Lazos, L., & Poovendran, R. (2006). HiRLoc: High-resolution robust localization for wireless sensor networks. *IEEE Journal on Selected Areas in Communications, 24*(2), 233–246.
8. Baggio, A., & Langendoen, Koen. (2008). Monte Carlo localization for mobile wireless sensor networks. *Ad Hoc Networks, 6*(5), 718–733.
9. Boukerche, A., Oliveira, H. A. B. F., Nakamura, E. F., & Loureiro, A. A. F. (2009). DV-Loc: A scalable localization protocol using voronoi diagrams for wireless sensor networks. *IEEE Wireless Communications, 16*(2), 50–55.
10. Abu-Mahfouz, A. M., & Hancke, G. P. (2013). An efficient distributed localisation algorithm for wireless sensor networks based on smart reference-selection method. *International Journal of Sensor Networks, 13*(2), 94–111.
11. Abu-Mahfouz, A. M., & Hancke, G. P. (2011). ns-2 extensi on to simulate localization system in wireless sensor networks. IEEE Africon.

A Scientometric Analysis of Smart Grid Implementation at Distribution Feeder

J.P. Sharma, Devendra Bhavsar and Laxmi Chand Sharma

Abstract This paper focuses on the development of smart grid implementation at distribution feeder in terms of publication output as reflected in the IEEE Xplore digital library. The IEEE Xplore digital library has total 46 publications on the above field during 2008–15. The highest number of publications of 13 was published in 2012. Maximum contribution was given by authors from the USA as compared to other countries. The relative growth rates (RGRs) have decreased from 2012 (0.624) to 2015 (0.022) in the span of 3 years. The doubling time (DT) has gradually increased from 1.11 in 2012 to 32.22 in 2015. The published research works of 21 IEEE publications out of aforesaid 46 were studied in the literature review.

Keywords Smart grid · Distribution feeder · Scientometric analysis · Relative growth rate · Doubling time

1 Introduction

This paper attempts to illustrate a scientometric analysis of smart grid implementation at distribution feeder for describing the innovation, development, or demise of a technology field. The burning issues for distribution utilities are shortage power, power quality, and renewable energy sources integration. Smart grid is a new and currently developing platform that integrates, monitors, and operates

J.P. Sharma (✉)
Electrical Engineering Department, JK Lakshmipat University, Jaipur, India
e-mail: jpsharma.jklu@gmail.com

D. Bhavsar
Computer Science and Engineering, JK Lakshmipat University, Jaipur, India
e-mail: devendrabhavsar@jklu.edu.in

L.C. Sharma
Learning Resource Center, JK Lakshmipat University, Jaipur, India
e-mail: lrcasst@jklu.edu.in

© Springer Science+Business Media Singapore 2016
S.C. Satapathy et al. (eds.), *Proceedings of International Conference on ICT for Sustainable Development*, Advances in Intelligent Systems and Computing 409, DOI 10.1007/978-981-10-0135-2_64

distribution system in real-time mode. Smart grids provide a better use of their technological capital to maintain their competitive edge. It is an application of information, communication, and sensor technologies for effective planning, forecasting, life cycle management, and road-mapping. The following factors emphasize the adoption of the smart grid for distribution feeder

- Integration of distributed energy resources
- Increase in energy trading
- Loss reduction
- Performance efficiency
- Peak load management

The integration of renewable sources to distribution system creates enormous dare for distribution system operators (DSOs). To overcome these challenges, coordination and simultaneous bilateral connection are required, which is the part of smart grid. Due to minimization of system vulnerability, increased security, reliability, and power quality characteristics of smart grid make one of the fastest-growing research topics. Total 46 publications on smart grid implementation at distribution feeder were available in the IEEE Xplore digital library and a scientometric analysis for all these 46 publications was carried out. We have studied 21 publications for literature review [1–21].

2 Literature Review

Smart grid is a multidisciplinary research area especially for electrical engineering, computer science, and electronics. The IEEE Xplore digital library has the best known bibliographic databases for these streams.

Shariatzadeh et al. [1] have developed an estimation method for real-time energy using Volt/Var control in smart grid environment. Voltage dependency load characteristic is also estimated in this paper. Yong Lin et al. [2] have developed an advanced strategy for automation of unbalanced distribution grid. This strategy includes four standardized parts, which provide reasonable development planning for future distribution automation.

Chen et al. [3] have improved reliability of supply using distribution automation system (DAS). Fault detection isolation and restoration (FDIR) is performed by smart grid. Advanced automation system is also proposed to photovoltaic (PV) inverter control and asset management. Aguero [4] discusses self-healing schemes, which represent the basis for automated system reconfiguration and optimization. Kim et al. [5] have explored a loop configuration for an advanced power distribution system (APDS). This configuration can integrate more renewable energy sources to improve voltage regulation. Uluski [6] facilitates implementation of distributed energy resources to advanced distribution automation (ADA).

Kim et al. [7] built an online grid data analytic system, data mining and analytics system (DMAS) using a set of real utility data. Haiyang and ShanDe [8] has discussed different types of traditional energy sources and new energy (solar, wind, tidal energy, etc.) with energy storage techniques. Ehsan ur Rahman et al. [9] present a prototype implementation of smart metering system for loss reduction and efficient load management in the power distribution system. Paudyal et al. [10] present a three-phase distribution optimal power flow (DOPF) model by transforming the mixed-integer nonlinear programming and this model can be used by local distribution companies (LDCs) to integrate their distribution system feeders into a smart grid. Cappelle et al. [11] investigate the possibilities to prevent over-voltages on a low voltage distribution feeder due to the simultaneous power injection of a considerable number of PV installations.

Zhifeng et al. [12] present an efficient strong real-time communication scheme used in intelligent distribution automation system. Aguero [13] has reviewed technologies, methodologies, and operational approaches aimed at improving the efficiency of power distribution systems, with emphasis on the accurate estimation and reduction of technical and non-technical power and energy losses. Sanchez-Ayala et al. [14] explore the contribution of phasor measurement units (PMUs) to handle challenges by large penetration of intermittent DG on smart distribution feeders. McBee and Simoes [15] defines a proactive approach for voltage investigations and describes the benefits associated with the approach. Argade et al. [16] have developed different charging patterns using a probabilistic model for vehicle arrival time and charge left at arrival.

Chai et al. [17] have introduced an ICN-based C-DAX communication platform, while maintaining the required hard real-time data delivery as demonstrated through field trials at national scale. Vukojevic et al. [18] have determined the optimal location and optimum number of fault circuit indicators (FCIs) on the distribution feeder. Gantz et al. [19] investigate the optimal implementation of distributed storage resources in a power distribution system or islanded microgrid in conjunction with an intelligent load shedding scheme to minimize the societal costs of blackouts. Manaz et al. [20] has studied feasibility of virtual power plant (VPP) implementation through a coordinated control scheme that coordinates the operation of distributed energy resources (DER) to meet utility's demand response (DR) needs effectively. Jauch [21] focuses on load-tap-changer transformer duties associated with smart grid (SG) integrated volt/var/kilowatt management functions.

3 Objectives

Scientometric analysis emerged as one of the necessary tools to avoid duplication in research subject. The objectives framed for the study are to:

- Explore the growth of literature on smart grid implementation at distribution feeder.
- Find the scattering of literature based on publication types.
- Identify the prolific authors in the aforesaid area.
- Analyze countrywise contributions of the publications.

4 Scientometric Analysis

The data for the present study was retrieved from the IEEE Xplore digital library, which is one of the largest-established libraries and has 3-million full-text documents. The IEEE Xplore digital library is also best known bibliographic databases for electrical engineering, computer science, and electronics. The content in IEEE Xplore comprises over 160 journals, over 1,200 conference proceedings, more than 3,800 technical standards, over 1,000 ebooks, and over 300 educational courses. Approximately 25,000 new documents are added to IEEE Xplore each month. With the aim of covering all the available citations on the subject, the database was searched with advanced search options. A total of 46 publications spanning over the years 2008–2015 were published. Each publication contains detailed bibliographic information. MATLAB package is used for the purpose of analysis.

5 Data Analysis and Interpretations

5.1 Publications Output and Types

The source of publications covered by the IEEE Xplore digital library on smart grid at distribution feeder is conference articles with 38 (82.61 %) followed by journal articles with seven publications (15.22 %) and one article one (2.17 %) in press (Table 1).

Table 1 Publications output and type

S. no.	Forms of publications	No. of publications (%)
1	Conference publications	38 (82.61 %)
2	Journal and magazines articles	7 (15.22 %)
3	Articles in press	1 (2.17 %)

Table 2 Relative growth rate (RGR) and doubling time (DT) of publications

Year	No. of publications	Cumulative total	Log_eW1	Log_eW2	RGR	DT
2008	1	1		0.000		
2009	1	2	0.000	0.693	0.693	1.000
2010	2	5	0.693	1.609	0.916	0.756
2011	10	15	1.609	2.708	1.099	0.631
2012	13	28	2.708	3.332	0.624	1.110
2013	11	39	3.332	3.664	0.331	2.091
2014	7	46	3.664	3.829	0.165	4.198
2015	1	47	3.829	3.850	0.022	32.223

5.2 Growth of Publications

During the period of 2008–2015, a total of 46 publications were published on smart grid at distribution feeder. The highest number of publications is 13 articles in 2012. The lowest publication is 1 in 2008, 2009, and 2015. But it is seen from Table 2 that there is a downward trend in 2014.

5.3 Relative Growth Rate and Doubling Time

Relative growth rate (RGR) and doubling time (DT) are used to compute the pace and weightage of published work on a particular area/topics [22]. The RGR is defined as increase in the number of articles or pages over a specified period of time. DT is used to quantify RGR on a nonlinear scale. There is a direct equivalence existing between the RGR and DT. If the number of articles or pages of a subject doubles during a specified period of time then the difference between the logarithms of numbers at the beginning and end of this period must be logarithm of number 2. "Both Relative RGR and DT is computed for each specific period of interval". It has been observed from Table 2 and Fig. 1, that the RGR has continuously decreased from 2013 (0.331) to 2015 (0.022). During this period, DT has increased from 2.091 in 2003 to 32.223 as shown in Fig.2.

5.4 Geographical Distribution of Publications

There are 11 countries involved in carrying out research in the field of smart grid at distribution feeder. It is seen from Table 3, the USA is ranked first followed by Canada.

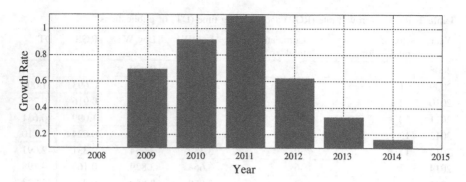

Fig. 1 Relative growth rate for research output

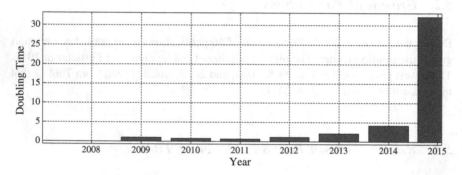

Fig. 2 Doubling time for research output

	S. no.	Country	No. of articles	No. of articles (%)
Table 3 Geographical distribution of publications time (DT)	1	USA	14	30.4
	2	Canada	2	4.3
	3	UK	1	2.2
	4	South Korea	1	2.2
	5	Taiwan	1	2.2
	6	China	1	2.2
	7	Switzerland	1	2.2
	8	Brazil	1	2.2
	9	Saudi Arabia	1	2.2
	10	Italy	1	2.2
	11	Sri Lanka	1	2.2

Table 4 Most prolific authors

S. no.	Country	No. of publications (%)
1	Bhattacharya, Kankar	4.35
2	Jauch, Erwin Tom	4.35
3	Paudyal, Sumit	4.35
4	Paolone, Mario	4.35
5	Canha, Luciane N.	4.35
6	Agüero, Julio Romero	4.35
7	Desmet, Jan J.M.	4.35
8	Debruyne, Colin	4.35
9	Vanalme, J.	4.35
10	Abaide, A.R.	4.35
11	Pereira, Paulo R.	4.35

5.5 *Most Prolific Authors*

Table 4 indicates the rank list of authors who have contributed more than one article to the IEEE Xplore digital library.

6 Conclusions

Smart grid implementation at distribution feeder is a rapidly developing field of research. In this paper, we conduct a scientometric analysis to comprehensively investigate the development and current state of smart distribution feeder related publications based on a large bibliographic data basis provided by the IEEE Xplore library. Relative growth rate reveals that publications on smart grid implementation at distribution feeder are continually decreasing, which is an alarming situation. Researchers have paid very little attention to smart grid implementation in distribution system as distribution system is highly complex and weak link between generation and transmission. Total 38 articles out of 46 were only published in the conference which is giving hope for more literature on this subject from all the countries in the world. Smart grid implementation on feeder will definitely give reduced aggregated technical and commercial (AT&C) loss.

References

1. Shariatzadeh, F., Chanda, S., Srivastava, A. K., & Bose, A. (2014). Real time benefit computation for electric distribution system automation and control. In *Industry Applications Society Annual Meeting, 2014 IEEE* (pp. 1, 8). 5–9 October 2014. doi:10.1109/IAS.2014. 6978421.
2. Lin, Y., You, Y., Liu, D., & Qu, Y. (2012). Current situation analysis and development strategies for distribution automation of guangdong grid. In *2012 China International Conference on Electricity Distribution (CICED)* (pp. 1, 8). 10–14 September 2012. doi:10. 1109/CICED.2012.650858.
3. Chen, C. -S., Lin, C. -H., Hsieh, S. -C., & Hsieh, W. -L. (2013). Development of smart distribution grid. In *2013 IEEE International Symposium on Next-Generation Electronics (ISNE)* (pp. 4, 6). 25–26 February 2013. doi:10.1109/ISNE.2013.6512272.
4. Aguero, J. R. (2012). Applying self-healing schemes to modern power distribution systems. In *Power and Energy Society General Meeting, 2012 IEEE* (pp. 1, 4). 22–26 July 2012. doi:10. 1109/PESGM.2012.6344960.
5. Kim, J. -C., Cho, S. -M., & Shin, H. -S. (2013). Advanced power distribution system configuration for smart grid. *IEEE Transactions on Smart Grid, 4*(1), 353–358. doi:10.1109/ TSG.2012.2233771.
6. Uluski, R. W. (2010). The role of advanced distribution automation in the smart grid. In *Power and Energy Society General Meeting, 2010 IEEE* (pp. 1, 5). 25–29 July 2010. doi:10.1109/ PES.2010.5590075.
7. Kim, Y. -J., Feather, F., & Thottan, M. (2014). Implementaton aspects of On-line grid data analytics systems. In *Innovative Smart Grid Technologies Conference (ISGT), 2014 IEEE PES* (pp. 1, 5). 19–22 February 2014. doi:10.1109/ISGT.2014.6816469.
8. Haiyang, Z., & ShanDe, L. (2014). Research on microgrid. In *2011 International Conference on Advanced Power System Automation and Protection (APAP)* (vol. 1, pp. 595, 598), 16–20 October 2011. doi:10.1109/APAP.2011.6180470.
9. Ehsan ur Rahman, G. M. A., Ahmed, K. I., Mostafa, R., & Khan, F. (2013) A novel smart metering system for loss reduction and efficient load management in the power distribution sector of Bangladesh. In *2013 International Conference on Advances in Electrical Engineering (ICAEE)* (pp. 207, 212). 19–21 December 2013. doi:10.1109/ICAEE.2013. 6750334.
10. Paudyal, S., Canizares, C. A., & Bhattacharya, K. (2011). Optimal operation of distribution feeders in smart grids. *IEEE Transactions on Industrial Electronics, 58*(10), 4495–4503. doi:10.1109/TIE.2011.2112314.
11. Cappelle, J., Vanalme, J., Vispoel, S., Van Maerhem, T., Verhelst, B., Debruyne, C., & Desmet, J. (2011). Introducing small storage capacity at residential PV installations to prevent overvoltages. In *2011 IEEE International Conference on Smart Grid Communications (SmartGridComm)* (pp. 534, 539). 17–20 October 2011. doi:10.1109/SmartGridComm.2011. 6102380.
12. Zhifeng, Z., Dong, A., Qincheng, Y., & Hongyuan, H. (2014). Communication research based on of distributed intelligent feeder automation system of the distribution network. In *2014 China International Conference on Electricity Distribution (CICED)* (pp. 1, 4). 23–26 September 2014. doi:10.1109/CICED.2014.6991661.
13. Aguero, J. R. (2012). Improving the efficiency of power distribution systems through technical and non-technical losses reduction. In *Transmission and Distribution Conference and Exposition (T&D), 2012 IEEE PES* (pp. 1, 8). 7–10 May 2012. doi:10.1109/TDC.2012. 6281652.
14. Sanchez-Ayala, G., Aguerc, J. R., Elizondo, D., & Lelic, M. (2013). Current trends on applications of PMUs in distribution systems. In *Innovative Smart Grid Technologies (ISGT), 2013 IEEE PES* (pp. 1, 6). 24–27 February 2013. doi:10.1109/ISGT.2013.6497923.

15. McBee, K. D., & Simoes, M. G. (2009). Benefits of utilizing a smart grid monitoring system to improve feeder voltage. In *North American Power Symposium (NAPS)* (pp. 1, 5). 4–6 October 2009. doi:10.1109/NAPS.2009.5483981.
16. Argade, S., Aravinthan, V., & Jewell, W. (2012). Probabilistic modeling of EV charging and its impact on distribution transformer loss of life. In *Electric Vehicle Conference (IEVC), 2012 IEEE International* (pp. 1, 8). 4–8 March 2012. doi:10.1109/IEVC.2012.6183209.
17. Chai, W. K., Wang, N., Katsaros, K. V., Kamel, G., Pavlou, G., Melis, S., Hoefling, M., Vieira, B., Romano, P., Sarri, S., Tesfay, T. T., Yang, B., Heimgaertner, F., Pignati, M., Paolone, M., Menth, M., Poll, E., Mampaey, M., Bontius, H. H. I., & Develder, C. An information-centric communication infrastructure for real-time state estimation of active distribution networks. *IEEE Transactions on Smart Grid*, (99), 1,1. doi:10.1109/TSG.2015.2398840.
18. Vukojevic, A., Smith, M., Frey, P., & Kuloor, S. (2014). The business case for smart fault circuit indicators. In *T&D Conference and Exposition, 2014 IEEE PES* (pp.1, 6). 14–17 April 2014. doi:10.1109/TDC.2014.6863154.
19. Gantz, J. M., Amin, S. M., & Giacomoni, A. M. (2012). Optimal mix and placement of energy storage systems in power distribution networks for reduced outage costs. *Energy Conversion Congress and Exposition (ECCE), 2012 IEEE* (pp. 2447, 2453). 15–20 September 2012. doi:10.1109/ECCE.2012.6342550.
20. Manaz, M. A. M., Liyanage, K. M., & Ekanayake, J. B. (2014). Enabling the participation of domestic consumer based VPPs in DR programs using near real time control over LTE networks. In *2014 9th International Conference on Industrial and Information Systems (ICIIS)* (pp. 1, 6). 15–17 December 2014. doi:10.1109/ICIINFS.2014.7036650.
21. Jauch, E. T. (2011). Possible effects of smart grid functions on LTC transformers. *IEEE Transactions on Industry Applications, 47*(2), 1013,1021, March-April 2011. doi: 10.1109/TIA.2010.2101993.
22. Santhakumar, R., & Kaliyaperumal, K. (2014). Mapping of mobile technology publications: A scientometric approach. *DESIDOC Journal of Library and Information Technology, 34*(4), 298–303. doi:10.14429/djlit.34.5825.

Enhancing Web Search Results Using Aggregated Search

Dhara Bakrola and Snehal Gandhi

Abstract Many emerging organizations are developing their applications on web. Search engine is an information retrieval system which is designed to rummage information over the World Wide Web (WWW). Commercial search engines such as Google, Bing, and Yahoo provide access to a wide range of specialized services that are called as Verticals. All the data in web are scattered in different types of Verticals like image, video, news, etc. Conventional information retrieval system docs not gives a blended results rather it gives a ranked lists of search results. Aggregated search is a current evolution in a Web search. It assembles information from different verticals and hooked on a single result page. This paper gives an overview of aggregated search and its existing limitations. It also contains exhaustive survey of the current evaluation on advance information retrieval. Our propose scheme satisfies user's need by placing the desired verticals on the top of the web result page. It predicts verticals based on the user's past behavior. Thus, our proposed scheme is highly user centric and also it reduces user's browsing time and efforts.

Keywords Aggregated search · Information retrieval

1 Introduction

The World Wide Web (WWW) is an incredible source of information, it can be considered as substantial distributed information system which provides access to shared data items through Information Retrieval system [1]. There are thousands of different search engines available with their own abilities and features. It contain

D. Bakrola (✉) · S. Gandhi
Department of Computer Engineering, Sarvajanik College of Engineering
& Technology, Surat, India
e-mail: bakrola.dhara@gmail.com

S. Gandhi
e-mail: snehal.gandhi@scet.ac.in

© Springer Science+Business Media Singapore 2016   675
S.C. Satapathy et al. (eds.), *Proceedings of International Conference on ICT for Sustainable Development*, Advances in Intelligent Systems and Computing 409, DOI 10.1007/978-981-10-0135-2_65

various documents related to education, news, scientific research, sports, stock exchange, entertainment, map, weather, shopping, etc.

The search engine aims to exhibit available links which are related to the query fired by the user. In current development, search engines have elongated their services that include search (known as vertical search), on specialized assemblies of documents that are termed as verticals, which focuses on precise domains (e.g., travel, shopping, news) or media types (e.g., video, blog, image) [2, 3]. Users believe related information that exists in vertical and can submit their queries directly to vertical search engine. Users are unsuspected or not willing to use a suitable vertical and therefore they submit queries directly to the *general* web search.

Aggregated search endeavors to attain variety by presenting search result from diverse source of information called as verticals (e.g., video, image, blog, etc.) and present them with standard web result on single result page [4]. This comes in division with the ordinary search standard, where users were made available with a list of information sources and they have to scrutinize on term, to discover related information.

This paper is further structured as follows: Sect. 2 represents the motivation toward aggregated search. Subsequent Sect. 3 describes theoretical background and survey and Sect. 4 illustrates various issues of aggregated search. We have put forward our proposed scheme in Sect. 5. Finally, Sect. 6 discusses experimental analysis and Sect. 7 illustrated the conclusion of the study.

2 Motivation

Most of the information retrieval systems offers information according to the rank retrieval (rank list) model. Generally, query response is arranged in a ranked on the basis of some scoring function. Scoring function combines different characteristics produced by the documents and query. But, there are some constraints of conventional information retrieval system which are as follows:

- *Rank retrieval* [1]: Results are represented according to their rank.
- *Scattered data* [2]: For particular query, single document is not enough, but related results are available on different document type. In such cases, user has to fulfill their need by finding information in different vertical.
- *Short of focus* [3]: For each user issued query, information retrieval system has to return related documents. For web search results, instead of serving whole document as response of query just provide a part of document.
- *Vague query* [1, 2, 5]: The reference example is *Saturn* which can be referred as the sixth planet from the sun, it is an Operating System, and it is also a car company. Ultimately, it should return single answer for each query interpretation and it can be several ranked lists or related sets of results.

These constraints are overcome by a novel paradigm called as aggregated search. In aggregated retrieval [5] there is no compulsion that final result should be the rank result, it can be any arrangement of useful content which is fruitful to find necessary information.

3 Theoretical Background and Survey

The goal of aggregated search is to provide integrated access to all these different sources from a single page. From a system perspective, this task is divided into two parts: First, Predicting verticals to present results (called as vertical selection) subsequent, predicting where to present them with web results (called as vertical presentation) [4]. Generally, selected vertical is blended with few of its top results and presented somewhere above, below, within the first page of the web results.

3.1 Typical Framework for Aggregated Search

The thought of aggregated search was unequivocally settled as universal search in 2007 by Google. Kopliku et al. [1] have proposed a framework for aggregated search which provide the study of various approaches which are related to aggregate search. Three main components of framework are: *Query Dispatching* (QD) It is an initial step that proceeds toward query matching and that will decide the solution for a given query, *Nugget Retrieval* (NR) It is an intermediate step which correspond with the meaning of a source which gets input as a query and matches with the relevant information nuggets (nuggets is a piece of valuable information), and *Result Aggregation* (RA) It starts when it will have possible relevant set of information nuggets. It involves different ways of gathering content by applying some actions (aggregation actions) on search result before presenting to the user and these actions are shorting, grouping, merging, splitting, and extracting. All these action can be achieved alone or in any combination. It means that each requested query processed with all the term, query will be dispatched in several sources to find relevant information for each source. All results are assembled in final result and answers can be organized irrespective of query sense. This makes a clear distinction of result aggregation process from prevailing approaches (Fig. 1).

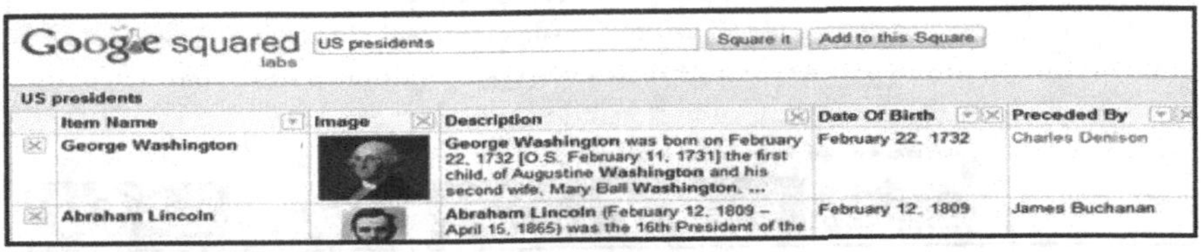

Fig. 1 Example of relational aggregated search

Table 1 Vertical description

Vertical	Descriptions	Vertical	Descriptions
Images	Retrieves online images	Music	Retrieves musician profiles
Videos	Retrieves online videos	News	Retrieves news articles
Local	Business listing	Job	Listing of job
Shopping	Reviews and product listing	Games	Retrieves online games
Movies	Retrieves movie shows times	Map	Retrieves maps and direction

The different search engine provides different specialized services called as verticals and its brief description is shown in Table 1.

3.2 Exploration of Various Aggregated Search Approaches

This section describes various types of aggregated search approaches. First of all, there are some approaches in natural language generation that focuses on result aggregation. Then, we have question answering approach in which there are rousing case studies with reverence to the query interpretation and result aggregation. Besides these, there are two prominent approaches such as *Cross-Vertical Aggregated search* and *relational aggregated search* which is described as follows:

- *Cross-Vertical Aggregated Search*: Cross-vertical aggregated search [6–8] is a task of diversifying search results with different vertical standards on a single result page (Fig. 2). The advantage of cross-vertical aggregated search is that the relevant verticals are represented in blended manner within a single result page. It will search relevant result in each vertical for each user issued query. This methodology can be considered as "divide and conquer approach."
- *Relational Aggregated Search*: Kopliku et al. [9, 10] have developed a framework which consider relations between results called as relational aggregated search (Fig. 1). It focuses on relation for example, consider a query *Us President* than relational aggregated search that provide relational result (date of birth, date of death, achievements, etc.) related to that query (Fig. 1). E.g., Google Squared, Wolfram Alpha.

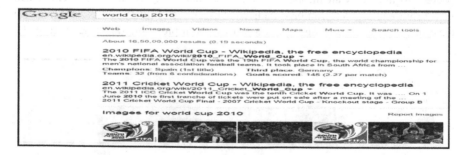

Fig. 2 Example of cross-vertical aggregated search

3.3 Literature Survey

In this exhaustive literature survey on aggregated search for different verticals, we have found that aggregated search is evaluated on the basis of vertical position [2], understanding user's sequence of action and simple action [3], predicting user's preferences on web vertical [7], effect of thumbnail and spillover effect [9], vertical position on different page [10], position of result [8] such as image, video, news, vertical presentation [11] of image, video, news, blog, etc., user's decision process on web [12], for improving the ranking results of web search [6] by considering dwell time and clicks.

Classification and ranking algorithm uses the features that can be turned from evidence and these features are divided into pre-retrieval features that are produced before issuing the query and post-retrieval features are produced after issuing the query [13]. Various pre-retrieval and post-retrieval features are shown in Table 2.

4 Issues of Aggregated Search

Aggregated search is an effective approach of presenting the search results from diverse sources into a single result page. But, there are some critical issues associated with it which are described as follows:

Table 2 Pre-retrieval and post-retrieval feature

Feature type	Features	Vertical
Pre-retrieval features [1, 8, 15]	Named entity	Named entity attributes shows the existence of named objects of several type in the query
	Click through investigation	These characteristics are created from the documents that users have been clicked for request and that click can be considered as implicit feedback
	Vertical intent	Various phrase point toward a query intent such as video, image, etc. Most of the time they provide query intent as well as source intent
	Category representation	With the help of classification of query into pre-defined classes such as technology, music, etc., these features can be generated
Post-retrieval features [8, 15]	Identical match score	This feature resembles to equivalent score on the results calculated reliably across various sources
	Source relevance score	This feature is measure of relevance of the different sources for user issued query
	Quantity of result	This feature is a count of result retrieved from different sources

4.1 Vertical Selection and Representation

Task of selecting the relevant vertical for each user issued query is called as vertical selection or source selection. Majority of the search engines are source selective in order to evade a long query response time. Vertical selection is one of the familiar issues in aggregated search with several verticals. Its focus is to select the vertical that is expected to answer the issued query. Aggregated search deals with extremely heterogeneous and it requires large access time than conventional system. Another side in vertical representation sources has internal representation in cross-vertical aggregated search. Representation of vertical should be in text description or in terms of some feature? How to assemble result that are coming from different verticals and how to represent them?

4.2 Result Representation

Result aggregation concerns with the ranking of results whereas, result presentation deals with presentation interface. Two types of result page designs are described by Arguello et al. [2] and Lalmas et al. [4] in aggregated search. One, in which results from diverse sources are blended onto a solitary interface (Fig. 3a) called as *blended design* and in addition, in which results from the different sources are accessible, separately in panel (Fig. 3b) called as *non-blended design*. In aggregated search, blended results of a same vertical are presented in a slot. In blended design, the core ranking criteria inside the verticals and athwart verticals are considered. Results from the similar verticals are positioned together and each result ranked with reverence to their expected relevance to that query nevertheless, whole slot is ranked with respect to one another. Lalmas et al. [4] defined non-blended design and results from each vertical are represented separately in panel. Panel is also

(a)   **(b)**

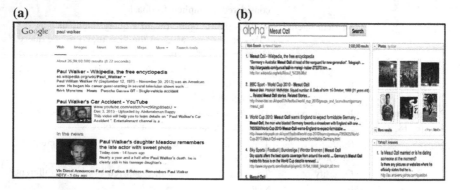

Fig. 3 **a** Blended result design and **b** non-blended result design [1]

referred as tile in search engine terminology. Examples of non-blended design are alpha yahoo, Kosmix, and Naver.

It is not easy to decide which source would be used and how the retrieved information (result) should be collected and presented. The task is distributed; the problem is far away from being solved. We enlist some of the major issues which have the consideration of the current research.

- *Vertical selection and representation*: which vertical ought to be utilized? In terms of features how vertical should be represented?
- *Aggregation of result*: In what way to assemble search results from diverse sources?
- *Result presentation*: which are the acceptable interface used for Cross-Vertical Aggregated Search? And how to arrange vertical in interface? A main problem is to discover the best position to place item retrieved from pertinent verticals on the final result page to exploiting click through frequency (e.g. blended design or non-blended design)

In order to resolve result presentation, we have to design a system which will identify user's interest on specific vertical for particular query. Proposed system will consider users past behavior with web and present that vertical on the top of the result page. It will arrange vertical on the basis of user's requirement, and vertical position is not predefined and not fixed.

5 Proposed Scheme

After extensive literature survey, we have found out various limitations of aggregated search. Among all the main constraint of aggregated search, result representation and we have focused on this issues. Previously, published aggregated search techniques are not explicitly designed to envisage vertical intent which will reduce cost of user inspection.

5.1 Proposed Idea

In result representation for each issued query, final arrangement of the blended result is done by machine learning techniques, probabilistic model (such as vertical being relevant with query, results in a vertical being pertinent, etc.), scoring function and features were estimated. This representation of vertical result is not user centric and increases the browsing time and efforts of user. In order to overcome this issue, we proposed our novel scheme in which the desired vertical of user's is placed on the top of the web result page. This is achieved by predicting verticals based on the user's past behavior. To the best of our knowledge, none of the research paper has focused on the user's past behavior for predicting verticals. Hence, our proposed scheme is highly user centric and also reduces browsing time and efforts. User's relevance measure is essential and it will assist to improve search engine performance. Search relevance can be measured by human evaluation and judgments [14, 16]. Human judgment or feedback (or ratings) can be obtained in two ways, one is explicit and another is implicit feedback.

In this explicit, ratings method system keep asking user to rate the document they have visited. User may stop providing explicit feedback, when he/she will not found beneficial [14, 16]. Explicit ratings of humans are expensive to obtain.

Implicit feedback is the normal activities which are generally performed by the user while browsing the Web such as mouse clicks, mouse movements, book-marking, dwell time, query reformulation, eye-tracking, keyboard activities, etc. Implicit feedback reduces the cost of user inspection [14]. We will use implicit feedback to identify which vertical is useful for what type of query. The main goal is to identify the best position to place item retrieved from related sources (verticals) on the result page to increase click through frequency.

5.2 Proposed Design and Methodology

There are various data mining algorithms available in literature. These algorithms are characterized as classification and clustering algorithm, we have used frequency term-based clustering algorithm and for classification Support vector machine algorithm. Our proposed scheme mainly comprises of several steps discussed as follows:

Step 1 Create a custom search engine. (we have created search engine using Bing search API).

Step 2 Query will be issued by user.

Step 3 Now, user's past behavior is measured using number of clicks as an implicit method of taking feedback.

Step 4 In this, system will fetch query and match with available clusters (on the basis of text similarity). If matched, that query is inserted into the matched cluster or new cluster is formed which contain this query using online clustering of text stream [17] clustering algorithm.

Step 5 Now, Support Vector Machine [18] classifier is used to classify the verticals on the basis of numbers of clicks. Whichever vertical (web/image) has higher clicks, that vertical will be predicted.

Step 6 Finally, the predicted vertical will be displayed on the top of the result page (Figs. 5b and 8).

6 Experimental Analysis

Searching is an art, different users have different ways of formulating queries to find the information over the search engine. Various users have diverse requirement but it is not possible to fulfil all of it. Thus, a prime solution is to perform search personalization. The result retrieved on target senses have higher chances to be clicked. In our proposed system we have observed different user's behavior and its experimental results and analysis have been further described in Figs. 4, 5 and 8. We have conducted lab experiment considering 20 persons who are graduate (in order to avoid fake clicks) to find how user deals with image and web results. For training the system we have to consider AOL Query log [19] in which, a total of 2265 queries were fired and each user had fired 112 common queries. Consider a *Query*: *Nepal Earthquake Reason*. For this query, user is interested to finding out the reason of the Nepal earthquake and only the web results are able to answer this query. The traditional system shows image vertical on the top of the result page followed by the web results. In our proposed system, we have considered click-through feature that will represent web result followed by the image result (Fig. 6).

Commercial search engine like Google, Bing, and Yahoo does not perform any search personalization. Our proposed system first analyzes the query, and if same or related query exist in database then it will analyze its number of clicks. Finally, it will predict appropriate vertical. For the above-mentioned query, our proposed system has decided to put web result on the top of the result page as shown in Fig. 5b. Now, we consider a scenario in which image result has higher impact on web results in such case image vertical presented on the top of the result page (Fig. 8). Moreover, if impact of image result and web result is equal then image vertical is presented on the top of the result page (Fig. 7).

Suppose for a Query *President of India* users are mostly interested in image results rather than web results. From users past behavior, we have found that users had clicked more on image results than on web results. So, our proposed system

(a)   **(b)**

Fig. 4 **a** Google results, **b** bing results for query *Nepal Earthquake reason*

(a)   (b)

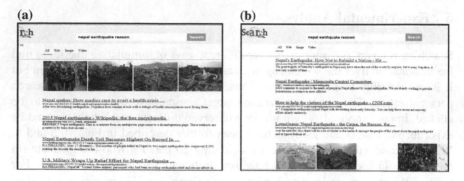

Fig. 5 a Proposed system result page, **b** proposed system has predicted web vertical for query *Nepal Earthquake reason*

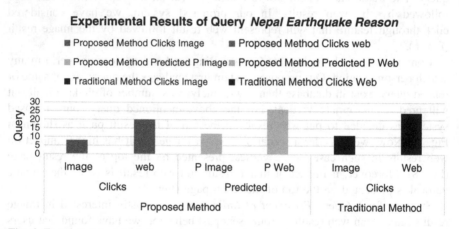

Fig. 6 Experimental analysis for query *Nepal Earthquake reason*

Fig. 7 Result page design

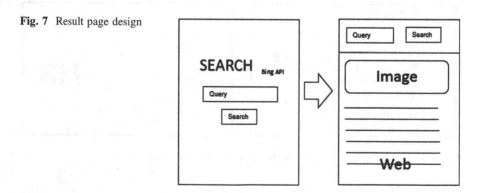

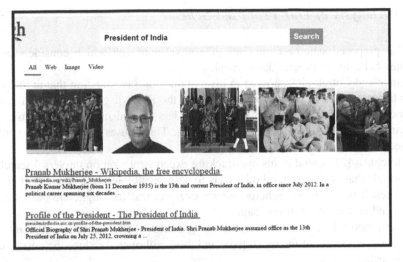

Fig. 8 Proposed system has predicted image vertical for query *President of India*

predicted image vertical for all the users who have search similar type of queries. From our experimental results, we have found that mostly all the users got their answer in web results as well as image results but impact of image results are more. Therefore, our proposed system had shown image vertical on the top of the result page (Fig. 8). In Fig. 9 traditional system depicts that image has higher impact than web, but does not perform vertical prediction and results are not being displayed on top of the web page.

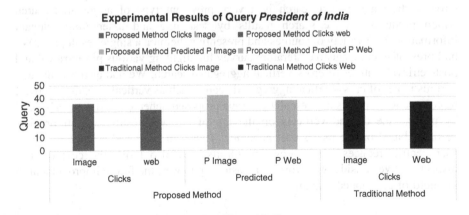

Fig. 9 Experimental analysis for query *President of India*

6.1   Analysis of Our Proposed Scheme

- Our proposed scheme comprises of a novel approach which considers user's past behavior to predict the vertical.
- Guan and Cutrell [20] showed in his eye tracking investigation that at the point when results were put moderately low in the result page, individuals requires more energy in finding answer and were less fruitful in their query task, and same is observed with aggregated search. This rouses us to predict vertical according to their user's need.
- Hotchkiss [21] found in his eye-tracking experimentation on universal search as Google that common trend of user is to scan result page from upper left corner of result page. In our scheme which ever vertical has higher impact will be placed on top of the result page.
- Our proposed scheme reduces browsing efforts of user as required result will appear on the top of the result page and thus, will overall reduce the cost of user inspection.
- Our proposed approach is a novel step toward user oriented search personalization.
- Our proposed scheme seems to be user centric as the search is designed to find the appropriate results in the top links of a web search result page.

7   Conclusion

Aggregated search is a novel paradigm of information retrieval which presents the search results from diverse sources and presents them in a single interface. Cross-vertical aggregated search is a very prevalent type of aggregated search which produces diverse search results by searching and assembling relevant information from variety of sources and presenting them on a single result page. We had presented an exhaustive literature survey highlighting various pre-retrieval and post-retrieval features of cross-vertical aggregated search. We had also accentuated various issues of cross-vertical aggregated search such as vertical selection, vertical representation, and result presentation. Our proposed scheme satisfies user's need by placing the desired verticals on the top of the web result page. It predicts verticals based on the user's past behavior. Thus, our proposed scheme is highly user centric, reduces user's browsing efforts, and also limits the cost of user inspection. We consider this work as a basic step toward the future improvement in the field of aggregated search.

References

1. Kopliku, A., Pinel-Sauvagnat, K., & Mohand, B. (2014). Aggregated search: A new information retrieval paradigm. In *ACM Computing Surveys (CSUR)* (vol. 46, no. 3, p. 41). New York: ACM.
2. Arguello, J., Robert, C., & Wan-Ching, W. (2013). Factors affecting aggregated search coherence and search behavior. In: *22nd ACM International Conference on Information and Knowledge Management* (pp. 1989–1998). New York: ACM.
3. Arguello, J., & Robert, C.: The effect of aggregated search coherence on search behavior. In: *21st ACM International Conference on Information and Knowledge Management* (pp. 1293–1302). New York: ACM (2012).
4. Melucci, M., & Ricardo, B. (2011). *Advanced topics in information retrieval* (vol. 33). Springer Science and Business Media.
5. Jiang, D., Jian, P., & Hang, L. (2013). Mining search and browse logs for web search: A survey. In *ACM Transactions on Intelligent Systems and Technology* (pp. 4–57). New York: ACM.
6. Sushmita, S., Hideo, J., Mounia, L., & Robert, V. (2010). Factors affecting click-through behaviour in aggregated search interfaces. In: *19th ACM International Conference on Information and Knowledge Management* (pp. 519–528). New York: ACM.
7. Arguello, J., & Robert, C. (2012). The effect of aggregated search coherence on search behavior. In *21st ACM International Conference on Information and Knowledge Management* (pp. 1293–1302). New York: ACM.
8. Arguello, J., Diaz, F., Callan, J., & Crespo, J. F. (2009). Sources of evidence for vertical selection. In *32nd international ACM SIGIR Conference on Research and Development in Information Retrieval* (pp. 315–322). New York: ACM.
9. Kopliku, A., Karen, P., & Mohand, B. (2011). Attribute retrieval from relational web tables. In *String Processing and Information Retrieval* (pp. 117–128). Berlin: Springer.
10. Kopliku, A., Karen, P., & Mohand, B.: Retrieving attributes using web tables. In *11th Annual International ACM/IEEE Joint Conference on Digital Libraries* (pp. 397–398). New York: ACM.
11. Arguello, J., Fernando, D., Jamie, C., & Ben, C. (2011). A methodology for evaluating aggregated search results. In *Advances in Information Retrieval* (pp. 141–152). Berlin: Springer.
12. Arguello, J., Fernando, D., & Jean-François, P.: Vertical selection in the presence of unlabeled verticals. In *33rd International ACM SIGIR Conference on Research and Development in Information Retrieval* (pp. 691–698). New York: ACM.
13. Arguello, J., Fernando, D., & Jamie, C. (2011). Learning to aggregate vertical results into web search results. In *20th ACM International Conference on Information and Knowledge Management* (pp. 201–210). New York: ACM.
14. Claypool, M., Phong, L., Makoto, W., & David, B.: Implicit interest indicators. In *6th International Conference on Intelligent User Interfaces* (pp. 33–40). New York: ACM.
15. Dou, Z., Ruihua, S., Xiaojie, Y., & Ji-Rong, W. (2008). Are click-through data adequate for learning web search rankings?. In *17th ACM Conference on Information and Knowledge Management* (pp. 73–82). New York: ACM (2008).
16. Joachims, T., Laura, G., Bing, P., Helene, H., & Geri, G. (2005). Accurately interpreting clickthrough data as implicit feedback. In *28th Annual International ACM SIGIR Conference on Research and Development in Information Retrieval* (pp. 154–161). New York: ACM.
17. Beil, F., Martin, E., & Xiaowei, X. (2002). Frequent term-based text clustering. In *8th ACM SIGKDD International Conference on Knowledge Discovery and Data Mining* (pp. 436–442). New York: ACM.

18. Cortes, C., & Vladimir, V. (1995). Support-vector networks. In *Machine Learning* (vol. 20, no. 3, pp. 273–297). Kluwer Academic.
19. Aol Query Log. http://www.cim.mcgill.ca/ ~ dudek/206/Logs/AOL-user-ct-collection/.
20. Cutrell, E., & Zhiwei, G. (2007). What are you looking for?: An eye-tracking study of information usage in web search. In: *SIGCHI Conference on Human Factors in Computing Systems* (pp. 407–416). ACM.
21. Hotchkiss, G., Tracy S., Rick T., Cory B., & Krista, B. (2010). Search engine results: 2010. *Enquiro Research*.

Managing Heterogeneity by Synthesizing Composite Data

Manjeet Kantak and Sneha Tiwari

Abstract The long-standing challenge in database management, information retrieval systems are Entity resolution (ER), the problem of extracting, matching and resolving entity mentions in structured and unstructured data. Getting the data in unambiguous form when fetched from integrated heterogeneous databases had become an important task when heterogeneous databases come into picture. In order to retrieve information from these database and to avoid the retrieval of multiple ambiguous information with same citation and algorithms have been proposed. The input to the algorithm is a query output, whereas the algorithm will return only feasible data required in the query.

Keywords Entity resolution · Confidence score · Advance search · Veracity

1 Introduction

With the ever increasing growth of information usage, storing the data into a system and retrieving the data is a huge task. A database is defined as a collection of related data [1] and in order to manage this data a database management system is designed. The drawback of the database system is that it retrieves multiple records of same match if present. Data mining [2] is defined as a process of finding a pattern if exist in the data and thus retrieve the data based on the required pattern. To avoid the redundant retrieval of data from the database data mining algorithms are applied on the database to avoid the redundant retrieval of data.

M. Kantak (✉) · S. Tiwari
Computer Engineering Department, Goa College of Engineering, Farmagudi, India
e-mail: manjeet959@gmail.com

© Springer Science+Business Media Singapore 2016
S.C. Satapathy et al. (eds.), *Proceedings of International Conference on ICT for Sustainable Development*, Advances in Intelligent Systems and Computing 409, DOI 10.1007/978-981-10-0135-2_66

An algorithm has been proposed which check for entity resolution and gives the unambiguous data. It calculates the confidence score and on account of that it tries to find the facts, in which all match with the facts made on confidence score and the search data.

The paper is organized as follows; Sect. 2 discusses the 'Related Work in Entity Resolution,' whereas Sect. 3 presents Proposed Algorithm, followed by Conclusion in Sect. 4.

2 Literature Review

The paper 'Entity Resolution: Theory, Practice and Open Challenges' [3] authored by 'LiseGetoor and AshwinMachanavajjhala' have focused on the various perspective for the Entity Resolution for the various fields. These fields include the database, natural language processing, and machine learning. In this paper, the authors have considered the theoretical aspects and the practical aspects and have also described the existing solution, the current challenges, and the open research problems associated with the Entity Resolution. Under the ER-theory section, the authors have categorized ER based on the input as single-entity, relational-entity, and multiple-entity. The authors have surveyed some algorithms which measure the similarity and the distance among the entities in order to eliminate the redundant retrieved data. The authors of the paper suggested the use of multi-relational clustering algorithm because of the poor performance of the single-relational clustering algorithm.

They propose to make use of Markov logic networks and probabilistic soft logic networks for eliminating the redundant entities. In practice for the ER theory, the complexity of comparison calculated was $O(n^2)$ which was very high. To reduce the aforementioned complexity, the authors propose the use of techniques like the efficient indexing or blocking or message passing. With the use of these techniques the authors believes in reducing the complexity to a nonlinear time. The challenges faced by the authors were the use of ER in a dynamic environment with a varying data, a proper and accurate query-driven ER, and efficient user learning based methods for ER. The paper 'Query-Driven Approach to Entity Resolution' [4] authored by 'Hotham et al.' have proposed a different query-driven technique that perform the data cleaning at the real-time in context of a query. In the proposed Query-Driven approach, the number of steps involved in the data-cleaning depends on the steps required to answer only to the selected query, thus reducing the steps needed to perform the data-cleaning and hence reducing the complexity in terms of efficiency compared to the traditional approaches. The reason for this approach is explained by the authors with an example. In their example, the authors have considered a case where in they want to retrieve the publications of a particular author in Google scholar's articles. The result obtained by the authors includes redundant publications. The authors encountered that this redundant information was obtained due to the citation criteria observed by the Google Crawler search engine. To avoid such a redundant retrieval of information, the authors state that the proposed Query-Driven Approach considers the exact semantics of the query to perform data-leaning so as to eliminate redundant data retrieval. The authors have used Relation-Clustering and Approach-Specific notations for the mathematical representation of problem definition and the proposed solutions in the QDA theory.

Conceptually, the proposed Query-Driven Approach first create a graph and labels the graph; next it chooses an edge to resolve and the edge based on the edge-picking policy which is followed by the edge removal technique. This technique performs optimization of the Query-Driven Approach. The vestigality testing avoids the call on an edge by checking if it is vestigial. The functioning of the approach stops if all the edges are resolved but if there still exist an edge that need to be resolved and then a call is made to the edge-picking policy. After all the edges are resolved, the final answer is computed using the required answer semantics. The proposed Query-Driven approach is analyzed against the answer correctness which checks the representation, the distinction, and the exact equivalence of the retrieved clusters.

The paper 'Pay-As-You-Go Entity Resolution' [5] authored by 'Steven ct al.' have proposed the use of Hints, to maximize the progress of an ER within the limited amount of work, and to provide the information that are related to the real-time world. The authors have proposed the technique that creates a hint and how it can efficiently use the hints for ER. The authors have proposed three types of hints namely (i) A Sorted list of record pairs, (ii) An ordered list of Records (iii) Hierarchy of likely record partitions, and (iv) An ordered list of records. For each hint-type, the authors have proposed different techniques to efficiently generate hints and investigate how ER algorithms have utilized these hints to maximize the quality of ER while minimizing the number of record comparison.

The Pay-As-You-Go-Model proposed by the author uses the likelihood matching criteria to pair the records and then it uses the ER algorithms for record comparisons. The use of Sorted list of Record Pairs, the hints are made of list of recorded pairs which are ranked on the basis of likelihood condition for the match pairs. The distance functions and the match functions are used for the ER algorithm. The author has also assumed the use of estimator function to compute that is much less expensive to compute compared to the other two factors. The author states that the use of estimator function approximates the distance function of the ER algorithm. Also according to the author, the smaller the values of the estimator function, the more the match function value increases.

The other alternative proposed by the author is the use of hints on demand rather than the use of fixed-pair hints. This results the ER algorithm to avoid the $O(n^2)$ complexity of generating the hints. Two methods are used to generate the concerned hints by the author. In the first method, 'Using Application Estimates' the authors have considered an application-specific estimate function to construct the hints. The estimations of the hints for the application-specific lead the ER algorithm to use estimator function for all record pairs where in each record-pair and its estimates are inserted into heap. Based on the estimates, the records are retrieved by reducing the complexity of search for ER algorithm. In the other method,

'Application Estimate not Available' the authors construct a generic but rough estimates based on sampling. The ER algorithm uses the distance function thus the computation for generating the hints using this method is expensive.

The other hint is the 'Hierarchy of Record Partitions' the author's partition hierarchy is one of the format for hints. The partition hierarchy method performs matching of records to provide information. These records are matched in the form of partitions with different levels of granularity where each partition represents a possible-word of an ER result. The authors have proposed the use of sorted records as a generation method for the hints. According to the author, the partition hierarchy is generated when the estimated distance between records can map into distances along a single dimension based on a certain attribute key. The third type of the hints is the 'Ordered List of records.' In this method, the matching constraint is maximized when the list is resolved sequentially. The authors have proposed the use of partition hierarchies for generating the record list. The ER algorithms are able to minimize the number of fully identified entities at any point if the record list is ordered from left to right.

The experimental results evaluate the pay-as-you-go ER on the real datasets and have showed how to create and use hints so as to improve the ER quality, given a limit on how much work can be done. The Real dataset is a shopping comparison set provided by Yahoo. The apace and time complexity of the use of hints in the various ER algorithm when used on the dataset was also computed. Also the figure plots have displayed the scalability results for generating hints. The author concludes that there still exist some problems that need to be solved which include more formal analysis of different types of hints, and a guidance of constructing and updating the hints that are best hint for any given algorithm.

3 Proposed Work

This section presents the proposed algorithm for type of issues faced while retrieving the data from a database or a website.

Illustration 1:

Query 1: To find who wrote the book Rapid Contextual Design (ISBN: 0123540518).

It is found that many sets of authors from different online bookstores, and several of them are in Table 1. It shows that A1 Books provides the most accurate information. In comparison, the information from Powell's books is incomplete, and that from Lakeside books is incorrect.

The reason A1 Books provides the most accurate information is due to the Algorithm 3.1 which is advance search algorithm, which works on confidence score that has been calculated in Algorithm 3.2. In the advance search, it tries to find the best match for the input keywords which is non-conflicted, trustworthy data.

Table 1 Websites and authors

Websites	Authors
A1 books	Karen Haltzblatt, Jessamyn Burns Wendell, Shelly Wood
Powell's books	Holtzblatt, Karen
Cornwall books	Holtzblatt-Karen, Wendell-Jessamyn Burns, Wood
Mellon's books	Wendell, Jessamyn
Lakeside books	Wendell, Jessamyn Holtzblatt, Karenwood, Shelley
Blackwell online	Wendell, Jessamyn, Holtzblatt, Karen, Wood, Shelley
Barnes and Noble	Karen Holtzblatt, Jessamyn Wendell, Shelley Wood

Figure 1 shows how exactly the data flows in the Algorithm 3.1. Initially, the input is given in the form of Keywords to Algorithm 3.1, which searches for the data in the dataset. If the selected option is 'Normal Search,' the output of the search is ambiguous, conflicted, and untrustworthy data. If the selected option is 'Advance Search,' then it goes through the 'Veracity Algorithm' (Algorithm 3.1) whose output is unambiguous. Veracity algorithm is advance, truth-finding algorithm where it tries to find out the trustworthy data by calculating the confidence

Fig. 1 Flow of data

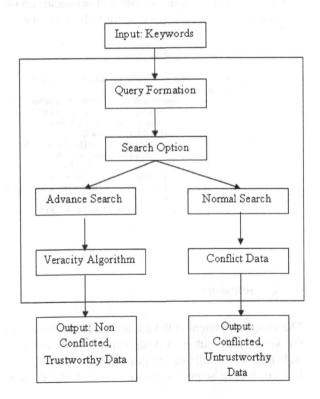

score depending on the accuracy and trustworthiness of a website. In Algorithm 3.1, it compare the url's from search table and url's from fact table so as to check which are true and correct websites or links.

Algorithm 3.1(Veracity Algorithm):
  1. Start
  2. Take input into the dataset will be dynamically taken from the web as we search the key words and accordingly the url fact tables will be formed.
  3. SearchKey is a variable used to differentiate between the Normal Search and Advance search.
  4. If (SearchKey == Normal Search) Then List of sites by Normal Search keywords.
  5. Else if(SearchKey == Advance Search)
    5.1 Search for the data in dataset.
    5.2 Call Algorithm 3.2 (Confidence Score), Calculate the confidence score for the searched websites.
    5.3 List sites in descending order by confidence score.
    5.4 Select url from url search table and url fact table, url search table will be depending on the number of Records retrieved while searching the keyword.
    5.5 If (url_search_table == url_fact_table)
      5.5.1 Update confidence score of url in fact table
      5.5.2 while(confidence score == 1) Display url in descending order giving the highest score to best website.
  6. Stop

The confidence score is calculated from the set of websites, Set of facts and links, it also take in consideration the page rank of a website in Algorithm 3.2. Every time when the advance search option is selected, the url's from the search and the facts table will be mapped and depending on the confidence score they will be ordered, giving the highest score to best website.

Algorithm 3.2 (Confidence Score):

Input: The set of websites W, Set of facts F, and links
Output: Confidence score
  1.   Initialize WR[w] to 1.0 for each website w in W.
  2.   For each pair of websites w1 and w2 belongs W do steps 3 to 8 until Accuracy is computed for all facts.
  3.   If WR[w1] > WR[w2]
  4.   WR[w1] = WR[w1] + WR[w2] * 10
  5.   If WR[w1] not equals to WR[w2] and WR[w1] < WR[w2]
  6.   WR[w1] = WR[w1] + WR[w2] / 10
  7.   If fact is positive, Increment the positive counter.
  8.   If fact is negative, Increment the negative counter.
  9.   For i from 1 to n
  10.   Update website rank i.e. UWR[i]=WR[i]

4 Conclusion

The proposed system is the advance search which searches the best website using the veracity algorithm. It deals with resolution of conflicting facts from multiple websites. Upon utilizing the interdependency between website trustworthiness and fact confidence score, the method finds feasible output. The confidence score is calculated on the basis of page rank of a website. Future work includes finding the new similarity measure in order to retrieve the correct and accurate trustworthy data in accordance with the confidence score.

References

1. Shibo, H., Gang, L., Zhewen, H., & Zheng Ping, W. (2010). Design and implementation of log management module in three-dimensional spatial database management system. In *IEEE Transaction, 2010, 18 International Conference on Geoinformatics*.
2. Ohmid, P., Amir, P., & Amin, P. (2010). Evaluating the data-mining techniques and their roles in increasing the search speed in data in web. In *3rd IEEE International Conference on Computer Science and Information Technology, IEEE Transaction, 2010*.
3. Lise, G., & Ashwin, M. (2012). Entity resolution: theory, practice and open challenges. In *38th International Conference on Very Large Databases, Proceeding of the VLDB Endowment* (vol. 5, no. 02).
4. Hotham, A., Kalashnikov, D. V., & Sharad, M. (2014). Query-driven approach to entity resolution. In 39th *International Conference on Very Large Databases, Proceeding of the VLDB Endowment* (vol 6, no. 14).
5. Steven, E. W., David, M., & Hector, G.-M. (2013). Pay-as-you-go-entity resolution. *IEEE Transaction on Knowledge and Data Engineering, 25*(05).

A Novel Approach to Filter Topic Related Important Terms Within Document

Payal Joshi and S.V. Patel

Abstract Primary goal of information retrieval system is to retrieve documents relevant to the user query. An advanced IR system should go beyond this. It should be able to retrieve document even if user does not know exact query terms to browse for. For this purpose, identifying important terms of document is very important. In bag of words mechanism, TF/IDF is a measure to give weightage of a term within document and at corpus level. Term frequency gives frequency of a term in a document, and inverse document frequency gives weightage of a term in corpus. Also, there exist query level weightage algorithms. However, these methods are not useful to obtain document's important terms related to topic or subject of a document when document contains thousands of terms or keywords. Further, all terms do not necessarily represent topic(s) of that document. To address this issue, we have developed a novel algorithm to return most significant subject-related topics of eBook. It makes use of LDA (Latent Dirichlet Allocation) and our earlier work known as AuTopicGen (Automatic Topic Generator) algorithms. These extracted terms will be very useful for automatic document classification as well as ranking.

Keywords Information retrieval · Term filtering · Natural language processing

1 Introduction

Main goal of information retrieval system is to retrieve documents relevant to the user query. IR system can go beyond this. It should be able to retrieve document even if user does not know exact query terms to browse for. Digital library is one of

P. Joshi (✉)
Veer Narmad South Gujarat University, Surat, Gujarat, India
e-mail: payaljoshi.mscit@gmail.com

S.V. Patel
Department of Computer Science, Veer Narmad South Gujarat University,
Surat, Gujarat, India
e-mail: patelsv@gmail.com

© Springer Science+Business Media Singapore 2016
S.C. Satapathy et al. (eds.), *Proceedings of International Conference on ICT for Sustainable Development*, Advances in Intelligent Systems and Computing 409, DOI 10.1007/978-981-10-0135-2_67

the applications of information retrieval. Digital library contains eBooks. To retrieve eBook(s) that most relevantly matches user requirement is an open research issue. In information retrieval, finding important terms is very important to meet this requirement. A document contains thousands of terms or keywords. But all terms do not represent topic(s) of that document. TF/IDF is measured to give weightage of a term within document and at corpus level. Term frequency gives frequency of a term in a document and inverse document frequency gives weightage of a term in corpus. Also query level weightage algorithms are available. These approaches are just number of occurrences based. Hence, they are less useful to find topic level relevant terms within a document.

In this paper, we have extended our work done in publication given in reference [1]. Algorithm developed in this paper combines use of LDA (Latent Dirichlet Allocation) and our previous research work of Automatic Topic Generator (AuTopicGen) and returns most of topic relevant terms within eBook. LDA algorithm is a statistical machine learning algorithm. LDA is a topic model and was first presented as a graphical model for topic discovery by David Blei, Andrew Ng, and Michael Jordan in 2003 [2, 3]. Automatic Topic Generator algorithm automatically collects most relevant topics of eBooks from its contents and indexes using rule-based positional patterns approach [1]. Our algorithm returns subject-related topics of eBook. These terms will be very useful for automatic document classification as well as ranking algorithm.

Rest of the paper is organized as follows: Section 2 describes related work. Section 3 describes our approach to find important topics in eBook. Section 4 shows experiments and results and Sect. 5 concludes the paper.

2 Related Work

Information retrieval involves various phases like document preprocessing, indexing, query expansion, query matching, ranking, etc. The document preprocessing phase is the most important phase to parse the document and collect keywords. Relevance of overall IR system improves if main topics of document are perfectly identified during this phase [1]. For this purpose, mechanism of term weighting is used.

Weighted terms become more useful if they are relevant to topic or subject within the document. If we do so, then at the time of classification, ranking, and retrieval, number of computational steps greatly reduce. Following points list various term weighting approaches.

2.1 Local-Term Weighting

Term frequency (tf) is a weight of a term in a document that depends on the number of occurrences of the term in the document [4]. For document weighting, these

Table 1 Local-term weighting schemes

Scheme	Description
Binary	$l_{ij} = 1$ if the term exists, or 0
Term frequency	$l_{ij} = \text{tf}_{ij}$, the number of occurrences of term i in document j
Log	$l_{ij} = \log(\text{tf}_{ij} + 1)$
Augnorm	$l_{ij} = \dfrac{\left(\frac{\text{tf}_{ij}}{\max_i(\text{tf}_{ij})}\right) + 1}{2}$

weights are generally not best because binary does not differentiate between terms that appear frequently and terms that appear only once and because tf gives too much weight to terms that appear frequently. The logarithm formulas offer a middle ground [5]. Table 1 shows list of local term weighting schemes.

2.2 Global-Term Weighting

2.2.1 Document Frequency (DF) and Inverse Document Frequency (IDF)

DF is number of documents in the collection that contain a term t [4].

The IDF is a statistical weight used for measuring the importance of a term in a text document collection. The DF of a term is defined by the number of documents in which a term appears [6].

2.2.2 TF/IDF

TF/IDF approach combines the definitions of term frequency and inverse document frequency to produce a composite weight for each term in each document tf–idf. The tf–idf weighting scheme assigns to term t a weight in document d given by

$$\text{tf–idf}t, \text{d} = \text{tf}t, \text{d}(6.8) \times \text{idf}t.$$

In other words, tf–idf$t$, d assigns to term t a weight in document d that is

1. highest when t occurs many times within a small number of documents (thus lending high discriminating power to those documents)

2. lowest when the term occurs fewer times in a document, or occurs in many
   documents (thus offering a less pronounced relevance signal)
3. lowest when the term occurs in virtually all documents [4].

2.2.3 Vector Space Model

Vector Space Model (VSM) represents documents as a vector that captures the
relative importance of the terms in a document [4].

2.2.4 Topic Model

Various topic models exist that find topics in document. Among them LDA is a
well-known topic model. But main issue with LDA is that we have to provide
number of topics to find in a document as a hyperparameter [3, 7, 8]. Moreover,
using LDA we may also get many terms which are not relevant as document topics.
We have done comparison of result of our approach and LDA, and have demonstrated that which extra keywords are generated by LDA in Table 3. For this we
have used some documents.

In information retrieval, retrieving eBook(s) or document that most relevantly
matches user requirement is an open research issue. Identifying important terms is
very important to meet this requirement. A document contains thousands of terms
or keywords, but all terms do not represent topic(s) of that document.
Above-mentioned methods are used in one or the other way by various researchers
till date to solve this issue. They are based on occurrences of a term in a document
or corpus level. But they may fail to assign topic level relevance for terms within
the document.

3 Methodology to Find Important Keywords

We have practically implemented an approach using Java to programmatically find
terms which are significantly relevant to document's topic(s) or subject. Our
algorithm combines use of LDA and Automatic Topic Generator and returns most
of topic relevant terms within eBook. LDA algorithm is a statistical machine
learning algorithm. LDA is an example of a topic model and was first presented as a
graphical model for topic discovery by David Blei, Andrew Ng, and Michael
Jordan in 2003 [2, 3]. Automatic Topic Generator algorithm automatically extracts
most relevant topics of eBooks from its contents and indexes using rule-based
positional patterns approach [1].

3.1 Algorithm

```
Program initiation
VAR str_document := text_ebook
VAR     array_keywords_frequency     :=     text_document_
keywords_stopword_filtered_with frequency
VAR R1 := Filter_terms (text_document_keywords_
stopword_filtered_with frequency)
VAR R2 := AuTopicGen_topics (text_ebook)
VAR R3 := LDA_topics (text_ebook)
VAR  Important_terms_set  :=  unique  ((R3  union  (R1
intersect R2)) AND POS=noun)
Function
Filter_terms(text_document_keywords_stopword_filtered_wit
h frequency)
    /* - Filter terms whose frequency is 1 or 2 because
    terms that occurs less number of times will not have
    topic level weightage in a document
    - Assign    part  of   speech(POS)   tag  to   each
    keyword.  Calculate num of resulting terms M. Call
    this set R1. */
          return array_refined_terms
End Function

Function AuTopicGen_topics (text_ebook)
    /* Find topics using AuTopicGen, tokenize them and
    calculate number of topics found N. Filter stopwords
    and terms with 1 or 2 frequency. Call this set R2 */
End Function

Function LDA_topics (text_ebook)
    /*Use LDA to find topics in document. LDA requires
    number of topics to get from document as an input
    parameter.  Again  this  is  an  open  research  issue
    because of size of a document and diversity of topics
    in a  document. In  our  algorithm, based  on  certain
    observations   we   have   applied   certain   rules   as
    experiment to determine this input number. We find
    unique topics from this result. Call this set R3. */

    End Function
    end.
```

4 Experiments and Result

Our system produced results as shown in Table 2.

Observing title and keywords, person acquainted with computer science can apparently relate book title with important terms. Further, Table 3 shows comparison of terms generated from one eBook using LDA topic model and our

Table 2 Books and terms obtained

No.	Book title	Important terms
1	NoSQL databases	data, databases, mongodb, nodes, nosql, read, server, operation, system, storage, distributed, query, relational, replication, consistency, vector, model, object, project, sql, master, updates, availability, concepts, techniques, sstables, transfer, type, dbms
2	Practical artificial intelligence programming in Java	class, search, mark, page, data, array, training, program, neural, simple, atn, database, network, prolog, hidden, nlp, classes, nlbean, systems, board, function, nodes, directory, genetic, uml, breadth, piece, instance, propagation, application, writing, model, crossover, shown, machine, elements, version, decision, database
3	The myths of security	security, people, bad, companies, system, google, vendors, computer, run, code, product, users, technology, internet, secure, microsoft, spam, windows, personal, click, passwords, spend, phone, message, false, detection, application, cloud, computers, write, vulnerability, services, call, positives, idea, updates, model, training, failure, types, hidden
4	A semantic web primer	rdf, xml, ontology, owl, schema, language, knowledge, logic, property, document, type, ontologies, rule, documents, predicate, syntax, statement, resource, book, types, applications, attribute, rdfs, instances, range, form, subclass, tools, agent, content, body, describing, agents, inference, object, process, instance, basic, world, existing, vision, program, function, modeling, enersearch, integration, site, names, rql, ideas, layer
5	Big data, data mining, and machine learning	data, time, mining, models, regression, network, sas, modeling, software, series, techniques, methods, clusters, line, learning, function, customer, clustering, response, networks, neural, machine, systems, observations, decision, level, advantage, distance, quality, hardware, future, vector, language, disk, study, distribution, support, company, development, distributed, incremental, source, application, services, content, squares, assessment, supervised, partition, online, factor

Table 3 Difference between keywords of LDA and our approach

No.	Book title	Important terms
1	A semantic web primer	Using our approach
		rdf, xml, ontology, owl, schema, language, knowledge, logic, property, document, type, ontologies, rule, documents, predicate, syntax, statement, resource, book, types, applications, attribute, rdfs, instances, range, form, subclass, tools, agent, content, body, describing, agents, inference, object, process, instance, basic, world, existing, vision, program, function, modeling, enersearch, integration, site, names, rql, ideas, layer
		Using LDA
		Rules, xml, monotonic, include, types, information, ontology problem, data, sources, expressive, chapter, online, power, limited, content, section, tag, work, meaning, tools, techniques, case, special, intelligence, important, life, makes, people, authors, printers, references, jet, projects, number, search, implied, correct, type, rdf, semantics, model, query, objects, writing, databases, software, domain, property, range, values, applications, made, documents, web, structured, http://www.w, syntax, owl, abstract, simple, individuals, ontologies, learning, engineering, classes, properties, statement, note, list, rql, user, make, knowledge, users, agents, semantic, van, harmelen, description, logic, document, function, represented, order, predicate, program, science, primitives, modeling, top, layer, vision, enersearch, site, elements, element, html, resources, describing, set, inference, facts, statements, billington, david, predefined, taught, subclassof, lecturer, names, answer, give, staff, members, university, courses, academic, class, defined, instances, rule, node, unique, resource, part, basic, book, ideas, object, systems, proof, support, representation, figure, shows, language, full, true, atomic, body, formula, application, process, size, integration, discuss, agent, instance, subclass, form, encoding, terms, world, attribute, concepts, nodes, schema, rdfs, oil, standard, area, existing

algorithm. For LDA we have made use of MALLET java library. Single occurrence of topic of LDA is considered in this algorithm.

From Table 3, it can be observed that our approach returns most of the important terms which are related to subject of eBook where as using LDA we also get keywords like http://www.w, true, etc., which are not relevant as document topics. In both LDA and our approach we have used the same ebooks and obtained these results. The comparison is also shown graphically in Fig. 1.

The usefulness of our approach is that topics generated can perform better for various subtasks of IR and digital library applications like classification and query recommendations.

Fig. 1 Comparison chart of
results generated by LDA and
our approach

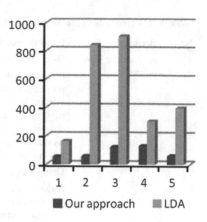

■ Our approach   ■ LDA

5   Conclusion and Future Work

The paper presented a novel approach to find set of terms related to topic or subject
of the document by extending our earlier work at reference [1]. Algorithm developed in this paper combines use of LDA and our earlier work Automatic Topic
Generator and returns most of topic relevant terms within eBook. These terms will
be very useful for automatic document classification as well as ranking algorithm.
The key challenge addressed in this paper is to find significant terms with respect to
topic or subject within eBook. Topics generated using our approach can perform
better for various subtasks of IR and digital library applications like classification
and query recommendations.

Our future work is further extension of the system for better performance and
development of digital library.

References

1. Joshi, P., & Patel, S. V. (2015). AuTopicGen: Rule based positional pattern approach for topic
   collection in IR. *International Journal of Computer Applications, 109.*
2. http://en.wikipedia.org/wiki/Latent_Dirichlet_allocation.
3. Blei, D. M., Ng, A. Y., & Jordan, M. I. (2003). Latent dirichlet allocation. *Journal of Machine
   Learning Research, 3.*
4. Manning, C. D., & Raghavan, P. (2009). An introduction to information retrieval (Cambridge
   UP Online Edition).
5. Polettini, N. (2004). The vector space model in information retrieval—term weighting problem.
6. Ounis, I. (2009). Inverse document frequency. In *Encyclopedia of Database Systems* (pp. 1570–
   1571). US: Springer.
7. Blei, D. M. (2012). Introduction to probabilistic topic models, Princeton University. *ACM
   Digital Library, 55(4),* 77–84.
8. Blei, D. M., & Lafferty, J. (2006). Correlated topic models. In *Advances in Neural Information
   Processing.*

Domain-Driven Density Based Clustering Algorithm

Neethu Antony and Arti Deshpande

Abstract Due to increasing demand to derive knowledge from data, there is need for efficient data mining algorithms. We have proposed an algorithm to get clusters of arbitrary shapes with the help of Density Based clustering algorithms. Density Based clustering algorithms need Epsilon Value (Eps) and Minimum Points Value (MinPt) to create clusters. Hence in this paper, a method is proposed which accepts the domain knowledge about the dataset as an input and calculation of Eps and MinPt is automated which helps to make the data certain to some extent. Domain knowledge adds some relevance to data, hence this data with knowledge will never be ignored during clustering. In this method, we first create grids for dataset as per user's requirement then it derives the default Eps and MinPt which are inputs for Density Based Clustering Algorithm for Large Datasets (DBSCALE) algorithm. The results taken after implementation shows the proposed method gives better clusters.

Keywords DBSCAN · DBSCALE · Density based clustering · Epsilon · Domain knowledge · Grid

1 Introduction

Clustering analysis is an active research area in the field of data mining and others [1]. Clustering algorithm can be categorized into five broad categories: density based method, model-based method, partitioning method, grid-based method, and hierarchical method.

N. Antony (✉)
Thadomal Shahani Engineering College, Mumbai, India
e-mail: neethuantony2006@hotmail.com

A. Deshpande
G. H. Raisoni College of Engineering, Nagpur, India

© Springer Science+Business Media Singapore 2016
S.C. Satapathy et al. (eds.), *Proceedings of International Conference on ICT for Sustainable Development*, Advances in Intelligent Systems and Computing 409, DOI 10.1007/978-981-10-0135-2_68

In *Partitioning Method*, a database having n objects is partitioned into k datasets, where $k <= n$ and each partition depicts a cluster. Hence, the data gets classified into k partitions satisfying the requirements of each group containing at least one object [2] and each object relating to not more than one group [3].

In *Hierarchical Method*, a given set of data objects are hierarchically decomposed. Based on the formation of hierarchical decomposition, it can be either agglomerative or divisive. The *agglomerative approach* is also called the *bottom-up* approach as the formation of a separate group which starts from each object. All the closely coupled objects or groups are successfully merged into one (the topmost level of the hierarchy), or until a terminating condition is reached. The *divisive approach* is also called the *top-down* approach as a single cluster has all the objects at the start. A cluster is split up into smaller clusters in each successive iteration, until a termination condition holds or each object is in one cluster.

In *Density Based Method* [4], the objects are clustered with respect to the distance between the objects like most partitioning methods. Clusters of arbitrary shape are derived from such methods. The principle behind this algorithm is to increase the size of the cluster until the density of the cluster or number of objects in the cluster or data points in the neighborhood exceeds some threshold. Such methods are beneficial in filtering out outliers and noise.

In *Grid-Based Method* [4], the object space is quantized to a particular number of cells to form a grid structure. The most important benefit of this algorithm is the quick processing time. It is so, because the processing is independent of the number of data points and only dependent on the number of cells in quantized space in a particular dimension [5]. In *Model-Based Method*, a model is hypnotized for a particular cluster and the best fit to given model is found for the data.

Many algorithms, such as DBSCAN [6], CURE [7], CLARANS [1], STING [8], K-MEANS [1], DENCLUE [9], DBRS [10], analyze high dimension and large data from different aspect. Every algorithm has benefits and drawbacks. The k-means clustering algorithm, the most simple and commonly used partitioning algorithm. K —points are randomly chosen as the cluster centers, and then each point in the dataset is assigned to the center closest to it. Then it re-compute the center of each and every cluster based on the objects available for the same cluster, the assignment process of the algorithm is repeated and computing steps until it meets the convergence criterion. It is simple and straightforward. However, it has some drawbacks like there is a strong dependency of the results on the k initial centroids and the other is the outlier sensitive process.

CURE [7] is a hierarchical method. Each cluster is represented by a certain fixed number of points that are taken by a selection process from a set of well scattered points and then they are accumulated toward the cluster's center by a specified fraction. To handle large databases, CURE employs a combination of partitioning and random sampling [5].

DBSCAN [6] is a density based clustering method. The working of this algorithm depends on the value of the Minimum Points Threshold given by the user. The value makes the cluster stronger and this is what represents the density of the object as the neighbors are checked for the count of the objects. Then clustering to objects which have density connected characteristic. In this methodology, the process of clustering is dependent on the fact that the cluster can be identified only by one of its core points that satisfies the Minimum Points Threshold. Arbitrary shaped clusters are mined with the help of DBSCAN, without a need to ordering of the input data and it can also classify noise and outliers from the data points. When using spatial index such as R^*-tree is used, its time complexity is $O(n * \log n)$ [5].

DENCLUE [9] is also a density based clustering method. The basic idea of it is to model the overall point density analytically and to assign the points to the same cluster if they belong to same local maximum. Density attractors helps in determining the clusters, and arbitrary shaped clusters can be described easily by using the simple equation based on the overall density function. The important benefits of it are that it has a sound mathematical basis and a compact mathematical description of arbitrarily shaped clusters is allowed in high-dimensional datasets. At the same time, it is significantly faster than many existing algorithms and it has good clustering properties in datasets with large amount of noise.

STING [8] is a variation of grid-based cluster method. High-dimension data are managed well with the help of grids and hence the efficiency improves but still the algorithm has some flaws. For example, the distribution of the data points are done only after the algorithm has the reference of the grid. It utilizes the statistical information of grid, ignoring the points in the grid. This is how the effect of the cluster results is reduced.

2 Literature Survey

The DBSCAN algorithm is a form of density based algorithm. Here, it divides the high density area into several defined clusters, and it can also help in forming arbitrary figure cluster in the database by taking the noise into consideration. The DBSCAN algorithm also lacks in many aspects. One is that the results of clustering are improper when there is a significant change in the density. The other is that the uncertain data is not handled well by the algorithm. Domain knowledge is unavailable in uncertain data. Considering all these, the researchers are giving out many solutions to make these better [11].

In the aspect of the clustering for certain data, Ankerst M has put forward OPTICS [12]. This algorithm provides an additional storage for the reachable distance as well as for the core distance so that it can give a cluster order alternatively and automatically. GDBSCAN [13] was proposed by Sander J., which uses the concept of polygon over point as a polygon helps to cluster lines and polygon as well along with points, which is not possible the other way round. The k-dist figure is used in VDBSCAN [14] algorithm and the DK (Distance from K) graph to analyze and select parameters suitable for varying densities and cluster varying density dataset was proposed by Dong. Ma put forward a CURD [15] algorithm, in order to solve the problems related to efficiency of the large size database, and parallel DBSCAN algorithm was proposed by Song [16]. Zhou put forward

FDBSCAN algorithm which uses a very few representative points in a core point's neighboring area as expansion seeds for the cluster such that there is a reduction in the execution frequency of region query and also in the cost of I/O [17].

In the aspect of the clustering of uncertain data, some researchers have taken the considerations of the characteristics of the uncertain data and have modified the existing algorithm to come up with a solution. Kriegel and Pfeifle came up with FDBSCAN [18] algorithm that uses the basic DBSCAN algorithm to comply with the requirements of clustering the uncertain data. The probabilistic is used to represent the outcomes of the clustering and to classify the points to proper cluster. This algorithm can form proper clusters by taking into consideration the neighborhood and density of the data points but the algorithm also depends on the parameters set by the user and is too sensitive to it. Any small change by the user in the parameters can bring about a huge difference in clustering outcomes. To solve this problem, FOPTICS algorithm [19] is put forward which uses the same way of measurement to improve the OPTICS [12] algorithm. This algorithm works well with large datasets and the output of the cluster is represented visually. Xu and Li in 2008 [20] proposed P-DBSCAN algorithm which is based on a probability index clustering algorithm and the DBSCAN algorithm. This algorithm uses MBR (Minimum Boundary Rectangle) and takes the minimum and maximum distance as the similarity module instead of the expected distance. It also uses the index technology to filter the objects that does not cater to the parameters' need, helping in reducing the time complexity. Analyzing the improved algorithm described above, these clustering algorithm covers up the limitations of the DBSCAN, but these algorithms have done nothing to handle the effects of data uncertainty leading to improper clusters. These algorithms failed to consider the effect of the exiting center point probability; what's more they did not judge the uncertainty of the uncertain data, so these algorithms are lacing and are not complete in its sense.

For the problems explained above, this paper comes up with a proposal for a density based clustering algorithm for converting the uncertain data into certain data by helping the system with the domain knowledge about the data. Placing and realignment of the uncertain data with respect to the domain knowledge will not make it certain completely, but will at least provide a direction to it.

3 Proposed Algorithm

Clustering with Density and Grid concept uses some reference points to create the clusters. Each reference point is evaluated against the concept of core point. A reference point becomes a core point in DBSCAN if it has MinPts satisfied in the given epsilon diameter. Not a single reference actually exists in the space and is fictitious. Eps a parameter of the algorithm decides the count of references, so the user need not control it.

3.1 Block Diagram of Proposed System

Each block of the overall block diagram given in Fig. 1 is explained below:

Preprocessing Dataset If there are any missing values in dataset, then in preprocessing phase those values should be handled.

Split the Dataset The grid is plotted on dataset after taking the domain knowledge as an input as per user's requirement.

Min Pt Calculator The subsection of grid with least number of points is selected as default MinPt value.

Eps Calculator The major diagonal of the subsection of grid is selected as default value for Eps by considering the largest subsection of grid.

Apply DBSCALE Finally DBSCALE [21] is applied which is the improvement of DBSCAN algorithm and consider the above calculated MinPts and Eps as inputs. This process expands the region of search for data points to form better clusters in less time.

Calculate Outlier Score and Cluster Count Outlier percentage is calculated and also the count of formed clusters as we need to maximize the count for better results.

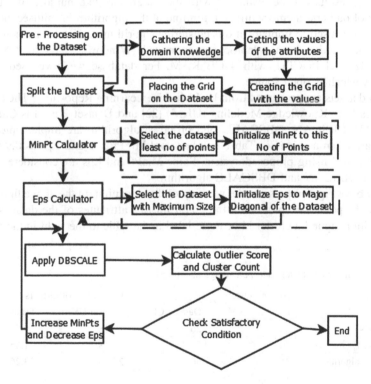

Fig. 1 Block diagram of proposed system

Increase MinPts and Decrease Eps If there is no outlier then the value of Eps is reduced to half of the current value to be used in the next iteration. This is done to increase the cluster count as well. But the reducing procedure stops when there is a significant decrease in the outlier and then the Eps value is set back to the value of Eps in last iteration. In the similar fashion, the value of MinPts is increased but not as Eps. MinPts value is made to increase after the Eps is set. This is done to test the Eps. Increasing MinPts would not result in maximizing the cluster count and hence it is just used to test the value of Eps. These testing checks, if the derived Eps can accommodate more data points and reduce the outliers created in the previous iterations. Hence this increment of Eps is done with scale of 2 %.

Check Satisfactory Condition The satisfactory condition is the stop condition for the algorithm where the system understands that the Eps and MinPts decided for the system has come to a perfect value, where any change in the value of Eps or MinPts gives and brings about a huge change in the number of outliers.

4 Experimentation Results

Clustering results can be evaluated with the parameters like number of clusters, number of outliers, memory utilized, runtime of the algorithm in milliseconds. C# language was used to implement this clustering algorithm in .Net 4.0 framework in MS Visual Studio 8 on a laptop computer with Windows 7, 64 bit OS, with 2.50 GHz Intel i5 CPU, with 4 GB RAM. For database we have used Mysql database which is open source.

Two datasets are processed from UCI Machine Learning Repository. The dataset 1 used is User Knowledge Modeling (UKM) [22] and Dataset 2 used is Car Data (CD) [23]. DBSCAN, DBSCALE, and proposed algorithm are implemented and results are taken as given in Table 1. It has used MinPt as 2 and Eps as 0.9 which was calculated using proposed system. Same MinPt and Eps are considered as an input for DBSCAN and DBSCALE algorithm.

The above Fig. 2 represents the working of the algorithm. In the above figure, we see that the points are plotted on the graph for two attributes of the database and each point assigned a cluster id or noise label in the table to the right in the figure.

Table 1 Number of clusters and percentage of outliers

	No. of clusters		Percentage of outliers	
	Dataset-UKM	Dataset-CD	Dataset-UKM	Dataset-CD
DBSCAN	40	26	13.18	1.55
DBSCALE	40	26	13.18	1.55
Proposed algorithm	45	46	27.13	23.26

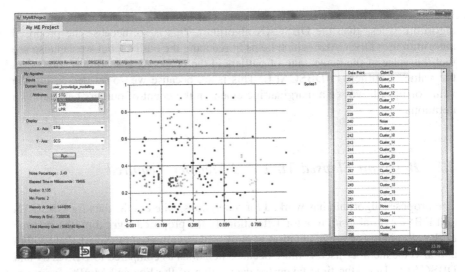

Fig. 2 The proposed algorithm results

4.1 Based on Number of Clusters and Percentage of Outliers

In the proposed algorithm, the time taken to decide on Eps and MinPt value is accountable, which is not in the case of DBSCALE and DBSCAN. It works on trial and error concept. We have to try different MinPt and Eps to get the desired number of resultant clusters. But the number of clusters generated in Table 1 is at the cost of outliers analysis. Hence the number of outliers for the same dataset is shown in Table 1. The more the number of clusters, the better is the differentiation between the data points. But the clusters should be high in density. Hence we use DBSCALE in proposed system, as the DBSCALE algorithm not only includes the neighbor in the cluster but also goes for neighbor of the core point. A core point is the data point that satisfies the MinPts condition with the given Eps value as radius for the region (Table 2).

The number of outliers generated is an important parameter as it is used for the stop condition of the algorithm. The algorithm proceeds with reducing the Eps value till it sees a marginal difference in the increment of the percentage of outlier.

Table 2 Number of clusters and percentage of outliers

	Elapsed time (ms)		Memory used in bytes	
	Dataset-UKM	Dataset-CD	Dataset-UKM	Dataset-CD
DBSCAN	97	56	2212,264	2729,308
DBSCALE	93	59	3068,640	676,744
Proposed algorithm	1821	1245	3349,392	1669,380

In Table 1, we clearly realize that percentage of outliers generated in the proposed algorithm is less than the DBSCAN algorithm. This is so, because the proposed algorithm uses DBSCALE which helps in reducing the outliers, but we can also see that the value of the percentage of outliers in the proposed algorithm is more than the value of outliers in DBSCALE. This is so, because we go on decreasing the value of Eps till we see a marginal increment in the count of outliers between two iterations.

4.2 Based on Elapsed Time and Memory Required

The proposed algorithm has worked for 5 iterations, whereas the data for DBSCAN and DBSCALE algorithm is for 1 iteration. In the proposed algorithm, the runtime of the algorithm for single iteration is same as the runtime of DBSCALE algorithm and also the memory used is more because iterations as compared to DBSCAN and DBSCALE. Here, the time taken for calculation of the Eps and MinPts for every iteration is the overhead but that is what makes the system independent of the user trial and error method for determining Eps and MinPts values in case of DBSCAN. The runtime of DBSCALE is more than DBSCAN because of the expand cluster function.

5 Conclusion

Hence, the algorithm concludes by making the uncertain data certain to some extent and by giving a start to the user for the process of clustering. The user may go ahead by changing the values of MinPts and Eps. The disadvantage of the system will be providing the domain knowledge. This system will not be able to provide much help in optimizing the process of clustering to the user who cannot provide the domain knowledge and will work as any other clustering algorithm works but reduces the time considerably in selecting the Eps and MinPt which otherwise would be a daunting task for the user.

6 Future Work

In the current system, the process of acquiring the domain knowledge about a particular domain is by taking the knowledge about the attributes and the values the attributes can hold in the form of ranges. The description to be filled for each range is optional. This process of acquiring the knowledge about the particular attribute can be relaxed or alternated for the user by adopting a simpler way.

References

1. Han, J., & Kamber, M. (2001). *Data mining concepts and techniques*. Beijing: Higher Education Press.
2. Shah, G. H., Bhensdadia, C. K., & Ganatra, A. P. (2012). An empirical evaluation of density based clustering techniques. *1*(2).
3. Santhisree, K., & Damodaram, A. (2011). SSM-DBSCAN and SSM-OPTICS: Incorporating new similarity measure for density based clustering of web usage data. *International Journal on Computer Sciences and Engineering*.
4. Shah, G.H. (2012). An improved DBSCAN, a density based clustering algorithm with parameter selection for high dimensional data sets. In *2012 Nirma University International Conference on Engineering, Nuicone-2012*, 06–08 December, 2012.
5. Zhiwei, S, Zheng, Z., Hongmei, W., Maode, M., Lianfang, Z., & Yantai, S. (2005). A fast clustering algorithm based on grid and density. In *IEEE CCECE/CCGEI*. Saskatoon, May 2005.
6. Ester, M., Kriegel, H.-P., Sander, J., & Xiaowei, X. (1996). A density based algorithm for discovering clusters in large spatial databases with noise. In *Proceedings of Knowledge Discovery and Data Mining* (pp. 226–231). Portland: AAAI Press.
7. Guba, S., Rastogi, R., & Shim, K. (1998). CURE: An efficient clustering algorithm for large databases. In L. M. Haas & A. Tiwary (Eds.), *Proceeding of the ACM SIGMOD International Conference on Management of Data* (pp. 73–84). Seattle: ACM Press.
8. Wang, W., Yang, J., & Muntz, R. (1997). Sting: A statistical information grid approach to spatial to spatial data mining. In *Proceedings of VLDB'1997* (pp. 186–195).
9. Hinneburg, A., & Keim, D. A. An efficient approach to clustering in large multimedia databases with noise. In *Proceedings of the 4th International Conference on Knowledge Discovery and Data Mining (KDD'98)* (pp. 58–65). New York: AAAI Press.
10. Wang, X., & Hamlton, H. J. (2003). DBRS: A density-based spatial clustering method with random sampling. In *Proceedings of 7th PAKDD* (pp. 563–575). Seoul, Korea.
11. Wang, H., Wang, Y., & Wan, S.: A density-based clustering algorithm for uncertain data. In *2012 International Conference on Computer Science and Electronics Engineering*.
12. Ankerst, M., Breunig, M. M., & Kriegel, H. P. et al. (1994). OPTICS: ordering points to identify the clustering structure [C]. In *Proceeding of 1999 ACMSIGMOD International Conference* [S.l.] (pp. 49–60). ACM Press.
13. Sander, J., Ester, M., Kriegel, H. P., et al. (1998). Density-based clustering in spatial database: The algorithm GDBSCAN and its applications [J]. *Data Mining and Knowledge Discovery, 2* (2), 169–194.
14. Zhou, D., & Liu, P. (2009). VDBSCAN: Varied density based clustering algorithm [J]. *Computer Engineering and Application, 45*(11), 137–141.
15. Ma, S., Wang, T., & Tao, S. (2003). A fast clustering algorithm based on reference and density [J]. *Journal of software, 14*(6), 1089–1095.
16. Song, M., & Liu, Z. (2004). A data-overlap-partitioning-based parallel DBSCAN algorithm [J]. *Application Research of Computers, 7*, 17–20.
17. Zhou, S., Zhou, A., & Fan, Y. (2000). FDBSCAN: A fast DBSCAN algorithm [J]. *Journal of Soft ware, 11*(6), 735–744.
18. Kriegel, H.P., & Pfeifle, M. (2005). Density-based clustering of uncertain data [C]. In *Proceedings of the 11th ACM SIGKDD International Conference on Knowledge Discovery and Data Mining, 2005* (pp. 672–677).
19. Kriegel, H. P., & Pfeifle, M. (2005). Hierarchical density-based probabilistic clustering of uncertain data [C]. In *Proceedings of the 5th IEEE International Conference on Data Mining, 2005* (pp. 689–692).

20. Xu, H. J., & Li, G. H. (2008). Density-based probabilistic clustering of uncertain data [C]. In *Proceedings of the 2008 International Conference on Computer Science and Software Engineering 2008* (pp. 474–477).
21. Tsai, C. F., & Sung, C.-Y. (2010). DBSCALE: An efficient density based clustering algorithm for data mining in large databases. In *2010 Second Pacific-Asia Conference on Circuits, Communications and System* (PACCS).
22. Dataset User Knowledge Modelling. https://archive.ics.uci.edu/ml/datasets/User+Knowledge +Modeling
23. Car Dataset. https://archive.ics.uci.edu/ml/datasets/Car+Evaluation

Adaptive Approach of AODV and DSDV Routing Protocols Using Optimal Probabilistic Logical Key Hierarchy in MANET

Harshit Prakash Patidar and Neetu Sharma

Abstract Mobile Ad-hoc Network is an automatic-configuring infrastructure less network of mobile nodes in wireless. Ad-hoc is a Latin word that means "for this purpose". Each node moves freely and independently in Mobile Ad-hoc Network. In MANET, the mobile nodes can perform the roles of both hosts and routers. Many MANET applications are used for Military Tactical Communications and Disaster Recovery are mostly dependent on secure node communication. For Secure Communication, we use various Logical Hierarchy Key Protocols in Mobile Ad-hoc Network. But group key management faces many problems because of unreliable media, less energy resources and mobile nodes failure. In this paper, analysis is done on the basic of new logical key with Optimal Probabilistic Technique. In logical key, all nodes are formed of tree structure. OPLKH reduces the Rekey Cost and Routing Energy Consumption in Mobile Ad-hoc Network. In simulation, we have calculated the numbers of Rekeys, Energy Consumption at Server and Energy Consumption for Key Generation.

Keywords Automatic-configuring infrastructure · Energy Consumption · Rekey Cost

1 Introduction

Mobile Ad-hoc Network is a new schema in wireless communication field where collections of mobile nodes are formed and destroyed without any centralized control. In this network, individual node can perform as both sender and receiver of data terminals. We can say that each node may act as an end node or intermediate

H.P. Patidar (✉) · N. Sharma
Department of Computer Science, Government Engineering College, Ajmer, Rajasthan, India
e-mail: harshitprakash@gmail.com

N. Sharma
e-mail: neetucom10@gmail.com

© Springer Science+Business Media Singapore 2016   715
S.C. Satapathy et al. (eds.), *Proceedings of International Conference on ICT for Sustainable Development*, Advances in Intelligent Systems and Computing 409, DOI 10.1007/978-981-10-0135-2_69

node which is responsible for sending and receiving packet. MANET mainly operates in bandwidth-constrained variable-capacity link.

The dynamic network can run as an independent network by which we can access other network through the multi-hop. In MANET, due to lack of energy, mobile nodes have the network topology volatile in the environment and face many problems in designing effective conservation in Energy Routing Protocol. In MANET, Vulnerabilities are possible because of dynamic topology, lack of a clear line of defense and limited resources. There may be various attacks like active attack and passive attack so security is major issue in Mobile Ad-hoc Network. Security is mostly based on secure routing, authentication and key management. In this issue, network management of key solves the most critical problems. Basically, Cryptographic techniques are used for Secure Communications in wired and wireless networks to achieve data confidentiality. The ad-hoc network is used in many applications like battlefield, moving vehicles, disaster management and rescue operations.

Harder et al. placed major issues in key management strategy for secure group communication in maintaining the forward and backward privacy. In other arguments, new joining members should not know about the previous communication and the old leaving members should not know about the future communication when they leave from the group. To provide forward and backward privacy, key server needs to change the group key for every joining/leaving of a member. It also encrypts the group key and sends it to every node individually [1] .

In this paper, analysis is done on the performance of AODV and DSDV Routing Protocols using Optimal Probabilistic Logical Key Hierarchy in Mobile Ad-hoc Network. We have tried to reduce Rekey Cost, Network Overhead and Energy Consumption in Mobile Ad-hoc Network.

2   Overview of AODV and DSDV Routing Protocols

Generally, a set of topology often called Routing Protocols transmit the packet from initial node to final node. Indicating paths in a network along which it is supposed to send packets, is called Routing. An Ad-hoc Routing Protocol controls how a node concludes which way to route packets amongst computing devices in a Mobile Ad-hoc Network [2].

Three types of routing protocols are available- Proactive Routing Protocol, Reactive Routing Protocol and Hybrid Routing Protocol. A Proactive Routing Protocol is also known as the Table Driven Routing Protocol because all paths are already allocated to send packet from source to destination and value can be defined in the table. Proactive Routing Protocol contains the routing information of all the working nodes. The main drawback of Proactive Routing Protocol is to control the messages in the network because it makes individual table for each protocol and creates heavy weight. Reactive Routing Protocol is also known as Dynamic Routing Protocol because all paths are dynamically generated when required to

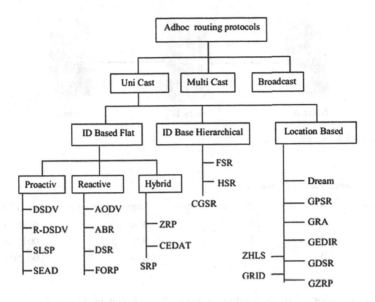

Fig. 1 Classification of Routing Protocols

send packet from source node to sink node. In Reactive Routing Protocol, complexity is more as compared to Proactive Routing Protocol due to dynamic path but packet transmission time is very low. A Hybrid Routing Protocol is a combination of both Proactive Routing Protocol and Reactive Routing Protocol (Fig. 1).

(a) *Table Driven Routing Protocols*

Proactive Routing Protocols is based on the periodically exchange of control message which is set locally or throughout in the network. Thus, a path is simply available when required. Once the routing tables are setup then packet transmission will be easy and efficient as in the traditional wired networks. Popular Proactive Routing Protocols are DSDV, OLSR, STAR, TBRPF and WRP.

- *Destination-Sequenced Distance Vector (DSDV)*

Destination Sequenced Distance Vector is a method which is Table-Driven Routing oriented approach in Mobile Ad- hoc Network based on Bellman-Ford algorithm. It was invented by C. Perkins and P. Bhagwat in 1994. The main role of algorithm is to solve routing loops problem. In this process, all paths to be defined for destinations are already available at all nodes for every times. The tables are interchanged between the neighbours in regular intervals in order to update view of the network. Missing transmission has been used by neighbour node in order to catch broken links in the topology [3] (Fig. 2).

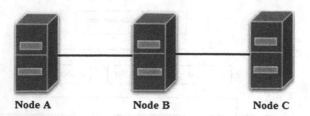

Node A   **Node B**   **Node C**

Fig. 2 Network of Three Nodes

Table 1 Routing Table of Node A

Destination	Next Hop	Number of Hops	Sequence Number	Install Time
A	A	0	A46	001000
B	B	1	B36	001200
C	B	2	C28	001500

The description of routing table of Node A is shown in Table 1.

Generally, the table holds description of all possible routes accessible by node A along with the next hop, number of hops, sequence number and install time.

Advantage: DSDV was one of the earlier procedures available. It is quite pertinent for generating ad-hoc networks with minor numbers of nodes.

Disadvantage: DSDV needs information uniformly of its routing tables which uses up the battery power and a small quantity of bandwidth even when the network is idle.

(b) *Dynamic Routing Protocols*

Dynamic Routing Protocols are better than Table Driven Routing Protocols and reactive in nature. On-Demand route discoveries are basis of this protocol. Hence, when source node requires then only the paths are determined. Path can be found by Reactive Routing Protocol when demanded by network flooding along with Route Request Packets. Popular Reactive Routing Protocols are AODV, DSR and DYMO.

• *Ad-hoc On-demand Distance Vector (AODV)*

Unicast and multicast routing can be performed by AODV. It is a Reactive Routing Protocol sensing that it establishes a route to a destination only on-demand. In AODV, unless the connection is required, the network is supposed to be silent. At that point, the network node that needs a connection, broadcasts a request for connection [4, 5] (Fig. 3).

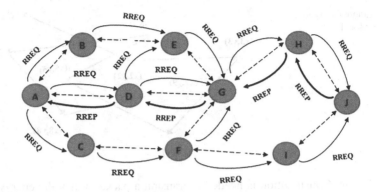

Fig. 3 AODV Protocol Messaging Processor

Advantage: The main pros of this protocol is that routes are recognized on-demand and destination sequence numbers are used to find the last route to the endpoint. It generates no additional traffic for communication along existing links. The connections setup delay is lower and also does not need any storage.

Disadvantage: AODV requires additional time in order to establish a connection and the complexity of finding first route is greater than other routes. Multiple Route Reply Packets answer to a single Route Request Packet and can lead to weight control overhead.

3 Description of Mobility Model

The movement pattern can be described by mobility model for users and their location, velocity and acceleration changes over time. Mobility is very essential to check the movement of routing protocols. In this paper, we have used Random Waypoint Mobility Model to move the nodes within the network.

(a) *The Random Waypoint Mobility Model*

Random Waypoint Mobility Model is processed by a default mode of random selection of mobile node. The Random Waypoint Mobility Model is supreme popular mobility model and very easy to implement [6] (Fig. 4).

4 Energy Consumption Model

We have calculated the Energy Consumption for Key Generation proposed by Potlapally Nachiketh (Nachiketh R. et al. 2003) and for Data Transmission and receiving as proposed by Dongkyun Kim (Dongkyun Kim et al. 2002) [7].

Fig. 4 Random Waypoint
Mobility Model

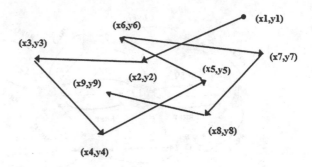

The Energy Consumption is needed to transmit a packet p then the energy E(p) =i*v*tp Joule where i is fresh value, v is the voltage and tp is the time taken to transmit the packet p. Energy Consumption for the key setup phase using AES of 128-bit key is 7.83 uJ/key. We use simulated symmetric key of AES (Advanced Encryption Standard) of 128-bit length.

5 Related Work

Nowadays, many key management methods have been proposed for secure group communication. Some of them are defined below-

In self-organized public-key management for MANET, to problem certificates, it enables users to produce their public-private key pairs without any centralized services. The CA (Certification Authority) functionality is totally distributed. All nodes have equal works in the network [8, 9].

Jun Li et al. introduced a group key management structure DVGKM in MANET which is depended on the secret sharing mechanism. In this, each node contains a secret share and multiple nodes in a local neighbourhood that can update the group key simultaneously [10].

Jayanta Biswas et al. introduced a topology aware key management and distribution approach for MANET. They have used overlay method for key distribution and their impartial is to keep message overhead small for key management and distribution [11].

K. Gomathi et al. introduced a cluster based key management structure for MANET In this approach, they separated the network into clusters. Each cluster-head will preserve the group key, it will inform the group key whenever there is a membership change [12].

R. Agee et al. introduced the LKH schema. In LKH schema, the key tree structure can be binary or k-ary. The basic LKH schema was not created exactly for ad-hoc networks [1].

Alwyn R. Pais [13] introduced a new probabilistic Rekeying technique for secure multicast groups in which they have optimized the logical key hierarchy which is known as OPLKH. They introduced the reduction of Rekey Cost by establishing LKH tree structure which is beneficial for Rekey Probabilities of members using new join and leave operations [14].

Selcuk A.A. et al. introduced Probabilistic Logical Key Hierarchy (PLKH), a refinement of basic LKH schema. PLKH scheme minimizes average Rekey Cost of LKH-based protocol by organizing the LKH tree structure with respect to Rekey likelihoods of members [15].

(a) *OPLKH Schema*

We have analyzed OPLKH approaches which are the optimization for PLKH that decreases the Rekey Cost further. We establish the LKH tree structure with respect to representative Rekey Probabilities as opposed to aggregate probability of PLKH. We focus on decreasing the number of Rekeys that are caused due to member negotiation or eviction [14, 15].

In tree structure, when we insert a member as a leaf node in PLKH, we arrange the new insert operation having position either as a leaf node or as an interior node in LKH tree structure positioned on the basic of their probabilities. When a new node M joins the group, we place member M at a position such that all ancestors of M will have greater probability and all descendants of M will have lower probability.

The LKH scheme aims to reduce the cost of an accommodation recovery operation by adding extra encryption keys into the system. The members of the group are organized as the leaves of a "logical key" which are controlled by the key manager. The internal nodes in this tree structure are logical entities which do not relate to any real life entities of the multicast group but are used for key distribution purpose only. There is a key related to all nodes in the tree structure and all the nodes grip a copy of every key on the route from its corresponding leaf node to the root node of the tree structure.

Each member contains the keys on the route from its leaf node to the root node. K_{Root} is the key shared by each group members.

In OPLKH schema, we proposed a new insert method called MPUT that is used to insert new member in a location which preserves relative locations of current members in the tree structure. It is comparable to PUT operation of PLKH but generates a logical node [15] (Fig. 6).

When the group is left by the fellow nodes then their corresponding physical node gets erased from the tree structure. The internal node may be termed as

Fig. 5 The description shown LKH tree structure with eight members

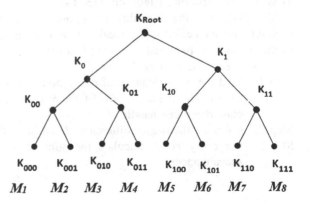

Fig. 6 MPUT operation
creates new logical node
N with M and X as its children

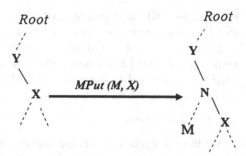

physical node in the tree structure depending upon the factor how it is inserted and whether it has any associated node or not. The physical node gets deleted if it is supposed to be leaf node in case of OPLKH. This replaceable node will be replaced whenever a node arises with suitable Rekey Probability. The unwanted logical and replaceable node can be removed by deletion operation.

The centralized key management was developed to reduce the cost of Rekeying and is better in case of tree structure keying scheme Probability 0 (n) to 0 (log n) (where n is the group size). We have adopted OPLKH method in MANET and have analyzed the Rekey Cost and Energy Consumption for Data Transmission and Routing in MANET [16].

6 Proposed Methodology for MANET

In this technique, we largely focus on minimizing the Rekey Cost of LKH placed protocols by organizing the tree structure based on Rekey Probabilities of the nodes.

As in OPLKH, we have implemented all the logical operations of OPLKH into MANET environment. In MANET, we have chosen clusterhead as Key-server because there is no Key-server. To select the clusterhead, we have used the Weighted Clustering Algorithm (WCA). As Rekey Probability is one of the issues to cause Re-clustering, we have considered Rekey Probability in be another factor to Weighted Clustering Algorithm [13, 14].

The WCA has the flexibility of appointing different weights and taken into account the united effect of the ideal degree, transmission power and battery power of the nodes. The modified Weighted Clustering Algorithm is as follows:

Clusterhead Selection Technique

Step 1: Find the acquaintances of every node v (i.e. nodes within its broadcast range). The degree is, dv, of the v node. H is the number of nodes, a clusterhead can handle.

Step 2: Calculate the degree-difference, $D_v = |d_v - H|$, for every node v.

Step 3: For every node, calculate the sum of the distances, S_v, with all its acquaintances.

Step 4: Calculate the running average of the speed for each node v. This provides the mobility of the node v and is denoted by M_v.

Step 5: Calculate the consumed battery power, T_v. Assuming that battery power utilization is more for a clusterhead in comparison of an ordinary node.

Step 6: Calculate a joined weight $I_v = c_1 * D_v + c_2 * S_v + c_3 * M_v + c_4 * T_v$, for each node v.

The coefficients c_1, c_2, c_3 and c_4 are the weighting factors for the corresponding system parameters.

Step 7: Calculate the average Weights of all nodes, AI, and also compute the average Rekey Probabilities of all nodes, ARP.

Step 8: Now check for each node v,

If (weight $I_v < AI$ and corresponding Rekey Probability, $RP_v < ARP$)

Then Calculate the new weight $NI_v = I_v * 0.001 + RP_v$.

Step 9: Select the node with minimum NI_v to be the clusterhead (Key-server).

Basis for Our Algorithm

To avoid Re-clustering, primarily we choose the best node as clusterhead from the existing nodes using the modified WCA algorithm. The following features are measured using Weighted Clustering Algorithm as given below:

(a) The procedure of clusterhead prediction is not a periodic method and a rarely invoked system update thereby reducing the computational and communication cost.

(b) A predefined system threshold node has been supported by each clusterhead to ensure the efficiency of mac functioning. By optimizing the number of nodes in each cluster, we can achieve a high throughput of the system.

(c) Certain transmission range has been allotted to use the battery power efficiently. If node is acting as clusterhead, the battery power would be enhanced as compared to ordinary node.

(d) In order to decide the clusterhead, the mobility factor is key factor when one of the ordinary node moves out of the cluster and joins other existing cluster if Re-affiliation is supposed to occur.

(e) If the clusterhead is closer in the transmission range, the communication between them would be more effective. The factor signal attenuation is increased with distance [13].

The Weighted Clustering Algorithm uses physical parameters like mobility, connectivity, energy and location. These parameters are modified in Weighted Clustering Algorithm and also considers the Rekey Probability because the server node should not be Rekeyed in early time. In some conditions, when the Key-Server (clusterhead) node energy may exhaust to reduce the threshold then the Key-Server node should be changed from clusterhead position and it leads to Re-clustering. In Re-clustering procedure, we again simulate the modified clusterhead selection algorithm and will select the best node as clusterhead among the available nodes and it will act as a Key-Server. This process continues till the simulation ends. After the clusterhead selection technique, the selected clusterhead acts as a Key-Server and responsible for key distribution in MANET.

To reduce the Energy Consumption in Mobile Ad-hoc Network while using OPLKH approach for key management, we use group oriented Rekeying which is better than key oriented and user oriented in the Mobile Ad-hoc Network. Because group oriented Rekeying is good for server side. We can reduce the message transmission as well as the receiving cost in the network and also at server [17].

It is significant to minimize Energy Consumption at Server because exhaustion of server energy will lead to change of Key-Server which increases the Rekey Cost and other overheads like Routing Overhead, Clusterhead Selection and Message Transmission Overhead.

7 Simulation Result and Analysis

We have Simulated Optimal Probabilistic Logical Key in Mobile Ad-hoc Network. Simulation is implemented in C++ language. We have performed experiments on groups of 128, 256, 512, 768 and 1024 nodes. For each experiment, we have created the joining/leaving of nodes randomly. In addition, some members may leave because of power exhaustion and some members may join/leave based on connection failure or availability. For each join/leave operation, we have recorded the numbers of Rekeys generated, Energy Consumption for Key Generation and Energy Consumption at Key-server.

In OPLKH approach, we have categorized three categories namely Static, Semi-Dynamic and Dynamic based on the number of leaves and Rekey Probabilities. But in MANET, we added some extra parameters to classify these categories. The additional parameters are pause time, node mobility and updating interval time. The additional parameters are listed in Table 2. In simulation, for every updating interval time, we have updated the node positions and routing tables.

Table 2 Simulation Parameters

Simulation Parameters	Static	Semi-dynamic	Dynamic
Mobility	0–5 m/s	0–10 m/s	0–20 m/s
Packet Size	256 bytes	256 bytes	256 bytes
Mobility Model	Random Waypoint	Random Waypoint	Random Waypoint
Pause Time	0–10 s	0–5 s	0 s
Updating Interval Time	10 s	5 s	1 s
No. of Leaves	¼ of Group Size	½ of Group Size	¾ of Group Size
Area (in sq. m)	800 × 800	800 × 800	800 × 800
Energy	0–1000 J	0–1000 J	0–1000 J

Fig. 7 Graph between
Number of Nodes and
Number of Rekeys in case of
DSDV

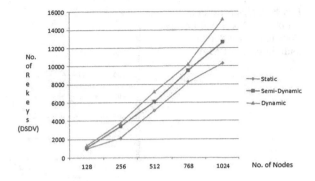

Simulation Results

In our simulation, we have calculated the numbers of Rekeys and Energy Consumption for Routing, Data Transmission and Key Generation in Static, Semi-Dynamic and Dynamic categories for each group size of 128, 256, 512, 768 and 1024 nodes

Figure 7 displays Number of Nodes versus Number of Rekeys in the network in the case of Destination Sequenced Distance Vector Routing Protocol. In DSDV, Rekey operation i.e. number of joining/leaving in the Static categories is less as compared to the Semi-Dynamic categories and Dynamic categories. Similarly, Rekey operation i.e. number of joining/leaving in the Semi-Dynamic categories is less as compared to the Dynamic categories.

Figure 8 displays Number of Nodes versus Energy Consumption at Server in the network in case of Destination Sequenced Distance Vector Routing Protocol. In DSDV, Energy Consumption at Server in the Static categories is less as compared to the Semi-Dynamic categories and Dynamic categories. Similarly, Energy Consumption at Server in the Semi-Dynamic categories is less as compared to the Dynamic categories. Energy Consumption at Server occurs because of key generation and key distribution. In case of DSDV, it is a Proactive Routing Protocol and computes routes for each node. It causes more energy depletion in the network.

Figure 9 displays Number of Nodes versus Energy Consumption for Routing in the network in case of Destination Sequenced Distance Vector Routing Protocol. In DSDV, Energy Consumption for Routing in the Static categories is less as compared to the Semi-Dynamic categories and Dynamic categories. Similarly, Energy Consumption for Routing in the Semi-Dynamic categories is less as compared to the Dynamic categories. Energy Consumption for Routing is greater in case of DSDV as compared to AODV.

Figure 10 displays Number of Nodes versus Energy Consumption for Data Transmission in the network in case of Destination Sequenced Distance Vector Routing Protocol. In DSDV, Energy Consumption for Data Transmission in the Static categories is less as compared to the Semi-Dynamic categories and Dynamic categories. Similarly, Energy Consumption for Data Transmission in the Semi-Dynamic categories is less as compared to the Dynamic categories. Energy

Fig. 8 Graph between Number of Nodes and Energy Consumption at Server in joule in case of DSDV

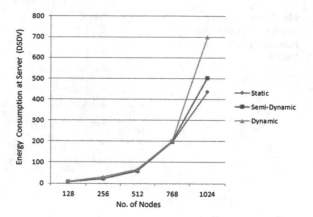

Fig. 9 Graph between Number of Nodes and Energy Consumption for Routing in joule in case of DSDV

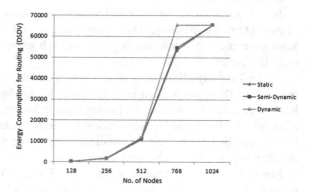

Fig. 10 Graph between Number of Nodes and Energy Consumption for Data Transmission in joule in case of DSDV

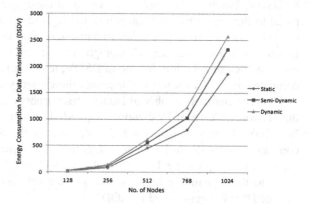

Consumption for Data Transmission is greater in case of DSDV as compared to AODV.

Figure 11 displays Number of Nodes versus Energy Consumption for Key Generation in the network in case of Destination Sequenced Distance Vector Routing Protocol. In DSDV, Energy Consumption for Key Generation in the Static

Fig. 11 Graph between Number of Nodes and Energy Consumption for Key Generation in joule in case of DSDV

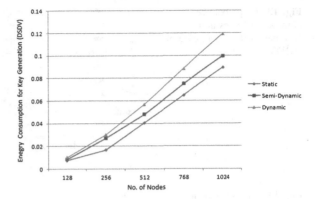

Fig. 12 Graph between Number of Nodes and Total Energy Consumption in Network in joule in case of DSDV

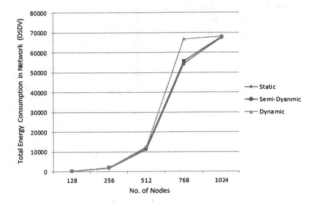

categories is less as compared to the Semi-Dynamic categories and Dynamic categories. Similarly, Energy Consumption for Key Generation in the Semi-Dynamic categories is less as compared to the Dynamic categories. Here, it is observed that if number of Rekeys increase, the Energy Consumption for Key Generation also increases.

Figure 12 displays Number of Nodes versus Total Energy Consumption in Network in case of Destination Sequenced Distance Vector Routing Protocol. In DSDV, Total Energy Consumption in Network in the Static categories is less as compared to the Semi-Dynamic categories and Dynamic categories. Similarly, Total Energy Consumption in Network in the Semi-Dynamic categories is less as compared to the Dynamic categories. Total Energy Consumption in Network is the sum of Energy Consumption for Key Generation, Energy Consumption for Routing and Energy Consumption for Data Transmission.

Figure 13 displays Number of Nodes versus Number of Rekeys in the network in case of Ad-hoc On-demand Distance Vector Routing Protocol. In AODV, Rekey operation i.e. number of joining/leaving in the Static categories is less as compared to the Semi-Dynamic categories and Dynamic categories. Similarly, Rekey operation i.e. number of joining/leaving in the Semi-Dynamic categories is less as compared to the Dynamic categories.

Fig. 13 Graph between
Number of Nodes and
Number of Rekeys in case of
AODV

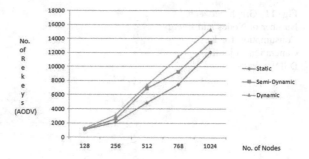

Fig. 14 Graph between
Number of Nodes and Energy
Consumption at Server in
joule in case of AODV

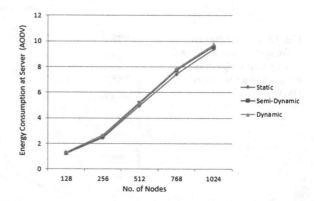

Figure 14 displays Number of Nodes versus Energy Consumption at Server in the network in case of Ad-hoc On-demand Distance Vector Routing Protocol. In AODV, Energy Consumption at Server in the Static categories is less as compared to the Semi-Dynamic categories and Dynamic categories. Similarly, Energy Consumption at Server in the Semi-Dynamic categories is less as compared to the Dynamic categories. Energy Consumption at Server occurs because of key generation and key distribution. In case of AODV, it is a Reactive Routing Protocol and computes routes only when required so Energy Consumption is very less.

Figure 15 displays Number of Nodes versus Energy Consumption for Routing in the network in case of Ad-hoc On-demand Distance Vector Routing Protocol. In AODV, Energy Consumption for Routing in the Static categories is less as compared to the Semi-Dynamic categories and Dynamic categories. Similarly, Energy Consumption for Routing in the Semi-Dynamic categories is less as compared to the Dynamic categories. Energy Consumption for Routing is lesser in case of AODV as compared to DSDV.

Figure 16 displays Number of Nodes versus Energy Consumption for Data Transmission in the network in case of Ad-hoc On-demand Distance Vector Routing Protocol. In AODV, Energy Consumption for Data Transmission in the Static categories is less as compared to the Semi-Dynamic categories and Dynamic categories. Similarly, Energy Consumption for Data Transmission in the Semi-Dynamic

Fig. 15 Graph between Number of Nodes and Energy Consumption for Routing in joule in case of AODV

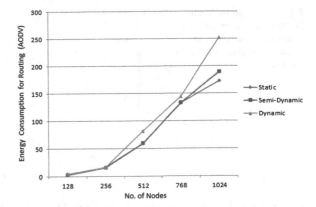

Fig. 16 Graph between Number of Nodes and Energy Consumption for Data Transmission in joule in case of AODV

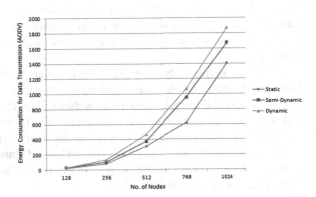

Fig. 17 Graph between Number of Nodes and Energy Consumption for Key Generation in joule in case of AODV

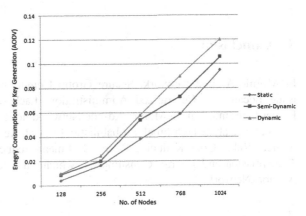

categories is less as compared to the Dynamic categories. Energy consumption for Data Transmission is lesser in case of AODV as compared to DSDV.

Figure 17 displays Number of Nodes versus Energy Consumption for Key Generation in the network in case of Ad-hoc On-demand Distance Vector Routing Protocol. In AODV, Energy Consumption for Key Generation in the Static

Fig. 18 Graph between Number of Nodes and Total Energy Consumption in Network in joule in case of AODV

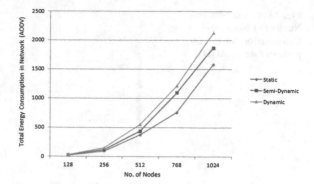

categories is less as compared to the Semi-Dynamic categories and Dynamic categories. Similarly, Energy Consumption for Key Generation in the Semi-Dynamic categories is less as compared to the Dynamic categories. Here, it is observed that if number of Rekeys increase, the Energy Consumption for Key Generation also increases.

Figure 18 displays Number of Nodes versus Total Energy Consumption in Network in case of Ad-hoc On-demand Distance Vector Routing Protocol. In AODV, Total Energy Consumption in Network in the Static categories is less as compared to the Semi-Dynamic categories and Dynamic categories. Similarly, Total Energy Consumption in Network in the Semi-Dynamic categories is less as compared to the Dynamic categories. Total Energy Consumption in Network is sum of Energy Consumption for Key Generation, Energy Consumption for Routing and Energy Consumption for Data Transmission.

8 Conclusion

In Mobile Ad-hoc Network, Secure Group Communication is the most focused issue because of Centralized Administration, Lack of Fixed Infrastructure and Power Consumption. In Mobile Ad-hoc Network, node has limited power resource. We have analyzed Optimal Probabilistic Logical Key Hierarchy schema which reduces Rekey Cost. Reducing Rekey Cost means reducing the cost of Energy Data Transmission and Energy Consumption which leads to long existence of Mobile Ad-hoc Network.

References

1. Wallner, D., Harder, E., & Agee, R. (1999). Key management for Multicast: Issues and Architectures. *IETF RFC* 2627.
2. Lee, F. *Routing in Mobile Ad-hoc Networks*.

3. Perkins, C. E., & Bhagwat, P. DSDV Routing Over a Multi hop Wireless Network of Mobile Computers. Technical Report, IBM *Research and University of Maryland*, USA.
4. Perkins, C. E., & Royer, E. M. (2000). The Ad-hoc On-demand Distance Vector Protocol. In C. E. Perkins (Ed.), *Ad-hoc Networking* (pp. 173–219). Addison-Wesley.
5. Perkins, C. E., Belding-Royer, E. M., & Das, S. (July 2003). Ad-hoc On-Demand Distance Vector (AODV) Routing. *RFC* 3561.
6. Bai, F., & Helmy, A. *A Survey of Mobility Models in Wireless Ad-hoc Networks*.
7. Potlapally, N. R., Ravi, S., Raghunathan, A., & Jha, N. K. Analyzing the Energy Consumption of Security Protocols. *Proceedings of the ISLPED'03*, ACM 1-58113-682-X/03/0008.
8. Capkun, S., Buttyan, L., & Hubaux, J.-P. (2003). Self-organized Public-key Management for Mobile Ad-hoc Networks. *IEEE Transactios on Mobile Computing*, 2(1).
9. Hegland, A. M., et al. (2006). Survey of Key Management in Ad-hoc Networks. *Proceedings of the IEEE Communications Surveys*.
10. Li, J., Cui, G., Fu, X., Liu, Z., & Su, L. (2005). *A Secure Group Key Management Scheme in Mobile Ad-hoc Networks*. IEEE Computer Society Press.
11. Biswas, J., & Nandy, S. K. (2006). Efficient Key Management and Distribution for MANET. *Proceedings of the ICC IEEE*.
12. Gomathi, K., & Parvathavarthini, B. (2010). An Efficient Cluster based Key Management Scheme for MANET with Authentication. *Trendz in Information Sciences & Computing (TISC), IEEE*.
13. Chatterjee, M., Das, S. K., & Turgut, D. (2000). An On-demand Weighted Clustering Algorithm (WCA) for Ad-hoc Networks. *Proceedings of IEEE Globecom'00*.
14. Pais, A. R., & Joshi, S. (2010). A New Probabilistic Rekeying Method for Secure Multicast Groups. *Proceedings of the International Journal of Information Security*, 9, 275–286.
15. Selcuk, A. A., & Sidhu, D. (2002). Probabilistic Optimization Techniques for Multicast Key Management. *Proceedings of the Elsevier Science*.
16. Sun, B., & Yu, B. *A Hierarchical Key Management Scheme for MANET*.
17. Wong, C. K., Gouda, M., & Lam, S. S. (2008). Secure Group Communications using Key Graphs. *Proceedings of the IEEE/ACM Transactions on Networking*, 8.

Re-Clustering Approach Using WCA in AODV and DSDV Routing Protocols in MANET

Harshit Prakash Patidar and Neetu Sharma

Abstract Many clustering patterns have been proposed for Mobile Ad-hoc Network. For better understanding and perfection in network system can be empowered by organized classification of clustering techniques. Growth of the overhead message in topology maintenance result of the movement of the network nodes in Mobile Ad-hoc Network. Protocols make an effort to keep the quantity of nodes in a cluster around a pre-defined threshold energy to expedite the optimal task of the Medium Access Control Protocol. The clusterhead selections are invoked on-demand and is targeted to decrease the computation and communication costs. A large variety of approaches like Weighted Clustering Algorithm in ad-hoc clustering have been established which focuses on different performance metrics. When executed, Weighted Cluster Algorithm takes care of the stability of the network and therefore, decreases the computation and communication costs linked with it. This paper represents a Re-clustering scheme in AODV and DSDV Routing Protocols in Mobile Ad-hoc Network. Re-clustering occurs because of changes in Key-Server. If Key-Server changes, the new Key-Server needs to generate and distribute the new keys to all the members in the group.

Keywords Mobile Ad-hoc Network · Clustering · Clusterhead · Key-Server

1 Introduction

Mobile Ad-hoc Network is a collection of mobile nodes which is automatic-configured and infrastructure less. These mobile nodes change their positions and topologies in the network without any centralized control. Every intermediate node works as an end node

H.P. Patidar (✉) · N. Sharma
Department of Computer Science, Government Engineering College, Ajmer, Rajasthan, India
e-mail: harshitprakash@gmail.com

N. Sharma
e-mail: neetucom10@gmail.com

© Springer Science+Business Media Singapore 2016   733
S.C. Satapathy et al. (eds.), *Proceedings of International Conference on ICT for Sustainable Development*, Advances in Intelligent Systems and Computing 409, DOI 10.1007/978-981-10-0135-2_70

and intermediate node which is responsible for sending packet and analyzing the network. An ad-hoc network is a group of mobile nodes without any infrastructure is previously defined. Mobile Ad-hoc Network is dynamic so the nodes can be used for some time in the network. In MANET, nodes move within the network or from one ad-hoc network to other ad-hoc network. In recent time, only two different types of wireless Mobile Ad-hoc Networks are used. The first one is called Base Station and second one is called Mobile Ad-hoc Network. The mobility model controls all dynamic locations. This mobile model uses specific parameters and checks the dynamic performances of various different routing protocols.

2   Overview of AODV and DSDV Routing Protocols

Routing Protocols are a set of topologies to broadcast the data from one source node to other destination node. Basically, three types of Routing Protocols are available— Proactive Routing Protocol, Reactive Routing Protocol and Hybrid Routing Protocol. A Proactive Routing Protocol is also known as the Table Driven Routing Protocol because all routes are pre allocated to send the data from source to destination. All values can be defined in the table so it is called Table Driven Routing Protocol. Proactive Routing Protocol contains the routing information of the entire working nodes. The main disadvantage of Proactive Routing Protocol is heavy weight generated by the network with the control messages. Reactive Routing Protocol is also known as Dynamic Routing Protocol because all paths are dynamically generated when need to send the data from source to destination. In Reactive Routing Protocol, complexity is more as compared to Proactive Routing Protocol due to the dynamic path but packet transmission time is very low. A Hybrid Routing Protocol is a combination of Proactive Routing Protocol and Reactive Routing Protocol.

Ad hoc On-demand Distance Vector (AODV)-

AODV is Ad-hoc On-demand Distance Vector Routing Protocol. It is a reactive routing protocol because paths are defined only when required. AODV does not preserve path and uses Destination Sequence Numbers (DNS) for each route entry [1].

AODV uses various different message type Route Request (RREQ), Route Error (RERR) and Route Response (RREP) to find path from source to destination by using UDP (User Datagram Protocol) packet (Fig. 1).

Destination-Sequenced Distance Vector (DSDV)-

DSDV routing is a Proactive Routing Protocol where all connection paths are already maintained in the table. It was invented by C. Perkins and P. Bhagwat in 1994. The main role of the algorithm is to explain routing loops problem. All the informations in the routing table maintaining a sequence numbers are generally even if a link is available otherwise odd sequencing will be used. The updation in the ad-hoc network is that routing loops are ignored. Each network node holds its own routing table. To reduce the cost of network traffic, table updates are sent as

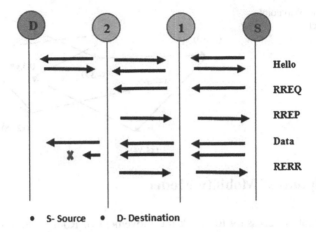

S- Source   •   D- Destination

Fig. 1 AODV Protocol Messaging Processor

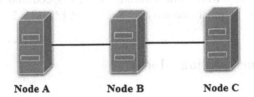

Node A   Node B   Node C

Fig. 2 Network of Three Nodes

smaller incremental updates during periods of low mobility. Destination Sequenced Distance Vector Routing Protocol is established on Bellman Ford Algorithm. In these protocols, paths to all destinations are available for each node at all times. The table is exchanged between neighbours at fixed regular intervals to keep up-to-date view of the network. Neighbour nodes are used missing transmission to detect broken links in the network. The main disadvantage of DSDV is that, it needs a regular update of its routing tables which uses the battery power and a small bandwidth of network even if the network is idle. Examples of Distance-Vector Routing Protocols include RIPv1, RIPv2 and IGRP [2] (Fig. 2).

The description of routing table of Node A is shown in Table 1:

Generally, the table holds a description of all possible routes accessible by node A along with the next hop, number of hops, sequence number and install time.

Table 1 Routing Table of Node A

Destination	Next Hop	Number of Hops	Sequence Number	Install Time
A	A	0	A46	001000
B	B	1	B36	001200
C	B	2	C28	001500

Fig. 3 Random Waypoint
Mobility Model

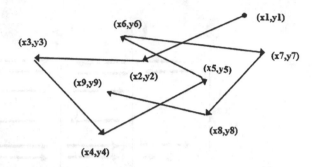

3 Description of Mobility Model

Mobility model is necessary to check the movement of Routing Protocols. In this paper, we have used Random Waypoint Mobility Model. The Random Waypoint Mobility Model is the standard mobility model. In this mobility model, all mobile nodes move randomly with some random velocity speed and changes direction randomly. It is very popular and easy to implement [3] (Fig. 3).

4 Energy Consumption Model

We have calculated the Energy Consumption for Key Generation proposed by Potlapally Nachiketch (Nachiketh R. et al. 2003) and for Data Transmission and receiving as proposed by Dongkyun Kim (Dongkyun Kim. et al. 2002) [4].

The Energy Consumption is needed to transmit a packet p then the energy $E(p) = i * v * t_p$ Joule where i is fresh value, v is the voltage and t_p is the time occupied to transmit the packet p. Energy Consumption for the key setup phase using AES of 128-bit key is 7.83 uJ/key. We use simulated symmetric key of AES (Advanced Encryption Standard) of 128-bit length.

5 Our Approach

Three experiments discussed above are used to optimized selection of clusterheads as each deals with one subset of parameters that imposes limitations on the system. Due to resource constraints, clusterhead might not handle the nodes even if the adjacent nodes are well within the transmission range. Therefore, an upper bound is enforced due to the load handling capacity of clusterhead. In simple terms, covering the area including least number of clusterhead will impose more pressure on clusterheads, but at the same instance, more clusterheads imply a costlier system. This might eventually lead to better throughput but it will also lead to high latency as the data packets need to go through multiple hops. Thus, it is still a problem to choose an optimal number of clusterheads as increasing those leads to high throughput but also result into high latency which is not desired. Thus, we suggest to use combined weighted metric which takes into consideration various parameters like ideal node degree, mobility, transmission power and battery power of the nodes [5].

We should have a fully dispersed system where all nodes share same accountability and act as clusterheads. However, more number of clusterheads means more number of hops from source to destination as the packet needs to go through larger number of clusterheads. This results into more power consumption, higher latency and more information processing per node. For maximize resource utilization, we need to have minimum number of clusterheads that shelters the entire geographical area over which the nodes are dispersed. The complete area can be divided into two zones, the size of which can be defined by nodes transmission range [6, 7].

Basis for Our Algorithm

To choose how appropriate a node is to be a clusterhead, we take its battery power, mobility, degree and transmission power as constraints.

The following features are considered in our Weighted Clustering Algorithm (WCA) as given below-

- The procedure of clusterhead election is not periodic and needs to be invoked as minimum as possible. It leads to reduction in system updates which results into optimized computation & communication cost.
- To guarantee efficient MAC functioning, each clusterhead can ideally back pre-defined threshold nodes. By optimizing the number of nodes in each cluster, we can achieve a high throughput of the system.
- If one normal node moves out of a cluster and join other prevailing cluster, it will result into Re-affiliation.
- A better communication is possible with clusterhead if the nodes are neighbours and within the transmission range. This is because of the signal weakening with increasing distance [8].

Clusterhead Selection Technique

Step 1: Find the acquaintances of every node v (i.e. nodes within its broadcast range). The degree is, d_v, of the v node. H is the number of nodes, a clusterhead can handle.

Step 2: Calculate the degree-difference, $D_v = |d_v - H|$, for every node v.

Step 3: For every node, calculate the sum of the distances, Sv, with all its acquaintances.

Step 4: Calculate the running average of the speed for every node v. This provides the mobility of the node v and is denoted by M_v

Step 5: Calculate the consumed battery power, T_v. Assuming that battery power utilization is more for a clusterhead in comparison of an ordinary node v.

Step 6: Calculate a combined weight $I_v = c_1 * D_v + c_2 * S_v + c_3 * M_v + c_4 * T_v$, for each node v. The coefficients c_1, c_2, c_3 and c_4 are the weighting factors for the corresponding system parameters.

Step 7: Calculate the average Weights of all nodes, *AI*, and also compute the average Rekey Probabilities of all nodes, *ARP*.

Step 8: Now check for each node *v*,

   If (weight $I_v < AI$ and corresponding Rekey Probability, $RP_v < ARP$)

   Then Calculate the new weight $NI_v = I_v * 0.001 + RP_v$.

Step 9: Select the node with minimum NI_v to be the clusterhead.

6 Simulation Result and Analysis

We have simulated Re-clustering in Mobile Ad-hoc Network. Simulation is implemented in C++ language. We have performed experiments on groups of 128, 256, 512, 768 and 1024 nodes.

For each experiment, we have created the joining/leaving of nodes randomly. In addition, some members may leave because of power exhaustion and some members may join/leave based on connection failure or availability. For each join/leave operation, we have recorded the numbers of Rekeys generated, Energy Consumption for Key Generation and Energy Consumption at Key-Server.

In Re-clustering approach, we have categorized three categories namely Static, Semi-Dynamic and Dynamic based on number of leaves and Rekey Probabilities. But in MANET, we added some extra parameters to classify these categories. The additional parameters are pause time, node mobility and updating interval time. The additional parameters are listed below in Table 2. In simulation, for every updating interval time, we have updated the node positions and routing tables.

Simulation Results

In our section, we present the Rekey Cost and Energy Consumption values for 0–5 times Re-clustering in Static, Semi-Dynamic and Dynamic categories. If the number of Re-Clustering increases, the Rekey Cost and other Energy Consumptions also increases for each group size of 128, 256, 512, 768 and 1024 nodes.

Table 2 Simulation parameters

Simulation Parameters	Static	Semi-dynamic	Dynamic
Mobility	0–5 m/s	0–10 m/s	0–20 m/s
Packet Size	256 bytes	256 bytes	256 bytes
Mobility Model	Random Waypoint	Random Waypoint	Random Waypoint
Pause Time	0–10 s	0–5 s	0 s
Updating Interval Time	10 s	5 s	1 s
No. of Leaves	¼ of Group Size	½ of Group Size	¾ of Group Size
Area (in sq. m)	800 × 800	800 × 800	800 × 800
Energy	0–1000 J	0–1000 J	0–1000 J

Figure 4 displays Rekey Cost in the network in case of Static category for 0–5 times Re-clustering in Ad-hoc On-demand Distance Vector Routing Protocol. Rekey Cost in the Static category is less as compared to the Semi-Dynamic category and Dynamic category. Here, it is observed that if the number of Re-clustering increases, the Rekey Cost also increases.

Figure 5 displays Rekey Cost in the network in case of Semi-Dynamic category for 0–5 times Re-clustering in Ad-hoc On-demand Distance Vector Routing Protocol. Rekey Cost in the Semi-Dynamic category is less as compared to the Dynamic category. Here, it is observed that if the number of Re-clustering increases, the Rekey Cost also increases.

Figure 6 displays Rekey Cost in the network in case of Dynamic category for 0–5 times Re-clustering in Ad-hoc On-demand Distance Vector Routing Protocol. Rekey Cost in the Dynamic category is more as compared to the Static category and Semi-Dynamic category. Here, it is observed that if the number of Re-clustering increases, the Rekey Cost also increases.

Figure 7 displays Energy Consumption at Server in the network in case of Static category for 0–5 times Re-clustering in Ad-hoc On-demand Distance Vector Routing Protocol. Energy Consumption at Server in the Static category is less as compared to the Semi-Dynamic category and Dynamic category.

Figure 8 displays Energy Consumption at Server in the network in case of Semi-Dynamic category for 0–5 times Re-clustering in Ad-hoc On-demand Distance Vector Routing Protocol. Energy Consumption at Server in the Semi-Dynamic category is less as compared to the Dynamic category.

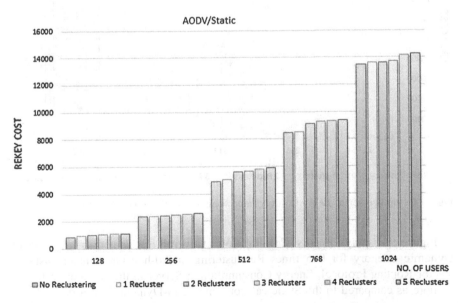

Fig. 4 Group size versus Rekey Cost (static scenario) for 0–5 times Re-clustering

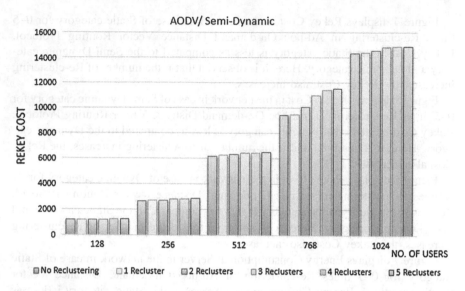

Fig. 5 Group size versus Rekey Cost (semi-dynamic scenario) for 0–5 times Re-clustering

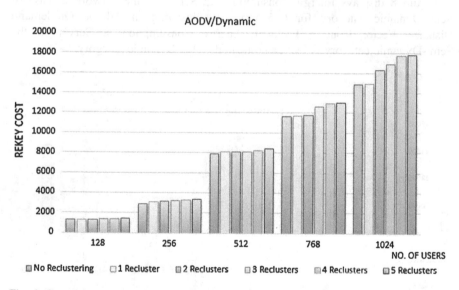

Fig. 6 Group size versus Rekey Cost (dynamic scenario) for 0–5 times Re-clustering

Figure 9 displays Energy Consumption at Server in the network in case of Dynamic category for 0–5 times Re-clustering in Ad-hoc On-demand Distance Vector Routing Protocol. Energy Consumption at Server in the Dynamic category is more as compared to the Static category and Semi-Dynamic category.

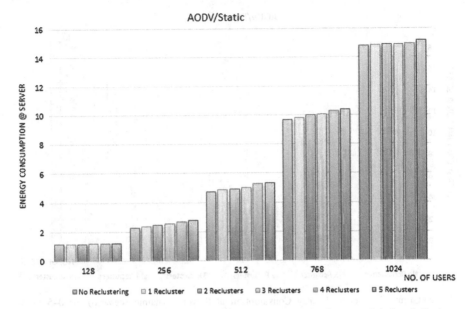

Fig. 7 Group size versus Energy Consumption at Server (static scenario) for 0–5 times Re-clustering

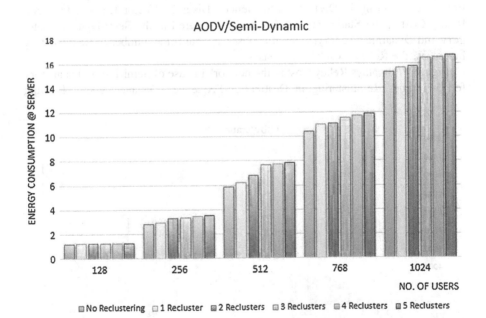

Fig. 8 Group size versus Energy Consumption at Server (semi-dynamic scenario) for 0–5 times Re-clustering

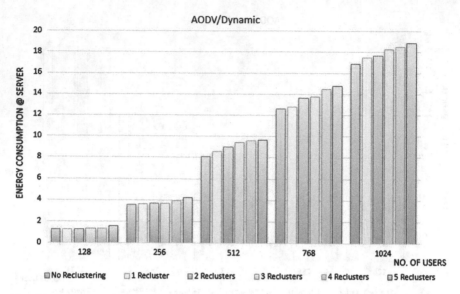

Fig. 9 Group size versus Energy Consumption at Server (dynamic scenario) for 0–5 times Re-clustering

Figure 10 displays Rekey Cost in the network in case of Static category for 0–5 times Re-clustering in Destination-Sequenced Distance Vector Routing Protocol. Rekey Cost in the Static category is less as compared to the Semi-Dynamic category and Dynamic category. Here, it is observed that if the number of Re-clustering increases, the Rekey Cost also increases.

Figure 11 displays Rekey Cost in the network in case of Semi-Dynamic category for 0–5 times Re-clustering in Destination-Sequenced Distance Vector Routing

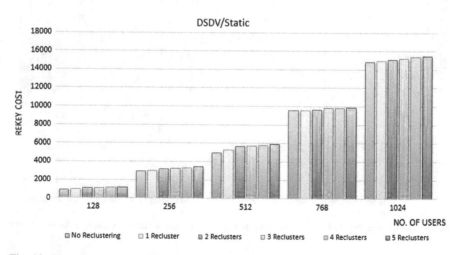

Fig. 10 Group size versus Rekey Cost (static scenario) for 0–5 times Re-clustering

Protocol. Rekey Cost in the Semi-Dynamic category is less as compared to the Dynamic category. Here, it is observed that if the number of Re-clustering increases, the Rekey Cost also increases.

Figure 12 displays Rekey Cost in the network in case of Dynamic category for 0–5 times Re-clustering in Destination-Sequenced Distance Vector Routing Protocol. Rekey Cost in the Dynamic category is more as compared to the Static category and Semi-Dynamic category. Here, it is observed that if the number of Re-clustering increases, the Rekey Cost also increases.

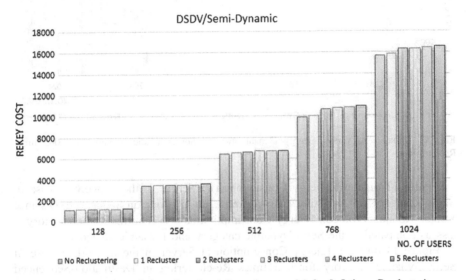

Fig. 11 Group size versus Rekey Cost (semi-dynamic scenario) for 0–5 times Re-clustering

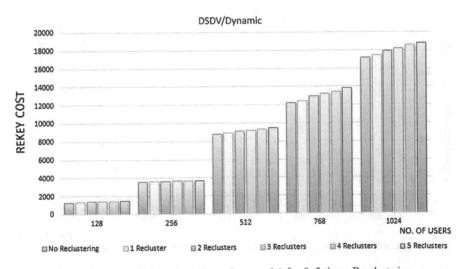

Fig. 12 Group size versus Rekey Cost (dynamic scenario) for 0–5 times Re-clustering

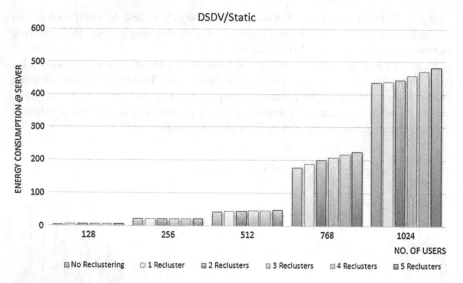

Fig. 13 Group size versus Energy Consumption at Server (static scenario) for 0–5 times Re-clustering

Figure 13 displays Energy Consumption at Server in the network in case of Static category for 0–5 times Re-clustering in Destination-Sequenced Distance Vector Routing Protocol. Energy Consumption at Server in the Static category is less as compared to the Semi-Dynamic category and Dynamic category.

Figure 14 displays Energy Consumption at Server in the network in case of Semi-Dynamic category for 0–5 times Re-clustering in Destination-Sequenced

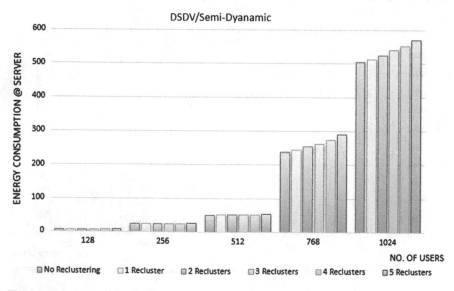

Fig. 14 Group size versus Energy Consumption at Server (semi-dynamic scenario) for 0–5 times Re-clustering

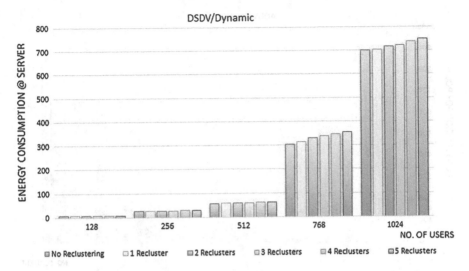

Fig. 15 Group size versus Energy Consumption at Server (dynamic scenario) for 0–5 times Re-clustering

Distance Vector Routing Protocol. Energy Consumption at Server in the Semi-Dynamic category is less as compared to the Dynamic category.

Figure 15 displays Energy Consumption at Server in the network in case of Dynamic category for 0–5 times Re-clustering in Destination-Sequenced Distance Vector Routing Protocol. Energy Consumption at Server in the Dynamic category is more as compared to the Static category and Semi-Dynamic category.

Figure 16 displays Energy Consumption for Routing in the network in case of Static category for 0–5 times Re-clustering in Ad-hoc On-demand Distance Vector Routing Protocol. Energy Consumption for Routing in the Static category is less as compared to the Semi-Dynamic category and Dynamic category.

Figure 17 displays Energy Consumption for Routing in the network in case of Semi-Dynamic category for 0–5 times Re-clustering in Ad-hoc On-demand Distance Vector Routing Protocol. Energy Consumption for Routing in the Semi-Dynamic category is less as compared to the Dynamic category.

Figure 18 displays Energy consumption for Routing in the network in case of Dynamic category for 0–5 times Re-clustering in Ad-hoc On-demand Distance Vector Routing Protocol. Energy Consumption for Routing in the Dynamic category is more as compared to the Static category and Semi-Dynamic category.

Figure 19 displays Energy Consumption for Routing in the network in case of Static category for 0–5 times Re-clustering in Destination-Sequenced Distance Vector Routing Protocol. Energy Consumption for Routing in the Static category is less as compared to the Semi-Dynamic category and Dynamic category.

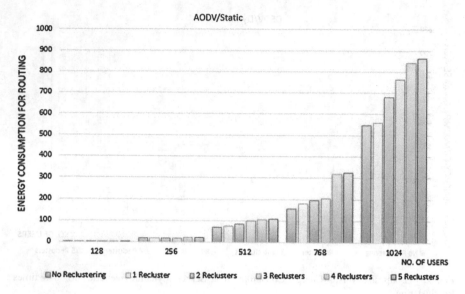

Fig. 16 Group size versus Energy Consumption for Routing (static scenario) for 0–5 times Re-clustering

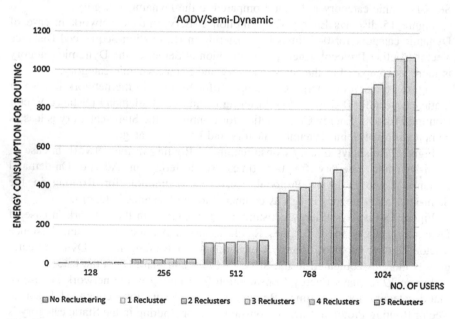

Fig. 17 Group size versus Energy Consumption for Routing (semi-dynamic scenario) for 0–5 times Re-clustering

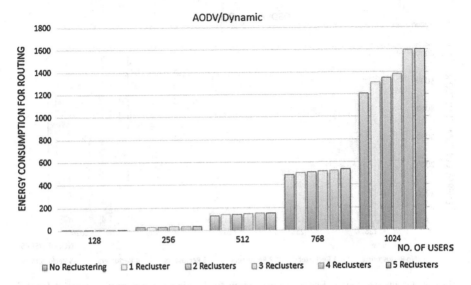

Fig. 18 Group size versus Energy Consumption for Routing (dynamic scenario) for 0–5 times Re-clustering

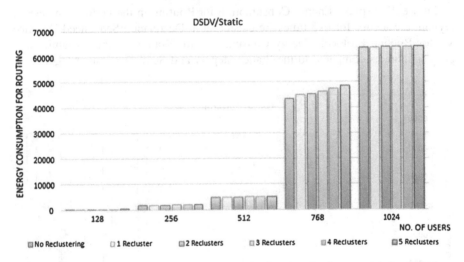

Fig. 19 Group size versus Energy Consumption for Routing (static scenario) for 0–5 times Re-clustering

Figure 20 displays Energy Consumption for Routing in the network in case of Semi-Dynamic category for 0–5 times Re-clustering in Destination-Sequenced Distance Vector Routing Protocol. Energy Consumption for Routing in the Semi-Dynamic category is less as compared to the Dynamic category.

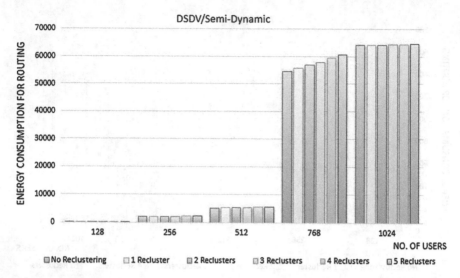

Fig. 20 Group size versus Energy Consumption for Routing (semi-dynamic scenario) for 0–5 times Re-clustering

Figure 21 displays Energy Consumption for Routing in the network in case of Dynamic category for 0–5 times Re-clustering in Destination-Sequenced Distance Vector Routing Protocol. Energy Consumption for Routing in the Dynamic category is more as compared to the Static category and Semi-Dynamic category.

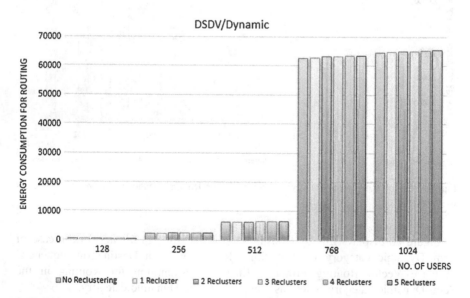

Fig. 21 Group size versus Energy Consumption for Routing (dynamic scenario) for 0–5 times Re-clustering

7 Conclusion

On-demand Weighted Clustering Algorithm is recommended because it is dynamically adapted by itself with the ever changing topology of ad-hoc network. The flexibility of handover of Weight Cluster Algorithm is differently weighted and taken into account of joined effect of the ideal battery power, mobility, degree and transmission power of nodes. The algorithm is performed only when there is a need i.e., when a node is no longer capable to attach itself to the working clusterhead. Re-clustering occurs because of change in Key-Server. If Key-Server changes, the new Key-Server needs to generate and distribute the new keys to all the members in the group. We present the Rekey Cost and Energy Consumption values for 0–5 times Re-clustering in Static, Semi-Dynamic and Dynamic scenarios, such that as the number of Re-clustering increases, the Rekey Cost and other Energy Consumptions also increases.

References

1. Perkins, C. E., Belding-Royer, E. M., & Das. S. (July 2003). Ad-hoc On-demand Distance Vector (AODV) Routing. *RFC* 3561.
2. Perkins, C. E., & Bhagwat, P. DSDV Routing Over a Multi-hop Wireless Network of Mobile Computers. *Technical Report, IBM Research and University of Maryland, USA.*
3. Bai, F., & Helmy, A. *A Survey of Mobility Models in Wireless Ad-Hoc Networks.*
4. Potlapally, N. R., Ravi, S., Raghunathan, A., & Jha, N. K. Analyzing the Energy Consumption of Security Protocols. *Proceedings of the ISLPED'03, ACM* 1-58113-682-X/03/0008.
5. Gomathi, K., & Parvathavarthini, B. (2010). An Efficient Cluster based Key Management Scheme for MANET with Authentication. *Trendz in Information Sciences & Computing (TISC), IEEE.*
6. Chatterjee, M., Das, S. K., Turgut, D. (2000). An On-demand Weighted Clustering Algorithm (WCA) for ad-hoc networks. *Proceedings of IEEE Globecom'00.*
7. Basagni, S. (June 1999). Distributed Clustering for Ad-hoc Networks. *International Symposium on Parallel Architectures, Algorithms and Networks, Perth* (pp. 310–315).
8. Chatterjee, M., Das, S. K., & Turgut, D. (2010). An On-demand Weighted Clustering Algorithm (WCA) for Ad-Hoc Networks, *IEEE.*

Issues and Challenges of Heterogeneous Datasets in MapReduce Framework of Big Data Environment

Saraswati Gupta, Vishal Bhatnagar and Ramneet Singh Chadha

Abstract In today's world, peta byte and more data is generated at very rapid pace. The collection of huge amount of data leads to problem of storage, finding of valuable information, etc. In today's scenario, term Big Data had emerged as a key technology to handle the problem of data processing. It is a collection of very huge amount of datasets which cannot be handled by the traditional data processing application. MapReduce is gaining popularity due to their excellent problem-solving capabilities in big data environment. MapReduce is a programming model for Hadoop type framework for manages big data. This paper provides brief introduction about MapReduce algorithm for solving the problem of MapReduce. At last, authors explained different issues and challenges of heterogeneous datasets in MapReduce framework.

Keywords Big data · MapReduce · Heterogeneous data sets · Hadoop · Distributed computing

1 Introduction

Big data is a term for collection of huge amount of datasets which is so large and huge and that which cannot be processed by traditional applications and on hand data analysis tools be it for structured or unstructured datasets. Big data analytics is used for processing and analyzing the large datasets collected over a span of time. It helps in uncovering hidden and valuable information from petabyte of data sets.

S. Gupta (✉) · R.S. Chadha
CDAC Noida, IP University, Delhi, India
e-mail: saraswatigupta89@gmail.com

R.S. Chadha
e-mail: rschadha@cdac.in

V. Bhatnagar
AIACT&R, IP University, Delhi, India
e-mail: vishalbhatnagar@yahoo.com

© Springer Science+Business Media Singapore 2016
S.C. Satapathy et al. (eds.), *Proceedings of International Conference on ICT for Sustainable Development*, Advances in Intelligent Systems and Computing 409, DOI 10.1007/978-981-10-0135-2_71

It is the technique which uncovers the hidden information and values from the datasets which are too complex and highly unstructured in nature. Big data analytics discloses dependencies, relationships, and behavior of the datasets which helps the organizations and entrepreneurs to take crucial strategic decisions with ease. For reliable and authentic information, data needs to be processed in real time which should be consistent in performance and which will enhance the productivity of the organization. The generation of huge volume of data in every field like telecommunication, banking, and financial had results the widespread usage of big data analytics in various sectors like business, government sector, bioinformatics, retail sector, and internet [1].

Big data has five dimensions over which the work and effectiveness of the big data rely. They are namely, velocity, variety, veracity, variability and volume. Veracity means to tackle different type of datasets. Velocity means at what frequency the data is generated from the internet. Volume means how the data is like terabyte or zettabytes of data. Variety means what verity of data coming from internet like video, audio, text, etc. Variability refers to unpredictability which can show in the data and hold data well.

Over the past year, digital content over the internet is increasing day-by-day and now it reach to petabytes and zettabytes of data. Therefore, any new technique which allows searching in huge files whether structured or unstructured is of tremendous interest. The growth of data is increasing day-by-day; for doing this task efficiently at low cost, we require a platform which is called as Hadoop. Hadoop is an open-source framework to handle large datasets for distributed computing in big data environment. Hadoop framework is implemented on Java. Hadoop makes it possible for running applications on systems with many nodes which involve the zettabytes of data. It facilitates the transfer of data to the nodes without interrupt even at the time of failure [2].

MapReduce is a programming model introduced by Google in 2004. It is used for programming and processing information in distributed environment of big data. MapReduce is gaining popularity as it is used for processing the large datasets with parallel computing. MapReduce provide greater scalability, fault tolerance, locality, task granularity, and batch processing which are needed in case of Big data analytics as: MapReduce for implementing big data problem like searching, capture, storage, sharing, transfer, and analysis. By mapper and reducer, it can easily be search and capture by user. For storage problem in previous tools, Hadoop distributed file system is capable for storing more than terabytes of data which was not possible in traditional systems. MapReduce has some problems like compound records, joins, sorting, and heterogeneous datasets [3].

This paper has been classified into different sections. Section 2 will elucidate the related research and motivation which prompted the authors to work on the said field. Section 3 explains the Hadoop framework which is the key in the principle understanding of the Big Data setup. Section 4 discusses issues and challenges of heterogeneous datasets. Section 5 describes the implication of the work carried by the authors in this study. In Sect. 6, we conclude by mentioning big data and its emerging technologies extensive potential for further research.

2   Related Research and Motivation

Big data is all about the large data sets which are too complex and require high-end processing for which the most significant model available is MapReduce model. MapReduce model approaches is used to solve the big data challenges and issues in better way in timely manner.

The MapReduce programming model has been used by Google for many purposes. Dean and Ghemawat [4], proposed the MapReduce which runs on large cluster and better than traditional system.

In Fig. 1, the user program by mapper splits the input files in M pieces of 64 MB per piece. One of the copies is special called master and other is workers, where workers are assigned work by the master. Input files are divided into the m pieces that are from 16 to 64 MB. These splitted input files goes to the worker and are written to the intermediate files called buffered pair. After local write, it removes the read component and goes to the reducer phase which reads all the intermediate data and writes to output files.

In this paper, authors argued for three parts namely: First, MapReduce model easy to use. Second, a huge variety of problems can easily be solved in MapReduce. Third, they have developed the implementation for large clusters.

In paper Yang et al. [5], they introduced a new algorithm for heterogeneous datasets as MapReduce merge.

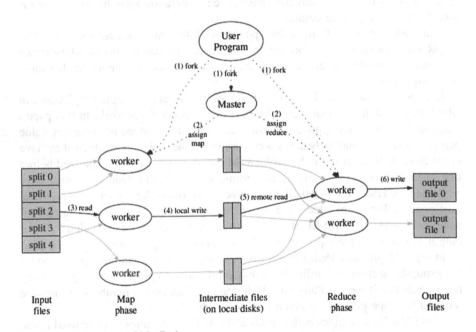

Fig. 1 Execution plan of MapReduce

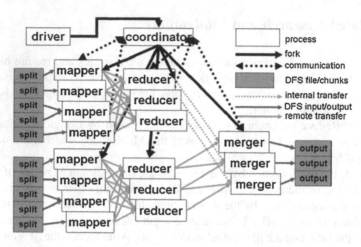

Fig. 2 MapReduce–merge framework

In Fig. 2, the coordinator manages the mapper and reducer. The mapper takes the input and further the reducers give the output in results. The merger then aggregates results and send it to the output file.

In the paper MapReduce–merge, the merge phase makes it more efficient. It process heterogeneous datasets. Mapper reads from GFS and reducer work on local or output sends to GFS. In this they have given an iteration logic for joins which is used for processing large datasets.

MapReduce programs are of two phase, workflow map and reduce. After this MapReduce–merge creates workflow combinations that can fit into the MapReduce framework. It enables many data processing patterns and it support parallel database functionality.

In paper Ferrera and de Pardo [3], they have introduced the tuple MapReduce in which they explained about the problem of MapReduce framework. In this paper, Pangool framework for application which can take tuple instead of using key value pair was discussed and its benefits were shown by the author's in which they have given the algorithm to solve the problem MapReduce which was not solved before like compound records, sorting, and joins. Pedro Ferrera Ivan de Pardo have explained the Hadoop projects like pig, hive which offers the higher level tool data manipulation but MapReduce is a low level tool. To process the data instead of using key value pair, tuple MapReduce takes a tuple as input not key value so as for output also it emits the input tuple and give tuple as output not as key value pair.

In tuple MapReduce Pedro Ferrera Ivan de Pardo have given three pseudocodes for group-by sorting and rollupfrom and proposed rollup API in Pangool. They have given that if we use Pangool API instead of Hadoop the numbers of lines are reduced by some percentage given in below Table 1.

Tuple MapReduce gives better result and it reduces the lines of code used in the Pangool framework as compare to Hadoop framework.

Table 1 3 LOC reduced between Pangool and Hadoop

	Hadoop codes lines	Pangool code lines	% of reduction
Secondary sort	256	139	45.7
URL resolution(join)	323	158	51

In paper Ferrera and de Pardo [6], they extended the Pangool API for bridging the gap between MapReduce and tuple MapReduce. In this paper, the authors had given more algorithms and explain the splout and Pangool API. In this paper, they have given more pseudocode for joins and page rank algorithm. They have given the details of Pangool and splout sql distributed database. Without modifying the key system of MapReduce, tuple MapReduce easily used for batch oriented application and we can use direct joins, sorting.

3 Hadoop: An Introduction

This section gives brief introduction about Hadoop which is an open-source framework for processing large dataset on clusters.

3.1 HDFS (Hadoop Distributed File System)

HDFS is made for holding large datasets and allow access to data simultaneously to many clients on distributed network. There are many traditional applications which solve the datasets but when we talk about the bulky dataset we require HDFS. HDFS is designed for information like terabytes to zettabytes of data. It spreads over the large number of cluster. HDFS stores any format of datasets. HDFS is integrated with the Hadoop MapReduce, which allow data to be read and compute on locally when require. In HDFS architecture, the name node which is the brain of the HDFS which maintains metadata information about files and many data node are there which is used to store the actual data. It divides the files into blocks. Each block in HDFS is replicated many times.

3.2 MapReduce Model

This section gives brief introduction about MapReduce. MapReduce paradigm is used in distributive environments. It is typically deployed on large clusters of computers for parallel processing of data. There are three stages of this paradigm: map, shuffle, and reduce.

3.2.1 MapReduce

MapReduce is programmable framework for polling data in Parallel. It is given by Google in 2004 for search engine-related processing of data. MapReduce is capable of handling homogenous datasets. MapReduce is used homogenous datasets but for heterogeneous datasets is not capable because it require memory. Heterogeneous datasets does not fit into MapReduce framework. It can be done using by more steps of MapReduce but it is takes more time and extra steps to process those datasets.

3.2.2 MapReduce Function

MapReduce work on key value pair. A MapReduce program includes two functions one is map and other is reduce value. Map function used to integrate the result and reducer is used to combine the result which came from mapper.

In MapReduce key value pair written by user has associated type [4]:

Map (K1, V1) → list (K2, V2)
Reduce (K2, (V2)) → list (K3, V3)

The input comes as file, etc., now input goes to map function then it will take input as key value pair and output of the one phase is the input of the other phase. After map function list the key value pair and goes to shuffle and sort phase then to the reducer phase and lists the key value pair (K3, V3) and gives the output to reducer task, the reducer then aggregate the result after the shuffle phase.

4 Issues and Challenges of Heterogeneous Datasets

Despite all the advantages of MapReduce in big data environment, there are certain issues and challenges pertaining to heterogeneous datasets.

They are as follows:

- **Compound Records**—Compound records are collection of data type. Data are not made up of single field. It is a collection of many fields. In MapReduce, the fields are the combinations of key and value pair. For processing many field records, we require compound records. To overcome this problem in MapReduce, custom data types are used. They are the data types which are in structured form which are easy for quick and easy processing. Also once the data are processed, they can be distributed quickly across the users. They are data type which is the sequence of data type like cust_name, cust_id, cust_email. They define the contiguous sequence of bytes which are easily accessible and require less time. Compound records can have any number of records, in any format, and any order. Each record of the compound data must have a unique name which is used as key for uniquely identifying the records. By this, we can group the variables and treat this as key value pair in MapReduce framework. Custom data types run faster than other data types because predefined data types does not fulfill the requirement of user.

- **Data Storage**—In big data, the main problem is storage of huge amount of data which are normally flooded through the Internet. This type of data has many problems like they are bulky and also highly unstructured. This creates a problem of opting for large clusters which are too many in number and machines to tackle large amount of data coming from different sources. We require disk space for storing the data. This also demands the highly sophisticated usage of the distributed environment.
- **Resource Management**—In today's modern day scenario, most of the applications are highly real time which demands the processing and the analytical results in real time without wasting too much of time. MapReduce is not capable for quickly solving the real-time applications like Amazon, retail sector, face book, and twitter data.
- **Security and Privacy**—Data sent on the network passes from many security concerns like authentication, access control, and privacy. The involvement of the distributed environment forces us to provide high security and privacy which is a matter of concern in present day scenario.
- **Joins**—In MapReduce when joining two heterogeneous datasets requires extra steps for processing dataset in MapReduce framework, because heterogeneous datasets does not fit into MapReduce memory as it requires extra disk space. Join are used for implementing a relational database in such cases. Using join algorithm, we can find the distinct value of the join attributes; it finds the set of row in each data which have that value.
- **Sorting**—In MapReduce there is no method available for sorting due to this we are unable to find out the data is arranged systematically in groups or not. To do so Pangool framework introduced, in which after grouping the datasets we can do sorting on the tuples. In MapReduce, the records are grouped with the key value pair but in which the sorting is not done by which the dataset are comes in order. This complexity is overcome by the Pangool framework. By sorting the records, we can easily find out the records from the large datasets. But in Pangool framework, it sorts the datasets in tuples not on key value pair.

There are more challenges like data storage for database and lack of sql like language support, scaling difficult algebra; lack of multiple data support, and privacy. Big data issues are auditing, security, and accountability (Table 2).

Table 2 Issues, problems and their solutions in tabular form

Name	Problem	Platform	Solution
Join	Extra space to fit in the MapReduce framework	Pangool solves the problem	We can use SQL type methods to solve the problem
Sort	No methods available for Sorting in MapReduce framework	Pangool solves the problem	Sorting methods need to be introduced in MapReduce to solve the problem
Resource management	MapReduce is not capable for real-time applications	YARN introduced to solve the resource management problem	Resource scheduling algorithm can be implemented
Security and privacy	Data pass through the network is not secured	Hadoop solves the problem	Security algorithms are needs to implemented to increase the security and privacy
Compound records	Only works on key value pair	Pangool solves the problem	SQL keywords to solve the problem

5 Implication of the Work

As data is spread over the multiple machines and data will be in different format like structured data, unstructured data, and semi-structured data, problem encountered is predominately of Heterogeneous data sets. The research toward finding the issues and challenges of heterogeneous datasets was carried to understand the difficulty and problems which are encountered during analysis of the heterogeneous data sets. The main research implications from the study are:

- The issues and challenges of heterogeneous datasets presented in the paper would help the researchers to work on the above said issues and challenges and work on the solutions for effective data analysis.
- Enormous amount of research is going on to overcome the problem of Heterogeneous datasets pertaining to sorting, join, compound records, etc.
- New software languages are used for better solutions to the above stated problems.
- It has also emerged from our study that the data set problem of heterogeneity is not confined to single area of application or domain but is widespread across all latest areas and the solution cannot be generalized to all the domains and area. This creates a problem to find a universal or general solution to the above stated problems.
- The study has led us to comprehend the importance of peta byte of data which is generated across the globe and that too heterogeneous in nature and which needs to be analyzed over different angle for effective future outcome.

6 Conclusions and Future Research

This papers reviewed about the MapReduce problem. MapReduce is capable of handling fault tolerance, scalability, and batch processing, but not solve the problem of heterogeneous datasets. MapReduce framework does not directly support joins because joining heterogeneous data does not fit in the MapReduce framework; for solving this issue, we can use join algorithm to solve the problem of MapReduce. Our efforts are going on to propose a scheme for MapReduce which aim to solve the problems of MapReduce. Our aim of humanizing and extending MapReduce to address challenges is presented in the paper. This paper provides an overview of the field facilitates for better planning for future research.

References

1. Jung, G., & Gnanasambandam, N. (2012). Synchronous parallel processing of big-data analytics services to optimize performance in federated clouds. In *2012 IEEE Fifth International Conference on Cloud Computing*. USA: Xerox Research Center Webster.
2. Liao, J. (2014). MRPrePost—A parallel algorithm adapted for mining big data. In *2014 IEEE Workshop on Electronics, Computer and Applications*. Computer Science and Engineering, South China, university of Technology Guangzhou, China.
3. Ferrera, P., & de Pardo, I. (2012). Tuple MapReduce: Beyond classic MapReduce. In *2012 IEEE 12th International Conference on Data Mining*.
4. Dean, J., & Ghemawat, S. (2004). *MapReduce: Simplified data processing on large clusters*. Google Inc.
5. Yang, H., Dasdan, A., Hsiao, R. -L., & Parker, D. S. (2007). Map-reduce-merge: Simplified relational data processing on large clusters. ACM.
6. Ferrera, P., & de Pardo, I. (2013). Tuple MapReduce and pangool: An associated implementation. London: Springer.

Strong Virtual Password Scheme Using Reference Switching on Coded User Parameters and Phishing Attack

Tank Himadri and Harsora Vinay

Abstract In today's technically advanced world, online services provided by commercial websites have become progressively popular. People have more convenience with online services like online shopping with credit card, mobile banking, or Internet banking. Prerequisite of user password is to provide strong security with some random salt and usage of additional special symbol. For this, multi-level security is needed because use of fake webpages to gain user-sensitive information is an easy task for phishers. In this paper, we propose a security mechanism for generating strong virtual password using reference switching on coded parameters involving zero human computing with differentiated virtual password. We also analyze our scheme against phishing attack.

Keywords Virtual password · Codebook and reference switching · Phishing attack

1 Introduction

In the present time, most of the people in the world keep their information online. Furthermore, people are facilitated by online apps in smart phones by commercial and financial organizations. For this reason the usage of online services is rapidly increasing. User password for authentication plays a critical role in using not only financial services but also other online services. There are many techniques to generate strong password with different encryption methods that offer sound level of protection and are hard to crack.

Another well-known issue is the use of static password that allows users to enter repeatedly the same password every time and it is a subject to be stolen once for the

T. Himadri (✉) · H. Vinay
RK University, Kasturbadham, Tramba, Rajkot, Gujarat, India
e-mail: himadritank@gmail.com

H. Vinay
e-mail: vinay.harsora@rku.ac.in

© Springer Science+Business Media Singapore 2016
S.C. Satapathy et al. (eds.), *Proceedings of International Conference on ICT for Sustainable Development*, Advances in Intelligent Systems and Computing 409, DOI 10.1007/978-981-10-0135-2_72

advantage of gaining access to the system; this is known as reply attack. One of the most popular attack nowadays known as phishing attack is a kind of social-engineering attack which allows user to log in some fake web page related with reputed organizations [1]. In contrast to phishing, shoulder surfing, malware and key-loggers referred to as "observer attack" [2] play an effective role in stealing password by any adversary.

Users are always advised by security experts to choose their passwords which have more number of characters, are hard to predict, and may have some random salt [3]. To overcome the password based on static, the scheme differentiated virtual password along with codebook and reference switching approach was proposed [4] by the concept of generating a user password each time differently when user logs into the system; this provides better security by using secret user defined function as encryption algorithm rather than conventional encryption algorithm. In the specified scheme, users are free to choose only one approach among different virtual password approaches to generate their virtual password.

1.1 Phishing Attack

Before defining any strong virtual password scheme we also stand our mind towards attacks of password cracking. Phishing attack is one of them which aimes to target users, not the system [5]. Phishers can acquire users' important information by instructing the users to enter their sensitive information in fraud messages which appear to be from trustworthy organization.

Phishers can have a large number of tools like botnets, phishing kits, and other malware components with them [6]. Phishing attack consists of two techniques including deceptive phishing which concerns with redirecting user to phishing websites by sending email containing the same message design as any financial institute. Another type is technical subterfuge scheme which contains a link with malicious code to get users online information [7].

Phishers are becoming increasingly successful in attacking by creating more number of phishing websites in 2011–2012 [8]. A number of techniques have already been developed to detect and prevent the fastest growing phishing attack including user awareness about fake pages, email spoofing, and instant messaging but still "how to deal with phishing" is one of the most popular areas of research.

1.2 Strong Virtual Password Scheme with Reference Switching on Coded Parameters

Strong user authentication requires dealing and protecting with users' sensitive information during online transactions. Our proposed strong virtual password scheme includes two approaches: codebook and reference switching [4] to generate virtual password including some special symbols to provide strong security. The scheme includes zero user computation burden.

The specified scheme allows the users to defend against some known attack like phishing, key logger, shoulder surfing, and malware by generating each time different input to log into the system. Among all attacks phishing attack is a social engineering technique that asks users financially sensitive information.

In this paper, we combine the idea of reference switching on coded user secret pin. In the first stage based on the random salt the codebook is generated.

2 Related Work

For passwords, security mechanism always includes multi-level authentication because a lot of fake elements are introduced from time to time and it may be challenging to detect and prevent them [9]. Well known encryption algorithms with conventional cipher are at the level of vulnerability [10]. People also suffer from junk mails and unwanted mails for marketing or online shopping purpose. One time password security (OTP) facilitates user for two-level authentication based on time synchronization technique but it can take some time to enter this password by users after getting it in their mobile [11].

Beginning with 1996, the effects of most phishing attacks have had impacts and are going on progressively increasing [8]. Mostly adversary attacks user with phishing techniques including "similar spoofing" by creating similar featured phishing web sites with identical URLs and using "instant spam messaging" in adversary may send the link associated with some important legitimate website [9].

Finite State Machine [12] is a fake website detection with majoring response values against user input, but it is limited only to some responsive input. By [13] using anti phishing tools to find appropriate valid website from fake websites using domain name server with URL-based deceiving methods. It is ideal to improve user identification about phishing websites but if a PC already hacked by an attacker the specified programs can not help the user. In 2011, IBM found some fake web server and log information files which contain some important information about the number of users who have been accessed the websites, the users' devices and inputted log in information [14]. Prediction of phishing attack based on neural networks was introduced by [5]. Heuristic based detection techniques [8] to identify web sites based on different parameters like IP address of a machine, URL of web pages.

In our review of literature most of the cases people suffer from static passwords. In [3] author proposed a virtual password scheme based on linear randomized function. One more approach differentiated virtual password that was introduced with secret little functions as encryption algorithms which requires small amount of user computation burden [4].

In this paper, first we review the concept of differentiated virtual password with codebook and reference switching approaches and discuss the issues with the current system. Second, we propose a virtual function based on reference switching performed on coded secret parameters of users. Next we analyze our proposed scheme with current codebook and reference switching against phishing attack because it is the most forceful attack to gain access on users' private information like password. Finally we conclude our work with future work.

3 Preliminary

In this section, we present a review of the different virtual password scheme proposed in [4].

User-specific ID and password both are mandatory to log into the system, which in turn further used by the system to validate the user for log-in. In online services like financial institution or online banking system, user static passwords are very insecure and vulnerable. User passwords defined by additional computation including some random salt can resolve above specified challenges.

A virtual password [3] is a concept of forming a user password which is generated differently each time when users log into the system. By the following formula, users' fixed alphanumeric part and system-generated random numbers are combined to form virtual passwords.

$$V = VS\_fun(H, R) \tag{1}$$

where H is a secret part and R is a random number provided by the system. Virtual password with differentiated approach [4] involves user choice to select one approach for their password generation among conventional scheme without using virtual password, selecting system suggested function and choice-based user defined function with an addition of two approaches: codebook and reference switching. This scheme also has a facility for advanced users to use their own user-defined program implemented in C or java.

A virtual function [4] is a small secret function, involves user computation on secret part as well as random parameters generated by the system, also called as secret encryption algorithms like flipping of digits in a password or the first digit of password is tripled and then add with $100\times$ + birthdate which can provide different output each time. Essential requirement for virtual functions is that they must use random parameters. Furthermore the function should be unobservable and unsolved since it is subject to stealing by phishing or any other attack.

Codebook and reference switching are very straight forward to generate virtual password for the user which facilitates user to avoid computation burden. Reference switching approach includes the following function [4] to calculate virtual password.

$$V_i = r_i x_{(x_i r_i \bmod n)} + 1 \mod 36 \tag{2}$$

3.1 Issues with Existing System

Though differentiated virtual password provides better security but still few points could be observed.

1. Extra time is required to register with the scheme because virtual function must be set during the registration phase.
2. It requires system overhead to store and define secret little functions.
3. Except system recommended and default approach among the scheme user computation burden increases with security level. However simplicity and complexity are inversely proportional [4].
4. Users are required to memorize their selected virtual function in addition to the secret pin.
5. Although codebook approach can generate virtual password automatically for the user, but the major problem is that one codebook is designed for a user and it generates virtual password based on codebook static digits. So after one successful attack, the adversary can guess rest of the digits [4] of password.
6. Reference switching protects the users by using reference code to hidden parameters, but the effect of phishing attack is described with one example [4] with length of password $X = 7$ of any alpha numeric digit, virtual password is calculated by 35 reference code. So, using a fake webpage, the adversary can get random number R and virtual password V from following formula.
   So in the worst case adversary may get all digits of hidden parameters. In that case the original secret pin is protected by its number of permutation. With the limitation of this authors in [4] suggested the length of the password to be at least 11. In practice it is difficult to remember 11 digits secret pin for all users.

$$X_i = r_i - 1 k_i \mod 36 \tag{3}$$

4 Our Proposed Scheme with Reference Switching and Codebook

We develop a smart function to create virtual password based on reference switching on coded user-specified secret parameters in addition to differentiated virtual password proposed by [4] with zero user computation. First, we define virtual password generation with different user registration approach. Then we develop a smart function to enhance simplicity for user involvement to compute virtual password. Finally, we examined our scheme against phishing attack and did a comparative study of our proposed scheme with existing differentiated virtual password for simplicity of a system.

4.1 Strong Virtual Password Using Reference Switching on Coded Secret Pin

Instead of directly deriving virtual password from hidden password and system generated random number, a strong virtual password V is computed within the following reference switching function

$$V = RS\_Fun(X\_code, R) \tag{4}$$

where X_code, from S to S where $S = \{0, 1, 2...9\}$, a coded parameter of hidden password which is entered by user is generated using codebook. R is a random number provided by the server. After entering the secret PIN by the user a strong password is automatically generated. Furthermore this scheme does not involve any kind of user computing. User authentication by the system is based on user ID, secret PIN and submitted strong virtual password by the user. If the submitted virtual password is same as system computed with secret PIN, the user is allowed to log into the system.

User can choose any number from digits 0 to 9 for secret PIN. To use strong virtual password scheme first users need to register themselves with user ID, password, and some necessary information.

After registration, the system will display log in screen in which user needs to input user ID, secret PIN, and random number provided by the server. In log in screen, users are required again to enter secret pin and then the system generates virtual password automatically.

Generation of strong password is done with following:

Step 1   Input user secret pin to the system X
Step 2   Input random number generated by system R
Step 3   Calculate codeX = coded parameter of secret pin X from the codebook
Step 4   Switch codeX to symbolX using defined reference
Step 5   Calculate temp_v with Eq. 3
Step 6   Reference the temp_v to virtual password V.

Here we use password length as 4 digit which is less than specified in [4]. Suppose we have hidden parameter $X = 1234$, random number $R = 2526$ then from our scheme we can calculate all the values in following form (Table 1).

Table 1 Calculation steps to determine virtual password

	x_i	codeX$_i$	symbolX$_i$	r_i	symbolX$_i$r$_i$	symbolX$_{ai}$	temp_v$_i$	v_i
x_1	1	0	3	2	0	4	8	7
x_2	2	8	7	5	2	7	35	T
x_3	3	7	6	2	2	7	14	G
x_4	4	1	4	6	2	7	2	1

4.2 Security Analysis of Virtual Function

From the above table virtual password with 4 digits is generated. By the fake page, a phisher can have random number and virtual password. From these two values they can calculate the value of codeXi by Eq. 3. They may get digits of codeX but by Eq. 3 the number of combination of codeX is still safe. Here we should note that our secret parameter is still protected using our dynamic codebook. Attacker cannot get the real parameters except that they may try for the random fake number by the combination of 4 digits.

We have also used 40 symbols including some special symbols with alphanumeric values to provide strong security to determine our final virtual password. In the proposed scheme, users are required to choose their secret part from numeric values of only 4 digits. This may be considered as effective parameter of our scheme. Furthermore, the proposed scheme automatically produces virtual password involving any user computation burden.

The following chart effectively shows the chance of cracking password using proposed virtual function with codebook and reference switching with formula specified in [4].

$$((1+p)/s - p/s^2)^n \tag{5}$$

where p = no. of phishing attack, s = symbol size, n = password length. Based on the above formula we can have following chart.

Figure 1 shows that codebook has a higher chance to crack the password among the three approaches. It also clear that if we increase the symbol size the possibility of password cracking is decreased. We can also set symbol size to 35 instead of 40 in our scheme because we reference our codeX, not the original secret parameters of password. But, we have added five extra special symbols to add some more complexity for the attacker. Furthermore, by entering fake numbers, they may get coded secret parameter, in that case the system can protect by allowing to enter secret pin only for three attempts.

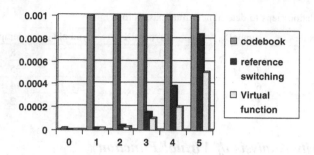

Fig. 1 Chance of cracking the password using proposed scheme, codebook, and reference switching approach for virtual password by number of phishing attack

5 Conclusion

We developed a smart calculation using small function to determine virtual password which provides strong security. In twenty-first century, security of user password has a need of multi-level authentication from thieving it by any adversary. Differentiated virtual password scheme offers users security by generating random password with user computation burden. In practice most users are expected to do some computation for password security for their sensitive online financial transaction. However, by generating smart function we can reduce computation burden of users. We can also free users to set their secret parameter to only four digit which is feasible to memorize.

Concept of phishing includes thieving of user password and other sensitive information from online user transaction. It is an essential requirement to deal with phishers. This scheme with automatic generation of virtual password enables attackers to acquire different password each time by fake page. In our future work, this scheme could be designed based on location or any time-based variable in alteration of random number to reduce system overhead for storing efficient random generator.

References

1. Shum, H.-Y., & Li, S. (2003). *Secure human-computer identification against.*
2. Li, S., Khayam, S. A., Sadeghi, A.-R., & Schmitz, R. (2010). Breaking randomized linear generation functions based on virtual password system. *IEEE ICC.*
3. Li, C.-C., Lei, M., & Vrbsky, S. V. (2008). Virtual password scheme to protect passwords communications, ICC '08. *IEEE International Conference.*
4. Xiao, Y., Senior Member, IEEE, Li, C.-C., Lei, M., & Vrbsky, S. V. (2014). Differentiated virtual passwords, secret little functions, and codebooks for protecting users from password theft. *IEEE System Journal, 8.*
5. Financial Fraud Action UK.
6. Hong, J. (2012). The state of phishing attacks. *Communications of the ACM,* 74–81.

7. Chawla, M., & Chouhan, S. S. (2014). A survey of phishing attack techniques. *International Journal of Computer Applications (0975–8887), 93*, 3.
8. Barraclougha, P.A., Hossaina, M.A., Tahirb, M.A., Sextona, G., & Aslama, N. (2013). Intelligent phishing detection and protection scheme for online transactions. *Expert Systems with Applications*.
9. Kamble, S., Malshikare, A., Gargund, P., & Bhagwat, C. Securing internet banking from phishing attack. *Multidisciplinary Journal of Research in Engineering and Technology, 2*(3), 562–567.
10. Nandikotkur, G. (2015). *RBI to Ease Transaction Security*.
11. https://www.wikipedia.org/wiki/One-time_password.
12. Liu, Y., & Zhang, M. (2012). Financial websites oriented heuristic anti-phishing research. *Cloud Computing and Intelligent Systems (CCIS), IEEE 2nd International Conference*.
13. Abbasi, A., Zahedi, F.M., & Chen, Y. (2012). Impact of anti-phishing tool performance on attack successes rate. *Intelligence and Security Informatics (ISI), 2012 IEEE International Conference, Arlington*.
14. Ollmann, G., Director of Security Strategy. *The phishing guide—understanding & preventing phishing attacks*. IBM Security System.

Need of ICT for Sustainable Development in Petroleum Industry

Amit Singh and Sandhya Singh

Abstract With increasing number of consumers, the issue of maintaining an ecological balance between consumers and resources has taken hours of discussions. A number of solutions for each sector have been proposed now and then. But, keeping a large number of factors in mind makes it a laborious task to accomplish. Thus, when we talk about sustainable development, the role of ICT becomes important. In one respect it supports innovation and efficiency of strategies and layouts; it does a remarkable work on grounds of economic growth and increased productivity. ICT tools do icing on cake with their powerful aim to support sustainable development with simplification, standardisation and giving a wonderful walkthrough of the whole life cycle of development of a product in an impressive computerised manner; wherein, ICT proves to be positively changing the meaning of provided services and the way they are produced and consumed.

Keywords Icing · Ecological

1 Introduction

A. What Is Ict?

Information and communications technology (ICT) emphasises communication devices, the software they are being operated on and the services they provide. Though it is normally seen as an extension of IT (information Technology), ICT states to be much more than that. On one side it involves management of transmission and telecommunication media, on the other side it involves

A. Singh (✉)
Vedic Gurukul Institute of Engineering and Technology, Jaipur, India
e-mail: ganeshnamah06@gmail.com

S. Singh
BS Anangpuria Institute of Law, Faridabad, India
e-mail: sandhyasing14@gmail.com

© Springer Science+Business Media Singapore 2016
S.C. Satapathy et al. (eds.), *Proceedings of International Conference on ICT for Sustainable Development*, Advances in Intelligent Systems and Computing 409, DOI 10.1007/978-981-10-0135-2_73

handling of audiovisual systems and transmission hardware leading to designing of intelligent and smart management systems.

B. **Sustainable Development**

Sustainable development means efficient consumption of precious resources in limited and finite manner so that there remains an ecological balance between resources and consumers so that the future consumers do not see any compromised use and depletion of natural resources. Thus, the most effective definition is given as "Sustainable development meets the needs of the present without compromising the ability of future generations to meet their own needs."

2 Problems that Are Yet to Be Looked At

For example, you need industrial setups and housing land that would eventually affect both flora and fauna of the place or looking at decomposable constraints, you choose paper over plastic but that would require chopping of trees. Acid rain and ozone layer depletion due to more electricity consumption, climatic changes and removal of top soil layer are yet other examples. Thus, it becomes a tedious task to meet our needs and save resources at same time and the big question is what do we choose over other? What is our priority?

3 Finding Solutions Using ICT

The development and applications of ICT are directly proportional to sustainable development, i.e. better the development of ICT, more will be the solutions to our economical and social problems so as to give people increased use of products and services and efficient use of precious and rare resources. Including the management of energy for its moderate and sensible use ICT involves least possible wastage of the same. Summing up, it can be said that good development in ICT will help in monitoring the efficient consumption of finite resources (Fig. 1).

4 How Is Petroleum Found

The terms petroleum and crude oil are often taken interchangeably. Crude oil is formed by the decomposition over years of dead flora and fauna into the sea that are buried under the soil on water bed or rocks. These remains or fossil are subject to biochemical reactions, temperature and pressure which over a long period of time result into fossil fuel.

Fig. 1 Shows side effects of industrilisation

Figure 2 the formation of petroleum. Figure 2a shows how mountains create anticlines and faults which trap oil-forming organic material. Figure 2b shows how petroleum and natural gas accumulate in the dome of the anticline.

5 Uses of Petroleum

- **Transportation**
  Not a new factor, petroleum is used as transportation fuel widely.
- **Plastic**
  The second major product made from petroleum products is plastic and other synthetic materials. It mostly comes from olefins that integrate within it, ethylene and propylene.
- **Synthetic Rubber**
  Petroleum has its application in making of synthetic rubber which is made from butadiene. Synthetic rubber used in making of tyres.

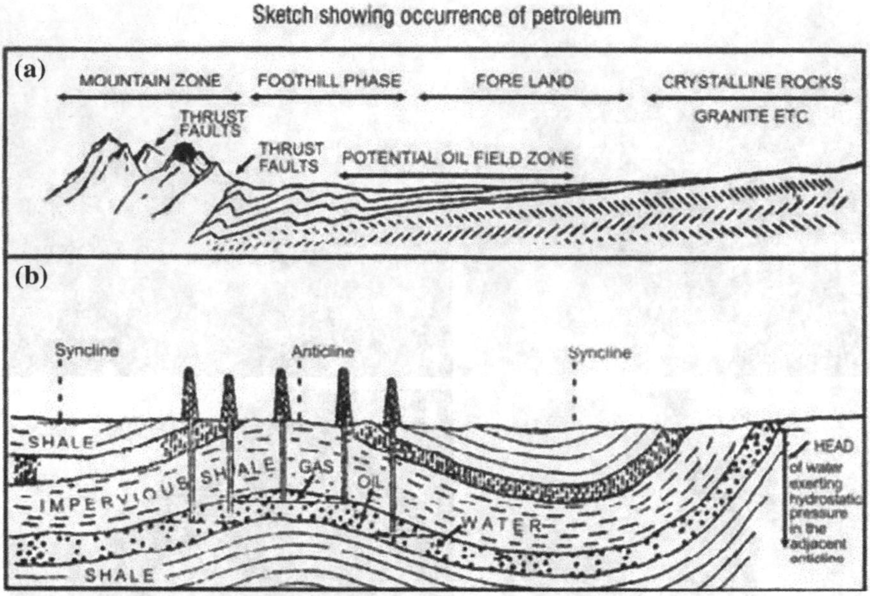

Sketch showing occurrence of petroleum

Fig. 2 Occurrence of petroleum

- **Ammonia**

  Petroleum also sees an important use in production of ammonia which is further used as nitrogen source in making of fertilizers. Thus it has an impact over the health of crop yields as they depend on the use of pesticides too.

- **Pharmaceuticals**

  One of the petroleum by-products is mineral oil which is used in pharmaceuticals, so petroleum also has an application in medical fields like in anaesthesia, vitamin capsule, etc.

- **Benzene**

  Benzene is used in preparation of dyes, fibres, lubricating oils and in varnishing of wood.

- **Cosmetics**

  Petroleum is also used in many of the cosmetics in the form of mineral oil. This oil is used in preparation of many creams, lotions, lip shades, hair colours, foundations and much more. Also aromas used in these cosmetics are result of aromatic hydrocarbons that are derived from petroleum (Fig. 3).

- **Other Uses**

  Petroleum is used for heating and electricity generation, making of ink, pillows, CDs, crayons etc.

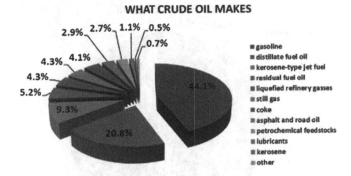

Fig. 3 Products of crude oil by distillation process

Thus it becomes clear that petroleum is too precious to be wasted and takes a major place in topic of sustainable development.

6 Statistics of Consumption of Petroleum

The following chart clearly shows various types of petroleum consumption all over the world where consumption form of gas and diesel takes more than half of place as per the chart (Fig. 4).

Crude oil accounts for 72 % of refinery cost to produce gasoline and 65 % of refinery cost to produce diesel as per statistics where both of them form a major part of yields from crude oil. So it gets clear that refinery cost to produce such an enormous amount would be no less in figures (Fig. 5).

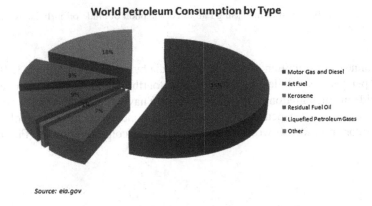

Fig. 4 Shows world petroleum consumption

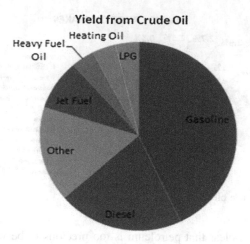

Fig. 5 Shows yield from crude oil

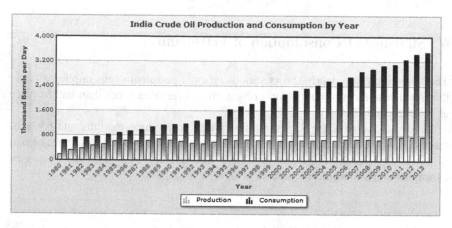

Fig. 6 The graph above shows increasing rate of consumption of crude oil in India as we move forward in years

The annual consumption of petroleum in India by year 2011 had been 32,92,000 barrels per year which leads India to rank fourth largest among the countries worldwide in consumption of petroleum. Despite having large reserves of coal and natural gas, India is dependent on imported fuel and when taking a look at the consumption of crude oil worldwide, the quantity becomes enormous (Fig. 6).

7 ICT for Sustainable Development of Petroleum

ICT is helping in providing efficient services, improved decision making, increased pace of new and useful products, and finding solutions to achieve sustainable development.

If it is applied properly, it can provide many ways for development.

It provides a way through green practices and efforts for development that would lead to sustainable and resource friendly environment.

Efforts are made by ICT for industries to adopt energy efficient methods and technologies so that industries:

- Reduce their overall consumption of raw resources.
- Reduce emissions or waste out of industry that results in pollution.
- Increase product quality.
- Increase economic growth.
- Move towards a green practice.

For achieving energy efficiency, ICT calls for many methods such as recycling possible products, replacing natural resource with some other possible source, switching between fuels.

8 Use of ICT Tools for Petroleum Industry

ICT tools such as ERPs and software would help in:

- Close monitoring of required parameters for design.
- Providing proper feedback.
- Achieving expected product.
- Risk management.
- Design of complete life cycle of product.
- Smart energy use.
- Efficient manufacturing process.
- Optimizing design.
- Reduced implementation cost.
- Surety that correct procedures are followed.
- Mapping of overall workflow.
- Decreased rate of human errors.
- Enhancing improvements in the industry.
- Standardised operations and procedures.
- Taking care of technical documentation.

The above processes can only be implemented by proper tracking, decision making, keeping stick to what is best for sustainable development, financing and proper measurements.

9 Challenges Faced by ICT

- Less awareness of ICT based solutions.
- Unclear results in terms of total energy savings.
- Dependence of ICT on respective industry.
- One way to be selected out of many possible solutions.
- Diversity and dynamicity of industries.

10 Results and Discussions

ICT can help with efficient use of petroleum and better go through of manufacturing processes if:

- All the existing ICT methods are provided an emphasis.
- ICT sees to dynamicity of petroleum industries.
- More and better tools are provided for each phase of life cycle of development of petroleum products.
- Awareness about all possible ICT methods is created using success stories.
- Promoted use of ICT by government and non-government agencies.
- ICT researches for development of new technologies.
- Preparation of feasible reports over which procedure is the best.
- Deploying cost-effective systems.
- Emphasising on reduced waste from petroleum industries and increased quality of end product.
- At last, keeping the motive of sustainable development at highest priority.

References

1. http://www.indexmundi.com.
2. http://www.petroleum.co.uk.
3. https://www.forumforthefuture.org.
4. http://www.teriin.org.

Hybrid *K*-Mean and Refinement Based on Ant for Color Image Clustering

Lavi Tyagi and Munesh C. Trivedi

Abstract By comparing the modified *K*-mean and improved *K*-mean algorithm, a hybrid *K*-mean algorithm is proposed for color image clustering. First, hybrid algorithm is applied to get color image clustering result and then ant-based refinement to refine the clustering result. In hybrid *K*-mean, modified *K*-mean is used to solve the problem of empty cluster formation and improved *K*-mean to reduce the calculation of distance between each data object and cluster centroid and then refinement will be done. Experimental result shows that proposed hybrid algorithm and refinement effectively and efficiently perform clustering.

Keywords Clustering · *K*-mean · Modified *K*-mean · Improved *K*-mean

1 Introduction

Clustering is a well-known unsupervised learning problem, which finds a structure in a collection of unlabelled data. Clustering is a process of organizing data objects into groups that are similar to one another within the same group and dissimilar to objects in the other groups. Clustering is used in data mining, machine learning, statistics, pattern recognition, and image processing as well. Clustering in image processing to perform segmentation, to identify hidden patterns, CBIR, and so on.

L. Tyagi (✉) · M.C. Trivedi
ABES Engineering College, Ghaziabad, India
e-mail: lavityagi15march@gmail.com

M.C. Trivedi
e-mail: munesh.trivedi@abes.ac.in

© Springer Science+Business Media Singapore 2016
S.C. Satapathy et al. (eds.), *Proceedings of International Conference
on ICT for Sustainable Development*, Advances in Intelligent Systems
and Computing 409, DOI 10.1007/978-981-10-0135-2_74

779

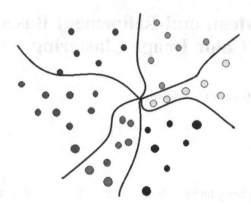

The main branches of clustering are: Hierarchical and partitioning. Each clustering type has its own peculiarities, but our main focus is on partitioning clustering, and in partitioning clustering, we are also interested in K-mean clustering.

1.1 K-Mean

This is the most commonly used clustering algorithm. The "k" in name refers to the fact that it looks for the fixed number of clusters. The value of "k" is specified by the user. It was first published by J.B Mac Queen in 1967. There are usually more than two input variables and are numeric. The goal of clustering is to find 'k' points that make good cluster centroids. In this, cluster centroids define the clusters. Data objects are assigned to cluster defined by its nearest cluster centroid. Best assignment of cluster centroids could be defined as that minimizes the sum of distance from each data object to its nearest cluster centroid. Finding optimal solution is difficult and K-mean does not attempt it. It starts with an initial guess and uses series of steps to improve it. There are various enhancements of K-mean like: Bi-level k-mean that forms cluster in two stages rather than one stage [1] performs effectively and efficiently on data. PBPA, i.e., the priority-based pheromone algorithm for clustering of image, it creates cluster using three information namely priority, pheromone, and heuristic. It is very complex as number of parameters need to be defined [2]. Modified K-mean to improve the sensitivity of initial centroid of clusters. This modified K-mean divides the data objects into different segments and the segments which show the maximum frequency have the maximum probability to contain the initial cluster centroid [3].

K-mean algorithm:

Input:

> D = { d₁, d₂, ...,dₙ} - Set of data objects
> k - Number of desired clusters

Output:

> K - A set of clusters

Algorithm:

> Assign initial values to the centroids $c_1, c_2, ..., c_k$;
> repeat
>> Assign each data object d_i to the cluster which has the closest centroid; calculate the new centroid for each
> cluster;
>> until   Convergence criteria is met;

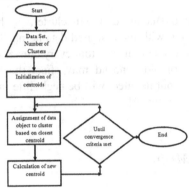

1.1.1   Properties of *K*-Mean Are

- Guaranteed convergence
- Guarantee for local optimal, not necessarily for global optimal
- Always '*K*' clusters
- Clusters are nonhierarchical and nonoverlapped

1.1.2   Shortcomings of *K*-Mean

- Necessity of specifying '*K*'
- Sensitive to noise and outliers (outliers are the data values that affect the mean value)
- Sensitive to initial assignment of centroids
- Not deterministic in nature
- Clusters are inconsistent from one run to another

1.2 Modified K-Mean

K-mean is the one of the partition clustering algorithm, i.e., used widely. Standard K-mean face various problems but one of the significant problem is empty cluster formation problem just because of cluster centroids are poorly initialized. To solve this problem, modified K-mean algorithm has been proposed, in this algorithm only the formula to update the cluster centroid has been modified. The updated formula is

$$\mathbf{Z}_k^{(\text{new})} \leftarrow \frac{1}{n_k + 1} \left\{ \sum\nolimits_{x_j \in C_k} (\mathbf{X}_j) + \mathbf{Z}_k^{(\text{old})} \right\}$$

In this formula, the old centroid of kth cluster, z_k, has been used as a data member of cluster k along with the assigned data items. This denies the formation of empty cluster. This formula indicates that every cluster contains at least one data element. The inclusion of old centroid may affect the rate of convergence and quality of final clustering but its effect will be negligible in few iterations, hence no significant effect on clustering [4].

1.3 Improved K-Mean

The only change in this improved K-mean is that, it makes use of a simple data structures to store the value of pixel label and minimum distance of that pixel, which is used in the next iterations. Storing these two information improved k-mean and it does not compute the distance between each pixel and cluster centroids repeatedly. Hence, save computation time [5].

To measure the similarity between data point and centroid, metric like Euclidean distance, Manhattan, and correlation can be used, but each has obtained similar result. No one is dominant so based on the application, type of data and complexity any of the metric can be used to measure similarity [6].

2 Hybrid K-Mean and Ant-Based Refinement

The proposed algorithm called hybrid k-mean, because we are making use of modified k-mean to compute the cluster centroids as its modified formula reduce the probability of empty cluster formation and improved k-mean to store two values. The cluster label and minimum distance in a data structure called an array.

By making use of these two *K*-means, performance will be enhanced in terms of time and after that refinement based on ant will be done to improve the performance in terms of time and accuracy.

2.1 Block Diagram of Proposed Method

Sum of squared error (SSE) is used as convergence criteria in hybrid *K*-mean. SSE is defined as

$$SSE(C_1, C_2, \ldots\ldots, C_k) = \sum_{k=1} \sum_{x_j \in C_k} \| x_j - c_k \|^2$$

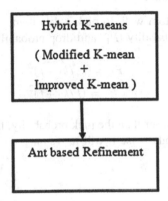

The procedure of hybrid *K*-mean and ant-based refinement is described as

1. Decide the value of '*K*', i.e., the number of clusters;
2. Choose '*K*' which belong to input data set, as initial means;
3. Compute the distance $d(x_j, c_k)$ between each data object x_j $(1 <= j <= n)$ and '*K*' cluster centroid C_k $(1 <= k <= K)$, and assign data object to cluster having closest cluster centroid;
4. For each data object store this label and closest distance in a data structure, i.e.,. an array, Cluster[] and the Dist[]. Set Cluster[*j*] = *k*, where '*k*' is the label of closest cluster and Dist[*j*] = $d(x_j, C_k)$, i.e., the closest Euclidean distance to cluster *k*;
5. For each cluster *k* $(1 <= k <= K)$, recompute the cluster centroid using:

$$C_k = \frac{1}{n_k + 1} \left\{ \sum_{x_j \in C_k} (x_j) + C_k^{(old)} \right\}$$

Repeat
6. compute the distance between each data object x_j and current cluster centroid;
7. (a) If this computed distance is less than or equal to Dist[j], the data object stays in the current cluster;
   (b) Else for every cluster centroid C_k ($1 <= k <= K$), Compute the distance $d(x_j, C_k)$ for each data object to each cluster centroid and assign data object x_j to closest center C_k;
   Set Cluster[j] = k;
   Set Dist[j] = $d(x_j, C_k)$;
8. For each cluster j ($1 <= k <= K$), recompute the cluster centroid using the formula i.e. given in step 5;
9. Until SSE is not stable

Ant-based Refinement
While entropy is not stable

1. Let the ant go on random walk to pick a data item;
2. Calculate the pick probability (P_1) and drop probability (P_2);

$$P_1 = (k_1/k_1 + f)^2$$
$$P_2 = (f/k_2 + f)^2$$

3. If drop probability is lower than the pick probability, then ant will drop the item in the current cluster otherwise it will move on;

3 Experimental Result

Standard K-mean, hybrid K-mean, and ant-based refinement are used to analyze clustering result of same data. In both methods, cluster centers are randomly chosen, convergence criteria for both methods are squared error criterion, one ant is used for refinement purpose. In ant-based refinement, two probabilities are used namely pick probability and drop probability. Two constants ($k_1 = 0.1$, $k_2 = 0.5$) are used, k_1 is used in pick probability and k_2 is used in drop probability and 'f' is the entropy value of the kth cluster calculated before the item is picked.

Entropy is the best measure to find out the amount of uncertainty in the data rather than certainty. It can be computed as (Figs. 1, 2 and 3)

Fig. 1 Original image

Fig. 2 Color image clustering using standard *K*-mean

Fig. 3 Color image clustering using hybrid *K*-mean and refinement based on ant

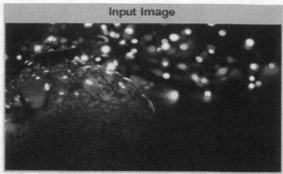

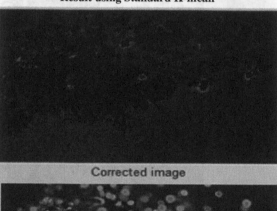

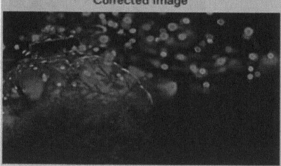

Table 1 Resulting table color image clustering

	Standard K-mean	Hybrid K-mean and ant-based refinement
No. of tested Images	100	100
Entropy	2.0957	0.6707
Accuracy	84	92

$$E_k = -\sum_j p_{ij} \log(p_{ik})$$

where E_k is the entropy for kth cluster, P_{jk} the probability, i.e., whether the data object j belongs to cluster k.

Two data sets are created randomly of different sizes 30 and 1000. Then both k-mean have been applied three times, one for 30 data items to make 2 clusters, second time for 1000 data items to make 2 clusters, and third time for 1000 data items to make 4 clusters. The values of k_1 and k_2 constants for picking and dropping probability are 0.28, 0.47. Resulting Table 1 shows the performance for both clustering algorithm (Figs. 4 and 5).

4 Conclusion

Experimental results show that proposed hybrid K-mean algorithm and ant-based refinement gives better results for image clustering as well as for randomly generated data than standard K-mean. This approach is tested on 100 color images of different sizes and on randomly generated data as well, resulting Table 2 shows that proposed hybrid K-mean and refinement give better results as compared with standard K-mean (Fig. 6).

Fig. 4 Accuracy graph for color image clustering

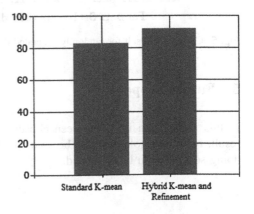

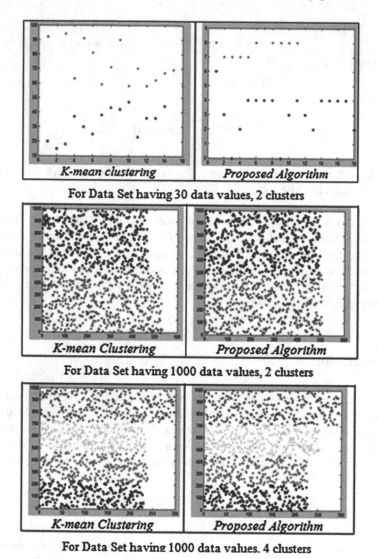

K-mean clustering   **Proposed Algorithm**

For Data Set having 30 data values, 2 clusters

K-mean Clustering   **Proposed Algorithm**

For Data Set having 1000 data values, 2 clusters

K-mean Clustering   **Proposed Algorithm**

For Data Set having 1000 data values. 4 clusters

Fig. 5 Clustering Result for randomly generated data

5 Future Scope

In this paper, data item has been chosen randomly for refinement of clustering result, but a threshold can also be used for choosing a data item for refinement by doing so result can be enhanced.

Table 2 Resulting table for randomly created dataset

	Standard K-mean	Hybrid K-mean and ant-based refinement
Number of data samples	30/1000/1000	30/1000/1000
Cluster	2/2/4	2/2/4
Entropy	1.5623	1.5026
Time	158.43/90.96/356.72	74.95/88.26/347.97
Iteration	2/10/11	0/4/6

Fig. 6 Entropy graph for randomly generated data

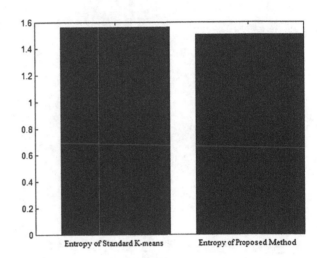

References

1. Yu, S.-S., Chu, S.-W., & Wang, C.-L. (2014). A modified K-means algorithms-Bi-level K-means algorithm. In *International Conference on Soft Computing in Information Communication Technology (SCICT)* (pp. 10–13).
2. Karthikeyan, T., Balakrishnan, R., & Karthick Kumar, U. (2012). Priority based pheromone algorithm for image cluster. In *3rd National Conference on Emerging Trends and Applications In Computer Science(NCETACS)* (pp. 230–239). IEEE.
3. Singh, R. V., & Bhatia, M. P. S. (2011). Data clustering with modified K-means algorithm. In *IEEE-International Conference on Recent Trends in Information Technology, ICRTIT* (pp. 717–721).
4. Pakhira, M. K. (2009). A modified k-mean algorithm to avoid empty clusters. *International Journal of Recent Trends in Engineering, 1*(1), 220–226.
5. Na, S., Xumin, L., & Yong, G. (2010). Research on k-means clustering algorithms. In *Third International Symposium on Intelligent Information Technology and Security Informatics* (pp. 63–67). IEEE.
6. Grabusts, P. (2011). The choice of metrics for clustering algorithm. In *Proceedings of the 8th International Scientific and Practical Conference* (Vol. I1, pp. 70–76).

A Framework for Secure Data Storage in Mobile Cloud Computing

Vinodray Thumar and Vipul Vekariya

Abstract In mobile cloud computing, data storage and its processing is done externally from the mobile devices. The mobile user can access the applications or data from cloud servers (Dinh et al., Wireless Commun. Mobile Comput. 13(8), 1587–1611 [1]). The client can store his/her multimedia data to the cloud storage server. The client may be given assurance that the access rights of data will only be restricted to authorized access. The cloud service provider assures the clients for proper security, data confidentiality, and privacy for data in their service level agreement (SLA). Clients may be given full assurance in proper privacy policies and procedures for data safety in cloud but there may be risk of unauthorized access of client sensitive data by cloud service provider or cloud attacker. Another risk is the mobility of data. Data may be transferred from one location to other locations. Frequently, data may be transferred from one place to another place so there may be security concerns of data while mobility. To secure the client's confidential data, we propose a framework designed with modified RSA encryption technique so that client's multimedia data may be preserved before storing on the cloud from client side.

Keywords Cloud computing · Cloud security · SLA · Encryption · Data privacy · Data confidentiality

1 Introduction

Smart phones, tablet PCs, and PDAs are mobile devices that have become very much popular in people to give them comforts and way to communicate in their daily lives. Mobile users are able to use the many services offered by service

V. Thumar (✉)
Faculty of Engineering & Technology, C. U. Shah University, Wadhwancity, Gujarat, India
e-mail: vinod.thumar@gmail.com

V. Vekariya
Noble Group of Institutions, Junagadh, Gujarat, India
e-mail: vekariya.vipul@gmail.com

© Springer Science+Business Media Singapore 2016
S.C. Satapathy et al. (eds.), *Proceedings of International Conference on ICT for Sustainable Development*, Advances in Intelligent Systems and Computing 409, DOI 10.1007/978-981-10-0135-2_75

providers. These services are able to function on many mobile devices using wireless networks and remote servers [2–4].

In mobile cloud computing, different kinds of security issues may often arise, which needs more security measures has to be taken. There are different security and privacy issues in data storage, mobile network and mobile terminal in cloud in mobile cloud computing [5].

Another security issue regarding cloud storage is data ownership. There is a possibility to store different kinds of media or text files like audio, video, database, or e-books which are bought by the user and store to the cloud located remotely. This gives rise to the issue of true ownership of those files. User may have lost access of those bought media because they are stored at remote place and the service provider may sell those media files to third party. Hence it may raise an issue of true ownership of those media files [3].

It may be risk of data theft and issues of security or privacy for mobile device users while storing data to the cloud [6, 7]. The users' important data files are stored arbitrarily on the cloud infrastructure all over the world, and users do not have any information regarding specific storage location of their data and the location of cloud servers. So there may be a risk of discloser of user's private information. Relocating of data from one cloud to another cloud at remote place will also be one of the issues related to security and privacy of user's data [2, 5, 8, 9, 10].

In this paper, we propose a framework for maintaining privacy of user data in mobile cloud during storage as well as mobility.

The paper is organized as follow: Brief overview of cloud computing and mobile cloud computing is given in Sect. 2. In Sect. 3, We discuss about security issues in cloud computing. We introduce proposed framework using modified RSA algorithm and comparative result analysis of it in Sect. 4, and finally we give conclusion of the paper in Sect. 5.

2 Overview of Mobile Cloud Computing

2.1 Cloud Computing

Cloud computing is a platform for providing on demand services and to share infrastructural resources, e.g., storage, networks, servers, and software. It can provide various services with minimal administrative efforts. We have three service models and four deployment models in cloud platform [11].

Service Models

1. Software as a Service (SaaS)

The SaaS service model provides various services to the clients. Client can access different applications running on a cloud infrastructure. User can access various applications from various devices. The clients need not have to worry about managing various cloud resources like operating systems, storage, network, and servers.

2. Platform as a Service (PaaS)

In PaaS service model, clients can use different services from service provider like programming languages, libraries, and tools supported by the provider. The clients need not have to worry about managing various cloud resources like operating systems, storage, network, servers but they have to control on various configuration settings.

3. Infrastructure as a Service (IaaS)

In IaaS service model, clients can use the services like storage, networks, and other fundamental computing resources. They can use operating system as well as other system software and required infrastructural resources from service provider.

Deployment Models

1. Private cloud

The cloud platform which is developed only for a single organization is called private cloud. The private cloud may be managed and executed by individual organization itself.

2. Community cloud

The cloud platform which is developed only for a specific community of clients of any organizations, group, or society is called community cloud. There is a common goal or purpose of the users of the community cloud. The community cloud may be managed and executed by certain community or group.

3. Public cloud

The cloud platform which is developed for open use by the general people or all the members of society is called public cloud. The public cloud may be managed and executed by academic institutions, business organizations, government organization, etc.

4. Hybrid cloud

The cloud platform which is combination of two or more different cloud platforms is called hybrid cloud.

2.2 Mobile Cloud Computing

The mobile cloud computing is a combination of mobile network and cloud computing [2]. This platform provides feasible services to mobile devices users. In cloud computing, environmental applications and data are stored on the internet instead of an individual device. User can access different applications which are running on a remote server.

Mobile cloud computing is a platform developed as a solution to overcome the mobile devices challenges using cloud computing services like storage and computing resources [12]. Cloud computing has certain limitations like limited bandwidth capacity and poor network connectivity but mobile cloud computing may provide solutions for these limitations.

We have seen that number of users of mobile devices have been increased during last few years. The reason is that there is a vast technological advancement in mobile technology. We can check that approximately all mobile devices have better quality of memory capacity, network connectivity, good quality of battery life, display, and many other features. Due to this enhancement in technology, the user can access numerous mobile apps and services on the mobile cloud [13, 14].

3   Security Issues in Data Storage in Cloud

Mobile cloud computing provides the advantage of storing a large amount of data outside the mobile device, in the cloud. But the cloud can be the target of various attacks concerning about data privacy, data ownership and location, data access and integrity [8, 15, 16]. Various security related issues in cloud computing are:

Data Integrity
Cloud service providers always give assurance to their clients that they have developed such system that they can ensure data integrity and they can tell what happened with their data stored in the cloud. They regularly provide information to their client that what particular data is hosted on the cloud and which type of integrity mechanisms put in place.

Data Privacy and Confidentiality
When the clients host data to the cloud then they can be given assurance that the access to that data will only be limited to the restricted access. There is one of the risk factor to access user's sensitive data by cloud personnel which can be crucial threat to cloud data. The client has been given assurance that the data stored on the cloud will be secured but it may be risk against unauthorized access.

Data Availability
Client's important data is usually stored in blocks or parts on different storage servers which are located in different clouds at different regions. In these circumstances, data availability becomes a major issue. The availability of client's data as on demand may arise some short of difficult situation for cloud service provider.

Data Mobility
Data mobility in cloud computing environment became one of the security issues for the clients. Clients are never aware about the location of their important data. Whenever certain organizations have stored their sensitive data in the cloud, they wish to know the location of the place where storage server is located. Another security issue is the mobility of data from one location to another. Initially, cloud

service provider stores client's data at a suitable location known to him only. But it is the situation that they often move client's data from one server to another. There may be a contract among various cloud storage providers for sharing their resources. Therefore, It might be very risk for clients to secure their data when there is mobility of cloud.

No.	Author	Year of publication	Security issue and other technical details	Current approach	Advantages	Limitations
1	Newaz Bahar [2]	2013	Data privacy and confidentiality	Data encryption with public key	Better services to clients from service provider side	It is third-party security frame work
			Data integrity			
			Data location and relocation	Two agents from client side and two service providers ACSP and DSP		
			Data availability			
2	Suo [5]	2013	Mobile terminal, mobile network and mobile cloud	Key management and data encryption	Integrating the current security technologies	Specific technique for data security is not specified
3	Jana [16]	2013	Data loss, loss of encryption key, control of resources in cloud, Malicious insiders and data breaches, data ownership	Secure multiparty computation (SMC) and homomorphic encryption (HE)	–	Lack of security in communication
4	Hamid [6]	2012	Data availability	Encryption schemes	No need of TTP verification for identity	–
			Data privacy and confidentiality	Homomorphic encryption		
			Disaster recovery and business continuity			
			Cloud Service provider viability			

(continued)

(continued)

No.	Author	Year of publication	Security issue and other technical details	Current approach	Advantages	Limitations
5	Chen [9]	2012	Multi tenancy	Data encryption with key management	Fast access of cloud storage with multi tenancy features	Service provider has to manage large no. of keys
			Data confidentiality, integrity and availability			
			Data encryption key management			
			Data destruction			

4 Proposed Framework

The proposed framework will be designed to overcome the security issues which have been faced by the clients, while preserving the data in cloud server and relocating data from cloud. It will provide the solution that allows mobile users to store data securely so that the privacy of their data is maintained. This is a client-side system to maintain privacy of data in cloud. There are various types of mobile user's multimedia data which he/she has to store on cloud. The main components in this security architecture consists encryption of data using proposed encryption techniques for multimedia files.

The flowchart of proposed framework is in Fig. 1.

In our proposed work, we have designed a framework for client using modified RSA algorithm to encrypt the data to preserve privacy and maintain confidentiality. User's important and confidential data is encrypted at client side and then it is stored on the cloud storage. When there is requirement of data, user places a request for the data and cloud service provider validates the authentic user and delivers the data. Client can retrieve his data after doing the decryption process.

RSA is an asymmetric cryptographic algorithm, in which all messages are mapped to an integer. RSA algorithm generates security keys called as public or private keys [17]. In our security framework, both encryption and decryption processes will be done by cloud user through software interface. First, the user data is encrypted with the receiver's public key, after that decryption process can be done with the corresponding key pair only. These two keys are generated and sent to receiver separately

Proposed modified RSA Cryptographic Algorithm

RSA is an asymmetric cryptographic algorithm in which the original text and encrypted text both are natural integer numbers between 0 to $n - 1$ for certain value

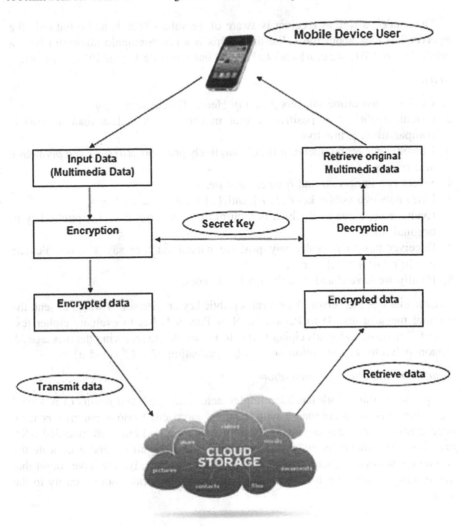

Fig. 1 Flowchart of proposed system

of n. Encryption process and decryption process are as per the given approaches for specific original message M and cipher text C,

Encryption process : Clipher Text $C = M^{b/a} \bmod n$

Decryption process : Original message $M = C^d \bmod n$, means $M = (M^{b/a})^d \bmod n$,

$$\text{therefore } M = M^{bd/a} \bmod n$$

The sender as well as receiver is aware of the values of a, b, and n but only the receiver has idea about the value of d. This is a cryptographic algorithm with a public key of PBK = {b, n} and {a} and it has a private key of PRK = {d, n}.

Steps:

1. Consider two prime integers p and q. Hence, Calculate n = pq
2. Calculate φ(n), It is positive natural number which is less than n. φ(n) is comparatively prime to n.
3. Consider integer number e. It is comparatively prime to φ(n).(i.e., gcd between e and φ(n) is 1)
4. Select two integers a and b where b = ae.
5. Formulate two public keys {b, n} and {a} using these numbers.
6. Evaluate the value of d which is multiplicative inverse of e. d is public key in original RSA.
7. Receiver has to consider any positive natural number say x and Calculate e = [((x * a) + b)/a] − x.
8. Finally we have d and e as the final outcomes.

Consider that the Person A generates public key and Person B wants to send the original message text M to Person A. Now Person B has to evaluate cipher text $C = M^{b/a}$ (mod n) and sends cipher text C to Person A. On receiving the message M, Person A has to do decryption process by evaluating $M = C^d$ (mod n)

Result Analysis and Implementation

The proposed framework has been implemented and simulated results of modified algorithm have been compared with existing approach. Various parameters have been analyzed and comparative analysis of existing algorithm with modified RSA based on performance is given in following Table 1. Figures 2 and 3 indicate the simulated process of encryption and decryption, respectively. We have found that the security aspect ratio has been raised and we can provide more security to the data.

Table 1 Comparative analysis

Sr. no	Parameter	RSA	Modified RSA
1	Public key	Only one	Two
2	Communication overhead	Less	High
3	Key transmission	Once	Twice
4	Security aspects	Less secure	More secure
5	Vulnerable to brute force attack	More	Less
6	Processing speed	High	Less

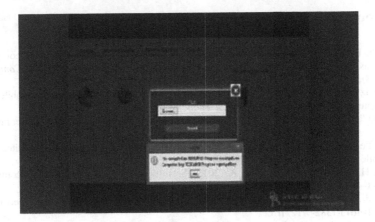

Fig. 2 File encryption process

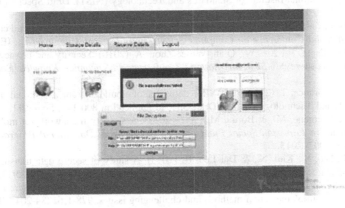

Fig. 3 File decryption process

5 Conclusion

With the development of this system, the client does not have to be dependent on the cloud service provider for privacy and confidentiality of data, while storing data on cloud or transmitting data over network or relocating of data from one cloud to another cloud. Client can store his important data to the cloud storage and maintain its confidentiality. Client-side data privacy and security will be provided through this system.

References

1. Dinh, H., Lee, C., Niyato, D., & Wang, P. (2013). A survey of mobile cloud computing: architecture, applications, and approaches. *Wireless Communications and Mobile Computing*, *13*(18), 1587–1611.
2. Newaz Bahar, A., Habib, A., & Islam M. (2013). Security architecture for mobile cloud computing. *International Journal of Scientific Knowledge*, *3*(3).
3. Alizadeh, M., & Hassan, W. (2013). Challenges and opportunities of mobile cloud computing. 978-1-4673-2480-9/13. IEEE.
4. Xiu-Feng, Q., Jian-wei, L., & Peng-chun, Z. (2011). Secure cloud computing architecture on mobile internet. 978-1- 4577-0536-6/11. IEEE.
5. Suo, H., Liu, Z., Wan, J., & Zhou, K. (2013). Security and privacy in mobile cloud computing. 978-1-4673-2480-9/13. IEEE.
6. Hamdi, M. (2012). Security of cloud computing, storage, and networking. 978-1-4673-1382-7/12. IEEE.
7. Horrow, S., Gupta, S., Sardana, A., & Abraham, A. (2012). Secure private cloud architecture for mobile infrastructure as a service. In *IEEE Eighth World Congress on Services*, 2012.
8. Jansen, W., & Grance, T. (2011). Guidelines on security and privacy in public cloud computing. National Institute of Standards and Technology (NIST), Draft Special Publication 800-144, Jan-2011.
9. Chen, D., & Zhao, H. (2012). Data security and privacy protection issues in cloud computing. In *International Conference on Computer Science and Electronics Engineering*. IEEE.
10. Zhou, M., Zhang, R., Xie, W., Qian, W., & Zhou, A. (2010). Security and privacy in cloud computing: A survey. In *Sixth International Conference on Semantics, Knowledge and Grids*. IEEE.
11. Mell, P., & Grance, T. (2011). The NIST definition of cloud computing. National Institute of Standards and Technology (NIST), Draft Special Publication 800-145, Sep-2011.
12. Popa, D., Cremene, M., & Borda, M. (2007–2013). A security framework for mobile cloud applications. In *European Social Fund through the Sectorial Operational Program Human Resources* 2007–2013.
13. Hong, J., Seo, S., Kim, N., & Dai Lee, B. (2013). A study of secure data transmissions in mobile cloud computing from the energy consumption side. 978-1-4673-5742-5/13. IEEE.
14. Qureshi, S., Ahmad, T., & Rafique, K. (2011). Mobile cloud computing as future for mobile applications—implementation methods and challenging issues. 978-1-61284-204-2/11. IEEE.
15. Sun, D., Chang, G., Sun, L., & Wang, X. (2011). Surveying and analyzing security, privacy and trust issues in cloud computing environments. In *Advanced in Control Engineering and Information Science, Elsevier*.
16. Jana, D., & Bandyopadhyay, D. (2013). Efficient management of security and privacy issues in mobile cloud environment. 978-1-4799-2275-8/13. IEEE.
17. Stallings, W. (2010). *Network Security Essentials Applications and Standards* (6th edn.) Pearson Education.

Hindi Word Sense Disambiguation Using Cosine Similarity

Sarika and Dilip Kumar Sharma

Abstract Hindi is the regional language of India. Most of the people access, retrieve, and share documents in Hindi language. As all the natural languages possess property of being ambiguous, so does Hindi language, which creates obstacles in usage of information technology properly. In order to remove ambiguity from Hindi language, we need a system called Hindi word sense disambiguation (HWSD). In this paper, we present a supervised method, called HWSD using cosine similarity in which vectors are created for testing query and sense knowledge data for the ambiguous word by considering weights. Experiment is performed on dataset consisting of 90 Hindi ambiguous words and it is found that this method outperforms Lesk's algorithm which is well known algorithm for Word sense disambiguation (WSD). We obtained an overall average precision of 78.99 % and average recall of 72.58 %.

Keywords Word sense disambiguation · Natural language processing · Ambiguity · Hindi WordNet · Cosine similarity

1 Introduction

Today is an era of information technology. Everyone is uses the web to share and find information but the information is present in natural languages. As we know that all natural languages have the fundamental characteristic of possessing ambiguity. So to use information technology efficiently we need to remove ambiguity from the sentences with the help of a system called word sense disambiguation.

Word sense disambiguation (WSD) is the computational identification of correct sense of a polysemous words in the context which they occur [1]. For instance

Sarika (✉) · D.K. Sharma
Department of Computer Engineering & Applications, GLA University, Mathura, India
e-mail: varshneysarika16@gmail.com

D.K. Sharma
e-mail: dilip.sharma@gla.ac.in

© Springer Science+Business Media Singapore 2016
S.C. Satapathy et al. (eds.), *Proceedings of International Conference on ICT for Sustainable Development*, Advances in Intelligent Systems and Computing 409, DOI 10.1007/978-981-10-0135-2_76

consider the following sentences-आपने मेरे प्रश्न का उत्तर नहीं दिया। and भारत के उत्तर में हिमालय पर्वत विराजमान है। Here, an ambiguous word is उत्तर which can be interpreted as 'answer' or as 'North direction' based on the context.

Unfortunately, the problem of identification of specific sense of a given word seems to be easy. As Humans easily detect specific meaning of a word given in a context but for a machine it is difficult. It is used in various applications [2, 3] like Machine translation, which is one of the most important applications of WSD. For example, Hindi word 'सोना' can be translated in English as 'Gold' or 'sleep' depending on the context, which results in wrong sentence in another language in information retrieval to retrieve relevant information from the web. In speech processing, it is required for correct phonetization of word in speech synthesis.

The structure of the rest of paper is as follows: Sect. 2 gives a brief review of work done in the field of WSD. In Sect. 3 we present a method for HWSD using cosine similarity. Section 4 explains dataset structure. Section 5 shows experimental results and discussion. Finally in Sect. 6 conclusion and future directions are discussed.

2 Related Work

Work done on knowledge-based approaches [4] includes [5–9]. Michael Lesk [6] in 1986, developed an algorithm called Lesk algorithm to determine the senses of polysemy words. He used machine readable dictionary to find the overlap of word definition and the context in which ambiguous words occur to disambiguate the word sense. Banerjee and Pederson [7] proposed an Adapted Lesk Algorithm for word sense disambiguation. In this approach instead of using a standard dictionary as a source of knowledge, the lexical database called WordNet is used. Work done by Sinha et al. [5] is the first effort for an Indian language. The main idea is to match a context in which an ambiguous word occurs with the context constructed from the Hindi WordNet [10] (developed at IIT Bombay) and chooses the winner based on the maximum overlapping.

Work done using supervised approaches includes [11, 12]. Singh et al. [11] used supervised approach for Hindi word sense disambiguation (HWSD). In this algorithm different weight is assigned to words which occur in the context of the ambiguous word by using sense-tagged training corpus, dictionary definition and semantic relations from Hindi WordNet [10]. In [12], naïve bayes classifier for Hindi Word sense disambiguation is investigated. They utilize 11 features like local context, collocations, unordered list of words, vibhaktis, nouns etc.

Work done using unsupervised approaches includes [13–19]. Yarowsky [14] has attempted to resolve a lexical ambiguity by using an unsupervised learning algorithm. In this, the author has used an un-annotated English text and its performance is equal to supervised algorithm which requires sense-annotated corpus. In [13], Mishra et al. attempt to resolve ambiguity by using an unsupervised approach. In this approach first, preprocessing is performed on the context in which the ambiguous word occur. Then, learning of decision list using untagged examples is performed. Few seed examples are provided manually. The decision list created is now used for depicting the sense to an ambiguous word. Singh et al. [15] proposed an algorithm for HWSD which resolves ambiguity by computing similarity, which is not based on the exact matching of context with the sense repository. Instead, it utilizes Hindi WordNet hierarchy to obtain a similarity based on meaning of words and then, uses it in disambiguation task. In [16], authors used an unsupervised approach based on probabilistic latent semantic analysis (PLSA) which does not require sense-tagged data. It uses PLSA method for making clusters of similar words and these clusters are further expanded using lexical database. This approach is language independent. Patwardhan et al. [17] proposed a method for WSD using semantic relatedness which generalizes the adapted Lesk algorithm. They evaluated different measures of semantic relatedness.

3 Proposed Methodology

In this paper, we proposed a method for removing ambiguity from Hindi language using cosine similarity which was earlier used for English language. We used supervised approach for finding cosine similarity between query containing ambiguous word and the sense knowledge text. The sense having maximum similarity with the query is the appropriate sense of that ambiguous word.

The steps for performing HWSD task are as follows and their framework is shown in Fig. 1.

3.1 User Query

First of all, user containing ambiguous word is given as query. There can be a multiple ambiguous word in the query.

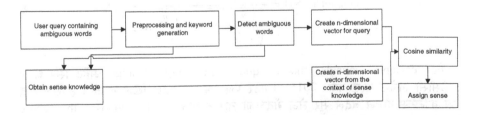

Fig. 1 Framework of proposed methodology

3.2 Preprocessing and Keyword Generation

Preprocessing is performed on query text which includes removal of stop words like 'के', 'थे', 'में' etc., removal of repeated words, punctuation marks like '/','?','%' etc. and keywords are generated from the text after preprocessing.

3.3 Detection of Ambiguous Words

Ambiguous word is detected from the generated keywords after preprocessing step with the help of dataset consisting of 90 ambiguous Hindi words.

3.4 Obtain Sense Knowledge

Sense knowledge corresponding to that ambiguous word can be obtained from the lexical knowledge base Hindi WordNet [10], from Hindi corpus [20] and from web by firing queries. Preprocessing is performed on this data also.

3.5 Cosine Similarity

Now, find cosine similarity between the query containing ambiguous word and the sense knowledge obtained for all sense of that ambiguous word. Vectors are created from the context in which ambiguous word occurs and from the sense knowledge's context. Then cosine similarity is calculated by formula shown in Eq. 3 and vector creation in Eqs. 1 and 2

$$V(S_1) = \{(W_1, Wt_{11}), (W_2, Wt_{12}), \ldots \ldots, (W_n, Wt_{1n})\} \tag{1}$$

$$V(S_2) = \{(W_1, Wt_{21}), (W_2, Wt_{22}), \ldots \ldots, (W_n, Wt_{2n})\} \tag{2}$$

$$\text{cosine}(S_1, S_2) = \frac{\sum_{K=1}^{n} Wt_{1K} * Wt_{2K}}{\sqrt{\sum_{K=1}^{n} W^2 t_{1k}} + \sqrt{\sum_{K=1}^{n} W^2 t_{2K}}} \tag{3}$$

For example: consider this as query after preprocessing—'महेंद्र सिंह धोनी आईसीसी क्रिकेट वर्ल्ड कप 2015 क्वार्टर फाइनल बांग्लादेश खिलाफ जीत हासिल बाद प्रेस कॉन्फ्रेंस दौरान बदले सुर तेज गेंदबाज़ों तारीफ थक' and suppose the sense knowledge vector is created from the context—'बंगलादेश जीत साथ पूल ए श्रीलंका क्वार्टर फाइनल पहुंच'.

Then n-dimensional vector is created which consist of unique words from testing and training data. As shown below:

$V(S_1)$ = {(महेंद्र,1), (सिंह,1), (धोनी,1), (आईसीसी,1), (क्रिकेट,1), (वर्ल्ड,1), (कप,1), (2015,1), (क्वार्टर,1), (फाइनल,1), (बांग्लादेश,1), (खिलाफ,1), (जीत,1), (हासिल,1), (बाद,1), (प्रेस,1), (कॉन्फ्रेंस,1), (दौरान,1), (बदले,1), (सुर,1), (तेज,1), (गेंदबाज़ों,1), (तारीफ,1), (थक,1), (साथ,0), (पूल,0), (ए,0), (श्रीलंका,0) (पहुंच,0) }

$V(S_2)$ = {(महेंद्र,0), (सिंह,0), (धोनी,0), (आईसीसी,0), (क्रिकेट,0), (वर्ल्ड,0), (कप,0), (2015,0), (क्वार्टर,1), (फाइनल,1), (बांग्लादेश,1), (खिलाफ,0), (जीत,1), (हासिल,0), (बाद,0), (प्रेस,0), (कॉन्फ्रेंस,0), (दौरान,0), (बदले,0), (सुर,0), (तेज,0), (गेंदबाज़ों,0), (तारीफ,0), (थक,0), (साथ,1), (पूल,1), (ए,1), (श्रीलंका,1) (पहुंच,1) }

$$\text{Cosine}(S_1, S_2) = (1.0 + 1.0 + 1.0 + 1.0 + 1.0 + 1.0 + 1.0 + 1.0 + 1.1 + 1.1$$
$$+ 1.1 + 1.0 + 1.1 + 1.0 + 1.0 + 1.0 + 1.0 + 1.0 + 1.0 + 1.0 + 1.0 + 1.0 + 1.0$$
$$+ 0.1 + 0.1 + 0.1 + 0.1 + 0.1)/\sqrt{24} + \sqrt{9} = 4/7.8989 = 0.50639.$$

3.6 Assign Sense

Sense is assigned to the ambiguous word on the basis of cosine similarity. The sense among all sense of that polysemy word having highest cosine similarity is the appropriate sense for that word.

4 Dataset

There is no standard dataset available for resource scarce language like Hindi. For the disambiguation task we create sense-tagged dataset consisting of 90 ambiguous Hindi words in which information is stored about their synonyms, and other semantic relations, gloss, examples extracted from Hindi corpus [20] and information from Hindi web pages. Some examples are manually sense-tagged with their correct sense and few examples are used to test the system.

5 Experimental Results and Discussions

5.1 Experimental Results

The system is evaluated with the help of manually created sense-tagged dataset and the Lesk's algorithm [5, 6] is also evaluated on the same dataset. For this we take 20 highly ambiguous Hindi words and test the system by firing queries. We have taken whole context window so that there will be more content words which may provide clue for disambiguation purpose. We have tested our system on total 1200 instances and calculated their precision and recall which is shown in Table 1, their comparison in Table 2 and comparison graph in Fig. 2.

5.2 Discussions

Table 2 shows the comparison of cosine similarity measure and Lesk's Algorithm and it is found that cosine similarity measure obtained an average precision of

Table 1 Precision and recall of 20 highly ambiguous words of Hindi

Ambiguous word	Cosine similarity measure (precision)	Cosine similarity measures (recall)	Lesk's algorithm (precision)	Lesk's algorithm (recall)
आम	0.8983	0.7294	0.6020	0.5939
चीनी	0.9834	0.9329	0.5332	0.3694
चैन	0.6421	0.4951	0.2746	0.2136
डिग्री	0.7418	0.5859	0.6784	0.4642
बिल	0.5409	0.5294	0.2834	0.2741
हार	0.9398	0.8429	0.9275	0.8419
फल	0.7952	0.7952	0.7952	0.7952
क्वार्टर	0.9387	0.8919	0.8349	0.7429
कलम	0.8946	0.7593	0.6183	0.5723
अशोक	0.4895	0.4895	0.4895	0.4476
तीर	0.9573	0.7452	0.8619	0.7034
डाक	0.6184	0.5962	0.5912	0.4956
जेठ	0.9147	0.9147	0.9147	0.8952
चंदा	0.8308	0.7047	0.8875	0.6732
गुरु	0.7519	0.7519	0.4937	0.4937
कोटा	0.8530	0.6490	0.6849	0.5938
उत्तर	0.9864	0.8038	0.9782	0.7396
कुंभ	0.5940	0.4927	0.2435	0.2109
खान	0.6197	0.6197	0.4567	0.4567
माँग	0.8092	0.6982	0.7853	0.5692

Table 2 Comparison on the basis of precision

Method	Average precision (tested on 20 highly ambiguous words)	Average recall (tested on 20 highly ambiguous words)
Cosine similarity measure	0.7899	0.7258
Lesk's algorithm	0.6467	0.5573

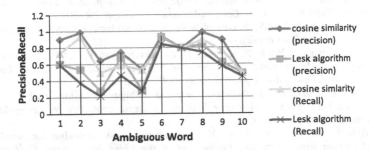

Fig. 2 Comparison graph on the basis of precision and recall by taking first 10 ambiguous words

78.99 % and average recall of 72.58 %; on the other hand Lesk's algorithm [5, 6] obtained average precision of 64.67 % and recall of 55.73 %. This difference in precision is due to the fact that Lesk algorithm has few content words for disambiguation as they utilize the gloss only. But cosine similarity measure utilizes information from Hindi WordNet [10], Hindi corpus [20] and the information from web. This method also consider different weights to different words, more important word is given more weight. Graph in Fig. 2 shows the comparison of these two methods on first 10 ambiguous words shown in Table 2. From this graph we see that cosine similarity measure mostly outperformed Lesk's algorithm in terms of precision and recall, but in some case it is same due to availability of clue words from the query in dataset. We clearly see that Lesk's algorithm never outperformed cosine similarity measure because it is also doing matching but with more content words and according to the weight of specific word [21].

6 Conclusion and Future Work

We have proposed the method for disambiguation of Hindi words using cosine similarity measure and its comparison is done with the well-known algorithm for WSD called Lesk algorithm [5, 6] and found that cosine similarity measure method outperformed Lesk algorithm (shown in Table 2). This method has a drawback that it does not disambiguate part of speech other than noun like adjective, adverb, etc. properly because these have shallow networks of relation stored in Hindi WordNet. In future, work can be done to utilize other similarity measures for disambiguation of Hindi words.

References

1. Navigli, R. (2009). Word sense disambiguation: A survey. *ACM Computing Surveys (CSUR),41*(2), 10.
2. Agirre, E., & Edmonds. P. (2006). *Word sense disambiguation algorithms and application* (Vol. 3). New York, NY: Springer.
3. Sarika, & Sharma, D. K. (May 2015). A comparative analysis of hindi word sense disambiguation and its approaches. *IEEE International Conference on Computation Communication and Automation 2015 (ICCCA-2015), Galgotia University, India* (pp. 296–302).
4. Zhou, X., & Han, H. (2005). Survey of word sense disambiguation approaches. *American Association for Artificial Intelligence.*
5. Sinha, M., Kumar, M., Pande, P., Kashyap, L., & Bhattacharyya, P. (2004). Hindi word sense disambiguation. *International Symposium on Machine Translation, Natural Language Processing and Translation Support Systems, Delhi, India.*
6. Lesk, M. E. (June 1986). Automatic sense disambiguation using machine readable dictionaries: How to tell a pine cone from an ice cream cone. *Proceedings of SIGDOC Conference, Toronto, Ontario.*
7. Banerjee, S., & Pederson, T. (2002). An adapted Lesk algorithm for word sense disambiguation using WordNet. *Proceedings of the Third International Conference on Computational Linguistics and Intelligent Text Processing.*
8. Mutlum, B. Word sense disambiguation. http://www.denizyuret.com/students/bmutlum/index.htm.
9. Agirre, E., & Rigau, G. (1996). Word sense disambiguation using conceptual density. *Proceedings of the International Conference on Computational Linguistics(COLING), Copenhagen, Denmark* (pp. 16–22).
10. HindiWordNet. http://www.cfilt.iitb.ac.in/wordnet/webhwn/wn.php.
11. Singh, S., & Siddiqui, T. J. (April 2003). A supervised algorithm for hindi word sense disambiguation. *International Journal of Systems, Algorithms & Algorithms, 3*(ICASE13). ISSN:2277-2677.
12. Singh, S., Siddiqui, T. J., & Sharma, S. (2014). Naïve Bayes classifier for hindi word sense disambiguation. *Proceedings of the 7th ACM India Computing Conference (COMPUTE'14).*
13. Mishra, N., Yadav, S., & Siddiqui, T. J. (2009). An unsupervised approach to hindi word sense disambiguation. *Proceedings of the First International Conference on Intelligent Human Computer Interaction* (pp. 327–335).
14. Yarowsky, D. (1995). Unsupervised word sense disambiguation rivaling supervised methods. *Proceedings of the 33rd Annual Meeting of the Association for Computational Linguistics*, Cambridge, MA (pp. 189–196).
15. Singh, S., Singh, V. K., & Siddiqui, T. J. (2013). Hindi word sense disambiguation using semantic relatedness measure. *7th International Workshop, MIWAI 2013* (pp. 247–256).
16. Tomar, G. S., Singh, M., Rai, S., Kumar, A., Sanyal, R., & Sanyal, S. (September 2013). Probabilistic latent semantic analysis for unsupervised word sense disambiguation. *International Journal of Computer Science Issues, 10*(5), 2.
17. Patwardhan, S., Banerjee, S., & Pedersen, T. (2003). Using measures of semantic relatedness for word sense disambiguation. *Proceedings of the Fourth International Conference on Intelligent Text Processing and Computational Linguistics (CICLING-03).*
18. Veronis, J. (2004). Hyperlex: Lexical cartography for information retrieval. *Computer Speech & Language, 18*(3), 223–252.
19. Lin, D. (1988). Automatic retrieval and clustering of similar words. *Proceedings of the 17th International Conference on Computational linguistics (COLING, Montreal, P.Q., Canada)* (pp. 768–774).
20. Hindi Corpus. http://www.cfilt.iitb.ac.in/Downloads.html.
21. Manning, C., & Schutze, H. (2002). *Word sense disambiguation based on foundations of statistical NLP.* MIT Press, Ch. 7.

A Multi-classifiers Based Novel DoS/DDoS Attack Detection Using Fuzzy Logic

Jatin Patel and Vijay Katkar

Abstract Intrusion detection systems (IDSs) have become an efficient defense tool against network attacks since they allow network administrator to detect policy violations. However, traditional IDS are vulnerable to novel malicious attacks. It is hard to make prevention mechanism to detect novel attack. It takes time to prevent from novel detected attack. This paper presents data mining and fuzzy logic-based mechanism for effectively identifying intrusion activities. The proposed fuzzy logic and data mining based mechanism can detect intrusion behavior of the networks intrusion and improve the detection rate of intrusion detection. The proposed mechanism identifies if the detected novel DoS attack is a variation of previously known DoS attack or not. If novel attack is identify as a variation of previous known attack then it is easy to make pretension mechanism in less time. The KDD Cup 99 intrusion detection dataset is used for experiments and evaluations of the proposed intrusion detection system. Experimental results are provided to support the proposed mechanism.

Keywords Intrusion detection system · Classification algorithm · KDD 99 dataset

1 Introduction

A denial of service (DoS) is an action that prevents or impairs the authorized use of network, system or applications by exhausting resources such as CPU, memory bandwidth, and disk space. Every attack uses any one of the following techniques:

J. Patel (✉)
Department of Computer Engineering, GPERI, Mevad, Mehsana, India
e-mail: jatinit2010@gmail.com

V. Katkar
Department of Information Technology, PCCOE, Pune, India
e-mail: katkarvijayd@gmail.com

© Springer Science+Business Media Singapore 2016
S.C. Satapathy et al. (eds.), *Proceedings of International Conference on ICT for Sustainable Development*, Advances in Intelligent Systems and Computing 409, DOI 10.1007/978-981-10-0135-2_77

(i) Consume server resources (ii) Consume network bandwidth (iii) Crash the server using vulnerability present in the server (iv) Spoofing packets.

Intrusion detection systems have become a needful component in terms of computer and network security. There are various approaches being utilized in intrusion detection, but unfortunately none of the systems so far is completely flawless. Current IDS has a drawback of highly false positive and false negative. Due to false positive and false negative, the intrusion detection rate becomes low. If the system is detected as a novel attack whose signature is not present in database, it is hard to make defense mechanism. It takes time to make prevention mechanism.

The proposed mechanism is developed using data mining and fuzzy logic concepts and also improves the intrusion attack detection rate. The mechanism is used to identify if the attack detected is a variation of previous attack or not. If the system identifies that the detected novel attack is variation of previous attack then its takes less time to build defense mechanism for novel attack and reduces the complexity for making defense mechanism. Using this mechanism IDS provides faster prevention for novel attack.

2 Intrusion Detection Attack Database (KDD 99 Data Set) [2]

The 1998 DARPA Intrusion Detection Evaluation Program was prepared and managed by MIT Lincoln Labs. The objective was to survey and evaluate research in intrusion detection. A standard set of data to be audited, which includes a wide variety of intrusions simulated in a military network environment, was provided. The 1999 KDD intrusion detection contest uses a version of this dataset. "10 % of KDD Cup'99" from KDD Cup '99 data set was chosen to evaluate rules and testing data sets to detect intrusion. The entire KDD Cup '99 data set contains 41 features. Connections are labeled as normal or attacks fall into four main categories.

1. DoS: Denial of Service
2. Probe: e.g., port scanning
3. U2R: unauthorized access to root privileges
4. R2L: unauthorized remote login to machine.

3 Features Selection (Attribute Selection)

Due to large amount of network traffic captured in terms of number of features and number of record, it is very difficult to process all the network traffic before making any decision about normal or abnormal. In order to achieve high detection rate and low false alarm rate, we first extract most relevant and effective features on the basis of information gain.

4 Proposed Method

The proposed mechanism is used to identify the detected intrusion DoS attack is variation of known attack or not. The work is carried out in two parts. In the first part we used KDD 99 data set as a benchmark and apply classification algorithm (SVM, Naïve Bayes, J48 and CART) on KDD 99 dataset, the outcome gives, which algorithm provides highest detection rate. In the second part our work goes towards our objective for finding if the new attack is variation of previous attack or not. In that we use one pass incremental association rule detection algorithm and the algorithm that gives the highest detection rate in the first part for finding variation of known intrusion attacks.

A. Comparative Analysis of Classification Algorithms for Intrusion Attack Classification Using KDD Cup Training and Testing Dataset:

(1) *Training DB and Testing DB* The training data set contains 42,674 connection records of the available 10 % of the training set as published by Lincoln Labs which contains 494,021 connections for training of the attacks and normal type and the testing data set contains 32,957 of the total connection records of the attacks and normal type. To test the performance of this model we used KDD 99 Cup corrected data set. The data set has been provided by MIT Lincoln labs. It consists of 41 features, 38 of them are numeric and 3 are symbolic (Fig. 1).

(2) *Pre-processing the data using fuzzy logic* Use fuzzy logic triangular membership function to fuzzify the training and testing data for getting correct results.

(3) *Attribute selection* Information gain is used to select the relevant features; it helps in faster processing.

(4) *Transformation of data into appropriate form* Convert the data into. Arff form for input to the weka tool.

(5) *Apply data mining classification algorithms (CART, J48, NAÏVE BAYES AND SVM)* Apply above four classification algorithm on fuzzified data for getting result of detection rate.

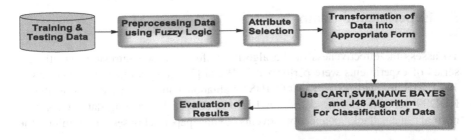

Fig. 1 Compression of classification algorithms

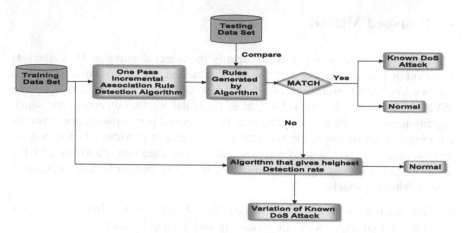

Fig. 2 Find out if the detected DoS attack is variation of previous DoS attack or not using classification algorithm that gives more accuracy

(6) *Evaluation of Result* Using evaluation parameter to analyze the result and identify the algorithm which gives higher accurate result.

B. Find out the detected DoS attack is variation of previous DoS Attack or not Using Classification algorithm that gives more accuracy:

- Train one pass incremental association rule detection algorithm using 10 % KDD 99 training data set (Fig. 2).
- Train classifier algorithm which gives the highest detection rate using 10 % KDD 99 training data set.
- Trained one pass incremental association rule detection algorithm [1] and generates rules.
- Compare corrected testing KDD99 dataset each record with rules. If record matches with rules, then it predicts either normal or known DoS attack. Otherwise pass that novel record to trained classifier algorithm for testing.
- The classifier predicts novel records either normal or variation of known DoS attack.

5 Experimental Setup

To assess the effectiveness of the algorithms for proposed intrusion detection, a series of experiments were performed in Weka [3]. The java heap size was set to 1024 MB for weka-3-7. KDD99 IDS evaluation dataset is used in this thesis. KDD99 contains training dataset and testing dataset; its training dataset contains normal and attack connection events. This paper chooses a training file kddcup.data_10_percent.gz as the training dataset. And chooses testing file corrected.gz that contains connect flags as the testing dataset.

A. Analysis of SVM, NAÏVE BAYES, J48 and CART Algorithms Output

Based on above output, we can say that CART algorithm with 16 interval training and testing dataset gives higher TPrate, FPrate and Precision and lower FPrate than other algorithms. So the detection rate of CART is high for DoS attack (Table 1).

B. Accuracy Measurement of IDS for Known DoS Attack Record Detection

Table 2 shows a list of known DoS attack, the records in dataset, how many records are correctly classified and other records that are incorrectly classified. Finally it shows the accuracy obtained by the IDS.

C. Accuracy Measurement of IDS for Novel DoS Attack Record Detection

Tables 3 and graphs show only known DoS attack accuracy. In our proposed mechanism, the IDS detects novel DoS attacks which are processtable, udpstorm, mailbomb and apache2. The detection accuracy of novel DoS attack is shown in below table.

Table 4 shows how many novel attacks are correctly detected. Our proposed method shows that if the attack detected is variation of known attack or not. Here we identify in the last column that the novel attack is variation of which known DoS attack. We can see that udpstorm is a variation of teardrop attack. The mailbomb attack is a variation of smurf attack. The process table attack is a variation of smurf and Neptune attack. Apache2 attack is variation of a back and Neptune attack.

Table 1 Result of combining all four algorithms, accurate output

Algorithm name-linguistic variables	TP rate	FP rate	Precision	Recall
J48-15	0.933	0.016	0.925	0.933
Naïve Bayes-5	0.97	0.009	0.949	0.97
SVM-5	0.972	0.007	0.951	0.972
CART-16	**0.973**	**0.007**	**0.951**	**0.973**

Table 2 Analysis of known DoS attack record detected by IDS

DoS attack type	Total no. of records	Correctly classified	Incorrectly classified	Accuracy (%)
Smurf	164,091	164,091	0	100
Neptune	58,001	58,001	0	100
Back	1098	943	155	85.88
Teardrop	12	9	3	75
Pod	87	83	4	95.4
Land	9	5	4	55.56

Table 3 Analysis of novel DoS attack record detected by IDS

Novel DoS attack type	Total no. of records	Correctly classified	Incorrectly classified	Accuracy (%)
Udpstorm	2	2	0	100
Mailbomb	5000	4959	41	99.18
Processtable	759	759	0	100
Apache2	794	786	8	98.99

Table 4 Final output of proposed mechanism (variation of Known DoS attack)

Novel DoS attack type	Variation of known DoS attack
Udpstorm	Teardrop
Mailbomb	Smurf
Processtable	Smurf, Neptune
Apache2	Back, Neptune

D. Justification for the Output of Proposed Mechanism

The detected variation is really related to novel attack or not that is identified by the standard document of MIT Lincoln Laboratory of DARPA Intrusion Detection Evaluation [4]. This document has description of various known and novel DoS attack.

From the DARPA Intrusion Detection Evaluation document [4] description of the attacks, we give the justification for the outputs of proposed mechanism as follows:

Udpstorm is variation of Teardrop attack
From the above description of Teardrop and udpstorm, we can say that both the attacks create malformed packets that confuse the TCP/IP stack of the machine. So we can say that novel teardrop DoS attack is a variation of udpstorm attack.

Mailbomb is variation of Smurf attack
From the above description of mailbomb and smurf attack, we can say that both the attack send more number of packets on the target machine, so the target machine (server) overflows by the number of spoofed packets. In a short period of time the target machine gets more number of connections on the same service on the same host also; both the attack have attack pattern similarity, so we can say that novel mailbomb DoS attack is variation of known smurf attack.

Processtable is variation of smurf and neptune attack
From the above description of processtable, neptune and smurf attack, we can say that all the attacks consume the resource and target system does not work properly.

Apach2 is variation of back and Neptune attack
From the above description of apache2 and back attack, we can conclude that both the attack take advantage of bugs in a particular network daemon. Both the attacks apply on apache web server. Apache2 and Neptune attack have similar effect on the system, the system may be crashed, or be rendered otherwise inoperative.

6 Conclusions and Future Work

In this paper, we describe a mechanism using data mining and fuzzy logic concept for identifying if the detected novel DoS attack is variation of known attack or not. In our proposed mechanism we used one pass incremental rule detection algorithm and cart algorithm. For the experimental purpose, we used the KDD 99 benchmark training and testing dataset. The rule generated by one pass incremental algorithm is matched with testing database file, if rule is matched, then it predicts either known DoS attack or normal, otherwise the records pass to the CART algorithm, The CART algorithm detects the novel DoS attack. We found that the novel apache2 DoS attack is variation of back and Neptune attack. Novel processtable DoS attack is variation of smurf and Neptune attack. Novel mailbomb DoS attack is variation of smurf attack. Novel udpstorm DoS attack is variation of teardrop attack. The proposed algorithm is implemented in java. Using the proposed mechanism we get 98.2 % detection accuracy.

As part of our future work, we shall implement the signature generation module for intrusion prevention system. The signature generation module is made by our proposed approach. So if it is found the attack is variation of known attack, it will be easy for creating prevention mechanism and in lesser time, we can build defense mechanism for novel attacks.

References

1. Katkar, V. (April 2011). One pass incremental association rule detection algorithm for network intrusion detection system. *International Journal of Engineering Science and Technology (IJEST), 3*(4). ISSN:0975-5462.

Websites

2. KDD99 Dataset. http://kdd.ics.uci.edu/databases/kddcup99/kddcup99.html.
3. Weka Tool. http://www.cs.waikato.ac.nz/ml/weka/.
4. http://www.ll.mit.edu/mission/communications/cyber/CSTcorpora/ideval/index.html.

Author Index

© Springer Science+Business Media Singapore 2016
S.C. Satapathy et al. (eds.), *Proceedings of International Conference on ICT for Sustainable Development*, Advances in Intelligent Systems and Computing 409, DOI 10.1007/978-981-10-0135-2